John A. Bingham

The trial of the alleged assassins and conspirators at Washington City, D.C.,

May and June, 1865: for the murder of President Abraham Lincoln : full of illustrative engravings - Vol. 3

John A. Bingham

The trial of the alleged assassins and conspirators at Washington City, D.C.,
May and June, 1865: for the murder of President Abraham Lincoln : full of illustrative engravings - Vol. 3

ISBN/EAN: 9783337814564

Printed in Europe, USA, Canada, Australia, Japan

Cover: Foto ©ninafisch / pixelio.de

More available books at **www.hansebooks.com**

FULL OF ILLUSTRATIVE ENGRAVINGS.

THE WHOLE COMPLETE IN THIS VOLUME.

THE TRIAL
OF THE
ASSASSINS AND CONSPIRATORS
AT WASHINGTON, D. C., MAY AND JUNE, 1865.
FOR THE MURDER OF PRESIDENT LINCOLN.

ONLY FULL, CORRECT, GRAPHIC, AND VERBATIM REPORT OF THE TRIAL PUBLISHED.

READ THIS FULL REPORT OF THE TRIAL AND SPEECHES OF COUNSEL AT ONCE.

JOHN WILKES BOOTH, THE MURDERER OF ABRAHAM LINCOLN.

Being a full and verbatim Report of the Testimony of all the Witnesses examined in the whole Trial, with the Arguments of Counsel on both sides, and the Verdict of the Military Commission: with a sketch of the Life of all the Conspirators, and Portraits and Illustrative Engravings of the principal persons and scenes relating to the foul murder and the trial. It also contains items of fact and interest not to be found in any other work of the kind published. The whole being prepared, on the spot, by the Special Correspondents and Reporters of the Philadelphia Daily Inquirer, expressly for this edition.

Philadelphia:
T. B. PETERSON & BROTHERS, 306 CHESTNUT STREET.

PRICE 50 CENTS.

The Cheapest place in the world to buy or send for books of all kinds, is at T. B. Peterson & Brothers, Philadelphia. Send for their Catalogue. Booksellers, News Agents, Sutlers, and all others, will be supplied with any Quantities of any Books published, at the lowest net cash price, on sending their orders to them. For a List of "Petersons' Popular Series of Novels," see the other pages of this cover.

T. B. PETERSON & BROTHERS' PUBLICATIONS.

The Books on this page will be found to be the very Best and Latest Publications in the world, and are Published and for Sale by T. B. PETERSON & BROTHERS, Philadelphia.

MRS. HENRY WOOD'S BOOKS.

The Earl's Heirs; or Lord Oakburn's Daughters, - - 75	The Runaway Match, 50
	A Life's Secret, - 50
	Better for Worse, - 75
The Mystery, - - 75	The Lost Bank Note, 75

Above are each in one volume, paper cover. Each one is also published in one volume, cloth, price $1.00 each.

The Channings, - 1 00 | Aurora Floyd, - 50

The above are each in one volume, paper cover. Fine editions are also published in one vol., cloth, price $1.50.

Oswald Cray, - - 1 50	The Castle's Heir, 1 50
Squire Trevlyn's Heir; or Trevlyn's Hold, 1 50	Shadow of Ashlydyat, 1 50
	Verner's Pride, - 1 50

The above are each in one volume paper cover. Each one is also published in one volume., cloth, price $2.00.

The Haunted Tower, 25	The Lawyer's Secret, 25
Foggy Night at Offord, 25	William Allair, 25

GUSTAVE AIMARD'S WORKS.

The Prairie Flower, - 75	Pirates of the Prairies, 75
The Indian Scout, - 75	Trapper's Daughter, - 75
The Trail Hunter, - 75	The Tiger Slayer, - 75
The Indian Chief, - 75	The Gold Seekers, - 75
The Red Track, - 75	The Smuggler Chief, 75

MRS. DANIELS' GREAT BOOKS.

Marrying for Money, 75	Kate Walzingham, - 50
The Poor Cousin, 50	

WILKIE COLLINS' BEST WORKS.

The Crossed Path, - 1 50 | The Dead Secret, - 1 50

The above are each in one volume, paper cover. Each one is also published in one volume, cloth, price $2.00.

Hide and Seek, - - 75	The Stolen Mask, - 25
After Dark, - - 75	The Yellow Mask, - 25
The Dead Secret, - 75	Sister Rose, - 25
Sights A-Foot, or Travels Beyond Railways,	50

MISS PARDOE'S WORKS.

The Jealous Wife, - 50	The Wife's Trials, - 75
Confessions of a Pretty Woman, - - 50	Rival Beauties, - - 75
	Romance of the Harem, 50

The five above books are also bound in one vol. for $3 00

The Adopted Heir. One vol., paper, $1.50; or cloth, $2 00
A Life's Struggle. By Miss Pardoe, cloth, - 2 00

G. P. R. JAMES'S BOOKS.

Lord Montague's Page, 1 50 | The Cavalier, - - 1 50

The above are each in one volume, paper cover. Each book is also published in one volume, cloth, price $2.00.

The Man in Black, - 75	Arrah Neil, - - 75
Mary of Burgundy, - 75	Eva St. Clair, - - 50

GOOD BOOKS FOR EVERYBODY.

Life and Adventures of Don Quixotte, - 1 00	Lola Montes Life, - 1 50
Adventures in Africa, 1 00	Currer Lyle, - - 1 50
Adventures of Peregrine Pickle, 2 vols., - 1 00	Wild Southern Scenes, 1 50
	The Quaker Soldier, 1 50
Adventures of To-a-Jones, 2 vols., - - 1 00	Humors Falconbridge, 1 50
Aftermath of Unmarried Life, - - 1 50	Secession, Coercion, and Civil War. - 1 50
Life and Beauties of Fanny Fern, - - 1 50	What I saw and Where I Went, - - 1 00
Lady Maud; or the Wonder of Kingswood Chase, 1 50	Life and Adventures of Wilfred Montressor, 1 50

The above are each in one volume, paper cover. Each one is also published in one volume, cloth, price $2.00 each.

HUMOROUS AMERICAN WORKS.

BEAUTIFULLY ILLUSTRATED.

Major Jones' Courtship, 75	Drama in Pokerville, 75
Major Jones' Travels, 75	The Quorndon Hounds, 75
Simon Suggs's Adventures and Travels, 75	My Shooting Box, - 75
	Warwick Woodlands, 75
Major Jones' Chronicles of Pineville, - 75	The Deer Stalkers, - 75
	Peter Ploddy, - - 75
Polly Peasblossom's Wedding, - - 75	Adventures of Captain Farrago, - 75
Widow Rugby's Husband, 75	Major O'Regan's Adventures, - - 75
Big Bear of Arkansas, 75	Sol. Smith's Theatrical Apprenticeship, 75
Western Scenes, or Life on the Prairie, 75	Sol. Smith's Theatrical Journey-Work, - 75
Streaks of Squatter Life, 75	
Pickings from Pleayune, 75	The Quarter Race in Kentucky, - 75
Stray Subjects, arrested and Bound Over, - 75	Life of Col. Vanderbomb, - - 75
Louisiana Swamp Doctor, - - 75	Percival Mayberry's Adventures and Travels, 75
Charcoal Sketches, - 75	Yankee Yarns and Yankee Letters, - 75
Misfortunes Peter Faber, 75	
Yankee among the Mermaids, - - 75	American Joe Miller, 50
New Orleans Sketch Book, - - 75	Adventures of Fudge Fumble, - - 75

D'ISRAELI'S WORKS.

Henrietta Temple, - 50	Young Duke, - - 50
Vivian Grey, - - 50	Miriam Alroy, - - 50
Venetia, - - 50	Contarini Fleming, - 50

FRANK FAIRLEGH'S WORKS.

Frank Fairlegh, - 75	Fortunes of Harry Racket Scapegrace, 75
Lewis Arundel, - 75	

Fine editions of above are issued in cloth, at $2 00 each.

Harry Coverdale's Courtship, $1.50; or cloth, 2 00 | Lorrimer Littlegood, - 1 50 or in cloth, - 2 00

C. J. PETERSON'S WORKS.

Old Stone Mansion, - 1 50 | Kate Aylesford, - - 1 50

The above are each in one vol., paper cover. Each one is also published in one volume, cloth, price $2.00 each.

Cruising in Last War, 50 | Grace Dudley; or Arnold at Saratoga, - 25
Valley Farm, - - 25 |

MAITLAND'S WORKS.

The Watchman, - 1 50	Diary of an Old Doctor 1 50
The Wanderer, - 1 50	Sartaroe, - - 1 50
The Lawyer's Story 1 50	The Three Cousins, - 1 50

Above are each in one vol., paper cover. Each one is also published in one vol. cloth, price $2.00 each.

LANGUAGES WITHOUT MASTER

French without Master, 25	German without a Master, - - 25
Spanish without a Master, - - 25	Italian without a Master, - - 25
Latin without a Master, 25	

The above five works on the French, German, Spanish, Latin and Italian Languages, without a Master, whereby any one or all of these Languages can be learned by any one without a Teacher, with the aid of this great book, by A. H. Monteith, Esq., is also published in finer style, complete in one large volume, bound, price, $2.00.

BOOKS OF FUN AND HUMOR.

Each one full of Illustrations, and bound in Cloth.

High Life in New York, by Jonathan Slick, 2 00	Piney Woods' Tavern, or, Sam Slick in Texas, cloth, - 2 00
Judge Halliburton's Yankee Stories, Illustrated, cloth, - 2 00	Major Jones' Courtship and Travels, Illustrated, cloth, - 2 00
The Swamp Doctor's Adventures in the South-West. 14 Illustrations, cloth, - 2 00	Simon Suggs' Adventures and Travels. Illustrated, cloth, - 2 00
Major Thorpe's Scenes in Arkansas, 16 Illustrations, cloth, - 2 00	Major Jones' Scenes in Georgia, cloth, 2 00
	Sam Slick, the Clockmaker, cloth, - 2 00
The Big Bear's Adventures and Travels. 18 engravings, cloth 2 00	The Humors of Falconbridge, cloth, - 2 00
Harry Coverdale's Courtship, cloth, - 2 00	Frank Forrester's Sporting Scenes and
American Joe Miller, 50	Characters, 2 vols., 4 00

DOW'S PATENT SERMONS.

Dow's Patent Sermons, 1st Series, 1.00 cloth, 1 50	Dow's Patent Sermons, 3d Series, 1.00, cloth, 1 50
Dow's Patent Sermons, 2d Series, 1.00, cloth, 1 50	Dow's Patent Sermons, 4th series, 1.00, cloth, 1 50

HENRY W. HERBERT'S BOOKS.

My Shooting Box, - 75	Warwick Woodlands, 75
Deer Stalker, - - 75	Quorndon Hounds, - 75

The Roman Traitor, 1 vol., cl., $2.00, or 1 vol., pap., $1.50.

ELLEN PICKERING'S WORKS.

Orphan Niece, - - 50	Quiet Husband, - 38
The Grumbler, - 38	Nan Darrell, - - 38
Ellen Wareham, - 38	Prince and Pedlar, - 38
Who Shall be Heir? 38	Merchant's Daughter, 38
Secret Foe, - - 38	The Squire, - - 38
Expectant, - - 38	

ETIQUETTE AND USEFUL BOOKS.

The Ladies Guide to True Politeness and Perfect Manners. By Miss Leslie. Cloth, full gilt back,	2 00
The Ladies Complete Guide to Needlework and Embroidery. 113 Illustrations. Cloth, gilt back,	2 00
Ladies Work Table Book, plates, clo' Princess gilt	1 50
The Gentlemens Science of Etiquette,	25
The Ladies Science of Etiquette,	25
Creation of the Earth,	2 00
The Laws and Practice of the Game of Euchre,	1 00
Laminger's, or Thousand Ten Things Worth Knowing,	25
Knowlson's Complete Farrier, or Horse Doctor	25
Knowlson's Complete Cow or Cattle Doctor,	25
The Complete Kitchen and Fruit Gardener,	25
The Complete Florist and Flower Gardener,	25
Arthur's Receipts for Preserving Fruits, etc.,	12

☞ Copies of any of the above works will be sent by Mail, free of Postage, to any part of the United States, on receipt of the retail price, by T. B. Peterson & Brothers, Philadelphia.

Complete and Unabridged Edition.—Containing the whole of the Suppressed Evidence.

THE TRIAL

OF THE ALLEGED

ASSASSINS AND CONSPIRATORS

AT WASHINGTON CITY, D. C., MAY AND JUNE, 1865.

FOR

THE MURDER OF PRESIDENT ABRAHAM LINCOLN.

FULL OF ILLUSTRATIVE ENGRAVINGS.

Being a full and verbatim Report of the Testimony of all the Witnesses examined in the whole Trial, with the Argument of Reverdy Johnson on the Jurisdiction of the Commission, and all the Arguments of Counsel on both sides, with the closing Argument of Hon. John A. Bingham, Special Judge Advocate, as well as the Verdict of the Military Commission; with a sketch of the Life of all the Conspirators, and Portraits and Illustrative Engravings of the principal persons and scenes relating to the foul murder and the trial. It also contains items of fact and interest not to be found in any other work of the kind published. The whole being complete and unabridged in this volume, being prepared on the spot by the Special Correspondents and Reporters of the Philadelphia Daily Inquirer, expressly for this edition.

Philadelphia:
T. B. PETERSON & BROTHERS,
306 CHESTNUT STREET.

Entered according to Act of Congress, in the year 1865, by
T. B. PETERSON & BROTHERS,
In the Clerk's Office of the District Court of the United States, in and for the Eastern District of Pennsylvania.

THE TRIAL

OF THE ALLEGED

Assassins and Conspirators.

THE COURT MARTIAL.

ON the first of May, 1865, President JOHNSON issued the following order for the trial of the criminals:

EXECUTIVE CHAMBER,
WASHINGTON CITY, *May* 1, 1865.

Whereas the Attorney General of the United States has given his opinion that the persons implicated in the murder of the late President, Abraham Lincoln, and the attempted assassination of the Hon. William H. Seward, Secretary of State, and an alleged conspiracy to assassinate other officers of the Federal Government at Washington city, and their aiders and abettors are subject to the jurisdiction of and legally triable before a military commission:

It is ordered: First—That the Assistant Adjutant General detail nine competent military officers to serve as a commission for the trial of said parties, and that the Judge Advocate General proceed to prefer charges against said parties for their alleged offences, and bring them to trial before said military commission; that said trial or trials be conducted by the said Judge Advocate General, as recorder thereof, in person, aided by such assistant or special judge advocates as he may designate, and that said trials be conducted with all diligence consistent with the ends of justice, and said commission to sit without regard to hours.

Second—That Brevet Major General Hartranft be assigned to duty as Special Provost Marshal General, for the purpose of said trial and attendance upon said commission, and the execution of its mandates.

Third—That the said commission establish such order or rules of proceeding as may avoid unnecessary delay and conduce to the ends of public justice.

ANDREW JOHNSON.

ADJUTANT GENERAL'S OFFICE,
WASHINGTON, D. C., *May* 6, 1865.

Official Copy:
W. A. NICHOLS,
Assistant Adjutant General.

In compliance with this order the following officers were detailed as members of the military commission:

PRESIDENT.
MAJOR GENERAL DAVID HUNTER.

MEMBERS.
MAJOR GENERAL LEW. WALLACE,
BREV. MAJ. GEN. AUGUST V. KAUTZ,
BRIG. GEN. ALBION P. HOWE,
BRIG. GEN. ROBERT S. FOSTER,
BRIG. GEN. JAMES A. EKIN,
BRIG. GEN. THOMAS M. HARRIS,
COL. CHARLES H. TOMPKINS,
BREVET COL. D. R. CLENDENIN.

The prosecution was conducted by Brigadier General JOSEPH HOLT, Judge Advocate General; assisted by Brevet Colonel H. L. BURNETT, of Indiana, and Hon. JOHN A. BINGHAM, of Ohio, Assistant Judge Advocates.

The prisoners selected for their counsel, REVERDY JOHNSON, of Maryland, THOMAS EWING, of Kansas, W. E. DOSTER, of Pennsylvania, FRED. A. AIKIN, District of Columbia, WALTER S. COX, JOHN W. CLAMPIT, and F. STONE, of Maryland.

The commission was composed of men of distinguished ability and intelligence. General HUNTER is known as a man of superior attainments, and had served on a large number of Courts

(15)

Martial. Major General LEW. WALLACE is not only one of the most gallant officers in the army, but he is also a lawyer of great eminence, ranking among the first legal minds at the bar of his native State, Indiana. He was originally Colonel of the celebrated 11th Indiana Zouaves, and was promoted to Brigadier General, and afterward to Major General, for gallantry in the field. At present he commands the Middle Department, headquarters at Baltimore, a position which he has held for nearly two years. General KAUTZ is the celebrated Cavalry leader, and a man of great decision of character. Brigadier General FOSTER, of Indiana, Brigadier General HOWE, of Maine, Brigadier General HARRIS, General EKIN, and Colonels TOMKINS and CLENDENIN are soldiers who have won most honorable distinction in the service during the past four years.

Hon. JOSEPH HOLT, Judge Advocate General of the United States, needs no eulogy. His reputation as a lawyer is known throughout the nation. He was ably assisted by Assistant Judge Advocate BINGHAM, of Ohio, and Assistant Judge Advocate BURNETT, of Indiana, the latter gentleman having conducted the prosecution of the famous Indiana conspirators, who were found guilty of treason and sentenced to death, but who ultimately had their sentences commuted to imprisonment for life in the Ohio Penitentiary.

Hon. REVERDY JOHNSON, of Maryland, has a national reputation for legal acumen, and was selected by Mrs. SURRATT as her counsel. His argument against the right of the Government to try the prisoners by Court Martial is an ingenious effort. Of the remaining gentlemen defending the accused little is known outside the immediate localities where they practice their profession.

LABORS OF THE COMMISSION.

The following interesting items will give the public some idea of the labor imposed on the Commission :

Total number of witnesses subpœnaed, ... 483
Number examined, . . . 361
Number examined, including recalls, ... 422
Number examined, subpœnaed for prosecution, ... 247
Number actually examined, . 198
Number subpœnaed for defence, . 236
Number actually examined, . 163
Total number of pages of testimony, legal cap, . . 4300
Making a solid pile of MSS. somewhat over 26 inches in height.

The arguments make in addition, 700 pages. The vast mass of depositions, &c., taken by three Judge Advocates, Colonels BURNETT, FOSTER and OLCOTT, *prior to the opening of the case*, employed five short-hand writers a fortnight, and will require two experienced clerks six weeks to brief and file away. In this, as in all State trials, the Government pays the expenses of the witnesses for the defence, as well as those for the prosecution, at the rate of $3 *per diem*, and the actual cost of transportation from and to the witnesses' homes.

JUSTICE is always sure, sooner or later, to overtake the murderer. For a brief time he may elude the pursuing fate, and perhaps, as it has often been the case, he may cover up for years his footsteps and be lost to the keen scent of the avenger. But the day must come, when he will meet his deserts. God's eye watches him, and when the hour arrives, the murderer is exposed and justice is at last satisfied.

In the case of the assassins of President LINCOLN and Secretary SEWARD, the criminals were brought, either to a speedy death or arrest. Their plans of escape were well laid and promised success. The first great danger was passed when BOOTH and PAYNE made good their escape from the theatre and from Mr. Seward's house. So far all seemed well; but BOOTH's fall on the stage, which broke his leg, sealed his fate certainly. It was decreed that he should not long elude the swift punishment due his horrible crime— a crime for which there is no name.

PAYNE thrown from his horse, found himself in the limits of the city, and in disguise sought the house of Mrs. SURRATT. The ministers of justice were there before him, and he fell into their hands unwittingly, though unwillingly, a couple of days after the assassination.

HAROLD followed BOOTH, and proved a coward in the last act of the tragedy in which his principal died the death of a dog; and, begging for life, surrendered.

Geo. A. Atzeroth, Michael O'Loughlin, Samuel Arnold, Samuel E. Mudd, and Mary E. Surratt were also duly arrested as accessaries to the villainous plot, and confined in prison to await their trial, which is fully reported in the succeeding pages.

Sketches of the Culprits.

Although justice decided that BOOTH should not be brought to formal trial, it is not foreign to the history of the great trial of the conspirators, that a sketch of the principal actor in the tragedy which amazed the world, should be given in this work.

John Wilkes Booth.

BOOTH was born on his father's farm near Baltimore. Like his two brothers, Edwin and Junius Brutus, he inherited and early manifested a predilection for the stage, and was well known to theatre-goers and the public generally as a very fine-looking young man, but as an actor of more promise than performance.

He is best remembered, perhaps, in "Richard," which he played closely after his father's conception of that character, and by his admirers was considered superior to the elder Booth. He was quite popular in the Western and Southern cities, and his last extended engagement was in Chicago.

Excellent actors say—and actors are not over-apt to praise each other—that he had inherited some of the most brilliant qualities of his father's genius. But, of late, an apparently incurable bronchial affection made almost every engagement of his a failure. The papers and critics apologized for his "hoarseness," but it was long known by his friends that he would be compelled to abandon the stage.

In the winter of 1863 and '64 he played an engagement in the St. Charles Theatre, in New Orleans, under the disadvantages of his "hoarseness," and the engagement terminated sooner than was expected on that account. He had many old friends in that city, but this was his first appearance there since the inception of the rebellion. On his arrival he called upon the editor of one of the leading journals, and in the course of conversation he warmly expressed his sympathy with secession. Indeed, he was well known as a secessionist, but he was not one of the "noisy kind."

His last appearance in New York was on the evening of November 23, 1864, at Winter Garden, when the play of *Julius Cæsar* was given for the benefit of the Shakspeare Monument Fund, with a cast including the three Booth brothers—Edwin as "Brutus," Junius as "Cassius," and John Wilkes as "Marc Antony." In the early part of 1863, during an engagement at McVicker's Theatre, Chicago, he made the remark one day, "What a glorious opportunity there is for a man to immortalize himself by killing Lincoln!"

"What good would that do?" he was asked. He then quoted these lines:—

"The ambitious youth who fired the Ephesian dome,
Outlives in fame the pious fool who reared it."

"Well, who was that ambitious youth—what was his name?" was then asked.

"That I know not," Booth replied.

"Then where's the *fame* you speak of?"

This nonplussed him.

From this it would seem that the assassin had the commission of this horrid crime in his mind for at least two or three years.

He was a young man of slender form, nervous and wiry. He often rendered himself obnoxious in the theatrical circles by the expression of his disloyal sentiments, and was a great admirer of Brutus, the assassin of Cæsar, Charlotte Corday, the assassin of Marat, Joan of Arc, and that class of historical characters. He was subject to occasional sprees of intoxication, and was generally regarded among actors as a reckless and erratic young fellow, though a tragedian of superior ability, originality and promise.

Lewis Payne.

A great mystery envelopes this man—a mystery which seems impenetrable. As the assassin who attempted the life of Secretary Seward, more than ordinary interest was attached to the testimony affecting his case. Who he is no one appeared to know on the trial. The nearest approach to any thing satisfactory is, that he is the son of a Rev. Mr. Powell, a Baptist minister, residing in Florida; but even this is not positively ascertained. Miss Brandon, a witness, produced in his behalf, remembered him as a nurse in one of the hospitals after the battle of Gettysburg. He then went by the name of Powell; but, early in 1865, while boarding with Mrs. Brandon's mother, in Baltimore, he assumed the name of Payne.

During the progress of the trial he remained apparently indifferent to all around, and was possessed of a most extraordinary control over his feelings. He maintained a dogged and sullen demeanor throughout; and when the colored waiter at Mr. Seward's was placed upon the witness stand, Payne was directed to stand up and face the witness. Both looked steadily at each other for a few moments, when the colored boy pointed to Payne, saying, "*That is the man!*" This positive recognition did not in the least disconcert the prisoner. But when Sergeant George B. Robinson, the nurse at Mr. Seward's, was called, and Payne was again directed to stand up and look at the witness while he detailed the circumstances attending the attempted murder, the prisoner grew red in the face at the recital of Robinson, particularly while he held in his hand the knife which Payne used on the occasion, and gave a demonstration of the manner in which the assassin had struck at the defenceless man as he lay upon his sick bed.

The court-room was almost breathless at this moment, every eye being turned upon the prisoner, to read in his countenance the confirmation of the truth of the witness' statement; but he not so much as stirred. His wild stare was fixed upon the witness. His mouth was closed tightly, as if his teeth were firmly clenched together, and he stood up as straight as a statue, with no sign of fear, trembling, or trepidation. Two coats worn by Payne on the night of the attempted murder were produced.

The irons were taken from Payne's wrists, and he was directed to put on both coats and the hat which he dropped at the Secretary's house when he fled. The colored boy was again brought in, and Payne stood up, dressed in the clothes he wore on that night, and he again identified Payne as the man who forced himself into Mr. Seward's house while in this dress. Facing the witness, Payne would occasionally betray a sneering defiant smile, and looked like a perfect desperado.

Major Seward, son of the Secretary, also positively identified Payne as the man who entered his father's house, and, in a tone of deep emotion, narrated the incidents of the stabbing of his father and brother, and pointed to Payne as the man who did it. He was positive as to his identity, and the counsel for the prisoner, after a short cross-examination, desisted, as a refutation of this evidence was hopeless. The sleeve of the woolen shirt which Payne had improvised into a skull cap on the night he visited Mrs. Surratt's house, and the pickaxe he carried, were exhibited.

The sleeve was put on Payne's head, and he was fully identified by the respective officers as the man who attempted to pass himself off as a laboring man when he was arrested by the detectives at Mrs. Surratt's. The boots he wore on that night were also given in evidence, and it was shown that the name originally inside of them had been blotted out to prevent identification, but being experimented upon with oxalic acid, the name of "J. W. Booth" appeared. This completed the chain of evidence connecting Payne with Booth.

An attempt was made by his counsel to prove him insane; but a rigid examination, under direction of Surgeon General Barnes, furnished conclusive evidence of his sanity.

The testimony against him during the trial brought out the fact that he was employed by the rebel plotters who had taken refuge in Canada to assassinate Secretary SEWARD. He was a fit tool for these persons—BEV. TUCKER, GEO. N. SANDERS, C. C. CLAY, JACOB THOMPSON, W. N. CLEARY, et al. BOOTH succeeded, but, thanks to kind Providence, PAYNE failed. If ABRAHAM LINCOLN was to be the MARTYR, WM. H. SEWARD, his trusty counselor and friend, was to live and behold the triumph of our cause.

Payne went on to play his part in the work on the 4th of March, but as the scheme was postponed, he found his way to the house of Mrs. Surratt. At her house he passed under the name of Wood. The part which he enacted in the assassination plot is explained in the testimony given during the trial.

Payne is a bad looking man, tall and of huge proportions, neck bare, face smoothly shaven, a shock of black hair over a low forehead, and fierce eyes with small corner, around which the white is always disagreeably visible. He leans his head straight back against the wall, and when looked at, glares the looker out of countenance.

David C. Harold.

HAROLD, the accomplice of Booth in the assassination of President Lincoln, is not over twenty-three years of age. He was born in Maryland, and received his education at Charlotte Hall, in St. Mary's County. His father, a most estimable man, resided for many years in Washington, and held the position of principal clerk in the Naval store. Young Harold was perfectly acquainted with the topography of the lower portion of the State, lying between the Chesapeake Bay and the Potomac River, and made an excellent guide for Booth, with whom he was on most intimate terms for several months previous to the assassination. Harold led a very dissipated life, and was notoriously indolent, while it was a matter of general surprise how he obtained means to live. It is probable now that money was furnished him from the secret service fund of the Rebel Government, as well as to Booth, Payne and the other conspirators.

Harold is an inveterate talker, and a great coward, as his anxiety to surrender when in Garrett's barn sufficiently proves. Since his capture he has been talkative and reticent by turns, and although wearing generally an indifferent air while in court, when in his cell he frequently gives way to fits of weeping.

John H. Surratt.

SURRATT, the son of Mrs. SURRATT, and one of the principal conspirators, made his escape, leaving Washington the morning after the murder, at 6.15 A. M., going via Philadelphia and New York to Springfield, Mass., where he was delayed by trains missing connection, and remained all day.

He then took the cars and went direct to Burlington, where, in getting his supper, he dropped his handkerchief with his name marked upon it; at St. Alban's he left the train and proceeded on foot to Canada, where he went part way by rail and part on foot to Montreal, where he was secreted by some of the sympathisers, and on the morning of the 2d of May, he had an interview with George N. Sanders. He then left and went in the direction of a monastery. He was known to be in that vicinity that day, and cannot since be found or heard of. It is probable that he is within its walls.

Mrs. Mary E. Surratt.

MRS. MARY E. SURRATT is the mother of JOHN H. SURRATT, and the evidence adduced during the trial, proves her to have been one of the most active and energetic of the conspirators. There is no doubt but that she aided them in every manner in her power. She had the carbines prepared and the bottles of whisky ready for Booth and Harold when they arrived at her old tavern in their flight. She is a woman of great nerve and energy, and an out and out rebel at heart. Mrs. SURRATT is a Marylander, about forty-five or forty-eight years of age. Mrs. Surratt shut up her house after the murder, and waited with her daughters till the officers came. She was imperturbable and rebuked her girls for weeping, and would have gone to jail like a statue, but that in her extremity Payne knocked at her door. He had come, he said, to dig a ditch for Mrs. Surratt, whom he very well knew. But Mrs. Surratt protested that she had never seen the man at all, and had no ditch to clean.

"How fortunate, girls," she said, "that these officers are here; this man might have murdered us all!"

Her effrontery stamps her as worthy of companionship with Booth.

Samuel A. Mudd.

SAMUEL A. MUDD is the person who set BOOTH's leg. MUDD lives in Maryland, about three miles from Bryantown, and has been known through the war as a strong sympathizer with the Rebellion.

Geo. A. Atzeroth.

ATZEROTH, who was to murder Mr. JOHNSON, is a vulgar-looking creature, but not apparently ferocious; combativeness is large, but in the region of firmness his head is lacking where Payne's is immense. He has a protruding jaw, and mustache turned up at the end, and a short, insignificant looking face. He is just the man to promise to commit a murder and then fail on coming to the point. Mrs. Surratt calls him a "stick," and she is probably right.

ATZEROTH was captured during the week which succeeded the crime, and was taken to Washington. He had a room almost directly over Mr. Johnson's. He had all the materials to do murder, but lost spirit or opportunity. He ran away so hastily that all his arms and baggage were discovered; a tremendous bowie-knife and a Colt's cavalry revolver were found between the mattresses of his bed. Booth's coat was also found there, showing conspired flight in company, and in it three boxes of cartridges, a map of Maryland, gauntlets for riding, a spur, and a handkerchief marked with the name of Booth's mother—a mother's souvenir for a murderer's pocket! Atzeroth fled alone, and was found at the house of his uncle in Montgomery county.

Edward Spangler.

SPANGLER appears to have been Booth's right hand man during the awful scene at the theatre. SPANGLER was employed as the carpenter of the theatre. He is about forty years of age and of a mild looking face.

Samuel Arnold.

ARNOLD is a native of Maryland, and originally entered the plot to carry off President LINCOLN and immure him in some out of the way house or take him to Richmond. He seems to have hesitated about committing murder and was anxious for BOOTH to get the consent of JEFF. DAVIS to the crime, before he lent it his countenance. He is a young man of some 28 years of age and of medium height.

SAM. ARNOLD (who was arrested at Fortress Monroe), as well as other witnesses, states that one plan was to capture Mr. Lincoln some night between the War Department and White House, where he was accustomed to go alone late at night. He was then to be hurried down through the garden of the White House, thence to what is known as the old Van Ness house on Seventeenth street, near the confluence of Tyber and Potomac rivers.

This house is built near the old homestead of David Burns, a Scotchman, whose plantation embraced about one-third of Washington City. He grew rich from the sales of land. About the year 1820, General Van Ness built a house on the old homestead. It is a large brick commodious house, two stories and a half high. The partition walls all run to the same depth as cellar walls. At some subsequent period the cellars made by these walls were dug out, and one of them has a trap door going down through the floor, and was formerly used for a wine cellar. Another was used for a slave prison, and still another for an ice house.

On the death of Van Ness, fifteen years ago, it was sold to one Thomas Green, who owned the Warrenton Springs in Virginia. Green's sons were all in the rebel army.

Had they been able to have gotten Mr. LINCOLN across the Potomac and into Moseby's hands, all well. But if not then he could have been secreted in this house.

There are about two acres around the house filled with high trees and close shrubbery, with a high brick wall along the street, shutting the house from the street, and any cries from it would be effectually drowned long before reaching the street.

Several times during the war was this house an object of suspicion, and several arrests were made there, but not until the murder were the secret vaults and passages found and the character of the place ascertained.

Michael O'Loughlin.

O'LOUGHLIN was designated to be the assassin of Lieut.-Genl. GRANT. He has much of Booth's appearance, with black hair, mustache and imperial. He does not look like one who would be selected for such desperate work.

TRIAL OF THE ASSASSINS AND CONSPIRATORS.

A Description of the Conspirators.

REVERDY JOHNSON AND GEN. HARRIS.

Examination of Witnesses

THE TESTIMONY IN DETAIL.

WASHINGTON, May 13.—The court is held at the Old Penitentiary, in an upper room, white walled, with two windows east and north. These windows are ironed with flat bars along the wall.

On the west side, on raised seats, were Dr. Mudd, David C. Harold, Lewis Payne, Edward Spangler, of Ford's Theatre, Michael O. Laughlin, Atzeroth and Samuel Arnold. Sitting outside the paling was Mrs. Surratt, leaning on a small green-baized table. Beyond her, on the other side of the table, near the northern windows, sat the counsel for the accused, Thomas Ewing, son of the Ohio ex-Senator, Attorney Stone, Walter S. Cox, Reverdy Johnson, Aiken and Clampet.

Running east and west, beside the northern wall, there is a long table, also covered with green baize. At this sit the Court.

Dr. Mudd looked calm, collected and attentive, leaning on the railing that surrounded him as if to relieve his wrists from the weight of the handcuffs that encumbered them.

Arnold was restless, raising his hand to his hair with a nervous twitching, and constantly varying the direction of his looks, now glancing from face to face, then bowing his head on his hand, which was supported on his knees. His handcuffs were somewhat peculiar, not being connected as usually a chain, but by a bar about eight inches in length.

Payne, dressed in grey woolen shirt and dark pants, seemed more intent in trying to obtain a full view of the sunny landscape through the barred windows than of confining his attention to the details of the proceedings. As he looked, a strange, listless dreaminess pervaded his face. His dark hair, irregularly parted, hung over his forehead and often clouded his dark blue eyes. His thick, somewhat protruding lips were as if glued together. His legs were crossed, and his ironed hands rested on the knee of the upper one. Laughlin was observant of every move in the Court. He leaned back, with his head against the wall, fully exposing his broad but not high forehead, crowned with a full bushy head of black hair.

Atzeroth, a man some five feet six or seven inches in height, might have been taken, had it not been for his manacles, as a mere spectator. He possesses a style of face most common in southern Germany, though his beard and hair are of a reddish sand color, and his eyes light. A police officer sat beside each prisoner.

Mrs. Surratt has already been correctly described; a stout, buxom widow, fitting Falstaff's ideal, fair, fat and forty; although it is ascertained she is far beyond that period of life, having nearly reached her grand climacteric. She was dressed in black, and looked a little flushed, but we failed to notice that cold, cruel gleam in her grey eyes, which some of the gentlemen of the press have attributed to her.

The court engaged in the trial of the conspirators altered one of its rules to-day, so as to admit reporters for the press. Hon. Reverdy Johnson appeared as counsel for Mrs. Surratt, whereupon an objection was raised to him by General Harris, and which was withdrawn after an earnest debate on both sides.

Detectives Lee and the clerk of the Kirkwood House, and the present proprietor of the house heretofore occupied by the Surratt family and others, were examined with reference to this house, and in relation to arms having been deposited there in order to facilitate the escape of the assassins. The court was in session until a late hour.

An Objection to Reverdy Johnson.

The first testimony taken in the case of the several parties arraigned, was a portion of that which the Government deems it necessary for the present to withhold from the public. When that testimony had all been rendered, Brigadier-General T. M. Harris stated that he rose to object to the admission of Mr. Reverdy Johnson as a counsel pleading before the Court, and that he did this upon the ground that in an opinion delivered by Mr. Johnson, that gentleman had expressed his disregard of the sanctity of an oath. General Harris then stated that he referred to the opinion expressed in a letter written by Mr. Johnson at the time of the Maryland Convention held with reference to the adoption of the new constitution of that State.

Mr. Johnson's Reply.

Mr. Johnson replied as follows:—It is difficult to speak to that objection; to speak as I feel, without having that opinion before me. That opinion cannot be tortured by any reasonable man to any such conclusions. There is not a member of this Court, either the President or the member who objects, who recognizes the obligation of an oath more absolutely than I do, and there is nothing in my life, from the commencement to the present time, which would induce me for a moment to avoid a comparison in all moral respects between myself and any member of this Court. In this Rebellion, which has broken down so many moral principles, it has been my pride to stand by the Government from the beginning to the present moment, and to take every obligation which the Government thought it necessary to impose, and to do my duty faithfully in every department of the public service as well as in my individual capacity.

If such an objection was made in the Senate of the United States, where I am known, I forbear to say how it would be treated, because I know the terms in which it would be decided. I have too long gone through too many trials, and rendered the country such services as my abilities enabled me, and the votes of the people in whose midst I am living, for me, particularly, to tolerate for a moment, come from whom it may, such an aspersion on my moral character. I am glad it is made now when I have arrived at that period of life when it would be unfit to notice it in any other way; but I repeat there is not one word of truth in the construction of what has been given in the opinion already referred to. I have it not by me, but I recollect substantially what it was.

The convention called to form a new Constitution for the State was called under the authority of an act of the Legislature of Maryland, and under that alone. By that Legislature their proceedings were to be submitted to the then legal voters of the State. The convention thought that they were authorized themselves to impose, not only as an authority to vote what was not imposed by the existing Constitution and laws, but that they had a right to admit to vote those who are prohibited from voting by said Constitution and laws; and I said, in company with the whole bar of the State, and what the whole bar throughout the Union would have said, that to that extent they had usurped the authority under which alone they were authorized to act, and that, so far, the proceeding was a nullity.

They had prescribed this oath, and all the opinion said, or was intended to say, was that to take this oath voluntarily was not a craven submission to usurped authority, but was necessary in order to enable the citizen to protect his rights under the then Constitution, and that there was no moral harm in taking an oath which the Convention had no authority to impose. I make it no reflection on any member of this Court when I, at least able to form as correct an opinion as any of the gentlemen around this table.

I am here at the instance of that lady (pointing to Mrs. Surratt), whom I never saw or heard of till yesterday, she being a Maryland lady, protesting her innocence to me, because I deem it a right, due to the character of the profession to which I belong, and of which you are members, that she should not go undefended. I was to do it voluntarily, without compensation. The law prohibits me from receiving compensation, but if it had not, understanding her condition, I should never have dreamed of refusing upon the ground of her inability to make compensation. I am now volunteering to do what evidence will justify me in doing for this lady, who is now being tried for her life. My detestation of every one concerned in this nefarious plot, carried out with such fiendish malice, is as great as that of any member of this Court. I am not here to protect any one who, when the evidence is heard, I shall deem to have been guilty—not even her.

Will the honorable member of the Court who has thought it proper or believed it his duty to make this objection, or the President, who said that if the honorable member had not made it he should have done so, will they understand that I am not pleading here for anything personal to myself? I stand too firmly settled in my own convictions of honor and in my sense of duty, public and private, to be alarmed at all at any individual opinion that may be expressed. I ask the Court to decide, and I have no doubt they shall decide as seems best to them, and if it shall be such a decision as the President of the Court sees inclined to make, I can take care of myself in the future.

Remarks of Brigadier-General Harris.

I trust it is not necessary I should assure you nor the gentleman to whom I feel it my duty to object, as counsel before this Court, that I should say that I desire, above all things, not to do injustice to any man, and I can assure you that, in doing what I feel it my duty to do, I have not been influenced by any personal considerations. Though I never had the pleasure of acquaintance of the gentleman to whom I object, I have known him long as an eminent public man of our country of whom I must say, that my impressions have been of a very favorable character. But in regard to the matter of the objection, if my recollection serves me right, I must contend that it is well founded.

It is due to the gentleman that I should say that I have made this objection simply from the recollection of this letter, which I read, perhaps, nearly a year ago, and of the effects of that letter upon the vote of that State. Now, if I understand the remarks of that gentleman in explanation of this "thing," I cannot say that it removes the difficulty, from my mind, at least. I understand him to say that the doctrine he taught the people of his State was that because the Convention had framed and required the taking of an oath as a qualification to the right of suffrage, which was unconstitutional and illegal, in his opinion, and, therefore, it had no moral binding force, and that people might take it and then go and vote without regard to the subject matter of that oath. If that does not justify my conclusion, I confess I am unable to understand the English language.

Now I wish the gentleman to understand me, that in regard to his ability to decide a legal question I do not intend to enter into any controversy. He remarked to the Court rather boastingly that he is as well able as any member of this Court to judge in regard to any legal point, but this is not a point of law. It is a question of ethics and of the morality of the thing; of the sanctity of an oath voluntarily taken, which I understand he taught his people might be set aside as having no force, because the convention had transcended its authority, and done something it had no right to do, and that consequently they might voluntarily take this oath to entitle them to go and vote without considering it to have any binding force; and I am much mistaken in the history of those days, and in the effect of that opinion upon the vote of that State if it was not so considered.

A large number cast their suffrages under that ethical doctrine taught by the gentleman against whom I have objected; but as I was about to remark, I would be sorry to do injustice to the gentleman, or any other man, and having made my objection simply from my recollection of this letter, it is, perhaps, due to the gentleman and the members of this Court, that the letter itself should be submitted to the scrutiny of the Court. I may be wrong; if so, none can be more ready than myself to acknowledge that fact.

Rejoinder of Mr. Johnson.

Mr. Johnson said:—I do not intend to make an extended reply to the gentleman's remarks. As to my boasting about my competency to decide any legal question, the gentleman is mistaken. I said as competent as any of the members of this court, they not being lawyers. Now the honorable member seems to suppose that because I said there was no harm in taking an oath, that I meant there would be no harm in breaking it, if it was taken. If that is the meaning of the terms, I am better informed in regard to it now than I ever was before. I have already said to the court that I had no idea of using them for any such purpose; that according to my interpretation of them they admitted of no such construction. When a gentleman is dealing with gentlemen, even if the words he used were liable to misrepresentation, his explanation of the intended meaning of them is held to be sufficient.

I submit that amongst gentlemen, and I hope I am not boasting that in that capacity I may consider myself equal to any member of this Court, I repeat, when, as a gentleman, I say they were not used for any such design as imputed to them, the gentleman to whom the explanation is given will not be disposed to repeat that they were in point of fact used with that design. Now as to the effect upon the people of Maryland, I don't know where the honorable member is from, but he is not a citizen of our State, I suppose.

General Harris—I am a citizen of Western Virginia.

Mr. Johnson—I supposed you were not a citizen of Maryland. I was about to say, whoever supposed, and I hope he will not repeat the letter, that the people of Maryland can be induced by individual opinion to take an oath in order to violate it is under a very great misapprehension. We have had, what I regret, hundreds and hundreds of our citizens who have left our borders and participated in the Rebellion; but hundreds and hundreds also of those who remained have proved true to their flag, and have evinced their loyalty upon the battle-field with their blood, and with their lives; and in the relation in which I stand to the people of Maryland, I may be permitted to say, they are the equals, morally and patriotically, of the people of Western Virginia.

There were other topics involved in the Constitution which influenced the votes of those who voted against it, to which it is unnecessary and useless here to refer. But I deny, and deny implicitly, that there was a single man who voted because of that opinion, or who took the oath with a view to vote, thereby to violate the obligation. But as a legal question it is something new to me. The objection made, if well founded in fact, is well founded in law. Are the members of this Court to measure the moral character of every counsel who may appear before them? Is that their function? What influence has that upon the Court by which their judgment could be led astray. His client may suffer

TRIAL OF THE ASSASSINS AT WASHINGTON.

from the possible prejudice it may create in the minds of the Court.

But how can the Court suffer? Who gives to the Court the jurisdiction to decide upon the moral character of the counsel who may appear before them? Who makes them the arbiters of public morality, or of my professional morality? What authority have they under their commission to rule me out, or any other counsel out, upon the ground that he does not recognize the validity of an oath, even if they believed it? But I put myself on no such grounds. I deem myself, in all moral respects, to be the equal of any member of this tribunal. They may dispose of the question as they please. It will not touch me.

Response of Mr. Harris.

The Court will understand me as not intending to cast any reflection upon the people of Maryland in regard to loyalty and morality, or in regard to patriotism. I am proud to say that they have a good record in this great contest through which our country has just passed. While it is true of Maryland. I am sorry to say it is equally true of my State, that many joined the Rebellion, and have made for themselves a terrible record. But the circumstances of this case were rather peculiar. The people of Maryland were about to vote upon an alteration in the fundamental law of the State, upon the adoption of a new constitution—a constitution which made some radical changes in regard to the social status of the people of Maryland.

Slavery was about to be blotted out, that was the purpose, and it is an unfortunate fact that that portion of the people interested in the proposed change were, as a general thing, the disloyal portion, and it was in reference to the effect which this opinion expressed by the honorable gentleman in the letter referred to had upon that vote, and upon the action of this portion of the people, that my objection was in part founded, for it did seem as though they understood it as I did. In regard to the right of the court to inquire into the moral standing of counsel we have no such right, but the order constituting this Court makes provision for the prisoners or the accused having the aid of counsel. The provisions in reference to that matter is that gentlemen shall exhibit a certificate of having taken the oath, or shall take it in presence of the Court, and thus the obligation of an oath is here a special question.

If it does not appear that he ignores the moral obligation, and we admit him, it defeats the very provisions of the order, hence I think that it is proper in me, as a member of the Court, to found an objection of that character upon such grounds, whether the objection is sustained or not. The gentleman disclaims any such intention, but that is a tacit admission that the language of that letter may have been unguarded, that it may have had the effect supposed, though it was not in accordance with the intention of his mind in writing it. It is an unfortunate thing if he wrote a letter so misconstrued, but if it was not the intention of the writer, that of course must exonerate him. He disavows having any such intention, and claims for himself a moral character, which he is not ashamed to put in comparison with that of any member of the Court.

Now it is not my purpose to measure characters at all, but simply to bring forward an objection. I felt it my duty to bring, and nothing else, an objection founded on the understanding I had of the letter referred to. I was sorry to have to do it, but I did it in no spirit of personal ill will or bad feeling. I was sorry that it was my duty to do such a thing, but I could not do anything else with the impression I had on my mind, and he, as an honorable gentleman, will understand what I mean by this. He understands, too, what the force of conscientious convictions must be, and that if a man acts from principle, this thing will occasionally impose upon him some unpleasant duties. His disavowal of any such intention as I derived from memory of his letter I am bound to take; but this I must insist upon, that there was some ground for the objection.

Reply of Mr. Johnson.

Mr. President, one word more. All I propose to say is that the order confers no authority to refuse me admission, on the grounds claimed by the honorable member, because you have no authority to administer the oath to me. I have taken it in the Senate of the United States, in the Circuit Court of my State, in the Supreme Court of the United States, and I am a practitioner in all the courts in nearly all the States; and it would be a little singular if one who has a right to appear before the Supreme Court of the land, and who belongs to the body that creates courts-martial, shall not have the right to appear before courts-martial.

Major-General Hunter.—Mr. Johnson has made an intimation as to holding members of the court personally responsible.

Mr. Johnson—I made no such intimation, nor intended it.

Major-General Hunter—I shall say no more than I was going to say. The day had passed when freemen from the North were to be bullied and insulted by the humbug chivalry of the South.

The Court here took a recess for half an hour, and when it returned, went into secret session, in order to deliberate upon the objection so lengthily discussed.

The Court being reopened, General Harris stated that he desired to withdraw his objection, as he considered Mr. Johnson's explanation a satisfactory removal of the grounds on which the objection was founded.

Mr. Johnson expressed his desire and willingness to take the oath, but the Court deemed it unnecessary, and the oath was not taken.

The Testimony.

A. W. Lee, being sworn, testified as follows:
Q. Do you belong to the police force? A. Yes sir, to the military police.
Q. State whether at any time you examined the room of Atzeroth, at the Kirkwood House. A. Yes sir. I was ordered by Major O'Beirne to go into the principal part of the building and see how the house was situated. I made the examination, and told him one could get from the roof to a stairway in the back of the building which would admit him into any part of the building. I told the Major the circumstances.
Q. When was that? A. (Here the witness looked at a paper.) It was the night of the 15th of April. I then went, and while there a friend came to me and said there was a rather suspicious looking man who had taken a room there the day previous, and I had better go and look. I went, and found in the register, badly written, the name of Atzeroth—E. A. Atzeroth—made it out; but in fact nobody could make it out until I asked the proprietor, and he made it out on the register.
Q. Where did you go after that? A. I went up stairs to the room, and saw one of the clerks, and I asked him to go up to the room with me; found the door locked, and he said the party had taken the key with him; I went to one of the proprietors and asked if he had any objections to my going into the room. If we could find a key to fit it; he said no; but though he tried his keys, we could not get in. I asked him if we might burst in the door; he said he had no objection, and we burst the door open; when we went in I saw a coat hanging on the wall.

Colonel Burnett here ordered a bundle to be passed to the witness. This bundle, on being opened by the Colonel, was found to be a coat, rolled in which were sundry small articles.

Witness—That coat was hanging upon the wall, just in that way as you go in, on the left-hand side. That's the coat, sir.
Q. State what examination you made of the room? A. Well. I saw that coat right opposite the bed stood on the right; I went towards the bed, and underneath the pillow or bolster found a revolver bound with brass.

Here a pistol was shown to witness, passing through the hands of Mr. Johnson, who remarked, "It is loaded."
Witness—I then went down stairs to find Major O'Beirne, and we went up stairs to the room again; I took the coat down and found this room and that also.
Q. In the pockets? A. Yes sir.
Q. Look inside that book and see what was written in it? A. Yes sir; there was an account, too, on the Ontario Bank of four hundred and fifty-five dollars; I then put my hand in the pocket again and found this handkerchief with the name of Mary E. Booth on it; I then pulled out this other handkerchief, and had some difficulty in making out the mark, but I think it is F. E. Nelson or F. A. Nelson upon it; I found this handkerchief with M. H. on the corner; I got this new pair of gauntlets; I labeled all these things myself, and I got these three boxes of Colt's cartridges.
Q. Do they fit the pistol? A. I never loaded the pistol, sir; I don't know; I found this piece of licorice and this brush.
Q. This writing was in the back of that book, Mr J. Wilkes Booth, in account with the Bank of Ontario, four hundred and fifty dollars? A. Yes, sir; I then got that spur and pair of socks; that is all I got out of the pockets.
Q. Do you remember the number of the room? A. It was room 126, sir.
Q. Was it over where Vice-President Johnson was at that time?

The witness here entered into an explanation of the locality totally unintelligible, but upon being shown a plan or sketch by Mr. Ben. Pittman, seemed to recognize the situation of the room. This plan, however, was not admitted in evidence.

A. I went around the room, took up the carpets, took out the washstand, moved the stove and made a thorough search, and then went to the bed again; took off the clothes piece by piece, and after I came down underneath the sheets and mattrasses I got those bowie knives.

Here a knife was shown the witness, and handed to the various members of the Court. It was long and stylus-shaped, like that used by Booth, horn handled and sheathed in red leather.
Q. You did not see him in the room yourself? A. No sir; he had left the day before; the clerk who was there said he would recognize the man.

Q. Go and get him after you have been examined, with or without a subpœna; bring him as soon as you can.

Here the examination in chief, which had been conducted by Judge Holt, Advocate-General of the United States, was closed.

Cross-examination—Q. What is your business? A. Detective officer of the Board of Enrollment of the District of Columbia, of which Major O'Beirne is Provost Marshal.

Q. How long have you followed the business? A. I have been in service ever since I left New York on the commencement of the war; I was in the Ninety-fifth New York Volunteers.

Q. How long have you been a detective in Washington? A. Ever since the burning of Aquia Creek; I had been discharged as a volunteer from the Ninety-fifth New York.

Q. You mentioned a conversation with some one in reference to a suspicious character at the Kirkwood House. Where did you first see the man who told you his name? A. I first saw him in the house.

Q. Was he a clerk? A. A night watchman, I think.

Q. What was his precise language to you? A. He said to me there was a suspicious, bad, villainous looking fellow came into the place and took a room, and he didn't like the appearance of him.

Q. When was it that person had come and taken a room? A. I think it was the day before.

Q. Can you say for certain? A. No sir; I would not be positive about it; I think to the best of my knowledge it was the day before.

Q. Did he describe his appearance to you? A. Yes sir, he did.

Q. Repeat his description. A. I don't think I could, as he described it to me; I don't recollect; I think he said he had a grey coat on.

Q. Have you ever seen, to your knowledge, Mr. Atzeroth? A. I don't know that I have ever seen him; I have seen most everybody knocking around about Washington; I don't know as I ever saw him to know him by name; can't say that I have or have not.

Q. What first brought you to the Kirkwood House? A. I was at home eating my supper; Mr. Cunningham came after me, one of our force; no, I had gone out after supper and I think I met him a square from the house; says he, you are wanted immediately at the Kirkwood House; I went, and there was Major O'Beirne; I found men all about there, detailed for duty to protect the President, or at that time the Vice President.

Q. Describe the appearance of the man who gave you the information. A. The man was about your build. He may be a little heavier, but about your height.

Q. How old does he look to be? A. Somewhere about your age.

Q. What is my age? A. I take you to be about thirty.

Q. Don't you know his name? A. No sir, I don't.

Q. Now will you describe the relative position of Johnson's room and the room in which you found this coat?

The witness here entered into a series of gesticulations and explanations, from which neither court, counsels or reporters could derive any understanding of his meaning or the locality he sought to describe.

Q. Did you find any signature of Atzeroth in the room? A. I did not.

Q. What made you think it was his room? A. Because it said so on the register. It was No. 126.

Q. Then you have no other evidence except the register? A. No sir, I don't know as I have any other evidence.

Q. That is all.

Testimony of Lewis J. Weichman.

Q. State to the Court if you know James H. Surratt. A. I do. I first made his acquaintance in the fall of 1852, in St. Charles county, Maryland, or in the fall of 1859, I should say.

Q. How long were you together then? A. Until 1862; I renewed my acquaintance with him in January, 1863.

Q. In this city? A. Yes sir.

Q. When did you begin to board at the house of his mother, the prisoner here? A. On the 1st of November, 1864.

Q. Where is her house? A. On H street, No. 541.

Q. See if that is Mrs. Surratt sitting by you there? A. Yes sir, that is Mrs. Surratt.

Q. Will you state when you first made your acquaintance with Dr. Mudd. A. It was on or about the 15th of January, 1865.

Q. State under what circumstances. A. I was passing down Seventh street, with Surratt, and when nearly opposite Odd Fellows' Hall, some one called out, "Surratt, Surratt." On looking around Surratt recognized an old acquaintance of his, of Charles county, Maryland; he introduced Dr. Mudd to me, and Dr. Mudd introduced Mr. Booth, who was in company with him, to both of us; they were coming up Seventh street and we were coming down.

Q. By the Court. Do you mean J. Wilkes Booth? A. Yes sir, J. Wilkes Booth.

Q. Where did you go to then? A. He invited us to his room at the National Hotel.

Q. Who? A. Booth: he told us to be seated, and ordered segars and wine to the room for four, and Dr. Mudd then went out to the passage and called Booth out and had a private conversation with him. Booth and the Doctor then came in and called Surratt out, leaving me alone.

Q. How long? A. Fifteen or twenty minutes.

Q. Do you know the nature of their conversation? A. No I was sitting on a lounge, near the window; they came in at last, and Mudd came near me on the sofee. and apologized for their private conversation, stating he had private business with Booth, who wished o purchase his farm.

Q. Did you see any manuscript of any sort on the table? A. No. Booth at one time cut the back of an envelope and made marks on it with a pencil.

Q. Was he writing on it? A. I should not consider it writing, but marks alone; they were seated at the table in the centre of the room.

Q. Did you see the marks? A. No sir; just saw motion of the pencil; Booth also came to me and apologized, and said he wished to purchase Mudd's farm; Mudd had previously stated to me that he did not care to sell his farm to Booth, as he was not willing to give him enough for it.

Q. You didn, t hear a word spoken between them in regard to the farm? A. No sir; I did not know the nature of their conversation at all.

Q. Did I understand you to say that you did not hear any of their conversation at the table, but only saw the motion of the pencil? A. Yes sir.

Q. You continued to board at Mrs. Surratt's? A. I boarded there up to the time of the assassination.

Q. After this interview at the National, state whether Booth called frequently at Mrs. Surratt's? A. Yes sir.

Q. Whom did he call to see? A. He generally called for John H. Surratt, and, in his absence, called for Mrs. Surratt

Q. Were those interviews held apart, or in presence of other persons? A. Always apart; I have been in company with Booth in the parlor with Surratt, but Booth has taken Surratt to a room up stairs, and engage in private conversation up there; he would say "John, can you spare me a word? come up stairs;" they would go and engage in private conversation, which would be a two or three hours.

Q. Did the same thing occur with Mrs. Surratt? A. Yes.

Q. Have you ever seen the prisoner Atzeroth? A. I have sir.

Q. Do you recognize him here? A. Yes sir; that is he.

Q. Have you ever seen him at Mrs. Surratt's? A. He came there about three weeks after I formed the acquaintance of Booth.

Q. Who did he inquire for? A. For Mr. Surratt, John H.

Q. Did you ever see him with Booth there, or only with Surratt? A. I have never seen him in the house with Booth.

Q. How often did he call? A. Some ten or fifteen times.

Q. What was the name by which he was known by the young Ladies of the house? A. They understood that he came from Port Tobacco, and instead of calling him by his own name, they gave him the nickname of Port Tobacco.

Q. Did you ever see him on the street? A. Yes sir. I have see him on the corner of Seventh and Pennsylvania avenue; it was about the time Booth played Pescara, in the Apostate; Booth had given Surratt two complimentary tickets, on that occasion, and we went down and met Atzeroth; we told him where we were going, and he said he was going too, and at the theatre we met David C. Harold.

Q. Do you know Harold? Do you see him here? A. Yes sir.

Here Harold bent forward, and laughingly inclined toward the witness.

Witness—We also met another gentleman there, named Hollahan, who stopped in the house; we met him in the theatre, and we remained until the play was over, and the five of us left together and went together as far as the corner of Tenth and E streets, but on turning around Surratt noticed that Atzeroth and Harold were not following, and I went and found them in the restaurant adjoining the theatre, talking confidentially with Booth; on my approaching they separated, and then we took a drink, and there was a gentleman there whose face I remember; we left and jo ned the other two gentlemen, and went to another restaurant to have some oysters.

Q. Do you know where Surratt left his horses in this city? A. He stated to me that he had two horses, and that he kept them at Howard's stable, on G street, between Sixth and Seventh.

Q. Did you ever see Atzeroth there? A. Yes, sir, on the day of the assassination.

Q. What time was it? A. About half-past two o'clock.

Q. What was he doing? A. He seemed to be hiring a horse; I had been sent by Mrs. Surratt to hire a buggy; when I got there I saw Atzeroth, and asked what he wanted; he said he wanted to hire a horse; he asked Brooks if he could have a horse, and he told him he could not; then we left, and both of us went as far as the Post Office; I had a letter to draw out, and after that he went off towards Tenth street.

Q. Was this horse that was kept there Surratt's or Booth's? A. I will state that on the Tuesday previous to the assassination I was also sent to the National Hotel to see Booth, and get his buggy for Mrs. Surratt. She wished me to drive to her into the country. Booth said he had sold his buggy, but he would give me ten dollars, and I should hire a buggy for Mrs. Surratt, and spoke of the horses he kept at Brooks' stables. I then said they were Surratt's; he said they "were mine."

Q. Did Booth give you ten dollars? A. Yes, sir.
Q. Did you drive her out? A. Yes, sir.
Q. To what point? A. To Surrattsville; we left at ten and reached there at twelve; that was on Tuesday, the 11th.
Q. Did you return that day? A. Yes sir; we only remained half an hour; Mrs. Surratt said she went for the purpose of seeing Mrs. Notby, who owed her money.

Q. You continued to board at Mrs. Surratt's? A. I boarded there up to the time of the assassination.
Q. After the interview at the National, state whether Booth called frequently at Mrs. Surratt's. A. Yes sir.
Q. Whom did he call to see? A. He generally called for John H. Surratt, and in his absence called for Mrs. Surratt.
Q. Were these interviews held apart or in presence? A. Always apart; I have been in company with Booth in the parlor, with Surratt, but Booth has taken Surratt to a room up stairs and engaged in private conversation up there; he would say, "John, can you spare a word?—come up stairs." They would go and engage in private conversation, which would last two or three hours.

Q. Did the same thing ever occur with Mrs. Surratt? A. Yes, sir.
Q. Have you ever seen the prisoner Atzerott? A. I have, sir.
Q. Do you recognize him here? Yes, sir, that is he.
Q. State whether on the following Friday, that is the day of the assassination, you drove Mrs. Surratt into the country? A. Yes sir.
Q. Where did you drive to? A. To Surrattsville; we arrived there about half-past four.
Q. Did she stop at the house of Mr. Lloyds? A. Yes sir; she went into the parlor.
Q. What time did you have to return? A. About half-past six.
Q. Can you go down there in two hours? A. When the roads are good you could easily get down there in two hours.
Q. State whether you remember, some time in the month of March, a man calling at Mrs. Surratt's, and giving himself the name of Wood, and inquiring for John H. Surratt? A. Yes, I opened the door for him. He asked if Mr. Surratt was in; I told him no, but I introduced him to the family; he had then expressed a wish to see Mrs. Surratt.
Q. Do you recognize him here? A. Yes, sir; that's he; that's the man Payne; he called himself Wood then.
Q. How long did he remain with Mrs. Surratt. A. He stopped in the house all night, and had supper served to him in my room; they brought him supper from the kitchen.
Q. When was that? A. As nearly as I can recollect, it was about eight weeks previous to the assassination, I have no exact knowledge of the date.
Q. Did he bring a package? A. Yes, sir.
Q. How was he dressed? A. He had a black overcoat on and a black frock coat with grey pants at the time.
Q. Did he remain till the next morning? A. Yes; he left in the earliest train for Baltimore.
Q. Do you remember whether, some weeks after, the same man called again? A. Yes. I should think it was about three weeks, and I again went to the door, I then showed him into the parlor, and again asked his name. That time he gave the name of Payne.
Q. Did he then have an interview with Mrs. Surratt? A. Miss Fitzpatrick, myself and Mrs. Surratt were present; he remained about three days, and represented himself to be a Baptist preacher; he said he had been in Baltimore about a week, had taken the oath of allegiance, and was going to become a good loyal citizen.
Q. Did you hear any explanation why he said he was a Baptist minister? A. No; Miss Surratt said he was a queer looking Baptist preacher.
Q. Did they seem to recognize him as the Wood of former days? A. Yes, sir; in conversation one of the ladies called him Woods, and then I recollected that on his previous visit he had given the name of Wood.
Q. How was he dressed then? A. In a complete suit of grey.
Q. Did he have any baggage? A. Yes sir; he had a linen coat and two linen shirts.
Q. Did you observe any trace of disguise or preparations for disguises? A. One day I found a false moustache on the table in my room; I threw it into a little toilet box, and Payne searched for it and inquired for his moustache; I was sitting in the chair and did not say anything; I retained it ever since; it was found in my baggage among a box of paints I had in my trunk.
Q. Did you see him and Surratt together by themselves? A. Yes; it was on the same day; I went to the third story and found them sitting on a bed playing with bowie knives.
Q. Did you see any other weapons? A. Yes, sir. Two revolvers and four sets of new spurs. Here the witness was shown a spur and identified it as one of those he had then seen, saying, "Yes, these are the spurs, three of those were in my room."
Q. By the Court. That is the spur found in Atzeroth's room?
The witness was then shown the knife which had been identified by Mr. Lee as the one found in Atzeroth's room. But witness stated that he did not recognize it, and that the knife that Payne had on the bed was a smaller one.
Q. They had a brace of pistols, did you say? A. They had two long navy revolvers.
Here the witness was shown the pistol produced during Lee's examination and said "that looks like one of them."
Q. Was the barrel round or octagonal? A. Octagonal.
Q. Do you remember having gone with Surratt to the Herndon House to hire a room? A. Yes, sir.
Q. What time was that? A. It must have been the 19th of March.
Q. For whom did he wish to rent this room? A. Well, he went and inquired for Mrs. Mary Murray, and when she came, he had a private interview with her, but said that she did not seem to comprehend, though he thought that a Miss Ward had spoken to her already on the subject, and he said to Mrs. Murray, Miss Ward may have spoken to you about the matter of hiring a room for a delicate gentleman, and Mr. Surratt added he would like to have the room by the following Monday, as the gentleman wanted to take possession on that day; I think that was the Monday previous; it was the 27th of March.
Q. The name of the person was not given? A. No, sir, no name was mentioned at all.
Q. Did you afterwards learn that Payne was at that house? A. Yes, sir. I met Atzeroth on the street, and asked him where he was going? He stated that he was going to see Payne. I asked him, is it Payne that is at the Herndon House, and he said yes.
Q. Did you ever meet Harold at Surratt's? A. Once.
Q. Where else did you see him? A. I met him on the occasion of the visit to the theatre, when Booth played "Pescara;" also, at Mrs. Surratt's, in the Spring of 1863, when I first made her acquaintance; he was there with some musicians who were serenading some county officers after an election; I next met him in 1864, at church; these are the only times I recollect.
Q. Do you know either of the prisoners, Arnold or Laughlin? A. No, sir.
Q. What knowledge, if any, have you of Surratt's having gone to Richmond? A. About the 23d of March —no, it was the 17th. There was a woman named Slader came to the house; she went to Canada and reder turned on Saturday, the 23d of March. Mr. Surratt drove her into the county, about eight o'clock in the morning, and I understood that he had gone to Richmond with Mrs. Slader. This Mrs. Slader was to meet a man named Howe, but this man was captured and could not take her.
Q. She was a blockade runner? A. Yes, sir, or the bearer of despatches.
Q. Did Mrs. Surratt tell you so? A. Yes, sir.
Q. When did he return? A. He returned on the third of April.
Q. Do you know of his having brought any gold with him? A. Yes, he had some nine or eleven twenty dollar gold pieces, and he had some greenbacks, about fifty dollars; he gave forty dollars in gold to Mr. Hollihan, and Mr. Hollihan gave him sixty dollars in greenbacks; he remained in the house about an hour, and told me he was going to Montreal; he asked me, however, to go and take some oysters with him, and we went down to the corner of Seventh street and Pennsylvania avenue, and took some oysters.
Q. And he left? A. Yes, he left that evening, and since that time I have not seen him.
Q. Have you seen any letter from him? A. Yes. I saw a letter to his mother, dated April 12th: it was received here on the 11th, I also saw another written to Miss Ward. I did not see the date, but the receipt of the letter was prior to the one of his mother.
Q. Did he have any conversation with you, as he passed through, about the fall of Richmond? A. Yes, he told me he did not believe it; he said he had seen Benjamin and Davis, and they had told him that it would not be evacuated, and he seemed to be incredulous.
Q. Have you been to Canada since? A. Yes, sir.
Q. What did you there learn of Surratt? A. That he had arrived at Montreal on the 6th, and returned for the States on the 12th, returning again on the 18th, and engaging rooms at the St. Lawrence Hotel. He left the St. Lawrence that night at half-past ten. He was seen to leave the house of a Mr. Butterfield, in company with three others, in a wagon.

Objected to, and the statement not insisted on as a part of the record.

Q. Do you remember earlier in April that Mrs. Surratt sent for you, and asked you to give Mr. Booth notice that she wished to see him? A. Yes, sir.

Q. What was the message? A. Merely that she wished to see him.
Q. Did she say on private business, or use any expression of that kind? A. Yes sir.
Q. Did you deliver the message? A. I did.
Q. What did Booth say? A. He said he would come to the house immediately, or as soon as he could.
Q. What time was this? A. Some time in April; it was the second; when she sent me I found in Booth's room Mr. McColiom, the actor; I communicated to Booth her desire, and he did come in the evening of the 2d.
Q. State whether he called on the evening of the 14th of April, the day of the assassination? A. Yes, sir; about half-past two, o'clock, when I was going out at the door I met Mrs. Surratt, speaking to Booth.
Q. Were they alone? A. Yes, sir; they were alone in the parlor.
Q. How long was it after that when you started for the country? A. He didn't remain more than three or four minutes.
Q. And immediately after that you set out for the country? A. Yes, sir.

This examination in chief, like the preceding one, was conducted by General Holt, Judge Advocate of the United States.

Cross examination by Reverdy Johnson:—
Q. How long have you been at Mrs. Surratt's? A. Since December, 1864; Mrs. Surratt at that time had moved to the city from the country; she had rented her farm.
Q. Did you ever live with her in the country? A. No, sir; but I had visited her.
Q. You knew her very well at that time? A. Not very well; I made her acquaintance through her son, who was a school-mate of mine; I sometimes went there, and always experienced kindness and courtesy.
Q. What sort of a house had she in the city here? A. It contained eight rooms—six large and two small.
Q. Was she in the habit of renting her rooms out? A. Yes sir.
Q. Did she furnish board, as well as rooms? A. Yes sir.
Q. Did you say that young Surratt told you in April he was going to Montreal; did you ever know him to go there before? A. No sir; he was there in the winter of 1864 and 1865; sometimes at home and sometimes not; during the winter of 1861, especially during November, he was in the country most of the time; his stay at home was not permanent; he was sometimes away for three or four weeks.
Q. During the winter, was he long enough away to have been in Canada without your knowing it? A. Yes, sir. He could have gone but not returned to the house without my knowledge.
Q. Have you any knowledge that he was then in Canada? A. No sir.
Q. Were you on intimate terms with him? A. Very intimate, indeed.
Q. Did he ever acknowledge to you any purpose to assassinate the President? A. No sir, he stated to me and to his sister, that he was going to Europe on a cotton speculation; he said he had had three thousand dollars advanced to him by a gentleman; that he would go to Liverpool, thence to Nassau, and from there to Matamoros, to find his brother, who was in the Rebel army—in Maurader's army.
Q. Did he go to Texas, before the Rebellion—the brother I mean. A. I don't know; never saw the brother.
Q. Were you in the habit of seeing young Surratt almost every day. A. Yes sir. He would be seated at the same table. We occupied the same room. He slept with me.
Q. During the whole of that period you never heard him intimate it was his intention to assassinate the President? A. No sir.
Q. Did you see anything that led you to believe?
Question was objected to by Colonel Burnett, Assistant Judge Advocate, and was waived by Mr. Johnson.
Q. You never heard him or anybody else say anything about it from the mouth of November to the time of the assassination? A. No sir; he said once he was going with Booth to be an actor, and he said he was going to Richmond; he was well educated, and was a student of divinity.
Q. Were you a student with him? A. Yes sir; I was in the College one year longer than he.
Q. During that period what was his character? A. It was excellent; when he felt he shed tears, and the Superior told him he would always be remembered by those who had charge of the Institution.
Q. When did you first drive into the country with Mrs. Surratt? A. The first occasion was on the 11th of April.
Q. Did she tell you what her object was in going? A. She said to see Nothy, who owed her some money and the interest on it for thirteen years.
Q. Is there such a man? A. Yes sir, there is.
Q. Do you know whether she then saw him? A. When we arrived at the village Mr. Nothy was not there and she told the bar-keeper to send a messenger for him, and he sent one; in the meantime we went to Captain Gwynne's house; remained there two hours

and took dinner; he said he would like to return with us, and he did, to Surrattsville; on returning we found Nothy and she transacted her business with him.
Q. Did you know the man? A. No; Mr. Nott, the barkeeper, said he was in the parlor; I didn't go in.
Q. State what her purpose was in the second visit. A. She said she had received a letter in regard to this money due her by Mr. Nothy.
Q. Was the letter of the same date? A. Yes, and she stated she was compelled again to go to the country, and asked me to drive her down, and I consented.
Q. Did you see the letter? A. No—no, sir; she said that she had received it, and that it required her to go to Surrattsville; that's all I know.
Q. Did you go in a buggy? A. Yes sir.
Q. Any one else go with you? A. No one but I and her went.
Q. Did she take anything with her? A. Only two packages, one with letters concerning her estate, and a smaller package, about six inches in diameter; it looked like two or three saucers wrapped in brown paper; this was put in the bottom of the buggy, and taken out when we got to Surrattsville.
Q. How long did you remain? A. Till half-past six.
Q. What time did you reach home? A. About half-past nine or ten.
Q. When did you hear, or did you hear of the assassination of the President or the attack on Secretary Seward? A. I heard it at three o'clock on Saturday morning.
Q. Who came to the house within the period from your return to the time you heard of the assassination of the President? A. There was some one rung the bell, but who it was I don't know.
Q. Was the bell answered? A. Yes sir.
Q. By whom? A. By Mrs. Surratt.
Q. Was there any one at the door? A. Yes sir; I heard footsteps going into the parlor, and immediately going out.
Q. How long was that after you got back? A. About ten minutes; I was taking supper.
Q. That was before ten o'clock? A. Yes sir.
Q. Then it was before the time of the assassination, which is said to have been about ten o'clock? A. Yes, sir.
Q. Had persons been in the habit of coming for rooms to the house? A. Yes; coming from the country they would stop at the house; she had many acquaintances and was always very hospitable, and they could get rooms as long as they chose.
Q. Did Atzeroth take a room? A. Atzeroth, to my knowledge, stopped in the house but one night.
Q. Did he take a room? A. Not that I know of.
Q. What room did he sleep in? A. On the third story.
Q. Then he had a room there that night? A. Yes.
Q. Did he leave next day? A. Yes.
Q. You saw Paine yourself when he came to the house? Yes sir; the first time he gave the name of Wood; I went to the door, and opened it, and he said he would like to see Mrs. Surratt.
Q. What was his appearance, genteel? A. Yes, he had on a long black coat, and went into the parlor; he acted very politely; asked Mrs. Surratt to play on the piano for him.
Q. Do you know why Atzeroth left the house? A. No sir.
Q. Was there any drinking in the house at the time that Atzeroth was there? A. Yes sir; in February there was a man there named Harland; John Surratt had been in the country, and had returned that evening; he slept that night with Howe.
Q. Was there any drinking in the room occupied by Atzeroth? A. Yes.
Q. Was he noisy? A. No sir.
Q. Have you any knowledge that he was told that he could stop there no longer? A. No.
Q. Did he leave there next day? A. Yes sir; his leaving was owing to the arrival of Surratt; he said he wanted to see John, and having seen him, he left; I heard them afterwards say they did not care to have him brought to the house.
Q. What reason did they give for that? A. Mrs Surratt said she did not care to have such ricks brought to the house; they were no company for her.
Q. He did not come any more? A. Not since the 2d of April.
Q. You say you found upon your own table a false moustache; what was the color of the hair? A. Black.
Q. Was it large? A. About medium sized.
Q. This you put into your own box? A. Yes, in a toilet box and afterwards in a box of paints; it was found in my baggage.
Q. When he came home he seemed to be looking for it? A. Yes, he said "Where is my moustache?"
Q. Why did you not give it to him? A. I suspected, I thought it queer.
Q. But you locked it up? A. Yes, I didn't like to have it seen in my room.
Q. But you could have got it out of your room by giving it to him when he asked for it? A. I thought no honest person had a reason to wear a false moustache. I took it and exhibited it to some of the clerks in the office. I put it on with specs, and was making fun with it.

TRIAL OF THE ASSASSINS AT WASHINGTON.

Q. Can you describe to the court young Surratt's height and general appearance? A. He is about six feet; prominent forehead and very large nose; his eyes are sunk; he has a goatee and very long hair, black.
Q. Do you recollect how he was dressed when he said he was going away? A. He had cream colored pants, grey frock coat and grey vest, and had a shawl thrown over him.
Q. One of those scotch shawls? One of those plaid shawls.
Q. When he returned from Richmond you say he had in his possession twenty gold pieces? A. No, sir; I say nine or eleven twenty-dollar gold pieces.
Q. Did he tell you where he got them? A. No.
Q. He said he had seen Davis and Benjamin; did you understand, by Benjamin, the person who acted as Secretary of State for the Rebel Confederacy? A. All I know is, he said he saw Davis and Benjamin, and that Richmond would not be evacuated.
Q. You didn't ask him, nor did he voluntarily tell you where he got that money? A. No, sir.
Q. Give the date of the letter his mother received from him since he left. A. It was dated Montreal, April 12th, and was received here April 14th.
Q. How did you become acquainted with the date of the letter; by the postmark? A. By the heading of the letter; the letter was written in general terms; it stated that he was much pleased with the Catholic Cathedral, and that he had bought a French pea-jacket and paid ten dollars for it, but that board was too high at the St. Lawrence Hotel (two dollars a day in gold), and that he would go to a private boarding house, or to Toronto.
Q. How was the letter signed? A. John Harrison; his name is John Harrison Surratt.
Q. Was the handwriting disguised? A. It was unusually good for him.
Q. Unusually good, but not disguised? You knew it at once, didn't you? A. Yes, and I remarked to Mrs. Surratt, John is improving in his writing.
Q. Do you know anything about the letter that was received by Miss Ward? A. I only know that a letter was received by her.
Q. Who is Miss Ward? A. A teacher in the school on Tenth street.
Q. What was the date of the letter? A. I did not see that letter, Sir. I was merely told that she received a letter, and came to the house.
Q. Did the letter go to her directly, or through any other person? A. I understand it went directly to her, and was received in the usual course.
Q. Do you know what that letter was about? A. No sir; I merely heard Mrs. Surratt say that Miss Annie Ward had received a letter from John, What it was about I don't know.
Q. You have known Mrs. Surratt since November? A. I have known her since the spring of 1863.
Q. And have been living there since November? A. Yes.
Q. What has been her character since that time? A. Her character was exemplary and ladylike in every particular.
Q. Is she a member of the church? A. Yes sir.
Q. Is she a regular attendant? A. Yes sir.
Q. Of the Catholic Church. A. Yes sir.
Q. Have you been with her to church? A. Every Sunday, sir.
Q. As far as you could judge her character in a religious and moral sense, it was every way exemplary? A. Yes, sir; she went to her duties every two weeks.
Q. Did she go in the morning? A. It was sometimes in the morning and sometimes in the evening.
Q. Was that the case all the time you knew her? A. Yes sir.
Q. If I understand you, then, she was apparently discharging all her duties to God and to man? A. Yes sir.

Mr. Reverdy Johnson here said:—"I am done, sir!" and rising, left the court room, and the cross-examination of the witness was continued by other counsel.

Question. What time was it you said Dr. Mudd introduced Booth to yourself and Surratt? Answer. On the 15th of January, I think.
Question. Have you no means of fixing the exact date? Answer. Yes, sir, if the register at the Pennsylvania House could be had; Dr. Mudd had his rooms there at that time.
Question. Are you sure it was before the 1st of February? Answer. Yes, sir. I am sure.
Question. Are you sure it was after the 1st of January? Answer. Yes.
Q. Why. A. From a letter received about that time, about the 6th of January, and from a visit I made there again; it was immediately after the recess of Congress, and the room of Booth had been previously occupied by a member of Congress, and Booth pulled down some Congressional documents and, remarked what good reading he would have when left to himself.
Q. You are certain it was after the Congressional holiday, of the occasion, and have no other means of knowing, A. No, sir.
Q. Did you ever have any means of knowing it was after Christmas? A. Merely that it was after the Congressional holidays.

Q. Well, who said anything about the member not having returned? A. Booth did.
Q. Do you know who the member was? A. No.
Q. How did you know that pretty much all the other members had returned? A. Because Congress was in session at the time.
Q. How do you happen to recollect Congress was in session at the time? A. Well merely by Booth's taking down the documents and saying what good reading he would have when left to himself.
Q. Was it the first day of Booth's arrival in the city? A. It was the first day of his taking possession of that room.
Q. Do you recollect that it was after the Congressional holiday as distinctly as any part of the conversation that took place? A. I don't recollect that fact as distinctly as I do the conversation about the purchase of the farm.
Q. Have you any memorandum of your own that will enable you to fix the date? A. The date could probably be fixed by the register at the Pennsylvania House.
Q. On what street was it that you met Mudd? A. On Seventh street opposite Odd Fellows' Hall
Q. What did Mudd say in explanation of the introduction? A. Nothing that I can remember. Surratt introduced me to him, and he introduced Booth to both of us.
Q. Which introduction came first? A. That of Mudd by Surratt to me.
Q. And did Booth immediately invite you all to his room? A. Yes.
Q. What was said while you were going to the room? A. Nothing that I know.
Q. Did he give any reason for wishing you to go? A. No. In going down Seventh street Surratt took Mudd's arm and I took that of Booth's.
Q. And you went directly to Booth's room, and how long in all did you stay there? A. That I can't say exactly.
Q. You say Mudd wrote something on a piece of paper? A. I say Booth traced lines on the back of an envelope, and that Surratt and Mudd were looking at it, and were engaged in a deep private conversation scarcely audible.
Q. Were you in the room all that time? A. Yes sir.
Q. How close to them? A. About as far as that gentleman is from me.
Q. Was the conversation in part audible? A. It was an indistinct murmur.
Q. You heard none of it? A. No.
Q. Who went out the door? Did Mudd go first? A. Booth went first.
Q. Are you sure? A. Yes sir.
Q. How long were they out together? A. As near as I can judge, not more than five or eight minutes.
Q. Where did they go? A. Into a passage that leads past the door.
Q. How do you know they stopped there? A. I don't know, for the door was closed after them, but by their movements I judge they stood outside.
Q. Why? A. I did not hear any retreating footsteps.
Q. Surratt went out with them? A. Yes.
Q. Are you sure Booth was with them when they went out the second time? A. Yes sir.
Q. Did Mudd say anything as to how he came to introduce Booth to Surratt? A. No sir.
Q. Which one of them said it was about the farm? A. Mudd apologised to me for the privacy of the conversation, and said that Booth wanted to purchase his farm, but that he would not give a sufficient high price and he did not care about selling it.
Q. You had never seen Mudd before? A. No sir.
Q. Had you heard him spoken of in the house? A. I had heard the name mentioned, but whether it was this particular Dr. Samuel Mudd, I cannot say.
Q. Did you hear it mentioned in connection with any visit to the house? A. No sir.
Q. Do you know whether he did visit the house during the time you were there? A. No sir.
Q. Where did Mrs. Surratt formerly live? A. At Surrattsville.
Q. On the road to Bryanstown? A. I can't say exactly. I am not sufficiently acquainted with the country.
Q. Do you know whether it is on the road leading to Mudd's house? A. There were several ways of arriving at Mudd's house. One road, called the Port Tobacco road, cut by Piscataway.
Q. How far is Mudd's house from the city? A. I don't know.
Q. How far is Surrattsville? A. About ten miles from the Navy Bridge.
Q. Did you ever hear his name mentioned in the family? A. Yes, I heard the name of Mudd; Dr. Samuel Mudd, only once, I think.
Q. After Booth, Surratt and Mudd returned from the passage outside, how long did you remain together? A. About twenty minutes.
Q. And then where did you all go? A. We left the hotel and went to the Pennsylvania House, where Dr. Mudd had rooms, and Mudd went into the sitting room and sat down with me and talked about the war, and expressed the opinion that it would soon come to an end, and spoke like a Union man; Booth was speaking

with Surratt; Booth left, and bade us good night and went out; Dr. Mudd remained there but left next morning; he said he was going to leave, whether he did or not I cannot say.
Q. What time was it when you separated? A. It must have been about half-past ten in the evening.
Q. Was Booth talking when drawing those lines? A. Yes sir.
Q. And Mudd and Surratt were attending? A. Yes; all three sat around the table, and looked at what Booth was marking.
Q. Are you sure they were looking at what he was drawing, or simply attending to what he was saying? A. They looked beyond Booth; their eyes on the envelope.
Q. How near were you to them? A. As I stated about as near as that gentleman over there, (pointing to Judge Holt).
Q. Well, now, what distance is that in feet? A. Perhaps eight feet.
Q. How large was the room? A. I have no means of arriving at that.
About how large? A. I could not tell exactly how large it was.
Q. Do not expect you to do that; about how large? A. About half the size of this room.
Mr. Pitman here asked the witness whether he meant half the room in length and half in breadth, which would be quarter of the room, or merely half the length, with the same width. The witness then pointed to a dividing railing in the room, and said about the size from there.
Q. Have you ever heard any conversation having reference to Payne's assignment to the murder of the Secretary of State? A. No sir.
Q. In what part of the room was the table situated? A. In the centre.
Q. You say you saw Mr. Harold in the summer of 1863, at Mrs. Surratt's, at Surrattsville? A. It was at the time of the election of county officers; a band had gone down to serenade the officers who had been elected, and in returning they serenaded us; I also saw him in July at Piscataway Church, and also the time at the theatre.
Q. When you left the theatre you all walked down the street together a portion of the way? A. Five of us left together, and when we came to the corner of Tenth and E streets, we turned around, at least Surratt did, and saw the other two were not following, and told me to go back and find them; I went back and found them engaged in close conversation with Booth.
Q. You saw them at the restaurant? A. Yes, sir, and on my approaching them Booth asked me to take a drink, and introduced me to a man whose name I do not remember, but whose face is familiar to me.
Q. Did you take a drink? A. (emphatically), Yes, sir.
Q. They were all standing together when you approached? A. Yes.
Q. Near the bar? No, sir, around the stove.
Q. Was it a cold evening? A. No, sir; there was no fire in the stove; it was a very pleasant evening.
Q. Do you know whether Harold and Atzeroth had taken a drink together before you came in? A. No, sir.
Q. When you left, did you all leave together? A. Harold, Atzeroth and I left together, and overtook Surratt on Seventh street; he invited us to take some oysters, but Harold went down Seventh street.
Q. Do you know where Harold lived? A. I was at the house only once; I don't know the precise spot.
Q. You remarked sir, that at some time when you were in company with Mrs. Surratt, a party would call to see her. Do you remember of Mrs. Surratt sending a request to have a private conversation with Booth? A. On the 2d of April she sent me to the hotel and told me to tell him that she would like to see him on some private business.
Q. In reference to that ten dollars given you by Booth to obtain the buggy? A. I thought it an act of friendship. Booth had been in the habit of keeping a buggy and had promised to let Mrs. Surratt have the loan of it, and when I went for it he said, "Here is ten dollars; go and hire one."
Q. You spoke of going to Montreal; at what time was that? A. On the 18th of April, the Monday after the assassination.
Q. What business had you there? A. I was seeking Surratt.
Q. Did you find him? A. No sir.
Q. Did you ever see Mrs. Surratt leave the parlor to have a private interview with Booth? A. Frequently; she would go into the passage and talk with him.
Q. How much time did these interviews generally occupy? A. Generally not more than five or eight minutes.
Q. Well, sir, by any conversation with her were you ever led to believe she was in secret conspiracy with Booth, or any of his confederates?
Here it was remarked by a member of the Court that the witness had better confine himself to a statement of facts, and the question was waived by the cross-examining counsel. It was also here stated by the Court that it was a rule in the examination of witnesses that each one should be examined by one Judge-Advocate and by only one counsel to each prisoner.

Q. Did you ever transact any business for Mrs. Surratt? A. I only wrote a letter to Mr. Nothy.
Q. What was that? A. It was as follows:—Mr. Nothy, unless you come forward and pay that bill at once I will begin suit against you immediately.
Q. Anything else? A. I figured some interest sums for her, the interest on $439 for thirteen years.
Q. Do you know of any interview between Atzeroth and Surratt? A. I have been there frequently at interviews with Surratt in the parlor.
Q. Do you know of any between Payne and Atzeroth? A. Yes; on the occasion of Payne's last visit to the house Atzeroth called to see Surratt once, and they were in my room.
Q. Do you know of any conversation in reference to the assignment of Atzeroth to the assassination of the Vice President? A. No sir.
Q. Now you say, that at 2½ o'clock on the evening of the 14th of April, you saw Atzeroth at a livery stable? A. Yes sir.
Q. Trying to get a horse; did he say what he was going to do with the horse? A. He said he was going to take a pleasure ride out in the country.
Q. You say he did not get the horse? A. The stable keeper refused to let him have one.
Q. Do you know whether he succeeded in getting one that day? A. No, sir.
Q. When did you part with him? A. Immediately after at the Post Office; I dropped a letter and came back to the stable.
Q. Was that the last interview you had with him until the assassination? A. Yes sir.
Q. Where did you see him again? A. In the dock there.
Q. To-day? A. Yes sir; to-day.
Q. You say you recognized that spur as having been seen by you on the bed of Payne at the house of Mrs. Surratt. What makes you recognize it? what marks are there that distinguish it from spurs in general? A. I had them in my hand.
Q. Was it the same with the knife? I understand you to swear you saw that knife there. A. No, not that knife.
Q. On the 4th of April do you know where Payne was stopping? Do you know anything about Payne on that day? A. Yes, sir, I remember that Atzeroth and I met and I asked him where he was going, and he said he was going to get a horse for Payne.
Q. But where was Payne? A. I don't know; I only saw him on those two occasions.
Q. Where then was Atzeroth stopping? A. I don't know.
Q. Did not he speak of the place where Payne was stopping? A. No, sir.
Q. Do you know of his having stopped at the Herndon House? A. I know it because Atzeroth told me; I met him one day on Seventh street; he said he was going to see Payne, and I asked him if it was Payne that was at the Herndon House, and he said yes.
Q. You said Payne paid a visit to Mrs. Surratt, and stopped only one night? A. Yes, sir.
Q. With whom did he appear to have business? A. He appeared to have business with Mrs. Surratt.
Q. Did he have any other dress, going to show that he wanted to conceal himself, that you saw? A. No, sir.
Q. Have you seen Payne since the assassination until to-day? A. No, sir, I believe not.
Q. Was he received by Mrs. Surratt as an intimate friend? A. He was by Mrs. Surratt; he was treated as an old acquaintance on his first visit.
Q. Now you say he represented himself to be a Baptist minister; did they regard him as a man in disguise, or as a minister? A. One of the young ladies remarked that he was a queer looking Baptist preacher; that he wouldn't convert many souls.
Q. Did you ever see Payne and Atzeroth in company? A. Yes; Atzeroth was at the house on the occasion of Payne's last visit.
Q. Were you, or were you not at Mrs. Surratt's when Payne was arrested? A. No sir.
Q. Were you in the house at 3 o'clock on Saturday morning, when the officers took possession? A. Yes sir.
Q. Was Payne not there then? A. No sir.
Q. I would like to know what professional employment you are in? A. Clerk in the office of the Commissary General of Prisoners, and have been since the 8th day of January, 1864.
Q. Colonel Hoffman's office? A. Yes sir.
It was here moved that the Court adjourn, but after some discussion the adjournment was postponed.

Testimony of Robert R. Jones.

Robert R. Jones, sworn:—Q. You are a clerk at the Kirkwood House? A. Yes sir.
Q. Look at that paper and say if it is a page taken from the register of that hotel? A. Yes sir.
Q. Do you read upon it the name of Atzeroth? A. Yes sir, A. G. A-t-z-r-r-o-u-t, I believe.
Q. From that register does it appear that he took a room there? A. Yes, on the 4th of April, I should think in the morning before 8 o'clock.
Q. What is the number of the room? A. No. 126.

J. WILKES BOOTH.—THE MURDERER OF PRESIDENT LINCOLN.

TRIAL OF THE ASSASSINS AT WASHINGTON.

Q. Have you any recollection of the man being seen by you that day? A. I saw him that day, sir.
Q. Do you recognize him amongst those prisoners?
A. That looks like the man.
Major-General Hunter to Atzeroth—Stand up.
Witness said, "I think that is him, sir."
Q. Do you know what became of him after he took the room? A. I do not know; it was between twelve and one o'clock when I saw him that day.
Q. Do you know anything of Booth having called that day to inquire the number of Vice President Johnson's room? A. I don't know that he inquired; I gave a card of Booth's to Colonel Browning, Vice President Johnson's Secretary.
Q. You did not receive it from him himself? A. I did not, I think, although I may have done so.
Q. You have not seen the prisoner till now? A. No sir.
Q. Were you present when the room was opened? A. I was not there when it was opened; I went up with Mr Lee after it was opened.
Q. Did you see anybody there during the day that Atzeroth was at the hotel? A. There was a young man spoke to him when I saw him at the office counter.
Q. Did you see any one go to the room with him? A. No sir.
Q. Would you know Booth? A. I don't think I would; he has been at the house, but I don't think I recollect him.
Q. Were you present when that bowie knife was taken from the bed? A. Yes sir; it was under the sheet.
Q. On what day was that? A. The day after the murder of the President, or on the evening after.
Q. Had the bed been occupied? A. No sir; the chambermaid had not been in there.
Q. W.s Atzeroth out the night of the assassination? A. Not that I know of; it was between 12 and 10 o'clock that I saw him; he asked if any one had inquired for him.
Q. This was the 14th day of April? A. Yes sir.
Q. He paid for one day in advance for his room? A. Yes sir. It appears on the book.
Q. He had never been to the hotel before to your knowledge? A. I had never seen him there before.
Cross-examined:—Q. Were you clerking the desk the day when he registered? A. I went off duty at 12 o'clock that day.
Q. Did you see him register? A. No sir.
Q. What reason have you for supposing that the person who wrote his name was the person you have identified? A. He called to the counter, pointed to his name on the register, and asked if any one had called.
Q. What day was that? A. On Friday, between twelve and one o'clock.
Q. Did you see him after that in person? A. No, not after he left the counter.
Q. Did you see him when his baggage came in? A. No sir.
Q. Had he any baggage when he arrived? A. I was not there when he arrived.
Q. Did he go to his room while he was there? A. I didn't go there till next evening, between six and seven o'clock.
Q. Do you know whether he slept there? A. No sir; the chambermaid could not get in; she could not find the key.
Q. Did you ever find the key? A. We never have seen it since.
Q. Did you have any conversation with a detective in the course of the evening of the 15th, in reference to a suspicious looking person at the Kirkwood House? A. On the 15th, the day after the murder, I think probably I had, but I don't recollect of any particular conversation with regard to it.
Q. Do you remember going with the detective to the room? A. I went with Mr. Lee to the room.
Q. Do you know whether the prisoner Atzeroth had expressed any choice of the room, or for the particular number, No. 26? A. I was not there when he was roomed.
Q. Did you inspect the different articles which were found in the pockets of that coat? A. Yes; I saw them as Mr. Lee took them out.
Q. Could you identify the pistol you saw on that occasion? A. I don't think I could; the particular one; it was a large pistol such as cavalry soldiers wear.
Q. Was it loaded or not? A. It was.
Q. How are the barrels, round? A. I think it was a round, single barrel, with chambers.
Q. Could you recognize the books? A. I think I could; the one that had "J. Wilkes Booth" on the outside the knife was a sheath-knife, the same as that one on the table, but I could not swear to the identity of it.
The assistant counsel for Mrs. Surratt then said:—Mr. President, I have to ask that the examination of Mr. Floyd may be postponed until Monday, as his testimony affects Mrs. Surratt and is of great importance, and I feel desirous that his examination may take place when her senior counsel, Mr. Reverdy Johnson, is present.
The Court refused the application to defer the examination of Mr. Floyd on the ground that it could not wait on the whims or conveniences of counsel, and that Mr. Johnson might have remained in Court had he so desired.

Testimony of Mr. Floyd.

Mr. Floyd sworn.
Q. Where do you reside? A. At Surrattsville.
Q. Are you acquainted with John H. Surratt? A. Yes, since the 1st of December, 1864, not much previous to that.
Q. Do you know the prisoner, Harold? A. Yes, sir.
Q. Do you know the prisoner Atzeroth? A. Yes sir.
Q. Will you state whether or not some five or six weeks before the assassination of the President any or all of these men came to your house? A. They were there, sir.
Q. All three? A. Yes, sir.
Q. What did they bring to your house? A. Atzeroth came first, went on to T. B., was gone about half an hour and the three of them returned, Surratt, Atzeroth, and Harold. I noticed nothing with them until all three came came, when John Surratt called me into the front parlor, and I seen on the sofa I saw two carbines and some ammunition.
Q. Anything else? A. A rope.
Q. How long? A. About sixteen to twenty feet.
Q. Were these articles left at your house? A. Yes; Surratt asked me to take care of them and I told him I did not like to have these things in the house; he then called me into a room I had never seen into before, and showed me where I could place them under a joist.
Q. Were they concealed there? A. Yes sir; I put them there myself.
Q. How much ammunition was there? A. Just one cartridge box.
Q. What kind of a carbine was it? A. Did'nt examine them; they had covers over them.
Q. State whether on the Monday preceding Mrs. Surratt came to your house? A. I met Mrs. Surratt on the Monday previous to the assassination; when she first broached the subject to me I did not understand her; she asked me about the shooting irons, or something of that kind, to draw my attention to those things; I had almost forgotten they were there, and I told her they were hidden away; she said they would be wanting soon; I don't recollect the first question she put to me; she only referred to it in a manner, and finally came out and said they would be wanted soon.
Q. Now will you state whether on the evening or day on which the President was assassinated Mrs. Surratt did'nt come to your house? A. Yes I was out attending a trial, and found her there when I came back; I judge it was about five o'clock; I met her at the wood pile, and she told me to have them shooting irons ready that night, and said there would be some parties call for them that night; she gave me something in a piece of paper to keep for her, and I found it was a field-glass; she asked me also to have two bottles of whisky ready, saying they would be called for at night.
Q. And were they called for by Booth and Harold that night? A. They both came, Both and Harold, and took their whisky out of the bottles; Booth did'nt come in but Harold did; It was not over a quarter after 12 o'clock; Booth was a stranger to me; Harold came in and took the whisky, but I don't think he asked for it; he said to me, get me those things.
Q. Did he not say to you what those things were? A. No; but he was apprised that already; I know they were coming for them; I made no reply, but went and got them; I gave him all the articles, with the field glass and a monkey wrench.
Q. She told you to give them the whisky, the carbines and the field glass. A. Yes sir.
Q. How long did they remain at your house? A. Not over five minutes.
Q. Did they take both the carbines, or only one? A. Only one; Booth said he could not take his, because his leg was broken.
Q. Did he drink also? A. Yes, while sitting in the porch; Harold carried the bottle out to him.
Q. Did he say anything about the assassination? A. As they were leaving Booth said, "I will tell you some news: *I am pretty certain we have assassinated the President and Secretary Seward."*
Q. Was that in Harold's presence? A. I am not certain. I became so excited that I am not certain.
Q. At what hour was the news of the President's assassination afterwards received by you? A. I suppose it was about nine o'clock.
Q. As the news spread was it spoken of that Booth was the assassin? A. I think it was, on several occasions.
Q. Did you see the prisoner, Dr. Mudd, before? A. I never saw him before. I am not acquainted with him at all.
Q. What was the exact language used when Harold asked you for those things? A. For God's sake make haste and get those things.
Cross examination.—Q. At what time did you rent the house? A. About the 1st of December last.
Q. At the time you commenced the occupation of the premises did you find any arms in the house? A. No sir.
Q. No guns or pistols? A. There was a broken gun, a double barreled gun.
Q. Do you keep a bar there? A. I do, sir.

Q. Detail the first conversation you had with Mrs. Surratt on the two last times you saw her. A. It was out of Uniontown; we had passed each other; I stopped and saw it was her and got out and went to her buggy and she spoke to me in a manner trying to draw my attention to those things, the carbines, but she finally came out plainer, though I am not quite positive, but I think she said shooting irons.
Q. Can you swear, Mr. Floyd, on your oath that she mentioned shooting irons to you at all? A. I am pretty positive she did on both occasions, and I know she did on the last.
Q. At what time on Friday did you meet Mrs. Surratt? A. I did not meet her on Friday at all; I was out and when I returned home I found her there.
Q. How long did she remain after you returned? A. Not over ten minutes.
Q. Now state the conversation between you and her during those ten minutes. A. The first thing she said was, "Talk about the devil and some of his imps will appear." Then she said, "Mr. Floyd, I want you to have the shooting irons ready, some parties will call for them to-night;" she gave me a bundle, but I didn't open it until I got up stairs, and I found it was a field-glass.
Q. At what time of day had you this conversation with M.s. Surratt? A. I judge it was about 5 o'clock, but it might have been later. She told me to have those shooting irons ready, and I carried them and the other things into the house. That is all the conversation I had with her in reference to that. I went into the barn and she requested me to fix her buggy, the spring of which had become detached from the axle.
Q. Was any other person present during this interview? A. Mrs. Offet was there.
Q. Was she within hearing distance? A. I don't know; I suppose she was.
Q. This was in the yard? A. Yes sir.
Q. Is Mrs. Offet a neighbor of yours? A. She is my sister-in-law.
Q. When did you first have occasion to recollect these conversations? A. When I gave all the particulars to Captain Burnett, the Saturday week following.
Q. Was that the first time you detailed those conversations? A. Yes.
Q. Did you relate any of the circumstances to any other person? A. Only to Lieutenant Lovett and Captain Cunningham. I told them it was through the Surratts I got myself into difficulty, and if they hadn't brought those arms to the house I would not have been in any difficulties at all.
Q. Were Lovett and Cunningham together when you told them? A. Yes.
Q. Did you talk to Mrs. Offet about it? A. I don't think I did; I am not so positive about that.
Q. How soon after Booth and Harold left did you learn positively of the assassination of the President? A. I got it from them.
Q. How soon after did you get it from other parties? A. About eight or nine o'clock the next morning.
Q. Did you have any conversation with the soldiers in regard to it? A. No sir.
Q. Did you tell them about Booth and Harold being at your place? A. I did not, and I am only sorry that I did not.
Q. Did Mrs. Surratt have any conversation with you in reference to any conspiracy? A. Never sir.
Q. Did Mrs. Surratt hand anything to you when she spoke about those shooting irons? A. Yes sir, the field glass.
Q. Have you any family? A. I have a wife.
Q. Have you a son? A. No sir.
Q. Does any person work for you? A. Yes sir, a couple of colored men.
Q. Were any of them present at the conversation between you and Mrs. Surratt? A. No sir.
Q. Was the package handed to you by Mrs. Surratt's own hand? A. Yes, by herself.
Q. Where were you standing when she handed it to you? A. Near the woodpile.
Here a different counsel entered upon the task of continuing the cross-examination rendered exceedingly tedious by the insufficient voice of the witness, whom the Court and counsel could scarcely hear.
Q. Mr. Floyd, can you recollect who it was, after Booth and Harold left the house, that first told you it was Booth who killed the President? A. I cannot; it was spoken of in the bar-room the next morning and throughout the day.
Q. Were the circumstances told, and the manner in which he did it? A. I don't remember any circumstances being told.
Q. Do you know whether the soldiers who first came to the house knew it was Booth? A. I do not; I suppose they knew it, as they brought the report from the city.
Q. Mr. Floyd, how long before the assassination was it that the three gentlemen you referred to came to your house. A. About six weeks; they had two buggies; Surratt and Payne and Harold were in the buggies; Atzeroth came on horseback.
Q. They all came together? A. Yes.
Q. Well who went down to this place called T. B? A. Surratt and Atzeroth.
Q. Did Harold go with them then? A. No; Harold was there the night before; he had gone down the country, and told me he had come from T. B., when they all three came back.
Q. How long were they gone? A. Not over half an hour.
Q. Who handed the carbines to you? A. John Surratt; when they all came into the bar. Surratt told me he wanted to see me, and took me to the front parlor, and there, on the sofa, were the carbines.
Q. Do you know which buggy they were taken from? A. I did not see anything of any arms at all until they were on the sofa.
Q. What became of the rope that was not taken away? A. It was put in the store-room with the monkey wrench. I told the Colonel all about it at the Old Capitol, and I suppose he sent for it.
Q. Did at any time any conversation pass between you and Harold about the arms. A. The night of the assassination when he got the carbines.
Q. Which road did they take? A. Towards T. B.
Q. Did Booth and he start off together? A. They did.
Q. Can you say whether it was in Harold's presence that Booth told you he had killed the President? A. I am not sure, because Harold rode across the yard like.
Q. Where? A. About fifteen hundred yards from T. B., on my way home.
Q. Did Harold take a drink at the bar? A. He did.
Q. Did he take the bottle back? A. He did.
Q. Did he pay for the drink? A. He said, "I owe you a couple of dollars, and he gave me one dollar.
Q. Was it light enough for you to observe the kind of horses they had? A. One was almost a white horse and the other was a bay. They bay was a large horse. Harold was riding on the bay.

Here another counsel took up the cross-examination, beginning with the oft repeated injunction to the witness to speak louder.

Q. Had you ever you met Atzeroth in company with Surratt and Harold? A. He came there five or six weeks before in company with Surratt.
Q. Did you ever see him before that time? A. Yes; he had been to my house before.
Q. Did he ever deliver to you anything? A. Never.
Q. Have you seen him since the assassination? A. Never till now.
Q. Did you ever see the prisoner Arnold? A. I don't know him.
Q. Did Booth take a rifle with him? A. No sir, but Harold did.
Q. Where were the arms, then? A. They were in my bed chamber.
Q. When did you bring them there? A. After Mrs. Surratt left, in consequence of her order.
Q. Did you give them the carbines before they said anything about shooting the President? No sir; afterwards.
Q. What time was it? A, A little after twelve; I woke up just before twelve o'clock; I had gone to bed about nine o'clock.
Q. When the soldiers searched did you give them aid? A. I told them I did not know anything about it; I should have been perfectly free if I had given them the information they asked for.
Q. Did you have any conversation with Mrs. Offet after Mrs. Surratt went away? A. I am not certain; I think I told her.
Q. Where were you standing? A. Near the woodpile.

The court adjourned till Monday morning.

WASHINGTON, May 15.—The witnesses examined this afternoon showed the intimacy of Booth, Arnold and O'Laughlin.

Mr. Cox, for the defense, objected to the whole of this evidence, on the ground that the mere fact of intimacy was not evidence of conspiracy.

Judge Advocate Holt said they had fully established the intimacy of the party in Washington, and simply proposed to show the intimacy which existed in Baltimore.

The Court overruled the objection; but ordered it to be put on record.

It appeared from the testimony of David Stanton that on the night of the illumination, the 13th of April, O'Laughlin was prowling in the house of the Secretary of War; but having no business there, he was ordered out. General Grant was in the parlor at that time.

The Court remained in session until 7 o'clock.

A number of witnesses were examined as to the occurrences at the theatre on the night of the assassination.

The Charges and Specifications.

The following is a copy of the charges and specifications against David E. Harold, Geo. A. Atzeroth, Lewis Payne, Michael O'Laughlin, John H. Surratt, Edward

TRIAL OF THE ASSASSINS AT WASHINGTON. 31

Spangler, Samuel Arnold, Mary E. Surratt, and Samuel A. Mudd:—

Charge 1. For maliciously, unlawfully, and traitorously, and in aid of the existing armed Rebellion against the United States of America, on or be ore the 4th day of March, A. D. 1865, and on divers other days between that day and the 15th day of April, A. D. 1865, combining, confederating, and conspiring together with one John H. Surratt, John Wilkes Booth, Jefferson Davis, George N. Sanders, Beverley Tucker, Jacob Thompson, William C. Cleary, Clement C. Clay, George Harper, George Young, and others unknown, within the Military Department of Washington, and within the fortified and intrenched lines thereof, Abraham Lincoln, late, and at the time of said combining, confederating and conspiring, President of the United States of America, and Commander-in-Chief of the Army and Navy thereof; Andrew Johnson, then Vice President of the United States aforesaid; William H. Seward, Secretary of State of the United States aforesaid, and Ulysses S. Grant, Lieutenant-General of the Army of the States aforesaid, then in command of the Armies of the United States, under the direction of the said Abraham Lincoln, and in pursuance of, and in prosecuting said malicious, unlawful, and traitorous conspiracy aforesaid, and in aid of said Rebellion, a terwards, to-wit:— On the 14th day of April, A. D. 1865, within the Military Department of Washington aforesaid, and within the fortified and intrenched lines of said Military Department, together with the said John Wilkes Booth, and John H. Surratt, maliciously, unlawfully, and traitorously murdering the said Abraham Lincoln, then President of the United States and Commander-in-Chief of the Army and Navy of the United States as aforesaid, and maliciously, unlawfully, and traitorously assaulting with intent to kill and murder the said William H. Seward, then Secretary of State of the United States as aforesaid; and lying in wait with intent maliciously, unlawfully, and traitorously to kill and murder the said Andrew Johnson, then being Vice-President of the United States, and the said Ulysses S. Grant, then being Lieutenant-General and in command of the armies of the United States as aforesaid.

Specification I. In this, that they, the said David E. Harold, Edward Spangler, Lewis Payne, John H. Surratt, Michael O'Laughlin, Samuel Arnold, Mary E. Surratt, George A. Atzerodt and Samuel A. Mudd, incited and encouraged thereunto by Jefferson Davis, George N. Sanders, Beverley Tucker, Jacob Thompson, William C. Cleary, Clement C. Clay, Geor. e Harper, George Young, and others unknown, citizens of the United States aforesaid, and who were then engaged in armed Rebellion against the United States of America, within the limits thereof, did, in aid of said armed Rebellion, on or before the 6th day of March, A. D. 1865, and on divers other day and time b tween that day and the 15th day of April, A. D. 1865, combine, confederate and conspire together at Washington city, within the Military Department, and within the intrenched fortifications and military lines of the said United States, there being unlawfully, maliciously, and traitorously to kill and murder Abraham Lincoln, then President of the United States aforesaid, and Commander-in-Chief of the Army and Navy thereof, and unlawfully, maliciously, and traitorously to kill and murder Andrew Johnson, then Vice-President of the United States, upon whom on the death of said Abraham Lincoln, after the 4th day of March, A. D. 1865, the office of President of the said United States, and Commander-in-Chief of the Army and Navy thereof, would devolve, and to unlawfully, maliciously, and traitorously kill and murder Ulysses S. Grant, then Lieutenant-General under the direction of the said Abraham Lincoln in command of the Armies of the United States aforesaid; and unlawfully, maliciously, and traitorously to kill and murder William H. Seward, the Secretary of State of the United States aforesaid, whose duty it was by law upon the death of said President and Vice President of the United States aforesaid, to cause an election to ne held for electors of President of the United States, the conspirators aforesaid designing and intend'ng by the killing and murder of the said Abraham Lincoln and Andrew Johnson, Ulysses S. Grant and William H. Seward aforesaid, to deprive the army and navy of the said United States of a constitutional commander-in-chief, and to deprive the armies of the United States of their lawful commander, and to prevent a lawful election of President and Vice President of the United States aforesaid, and by the means aforesaid to aid and comfort the insurgents engaged in armed rebellion against the said United States as aforesaid, and thereby to aid in the subversion and overthrow of the said United States.

And being so combined, confederated, and conspiring together in the prosecution of such unlawful and traitorous conspiracy, on the night of the 14th day of April A. D. 1865, at the hour of about 10 o'clock and 15 minutes P. M., at Ford's Theatre on Tenth Street, in the city of Washington, and within the Military Department and military lines aforesaid, John Wilkes Booth, one of the conspirators aforesaid, in pursuance of said unlawful and traitorous conspiracy, did then and there unlawfully, maliciously, traitorously and with intent to kill and murder the said Abraham Lincoln, discharge a pistol, held in the hands of him, the said Booth, the same being then loaded with powder and a leaden ball, against and upon the left and posterior s de of the head of Abraham Lincoln, and did thereby then and there inflict upon him, the said Abraham Lincoln, then President of the said United States and Commander-in-Chief of the Army and Navy thereof, a mortal wound, whereof afterwards, to wit, on the 15th day of April, A. D. 1865, at Washington City aforesaid, the said Abraham Lincoln died, and thereby then and there, in pursuance of said conspiracy, the said defendants, and the said John Wilkes Booth, did unlawfully, traitorously, and maliciously, and with the intent to aid the Rebellion as aforesaid, murder the President of the United States as aforesaid.

In further prosecution of the unlawful, traitorous conspiracy a'ores iid, and of the murderous and traitorous intent of said conspiracy, the said Edward Spangler, on the said 14th day of April, A. D. 1865, at about the same hour of the same day as aforesaid, within said military department and the military lines aforesaid, did aid and assist the said John Wilkes Booth to obtain entrance to the box in said theatre in which said Abraham Lincoln was sitting at the time he was assaulted and shot as aforesaid by John Wilkes Booth, and also d d then and there aid said Booth in barring and obstructing the door of the box of said theatre so as to hinder and prevent any assistance to or rescue of the said Abraham Lincoln against the murderous assault of the said John Wilkes Booth, and did aid and abet him in making his escape after the said Abraham Lincoln had been murdered in manner aforesaid.

And in further prosecution of said unlawful, murderous and traitorous conspiracy, and in pursuance thereof, and with the intent as aforesaid, the said David E. Harold, on the night of the 14th of April, A. D. 1865, within the Military Department and military lines a oresaid, abet and assist the said John Wilkes Booth in the killing and murder of the said Abraham Lincoln, and did then and there aid, a d abet and assist him, the said John Wilkes Booth, in attempting to escape through the military lines aforesaid, and accompany and assist the said John Wilkes Booth in attempting to conceal himself and escape from justice after killing and murdering the said Abraham Lincoln as aforesaid.

And in further prosecution of said unlawful and traitorous conspiracy, and of the intent thereof as aforesaid, the said Lewis Payne did, on the same night of the 14th day of April, A. D. 1865, about the same hour of 10 o'clock 15 minutes P. M., at the city of Washington, and within the military department and military lines aforesaid, unlawfully and maliciously make an assault upon the said William H. Seward, Secretary of State as aforesaid, in the dwelling house and bed-chamber of him, the said William H. Seward; and there, with a large knife held in his hand, to k ll and murder Frederick W. Seward, Augustus W. Seward, Emerick W. Hansell, and George F. Robinson, who were then striving to protect and rescue the said Will am H. Seward from murder by the said Lewis Payne, and did then and there, with the said knife and pistol held in his hand, inflict divers wounds upon the head of the said Frederick W. Seward, and upon the persons of the said Augustus W. Seward, Emerick W. Hansell, and George F. Robinson.

And in the further prosecution of the said conspiracy and its traitorous and murderous designs, the said Geo. A. Atzerodt did, on the night of the 14th of April, A. D. 1865, and about the same hour of the night aforesaid, within the military department, and the military lines aforesaid lie in wait for Andrew Johnson, then Vice President of the United States aforesaid, with the intent unlawfully and maliciously to kill and murder him, the said Andrew Johnson.

And in the further prosecution of the conspiracy aforesaid, and of its murderous and treasonable purposes aforesaid, on the night of the 13th and 14th of April, 18 5, at Washington City, and within the military lines aforesaid, the said Michael O'Laughlin did then and there lie in wait for Ulysses S. Grant.

And in the further prosecution of the said conspiracy, the said Samuel Arnold did, within the military department and military lines aforesaid, on or about the 6th day of March, A. D. 1865, and on divers other days and times between that day and the 15th day of April, A. D. 1865, combine, conspire with and aid, counsel and abet, comfort and support the said John Wilkes Booth, Lewis Payne, George A. Atzerodt, Michael O'Laughlin, and their confederates in the said unlawful, murderous and traitorous conspiracy, and in the execution thereof as aforesaid.

And in the further prosecution of the said conspiracy, Mary E. Surratt did, at Washington City, and within the military department and military lines a'oresaid, on or be ore the 6th day of March, A. D. 1865, and at divers other days and times between that day and the 20th day of April, A. D. 1865, receive, enter ain, harbor and conceal, aid and assist, the said John W. likes Booth, David E. Herold, Lewis Payne John H. Surratt M'cha'l O'Laughlin, George A. Atzerodt Samuel Arn'ld, and their confederates, with a knowledge of the murderous and traitorous conspiracy a'cre aid, and with intent to aid, abet and assist them in the execution thereof, and in escaping from justice after the murder of the said Abraham Linco n, as a'oresaid, with intent to aid, abet and assist them in the execution thereof, and in escaping from justice after the murder of the said Abraham Lincoln, in pursuance of the said conspiracy, in the manner a'oresaid.

By order of the President of the United States,
J. HOLT, Judge Advocate-General.

Proceedings of Monday, May 15.

On Saturday it was moved that if the record created no objection on the part of the Judges Advocate, or of the counsel for any or all of the accused, the presence of the several witnesses need not be considered of material necessity.

Mr. Aiken, assistant counsel for Mrs. Surratt, expressed his willingness to accede to such an arrangement, except in the case of Welchman, whom he desired present not, however, that the witness might hear the record of his testimony read, but that he might re-examine him on new ground, which, as he alleged, had been brought forth in the examination of the subsequent witnesses.

It was decided by the Court that the reason so stated did not justify the delay that the finding and reading of Welchman would occasion, and the reading of the record was proceeded with.

After a time Mr. Weichman entered and heard the reading of the portion of his cross-examination conducted by Mr. Ewing, and several corrections made.

Mr Johnson, the senior counsel of Mrs. Surratt, when the whole of the testimony rendered by Mr. Welchman had been read from the record, applied to be permitted to ask of him some questions before he retired. This was objected to by Major-General Wallace. The President then remarked that the witness had been already examined by the counsel, and a fair opportunity afforded. The Justice Advocate General then asked whe her it were to be a cross-examination, and being to'd by the counsel that it was, the Court, under the Advocate's suggestion, determined that as he could call up the witness hereafter of the case, it would be an economy of time, General Wallace withdrew his objection, add ng, however, that he did so only for this time. He said—"I placed my objection on the ground that these objections would prove interminable, unless stopped by some rule, a ter counsel have once had a full opportunity for cross-examination.

Examination by Hon. Reverdy Johnson—Q. I understood you to say on Saturday t at you went with Mrs. Surratt the first time, on Tuesday before the assassination, in a buggy. Do you recollect whether you stopped on the way to Surrattsville? A. Yes sir.

Q. Where? A. We stopped on two or three occasions.

Q. Did you stop at Uniontown? A. I do not know the particular point, whether it was at Uniontown or not.

Q. Did you stop at a village? A. We stopped on the road at no partic alar village that I remember.

Q. How do you know Mr. Floyd? A. I have met him three times.

Q. Did you know him as the keeper of the hotel? A. I knew him as the man who ha I rented Mrs. Surratt's house from her, because I copied off the instrument.

Q. Do you recollect seeing him buy a buggy on the way from Washington to Surrattsville, on Tuesday? A. Yes sir; we met hi carriage; it drove past us; Mrs. Surratt called to Mr. Floyd; Mr. Floyd got out and approached the buggy; Mrs. Surratt put her head out and had a conversation with him.

Q. Did you hear it? A. No sir.

Q. Did you hear anything about shooting-irons?
Question objected to by Assistant Judge Advocate Bingham. The question was then withdrawn.

Witness—I heard nothing mentioned about shooting irons; Mrs. Surratt spoke to Mrs. Offatt about having this man, Howell, take the oath of allegiance and get released, and said she was going to apply to General Augur or Judge Turner for that purpose.

Q. How len t was that interview between Mr. Floyd and Mrs. Surratt on that occasion? A. That I couldn't say exactly; I don't think it was more than five or eight minutes; I don't carry a watch myself, and I have no precise means of knowing.

By Judge Holt—Q. I understood you to say you did not hear the whole of this conversation? A. I did not hear the conversation between Mr. Floyd and Mrs. Surratt; Mrs. Surratt spoke to Mr. Floyd at some distance from the buggy, and I couldn't hear it.

By Mr. Johnson—Q. Do you recollect whether it was raining at that time? A. I don't think it was raining at that particular time; it was a cloudy, murky day; I cannot say whether it was raining or not; I don't remember.

The reading of the record was resumed, and being finished by half-past one, the Court took a recess.

After the recess, John M. Lloyd was recalled, and asked if he could identify the carbines shown to him as the ones referred to in his previous testimony?

Witness—The one with the cover on I do not recognize; I do not think the cover looks like the same; it was a kind of grey cloth; the other looks like the one I saw; I recogn ze the fixture or breech-loading, which attracted my attention, and which I examin d; t the Court will allow me a wish to make a statement. When I was examined before I stated that it was on Monday when I met Mrs. Surratt at Uniontown, I was consulting my being summoned to Court on two successive Mondays. The first Monday I was summoned to Court I did not go. I met Mrs. Surratt at Uniontown the next day after I went to Court, and consequently it must have been on the Tuesday after the second Monday I was summoned. I also wish to make another s atement. I testified in my last examination that I was not certain whether I carried the bundle given me by Mrs. Surratt upstairs or not. I cannot now recollect distinctly, but I think it likely I laid it on the sofa in the dining room.

By Judge-Advocate Holt.—Q. You are sure it was the same bundle you examined Lere? A. Yes, sir, I am sure it was the same bundle.

By Mr. Aiken.—Q. D d I understand you to say you were in liquor at the time you had this conversation with Mrs. Surratt? A. I was somewhat in liquor, as I think I told you on Saturday.

Q. And on that account is it that you are at fault in your testimony, and wish to make this explanation? A. I was not pos tive whether I carried the bundle up stairs or not. The question was unexpected, If I had expected it, I might have recollected more distinctly in my former examination.

Testimony of Mary Vantine.

Examined by Judge Holt.—Q. Do you reside in the city of Washington? A. I do; at No. 420 G street.

Q. Do you keep rooms for rent? A. I do.

Q. Will you look at the prisoners at the bar and state whether, in the month of February last, you saw any of them; and if so, which? A. Two of those gentlemen had rooms at my house, Arnold and O'Laughlin.

Q. What time in February did they take rooms in your house? A. As near as I can recollect it was on the 7th. I cannot state positively the date.

Q. Did you know J. Wilkes Booth in his lifetime? A. I knew him by his coming to my house to see gentlemen who had rooms there.

Q. Did he er not come very often to see the prisoners, O'Laughlin and Arnold? A. Yes, frequently.

Q. Would he remain for a good while in conversation w th them? A. As a general thing he would go into their rooms and I could see nothing further of them.

Q. Did these prisoners leave the city and return several times? A. They left on Saturday to go to their homes, as I understood, in Baltimore.

Q. Do you know whether Booth accompanied them or not? A. I think not.

Q. Were these interviews between Booth and them alone or was Both accompanied by other persons? A. I never saw any one with him.

Q. They told you his name was J. Wilkes Booth, did they? A. Yes, Arnold did; I inquired who he was and he said J. Wilkes Booth.

Q. D d he call for them frequently and not find them in? A. Yes sometimes.

Q. Did he manifest much anxiety to see them on these occasions? A. Frequently; when they were away he would call three or four times before they would return; he would appear very anxious to see them.

Q. Would he on such occasions leave messages for them? A. Sometimes he would request, if they came in before he called again, to say that they would find him at the st ables sometimes he would go into their room and write a note.

Q. Look at the photograph now shown you, and say if you recognize it as the man you call Booth? A. I cannot see without my glasses (glasses brought in and handed to witness; I should not call it a good likeness; I recognize it as Booth, but like a very poor likeness.

Q. Do you remember the last time Booth played in this city, about the 18th or 20th of March, A. Yes.

Q. Did these prisoners present you with complimentary tickets for the play that night? A. Yes. I expressed a wish to see him, and O'Laughlin gave me the tickets.

Q. Did there seem to be any difference in the intimacy of his association with these two men, and if so, with which was he the most intimate? A. I can't say. They would sometimes inquire for one, and sometimes for the other, though I think he more frequently inquired for O'Laughlin.

Q. Did you ever see any arms in their room? A. I saw a pistol once, and but once.

Q. Do you remember at any time seeing a man call. A very rough looking person—a laboring man or mechanic? A. Not a laboring man. There was a man who used to come sometimes. I think he passed one

TRIAL OF THE ASSASSINS AT WASHINGTON. 33

night with them, from his coming out very early in the morning.
Q. Do you know his name? A. I would know him if I saw him; he was what would be called a respectable-looking mechanic, not what you would call a gentleman.
Q. Could you describe him at all? A. Not very minutely; his skin was hard, as if it had been exposed to the weather.
Q. Do you recognize him as among the prisoners at the bar? A. No.
Q. Did these prisoners seem to have any business transactions with Booth, and if so, of what character? A. They said they were in the oil trade.
Q. Did they seem to have an extensive correspondence? Did many letters come to them? A. Not a great many.
Q. Where did they generally come from? A. I never noticed; they were brought in and laid down.
Q. They were addressed to the names of O'Laughlin and Arnold, were they? A. Yes; sometimes to one and sometimes to the other.
Q. You say Booth came sometimes by day and sometimes at night? A. Not frequently at night; I do not know as ever I saw him at night; he might have come there without my seeing him; I slept in the back part of the house and persons might come out the front part of the house without my seeing them.
Q. You do not know whether, when they went out and stayed late at night, they were with Booth or not? A. No.
Q. You have not seen them since the time they left your house? A. No.
Q. Which was about the 20th of March? A. I think so; it was the Monday after the Saturday on which Booth played.
Q. Did you ever see Booth ride out in the evenings with these men? A. No, I do not think I ever did. I could not positively say whether I did or not. I frequently came to my house in a carriage and inquired for them. I never saw them, that I recollect, ride out together.
Cross-examined by Mr. Coxe.—Q. Did these prisoners say they were or had been in the oil business? A. They said that they were in.
Q. Was that during the first or latter part of the time they occupied a room at your house? A. I think they had been there two or three weeks.
Q. Did they say anything when they went away from your house, where they were going? A. To Pennsylvania.
Q. Did they say anything about having abandoned the oil business? A. No; not that I recollect.
Q. Were they much in their rooms, or were they moving about? A. They were not in their room a great deal.
Q. Did they occupy it regularly at night? A. They were out sometimes.
Q. Do you fix the 20th of March as the day they left? A. If you can ascertain what night Booth played I can tell you; it was the Monday following:
Q. Was Pescara the play? A. Yes.
Q. You cannot speak with certainty of anybody being with them besides Booth? A. No, not anybody that I know; others may have gone into their room, I could not say in regard to that.
Q. I ask you whether Booth's visits were most frequent in February, or the latter part of the time they were there in March? A. I think they were pretty much the same all through the time they were there; he was a pretty constant visitor.
Q. Were you present at any conversations between them? A. No, I was not.
Q. You never heard any of their conversations? A. No.
Q. Did they room up stairs? A. No, in the back parlor.

Testimony of Henry Williams (Colored).

Q. State to the Court whether you are acquainted with the prisoners O'Laughlin and Arnold; look and see if you remember to have seen them before? A. I know Mr. O'Laughlin, but not Mr. Arnold.
Q. Did you ever meet Mr. O'Laughlin, and where? A. In Baltimore.
Q. When was that? A. In March last; I carried a letter to him.
Q. From whom did you carry the letter to him? A. From Mr. Booth.
Q. John Wilkes Booth, the actor? A. Yes sir.
Q. Did you carry the letter to him alone, or to him and Arnold? A. I carried one to Arnold and gave it to a lady, and she said she would give it to him.
Mr. Coxe here said that unless this question was to be followed up he would object to it.
The objection of the counsel was overruled, and the examination proceeded.
Q. So you delivered it at the boarding house of O'Laughlin? Did he tell you where O'Laughlin lived? A. He said on Exeter street.
Q. But did you carry a letter to Arnold? A. No, sir, I carried one up there to the house; I did not know who it was for, myself.
Q. Who from? A. Mr. Booth gave it to me; he first called me and asked me if I would take a letter down there; I didn't know for whom it was; he first told me to carry it to the number that was on the letter.

Q. You carried more than one? A. Two.
Q. To whom did you deliver the second? A. To Mr. O'Laughlin.
Q. Do you know for whom it was? A. He told me it was for Mr. O'Laughlin; I know Mr. O'Laughlin, and was glad when I saw him in the theatre, because it saved me night walking.
Q. For whom did O'Laughlin say the letter was. A. Well, I said here is a letter Mr. Booth gave me for you, and that was all.
Q. Booth told you then this letter was for O'Laughlin? Mr. Cox here remarked again. I must object to this evidence, as it is not followed up as to what he did after the receipt.
The Judge Advocate-General remarked that the object was simply to show the intimacy of those men by their correspondence.
Mr. Coxe said he objected to any evidence of Booth's sending a letter to any individual. It was simply an act of Booth's own, to which the defendant was not privy.
The Judge Advocate-General then said that they did not offer the letter in evidence at all, but simply their correspondence with each other. The objection was finally entered upon the record, but was overruled by the Court.
Q. When did I understand you to say this letter was carried? A. It was in March.
Q. Are you sure? A. Yes sir, in March last.
Q. Late or early in March? A. About the middle of the month; I was coming along there near the mineral water store, and he said, couldn't I take a note for him: I said I could; I had to go in front; he said for me to take the note and he would pay me; I asked him where, and he said to Fayette street.
Q. You said something about the theatre; what theatre? A. The Holliday Street Theatre.
Q. You say you found O'Laughlin in the theatre; what part of the theatre? A. In the dress circle, in the afternoon.
Q. How did you find him? A. I went up with Pitch, and found him there.
Q. All you know about it is that you just gave the note to him and came away? A. Yes, sir.
Q. When Booth gave you the other letter, that was not for O'Laughlin? A. No, sir; that was for a house in Fayette Street. He just gave me the number of the house.
Q. He did not tell you who it was addressed to? A. No, sir.

Testimony of J. P. Early.

J. P. Early sworn.
Q. Do you know the prisoners, O'Laughlin and Arnold? A. I know O'Laughlin.
Q. Have you been on the cars with them coming from Baltimore to this city? A. Yes, with O'Laughlin, on the Thursday previous to the assassination.
Q. Was Arnold on the cars? A. No sir, not to my knowledge at least.
Q. That was the day previous to the assassination? A. Yes, Thursday, the night of the illumination.
Q. Do you know where he went to stay after you arrived? A. There were four of us, and when we stopped to get shaved between Third and Four-and-a-half streets, he asked me to walk down as far as the National Hotel with him.
Q. Did he take a room there? A. No sir, he did not.
Q. Did you see him associate with Booth? A. No sir, I never saw Booth but once, and that was upon the stage.
Q. Did he make any inquiry for Booth? A. I did not hear him.
Q. Did you see O'Laughlin during that day? A. I was with him the greater part of that day.
Q. Where? A. We slept at the Metropolitan that night, and then went to Welch's and had breakfast for four of us; as we were passing the National Hotel, I stopped to go to the water-closet; when I came out I met Mr. Henderson, who said he was waiting for Mr. O'Laughlin, who had gone up stairs to see Booth; we waited three-quarters of an hour, and he not coming down, we went out.
Q. When did you see him again? A. About four o'clock.
Q. What time did he go to see Booth? A. I should say it was about noon, perhaps.
Q. What was the latest hour at which you saw him on Friday? A. I don't recollect exactly; I had been drinking considerably, but I distinctly recollect I saw him come out of a restaurant pretty late; I can't say whether it was after the assassination.
Q. Can you give the name of the restaurant? A. I believe the name, at present, is "Lee Shore."
Q. Did you see him at the time or immediately after you heard of the assassination of the President? A. I can't say I did; I went to bed shortly after that; I think I distinctly recollect his coming out with Fowler.
Q. Who is Fowler? A. I don't know exactly; he used to be employed by O'Laughlin's brother once.
Q. Did O'Laughlin go to Baltimore the next day? A. Yes, on the three or half-past three o'clock train; I forget which it is.
Q. Where did he go to in Baltimore? A. Well, after we arrived we went down Baltimore street, as far as High, down to Fayette, and from there we went and

asked to see a gentleman's wife who was lying here sick in Washington; and then we came down and went to O Laughlin's; going down, we met his brother on the way, who told O'Laughlin that there had been parties looking for him; he asked me if I would wait, and then he asked me in; he then went up, and said he was not going to stay home that night.

Q Did he show much excitement about the assassination? A. I can't say he did, but his brother said he would be after him on account of his intimacy with Booth.

Cross-examination by Mr. Cox.—Q. Who was with O'Laughlin besides yourself? A. There was Henderson, Edward Murphy and myself.

Q. What was your purpose in coming down? A. We came to have a little good time, and to see the illumination.

Q. Did he join you in Baltimore? A. He came with Henderson.

Q. Where did you stay on Thursday night? A. At the National Hotel. Henderson, me and Smith stopped in one room, and as O'Laughlin signed the register last they gave him a room to himself.

Q. Who arranged to sleep separately? A. Well, he was the man who signed last, and the clerk gave him that room.

Q. How late were you up that night? A. It was about 2 o'clock on Friday morning.

Q. Was it you who woke him in the morning? A. Yes, sir, and then we went down and got breakfast.

Q. Where? A. At Welch's, on the avenue, near Tenth street, and after breakfast we went back, about 10 o'clock, to the National Hotel.

Q. Did you hear him state what he was going to see Booth for, or that he was going to see Booth at all? A. No sir. not at that time.

Q. Did Booth come down? A. He did not.

Q. You don't know whether he actually saw Booth or not? A. I do not,sir; we remained in the hotel three-quarters of an hour waiting for him, and he not coming down, Henderson concluded to go, but as we went out he had some cards written by the card-writer there; we walked down the avenue, I think, as far as the "Lee Shore," and he not being there we went back and got the cards that the writer had written for Henderson; he wrote my name on a samplecard; we then proposed to send cards to Booth's room as a hint to O'Laughlin to come down; the cards were returned, as there was nobody in the room.

Q. How long during that day was O'Laughlin in your company? A. We took a stroll around the city, in different parts of it, and had dinner again at Welch's.

Q. Did you stroll around together? A. Yes sir.

Q. You dine I at Welch's? A. Yes sir.

Q. At what hour? A. Between twelve and two.

Q. Do you know Stern's clothing store? A. Yes sir.

Q. Was it over that? A. No sir. I think it was further up the avenue.

Q. What time did you get through dinner? A. It took us over an hour.

Q. Where did you go after dinner? A. Around town again, and we went on a visit.

Q. Was O'Laughlin with you all the time? A. I can't say he was after dinner, but I recollect that between four and five o'clock he went with me to a friend's house.

Q. To pay a visit? A. Yes sir; and we had dinner a second time.

Q. That was on Friday? A. Yes sir.

Q. How soon did you leave there? A. We left there about 6 o'clock.

Q. You are not certain that O'Laughlin was with you all the afternoon? You don't suppose he was with you between the first and second dinners? A. I am not positive; I think we separated; O'Laughlin and Henderson going one way, and Michael and myself another.

Q. You are not certain? A. No sir.

Q. After 6 o'clock where did you go? A. After we came up from the place near the Baltimore depot, where we had paid the visit, we returned to the Lee Shore House, and were then joined by the other two.

Q. How late was that? A. I don't exactly recollect. We stayed around there until between 7 and 8 o'clock, and then went back to Welch's and had supper. We were there at the time the procession passed up the avenue to the Navy Yard.

Q. What time was that? A. Between eight and nine o'clock.

Q. How late did you stay there? A. Until our supper was ready; we then went to the Lee Shore House.

Q. Did you stay there till you went to bed? A. I did, sir.

Q. Do I understand you to say you were there after the assassination? A. Yes sir.

Q. Where is the house? A. Between Third and Four-and-a-half streets, near the Globe office; the second door I believe from the Globe office.

Q. Did you speak to O'Laughlin when he was in company with Fowler? A. Yes sir.

Q. Was not that after you received the news of the assassination? A. I am not certain.

Q. Were you all there? A. Yes sir.

Q. Where did you stay that night? A. I staid at that house.

Q. Did O'Laughlin? A. Not that I know of.

Q. Had you been drinking? A. Yes sir.

Q. Now charge your memory whether it was after the news of the assassination reached you or not? A. I should judge it was about 10 o'clock.

Q. Where was Murphy? A. He had left us in the avenue.

Q. He was not with you at that time? A. No sir.

Q. Where was Henderson? A. In the bar-room, I believe.

Q. Now I will ask you when you came down on Thursday, whether the whole party had not arranged to go back on Friday? A. Yes, that was the intention; at least I understood so.

Q. During this visit did you see anything in O'Laughlin—anything desperate, which would lead you to suppose—

Objected to by the Assistant Judge Advocate Brigham.

Q. How was his conduct? A. The same as I ever saw; he was rather jovial.

Q. Was he in good spirits? A. Very much so, coming down to the cars.

Q. Any nervousness? A. No sir.

Q. I will ask you whether you were near Willard's Hotel during Friday, or Friday evening? A. We were not as far up as Willard's, I think; I don't recollect passing there.

Q. What induced you to stay later than you Intended? A. Well, it was the liquor.

Q. Didn't Lieutenant Henderson press you to stay? The question was objected to by Assistant Judge Advocate Bingham, on the ground that it was a cross-examination as to Henderson, whose name was not on the record yet.

Major-General Lew Wallace remarked that Mr. Henderson himself could be brought into Court.

The Court asked Mr. Cox if the question was withdrawn, to which Mr. Cox replied—No, sir.

The objection, however, was sustained by the Court.

Q. You stated that probably the liquor kept you there. Now I will ask you if anything else did? A. I cannot say.

Q. State what time you went up to the depot in the morning? A. We did start to go at eleven on Saturday morning, and went as far as the depot, and Henderson went and got the tickets, but Henderson finally concluded to stay over the afternoon; O'Laughlin was wanting to go up to Baltimore, and said I to Henderson, if you press him to stay, he will, and so we all concluded to stay until three in the evening.

Q. Then you went up at three in the evening? A. Yes sir.

Q. You say you met his brother, and that he said parties were looking for him? A. Yes, I remember the remark he made, that he would not like to be arrested in his honor that it would be the death of his mother; his brother-in-law went with me to the corner of Fayette and Exeter streets; we stopped there and had a conversation, and I told him he had better stay at home, and that those parties would probably come again. He said—No, it would be the death of his mother, and asked me to go up town with him, and I went up, but I do not recollect the name of the street; we got into the cars, and then got out we returned home.

Examination in Chief Resumed.

By Judge Holt:—Q. Do you know the hour that O'Laughlin joined you on Thursday? A. We all four went into the hotel together.

Q. At what hour? A. About one or two o'clock.

Q. On Friday morning? A. Yes.

Q. Where had you been the previous part of the night? A. After supper we went to see the illuminations, and went a considerable distance up the avenue, and then turned back, and, at the invitation of Mr. Henderson, went into the Canterbury Music Hall.

Q. All of you? A. All of us.

Q. Did you all continue together? A. Yes sir.

Q. Did you go any where else? A. No sir.

Q. Didn't you go on K street or L street? A. No sir; I can't say; I don't know where that street is myself.

Q. Can you state where you were besides at the Canterbury? A. Afterwards.

Q. Not before that. A. We had supper previous to that and took a walk up the avenue.

Testimony of Lieutenant Henderson.

Q. State whether you are acquainted with the prisoner O'Laughlin? A. Yes sir.

Q. Did you see him in this city on Friday, April 14th? A. Yes sir, on Thursday and Friday.

Q. Do you know whether on either of those days he visited Booth? A. He told me on Friday that he was to see him in the morning.

Cross-examination by Mr. Cox.—Q. Did he tell you he was to see him, or that he went to see him? A. He said he was to see him on Friday.

Q. As if he had an engagement to see him? A. He only said he was to see him; I can't say whether he had an engagement or not.

Q. Did he tell you what for? A. No sir.

Q. That is all you know about it? A. That is all, sir.

Testimony of Samuel K. J. Stregg.

Q. Explain to the Court how long you have known O'Laughlin? A. I have known him for years.

TRIAL OF THE ASSASSINS AT WASHINGTON. 35

Q. Did you see him in the month of April last before the assassination? A. I can't be positive about its being April, but it was well on to the 1st of April.
Q. Did you see him with Booth? A. I did.
Q. Did the association between them seem to be of an intimate nature? A. It did.
Q. Did you see them converse in an intimate manner? A. I did.
Q. Where was that? A. I don't know the house; it was on the right hand side of the avenue as you go up to the Treasury Department.
Q. Inside? A. No, outside.
Q. Were they alone by themselves? A. There were three of the party.
Q. Did the third party take any part in the conversation? A. I think Booth was the speaker, and the other party the listener.
Q. Did they suspend their conversation when you approached? A. O'Laughlin did. He called me on one side and said Booth was busy with his friend talking privately.
Q. Do you know this man? A. No sir.
Q. Describe him. A. He was about my height, with curly hair; he was in a stooping position, as if talking to Booth; I thought it ill manners to go too near them.
Q. Do you recognize any of the prisoners as being the man?
The witness scrutinized the prisoners in the dock, and answered:—
In their present dress, I would'nt swear to any.
The question was objected to, and the objection was sustained.
Q. Have you any opinion as to whether either of these is the man? A. I feel it my duty to detect the man, but it is a delicate question. No sir, I will not swear that the man is there.
Q. State whether you are the person reported to have seen Booth and Harold on the night of the assassination? A. I don't know Harold and I never saw Booth but once after that.

Cross-examination by Mr. Cox.—Q. You say you saw this conference at the house on the avenue? Can you tell where the house is? A. I paid no attention to the locality; it is between Ninth and Eleventh streets, to the best of my recollection; I know I was going up to Eleventh street.
Q. Can you speak with any certainty as to the date? A. I could if I had the papers that I obtained. Then I could come nigh to it; but I can't now say positively as to the date.
Q. Might it not have been that you asked O'Laughlin to take a drink, and he have replied that Booth was busy with a friend? A. Well, I am in no ways stingy; I might have done so.
Q. And what was his answer in reply to your invitation to take a drink? A. I don't know.

Testimony of L. S. Sprague.

By Judge Holt.—Q. You have been a clerk at the Kirkwood House? A. Yes sir.
Q. Were you present when the room was broken open after the assassination? A. Yes sir.
Q. State what was found there? A. All I saw was a revolver.
Q. Do you recollect that in the course of the day some men called to inquire for Atzeroth? A. No sir, I do not.

Cross-examination by Mr. Doster.—Q. When were you at the desk? A. I came off duty at 12 in the morning.
Q. Did you observe anybody calling and asking for Atzeroth? A. No sir.

Testimony of David Stanton.

Q. Look upon the prisoner, O'Laughlin, and state to the Court whether you ever saw him before, and if so, when and where. A. I have seen him.
Q. Which is he? A. That is him; he sits there between two soldiers.
Q. State when and where you saw him? A. The night before the assassination; at the house of the Secretary of War; I simply saw him there; he remained some moments, till I requested him to go out.
Q. Did you have any conversation with him in the house? A. I asked him what his business was, and he asked where the Secretary was; I said he was standing on the stoop.
Q. Did he ask for anybody else but the Secretary? A. No.
Q. Did he offer any explanation while there? A. No; at first I thought he was intoxicated; but found afterwards that he was not.
Q. Was General Grant there that night? A. Yes, in the room.
Q. Did he ask in regard to him? A. I don't recollect that he did.
Q. Did he go when you told him? A. Yes, sir.
Q. At what hour was that? A. At 10½ o'clock; there was a crowd there, and a band there serenading Gen. Grant and the Secretary of War.
Q. Do you know anything of a man being seen lurking about the premises? A. No sir, it was eleven o'clock before I got there; his inquiry was simply where the Secretary of War was; I pointed him out to him, but he did not go to see him, nor did he tell what his message was.

Cross-examined by Mr. Cox.—Q. Was that the first time you saw this man? A. Yes.
Q. Have you never seen him since? A. Yes, on the Montauk, as a prisoner.
Q. How long after was that? A. I don't remember the date, but it was the day they took Booth's body away from the vessel.
Q. Was it dark or light? A. Not very dark.
Q. Moonlight? A. No sir, dark.
Q. How was he dressed? A. In black.
Q. What kind of hat had he? A. A slouched hat.
Q. Did he have a whole suit of black? A. Yes sir.
Q. What kind of a coat? A. A dress coat.
Q. Was his vest black? A. Yes sir.
Q. Where does the Secretary live? A. On the corner of Fourteenth and K; the second house from the corner of Fourteenth.
Q. What peculiarity about the man enabled you to identify him? A. The hall was well lit up, and I was directly in front of him.
Q. How far inside the door were you? A. About ten feet, next to the library door.
Q. What do you suppose his size was, standing in the hall? A. About my height; four foot five, or five feet four I should say.
Q. When you saw him on the monitor was he standing or sitting? A. He stood up; I had an indistinct view of him on the monitor, it was so dark.
Q. You at first thought he was intoxicated, and then that he was not? A. Yes sir.
Q. There were a good many people in front of the door. A. Yes sir.
Q. Was there any one else about the hall? A. No sir.
Q. Who was on the door-step? A. The Secretary and another gentleman were on the door-step.
Q. He had got behind them? A. Yes sir.
Q. Was General Grant in the parlor? A. Yes sir.
Q. Was that lit up? A. Yes sir.
Q. Did he have the same beard as he has now? A. I see no change except from the want of shaving.

Testimony of Mr. D. C. Reed.

Q. State whether you were acquainted with Mr. John N. Surratt, in this city. A. I had no personal acquaintance with him.
Q. Do you know him when you see him? A. Yes sir.
Q. When did you last see him? A. On the 14th of April, the night of the assassination.
Q. In this city? A. Yes sir.
Q. Where did you see him then? A. He was standing on the street below the National, when he passed; it was about 2½ o'clock.
Q. Was he alone? A. Yes sir.
Q. Do you remember how he was dressed? A. Yes sir; in a country cloth suit, varied in texture and appearance; it was genteely got up; he had a round crowned hat; I noticed his spurs as he passed me particularly; he had on a pair of new brass-plated spurs, with a very large rowel.
Q. He was on foot was he? A. Yes, sir.
Q. What did you say was the color of his clothes. A. They were drab.
Q. Did you speak to him? A. I bowed to him as he passed.
Q. You stated you knew him quite awhile? A. I knew him when a child; he had grown pretty much out of my recollection; still I knew him when I saw him.
Q. You have no doubt you saw him on that day? A. I am very positive I saw him.

Cross-examination by Mr. Aitken.—Q. How long have you known Surratt? A. I could not state positively the length of time.
Q. Have you been in the habit of seeing him frequently during the past year? A. I cannot say that I have.
Q. When did you see him? A. I could not say positively; I think I saw him some time last fall, I think in October.
Q. Describe his appearance? A. He was a light-complected man; his hair was rather singular like; it is not red nor burned, but rather sandy; it was cut round so as to lay it low down on his collar.
Q. Did he wear any whiskers when you last saw him? A. I don't recollect seeing any hair on his face at all; if he had any, it was very light.
Q. Did you see anything of a goatee or moustache on him? A. No; I did not notice his face so much; I was more attracted by the clothes he had on.
Q. What do you mean by drab or grey clothes? A. I mean regular country cloth.
Q. Did I understand you to say you were standing on the steps of the National Hotel? A. No, as it was two doors below.
Q. You had no talk with him? A. No sir.
Q. Can you swear positively it was Surratt? A. I may be mistaken, but I am as certain it was he as that I am standing here.
Q. What is the state of his forehead? A. I could not say. He had his hat on. My attention was attracted to his clothes and spurs.
Q. You observed the clothes and the rowel more than his face? A. I can't say my attention dwelt upon his face at all.
Q. How large a man is he; I dont mean his height? A. He is not a stout man, but rather delicate; he would

not weigh over one hundred and forty pounds; he walks a little stooped.
Q. How long did you have your eyes upon him? A. I saw him as he passed, and I turned and looked.
Q. Did you see him again during the day? A. No sir. By Judge Holt.—Q. Did Surratt recognize you? A. He bowed to me as he passed.
Q. You say you gave a particular attention to his clothing. Are you in the habit of judging of these things? A. Yes, sir: I make them myself.

Testimony of James W. Pomephrey.

Q. You reside in Washington? A. I do.
Q. What is your business? A. I keep a livery stable.
Q. Are you acquainted with Booth? A. I was sir.
Q. Do you remember to have seen him on Friday, April 14th? A. Yes sir; he came to my stable about twelve o'clock and again at four o'clock; he said he wanted a horse at four o'clock on that day; he wanted a sorrel that he used to ride, but I could not let him have it, and I gave him a bay mare about thirteen or fourteen hands high.
Q. Was it returned to you? A. I have never seen her since.
Q. Describe the mare. A. She was a small mare; a little rubbed behind; she was a blood-bay, black tail, with a little star on her forehead.
Q. Was he in the habit of hiring horses from you? A. Yes; he first came in company with Surratt; he asked me if I was the proprietor, and I said yes; he wanted a horse; says I, "you will either have to give me reference or security; I don't know you; well," says he, "you have read about me;" "well," says I, "who are you, if I have read about you?" He said he was John Wilkes Booth: I said I didn't know whether he was John Wilkes Booth, and Surratt spoke up and said, "this is John Wilkes Booth," and I let him have the horse.
Q. How long was this before the assassination? A. One month or six weeks.
Q. Look at that photograph, do you recognize it? A. That is the man, sir.
Q. Did he ask for anything else? A. Only a tie-rein; I told him not to hitch her by the bridle, but to get a boy to hold her if he should happen to stop: he said he was going to Grover's Theatre to write a letter, and he would put her in a stable back of that; I told him if he could not get a boy, he could get a bootblack; he said he was going to take a pleasure ride, and asked "How is Chrystal Springs?" I told him it was a good place, but rather airy to go in.
Q. That was between four and five o'clock. A. Yes, I have never seen Booth since.
Q. Do you know any of the other prisoners? A. No; I don't know any of them at all.
Cross-examined by Mr. Aiken.—Q. Was Surratt with Booth? A. Yes, sir, the first time I saw him; he never came with anybody else.
Q. When was that? A. Six weeks before the assassination.
Q. He was not with him on the Friday? A. No; Booth was always alone after that.
Q. What kind of a looking man was Surratt? A. He was about five feet, ten or eleven inches; a light sandy hair and a light goatee; his eyes were sunken; he was thin in feature.
Q. How was he dressed? A. He had on a grey shirt, I think; I am not certain.
Q. All the remarks he made was that one in reference to Booth? A. That was all, sir.
Q. Did Booth ever refer to his introduction by Surratt? A. Not at all, sir.

Testimony of Rufus Stables.

Rufus Stables sworn.—Q. Do you live in Washington city? A. Yes sir.
Q. What is your business? A. I keep livery stable only.
Q. State whether you were acquainted with Booth? A. Yes sir.
Q. Also with Surratt? A. Yes sir.
Q. Also with Atzeroth? A. Yes sir.
Q. Did you see them together at your stable? A. Yes, frequently.
Q. During what month? A. Down to about the 21st or 20th of April.
Q. March you mean? A. Yes sir, March.
Q. Were they unusually intimate? A. They would come together three or four times a day sometimes.
Q. Did they keep horses there? A. Surratt kept two.
Q. Did he allow Atzeroth to use his horses? A. No sir, he rode out occasionally with him.
Q. Did you ever see this note, "Mr. Howard will please let Atzeroth have my horses and also my gloves whenever he wishes to ride?"
Q. Who is Mr. Howard? A. He is the proprietor of the stable.
Q. Do you know whether under that order he rode Surratt's horse? A. Several times; but after that date I think the order was rescinded.
Q. Look at that paper, and see if you can identify it in any way? A. I know this note; it came through my hand.
Q. How did the note reach the hands of Howard? A. It was sent by Mr. Surratt, and I put it on file.
Q. Did you let the horse go, accordingly? A. Yes sir.

Q. Do you remember what Atzeroth said in regard to Surratt's visit to Richmond? Did he speak to you of his having been there, or of any trouble he was involved in in consequence? A. He told me he had been to Richmond and coming back got into difficulty, and that the detectives were after him.
Q. Do you remember what time that was in April? A. In the early part.
Q. Did Atzeroth himself hire horses of you? A. No sir. I think not at that stable.
Q. Did he, or did he not take away a horse blind of an eye? A. Yes; under the owner's orders.
Q. Who was the owner? A. Surratt.
Q. When did he take that horse away? A. On the 31st; it was paid for on the 29th.
Q. Describe the animals taken? A. They were both bay; one was darker than the other; the one that was blind of one eye was the smaller horse.
Q. Were you paid for keeping them? A. Yes; Booth paid their keep.
Q. Did you see the horse afterwards? A. Yes; at the stable; he took him there to sell him to Mr. Howard.
Q. Who, Atzeroth? A. Yes; and he took him away.
Q. Who claimed the horses? A. Surratt; Surratt claimed them, Booth paid for their keeping, and Atzeroth took them away; there was another gentleman who came and rode one of them away.
Q. Who was he? A. I don't know.
Q. Do you think you would recognize the horse that was blind of one eye, if you were to see him? A. Yes sir.
The Assistant Judge Advocate then ordered that the witness be taken in an ambulance to see the horse of Ninteenth and I streets; the Judge Advocate-General remarking that they wished to examine him further when he returned.

Testimony of Peter Flatterkelt.

Peter Flatterkelt, sworn—By Judge Holt—Q. Please state to the Court whether you knew J. Wilkes Booth. A. Yes.
Q. What is your business? A. I keep a restaurant near Ford's Theatre.
Q. State whether or not you saw Booth in your restaurant on the evening of the 11th of April. A. Yes; he was there just about ten, or a little after, that night.
Q. State what occurred, and under what circumstances you saw him? A. He just walked into the bar, and called for some whisky; I handed him the bottle of whisky and a tumbler; I did not give him water at once, as is usual; he called for water, and I gave it to him; he put some money on the counter, and went right out.
Q. Was your restaurant under Ford's Theatre? A. It is on this side of Ford's Theatre, adjoining it.
Q. Did you observe where he went from there? A. I only observed him to go out from the bar.
Q. Was he alone? A. Yes, sir.
Q. Was he there in the afternoon? A. I did not see him.
Q. How many minutes was it after he went out before you heard the report of a pistol? A. I did not hear the report of a pistol.
Q. How long before you heard the President was assassinated? A. I think from eight to ten minutes, as near as I can come at it.
Q. Are you acquainted with the prisoner Harold? A. Yes sir.
Q. When did you see him? A. I saw him either the night of the murder or the night previous to that; he came into my place; I was behind the bar, and he asked me if John Booth had been there that afternoon; I told him I had not been there myself all that afternoon; he asked if I had not seen him, and I said no; he then went right out.
Cross-examined by Mr. Stone.—Q. You cannot fix distinctly whether this was on Thursday or Friday? A. I cannot.
Q. Were there not two other gentlemen with Harold the evening he came to your place? A. I did not see them.
Q. Did he come alone? A. I think he came alone; there may have been some one outside of the restaurant, but I did not see any one come in.
Q. How long have you known Harold? A. Ever since he was a boy.
Q. What time in the evening did you see him on this occasion? A. I judge it must have been between six and seven o'clock, as near as I can recollect.

Testimony of James M. Dye.

Sergeant James M. Dye sworn—By Judge Holt. Q. State whether or not on the evening of the 14th of April last, you were standing in front of Ford's Theatre. and if so, at what time? A. I was sitting in front of Ford's Theatre about half past nine on that night.
Q. State whether or not you observed several persons whose appearance excited your suspicions, conferring together on the pavement in front of the theatre. A. Yes sir.
Q. Describe their appearance and what they did. A. The first that attracted my notice was an elegantly dressed gentleman that came out of the passage and commenced conversing with a rough looking party; then there was another joined them and the

TRIAL OF THE ASSASSINS AT WASHINGTON. 37

three conversed together; after they had conversed a while and it was drawing near the end of the second act, the well dressed one, who appeared to be the leader, said:—"I think he will come out now," referring, I supposed, to the President.

Q. Was the President's carriage standing there? A. Yes; they waited awhile, and several gent'emen came down and went into the saloon below and had drinks; then a ter they went up the best dressed gentleman stepped into the saloon and waited long enough to take a drink. He came out in a style as though he was becoming in oxidized and stepped up and whispered to the roughs, took ne one of the three, and went into the passage that leads from the stage to the street.

Then the smallest one stepped up just as the well-dressed one appeared again and called out the time. He started up the street and remained awhile, and came down again, and called the time again. Then I began to think thereo was something wrong. Presently he went up and called the time again, louder than before. I think it was ten minutes after ten.

Q. He was announcing it to them all, was he not? A. Yes sir. Then he started at a fast walk up the street; the best dressed one then then went inside the theatre. I started for a saloon, and had just time to get down to it and order oysters, when a man came running in and said the President was shot.

Q. Do you recognize the well dressed person from the photograph I now show you? (Photograph of Booth shown witness.) A. That is the man; his moustache was heavier and his beard longer though.

Q. Do you recognize his features? A. Yes; that is the man.

Q. Which restaurant did the well-dressed man go into? A. Into the restaurant just below the theatre towards the Avenue.

Q. Did he go in there alone? A. Yes.

Q. I wish you to give, if you can, a more particular description of this rough looking man; what was his size; what gave him the ruffianly appearance you spoke of; what is his dress? A. He was not as well dressed as the rest of them.

Q. Was he shabbily or dirtily dressed? A. His clothes were more worn and shabby.

Q. Was he a stout man? A. Yes, rather.

Q. Which way did he go? A. He remained at the passage, while the other one started up the street.

Q. The time was announced to these other two men, three times, was it? A. Yes sir.

Q. Did he immediately go into the theatre after announcing the time on the last occasion? A. Yes sir.

Q. Will you look at the persons, as I see whether you recognize any of them as persons you saw on that occasion? A. If that man (pointing to Spangler) had a moustache, he has exactly the appearance of the rough looking man standing at the end of the passage. It was rather dark, and I could not see him distinctly; but he had a moustache.

Q. You state that the last call was made ten minutes after ten. Can you state when the other calls were made? A. They were all made between half past nine and ten minutes past ten.

Q. Do you think you recognize either of the other persons here as among the ones you have mentioned? A. No, the third one was a very neat gentleman, well dressed, and with a moustache.

Q. You do not see him here? No sir; he was better dressed than any one I see here; he wore one of those fashionable hats they were in Washington, with round tops and stiff brims.

Q. Can you describe his dress in color? A. No not exactly.

Q. How was he in regard to his size? A. Not very large; about five feet six inches high.

Q. And you have never seen that man before or since? A. No, never.

Q. Do you remember now the color of his clothes? A. His coat was a kind of a dead color; his hat was black.

Q. Did you observe these men whether any of them had spurs on? A. I did not observe that.

Examined by Mr. Ewing.—Q. How long did you observe the slouchy man? A. While I was sitting there until I left; I was there from twenty-five minutes or half-a ter nine till the last time was called.

Q. Was the slouchy man there during the whole of that time? A. He remained at the passage during the whole of that time.

Q. Will you please describe the several articles of dress as nearly as you can? A. I cannot particularly; it was so dark.

Q. Could you see his countenance? A. Yes.

Q. Could you see the color of his eyes? A. I did not observe that.

Q. Did you notice the color of his moustache? A. His moustache was black.

Q. Did you observe the color of his hair? A. No. I did not; he remained in one position.

Q. What kind of a hat had he? A. A slouch hat, that had been worn some time.

Q. Had he an overcoat? A. I did not observe.

Q. Did you notice anything as to the color of his coat? A. I did not; I witnessed the well-dressed man whispering to him.

Q. Where did he stand? A. Right at the end of the passage on the pavement.

Q. Near the President's carriage? A. No; the President's carriage was near the curbstone.

Q. Did he keep the same position during the whole of this time? A. Yes; the man with the slouch dress did.

Q. Which way did Booth enter the theatre the last time? A. He just stepped into the front door.

Q. Was he the man with the slouch dress standing there at that time? A. When Booth whispered to him and left him, I did not see him change his position; I was observing Booth.

Q. You do not know whether the man with the slouch dress stood there after Booth went into the theatre or not? A. I d d not.

Q. Are you sure he did not go out on the pavement before Booth went in? A. I do not recollect his going out on the pavement.

Q. What first attracted your attention to that man? A. I observed the well dressed gentleman speaking to him.

Q. When did you notice that first? A. About twenty-five minutes or half-past nine.

Q. How long after Booth entered the theatre was it that you heard the news of the assassination? A. I could not tell positively; it might have been fifteen minutes; it may have been less.

Q. State what you done in the meantime? A. I started down and went around the corner and into a saloon, debated a while which saloon to go into; I had only just got in and had oysters ordered.

Q. About how tall do you think the man with the slouch clothes is? A. He was about five feet eight inches.

By the Court.—Q. I understand you to say that the prisoner you have identified (Spangler) was the man? A. I say that was the countenance with a moustache; that is the very face.

By Mr. Ewing.—Q. Have you seen the man since the assassination of the President before now. A. Yes; in the old Capitol Prison.

Q. In the presence of what persons? A. Of the proprietor of the theatre, Sergeant Cooper and another person.

Q. Did it seem to you that he was the man? A. All but the moustache.

Testimony of John M. Buckingham.

John M. Buckingham sworn.—By Judge Holt.—Q. In what business were you engaged during the month of April? A. At night I was door-keeper at Ford's Theatre; during the day I was employed in the Navy Yard.

Q. Were you acquainted with J. Wilkes Booth during that time? A. Yes; I knew him by his coming to the theatre.

Q. State if you saw him on the evening of the 14th of April, at what hour and what occurred? A. I judge it was about 9 o'clock. He came into the theatre and walked in and out again, and he returned in about two or three minutes. He came to me and asked what time it was. I told him to step into the lobby leading into the street, and he could see. He stepped out and walked in at the door leading to the parquette; came out immediately and walked up the stairway leading to the dress circle; that was the last I saw of him until I saw him leap on the stage and run across the stage with a knife in his hand; he was uttering some sentence, but I could not hear what it was so far back.

Q. He went into the President's box did he? A. The dress circle extends over my door so I could not see.

Cross-examined by Mr. Ewing.—Q. Are you acquainted with the prisoner, Edward Spangler? A. Yes, I have known him at the theatre.

Q. Did you see him enter and go out at the front entrance during the day? A. No.

Q. State your position there. Is it such that you would he likely to see any person who entered from the front of the theatre? A. Yes. Every person has to pass me entering the lower part of theatre for the parquette, the dress circle and the orchestra.

Q. Did you observe all persons who came in? A. I did not take special notice of them. I saw that no person came who was not authorized.

Q. If this man Spangler had gone in from the street would you have been likely to have seen him? A. Yes; he could not have passed me without my seeing him.

Q. Are you certain that he did not pass? A. I am perfectly satisfied he did not pass in that night.

Q. Did you see him that night at all? A. Not to my recollection.

Q. Did you ever see him wear a moustache? A. No sir, not that I can recollect.

James P. Ferguson Sworn.

By Judge Holt.—Q. State your business. A. The restaurant business, No. 452 Tenth street, adjoining Ford's Theatre on the upper side.

Q. Do you know J. Wilkes Booth? A. I do.

Q. Did you see him on the evening of the assassination of the President? A. I saw him that afternoon; I do not recollect exactly what time it was; perhaps between two and four o'clock; he came up just below my door in the street; he was sitting on a horse; I walked out and saw Mr. Maddox standing by the horse, with his hand on the mane; he looked round and said to me, "Ferguson, see what a nice horse I have; he will run just like a cat;" with that he stuck his spurs in the horse, and run off, and I saw no more of him till that night at ten o'clock; along in the afternoon, about one o'clock, I was told that my favorite, General Grant, was going to be at the theatre, and if I wanted to see him I had better go; I got a seat directly opposite the President's box, in the dress circle; I saw the President and his family when they came in with some gentlemen in citizen's clothes, whom I did not recognize; I supposed that General Grant had remained outside, intending to come in alone, and not create an excitement in the theatre, and I made up my mind that I would see him, and I watched every one who passed around that side of the dress circle. Somewhere about ten o'clock I saw Booth pass around in that direction. Something attracted my attention towards the stage, I then saw him push upon the door leading to the boxes. I did not see anything more of him until I saw him rush to the front of the box, and jump over, and as he jumped I could see the knife gleaming in his hand; at that time the President was sitting, leaning on his hands, towards the right, looking down on some person in the orchestra; he was not looking on the stage; he was looking between the post and the flag decorating the box; as he jumped over I saw it was Booth; I saw the flash of the pistol right in the box, and heard him exclaim *Sic Semper Tyrannis;* he ran right across the stage to the door; where the actors come in, and I saw no more of him; I ran as quickly as I could to the Police office, on Tenth street, and told the Superintendent; I then ran up Tenth street, for the purpose of seeing General Augur, or Colonel Wells; Colonel Wells was standing on the steps; I told him I had seen it all; he told me the guard to pass me in, and I went in and told him the story; I went home and went to bed; the next morning I got up and Mr. Gifford said to me it was a hell of a statement I had made last night, about seeing the flash of the pistol in the box, when the pistol was fired outside of the door; I told him it was fired inside the door, and afterwards went round to the theatre to examine the hole where the ball was supposed to have gone through the door; the hole was evidently bored with a large gimlet and whittled with a knife; the scratches of the knife could plainly be seen.

Q. Is Mr. Gifford the other carpenter? A. Yes; he had charge of the theatre altogether; he was the chief carpenter and had full charge there, as I always understood.

Q. Was the President's box on the south side of the theatre? A. Yes; he always had the same box, every time I saw him there.

Q. Did you hear any other expression except "Sic Semper Tyrannis?" A. I heard some one call out of the box, I do not know who, but I suppose it must have been Booth, "Revenge for the south!" just as he jumped; as he went over on to the stage I saw the President raise his head, and saw Mrs. Lincoln catch him by the arm; then I understood Mr. Lincoln had been shot; by that time Booth was across the stage.

Q. Did Booth's spur catch into the flag? A. His spur caught up the flag. It was the blue part of the American flag. As he went over his spur caught the moulding on the edge of the box, and also the flag. It tore a piece of the blue off, and carried it half across the stage. The spur was on his right heel.

Q. Did you observe the hole in the door only enough to see whether it had been freshly cut out? A. No, sir; not particularly; jailor noticed a hole cut in the wall, looking as if done by a knife to admit the end of a bar of wood, with which he had fastened the door.

Q. Could you observe the spur at all, as to the character of it? A. No, I could not observe that; I noticed it particularly, because it caught in the flag as he went over the boxes.

Cross-examined by Mr. Ewing.—Q. Did you see the bar with which the door was fastened. A. I did not; we could not find it the next day.

Q. Did you know Spangler, the prisoner? A. Yes.

Q. Did you see him on that night? A. I do not recollect seeing him. I was in the theatre that night, I went in about twenty minutes of eight o'clock. I wanted to get there be ore this party came in.

Q. Do you know him well? A. Yes; he worked in the Theatre.

Q. Did you ever see him wear a moustache? A. I do n't think I ever did; I do not think he ever wore a moustache since I have been there.

THE PRIVATE TESTIMONY.
Important Evidence of an Officer of Gen. Johnston's Staff.

The testimony taken before the doors were opened to reporter for the press includes that of a man who was for several years in the military service of the so-called Confederate States, employed in the topographical department, on the staff of General Edward Johnston. He was in Virginia in the summer of 1863, twenty miles from Staunton.

He became acquainted with three citizens of Maryland, one of whom was Booth and the other named Shepherd. He was asked by Booth and his com- panions what he thought of the probable success of the Confederacy, and he told them that after such a chase as the Rebels had then got from Gettysburg, he believed it looked rather gloomy.

Booth told him that was nonsense, and added: "If we only act our part right the Confederacy will gain its independence, and old Abe Lincoln must go up the spout." The witness understood by the expression "must go up the spout" that it meant he must be killed. Booth said that as soon as the Confederacy was nearly whipped, that was the final resource to gain the independence of the Confederacy.

The companions of Booth assented to his sentiments; the witness was at the camp of the Second Virginia Regiment, and there was a second meeting of Rebel officers on that occasion. He was not present at the meeting, but one of the officers who was, stated its purport; he believed that Booth was at that meeting. The purpose was to send certain officers on detached service to Canada and the borders to deliver prisoners, to lay the Northern cities in ashes, and finally to get after the members of the Cabinet and kill the President. The name of the officer who gave him the information was Lieutenant Cockerill.

Booth was associating with all the officers. He heard very often that the assassination of the President was an object finally to be accomplished. He had heard it freely spoken of in the streets of Richmond. This necessity was generally assented to in the service.

A lady from New York testified to having met Booth and a man named Johnson, and overheard their conversation. She picked up two letters which they had dropped, and one of them was addressed "Dear Davis," saying that the "lot had fallen upon him" to be the Charlotte Corday of the nineteenth century. Ahe must drink the cup; you can choose your own weapons, the knife, the bullet, &c. The letter is signed Chas. Selby.

Two other witnesses testified that they were in Canada, and saw Booth in conversation with George Sanders, and believed they also saw Booth talking with Clay, Halcomb and Thompson.

Testimony of Captain Theo. McGovern.

By Judge Advocate Holt—Q. Did you know J. Wilkes Booth? A. I knew him by sight.

Q. Did you see him the night of the assassination of the President? A. Yes.

Q. Describe what you saw on that occasion. A. I was sitting on a chair in the little aisle by the wall leading towards the door of the President's box on the night of the murder, when a man came up behind me in my seat, causing me to push my seat forward to permit him to pass; he then stepped about two or three feet from where I was, and stood leisurely taking a survey of the house; I looked at him, because he happened to come almost in my line of sight; he took a small pack of visiting cards from his pocket, and selecting one replaced the others; he handed the card to the President's messenger, who was sitting just below; whether the messenger took the card into the box, or after looking allowed him to go in, I do not know, but in a moment or two I saw him go into the box and close the door of the lobby leading to the box.

Q. Did you see him after the pistol was fired? A. Yes, I saw the body of a man descend from the front of the box to the stage, and he was out of my sight in a moment; in another moment he re-appeared, and strode across the stage, and as he passed I saw the gleaming blade of a dagger in his right hand.

Q. Was it a large weapon he held in his hand? A. Yes, the blade I should suppose to be five or six inches in length, from the length of the gleam I saw.

Q. Did you see whether it was Booth? A. I know Booth, but I did not recognize him.

Testimony of Major Henry R. Rathbun.

By Judge Holt.—Q. Please state to the Court whether or not you were in the box with the President on the night of the assassination. A. Yes.

Q. State all the circumstances that came under your observation in connection with that assassination. A. With the permission of the Court, I will say that I prepared a little statement at the time, which I would like to read in preference of giving the testimony here. It was made when the details were fresh in my mind. Permission having been given, witness thereupon read the statement to the Court. This has heretofore been published.

Q. You did not know Booth yourself? A. No.

Q. Could you recognize him from this photograph? A. I should be unable to recognize him as the man in the box; I myself have seen him on the stage some time since.

By the Court—Q. What distance was the assassin from the President when you first saw him? A. The distance from where the President was sitting was four or five feet, to the best of my recollection; this man was standing between him and the door.

By Judge Holt—Look at that weapon and see if it is about such a one as appeared to be used by Booth that night. A. I think it might have made a wound similar to the one I received; I could not recognize the knife; I simply saw the gleam.

By Colonel Burnett—Q. Did you notice how the blade

TRIAL OF THE ASSASSINS AT WASHINGTON.

was held in the hand of the assassin? A. Yes; the blade was held flat and horizontal; the entry of the wound would indicate it came with a sweeping blow from above.

Testimony of William Withers, Jr.

Examination by Judge Holt.—Q. Do you belong to the orchestra of Ford's Theatre? A. Yes.
Q. Were you there the night of the assassination of the President? A. Yes.
Q. Did you see J. Wilkes Booth there that night? A. Yes.
Q. State what you saw. A. I had some business on the stage with the stage manager, in regard to a national song I had composed; I wanted to see in what costume they were going to sing it; I learned from the manager that they would sing it in the costume they wore at the close of the piece; after that I was returning under the stage to the orchestra, when I heard the report of a pistol; I was astonished that a pistol should be fired while playing *The American Cousin*; I never heard one before; just then I met a man running before me; I stopped, completely paralyzed; I did not know what was the matter; he hit me on the leg, turned me round, and made two cuts at me, one on the neck and one on the side; as he went past, no I said that is Wilkes Booth; with that he made a rush for the door, and out he went; just then I heard the cry that the President was killed, and I saw him in the box, apparently dead.
Q. Which way did he go out of the theatre? A. Out of the back door.

Cross-examination by Mr. Ewing.—Q. Are you acquainted with the prisoner, Spangler? A. I have known him ever since I have been in the theatre.
Q. Did you see him that night? A. No, sir; I do not recollect seeing him that night; I only happened to go on the stage to see the manager.
Q. Which side of the stage did you go on? A. The right hand side facing the audience, furthest from the President's box.
Q. What was the position of this man? A. His position ought to have been there when the scene was to be changed; right in the centre of the stage; his business was to change the scenes, and he ought to have been right behind the scenes.
Q. On which side? A. I do not know on which side his position was.
Q. Do you know whether the passage through which Booth passed out of the door is generally obstructed? A. Sometimes there are a great many persons there, so that you cannot pass, but that night everything seemed to be clear; I met nobody that night until I met Wilkes Booth.
Q. Were they playing a piece requiring much shifting of the scenes? A. I think at that point of the play it could not be many minutes before the scene would require to be changed.
Q. Was it a time when the passage-way, in the ordinary course of things, would have been obstructed? A. Some of the actors might have been there waiting to go on the next scene. (Witness here described at length the various localities in connection with the stage.)
Q. Did you ever see Spangler wear a moustache? A. No, I have always seen him as he appears now; I do not think I ever saw him with a moustache.
Q. How long have you known him? A. Ever since Ford's Theatre has been going, nearly two years.
By Judge Holt.—Q. Is there not a side way by which the theatre can be entered without passing in from the front? A. No, not as I know of; there is one little passage where the actors and actresses get in, but that is the front way.
Q. That is used exclusively by the actors? A. Yes sir, it was used when the theatre was first opened by actors when they wanted to go out to take a drink without being observed.
By the Court—Q. When you met Booth on the stage as he was passing out, could you see the door as he went out? A. Yes sir.
Q. Was there any doorkeeper standing there that you could see? A. I did not see any.
Q. Was the door open? A. No, I think not.
Q. Was there anything to obstruct his passage out? A. No.
Q. Was that not an unusual state of things? A. It seemed strange to me; it was unusual.
Q. Was there any check at all as the door as he went out? A. No; it seemed to me after he gave me the blow that knocked me down, and in which he came very near going under, he made one plunge and was out.
Q. Was it your impression that the door was opened for him, or that he opened it himself? A. I don't know; I tried it myself, to see if it could be opened so easily; it surprised me.
Q. Was it your impression that some one assisted him in going out, by opening the door? A I did not see anybody; I only saw him go out.
Q. Do the scenes stand at this time just as they were left, or have they been changed? A. I really do not know.
Q. Do you say there is no passage out of the theatre except in front? A. No; you have to go from the alley round and come in front.

Re-examination of Stabler.

By Judge Holt.—Q. State to the Court whether since your examination you have been to a stable in the city and found the horse referred to? A. Yes, I have.
Q. Do you recognize that as the horse you referred to? A. Yes; that is the bay horse that Atzeroth took away on the 29th of March, and brought back some days afterwards, for sale.
By the Court—Q. That was the horse held at your stable at the Surratt House? A. Yes, until Booth paid the livery and took him away.
Q. Where is he kept now? A. On the corner of Seventeenth and I streets.
Q. Whose stable is it? A. A Government stable, by Mr. Dosier.
Q. Are you the owner of the place where these horses were kept? A. No, sir.
Q. What was your business there? A. The reception of livery horses, the hiring to parties, and a general oversight.
Q. Are you certain Surratt owned these horses? A. I supposed he did; he brought them there in his name and paid the livery.
Q. Did not you say that somebody else paid the livery? A. When they were taken away finally Booth paid it.
Q. Did you not say Surratt paid the livery? A. Surratt paid down to the end of the month previous.
Q. When Booth settled the bill, did he claim the horse as his? A. No.
Q. Did he state who they belonged to at that time? A. He gave the order of Surratt to pay for the horses and take them away.
Q. Did you say this horse you have just described was sold from your stable? A. No sir; he was not sold; he was brought there on livery, and on the 29th of March Booth paid the livery for the month ending March 31, and some days afterwards Atzeroth brought them there to sell.
Q. When did you see this horse last before to-day? A. About the 4th or 5th of April, when he was brought there to sell.
Q. Have you seen that horse in the possession of Atzeroth since that time? A. Not since he brought him there to sell.

Testimony of Joe Simms (Colored.)

Examined by the Judge Advocate.—Q. What connection have you at Ford's Theatre? A. I have worked there two years; I went there when I first came to Washington.
Q. Were you there the night the President was assassinated? A. I was up at the fly where they hang up the curtains.
Q. Did you see Booth there that evening? A. I saw him there between five and six o'clock.
Q. State where you saw him, and what he did? A. When I saw him he came in the back part of the stage; he went out and went into a restaurant beside the theatre; I saw him no more that night until after the performance commenced; during the performance I heard a pistol fired, and looked immediately to see what it was; I saw him jump from the private box on to the stage and make his escape across the stage; I saw no more of him.
Q. Who was with him when he went out in the afternoon? A. There was no one; Mr. Spangler was standing out in front, and he invited him in to take a drink.
Q. Is this the man here, pointing to Spangler? A. Yes, that is the man.
Q. Did you hear anything said between them? A. No; they went in to take a drink; that is all I heard.
Q. Did you see Booth when he came up back of the theatre with his horse? A. No; the other colored man who works with me saw him.
Q. Did you know Spangler very well? A. Yes.
Q. Were he and Booth very intimate? A. They were quite intimate.
Q. You saw them go and drink together? A. Yes; that is all.

Cross-examined by Mr. Ewing.—Q. Had Spangler anything to do with Booth's horses? A. Nothing more than that he would have them attended to when Booth was away.
Q. He saw to their being fed and watered, didn't he? A. Yes.
Q. Was he hired by Booth? A. No, not Spangler; the other young man Booth hired, but I suppose Booth thought he would not do justice by his horse and got Spangler to see to it, when he was not there.
Q. What position did Spangler hold in the theatre? A. He was one of the stage managers; he shifted scenery at night and worked on the stage during the day.
Q. What was his position on the stage at night? A. On the right hand of the stage as you face the audience.
Q. That was the side of the President's box, was it not? A. No; the President's box was on the left hand side of the stage, as you look out opposite Spangler's place.
Q. Where was your position? A. My position was up in the flyers where they wind the curtain up on the third story.
Q. Did you see Spangler that night after five o'clock? A. Oh, yes; he was there on the stage attending to his business as usual.

TRIAL OF THE ASSASSINS AT WASHINGTON.

Q. What time did you see him? A. It was in the early part of the evening; I never inquired the time; we had no time up where we were.
Q. How long did you see him before the President was shot? A. I did not see him at all before the President was shot; I was looking at the performance until I heard the report of a pistol.
Q. Did you see him during the play that night? A. Yes; he was obliged to be there.
Q. Did you see him in the first act? A. Yes.
Q. Did you see him in the second act? A. I do not remember seeing him in the second.
Q. Could you have seen him where you were up in the fly? A. Yes, sir; I could see him from my side over on the other side of the stage.
Q. Was Spangler's place on the opposite side? A. Yes sir, on the opposite side below.
Q. Were you looking for him during the second act? A. No.
Q. Was he a sort of assistant stage manager? A. He was a regular stage manager to shift the scenes at night.
Q. From where you were could you see the President's box? A. I could, plain.
Q. What time in the first act did you see Spangler? A. In the first act I saw him walking about the stage looking at the performance.
Q. Had he his hat on? A. No.
Q. How was he dressed? A. I could not tell exactly what kind of clothes he had on.
Q. Did he look just as he does now as to his face? A. Yes, just as natural as he does now.
Q. Did you ever see him wear a moustache? A. No.
Q. From where you were on the fly would not the scenes change so that sometimes you could not see him? A. Sometimes I could only see him occasionally.

Testimony of John Miles (Colored.)

Examined by Judge Advocate Holt.—Q. State whether you belong to Ford's Theatre. A. I do.
Q. Were you there on the night of the assassination of the President? A. Yes.
Q. Did you see J. Wilkes Booth there? A. Yes; I saw him when he came there.
Q. Tell the Court all about what you saw? A. He came there about nine or ten o'clock; he brought a horse up from the stable down there to the back door, and called to Ned Spangler to come out from the theatre three times; then Spangler came across the stage to him; after that I did not see what became of Booth any more till I heard the pistol go off; then I went up in sight of the President's box; I heard some man say he believed somebody had shot the President; when I got there the President had gone out, or I could not see him; I went in a moment to the window and heard the horses' feet going out of the alley.
Q. Did you see any one holding the horse? A. Yes, I saw the boy after the hand called for Ned Spangler.
Q. You do not know what was said between them? A. No; I only heard him call for Ned Spangler.
Q. You say he came up to the door with his horse, between 9 and 10 o'clock. Do you know where he kept his horse? A. Yes, in a little stable close by there; I saw him come from there about 3 o'clock with Ned Spangler and Joseph Maddox.
Q. How far is the little stable where he kept his horse from the theatre? A. I do not think it is more than fifty yards.
Cross-examined by Mr. Ewing.—Q. Was the play going on when Booth rode up and called for Spangler? A. Yes; they were just closing a scene, and getting ready to take off that scene; Spangler was pushing the scene across the stage when Booth called to him three times.
Q. Where were you? A. I was up on the fly, three stories and a half from the stage.
Q. In what act was that? A. I think in the third act.
Q. How long before the President was shot? A. The President came in in the first act; I think it was in the third act he was shot; from the time he brought the horse there until he was shot I think was about three-quarters of an hour.
Q. Do you know who held the horse? A. John Peanut held the horse from the time Booth left him until he went away; every time I saw him John was holding the horse.
Q. Was John Peanut there when Booth came up? A. I did not see him there; there was no one there when Booth came up.
Q. Do you know whether Spangler went out of the door when Booth called him? A. He ran across the stage; I did not see them go out.
Q. How long did Spangler stay there? A. I don't know; the next time I looked this boy was holding the horse.
Q. How long was this after he called Spangler? A. Perhaps ten or fifteen minutes.
Q. Did you know what Spangler had to do with Booth? A. No; he appeared to be familiar with him.
Q. Did Booth treat him? A. I never saw him treat him.
Q. Did Spangler have anything to do with Booth's horses? A. I have seen him hold them up at the stables.
Q. Did you know anything about his hitching the horses or holding them up? A. No, sir; I never saw him hitch them up to the buggy; John Peanut always did that.
Q. Do you know what place Spangler occupied on the stage? A. On the right hand side, next to E street; on the side the President's box was.
Q. Could you see him from where you were, three stories above? A. Yes; I could see right straight through the scenes on that side of the stage; I always saw him at work on that side.
Q. Was he on that side when Booth called him? A. Yes.
Q. What was Spangler's business there? A. To shift the scenes at night across the stage.
Q. Was there another man shifting them from the other side? A. Yes, there was a man opposite to him.
Q. Did you see Spangler after Peanut John held Booth's horse? A. I never saw him any more until I came down after the President was shot; Spangler was then outside of the same door Booth went out at.
Q. Were the others out there? A. Yes, there were some more men out there; I did not notice who they were.
Q. Men of the theatre? A. Yes; men who were at the theatre that night; there were strangers there too.
Q. How many men were out at the back door at that time? A. Not more than three or four when I came down; I came down in a very short time after I understood what it was; I asked Spangler who it was that held the horse; he told me not to say anything; I knew it was the same person who brought the horse there that rode him away.
Q. Could you see Spangler all the time that he was on the stage? A. When he was working; in that time I could see him.
Q. Did you look at him that night? A. I did not notice him particularly that night any more than I usually did; I would not have noticed him had not Booth called him.
Q. You do not know whether he was on that night or not? A. He was when I saw him.
Q. What was it you asked Spangler when you came down? A. I asked him who it was holding the horse at the door; he told me to hush, and not say anything at all to him; and I never said any more to him.
Q. Was he excited? A. He appeared to be.
Q. Was every person excited? A. Everybody appeared very much excited.
Q. Did you not say he replied to you hush, and not say anything to him? A. I should have said he told me not to say anything about it.
Q. Do you know Spangler well? A. I know him when I see him.
Q. Did you ever see him wear a moustache? A. No sir, I do not think I ever saw him wear a moustache. By Judge Holt—Q. This remark which he made to you, "hush, do not say anything about it," was immediately after the killing of the President, wasn't it? A. Yes, right at the door, as I went out.
Q. Did he make any further remarks as a reason why you should not say anything to him? A. No, not a word to me.
Q. Did you see Booth go out of the door? A. No; I heard the horse go out of the alley; which way he went, right or left, I cannot tell; I heard the rattling of his feet on the rocks in the alley.
Q. Was the door left open at that time when Booth had gone out? A. It was open when I went down; whether it was open from the time he went out I do not know; I had come down three stories before reaching the door.
Q. Do you know of anybody who probably heard your remark to Spangler and his reply? A. No sir; I do not know that any person was noticing it at all; there were a good many persons round by the court.
Q. When Booth called to Spangler, the first time, did you see where he was? A. No, when he called the first time I did not notice where he was; when he called the second and third times I noticed where he was standing.
Q. Where did he go? A. He went towards the door and got underneath the fly, so that I could not see him any more until I looked out of the window.
Q. How long was he with Booth? A. I could'nt tell I never saw him any more until I came down stairs from the fly.
Q. When Spangler told you to hush and not say anything about it, was he near the door? A. He was, I suppose, a yard and a half from the door.
Q. Was anybody else near the door? A. Not as I know of; there was nobody between him and me and the door.
Q. Did he have hold of the door at the time? A. No, he was walking across in front of the door.
Q. Was anybody else between him and the door? A. No.
Q. Was it light or dark? A. It was right dark; it was a dark night any way, and there was no light right there.
Cross-examined by Mr. Ewing.—Q. Were you and Spangler in, do the door or outside? A. Outside.
Q. Where were the other people who you say were about there? A. Standing just around; some of them a little further from the door; I was between those people and the door; they were in the alley.

By the Court.—Q. Did they appear to be guarding that door? A. No.
Q. Did he act as if he was trying to prevent persons from getting in and out of the door? A. No; he appeared to be very much excited; that was all I noticed; at that time Booth had gone out of the alley.

Testimony of John Seleeman.

By Judge Holt.—Q. Are you connected with Ford's Theatre? A. I am.
Q. Were you present on the night of the President's assassination? A. I was.
Q. Did you know J. Wilkes Booth? A. Yes.
Q. Did you or did you not see him on that night; if so, at what hour, and under what circumstances? A. I saw him about nine o'clock; he came up on a horse to the back door of the theatre; Spangler was standing there, and Booth said, "Help me all you can, won't you?" he replied, "Oh, yes."
Q. Did he say that as he came up to the door on his horse? A. Yes, when he came up on his horse.
Q. Was that the first remark he made? A. The first words I heard him say were: "Ned, help me all you can, won't you?"
Q. How long was that before the President was shot? A. About an hour and a half, I should judge.
Q. Did you observe the horse afterwards? A. No, I did not.
Q. You did not see Booth in front? A. I just caught a glimpse of him as he was going out of the first entrance, right hand side.
Q. What hour did you see him going out at that entrance? A. It was half-past ten, I judge, after he shot the President.
Q. Do you mean that he went out of the back door? A. Yes.
Cross-examined by Mr. Ewing—Q. Did your hear him calling Spangler? A. No; the first I heard him say was "Help me all you can."
Q. Where was that? A. Out of the back door.
Q. Did you see Booth ride up? A. No sir; the horse was standing there.
Q. Was anybody holding the horse then? A. I didn't see anybody at all.
Q. Did you see the horse? A. Yes; I could not see whether anybody held him or not, it was so dark.
Q. What is your place in the theatre? A. Assistant property man.
Q. What is your position on the stage? A. We have to set the furniture and all such work as that, on the stage.
Q. What was Spangler's position on the stage? A. Stage carpenter.
Q. Was he the principal carpenter? A. No, Gifford was the principal carpenter; Spangler was hired by Gifford.
Q. What was his duty during the performance? A. To shift the scenes.
Q. On which side was his position? A. I do not know.
Q. Were you about that night? A. Yes.
Q. Were you on the stage during the whole day? A. Except that I went down to the apothecary's store once, and I believe I was before that in a restaurant next door.
Q. Did you notice the employees so that you could say whether Spangler was there through the play? A. No, I could not; I saw him after the assassination; he was standing on the stage; he had a white handkerchief in his hand, and appeared to be wiping his eyes.
Q. Was he crying? A. I do not know.
Q. How long was that after the President was shot? A. About ten minutes.
Q. Did not Spangler frequently have Booth's horses? A. I didn't see him at all.
Q. Was Booth a hab tue at the theatre? Did he go back and forth frequently? A. Yes.
Q. Was he familiar with the actors and employees? A. I think he was.
Q. Knew them all pretty intimately? A. Yes.
Q. Did he not have access to the theatre at all times? A. Yes.
Q. And went behind the scenes in the green-room? A. Yes, anywhere at all about the theatre.
Q. Is Spangler a drinking man? A. I think he is.
Q. Did Booth treat him much? A. I don't know.
Q. Were you round in front of the theatre at any time during the performance? A. Yes, I was on the pavement in front.
Q. Did you see anything of Spangler in front? A. No.
Q. At what time were you there? A. I was there from about, or half-past 7 o'clock, until after the assassination.
Q. Did you know the people who were about there? A. No.
Q. If Spangler had been there would you probably have noticed him? A. I guess I would.
Q. Did you notice the President's carriage there? A. Yes.
Q. Did you ever see Spangler wear a moustache? A. No, I don't think I ever did; I have seen him wear side whiskers.
Q. How was his face at that time? A. I think he was smooth shaved.

Q. You say you were in front of the theatre constantly? A. Oh no; not constantly.
Q. But frequently? A. No sir; I got to the theatre about half-past seven or eight o'clock, and was about the theatre until after the assassination; I was in front two or three times.
Q. Were you there during the third act? A. No; I was on the stage during the third act.
Q. Were you in front during the second act? A. I think I was in the restaurant next door.
Q. How long before the close of the second act? A. About ten or fifteen minutes.
Q. And you think if Spangler had been there you would have seen him? A. Yes.
By the Court.—Q. How did you get from the rear to the front of the theatre? A. There is a side entrance from the alley.
Q. You did not go, then, through the front door? A. No.
Q. Did you see Booth in front of the theatre? A. I saw him that afternoon between 4 and 5 o'clock in a restaurant next door; he with several others were there drinking; I saw Ned Spangler, Maddox, Booth, Peanuts, and a young gentleman by the name of Malden, were there; Maddox asked me if I would not take a drink; I said yes, and went up and took a glass of ale.
Q. You did not see Booth out on the pavement when you were out on the pavement that night? A. Not after he rode up that afternoon.
Cross-examined by Mr. Ewing.—Q. How far were you from Booth and Spangler when Booth made the remark you have stated? A. About as far as from here to you; about ten feet
Q. How far was Spangler from him? A. About as far as this gentleman here is from you; about two or three feet.
Q. Then Booth spoke in a loud voice? A. Yes.
Q. Did Booth see you? A. I don't know; he went right behind the scenes.
Q. Could he have seen you from where he was standing? A. Oh yes.
Q. Was there anybody by except you? A. I didn't notice at that time.
Q. Was not Spangler in liquor that night? A. That I cannot say.
Q. Did you often see him drunk or in liquor? A. I could not tell whether he was drunk or not.
Q. Was not he habitually pretty well soaked? A. I do not know, indeed.
By the Court.—Q. Was there anything unusual in the arrangement of the furniture that night on the stage? A. Yes sir.
Q. Was it all in its proper place according to the performance going on? Yes.
Q. The scenes and everything? A. Yes.
By Judge Holt.—Q. Do you know whether the scenes remain now about as they were that night? A. I do not know; I have not been in the theatre but once or twice since the assassination.
Q. Do you know what Spangler had to do with the decoration or arrangement of the President's box? A. No sir, I do not.

The Judge Advocate-General remarked that to enable the Court to understand perfectly the testimony of witnesses relative to the occurrences in the theatre, it would be proper for them to visit the theatre, and observe for themselves the different localities. It was therefore determined that the members of the Court meet informally at Ford's theatre, on Tenth street, to-day, at half-past nine o'clock A. M. The Court adjourned formally until ten this morning.

SUPPRESSED TESTIMONY OF FRIDAY

Henry Van Steinacker.

A witness for the prosecution, being sworn, deposed as follows:—
By Judge Advocate Holt.—Q. Have you or not for several years been in the military service of the so-called Confederate States? A. Yes sir, I have been.
Q. In what capacity? A. I was employed in the Topographical Department, ranking as engineer officer, with the pay of an engineer officer.
Q. On whose staff? A. The staff of General Edward Johnson.
Q. Were you or not in the State of Virginia in the summer of 1863, and at what point? A. When we came back from Pennsylvania, after the battle of Gettysburg, I was ordered with another engineer lieutenant, who was very sick, to convey him to his home at Staunton, in the Valley of Virginia; and from there I took my way back to find the army again; and near Harrisonburg, twenty-five miles from Staunton, at Swift Run Gap, I was overtaken by three citizens, with whom I got better acquainted, after having ridden a while with them; and I found them out to belong to Maryland; the name of one was Booth, and the other one's name was Shepherd.
Q. Do you remember the features of Booth? A. I do not remember the features of all of them.
Q. Look at that photograph (handing to the witness a photograph of J. Wilkes Booth). A. There is a resemblance, but the face was fuller.
Q. You think it is the same person, but he had a fuller face than this? A. I believe it is.

Q. Did you learn at that time that it was John Wilkes Booth, the actor? A. I heard the other gentlemen call him Booth; I thought first it was a nickname, but afterwards I found out that it was Booth?

Q. How far did you ride with those persons? A. We stayed at the tavern at the foot of the mountain until the next day; there I got better acquainted with them.

Q. How long were you together; how many hours do you suppose? A. Eighteen or twenty hours.

Q. Did you have any free conversations in regard to public affairs while you were with him? A. Yes sir.

Q. Will you state what Booth said to you in regard to any contemplated purpose of attack upon the President of the United States; state all that he said? A. I was asked by Booth and by those others, too, what I thought of the probable success of the Confederacy, and I told them that after such a chase as we had then got from Gettysburg I believed it looked rather gloomy, and then Booth told me, "that is nonsense; if we only act our part right the Confederacy will gain their independence; old *Abe Lincoln must go up the spout, and the Confederacy will gain their independence anyhow;*" that was the expression at the time.

Q. What did you understand by the expression, he "must go up the snout," from all that Booth said? A. It was a common expression, meaning he must be killed; that I understood always.

Q. Did he state under what circumstances that would become necessary? A. He said so soon as the Confederacy was near giving out, so soon as they were nearly whipped, that must be done; that would be the final resource to gain the independence of the Confederacy.

Q. Did the citizens who were with him engage in conversation? A. Yes sir.

Q. Did they seem to assent to his sentiments? A. Certainly.

Q. Did not Booth know that you were a Confederate soldier? A. Yes sir; they asked when they overtook me on the road, where I was going to; I told them I belonged to General Edward Johnson's Staff, and was going to the army, coming from Staunton.

Q. At what point did you arrive together? A. I do not know the name of the place; it is near the foot of the swift Run Gap.

Q. Did you meet there a number of Confederate officers—I speak of the end of your ride—with the Stonewall Brigade? A. Yes sir; that was about three or four days afterwards; they went from me the next day; my horse could not keep up with the other horses; they were splendidly mounted, and my horse was nearly broken down; so they waited three or four days afterward. I was called to some of the regimental camps and told that some strangers, friends of mine, wanted to see me; I did not know who it was; when I came to camp I found those three citizens, and was introduced by Captain Randolph personally, formally to Booth and Stephens.

Q. Was that the Stonewall Brigade? A. It was at the camp of the 2c ond Virginia Regiment.

Q. Do you, or do you not know, whether there was a secret meeting of Rebel officers on that occasion? A. That evening there was a secret meeting, where I was not admitted.

Q. Did they state to you the purpose of that meeting, and what conclusion they reached? A. Some officer afterwards, who was about the meeting, stated to me what was the purpose of it.

Q. Was Booth in that meeting? A. I believe so. They were all in together.

Q. What did he state to you was the determination and purpose of that meeting? A. The purpose of the meeting was, as I was informed afterwards, to send certain officers on detached service to Canada and the borders, and to deliver prisoners, *to lay Northern cities in ashes, and finally, to get after the members of the Cabinet, and kill the President;* that was the main purpose. I heard that more than a thousand times, but never so much as at the time when I was informed it was the purpose of the meeting; I always considered it common braggadocia before.

Q. What was the name of the officer who gave you this account of the proceedings of the meeting? A. Lieutenant Cockerill.

Q. To what portion of the service did he belong, do you know? A. To the Second Virginia Regiment, I believe, and the same Company that Captain Beall belonged to; the captain who was executed at Governor's Island.

Q. Was anything said as to what part Captain Beall, the one afterwards executed, was to play in these movements at the North? A. Cockerill told me Beall was on detached service, and we would hear of him.

Q. Cockerill was a member of that meeting, I understood you to say? A. Yes sir.

Q. Did you while there see Booth and Cockerill associated together? A. I did not see them particularly; I saw them all in a crowd together.

Q. Booth was associating with all the officers? A. He was associating with a good many of them.

Q. Did you know of any other secret association or meeting, having similar objects, at any time in the service with which you have been connected? A. I heard of the existence of secret orders for certain purposes to assist the Confederacy; I heard one name very frequently called, the name of one order, the "Golden Circle," and several times I heard the name of the "Sons of Liberty."

Q. How many years do you state you were in the Confederate service? A. Not quite three years.

Q. State whether, during the last year or two, since the reverses of the Confederacy have commenced, it has not been freely and frequently spoken of in the Rebel service, as an object finally to be accomplished, the assassination of the President of the United States? A. Yes sir, I heard that very often.

Q. Have you not heard it spoken of freely in the streets of Richmond, among those connected with the Rebel Government? A. Yes sir.

Q. About what time; when is the latest you can now recall having heard declarations of that sort at Richmond? A. At the time after the battle of Chancellorsville, when I do not know what General it was, but believe it was General Kilpatrick, was on a raid near Richmond; at that time I heard it; I was in Richmond on a furlough at the same time.

Q. Whenever and wherever spoken of, do I understand you to say that this sentiment of the necessity of the assassination of the President of the United States was generally assented to in the service? A. Yes sir.

Q. The "detached service" of which you speak, on which these parties were to be sent, you say related to Canada, and the destruction of the Northern cities along the Canada frontier? A. It was outside of the Confederate lines—either here in the Northern cities or in Canada.

Q. Did you understand that the "detached service" was to be performed in that direction along the Canada frontier and in our Northern cities? A. This "detached servic " was a nickname in the Confederate army for such purposes.

Q. It meant that sort of warfare? A. Yes sir.

Q. You spoke of laying the Northern cities in ashes; did you understand that that was the mode in which that warfare was to be conducted, by firing our cities? A. *Yes, sir; by firing the cities down and getting the people dissatisfied with the war, and by that means to bring forward a revolution among the people in the North.* That was the purpose.

Necross-examination.

The Judge Advocate offered in evidence, without objection, the photograph of J. Wilkes Booth, shown to the witness Van Steinacker. It is attached to this record, and marked Exhibit No. 1.

Mrs. Mary Hudspeth,

A witness called for the prosecution, being duly sworn, testified as follows:—

By the Judge Advocate.—Q. Where do you reside? A. At Harlem, New York.

Q. Will you state whether or not in the month of November last you were riding in the railroad cars of New York city, the Third avenue cars, and whether you observed that there were two men in the cars that attracted your attention, one of whom, on leaving the cars, dropped a letter which you picked up? A. I was going down to the city; there were two gentlemen in the car; whether they were or not when I got in I am not confident; I overheard their conversation; they were talking most earnestly; one of them said he would leave for Washington the day after to-morrow, and the other was going to Newburgh or Newbern that night; they left the car; the man that was sittting near me pushed his hat forward, and with that pushed his whiskers at the same time; they were false whiskers; the front face was much darker than it was under the whiskers.

Q. Was he a young man? A. He was young.

Q. Do you think you would recognize his features again? A. I think I should.

Q. [Exhibiting to the witness the photograph of Booth, Exhibit No. 1.] Loo at that and say whether it recalls him to you? A. The face is the same; he had a scar on his right cheek.

Q. Was it on the cheek or neck? A. It was something like a bite, near the jaw bone.

Q. Did you judge from his conversation that he was a man of education and culture? A. He was a man of education, and the other was not; the other's name was Johnson.

Q. Did you observe his hands; did he seem to have been a man who had led a life of ease or not? A. The hand that was ungloved was very beautiful; the other hand had a gauntlet on; they exchanged letters in the cars; the one who had false whiskers put back the letters in his pocket, and I saw a pistol in his belt.

Q. Did any of the conversation fall on your ears, were you able to hear it? A. I overheard him say he would leave for Washington the day after to-morrow.

Q. That is the one who had the unloved hand and false whiskers? A. Yes; and the other was very angry because it had not fallen on him to go to Washington; he had been sent for to some place by a messenger.

Q. You say he seemed very angry because it had not fallen to his lot to go to Washington instead of his other? A. Yes sir; I had letters of my own to post at the Nassau street post office; one of them left about Twenty-sixth or Twenty-seventh street, and as he left I moved up into his place; the car was crowded; my daughter said that I had dropped one of my letters; she picked up something and gave it to me; when I went down to the brokers', where I was going with

TRIAL OF THE ASSASSINS AT WASHINGTON.

BOSTON CORBETT—THE EXECUTIONER OF BOOTH.

some gold. I went to take out my pocket-book, and I saw an envelope with two letters in it; I thought it of importance because of the conversation.
Q. Are you certain it is the envelope with the letters dropped by one of these men? A. It must have been because I saw them exchange letters, and there was no one else at that seat.
Q. Was it picked up at the point where they were sitting? A. Yes, just at the end of my dress.
Q. Would you recognize the envelope if you were to see it? A. Yes sir.
Q. [Exhibiting an envelope with two letters.] Look at that, and see if it is the same envelope and letter.
A. It is the same.
Q. Were both letters in that envelope as you now have them? A. Yes sir.

The letters were then presented and read to the Commission, as follows:—

"DEAR LOUIS:—The time has at last come that we have all so wished for, and upon you everything depends. As it was decided before you left, we were to cast lots. Accordingly we did so, and you are to be the Charlotte Corday of the nineteenth century. When you remember the fearful solemn vow that was taken by us, you will feel there is no drawback; *Abe* must die, and now. You can choose your weapons. The cup, the *knife*, the *bullet*. *The cup failed us once, and might again*. Johnson, who will give *this*, has been like an enraged demon since the meeting, because it has not fallen upon him to rid the world of the monster. He says the blood of his gray-haired father and his noble brother call upon him for revenge, and revenge he will have; if he cannot wreak it upon the fountain head, he will union some of the blood-thirsty generals. Butler would suit him. As our plans were all concocted and well arranged we separated, and as I am writing, on my way to Detroit, I will only say that all rests upon you. You know where to find your friends. Your disguises are so perfect and complete that without *one know your face* no police telegraphic despatch would catch you. The English gentleman, *Harcourt*, must not act hastily. Remember, he has ten days. Strike for your home, strike for your country; bide your time, but strike sure. *Get introduced, congratulate him, listen to his stories; not many more will the brute tell to earthly friends.* Do anything but fail, and meet us at the appointed place within the fortnight. Enclose this note together with one of poor Leenea. I will give the reason for this when we meet. Return by Johnson, I wish I could go to you, but duty calls me to the *West*; you will probably hear from me in Washington. Sanders is doing us no good in Canada.
"Believe me, your brother in love,
"CHARLES SELBY."

[The original of the foregoing is attached to this record, and marked Exhibit No. 1.]

"ST. LOUIS, Oct. 21, 1864.—Dearest Husband:—Why do you not come home? You left me for ten days only, and you now have been from home more than two weeks. In that long time only sent me one short note, a few cold words, and a cheek for money, which I did not require. What has come over you? Have you forgotten your wife and child? Baby calls for papa until my heart aches. *We are so lonely* without you. I have written to you again and again, and, as a last resource, yesterday wrote to Charlie, begging him to see you and tell you to come home. I am too ill, not able to leave my room; if I was I would go to you wherever you were. If in *this world*. Mamma says I must not write any more, as I am too weak. Louis, darling, do not stay away any longer from your heartbroken wife.
"LEENEA."

[The original of the foregoing is annexed to this record, and marked Exhibit No. 2.]

Q. At what time in November did you pick up this envelope and these letters? A. The day Gen. Butler left New York; I cannot tell the precise date, but General Scott told me he had left that morning.
Q. Was that after the Presidential election in November? A. Yes sir.
Q. What did you do with these letters after you examined them and found their character? A. I took them first to General Scott, who asked me to read them to him. He said he thought it was of great importance, and asked me to take it to General Dix; I did so, and gave it to General Dix.
Q. You say the men exchanged letters; which was giving letters to the other, the large or the small man? A. They exchanged twice; the larger one gave them to the one next to him, and he handed them back, and they were exchanged again.
Q. Did you see more than one? A. Yes sir.
Q. The small er one, or educated one, said he would leave for Washington the second day after. A. Yes; "the day after to-morrow."

No cross-examination.

G. W. Bunker,

a witness called for the prosecution, being duly sworn, testified as follows:—

By the Judge Advocate—Q. Will you please state whether you were, during the last fall, and still are, clerk at the National Hotel in this city? A. I have been connected with the National Hotel nearly five years.

Q. Did you know John Wilkes Booth? A. I did.
Q. Was he in the habit of stopping at that hotel when he came to the city? A. I think he made that his home when in the city.
Q. Have you the hotel books here for November last? A. Three of them are here.
Q. I wish you to examine them and state whether John Wilkes Booth was a guest at the National Hotel, and was in the hotel in the month of November and if so, at what time, and at what time he left? A. He arrived at the National Hotel Wednesday, November 9, in the evening.
Q. When did he leave? A. The memorandum states that he left on the morning of the 11th. I see that one cash-book, which I supposed was here, is not, but the memorandum is correct, as it was made out in the hotel and receipted; but I have not the book to refer to.
Q. When does it appear that he returned again? A. He returned November 14th, in the early part of the evening, and left again on the 16th.
Q. Does it appear at what time he left on the 16th? A. I have not the book that I could refer to for that; as it is not here, I am not able to state.
Q. Was he there during the month of October? A. His name does not appear on the books for October, I believe; I have not looked that book through fully, as I was not so requested by the parties who came to the hotel.
Q. Have you taken from the books memoranda to enable you to state as to his subsequent arrivals and departures during the following months? A. They are all contained in this memorandum from November 9th.
Q. When was his next return after leaving on November 16th? A. They are all included in this memorandum from November 9, 1864, to April 8, 1865.
Q. That paper, then, as you hold it in your hand, you state to be an accurate transcript from the books? A. Yes sir, from our books at the hotel.
Q. Do you know who were his associates in the hotel generally when he was there—his room-mates? A. His most intimate friends? one was John McCullough, an actor.
Q. Was he his room mate? A. He roomed with him a portion of the time.
Q. Could you name any other of his room mates during that time? A. John P. Wentworth, of California; he also roomed with Mr. McArdle, agent of Edwin Forrest, while he was rooming with Mr. McCullough; the three occupied the same room.
Q. That memorandum which you now brings him down to the 8th of April, you say? A. Yes sir.
Q. Did he leave on that day? A. That was his last arrival at the hotel.
Q. He remained there until the assassination of the President? A. Yes sir.
Q. Had he a room there at the time the President was assassinated? A. He had.
Q. Were you present when his trunk was opened by the officers? A. I was not; I packed his baggage the next day and had it removed to our baggage-room.
Q. Do you know John H. Surratt, of this city? A. I do not by name; Booth had a great many callers that I knew by sight, did not know their names.
Q. Have you seen any of these prisoners before? A. I know this small one with black whiskers and imperial; I do not know his name, but know him by sight. [Pointing to Michael O'Laughlin.]
Q. Did you see him at the hotel? A. Very often; he frequently called on Booth.
Q. Look at all the rest, and see if you recollect any of the others? A. No sir, [after looking at the various accused.]
Q. You say he called frequently. Would he remain with Booth in his room; did he remain at night at any time? A. We were so busy during the winter that I never paid much attention to these things.
Q. Do you know how long these calls were continued; whether they were up to the last moment of Booth's stay? A. I do not think I saw him the last few days of Booth's remaining there; I do not recollect that he called then.

— No cross-examination.

The Judge Advocate offered in evidence, without objection, the following portions of the memorandum spoken of by the witness Bunker:—

J. Wilkes Booth was not at the National Hotel during the month of October, 1864.
He arrived there November 9; occupied room 20; left on early train morning of 11th.
Arrived again November 14th, and left on the 16th. His next arrival was December 12th; left December 17th, morning train.
Arrived again December 22d; left 24th, 11·15 A. M. train.
Arrived again December 31st; left January 10th, 1865, 7·30 P. M.
Arrived again January 12th; left 28th, 7·30 P. M. train; occupied room 50½.
Arrived again February 22d; occupied room 231, in company with John P. H. Wentworth and John McCullough. Wentworth went into this room at the suggestion of Mr. Merrick, clerk, as they were short of rooms. Booth left February 18, 8·15 A. M. train, closing his account to date, inclusive. His name does not appear on the register, but another room is assigned

him, and his account commences March 1st, without any entry upon the register of that date; 2d, 3d and 4th he is called at 8 A. M.; 21st March, pays $30 on account, and left on 7:30 P. M. train.
Arrived, March 23th; room 231—to tea, and left April 1st, on an afternoon train.
Arrived again April 8th; room 228. Directly below Booth is registered, of that date, the name of A. Cox; residence not known; it was cut out by some one who cut out the name of Booth.
[The original memorandum is annexed to this record, marked Exhibit No. 4].

William E. Wheeler.

A witness called for the prosecution, being duly sworn, testified as follows:—
By the Judge Advocate:—Q. Where do you reside? A. My home is in Chicopee, Massachusetts.
Q. Were you in Canada during the last autumn? A. Yes sir.
Q. At what point in Canada? A. Montreal.
Q. Did you meet there citizens of the United States from the Southern States? A. I met some.
Q. Will you mention some whom you met there, and when? A. The only one there that I know the name of to swear to was Mr. Booth.
Q. Do you mean John Wilkes Booth, the actor? A. Yes sir.
Q. Where did you meet him? A. I was standing in front of the St. Lawrence Hall, Montreal, and saw him go across from a broker's office on the opposite side.
Q. What time was that? A. I cannot say the day exactly, but it was in October or November last.
Q. Did you see any others who were pointed out to you by name? A. There was another man who came across with him; who he was I do not know, and never heard his name; I spoke to Mr. Booth when he came across, and asked him if he was going to open the theatre there; he said no, he was not, and left me directly, and entered into conversation with a third man who was there, and some time after that, as I was walking along with a gentleman, he pointed him out to me as George Sanders.
Q. You saw Sanders and Booth in conversation together? A. Yes sir.
Q. You did not see Clement C. Clay or Jacob Thompson? A. No sir, not to know them.
Q. You had met Booth before, and knew him? A. I had seen him play on the stage, in Springfield, Massachusetts.
No cross-examination.

John Deveney.

A witness called for the prosecution, being duly sworn, testified as follows:—
By the Judge Advocate—Q. Where do you reside? A. I am living in Washington at present; my home is in Philadelphia; at least my father lives there.
Q. Were you during the past autumn or winter in Canada? A. I was.
Q. At what point? A. At Montreal.
Q. In what month were you there? A. I went over there in July, and left there on the 3d or 4th of February; I forget which.
Q. Were you, or not, acquainted with John Wilkes Booth? A. Very well.
Q. Did you meet him there? A. I did.
Q. In company with whom did you see him there? A. The first time I saw him in Canada, I saw him standing in the St. Lawrence Hotel, Montreal, talking with George N. Sanders.
Q. Can you tell about what time that was? A. I cannot tell you the month, but from what I have seen in the papers I am constrained to believe it was in October; but I am not willing to swear it was in that month.
Q. Did they, or not, seem to be intimate? A. They seemed to be talking very confidentially.
Q. Were they drinking together? A. Yes; I saw them go into Dowley's and have a drink together.
Q. You mean George N. Sanders? A. Yes; George N. Sanders, who used to be Navy Agent at New York.
Q. Did you see in Canada, at the same time, Jacob Thompson, of Mississippi, who was secretary of the Interior under the Administration of President Buchanan? A. I saw Mr. Thompson, Mr. Clay, Mr. Tucker and several others; they were pointed out to me, but I was not acquainted with those gentlemen.
Q. You mean Clement C. Clay, of Alabama, formerly United States Senator? A. That was the man; I mean him; I presume he was the man; he was pointed out to me as that person.
Q. Did you have conversations with Booth? A. Yes, I spoke to him; I asked him what he was doing there; I asked him, "Are you going to play here?" knowing that he was an actor; he said no, he was not; said I, "What are you going to do?" said he, "I just came here on a visit, a pleasure trip;" I saw in the papers afterwards that he had been trying to make an engagement with Buckland, of the Theatre Royal there; but I do not believe it.
Q. You say you saw him talking to Clay, Sanders, Holcomb and Thompson? A. I believe I did; I am not very positive that I saw him talking to those parties, but I did see him talk to Sanders; that I can swear to, because I was standing up against a pillar in the hotel,

and it was right in the hotel; Sanders was leaning against a pillar and Booth standing in front of him.
Q. You say you have seen others with Sanders? A. Yes sir. I do not know that I saw them there standing talking to Sanders that day, but I have seen those other men with Sanders at different times, talking to him.
Q. And with Booth? A. I will not say that. I saw Booth talking to Sanders, though. Of that I am positive, because these two were standing together when I came up; I just came from the post office, which is opposite the hotel; I came over and saw them talking there; I was surprised to see him, and that is what made me take particular notice of it; I thought, as a matter of course, he came there to play.
Q. When was the next time you saw Booth? A. The next time I saw Booth was on the steps of the Kirkwood House, in this city, the night of the 14th of April, a few minutes before five, or between five and six o'clock.
Q. What occurred then? A. He was going into the hotel; I was standing talking to a young man named Callan. I think, who works in one of the Departments; he was formerly a sergeant of cavalry, I think; I said to Callan, "I would like to go up to Willard's Hotel and see if we can see General Grant;" I had never seen him; said I, "Will you come and go along?" He said "No; I have got an engagement to be here at five o'clock, to meet some person." So I did not go, but went into the hotel, saying, "I wonder what time it is now; it must be time for your friend to come, if he is coming." I went in and found it was five, or five minutes off it, and said I, "I guess you can go now; that engagement is up;" he said, "No; I will wait a little longer." Just then Booth passed me going into the hotel, and turned around and spoke to me I asked him when he came from Canada, for I did not know he had left there. He said he had been back for some time, and was going to stay here some time, and would see me again; I asked, "Are you going to play here again?" said he, "No, I am not going to play again; I am in the oil business;" I laughed and joked at that, it being a common joke to talk about the oil business; a few minutes afterwards I saw him coming down street on horseback, on a bay horse; I took particular notice what kind of a looking rig he had on the horse; I do not know what made me do it; the next I saw of him I heard the speech and saw him jump out of the box at the theatre, and when he fell he fell on one hand and one knee, and I recognized him; he fell with his face towards the audience; I said, "He is John Wilkes Booth, and he has shot the President;" I made that remark right there; that is the last ever I saw of him, when he was running across the stage.
Q. You say you are certain you saw him and Sanders drinking together, as well as talking? A. Yes sir, I did; I am sure of it; Sanders says he never saw him; but Sanders tells a lie, because he did see him; I saw him talking to him.
Cross-examined by Mr. Aiken.—Q. How long have you resided in this city? A. I have been off and on here for a year or two; I was formerly an officer in the army, Fourth Maryland Regiment, as lieutenant in Company E; I was in the employ of Adams' Express Company a good many years, and worked with them in Washington for some time.
Q. Are you acquainted with any of the prisoners? A. Not that I know of.
Q. You are not acquainted with John H. Surratt? A. No, sir, I never saw him in my life to my knowledge.
By the Court.—Q. Why did you say it was John Wilkes Booth, and that he had shot the President? A. I did not know Mr. Lincoln had been shot, but it flashed on my mind when Booth jumped out of that box that he had done such a thing, because I knew the President was in the box; I saw him go in, and I heard the pistol shot and the words, "Sic Semper Tyrannis," and I knew from my school-boy knowledge that was the motto of the State of Virginia.
By the Judge Advocate.—Q. You say Booth shouted "Sic Semper Tyrannis?" A. I heard the words in the box; I think it was Booth said that; I heard the words before I saw the man.
Q. Had he his knife in his hand as he went across the stage? A. He had.
Q. Did he make any remark as he crossed the stage? A. It is said he did, but I did not notice it; the excitement was so great that I did not notice it; I can safely swear that I did not hear any remark; at least, I cannot call to mind that I did.

Lieutenant-General Ulysses S. Grant,

A witness called for the prosecution, being duly sworn, testified as follows:—
By the Judge Advocate.—Q. Will you state whether you are acquainted with Jacob Thompson, formerly Secretary of the Interior under President Buchanan's administration? A. I saw him once; that was when the army was lying opposite Vicksburg, at what is called Milliken's Bend and Young's Point; a little boat was discovered coming up on the opposite shore, apparently surreptitiously, trying to avoid detection, and a little tug was sent out from the navy to pick it up when they got to it they found a little white flag sticking out of the stern of the row-boat, and Jacob

Thompson in it; they brought him to Admiral Porter's flag-ship, and I was sent for and met him; I do not recollect now the ostensible business he had; there seemed to be nothing important at all in the visit, but he pretended to be under a flag of truce, and, therefore, he had to be allowed to go back again.
Q. When was that? A. I cannot say whether it was in January or February, 1863; it was the first flag of truce we had, though.
Q. Did he profess to be, and seem to be, in the military service of the Rebels? A. He said he had been offered a commission—anything he wanted, but knowing that he was not a military man, he preferred having something more like a civil appointment, and he had taken the place of an Inspector-General in the Rebel service.
Q. Did he then hold that position? A. That was what he said, that he was an Inspector-General, or Assistant Inspector-General, with the rank of Lieutenant-Colonel, I think he said.
Q. The Military Department of Washington, as it is spoken of in military parlance, embraces the city of Washington, does it not, and did it not during the past year? A. Yes sir.
Q. And all the defenses of the city? A. Yes sir, and on the other side of the river and Alexandria.
Q. It embraces all the fortifications on both sides? A. Yes, sir.
Q. I have in my hand a copy of your commission as Lieutenant-General of the Armies of the United States, bearing date the 4th day of March, 1864; will you state whether or not since that time you have continued to be in command, under that commission, of the Armies of the United States? A. I have.
[The Judge Advocate offered in evidence, without objection, the commission of Lieutenant-General Grant, dated March 4, 1864, accompanied by General Orders No. 98, March, which are appended to the record, marked Exhibit No. 6.]
Cross-examined by Mr. Aiken.—Q. Are you aware that the civil courts are in operation in this city, all of them? A. Yes, sir.
Q. How far towards Baltimore does the Department of Washington extend? A. I could not say exactly to what point; any troops that belong to General Augur's command, however, that he sends out to any point would necessarily remain under his command; he commands the Department of Washington.
Q. Is any portion of the State of Maryland in the Department of Washington? A. Oh yes sir; martial law, I believe, extends to all the territory south of the railroad that runs across from Annapolis, running south to the Potomac and the Chesapeake.
Cross-examined by Mr. Ewing.—Q. By virtue of what order does martial law extend south of Annapolis? A. I never saw the order; it is just simply an understanding.
Q. It is just an understanding? A. Yes sir, just an understanding that it does exist.
Q. You have never seen any order? A. No sir.
Q. And do not know that such an order exists? A. No sir, I have never seen the order.

Joseph H. Simonds,

A witness called for the prosecution, being duly sworn, testified as follows:—
By the Judge Advocate:—Q. Were you acquainted with J. Wilkes Booth, in his lifetime? A. I was.
Q. What relation did you sustain to him—were you his agent? A. I was his business agent, really.
Q. In what region of country, and in connection with what business? A. I was principally in the oil region; I did some little business for him in the city of Boston, but very little, which was entirely closed up before I left there.
Q. What was the character of his interest there in the oil region? A. He owned a third undivided interest at first in a lease of three-and-a-half acres on the Alleghany river, near Franklin.
Q. For which he paid how much? A. It was bought by means of contracting to pay off the old debts of that lease and carry on the work; afterward the land interest was bought, he furnishing one-half of the purchase money of the land interest, and owning one undivided third as above stated.
Q. How much did he pay? A. The land interest cost $4000; he paid $2000, one half of it.
Q. Did he make any other investments on which he paid money? A. Yes sir,
Q. What was the total amount of them? A. He purchased, for $1000, an interest in an association there owning an undivided thirtieth of a tract.
Q. What other purchases did he make? A. That is all that he ever absolutely purchased; there was money spent in carrying on the expenses of this lease previous to his purchase of the land interest; at the time of the purchase of the land interest the work was stopped, and there were no more expenses.
Q. These interests of which you speak were all that he possessed in the oil regions? A. Yes sir; all that he ever possessed in Venango, to my knowledge.
Q. Did he ever realize anything from them? A. Not a dollar.
Q. They were a total loss? A. Yes; as far as he was concerned.
Q. When did this occur? In what year? A. The first interest he acquired in any way was either in December, 1863, or January, 1864; I cannot say as to the date; it was only from his report to me that I knew of it; my first knowledge of it was in May, 1864; I accompanied him to the oil regions in June, 1864, for the purpose of taking charge of his business there.
Q. Have you given the total amount of the investment that it both made? What do you consider the total amount? A. The whole amount invested in this Alleghany river property, in every way, was about $5000; I cannot give the exact figures in dollars and cents.
Q. And the other investment was about $1000? A. Yes, sir.
Q. Making $6000 in all? A. Yes, sir.
Q. And that you know to have been a total loss to him? A. Yes, sir, that is, it was transferred; his business was entirely closed out there in the latter part of September, 1864; I think on the 27th of September.
Q. Was it placed in your hands as trustee, or to whom was it transferred? A. There were three owners, as I have told you. He held an undivided third. The three owners all decided to place the property in my hands as trustee to hold for them. It was so mentioned in the deed, and their several names were mentioned in the deed. Immediately upon the execution of that deed he asked me to make a deed conveying his interest away, which I did in accordance with his instructions. These deeds were properly executed, conveying his whole interest away in that way. At the same time, this other interest in a different portion of the country, on a different stream, for which he had paid $1,000, he also transferred, which was done by a different process, by assignment on the receipt which he held for his interest.
Q. This was all done last fall? A. It was done in September; I think the 27th or 28th of the month, I cannot be exact as to the date. It was done the day he left Franklin, the last time I ever saw him.
Q. Were the conveyances without compensation or voluntary gifts? A. One was made to his brother, Junius Brutus Booth; which was without compensation, but a consideration was mentioned in the deed.
Q. But there was none in fact? A. No sir; none in fact; the other was to me, and the same consideration was mentioned, but it was done in consideration of my services, for which I have never received any other pay.
Q. There was nothing paid him at all on either of them? A. No sir; not a dollar; and he paid all the expenses of the transfer and the conveyances.

Samuel P. Jones, (blind,)

a witness called for the prosecution, being duly sworn, testified as follows:—
By the Judge Advocate.—Q. Have you resided in Richmond at any time during the war? A. I have.
Q. State any conversations you may have heard there, to which officers of the Rebel Government were parties in regard to the contemplated assassination of the President of the United States. A. The nearest I know anything to that point among the officers there, is their common conversation in camp, as I would go about amongst them, and their conversations would be of this nature:—That all suspicioned persons, or those kind of people they were not certain were of their way of thinking, they would assassinate as soon as they came near them; but after I found out what I could learn in reference to these things, they were desperately anxious that any such thing as this should be accomplished.
Q. Will you state any particular occasion? A. In a general way I have heard sums offered, to be paid with a Confederate sum, for any person or persons to go North and assassinate the President.
Q. Do you remember any occasion when any such offers were made or any amount named, and by what kind of officers? A. At this moment I cannot tell you the particular names of shoulder-straps, &c.
Q. Do you remember any occasion—some dinner occasion? A. I can tell you this; I heard a citizen make the remark once that he would give from his private purse $10,000 in addition to the Confederate amount to have the President assassinated, to bring him to Richmond, dead or alive, for proof.
Q. What was meant by that phrase, "In addition to the Confederate amount?" A. I know nothing about that, any more than the way they would express it; I should judge, from drawing an inference, that there was any amount offered by the Government, in that trashy paper, to assassinate any officials that were hindering their cause, and even I have heard it down as low as a private or citizen; for instance, if it is not digressing from the purpose, I know of a Kentuckian, but cannot tell you the name now, that was putting up at the Exchange Hotel, or otherwise, Ballard House, (they belong to the same property and are connected by a bridge over Franklin street); he was arrested under suspicion of being a spy; I can tell you the name now, his name was Webster, if I remember rightly; I always supposed, from what I understood, that he came down to buy goods; but they took him as a spy and hung him; whether it was in reference to this assassination I cannot say.
Q. I understood you to say that it was a subject of general conversation among the Rebel officers? A. It

was; the Rebel officers, as they would be sitting around their tent doors, would be conversing on such a subject a great deal; they would be saying they would like to see his head brought there, dead or alive, and they should think it could be done, and I have heard such things stated as that they had certain persons undertaking it.

Samuel Knapp Chester.

A witness called for the prosecution, being duly sworn testified as follows:—
By the Judge Advocate.—Q. Your profession is that of an actor? A. Yes sir.
Q. Have you known J. Wilkes Booth a good many years? A. I have known him about ten or eleven years, since I first met him.
Q. Quite intimately, I suppose? A. For about six or seven years intimately.
Q. Can you recall a conversation which you are supposed to have had with him in November last in New York? Yes sir.
Q. What time in the month was it? A. I think it was in November that I had a conversation with him.
Q. What time in November? State about the period of time. A. I cannot think of the exact date, but it was in the early portion of November; one day we were in conversation, and I asked him why he was not acting, and he told me that he did not intend to act in this portion of the country again: that he had taken his wardrobe to Canada, and intended to run the blockade.
Q. Did you meet him after that, and have some conversation with him in regard to oil speculations, or was it at the same time? A. No sir; the next time I met him was about the time we were to play Julius Cæsar, which we did play on the 25th of November; and it was either on the 24th or 25th that he asked me to take a walk with him, or asked if I knew some customers, where he might get some dresses for his character in that play; and I asked him where his own wardrobe was.
Q. Was that in the city of New York? A. Yes; I never had any conversation with him relative to this affair out of New York; he said it was still in Canada, in charge of a friend, and I think he said, named Martin; I will not be positive, but I think he said it was in Montreal; he did not say anything to me at all about the oil business then, that I remember.
Q. Did he not ask you how you would like to go into the oil business with him? A. Not in the oil business; he never mentioned that.
Q. He told you he had a big speculation on hand? A. Yes, sir.
Q. Did he ask you to go in with him? A. Yes sir; I met him, and he was talking with some friends, and they were joking with him about the affair; I met him on Broadway; after he left them he said he had a better speculation than that on hand, and one they would not laugh at some time after that I met him again and he again talked of this speculation, and aske I me how I would like to go in with him; I to'd him I was without means, that I could not; and he said it did not matter, he always liked me and would furnish the means; the next time I heard from him he was in Washington.
Q. State the whole of the conversation in which he urged you to go into this speculation in New York. A. As well as I can remember, I will tell you from beginning to end. He left me then in New York, and I received several letters from him from Washington, telling me he was speculating in farms in lower Maryland and was sure to coin money; that I must go with him to Virginia, and still telling me that I mustjoin him; that I paid very little attention to it. Then about the latter part of December or early in January, I will not be positive which it was, but late in December or early in January, he came to New York; I then lived at No. 45 Grove street; he asked me to take a walk with him; I did so; we went out and went into a saloon known as the House of Lords, on Houston street; we remained there a considerable time; I suppose an hour, eating and drinking; he had often mentioned this affair to me, his spe culation; but would never say what it was; if I would ask him what it was he would say he would tell me by-and-by. We left there and went to another saloon under the Revere House, and ate some oysters. We then started up Broadway; I thought it was time to go home, and my way was down Bleecker street, that is, up Broadway from the corner of Houston, and I had to turn down Bleecker street to get to Grove street; I bade him good night. He asked me to walk a piece further up the street with him, and I did so; I walked a square, that is, to Fourth street, or next street; he asked me to walk up there with him, and I did so; he asked me to walk up Fourth street because Broadway was crowded; he said Fourth street was not so full of people as Broadway, and he wanted to tell me about that speculation; I walked up there with him, and when we got into an unfrequented portion of the street, he stopped and told me then that he was in a large conspiracy to capture the heads of the Government, including the President, and take them to Richmond; I asked him if that was what he wished me to go in; he said it was; I told him I could not do it, that it was an impossibility; only to think of my family; he said he

had two or three thousand dollars that he could leave them; I still said I could not do it; he urged it, and talked with me for, I suppose, twenty minutes or half an hour, and I still refused; he then told me that at least I would not betray him, and said I dare not; he said he could implicate me in the affair, any how; he said that the party were sworn together, and that if I attempted to betray them I would be hunted down through life, and talked some more about the affair; I cannot remember it now; but still urging me, saying I had better go in; I told him no, and bade him goodnight, and I went home.
Q. Did he indicate to you what part he wished you to play in carrying out this conspiracy? A. Yes sir.
Q. What did he say? A. That I was to open the back door of the Theatre at a signal.
Q. Did he indicated what Theatre this was to occur? A. Yes; he told me Ford's Theatre; because it must be some one acquainted or connected with the Theatre who could take part in it.
Q. Ford's Theatre in Washington? A. Yes sir.
Q. Did he urge you upon the ground that it was an easy affair, and that you would have very little to do? A. Yes, he said that; that was all I would have to do, he said. He said the thing was sure to succeed.
Q. What preparations did he say, if any, had been made toward the conspiracy? A. He told me that everything was in readiness; that it was sure to succeed, for there were parties on the other side ready to co-operate with them.
Q. Did you understand from him that the Rebel Government was sanctioning what he was doing? A. He never told me that.
Q. What do you mean by parties on the other side? A. I imagined that they were on the other side, but he did not say who they were; I mean they were those people he said on the other side.
Q. Did he mention the probable number of persons engaged in the conspiracy? A. He said there were from fifty to a hundred; he said that when he first mentioned the affair to me.
Q. Did he write to you? A. He wrote about this speculation, and then he wrote to me again; that must have been in January.
Q. Have you those letters? A. I never kept my letters; every Sunday I devote to answering my correspondents, and generally destroy their letters then.
Q. Did he or not make you any remittance with a view of enabling you to come to Washington? A. Oh yes sir; after I had declined going, had refused him, I got a letter from him stating that I must come; this was the letter in which he told me it was sure to succeed; I wrote back that it was impossible; I would not come; then, by return mail, I think, I got another letter, with $50 inclosed, saying I must come, and must be sure to be there by Saturday night; I did not go; I had not been out of New York since last summer.
Q. Can you remember the time you received the last letter with the $50 in it? A. That was in January, I think.
Q. You say he said he had $1000 to leave to your family? A. That was before, at the first interview.
Q. Did he, at the time he sent you the first $50, mention any more? A. In the letter he did not.
Q. Did he speak of having plenty of funds for the purpose? A. Not in his letter.
Q. Did he in his conversation? A. In his conversation after he came to New York again.
Q. What did he say then? A. When he came to New York he called on me again and asked me to take a walk with him, and I did so; he told me that he had been trying to get another party to join him named John Matthews, and when he told him what he wanted to do that the man was very much frightened, indeed, and would not join him, and he said he would not have thanked him if he had sacrificed him; I told him I did not think it was right to speak in that manner; he said no, he was a coward, and was not fit to live; he then asked me again to join him; he told me I must do so; he said that there was plenty of money in the affair; that if I would do it I would never want again as long as I lived; that I would never want for money; he said that the President and some of the heads of the Government, and the entire theatre very frequently during Mr. Forrest's engagements; I still urged him a it to mention theatfair to me; to think of my poor family; he said he would provide for my going with him; I still refused; he said he would ruin me in the profession if I did not go; I told him I could not help that, and begged of him not to mention the affair to me; when he found I would not go, he said he honored my mother and respected my wife, and he was sorry he had mentioned this affair to me, and told me to make my mind easy, he would trouble me about it no more; I then returned him the money he sent me; he said he would not allow me to do so, but that he was very short of funds—so very short that of her himself or some of the party must go to Richmond to obtain means to carry out their designs.
Q. He said, however, that there was plenty of money in the enterprise? A. Yes sir.
Q. When did this last conversation occur? A. That, I think, was in February.
Q. Did he have any conversation with you at a later period, after the inauguration, as to the opportunity which he had for the assassination of the President? Did he speak of that? A. Yes sir; on Friday, one

TRIAL OF THE ASSASSINS AT WASHINGTON. 47

week previous to the assassination, he was in New York.
Q. What did he say then? A. We were in the House of Lords at the time, sitting at a table, and had not been there long before he exclaimed, striking the table, "*What an excellent chance I had to kill the President, if I had wished, on Inauguration Day!*" that was all he said relative to that.
Q. Did he explain what the chance was? A. No; he said he was as near the President on that day as he was to me; that is all he said.
Q. Can you tell at what time in February he said it would be necessary to send to Richmond for money? A. No sir; I cannot tell positively.
Cross-examined by Mr. Clampitt.—Q. Did he mention any names of those who were connected with him in this plan as communicated to you in reference to the assassination of Mr. Lincoln? A. No, sir, not that I am aware of.
Q. You never heard him mention any names? A. I never did.
Cross-examined by Mr. Ewing.—Q. Do I understand you to say that he spoke to you of a plan to assassinate the President and to capture him? A. To capture him.
Q. Did he say anything to you as to how he would get him off? A. No.
Q. As to where he would take him? A. To Richmond.
Q. By what route? A. He did not say.
Q. He spoke of there being persons on "the other side?" A. Yes, sir.
Q. Did he use just simply that expression, or did he explain what he meant by the "other side," What did you understand him to mean? A. He did not explain it at all, but I supposed it was in the South.
Q. Across the lines? A. Yes, sir.
Q. Across the river? A. Across the Potomac.
Q. Did he say nothing to you as to the means he had provided or proposed to provide for conducting the President after he seized? A. No, sir; on one occasion he told me that he was selling off horses after he had told me that he had given up this project.
Q. When did he say to you that he had abandoned the idea of capturing the President? A. In February, I think.
Q. Did he say why he had abandoned it? A. He said the affair had fallen through owing to some of the parties backing out.
Q. On what day was it that he said to you what an excellent chance he had for killing the President? A. That was on a Friday, one week previous to the assassination.
Q. On what day of April was that? A. The 7th.
Q. Did he say anything to you as to his then entertaining, or having before that entertained, the purpose to assassinate the President? A. No, sir.
Q. Did he say anything to you then as to why he did not assassinate the President? A. No, sir; that was the only exclamation he made use of relative to it.
Q. State his exact words if you can? A. He said, "what an excellent chance I had, if I wished to kill the President on Inauguration day; I was on the stand as close to him nearly as I am to you." That is as near his language as I can give.
Q. State how far he explained to you his project for capturing the President in the theatre? A. I believe I have stated as far as I know.
Q. Did he ever indicate how he expected to get him from the box to the stage without being caught? A. No, sir.
Q. Did he say how many were to help him in seizing the President? At No sir.
Q. Did he name any other officials who were to be seized besides the President? A. No; the only one he told me, he said "*the heads of the Government, including the President.*"
By the Judge Advocate.—Q I understood you to say that he stated that the particular enterprise of capturing the President and heads of the Government had been given up, and that in consequence he was selling off the horses he had bought for the purpose? A. Yes sir.
Q. He did not state to you what mode of proceeding had been substituted for that, but simply that that one had been given up? A. He told me they had given up the affair.
Q. That it had fallen through? A. Yes sir.
The Commission then adjourned until to-morrow, Saturday morning, May 13th, at 10 o'clock.

THE PROCEEDINGS OF TUESDAY.

WASHINGTON, May 16.—According to the intention declared at the closing of the preceding session, the Court paid an informal visit, at half-past nine o'clock this morning, to the scene of the President's assassination. The visit was made at the suggestion of the Judge Advocate-General, with the object of enabling the Court to acquire, by visual observation of the now historic locality, such a knowledge of it as would render a more perfect understanding of all the evidence dependent upon its intricacies accurate and more easy.

The Court arrived at the appointed hour. Through the usual courtesy of the Judge Advocate-General, and of the President of the Court, the reporters of the Press were admitted. The announcement of the intended visit caused quite a crowd to assemble at the front of the theatre. Nothing is changed there. Having seen all there was to be seen, the several members started for the Court room at the Penitentiary, and, on their entering it, the prisoners were brought into the dock, and many eyes instinctively turned towards Spangler, who sat down listlessly and leaned back against the wall, staring vacantly.

During the reading of the record, Mr. Daniel Stanton, who was present, was permitted to amend the record of his own testimony delivered on the previous day. In the amendment, his answer to the question, "Did he ask in regard to General Grant?" now reads, "I meant to say that the man did ask for General Grant," in lieu of "I don't recollect that he did." Mr. Stanton also added, that the man referred to said he was a lawyer, and knew Mr. Stanton very well.

The Court took its usual recess, after which the reading of the lengthy record was resumed by Mr. D. F. Murthy. The reading being concluded, the Court proceeded to the reception of testimony for the prosecution.

Examination of John Burrow, alias "Peanuts."

Q. State whether or not you have been connected with Ford's Theatre, in this city? A. Yes sir.
Q. In what capacity? A. I used to attend to the stage door and carry bills in the day time; I attended to Booth's horse, stabling and cleaning him.
Q. Do you know John Wilkes Booth? A. I knew him while he kept his horse in the alley in that stable there.
Q. Immediately back of the theatre? A. Yes sir.
Q. Did you see him on the afternoon of the assassination? A. I saw him bring a horse into the stable, about five or six o'clock.
Q. State what he did? A. He brought him there and halloed out for Spangler.
Q. Did Spangler go down to the stable? A. Yes, sir; he asked him for a halter, and he went down for one.
Q. How long did he remain there? A. I don't know; I think Maddox was there, too.
Q. Did you see him again that evening? A. I did, on the stage, that night.
Q. Did you, or not, see him when he came with his horse, between nine and ten o'clock? A. No, sir, I did not.
Q. Did you see the horse at the door? A. I saw him when Spangler called me out to hold him.
Q. State all that happened at that time; did you see Booth when he came with his horse? A. No, sir.
Q. Did you hear him call for Spangler? A. No sir; at I heard a man call Ned, and tell him Booth wanted him.
Q. Who held Booth's horse that evening? A. I held him that night.
Q. Who gave you the horse to hold? A. Spangler.
Q. What hour was that? A. Between nine and ten.
Q. How long before the curtain was up? A. About fifteen minutes.
Q. What did Spangler say to you? A. He told me to hold the horse; I told him I had to attend to my door; then he said if there was anything wrong, to lay the blame of it on him.
Q. Did you hold him near the door? A. Against the bench near there.
Q. Did you hear the report of the pistol? A. Yes.
Q. Were you still on the bench when Booth came out? A. I got off the bench then.
Q. What did he say when he came out? A. He told me to give him his horse.
Q. Did you go again to the door? A. No, I was still against the bench.
Q. Did he do anything else? A. He knocked me down.
Q. With his hand? A. No, with the butt of his knife.
Q. Did he strike you again or kick you? Did he say anything else? A. He only halloed "Give me the horse."
Q. And rode off immediately? A. Yes sir.
Q. State whether or not you were in the President's box that afternoon? A. Yes sir.
Q. Who decorated or fixed the box that afternoon? A. Harry Ford put the flags around it.
Q. Was or was not the prisoner, Spangler, in the box? A. Yes sir, he was there with me.
Q. What was he doing? A. He came to help me to take the partition out of the box.
Q. Do you remember Spangler saying anything? A He damned the President and Gen. Grant.

Q. Did he say anything in addition to that? A. No sir; I told him he should not curse a man that way, that he did him no harm; he said he ought to be cursed for getting so many men killed.
Q. Did he or did he not say what he wished might be done to General Grant and the President? A. No sir; I don't remember that he did.
Q. Was there or was there not anything said in the course of that conversation as to what might or might not be done to the President or General Grant? Mr. Ewing objected to the last three questions, and insisted on his objection being entered upon the record, which it was.

Cross-examination by Mr. Ewing.—Q. Did you say you did not hear anybody calling out for Spangler? A. I heard Deverney call him, and telling him that Mr. Booth wanted him out in the alley.
Q. Who is Deveraey? A. An actor in the theatre.
Q. How long was it after that before Spangler called you? A. Not very long; about six or seven or eight minutes.
Q. What were you doing when Spangler called you? A. Sitting in front of the door entrance on the left.
Q. What business were you doing? A. I was attending to the stage door.
Q. What had you to do at the stage door? A. To keep strangers out, and not allow them in unless they belonged there.
Q. And you told him you could not hold the horse, and had to attend the door; and he said if anything went wrong to lay the blame on him? A. Yes sir.
Q. Were you in front of the theatre that night? A. I was out there while the curtain was down.
Q. You went out at every act? A. I go out every night every time the curtain is down.
Q. Was Booth in front of the theatre? A. No sir; I did not see him.
Q. Was Spangler in front of the theatre? A. No sir.
Q. Did you ever see Spangler wear a moustache? A. No sir.
Q. Do you know whether Spangler had on any whiskers that night? A. No sir, I did not see any.
Q. Was not Spangler in the habit of hitching up Booth's horse? A. Yes, he wanted to take the bridle off, and Booth wouldn't let him.
Q. When? About six o'clock; he didn't take it off, but he put a halter round his neck, and took the saddle off.
Q. Was not Spangler in the habit of bridling, saddling and hitching up Booth's horse? A. Yes, when I was not there he would hitch him up.
Q. Was he in the habit of holding him when you were not about? A. Yes, and he used to lead him when I was not there.
Q. You and Spangler together attended to Booth's horse? A. Yes; Mr. Clifford said he would give me a good job if I knew how to attend to horses; I said I knew something about it, and that is how I got to attending on Booth's horse.
Q. Do you know the way Booth went out after he jumped out of the President's box? A. No sir; I was out at the time.
Q. Do you know that passage between the green room and scenes, which leads to the back door? A. Yes, on the other side of the stage.
Q. The one that Booth ran through? A. I don't know which entrance Booth ran through.
Q. Was Booth about the theatre a great deal? A. He was'nt about there much; he came there sometimes.
Q. Which way did he enter generally? A. On Tenth street.
Q. Didn't he sometimes enter the back way? A. Sometimes.
Q. How far is the stable where Booth kept his horse from the back entrance of the theatre? A. Two hundred yards.
Q. Do you recollect what act was being played when you first went out to hold Booth's horse? A. I think it was the first scene of the third act; the scene at curtains across the door; it was the first scene.
Q. Was that scene being played when you went out? A. Yes, sir; they had just been closing in.
Q. Did you ever have the name of "Peanuts?" A. That's a name they gave me when I kept a stand there. By Judge Holt.—Q. Did Booth have more than one horse there? A. No sir.
Q. But I understand you to say there was only one horse in the stable that afternoon? A. That is all I saw, and I was there between five and six o'clock.
By Mr. Ewing.—Q. Do you know what side of the theatre Spangler worked on? A. On this side, on the left; he changed the scenes on the left.
Q. Is that the side the President's box was on? A. Yes sir.
Q. Was that the side you attended the door on? A. Yes sir, that's the side.
Q. When you were away didn't Spangler attend to the door for you? A. Yes sir.
Q. His position was near where your position was? A. Yes sir.
Q. What door was that; was it the door that went into the little alley? Yes sir; the alley from Tenth street.
Q. You attended there to see that nobody came in who was not authorized? A. Yes sir; when the curtain was down I used to go outside.
Q. When the play was going on who was there on that side who shoved the scenes except Spangler? A. There is another man on that side; two work on that side, and three on the other.
Q. Who was the man that worked with Spangler on that side? A. I think his name is Simonds.
Q. Who works on the other side? A. One is Sukay.
Q. When the play is going on do these men always stay there? A. Yes sir.
Q. They had to stay to shove the scenes? A. Yes sir; always so as to be there when the whistle blows, but sometimes when the scene would last a whole act they would go on the other side.
Q. Did they not go out? A. Sometimes they would go out not very often though.
By Judge Holt.—Q. Was there another horse in that stable any day before? A. There were two on one day.
Q. How long before that was it that there were two? A. Booth brought a horse and buggy there on Sunday.
Q. What was the appearance of the horse? A. It was a little horse; I don't remember the color.
Q. Do you remember whether he was blind of one eye? A. No sir; the fellow who brought the horse there used to go with Booth very often.
Q. Do you see that man among the prisoners here—I mean the man that brought the horse? A. No sir, I don't see him here; this fellow, I think, lives in the Navy Yard; I saw him go in a house one day there when I carried the bills down.
By the Court.—Q. Did you see Booth the instant he left the back door after the assassination of the President? A. Yes sir, when he rode off.
Q. Now which door was it, the small or the large one that he came out? A. The small door.
Q. Was anybody else at that door? A. I didn't see anybody else.
Q. Did Spangler pass through the door into the passage and back again while you were sitting at the door? A. I didn't take notice.
Q. You didn't see him go out or come in while you were there? A. No sir.
Q. You say he was in the President's box the day of the murder. What time of day was that? A. ——
Q. Did all of you know that the President was to be there that night? A. I heard Harry Ford say so.
Q. Did you hear Spangler speak of it? A. I told him the President was to come there.
Q. What time was that? A. About three o'clock, when we went to take the partition out.
Q. Who went into the box with you at that time? A. There was me, Spangler and Jake.
Q. Who is Jake? A. They call him Jake, that's all I know.
Q. Is he a black or a white man? A. A white man.
Q. How was he employed in the theatre? A. He is a stage carpenter.
Q. Is he employed there regularly? A. He was at work there night and day.
Q. He had been there for some time? A. For three weeks.
Q. How long did you stay with them in the box? A. Till we took the partition out, and after that we sat down in the box.
Q. Did you observe what else they did in the box? A. No; Spangler said it would be a nice place to sleep in.
Q. Did you observe anybody hankering with the lock of the interior door? No, sir.
Q. Do you know anything of the preparation of that bar inside? A. No sir; there were three music stands there and I threw them down on the stage; they were left there the night there was a ball in the theatre.
Q. Do you know whether it is customary to have that bar there? A. No sir.
Q. There never was anything of that kind there before. A. No sir.
Q. You don't know who put the bar there? A. No sir.
Q. Nor who made the preparation for it? A. No sir; I brought the flags in a box and left them there; after we got through that I brought the box that had contained the flags and came down.
Q. Who carried the keys of the private box? A. They were always left in the box office.
Q. Do you know who besides had been there that day? A. No sir, I do not.
Q. Did you see anybody in the box occupied

TRIAL OF THE ASSASSINS AT WASHINGTON. 49

by the President during the day except when Spangler and yourself were there? A. No sir.
Q. Who fixed and repaired the locks on the private boxes generally? A. I don't know sir.
Q. Were there locks on the private boxes? A. Yes sir.
Q. Inside or outside? A. Inside.
Q. When you went down after you left the flags there, did you leave Spangler and the other man at work then? A. No sir; they went down on the stage.
Q. Did you see anybody at work in that box on that day? A. Nobody only Harry Ford, fixing the flags.
Re-cross-examined by Mr. Ewing.—Q. When you went for the flags, did Spangler and Jake leave the box at the same time? A. Yes sir, they went down at the same time.
Q. Where did you go then? A. I went home.
Q. How long were you gone? A. No more than to go down stairs and bring the flags and leave them in the box.
Q. Who next went in? A. Harry Ford was there fixing the flags, and that's all I saw.
Q. What time was that? A. About half-past four o'clock he was fixing the flags.
Q. Do you know whether Spangler went there then? A. No sir.
Q. What furniture was in the box then? A. Those cane-seated chairs.
Q. Were there any red cushioned chairs, high backed? A. I didn't see any.
Q. Didn't you see Spangler in the box after that? A. No; the last I saw was Harry Ford in the box.
Q. Do you know where Spangler went to? A. No sir.
Q. Where did you see him next? A. When Booth called him.
Q. Where did you go? A. I went to the front of the house, on the steps.
Q. How long did you stay there. A. Not very long.
Q. Where did you go then. A. I came inside.
Q. Did you see Spangler inside then? A. No sir; that was about the time he went to the house, and I went there too.
Q. What time was that? A. Between five and six o'clock.
Q. Are you acquainted with Surratt? A. No sir; I may have seen him, but I never heard of his name.

Mary Ann Turner (Colored) Sworn.
By Judge Holt.—Q. State to the Court where you reside in this city. A. In the rear of Ford's Theatre, about as far from it as the gentleman who sits there is from me, about ten feet.
Q. Did you know J. Wilkes Booth? A. I knew him when I saw him.
Q. When you saw of him on the afternoon of the 14th of April last? A. I saw him between three and four o'clock, to the best of my recollection, standing in the back door of Ford's Theatre, with a lady standing by him; I did not take very particular notice at that time, and saw no more of him till, I suppose, between seven and eight o'clock that night; he was carrying a horse up to the back door; he opened a door and called for a man by the name of Ned three times, if not more; this Ned came out, and I heard him in a low voice tell Maddox to stop here; Maddox came, and I seen him reach out his hand and take the horse away; Ned then went on into the theatre.
Q. Did you see him or hear him when he came out after the assassination? A. I only heard a horse going out of the alley; I did not see him at all.
Q. Did you see the man Ned? A. Yes, I rushed out to the door, a crowd had come out at this time, and Ned came out of the door.
Q. Do you recognize "Ned" among the prisoners at the bar? A. Yes, I recognize him there (pointing to Spangler who, by direction of the Court, stood up), said I. "Ned, you know that man who called to you?" said he, "No, I know nothing about it," and went off down the alley.
Q. Was that all that occurred between you and him? A. That was all.
Cross-examined by Mr. Ewing.—Q. How far is your house from the back door of the theatre?

A. My front door opens on the back of the theatre; there is another house adjoining mine between it and the theatre, so that the distance from my door to the back door of the theatre is about twenty feet.
Q. Did you see where Spangler went when he called Maddox? A. I did not see where he went.
Q. Did he go off? A. I disremember, I didn't see him any more.
Q. Did you see him go in and call Maddox? A. Yes, he went to the door and called Maddox.
Q. Did you hear him call Maddox? A. No.
Q. Did you see Spangler come out again? A. I disremember whether he came out again; I do not think he did.

Mary Jane Anderson (colored) Sworn.
By Judge Holt—Q. Where do you live in this city? A. I live between E and F, and Ninth and Tenth streets, right back of the theatre.
Q. Is your room adjoining that of the woman who has just testified? A. Yes; my house and hers join.
Q. Did you know John Wilkes Booth? A. Yes, by sight.
Q. Did you see him in the afternoon or night of the 14th of April? A. Sir, I saw him in the morning, down there by the stable; he went out of the alley and I never saw him any more till between two and three o'clock in the afternoon; he was standing then in the theatre door in the alley that leads out back, him and a lady standing together, talking; I stood in my gate and looked right over at them a considerable while; they turned into the theatre then and I never seen him any more till night; I went up stairs pretty early that night,
night; there was a carriage drove up the alley after I went up, and after that I heard a horse stepping down the alley, and looked out of the window, and it seemed as though the gentleman was leading a horse down the alley; he did not get further than the end of the alley, when he turned back again; I still looked to see who it was, and he came up to the theatre door, and pushed the door open; he said something in a low tone, and then halloed in a loud voice, calling "Ned" four times; there was a colored man who sat at a window, and he said, "Mr. Ned, Booth calls you;" that's how I came to know it was Booth; it was pretty dark, and I could not see what kind of face he had; Mr. Ned came, and Booth said to him in low tone, "Tell Maddox to come here;" Mr. Ned went back, and Mr. Maddox came out; they said something to each other, but I could not understand from my window what the words were; after that Mr. Maddox took hold of the horse, and he and Mr. Ned between them had the horse and carried him round the corner, where I could not see him; Booth returned back into the theatre, and *this man who had carried the horse went in at the door*, too; the horse stayed out there a considerable while and kept a considerable stamping on the stones; I said, "I wonder what is the matter with this horse;" after a while I saw two persons who had the horse walking backwards and forwards; I supposed the horse was there an hour and a half altogether; in about ten minutes I saw this man come out of the door, with something in his hand glittering, but I do not know what it was; he jumped on the horse as quick as he came out of the theatre door, and was gone as quick as a flash of lightning; I thought the horse had certainly run off with the man; then I saw them running out of the door, and asking which way he had gone; still I did not know what was the matter; one man said the President was shot; I said, "by that man who went off?" he said, "yes; did you see him?" I said, "yes, I saw him when he went off;" this was the last time I saw him.
Q. Did you see the prisoner, Spangler, at that time? A. Yes, I saw him after that; after awhile I came down stairs and they were outside talking; I went up to the theatre door, and Spangler was standing there; I said to Spangler, "that gentleman called you;" he said "no he didn't;" said I, "yes he did;" said he, "no he didn't;" I said he did and kept on saying so, and with that he walked away, and I did not see him any more till Sunday, and then I didn't speak to him at all.

Cross-examined by Mr. Ewing.—Q. Do you know Maddox? A. Yes sir.
Q. What kind of a looking man is he? A. Well, he has a kind of reddish skin, and a kind of pale and light hair.
Q. How old a man is he? A. I suppose 25 or 30 years.
Q. Have you seen him often? A. Yes, I have seen him very often; I live close there, and I used to work for him.
Q. Did he hold the horse all the time after he was brought there? A. No, not all the time; he took hold of the horse and it seemed as though he held him a little while; he moved him out of my sight; then he returned and went into the theatre; he had on a light coat.
Q. Then who held the horse when he went in? A. I did not see; as it was carried out of my sight I heard a commotion, and it seemed as though a man had it, but I could not tell who it was; the horse made a great noise stamping about.
Q. I understand you that Spangler just came to the door, that Booth asked him to tell Maddox to come out, and then it seems as if he came out again? A. Whether he did or not I am not certain; Maddox came out, and Booth then had some conversation; I could not tell what it was.
Q. How long from the time Booth first rode up till the people said he had shot the President? A. I suppose a little less than an hour.
Q. Did you see the man who held the horse at the time Booth ran out and rode away? A. Yes; I saw him holding the horse when Booth came out; I could not tell who it was; he was walking the horse up and down; Booth came out, mounted, and it seemed as if, as soon as he touched the horse, he was gone; I was looking down the alley to see which way he went.
Q. Did that man look like Maddox? A. Very much so to me. I know Maddox wears a light coat, and this man seemed as though he had a light coat on; it was pretty dark that night and I could not see distinctly from my window.
Q. How far was he from you when you saw him? A. About as far as from here to that window, about fifteen feet, or a little further.
Q. It was not Spangler holding the horse? A. I do not know; it seems as though it was between three—I am not certain; there were three men altogether who held him.

Wm. A. Browning, sworn.

By Judge Holt.—Q. Will you state if you are the Private Secretary of the President? A. Yes.
Q. Were you with him on the night of the 14th of April? A. I was.
Q. What knowledge have you of the card having been sent by J. Wilkes Booth? A. Between the hours of four and five o'clock I left Vice-President Johnson's room in the Capitol; I went into the Kirkwood House, where I was boarding with him; went up to the office, as I was accustomed to do, and saw a card in my box; Vice President Johnson's box and mine were adjoining; mine was No. 67 and his 68; the clerk of the hotel, Jones, handed me the card.
Q. What was on it? A. (Reading from the card), "Don't wish to disturb you; are you at home? J. Wilkes Booth."
Q. You don't know the handwriting of Booth, do you? A. No sir.
Q. And had no acquaintance with him whatever? A. Yes, I had known him when he was playing in Nashville, Tenn.; I met him several times there; that is the only acquaintance I had with him.
Q. Did you understand the card as sent to the Vice-President or yourself? A. At the time I attached no importance to it; I thought perhaps Booth was playing here, and had some idea of going to see him; I thought he might have called on me as an acquaintance, but when his name was connected with this affair, I looked upon it differently; it was a very common mistake in the office to put the Vice-President's cards in my box, and my cards in his box.
Cross-examined by Mr. Doster—Q. State if you know, what time the Vice President was in his room that day? A. I do not know really at what hour; he was at the Capitol the greater part of the forenoon every day; he was at dinner at five o'clock; I do not think he was out afterwards; I was out myself, and did not return until after the occurrence at the theatre.
Q. Do you know at what time he left his room in the morning? A. I do not.
Q. But he returned at five o'clock. A. I do not know when he returned; he was there at five o'clock, and remained in his room the balance of the evening.
Q. Were you in his room in the course of the afternoon? A. I was there I think about seven or eight o'clock; I was not there afterwards till about eleven o'clock after the assassination.

Major Kilburn Knox, sworn.

By Judge Holt.—Q. State whether or not on the evening of the 14th of April you were at the house of the Secretary of War in this city? A. I was.
Q. Do you see among the prisoners at the bar any person you saw there on that occasion? A. Yes; I recollect that one, (pointing to O'Laughlin, who, by order of the Court, stood up.)
Q. State under what circumstances you saw him; at what hour, and what occurred? A. I was at the house of the Secretary of War about half-past ten o'clock; I had been at the War Department, and left there about ten that evening, and walked up to the Secretary's house; General Grant and Mrs. Grant, the Secretary, General Burres and his wife, Mr. Knapp and his wife, Miss Lucy Stanton, Mr. David Stanton, and two or three small children were there; there was a band playing in front of the house; I was talking to Mrs. Grant; the others were standing on the upper steps; they set off some fireworks on the square opposite, and I stepped in to let the children see them; I stood on the next to the lower step, and was leaning against the railing, when this man came up; he said to me, "Is Stanton in?" I said, "I suppose you mean the Secretary of War?" he said "Yes;" and I think he said "I am a lawyer in town and I know him very well;" I had the impression that he was under the influence of liquor, and told him I did not think he could see him then; he went on the other side of the steps and stood there perhaps five minutes; I still stayed in the same position, and he came over and said again, "Is Stanton in?" and then said "excuse me, I thought you were the officer of the day;" I said then "there is no officer of the day here;" he then walked up the steps into the hall, and stood there some minutes; I went over to David Stanton and said, "do you know that man;" he said he did not; I remarked that the man said he knew the Secretary very well, but that I thought he was drunk, and said to Mr. D. Stanton he had better take him out; Mr. Stanton walked in and talked with him a few minutes and took him out, and he went off.
Q. Did he say anything about General Grant in the course of the conversation? A. He did not; I think General Grant had gone into the parlor.
Q. Was he looking in to see the Secretary from his position? A. I think the Secretary stood on the steps outside, and that this man stood behind him where he could see in the parlor and in the inside of the house; there is a library on one side of the hall and a parlor on the other side; he stood on the side next to the library, from which position he could look into the parlor and see who was in there.
Q. Do you feel perfectly certain that the prisoner here is the man you saw on that occasion? A. Yes; I feel perfectly certain that he is.
Cross-examined by Mr. Cox.—Q. Was it moonlight or dark? A. I do not recollect; there was quite a large crowd there.
Q. Was the crowd close up to the steps? A. Yes.
Q. Did the person you saw mingle with the crowd? A. I did not notice him at all until he walked up the steps and spoke to me.
Q. You did not go inside the hall while he was there? A. No.
Q. Did I understand you to say the Secretary was standing on the steps? A. Yes, he was standing on the left-hand side, talking with

Mrs. Grant, and the man passed right by him on the right-hand side.
Q. How was he dressed? A. He had on a black slouch hat, a black frock coat and black pants; I cannot say as to his vest.
Q. Had you ever seen him before? A. I had not.
Q. Have you ever seen him before? A. I had not.
Q. Have you since? A. I have; I saw him a week ago last Sunday, here in the prison.
Q. Did you come for the purpose of identifying him? A. I did.
Q. Did you come in company with Mr. Stanton? A. No; I came in company with other persons.
Q. Can you fix the hour at 10½ o'clock, certainly? A. It must have been about that; I left the War Department at 10, walked up and had been there about ten minutes.

Testimony of John C. Hatter.

Examined by Judge Holt.—Q. State whether you knew the prisoner O'Laughlin? A. I know a man by that name.
Q. Do you recognize him here? A. Yes (pointing to the prisoner).
Q. Will you state whether or not you saw him on the 13th of April last, and if so, where, and under what circumstances? A. I seen him the night of the illumination, I suppose the night General Grant came from the front, at Secretary Stanton's house.
Q. State what occurred there. A. I was standing on the steps looking at the illumination; this man approached me, and asked if General Grant was in; I told him he was; he said he wished to see him; said I, this is not an occasion for you to see him; if you wish to see him, step out on the pavement, or carriage stone, and you can see him.
Q. What time of the night was it? A. I should judge it was about 9 o'clock, or a little after.
Q. Was that all that occurred between you? A. Yes.
Q. He did not go in the house or attempt to go in? A. No.
Q. Were you on the steps at Secretary Stanton's house? A. I was near the top.
Q. Was he on the steps? A. He was; I should judge, about two or three steps below me, about the third step from the pavement.
Q. Did he leave the step while you were there? A. He left the step after I spoke to him; he was talking; I did not quite understand what he was saying; he walked away towards the tree-box, and seemed to reflect on something; I then turned my eyes off and didn't see him any more.
Q. Are you certain you did not see anything more than that? A. Nothing more.
Q. The house was illuminated, was it? A. Yes; it was very light; it was lighted from the inside, and pretty light outside too.
Cross-examined by Mr. Cox.—Q. What is your business? A. I am employed at the War Department, in the Secretary's room.
Q. Had you ever seen the man you mention before that evening. A. I do not think I have to my knowledge.
Q. Have you ever seen him since? A. Yes, in prison; in this prison, or the one adjoining, on last Sunday week.
Q. Did you come down to see if he was the same man? A. When I first started to come down I did not know it was for that purpose; I was with Major Eckert and Major Knox; I inquired when we arrived at the prison if I was to come in; the Major told me to come in; when I was inside the building I did not know the purpose until Major Eckert called in the prisoners the moment I saw that man I thought I knew the object of my coming down.
Q. And this is the only occasion you recollect of having seen him? A. That is the only time except to-day.
Q. What made you think it was the same man? A. The first time I saw him it was very light; he had on a dark suit of clothes and a heavy moustache; while I was speaking with him I was looking right sharp in his face; he had on a dark slouch hat, not very high, and a dark dress coat; his pantaloons were dark; I could not say whether they were black or brown.
Q. What was his size? A. I should judge he was about my size; though, as he was standing on the steps below me, he might seen lower; I should judge he was about 5 feet 4 or 5 inches high.
Q. Had a crowd come there to serenade the Secretary at that time? A. Yes; there were three or four bands there.
Q. Was the Secretary on the steps at the time? A. No; he was inside the house; General Grant also; there was nobody on the steps but myself.
Q. Were the crowd close up to the steps? A. Yes; up to the lower steps.
Q. Was the door open at the time? A. Yes; the front door and the inner door, and the gas was fully lighted all around.

Testimony of Dr. Robert King Stone.

Examined by Judge Holt.—Q. State to the Court if you are a practising physician in this city? A. I am.
Q. State whether or not you were the physician of the late President of the United States? A. I was his family physician.
Q. State whether or not you called to see him on the evening of the assassination. If so, state the examination and the result. A. I was sent for by Mrs. Lincoln immediately after the assassination and was there within a few minutes; the President had been carried from the theatre to the house of a gentleman who lived directly opposite, and placed upon a bed in the back part of the house; I found several citizens there, and among others two assistant surgeons of the army, who had brought him over; they immediately gave over the case to my care in consequence of my professional relation to the family. I proceeded to examine him, and instantly found that the President had received a gunshot wound in the back part and left side of his head, into which I carried readily my finger, and at once informed those around that the case was hopeless; that the President would die; that there was no positive limit to his life, as his vital tenacity was very strong; that he would resist as long as any one, but that death would certainly follow; I remained with him as long as it was of any use to do anything for him, but of course nothing could be done; he died the next morning about half-past seven; it was about half-past ten when I first saw him that night.
Q. Did he die from that wound? A. Yes.
Q. Did you extract the ball? A. I did the next day when the body was ready to be embalmed, in the presence of Dr. Barnes, the Surgeon-General, and others; when the examination was made I traced the wound through the brain; the ball was found in the interior part of the left side of the brain; it was a large ball, resembling those shot from the pistol known as the Derringer; an unusually large ball, that is a larger ball than those used in ordinary pocket revolvers.
Q. Was it a leaden ball? A. Yes, a handmade ball, from which the tag had been cut from the side; the ball was flattened or compressed somewhat in its passage through the skull, or a little portion had been cut in its passage through the bone; I marked the ball with the initials of the President, in the presence of the Secretary of War; sealed it up with my private seal, and indorsed my name on the envelope; the Secretary inclosed it in another envelope, which he also indorsed and sealed with his private seal; it is still in his custody, having been ordered to be placed among the archives of his Department.
Q. Did you see the pistol from which the ball was fired? A. I did not.

Testimony of Sergeant Silas D. Coff.

Examination by Judge Holt.—Q. State whether or not on the night of the assassination of the President you were on duty at the Navy Yard Bridge? A. I was.
Q. Do you remember to have seen one or two men passing rapidly on horseback, and if so at what time? A. I saw three men approach me rapidly, on horseback, between 10½ and 11 o'clock, I should think.
Q. Did you challenge them? A. Yes; I challenged them and advanced to recognize them.
Q. Did you recognize them? A. I satisfied myself

that they were proper persons to pass, and passed them.
Q. Do you recognize either of these persons as among the prisoners here? Look the entire distance of the box, from one end to the other. The witness scrutinized each of the prisoners closely, and replied, No sir.
Q. Could you describe either of these men, or both of them? A. I could.
Q. Do you think you would recognize either of them by a photograph? A. I think I would; (a photograph of Booth was shown to the witness;) yes, that man passed first.
Q. Alone? A. Yes.
Q. Did you not say that three came together? A. No; three passed, but they were not together.
Q. Did you have any conversation with this first man as he passed? A. Yes, for three or four minutes.
Q. What name did he give? A. He gave his name as Booth.
Q. What did he say? A. I asked him what his name was; he answered Booth; I asked him "where from?" he answered, "from the city;" I asked him, "Where are you going?" "Going home;" I asked him where his home was; he said in Charles county; I understood to mean Charles county; I asked him what town? he said he didn't live in any town; I said you must live in some town; he said, "I live close to Bryantown, but I do not live in town;" I asked him why he was out so late; if he did not know that persons were not permitted to pass after that time of night; he said it was news to him; he said he had some ways to go, that it was dark, and that he thought he would have a moon.
Q. How long before the other two men came? A. The next one came up in five or seven minutes, or possibly ten minutes.
Q. Did they seem to be riding rapidly or leisurely? A. The second one who came up did not seem to be riding so rapidly.
Q. What did he say? A. I asked who he was; he said his name was Smith; that he was going to White Plains; I asked him how he came to be out so late; he made some or a rather indelicate reply, from which I should judge he had been in bad company.
Q. Was he a large or small sized man? A. A small sized man.
Q. Did you have a good view of his face? A. I did; I brought him up before the guard-house door so that the light could fall on his face.
Q. How would he compare in size with the last man among the prisoners (Harold)? A. He is very nearly the size, but I should not think he was the man; he had a lighter complexion than that man.
Q. Did you allow him to pass after that explanation? A. Yes.
Q. What became of the other man? A. The other man I turned back; he did not seem to have sufficient business to warrant me in passing him.
Q. Was he on horseback also? A. Yes.
Q. Did he seem to be a companion of the prisoner who had gone before? A. I do not know.
Q. Did they come up together? A. No; they were some distance apart.
Q. Did this man make any inquiry for Booth? A. He made an inquiry whether a man had passed on a roan horse?
Q. Did the second one who had come up make any inquiry in regard to another horseman? A. No sir, none whatever.
Q. What was the color of the second horse? A. It was a roan horse.

Testimony of Polk Graham.

Examined by Judge Holt.—Q. State whether you were on the road between Washington and Bryantown on the night of the 14th of April last? A. Yes, sir.
Q. You were going to Washington? A. Yes.
Q. State if you met one or more horsemen, and if so, at what hour and under what circumstances. A. I met two about 11 o'clock, riding very fast.
Q. In what direction? A. Going to Marlboro; I met the first one on Good Hope Hill, and the last one about half a mile beyond.
Q. Did they say anything to you? A. They first stopped me and asked me the road to Marlboro; he first asked me if the road did not fork a little ahead, and if he did not turn to the right; I told him no, to keep straight ahead.
Q. Was it light enough for you to see his horse? A. He rode a dark horse; I think it was a bay.
Q. What did the other one say? A. He said nothing to me; I heard him ask a question, whether it was of me or of the teamsters on the road, I do not know; I did not answer him.
Q. How far was he behind the first one? A. About half a mile, I reckon.
Q. What was the appearance of the horse? did you notice? A. It was a roan or iron-grey.
Q. Was the man large or small? A. I never noticed the man.

Cross-examined by Mr. Stone.—Q. How far was this from the city? A. I suppose two and a-half or three miles from the city.

Q. Was he the one who inquired the road to Marlboro? A. Yes.
Q. How long after the first man passed was it before the other came along? A. I do not suppose it was more than five or ten minutes; I do not know exactly.
Q. What did you say the second asked you? A. I do not know whether it was asked of me; he asked whether a horseman had passed ahead; I did not answer him.
Q. The road forks at Good Hope Hill, does it not, one turning to the right and the other to the left? Were they beyond the forks? A. I think so, but I am not acquainted with the road.
Q. Was the last man riding at a rapid gait? A. Yes; both were riding very fast.
Q. Was it at the top of the hill? A. No; about the middle of the way up; I suppose I had got off that hill entirely before I met the second man.

Re-Examination of Dr. Stone.

The ball extracted from the wound of President Lincoln having been received from the War Department, Dr. Stone was again called on the stand, and on examining it identified it fully as the ball extracted by him.

Testimony of Wm. F. Kent.

By Judge Holt.—Q. State whether or not the pistol you now have before you was picked up by you in the box of the President on the night of the assassination? A. Yes, sir; this is the pistol.
Q. What is it called? A. A Derringer, I believe, and I see that name marked on it.
Q. How long after the President was shot did you pick it up? A. I do not know exactly how long; I suppose about three minutes after the President was shot; when I went into the box, there were two persons in there then; the Surgeon asked me for a knife to cut open the President's clothes; I handed him mine, and with it I cut up President's clothes open; I left the theatre afterwards; I missed my night key and thought I had dropped it there; I turned back to go to the theatre, and when I went into the box my foot knocked against a pistol lying on the floor. I picked it up and cried out "I have found the pistol;" some persons told me to give it to the police; but there was a gentleman who said he represented the Associated Press, and I handed it to him; the next morning I went around to the police station and recognized it as the pistol I had picked up.

Testimony of Lieut. Alex. Lovett.

Examined by Judge Holt.—Q. Will you state whether or not, after the assassination of the President, you and others were engaged in the pursuit of the murderer? A. Yes.
Q. What route did you take? A. The route by Surrattsville.
Q. State whether or not in pursuing that route you came to the house of Dr. Samuel Mudd? A. I do, and recognize him as one of the prisoners at the bar.
Q. Did you stop there and make any inquiries? A. I stopped there and made inquiries of his wife first. He was out.
Q. State what questions were addressed by him to you and other members of your party, and what was said. A. We first asked him whether there had been any strangers at the house; he said there had; at first he did not seem to care about giving us any satisfaction; then he went on and stated that on Saturday morning, at daybreak, two strangers came to his place, one came to the door and the other sat on his horse; that he went down and opened the door when the other man got off his horse and came into the house; that one of them had a broken leg, and that he had set the leg; I asked him who the man was; he said he did not know, he was a stranger to him; he stated that they were both strangers; I asked him what kind of a looking man the other was; he said he was a young man about 17 or 18 years old.
Q. How long did he say they remained there? A. He said they remained a short time; this was the first conversation I had with him.
Q. You stated that Dr. Mudd said they were there a short time; do you mean they went away in the course of the morning? A. That is what I understood them.
Q. On what day was this? A. On Tuesday, the 18th.
Q. Did he state to you whether at that time or before he had heard anything in regard to the assassination of the President? A. He said he had heard it on Sunday at church.
Q. What distance is the house from Washington? A. By way of Bryantown it is about thirty miles, I suppose.
Q. Is it on one of the highways of the country? A. It is off the public road, running from Georgetown about a quarter of a mile.
Q. Did you have a considerable conversation with him in regard to the assassination of the President? A. We did not talk much about that. I was making inquiries more about these men than anything else.
Q. How long were you at his house? A. Probably an hour.
Q. Did he continue until the last to make the same representations to him? A. Yes, sir; that he knew nothing of them. He said one of them called for a razor, soap and water, to shave his moustache off. I asked him if he had any

TRIAL OF THE ASSASSINS AT WASHINGTON. 53

other beard; he replied, "Yes, a long pair of whiskers."

Q. Did he state that Booth had left there that morning on horseback? A. He said one of them went away on crutches, and that he showed them a way cross the swamp.

Q. Did he state what the wounded man had done with his horse? A. He said the other one led his horse and that he had a pair of crutches made for him; I was entirely satisfied that these parties were Booth and Harold.

Q. Did you arrive at the conclusion from the description given of the men? A. Yes.

Q. Did he state to you the reason these men had gone into the swamp? A. He said they were going to Allan's Fresh.

Q. Did he state for what purpose this man had shaved off his moustache? A. No; some of the other men along with me made the remark that it looked suspicious, and Mr. Mudd then also said it looked suspicious.

Q. Will you state whether you had a subsequent interview with Mr. Mudd? A. Yes sir.

Q. How long after the first one? A. At the first interview I had my mind made up to arrest him when the proper time came; the second interview occurred on Friday, the 21st; I went there for the purpose of arresting him.

Q. State what he then said in regard to these men? A. When he found that we were going to search the house he said something to his wife and then brought down a boot and handed it to me; he said he had to cut it off in order to set the man's leg; I turned the boot down and saw some writing on the inside, "J. Wilkes;" I called his attention to it; he said he had not taken notice of that before. [A large country boot slit down the leggings brought in and passed round and examined by the members of the Court; on the inside near the top of the leg, under the name of the maker, were the words "J. Wilkes," written plainly in ink.]

Q. Did he at that time still insist that they were strangers to him? A. Yes.

Q. Did he acknowledge at any subsequent period that he knew Booth? A. Yes; he said subsequently that he was satisfied it was Booth.

Q. When was that? A. That was on Friday, the same day; he made the remark that his wife had told him she saw the whiskers at the time became disconnected from the man's face.

Q. But he had stated to you distinctly before that he had not known this man? A. Yes sir.

Q. Did he or not at any subsequent conversation state that he had known this man Booth? A. After I had arrested him and we had got on our horses and were going out, some of the men gave him Booth's photograph; they held it up to him and asked if it did not look like Booth; he said that it was not like Booth; that it looked a little like him across the eyes shortly after that he said he had an introduction to Booth last fall; he said a man by the name of Johnson gave him an introduction to him.

Q. Did he state where he met Booth? A. No; on being questioned by one of the other men he said he had r de with him in the country, looking up some land, and when he bought a horse.

Q. Did he state the price? A. It was last fall I believe he said.

Q. Did he give you any description of the horse he bought? A. He said he wanted a good road horse.

Cross-examination by Mr. Ewing Q. You say that Dr. Mudd gave you a description of these two persons? A. Yes sir; he gave me a partial description of them; he said that one was quite a young man, and the other had large thin whiskers.

Q. What did he say to you as to the resemblance between the photograph and its original? A. In the first place he said that it did not look like Booth; then he said it looked like him across the eyes.

Q. Did you tell him about your tracking Booth from Washington? A. I do not think up to that time I had mentioned Booth's name at all.

Q. Where was Dr. Mudd when you called at his house the second time? A. He was out some place and his wife sent for him; I walked out and greeted him.

Q. Did you not say to him that you wanted the razor with which the man who stopped at his house shaved himself? A. Yes sir; I demanded that after we went into the house.

Q. Did not Dr. Mudd then tell you that since you were there before the boots had been found in the room? A. Not until after we were in the house some time.

Q. He then volunteered the statement? A. Yes, he said something to his wife, and sue went up stairs and brought it down.

Q. But did he not make the statement voluntarily? A. He did after one of the men told him that we would have to search the house.

Q. Are you sure he did not make the statement until after that was said? A. I am.

Q. He said that he had shown those men the way across the swamp? A. So I understood him.

Q. To what swamp did he allude? A. The swamp in the rear of his house, I believe.

Q. Is there a swamp immediately in the rear of his house? A. There is one about a thousand yards below his house.

Q. What else did he say in describing these men? A. I asked him if the whisker of one of the men spoken of by him might not have been false, and he said he did not know; it appeared afterwards that Booth had gone up stairs, but the doctor did not tell me of that.

Q. He did not say where Booth had been? A. He told me that he had been on the sofa.

Q. When you asked the Doctor how long those two men had stayed, he said they did not stay long? A. At our first interview he told me they stayed but a short time, and afterwards his wife told me that they stayed until three or four o'clock, on Saturday afternoon.

Q. You need not state to the Court what his wife said. A. Well, I think I.o to'd me that himself, afterwards.

Q. Did he not ask Dr. Mudd whether he charged anything for setting the leg? A. Yes sir.

Q. What did he say? A. I did not ask him whether he charged anything; my question was whether the men had much money? he said they had considerable of greenbacks; I then asked him if they had arms about them; to which he replied the wounded man had a brace of revolvers.

Q. Did he say anything about having been paid for setting the leg? A. I did not ask him about that; he went on to say that it was customary for men to make a charge to strangers.

Q. He spoke of that in connection with the fact of their having money? A. Yes sir.

Q. Did he not say to you that those men arrived at his house before daylight? A. He said about daybreak.

Q. Who went with you to his house, on the occasion of your second visit? A. There were three special officers, besides some cavalry.

Q. Who were the officers? A. Simon Galligar, Joshua Loyd, and William Williams.

Q. What civilian went with you the first time? A. Dr. George Mudd.

Q. When you were at Dr. Mudd's the second time do you not recollect that he told you the two men started from his house to go to Rev. Mr. Wilmer's? A. Yes sir, but I paid no attention to that; I thought it was a blind for the purpose of throwing us off the track.

Q. But he said that? A. Yes sir, he stated that they inquired for Parson Wilmer's, and that they said they were on their way to Allen's Fresh.

Q. Did he mention that both times you were there? A. I think only the first time.

Q. Are you sure it was not out of doors that you first asked Dr. Mudd for the razor? A. I might have spoken to him about it out of doors, but I remember having made the demand in the house.

Q. Are you sure that it was not before he got to the house he told you the boot had been found since you were there before? A. He told me that in the house, not outside.

Q. Was there not a citizen named Hardy with you at that time? A. N t that I know of.

Q. Was there not a citizen with Dr. Mudd? A. There was a citizen, who stood outside the door after we went into the house; I do not know his name.

Q. Was Dr. Mudd alone when you met him coming to the house? A. There was a citizen walking with him I think.

Q. Was it this man you speak of as having subsequently stood outside the door? A. It was.

Cross-examined by Mr. Stone.—Q. When you went to Dr. Mudd the first time did you have any conversation with him before you went into the house? A. I think not; I had a conversation with his wife.

Q. As soon as you asked him whether two strangers had been there, he told you at once they had? A. Yes sir; he was made aware of the nature of our errand, I suppose, by a friend; he seemed very much excited, and turned very pale when he was first asked about the two strangers, though he admitted they had been there.

Q. You asked him to describe them, and he gave you the description? A. Yes sir.

Q. By whom did he say he was introduced to Booth last fall? A. A man by the name of Johnson.

Q. He told you he was introduced to Booth by Johnson at church? A. He did not tell me that in the first place; he told me he did not know Booth at all.

Q. When, on the occasion of your second interview, you mentioned the name of Booth, he then told you he had been introduced? A. I did not mention it until we were on horseback, though I had previously mentioned Booth's name to the other doctor.

Q. You say that Dr. Mudd seemed to be very much alarmed? A. Yes; he turned very pale in the face and blue about the lips, like a man who was frightened at the recollection of something he had done.

Q. Did he mention, in connection with his introduction to Booth, the name of Thompson? A. I understood him to say Johnson, but Thompson might have been the name.

By Judge Advocate Holt.—Q. You state that Dr. Mudd appeared very much frightened; did you address any threat to him? A. No sir; I was in citizen's clothes at the time.

Q. His alarm then was not in consequence of anything that you said or done? A. No sir; he seemed very much concerned when I turned the boot inside out; some of the men present said that the name of

Booth had been scratched out, when I suggested that it had not been written.

Q. You have stated that when you asked Dr. Mudd whether the two strangers had any arms, he replied that the one with the broken leg had a brace of revolvers; did he say anything about the other having a carbine or a knife? A. No sir.

Q. Did you understand him to say that this brace of revolvers was all the arms the stranger had?

The question was objected to by Mr. Ewing as being a leading question. The following was then put:—

Q. Will you state what was his manner? Was it frank or evasive? A. Very evasive; he seemed to be very reserved.

Q. Did he speak of these men as having any other weapons than the brace of pistols of which you have spoken? A. To my knowledge one of the officers spoke to him on that point.

Q. Which one? A. I think it was Williams.

Q. I understand you to say that Dr. Mudd stated that he did not hear the news of the assassination of the President until Sunday morning, at church. At the time of this statement to you did he mention the name of the assassin? A. No sir.

By Mr. Ewing.—Q. Did not Dr. Mudd, at your first interview, state that he heard the details of the assassination while at church, on Sunday morning? A. I do not recollect that he did. I made a remark to one of the officers, at the time, that he must have been aware of the assassination, because the cavalry were all along the road, and everybody in the neighborhood knew it on Saturday.

Q. Did Dr. Mudd state to you that the strangers were going in the direction of Allen's Fresh, in connection with his statement that they had gone to the Rev. Dr. Wilmer's? A. He said that they inquired for Mr. Wilmer; that he took them across the swamp, and that they were going in the direction of Allen's Fresh. I went to Mr. Wilmer's, and searched his house, but I was satisfied we would find nothing there, as I looked upon it as a blind to draw us off that way.

Q. In going from Dr. Mudd's to Dr. Wilmer's, would you cross the swamp? A. Yes sir; you can go that way.

Q. Did you follow the track of this man Booth and his companion? A. Yes sir; as far as I could.

By the Court.—Q. When you reached Mudd's house on Tuesday morning after the assassination was it generally understood there that Booth was the man who killed the President? A. Every person around Bryantown and along the way understood so.

Q. Is there a telegraph line in that section? A. The only telegraph of which I have any knowledge is the one that runs to Point Lookout; I do not know the exact distance to that place; there was a telegraphic connection with Port Tobacco, but if any person who saw these men wanted to give information concerning them they need not have gone far; by merely going out on the public road they could have given it, as the cavalry were all along there.

Q. What is the distance from Washington to Surrattsville? A. About ten miles, I should judge.

Q. What is the distance from Surrattsville to Dr. Mudd's? A. By the way we first went, it was about sixteen miles to Bryantown, and about four and a half miles from there to Dr. Mudd's.

Q. In going to Mudd's, do you go through Surrattsville? A. Yes. There is a road running from Port Tobacco, by which you can go there. Dr. Mudd's is about twenty miles beyond Surrattsville by way of Bryantown.

Mr. Eakin.—Q. Are you acquainted with Mr. Floyd, who keeps the hotel at Surrattsville? A. I arrested him on Friday, the 18th of April.

Q. Did he make any statement to you? A. Yes, sir.

Q. What did he say concerning his connection with the affair?

Judge Advocate Bingham objected to the question on the ground that it was an attempt to discredit the testimony of Floyd, by showing that he had made statements in conflict with representations made before the Court. The question was understood to be withdrawn by Mr. Ewing.

Q. From whom did you first hear that two men had stayed at Dr. Mudd's house? A. I heard it from a soldier.

Q. Do you know his name? A. Yes sir; his name was Lieutenant Dana.

Q. Did Dr. Mudd say anything to you about it? A. He did; I sent for him, took him up into a room of the hotel and asked him to make his statement, which he did.

Joshua Lloyd, Sworn.

Q. State whether or not some day after the assassination of the President you were engaged with others in pursuing the assassins? A. I was.

Q. Did you, in the course of your pursuit, go to the house of the prisoner, Dr. Samuel Mudd? A. Yes sir.

Q. On what day did you go there? A. On Monday, April 18th.

Q. State what reply he made to your inquiry in regard to the object of your pursuit. A. I asked him if he knew that the President had been assassinated; he replied that he did; I then asked him if he had seen any parties looking like the assassins pass that way, and he said he had not.

Q. That was at the first interview? A. Yes sir.

Q. What did he state at the second interview? A. He then acknowledged that two men had stopped there, and that he had set the broken limb of one of them; wo showed him the likenesses, and he said he had seen them before; I then asked him had we been introduced to Booth last fall, and he said he had.

Q. How long did he say these men remained at his house? A. I think he said they remained there from four o'clock in the morning until 4 P. M.

Q. Did he say they were on horseback or on foot? A. He said that one was on horseback and the other was walking and leading a horse.

A photograph of Booth was shown to witness, and recognized by him as the one which he had in his possession, and which he exhibited to Dr. Mudd.

Q. What was the Doctor's manner? A. He appeared to be very much excited; when we went there the second time he was not in, and his lady sent for him; she appeared to be greatly worried.

Q. What did you say to him at the second visit? A. Very little conversation took place on my part, as I did not feel very well.

Q. Did he make any reference to his previous denial of having seen these men? A. I do not know that he did; after we found the boot he owned up, and said that he had formerly been introduced to Booth by a man named Thompson; he did not say anything about being in company with him in Washington city.

During the cross-examination the witness stated that Mudd at first denied having seen the supposed assassins, or even any strangers. The prisoner stated when arrested that at the time of his introduction to Booth by the man Thompson he was informed that Booth came there to buy some property; at the time of the witness' first visit to Mudd, the latter stated that he had heard of the President's assassination at the church on Sunday. Dr. George Mudd was then present. On Friday, the day of the second visit, the boot found in the house was produced upon the arrival of the prisoner at his home and while the party were waiting for him.

Colonel H. H. Wells, sworn.—Q. Are you Provost Marshal of the defences south of Washington? A. Yes sir.

Q. State to the Court whether, in the week subsequent to the murder of the President, you had an interview with the prisoner, Dr. Mudd? A. Yes sir; I had an interview with him on Friday, April 21st.

Q. State all that he said to you in regard to the men who called at his place on Saturday morning after the murder. A. I had three definite conversations with him; the first occurred, I think, about noon on Friday; I had the doctor brought to my head-quarters, and took his statement; he commenced by remarking that on Saturday morning, about 4 o'clock, he was aroused by a loud knock at his door; he was surprised at the loudness of the knock, and inquired who was there; receiving some reply, as I understand he looked from the window or went to the door, and saw two horses and a second person sitting on one of the horses; he described the appearance of the persons, and said that the youngest of the two was very fluent in his speech, and that the person on horseback had broken his leg, and desired medical attendance; he assisted in bringing the person who was on horseback into his house and laying him upon the sum in the parlor, and after some time he was carried up stairs and laid on a bed, in what was called the front room; he then proceeded to examine the leg and discovered that the outward bone was broken nearly at right angles across the limb, about two inches above the instep; he said it was not a compound fracture, and that the patient complained of pain in his back, but he found no apparent cause for the pain, except as proceeding from the effect of a fall from a horse, as the patient stated he had fallen; he said that he dressed the limb as well as he was able to do with the limited facilities at his command, and called a white hired servant to make a crutch for the patient; the crutch was made and breakfast was then prepared, and the younger of the two persons, the one who was uninjured, was invited to breakfast with them; the prisoner further stated that after breakfast he noticed his patient to be much debilitated and pale; the young man made some remarks in relation to procuring some conveyance for taking his friend away, and that some time after dinner he started with him to see if a carriage could be procured; after travelling for some distance and failing to procure a carriage, the young man remarked that he would not go any further, but would return to the house and see if he could not get his friend away; the doctor stated also that after going to the town, which was the farthest point of his journey, he returned to his house about 4 P. M.; in speaking of the wounded man I asked him if he knew who the person was, to which he replied that he did not recognize him; I then exhibited to him what was said to be a miniature of Booth, and he said that from the miniature he could not recognize him; he stated, however, in answer to another question, that he met Booth sometime in November; I think he said that he was introduced by a Mr. Thompson to Booth; I think the introduction to Booth took place at church on a Sunday morning, and after the introduction had been given, Thompson said that Booth wanted to purchase farming lands; they had some conversation on the subject of lands, and then Booth asked the ques-

TRIAL OF THE ASSASSINS AT WASHINGTON. 55

tion whether there were any desirable horses that could be bought cheap in that section, and he mentioned the names of several dealers in desirable stock in the neighborhood; I asked him if he could recognize again the person whom he then met under the name of Booth; he said he could, and I asked him if he had seen Booth at any time after the introduction in November and prior to his arrival there on Saturday morning; he said he had not; I asked him if he had any suspicions of the character of Booth, or either of these persons; he said he had not, but that after breakfast he thought there was something strange about their actions in view of the fact that the young man came down stairs and asked for a razor, and said his friend wanted to shave himself, and that shortly afterwards he noticed that the person answering to the name of Booth had shaved off his moustache; I asked him if the man had a beard, when he said that he had, and that it was larger than my own, but he could not determine whether it was natural or artificial; that he kept a shawl about his neck and seemed to desire to conceal the lower part of his face; I asked him at this time if he had heard of the murder of the President; he replied that he had not; I think, however, he remarked to me in one of his interviews, that he heard of the assassination for the first time on Sunday morning, or late in the evening of Saturday; my impression is that he did not hear of it until after these persons had left his house.

The witness stated further, that when leaving, Harold inquired for the most direct route to Mr. Wilmer's house, and that the prisoner gave him the desired information. The prisoner also communicated to the witness all the particulars concerning the discovery of the boot found in the house occupied by him.

Cross-examination by Mr. Ewing.—Q. At the time that Mudd gave you this information did you see anything that was extraordinary? A. He did not seem willing to answer a direct question, and I saw that unless I did ask direct questions all important facts were omitted by him.

Q. Was he alarmed? A. He was much excited.
Q. And alarmed? A. Not at the first or second interview, but at the third he was.
Q. What time of Friday did you pay your first interview with him? A. Not far from midday; it might have been before or in the afternoon.
Q. How long after was it that Lovett was gone for Dr. Mudd? A. I am not certain; I don't think I sent Lovett for Mudd.
Q. It was on the Friday after the assassination? A. I think it was, sir; on the 21st.
Q. At the first interview did you have any written statement made? A. No sir; I kept on talking with him, and, after I thought I had the facts, I had it taken down in writing; we had a dozen interviews at least.
Q. When was the last interview? A. On Sunday, I think.
Q. Did you have any more than one on Friday? A. Yes; he was in my presence for almost five hours; we were taking there from time to time.
Q. You said that at the last interview he was much alarmed from some statement you made? A. I said to him that he was concealing the facts, and that I did not know whether he understood that was the strongest evidence that could be produced of his guilt at that time, and might endanger his safety.
Q. When was it you went off with Dr. Mudd, and he took you along the route which these two men took? A. On Sunday morning, I am quite confident.
Q. He spoke of their taking the direct road to Piney Chapel? A. Yes sir, to Dr. Wilbur's, of Piney Chapel.
Q. You spoke of tracks on the direct road to Piney Chapel till they turned off? A. No; they took the direct road, coming out by the doctor's house, till they came to the wall, with this exception; the marsh was full of holes and bad places, and I remember thinking they had got lost, as they went from right to left, and kept changing on that way till they lost the general direction.
Q. Did you say that the Doctor said to you that he had heard of the assassination of the President on Saturday evening or on Sunday? A. My impression is that he said not till Saturday afternoon or Sunday morning.
Q. You think he said Saturday evening? A. Yes.
Q. Did he mention how and whence he heard it? A. No sir; I can't say that he did, but I have an indistinct idea that he heard it at the town, but am not sure; over in Bryantown.
Q. Did he say when it was that Johnson introduced him to Booth? A. He said it was about November.
Q. Did he say whether it was before daybreak when they came to his house? A. He said it was before daybreak; about four o'clock.
Q. Did you ask whether they paid him anything for setting the broken leg? A. I think he said they paid him twenty-five dollars. I think that statement was made to one of the men that was with me, but not to me directly.
Q. Didn't Samuel Mudd say to you that there had been two suspicious men at his house? A. Yes, sir.
Q. Did he not say to you that he told that on Saturday evening? A. I can't remember; but I think not.
Q. Was it on Sunday evening? A. I think it was later than that.

Q. Did he not say to you in some one of your interviews that he told you that on Sunday? A. My impression is that he told Dr. Mudd on Monday.
Q. You recollect his having said that he told Dr. Mudd? A. Yes; in this connection I said, "one of the strongest circumstances against you is that you have failed to give the fullest information of this matter." Then it was he said he told Dr. George Mudd.
Q. Did he examine the likeness of Booth in your possession? A. Yes sir.
Q. Did he recognize it as the man who he had been introduced to? A. My impression is that he said that he could not from the photograph recognize the man.
Q. Did he not say that he could not recognize it as the man whose leg was broken? A. He said, "I should not have known Mr. Booth from the photograph;" he said also he did not recognize the man when he first saw him, but that on recollecting he knew it was Mr. Booth, the person to whom he had been introduced.
Q. Did he not say that that was like a likeness that he had already seen of Booth, with his name marked upon it? A. I don't remember that.
Q. Was there not intense excitement in the town among the soldiers and the people? A. Not among the soldiers, they were calm enough; but among the people there was; they were going and coming all the time.
Q. In a state of angry and excited feeling? A. There was no angry feeling exhibited, but there was an excited state of feeling evident.
By the Judge Advocate.—Q. Can you state at what time Dr. Mudd professed to have recognized Booth as the man he had been introduced to? A. During their stay at his house.
Q. So you understood him to admit that he recognized him before he left? A. Yes; his expression was, that he did not know him at first, but that on reflection he recognized him.
By Mr. Ewing.—Q. Please state as nearly as you can Mudd's exact words when he spoke on reflection of recollecting "that it was Booth who was at his house on showing him the picture; that he should not have recollected the man from the photograph, and that he did not remember him when he first saw him, but that on reflection he remembered he was the man he was introduced to in November last, or in the fall." A. I won't say these are the exact words, but that is the substance of his words, as nearly as I can recollect them.
Q. There was nothing but that in his conversation upon that point? A. That was the substance of it, and it was said over and over again.
Q. Didn't he say whether this reflection on which he could recognize the man with the broken leg, as the man to whom he had been introduced, was a reflection which arose after the man had left his house? A. He left the impression clearly upon my mind that it was before the man left the house; he gave it as a reason why he didn't remember him at the first, that the man was much worn and debilitated; that he seemed to make an effort to keep the lower part of his face disguised; but when he came to reflect he remembered it was the man he had been introduced to.
Q. Did he speak of this disguise as having been thrown off or discontinued at any time during the man's stay at his house? A. No; but in the light of the day, the shaving of the face, the fact that he sometimes slept and at others was awake, gave him opportunities to recognize the man; but I do not recollect that he said the disguise was entirely thrown off.
Q. Did he admit to you having denied any person having been at his house? A. He certainly did not deny it to me.

The Court then adjourned to 10 o'clock to-morrow.

WASHINGTON, May 17.—General Harris said that on Saturday, for what he deemed justifiable reasons, he had objected to Hon. Reverdy Johnson appearing here as counsel. He now asked to have read a letter from Reverdy Johnson, dated Baltimore, October 7, 1864, addressed to William D. Bowie, C. C. Magruder, John D. Bowling, Prince George's county, in which he takes the ground that the oath prescribed by the Constitutional Convention was illegal, and concludes as follows:—"It is indeed the only way in which the people can protect themselves, and no moral injunction will be violated by such a course, because the exaction of the oath was beyond the authority of the Convention, and as a law therefore void."

Testimony of William Williams.

William Williams was called as a witness, and testified as follows:—
Q. Will you state to the Court whether, after the assassination, you were ever engaged in the pursuit of the assassins? A. Yes sir; I started on April 17th with Major O'Beirne, and pursued to Surrattsville.
Q. State whether, in the course of that pursuit, you went to the residence of the prisoner, Dr. Mudd? A. Yes sir; we went there on Tuesday, the 18th; when we arrived there Dr. Mudd was not at home, but we saw

his wife, and she told us she would send for him, that he was in the neighborhood; when he came I asked him whether any strangers had been that way; he said not; we questioned him about two men having been at his house, one with a broken leg, and he denied that they had; he spoke to some other officers.
Q. Did you mention the time when you supposed these men had been there? A. Not on our first visit; I did not.
Q. Did you have any further consultation with him upon that? A. No sir, not on our first visit.
Q. He denied altogether that there had been any strangers there, you say. A. Yes.
Q. Who made the remark about the man with the broken leg having been there? A. One of the other officers.
Q. Did you hear his reply? A. I am not positive what it was, but he made a reply.
Q. Did he on that occasion state to you when he heard for the first time of the assassination of the President? A. Yes sir; he said it was in church Sunday morning.
Q. Did he converse freely with you; was his manner frank or evasive? A. He seemed to be a little uneasy, and not willing to give us the information without being asked for everything.
Q. When did you see him the second time? A. On Friday, the 21st.
Q. What occurred then? A. We went there for the purpose of arresting him; he was not at home, but Mrs. Mudd sent for him; when he arrived at the house Lieutenant Lovett asked him a question or two, and then I asked him about the two men being at his house, and whether he had seen them, and then he said that he had; I asked him, also, if they were Booth and Harold; he said they were not; that he was introduced to Booth last fall, and knew him; he had been introduced to Booth by Mr. Thompson; after we arrested him we showed him his picture, and after looking at it a little while he said at first he did not recollect the features, but that it looked like Booth across the eyes; I informed Mrs. Mudd that we would have to search the house, and then she said that one of the men had left a boot up stairs in bed, and she went for and brought the boot; it was a long riding boot, with the New York maker's name and the name of J. Wilkes written inside; the boot was cut about two inches up from the instep.
Q. Did she say that the doctor had set the leg of the man? A. Yes sir.
Q. How long did he say they remained at the house? A. He stated to me they left between three and four in the afternoon on Saturday.
Q. Did he state to you at what hour they came? A. About daybreak.
Q. Did they leave on horseback or on foot? A. He said they left on horseback; Mrs. Mudd said they left on foot.
Q. Did you understand her to be speaking of one or both of them when she said they went on foot? A. I understood her to say Booth, and I believe it was Dr. Mudd who said the injured man went away on crutches, which he said had been made for him by one of his men.
Cross-examination by Mr. Stone—Q. Was Lieut. Lovett present? A. Yes sir.
Q. On both Tuesday and Friday? A. Yes sir.
Q. Was Mrs. Mudd in the parlor when she made this declaration about the boot? A. She was standing at the door.
Q. Where was Dr. Mudd? A. He was in the parlor.
Q. Could he hear what Mrs. Mudd said? A. I judge he could; he was no further than where you are sitting there.
Q. She was the first one who mentioned about Booth to you? A. Yes; I told her we should be compelled to search the house, and then she saw that the men had left the boot there, and went up and brought it down.
Q. Was it on Tuesday or Friday that he told you the first knowledge he had of the death of the President was derived at church the Sunday before? A. On Friday, I think.
Q. Do you remember that any one asked him in your presence? A. I do not.
Q. You were all together in one room? A. Yes sir.
Q. Did you or Lieutenant Lovett ask him about two strangers who had been at his house any time previous? A. We both asked him.
Q. Which asked him first? A. I don't remember.
Q. Did he give the same reply to both? A. I think he did, sir.
Q. Do you feel confident of that? A. His reply to me, on Tuesday, was that they had not been there; I think it was the same he said to Lieutenant Lovett.
Q. Do you remember on the Friday of the examination who asked him first? A. I think it was Lovett.
Q. Do you remember whether he asked about two strangers, or about Booth and Harold? A. About strangers, I think.
Q. What answer did he make on Friday? A. The question was whether two strangers had been there, one with a broken leg; and then he said he had set the man's leg; that one of them was, apparently, about seventeen or eighteen years of age; that they had knocked at the door, and he had looked out at the window and asked who they were; they replied that they were friends, and wanted to get in; and Dr. Mudd came down stairs, and with the assistance of the young man, helped the injured man from his horse and took him to his parlor and placed him on the sofa.
Q. Did he describe the strangers? A. He said one was about seventeen or eighteen; that the other had a moustache and long thin whiskers; I asked him if they were natural whiskers; he said he could not tell.
Q. Did he tell you the color of the other man's hair? A. No; not that I remember.
Q. Did he tell you his height? A. I am not positive.
Q. Did he give any description of his dress? A. I think he said the injured man had a shawl; I am not certain.
Q. Did he describe the dress of the younger man? A. I don't remember his saying anything about it.
Q. Did he describe his height and general appearance? A. He said he was a smooth-faced young man, about seventeen or eighteen.
Q. Did he tell you the direction they took, and did you search for tracks in the direction indicated, and if so, did you find any? A. Yes, we found tracks, but other teams were constantly passing, and the road is not much traveled.
Q. Did you go on Tuesday across the swamp? A. Yes; we went; it through the swamp on Tuesday and Friday, after we came back.
Q. Were you one of the party who went to see Mr. Wilmer's house? A. Yes sir.
Q. What time did you get there? A. Thursday or Tuesday night; I think it was late in the evening when we got there.
Q. What time did you say you got to Wilmer's? A. I think it was Wednesday evening.
Q. Did you hear anything of them on the road? A. I did not.
Q. This was before the doctor was carried to Bryantown? A. Yes sir.
Q. Were you and Mr. Lloyd under Lieutenant Lovett's orders? A. I was acting under Major O'Beirne's orders, but in his absence was under Lieutenant Lovett, who had charge of the squad, I suppose.
Q. Was Mr. Lloyd with you? A. Yes sir.
Q. Were you in the Court when his testimony was read? A. I was not.
The Court here took a recess.
On the Court reassembling the testimony was continued.

Testimony of Simon Gavasan.

Q. Will you state whether you are acquainted with Dr. Mudd? A. Yes sir.
Q. Were you not at his house the Tuesday following the assassination? A. Yes sir, I was.
Q. State what inquiries you made of him there to aid you in the pursuit of the murderers, and what replies he made? A. We went there on the forenoon of that Tuesday, the 18th; we went to his house, and we made inquiries whether any two men had passed there on the morning of Saturday, after the assassination; he said "no," and then, when we asked more particularly whether two men came, one of them having his leg fractured, he said "yes" we asked him what time, and he said, "at four or half-past four in the morning they rapped at his door, and he being alarmed at the noise came down and let them in; he said another man assisted the injured man into the house; he said he attended to the fracture as well as he could, but that he had not much fracture; the person with the fractured leg stayed in the parlor at first, but after that was taken up to one of the rooms up stairs, and remained there till between three and five o'clock in the afternoon on Saturday; he said they then left there, and he went part of the way with them, but that previous to that he went to look for a buggy, with the other man, to have the wounded man taken away, but that he could not find one; he said he went part of the way on the road with them, but they first inquired the way to Dr. Wilmer's, and he said he showed them the roads.
Q. Did you ask him whether he knew these persons? A. He said at first "No, not at all."
Q. On the subsequent days did you have any interview with him, and if so when? A. On Friday, the 21st.
Q. State what occurred then? A. We went there to arrest him and search his house. He was not in, but his wife sent for him; when he came we informed him that we would have to search his house; his wife then went up stairs and brought a boot down; we examined the boot and found "J. Wilkes" marked on the leg of the boot. She also brought a razor down, which one of the party took in charge.
Q. Did you repeat your inquiry as to who they were? A. We asked him if it was, not Booth? he said he thought not.
Q. Did you get any reason for his so thinking? A. He said he had whiskers on, and also had his moustache shaved off; probably he shaved it off up stairs.
Q. Did he speak of having known him before? A. Yes; when we made inquiries he said he was introduced last fall by a man named Thompson.
Cross-examination by Mr. Ewing.—Q. Who was the chief of the party who were with you? A. We had no chief.

TRIAL OF THE ASSASSINS AT WASHINGTON.

COL. LAFAYETTE C. BAKER.

TRIAL OF THE ASSASSINS AT WASHINGTON. 57

Q. Who was in charge of the party? A. Lieutenant Lovett came in charge of a cavalry detachment, but we went under the orders of Major O'Beirne.
Q. In the absence of Major O'Beirne, were you not under the order of Lieutenant Lovett? A. Yes sir, partly.
Q. Who commenced the conversation with Mudd on Tuesday? A. That I am not able to say.
Q. How long did the conversation last? A. Probably one hour.
Q. In your presence? A. Yes sir.
Q. Did not Lieutenant Lovett conduct the inquiries chiefly? A. No sir; the doctor was asked questions by all of us.
Q. Did not Dr. Mudd himself bring the boot down to you? A. No sir; his wife brought it down.
Q. Who was it given to? A. The one nearest the door.
Q. Did you, in point of fact, make a search of the house? A. We did not go up stairs; when we found the boot and razor we considered it satisfactory evidence that Booth and Harold had been in the house.
Q. Did you go to meet Mudd on Friday as he was going to the house? A. No sir.
Q. Did Lieutenant Lovett? A. There might have been one or two other officers; I am not sure.
Q. Did you ask him on Tuesday for a description of the party? A. No sir; I believe the photograph of Booth was shown to him and that he did not recognize it as one of the parties that was at his house, but that there was something about the forehead and eyes that resembled one of them.
Q. Did he point out to you the road they went across the swamp? A. No sir, he said he had made inquiries how they would get to the Rev. Dr. Wilmer's.
Q. He mentioned that on Tuesday? A. Yes sir.
Q. Did he tell you how to get to Dr. Wilmer's? A. Yes sir.

Testimony of Mrs. Emma Offutt.

Q. State whether or not you are the sister-in-law of John Floyd? A. Yes sir.
Q. State whether or not, on the Tuesday, the 11th of April, you were at his house? A. Yes sir.
Q. You saw Mr. Floyd on that day? A. Yes sir, I was in the carriage with Mr. Floyd.
Q. On that occasion did you happen to meet Mrs. Surratt? A. Yes sir.
Q. State to the Court where the meeting took place? A. Somewhere near Uniontown.
Q. State whether or not a conversation took place between Mr. Floyd and Mrs. Surratt on that day? A. Yes, they talked together.
Q. Did you hear any of the conversation? A. Yes sir, some of it.
Q. Under what circumstances did the conversation take place? A. Our carriages passed each other before we recognized who it was, and Mr. Floyd went out to her carriage, and they had a conversation which took place at her carriage, and not at ours.
Q. Were you at Mr. Floyd's again on Friday, the 14th of April? A. Yes sir.
Q. State whether you saw the prisoner, Mrs. Surratt, there? A. Yes sir.
Q. Did you observe any conversation between her and Mr. Floyd on that day? A. Yes; I saw them talking together, but I did not hear them at all, I had occasion to go to the back part of the house.
Q. Did the conversation take place in the back part of the house or in the yard? A. In the yard, sir.
Q. Had Mr. Floyd been to town that day? A. No sir, he had been to Marlborough, attending court.
Q. What did he bring with him when he came back? A. Some oysters and fish, and that is how he came to drive into the back part of the yard.
Q. Was any one else in the yard at the time of this conversation? A. No sir.
Cross-examination by Mr. Aiken.—Q. How far apart were the two carriages when you went past each other? A. Two or three yards; I think they talked but a very few minutes together.
Q. Did Mr. Floyd state what the conversation was? A. No sir.
Q. Nor what the conversation on the 14th was about? A. No; he did not.
Q. Have you been acquainted with Mrs. Surratt for some time? A. Eversince last summer, I believe.
Q. What time did she arrive at Mr. Floyd's on the 14th? A. At about 4 o'clock, I think
Q. Did you hear any conversation with her previous to Mr. Floyd's coming home? A. Yes sir; in the parlor.
Q. Did you learn what the conversation was on that day?
Question objected to and waived.
Q. Did Floyd make any statement in reference to his business with Mrs. Surratt? A. No sir.
Q. Did Mrs. Surratt have any business with you on that day? A. No sir.
Q. Did Mrs. Surratt place in your hands any package? A. No sir.
Q. During your visit to Mr. Floyd's did you hear anything about shooting irons?
Assistant Judge Advocate Bingham objected, and the objection was sustained by the Court.

Testimony of William P. Jebb.

Q. Look at the prisoners and see if you recognize any or all of them? A. Only one of them, sir.
Q. Which one? A. Harold.
Q. State when you first saw him? A. Since the 25th of last October I have been in Caroline county, Maryland, as commissary agent in the Confederate service; I was in the cavalry service, but was wounded on the 9th of January, and after that was appointed commissary agent; when I was on my way, in April, to Fauquier county I got down to Port Conway and saw a wagon on the wharf.
Q. When was that? A. On the 18th of April.
Q. The Monday after the assassination? A. No sir; the Monday week after the murder; there were three of us together; we saw the wagon and rode down on the wharf, and before we reached the wagon we saw a man get out of it and it seemed to us as if he put his hand into his bosom; I don't remember whether we hailed the ferry or not; this one man got out of the wagon and came where we were and said "What command do you belong to?" Ruggles said Mosoby's command; then he said, "Where are you going?" I said. "It is a secret; where are you going?"
Q. Did you ask him what command he belonged to? A. He said he belonged to A. P. Hill's Corps. He said his brother was wounded below Petersburg, and asked if we would take him down to the lines. Harold asked us then to take a drink, but none of us drank, and we declined. I got down and carried out three horses and tied them up, and Harold came and touched me, and said he wanted to speak to me, and said, "I suppose you are raising a command to go South;" and then said he would like to go with us. I said that I could go with no man that I didn't know anything about, and then he made this remark:—"We are the assassinators of the President." I was so shocked that I did not know what to say, and I made no reply. Lieutenant Ruggles was near by, watering his horse, and I called to him; became there, and then Booth came up and Harold introduced him; after introducing himself Booth had a mark upon his hand, I remember, J. W. B.; we went across the river, Booth riding on Ruggles' horse, and he said he wanted to pass under the name of Boyd; we went to a lady's house, and I asked her if she could take in a wounded soldier; she at first consented, and then said she could not; we then went up to Mr. Garrett's, where we left Booth; Harold and the rest of us went on within a few miles of Bowling Green; the next day Harold returned towards Garrett's, and that was the last I saw of him till after he was captured.
Q. Did I understand you that Booth went alone to Garrett's? A. No sir; Ruggles, Booth, Bainbridge and I rode up to Garrett's and we left Booth there and Harold came on with us to Bowling Green and had dinner.
Q. Do you know where Harold went to from Bowling Green? A. No sir; he left us the next day at two or three o'clock.
Q. Now when you saw him on Wednesday morning he was in custody then? A. Yes sir.
Q. Before he told you he was "we are the assassinators of the President," had you told him you were in the Confederate service? A. Why he could see that, because we were in Confederate uniform.
Cross-examined by Mr. Stone.—Harold wanted you to aid him in going further South? A. Yes; but we had no facilities to aid him.
Q. Did he seem disappointed? A. Yes sir.
Q. Was Booth present when you were talking with Harold about their being the assassinators of the President? A. Not when he first told me; he and Bainbridge came up after.
Q. Did he seem to be much agitated? A. Yes sir.
Q. What did Booth say? A. He said "I didn't intend telling that."
Q. But Harold did tell? A. Yes, he had told before Booth came up.
Q. Can you recollect whether he said that he had killed the President? A. No; he said, "We are the assassinators of the President;" then a few moments afterwards he said, "Yes, he is, the man, J. Wilkes Booth, who killed the President."
By Mr. Aiken.—Q. Have you ever taken the oath of allegiance? A. No, sir; but I am perfectly willing to do so.

Testimony Lieut.-Colonel C. J. Congers,

By Judge Holt—Q. State to the Court whether you and others were engaged in the pursuit of the murderers of the President. If so, please take up the narrative at the point where you met the Confederate soldier Jebb, who has given his evidence, and state what occurred afterwards. A. I found him in a room in the hotel in Bowling Green, in bed; I expected to find somebody else; as I went in he began to get out of ned; I said, "Is that you, Jebb?" he said, "Yes;" I said, "Get up, I want you;" he got up, and I told him to put on his clothes, and come into the part of the room where I was; I said to him. "Where were the two men who came with you across the river at Port Royal?" there were two men in the room with me; Jebb said to me, "can I see you alone;" I said yes, and Lieuts. Baker and Doherty went out of the room. He reached out his hand to me and said, "I know who you want, and I can tell you where they are now; they are on the road to Port Royal, about three miles from here, at the house of Mr. Garrett, and if I show you where they are now you can get them; I said "have you a hat?" he replied he had; I told him I had just come from there, and he seemed for a moment to be considerably embarrassed; he said he thought it we came from Richmond, but if we had passed by Garrett's he could not tell me whether the men were there or not; I told him it did not make any difference, we could go back and see; he got out his horse and we started; just before we got to the house Jebb, who was riding with me, said "we are near where we go through a gate, let us stop here and look round;" I rode, in the first place, alone, to find the gate, about as far as I under t od him to say it was, but did not see any opening there wa a hedge, or ra' her a bushy fence that side of the road; I turned round and went back, and told him I did not see; my gate in that direction; we then rode on some three hundred yards further and stopped again; Jebb went with Lieutenant Baker and myself to find the gate; I sent Lieutenant Baker on to the gate while I went back myself for the cavalry; we returned rapidly, and a guard was stationed round the building; when I went to the house Lieutenant Baker was telling some one to strike a light and come out; I think the door was open when I got there; the first individual I saw when I got there, whose name was said to have been Garrett; I said to him, "Where are the men who stopped at your house?" "They have gone," "Gone where?" "Gone to the woods," "Whereabouts in the woods have they gone?" he then commenced to tell me that they came there without his consent, and that he did not want them to stay; I said, "I don't want any long stories from you, I just want to know where those men have gone;" he commenced to tell me over again the same thing, and I turned to one of the men and told him to bring me a lariat, and threatened to hang the man to a locust tree because he did not tell me what he knew; one of his sons then came in and said don't hurt the old man, he is scared; I will tell you where these men are; I said that is what I want; he said they are in the barn, and as soon as I got there I heard somebody walking about on the hay; I stationed men around the barn, and Lieutenant Baker said to one of the young Garretts (there had two or them appeared by this time) "you must go in the barn and get the arms from that man;" I then said, "They know you, and you must go in;" Baker then said, "They know yo, and you must go in" Baker replied, "The men inside it at one of the men with whom they had been stopping was coming in to get their arms and they must deliver them up; Garrett went in, but came out very soon and said, "This man says, '—— you, you have betrayed me, and threatened to shoot me," I asked him how he knew the man was going to shoot him; he said, "He reached down in the hay and got the revolvers;" I directed Baker then to tell the men inside that they were to come on and deliver themselves up, and that if they did not in five minutes we would set the barn on fire; Booth said, "Who are you? what do you want?" Lieutenant Baker answ red. "We want you; we know who you are; give up your arms and come out;" Booth replied, "Give us a little time to consider;" Baker said, "Very well," and some ten or fifteen minutes elapsed, probably, before anything further was said, when Booth again asked, "Who are you? what do you want?" I said, to Baker, do not by any possible intimation or remark let him know who we are; he knows we take us for Rebels or friends; we will take advantage of it; we will not lie to him about it, but we will not answer any questions on that subject; stop, I insist on his coming out if he will, Baker replied to Booth, "It don't make any difference who we are; we know who you are and we want you;" Booth said, "This is h rd, because it may be I am to be taken by my friends;" some time during the conversation Booth said, "Captain, I know you to be a brave man, and I believe you to be h n'r able; I have got but one leg; I am a cripple; if you will withdraw your me 1 00 yards from the door I will come out and fight you;" Lieutenant Baker re died, "we did not come here to fight, we simply come to make you prisoner;" once after that he s id, "If you will take your men 50 yards from the door I will come out and fight; give me a chance for my life;" there was the same reply, and with a singularly theatrical voice, Booth called out, "well, my brave boys, you may prepare a stretcher for me;" I requested one of the Garretts to pile some pine boughs against the barn; he soon came to me a id said, "the man says if I put any more brush up there he wi l put a ba l throu h me;" said I, "very well, you need not go there any more;" After a wh le Booth s d:—"There is a man here who wants to come out;" Lieutenant Baker said "very well; let him take his arms and come out;" some talk passed between them in the barn; one of the expressions I heard Booth use to Harold was, "You —— coward, will you leave me now! but go, go I would not have you stay with me;" further words ensued between them, which I supposed had re erence to bring.ng out t e arms, which was one of the conditions on which I ar l was directed to come out; what the words were wa not heard; he came to the door and said, "Get me out;" Lieutenant Baker says to him, "Hand out your

TRIAL OF THE ASSASSINS AT WASHINGTON. 59

miles south of Port Royal, on the road to Bowling Green.
Q. Do you recognize the prisoner Harold as the one you took out of the barn? A. I do.
Q. What articles did you take from Harold, if any? A. I took a little piece of a map of the State of Virginia, including a part of Chesapeake B..y.
Q. Do you remember whether the map embraced the part of Virginia where they were? A. I. did; it covered that portion of Virginia known as the Northern Neck.
Q. Was it a map prepared in pencil? A. No; it was part of an old school map that had been originally sixteen inches square; (portion of a map shown to witness); yes, that is it; that is the only property found on him.
Cross-examined by Mr. Stone.—Q. Did you find any arms on Harold? A. No.
Q. You stated that Booth had some conversation in the barn before he came out; did you observe whether in that conversation Harold seemed willing to surrender himself? A. I do not know anything about it, except from the remark I have stated that Booth made; I did not hear any part of the conversation.
Q. In that remark Booth spoke harshly to Harold, and called him a coward, did he not? A. Yes.
Q. How long were you at the barn? A. I think I looked as soon as I conveniently could after we got to the barn, and it was about two o clock in the morning; Booth was shot and carried on the grass about fifteen minutes past three, so that we must have remained there about an hour and a quarter.
Q. Was he carried almost immediately on to the grass after he was shot? A. Yes.
Q. Did you hear Booth say anything else in relation to Harold than you have stated? A. No.
Q. Do you remember hearing him say that Harold was not to blame? A. I have an indistinct recollection of something of that kind; I will tell you as near as I can what it was; he said, "Here is a man who wants to come out," and I think he added, "who had nothing to do with it;" that is at near as I can remember what he said; after that Harold came out.
By Judge Holt.—Q. Had you seen Booth previously, so that you could recognize the man who was killed as the same person? A. I thought I could recognize him from his resemblance to his brother; I had often seen his brother, Edwin Booth, and was satisfied this was the man, from his resemblance to him.

Testimony of Sergeant Boston Corbett.

Examined by Judge Holt.—Q. You may state what part you took in the pursuit, capture and killing of Booth, beginning the narration at the point when you arrived at the house. A. When I arrived at the house my superior officer, Lieutenant D. ngnerty, told me that Booth was there and directed me to deploy men to the right and left around the building, and see that no one escaped; by this time inquiries had been made at the house and it was ascertained that Booth was not in the house, but in the barn; the greater part of the guard were then withdrawn from the house and placed around the barn and orders were given unknown to me not to escape; we had been previously cautioned to see that our arms were in readiness for use; after being ordered to surrender and told that the barn would be fired if they did not, we remained there for some minutes; Booth inquired who we took him for; he said his leg was broken, and what did we want with him; he was told that it made no difference who we were; that we knew who they were, and that they must surrender themselves as prisoners; he wanted to know where they would be taken to if they gave themselves up; no reply was given; the parley lasted nearly longer than the time first stated, probably, I should think, fully half an hour, more or less; in the course of that time many words passed, and Booth positively declared he would not surrender; at one time he said, "Well, my boys, you may get a stretcher for me;" at another time he said, "Well, Captain, make quick work; shoot me through the heart," or words to that effect, so that I knew he was perfectly desperate, and would not surrender; after a while I heard whispering there; Booth had previously declared there was no other person in there; the other person, who proved to be Harold, seemed to be trying to persuade Booth to surrender; we could not hear the words; after a while, Booth sang out, "Captain, there is a man in here who wants to surrender;" words followed; I could not hear what they were; Booth said, "Oh, go out, and save your life;" he then called out, "I declare before my Maker, this man is innocent of any crime whatever," or words to that effect; further words followed, in which Harold seemed to tell Booth that he would not surrender; he was told to take his arms and come out; Harold declared he had no arms; Booth also declared that this other man was unarmed; that the arms belonged to him; immediately after this, Harold having been taken out with arms, detective Lieutenant-Colonel Conger came over to the side where I was, and directed the barn to be fired; I had been previously standing before a crack in the boards, large enough to put in your hand; I knew that Booth could see us and could have picked us off, and he, in fact, once made the remark, "I could have picked three or four of your men off," "Just draw your men off

fifty yards and I will come out;" he used such words many times; when the fire was lighted, which was almost immediately after Harold had been taken out of the barn, I could then see him distinctly in about the middle of the barn; he started at first towards me, and I had a full front dress view of him; I could have shot him much easier than at the time I did, but as long as he made no demonstration I did not shoot him; I kept my eye on him steadily; he turned towards the other side; he brought his piece up to an aim and I supposed was going to fight his way out; I thought the time had come, and I took a steady aim upon him and shot him; the ball entered his head a little back of the ear and came out a little higher on the other side of the head. he lived, I think, until about seven o'clock that morning, perhaps two or three hours after he was shot; I did not hear him speak after he was shot, except to cry out when he was shot; others stated that he did utter words after that, but I did not hear any after I shot him.
Q. State whether you recognize the prisoner Harold as the man you took out of the barn? A. Yes, that is the man.
Q. Did you know Booth before? A. No; but I was perfectly satisfied from the first, when Booth said his leg was broken, and also from his desperate replies that he would not be taken alive, that he was the man; I knew no other man would act in such a way.
Cross-examined by Mr. Stone.—Q. You say that you judged from the conversation between Booth and Harold in the barn that Booth was anxious to surrender? A. I rather thought so.
Q. But that after Booth refused to surrender, Harold seemed to speak as if he desired to stay with him? A. Yes.
Q. And it was after that that Booth made his declaration ? A. Yes; he declared before his Maker that the man with him was innocent of any crime: I also wish to state, with permission of the Court, as improper motives have been attributed to me, that I offered twice to Lieutenant-Colonel Conger and Lieutenant Baker to go into the barn and take these men, telling them that I had rather go in than stand there before the crack exposed to his fire; I thought it was less dangerous, for while I could not see them they could see us; I did not fire the ball from fear, but because I was under the impression at the time that he had started to the door to fight his way through and that I thought he would do harm to our men if I did not.

Testimony of John Fletcher.

Examined by Judge Holt.—Q. State your business? A. I am the foreman of the Naylor's livery stable.
Q. Do you know the prisoner Atzeroth? A. Yes.
Q. State whether or not you seen him about the third of April last? A. Yes; he came to the stable at that time, between six and seven o'clock, with another gentleman and two horses; they said they wanted to put up their horses there; I ordered their horses down into the stable; the other gentleman who was with Atzeroth, told me he was going to Philadelphia, and that he would leave these horses in Atzeroth's care to sell; I have never seen that man since we kept the horses at the stable, and sold one of them to a Mr. Thompson, a stage contractor. We kept the brown horse at the stable until the 13th of the month, when Atzeroth took him away I didn't see him again until one o'clock on the 14th of April; he came in then with a dark bay mare: If asked him what he had done with the roan horse; he said he sold him in Montgomery county, and that he had bought this mare, saddle and bridle; he wished me to get the mare, which I did.
Q. State the character of the horse he said he had at his was one eye but? A. Yes; he was a very heavy common work horse, blind in one eye; a dark brown horse: heavy tail and mane; very heavy feet; I went to supper at 6½ o'clock on the 14th, and when I came back, the colored boys had the mare saddled and bridled; he paid the colored boy fifty cents for the keeping; and said "What that right?" I said "Yes;" he asked how much I would charge if he stayed till morning; I said fifty cents more; he went out and stayed three-quarters of an hour, and returned with the same mare; he told me not to take the saddle and bridle off the mare, and asked if I could keep the stable open for him till ten o'clock; I told him yes, I should be there myself at ten o'clock became after the mare; he asked me if I would have a drink with him; I told him I had no objection; we went down to the Union Hotel, corner of Thirteen-and-a-half street and E street, and took a drink; we returned to the stable, and he said to me, "If this thing happens to-night you will hear of a present." It seemed to me he was about half tight, and I paid no attention to him; he mounted the mare; I remarked that I would not like to ride that mare, that she looked too skittish like; he said she is good upon a retreat; I spoke to him of the other man, meaning Harold, staying out very late with the other horse; of he says he will be back after awhile; I watched him until he went down E st., past Thirteenth-and-a-half st., and I followed him down until I saw him go into the Kirkwood House; I watched him until he came out, mounted the mare again, went along D street, and turned up Tenth. when I returned to the stable again; I did not go to the

office; I was think'ng about his living so far off, and of the horse Harold had; I had su-picions that he was not going to bring the horse back; I went across E street again, and went up Fourteenth street and came on Pennsylvania avenue again, towards Willard's; I saw Harold riding the horse; I hailed him; the horse was going towards the stable; I started towards him to take the horse from him; I suspect that he saw me by the gaslight and knew me, for he began to move the horse away a little; I said "You get off that horse now, you have had that horse long enough;" he put spurs into the horse and went up Fourteenth street; I kept sight of him until he had gone up Fourteenth street as far as F street; I then returned to the stable and saddled a horse for myself; I went along the avenue, passed down E street, and turned down Ninth to Pennsylvania avenue again; I went along the avenue, and past the south side of the Capitol; I met a gentleman coming down, and asked him did he see any man riding on horseback; he told me yes, he saw two; that they were going very fast; I followed on till I came to the Navy Yard bridge; the guard there halted me and called for the Sergeant of the guard; I asked him if the man had passed, giving a description of the man, horse, saddle, and brid e; he said yes, he had gone across the bridge, that he waited a little for an acquaintance, but after a while went on; that another one came up riding a bay horse; I asked him if the first one gave his name, he said yes, Smith; I asked the Sergeant if I cou d cross the bridge; he said yes, but I could not get back; I said I would not go over so, and I turned round and came back to the city again; I looked at my watch when I had got back to Third street, and it was ten minutes past 12; I rode rapidly down to the bridge, but slowly back; when I got to the stable the foreman told me the President was shot; I put up the horse and sat down outside the office, it was then 1 o'clock; I heard peop e passing on the sidewalk say that it was a man who rode off on horseback that shot President Lincoln; I went across E street to Fourteenth, and asked a sergeant if they picked up any horse; he told me he had picked up some horse, and that I could go down to the police station on Tenth street; I went there and saw a detective by the name of Charley Stone, who told me that some horse had been taken up and taken to General Augur's Head-quarters; we went along together up to General Augur's office; I gave General Augur Harold's description and age as far as I could; I to d him I had put me I Harold to the Navy Yard bridge; a saddle and bridle were lying quite close to his desk, which I recognized as the saddle and bridle Atzeroth had on the horse he sai'd he had sold; he asked me what kind of a horse he had; I described him as a big brown horse, blind in one eye; I did not remember the man's name then; I had his name in the office; he sent the detective, Charley Stone, down to the office, who brought up the name and gave it to the General,

A saddle and bridle were here brought into Court, wh ch were identified by the witness as those he recognized at General Augur's office.

Q. Did he call at 10 o'clock precisely? A. Yes.

Q. Did he speak about anything wonderful that night? A. He said if this thing happened I would hear of it at present.

Q. Had he been talking to you of anything before? A. No, but he seemed to be very much excited.

Q. When you left the city was he going up Tenth street towards Ford's Theatre? A. Yes.

Q. You spoke of Harold's having a horse from your stables? A. Yes; he hired him on the 14th, about a quarter to ten o'clock, and said he would be after him at four o'clock; he came after the horse at a quarter past four o'clock; he asked me how much I would charge for the hire of the horse; I told him $5; he wanted him for $4; I told him he could not have it for that; he knew this horse and inquired for this particular one; I told him he might take a mare in the stable, but he said he would not take her; he wanted to see the saddle and bridle; I showed him the saddle; he said it was too small; I gave him another saddle; that did not suit him; they were not the kind of stirrups he wanted; they were covered with leather; he wanted English steel stirrups; he wanted to see the bridles, and I took him into the office and he picked out a white-eyed br dle; be'ore he mounted the horse he aske i me how late he could stay out; I told him he could not stay later than 8 or 9 o'clock at the furthest.

Q. At what hour did you see Harold riding that night? A. About half past ten o'clock; I was crossing down from towards the Treasury on the Avenue; I met him along by Willard's, as he was passing Fourteenth street when I spoke to him he rode off rapidly.

Q. Did he have a fast horse? A. Not very fast; he was a ladies' horse; any one could ride him; he was gentle and sure.

Q. Did he trot or pace? A. He had a single rack.

Q. Did he make any reply when you called him? A. Not the slightest.

Q. You had not then heard of the President's assassination? A. Not a word.

Q. Have you seen the horse Harold rode since that time? A. I have not.

Q. Did you see a saddle and bridle at General Augur's on the night of the 14th? A. Yes, at two o'clock that night I did.

Q. Have you seen that one-eyed horse since? A. No.

Cross-examined by Mr. Stone.—Q. At the time Harold c. d o jew you down in price was it when he ca led at one or four o'clock? A. When he engaged the horse at one o'clock.

Q. When you saw him again at Willard's did the horse seem to be tired? A. Not very; he seemed to kind to want to come to the stable.

Q. How near were you to him when you first saw him? A. Not fifteen yards; he was letting the horse go slow; then, as it to bring him up standing.

Q. Did you call him by name? A. I did not; it was then about twenty-five minutes past ten o'clock.

Q. Are you satisfied it was the same man now in the box? (pointing to Harold.) A. Yes, very well satisfied.

Q. Were you acquainted with him before? A. The way I got acquainted with H. rold was his coming to the stable, about the 5th or 6 h of April, and inquiring for Atzeroth; he did not give his name, but inquired or the gentleman who kept his horse in a particular stable; I saw him nearly every day until the 12th, coming there for Atzeroth, and sometimes riding with him.

Q. Did you notice the horse or man particularly, or both? A. I not ced the horse and man both.

Q. What time in the evening of the 14th of April was it that Atzeroth came to your stable? A. He le t there at 7 o'clock and came back at quarter to 8 o'clock; the last time he came there was at 10 o'clock; we went to the hotel, an I said, and took a drink, and it must have been ten minutes before he le t; the Union House is about 100 yards distant from the stable, as far as I could judge.

Q. You took a drink with Atzeroth; did he seem as though he had taken a good many more? A. Yes.

Q. What did you understand by the remark he made, you would hear of a present at? A. I did not pay much attention to that remark.

Q. What made you follow Atzeroth that night? A. On account of his acquaintance with Harold, who had rode away one of my horses.

Q. Did you suppose Atzeroth was going where Harold was? A. I supposed he lived so far away that he was not going home; I knew that he lived down at T. B., in Maryland; I followed him for the purpose of finding Harold.

Q. Were you called on to identify a horse at General Augur's stable? A. No.

Q. What did Harold tell you when he engaged the horse on the 14th? A. He told me he wanted to go riding with a Lady; I did not ask him with whom, and he did not tell me.

Q. How fast was Atzeroth in the Kirkwood House on the night of the 14th before you saw him come out? A. He did not stop there more than five minutes; I was watching the horse outside.

Q. If you followed him on foot, how did you manage to keep up with him? A. He started away from the stable rapidly, but soon after rode slowly and I could keep up with him; I reached the Kirkwood House just after he dismounted from the mare; the Kirkwood House is distant from the stable about two squares.

Q. Did you keep up with Atzeroth afterwards? A. No, I kept in sight of him; he rode away in a walk.

Q. How far did you follow him? A. I just kept in sight until he turned into Tenth street, and I never saw him again until to-day.

The witness, by direction of the court, was sent to the stable for the purpose of identifying the blind horse referred to in his testimony.

Testimony of John Greenawalt.

Q. State whether or not you are the keeper of the Pennsylvania House in this city? A. I am.

Q. Are you acquainted with the prisoner, Atzeroth? A. I am.

Q. Were you not acquainted with J. Wilkes Booth? A. I was not well acquainted with him; he came to the house. (A photograph was exhibited to the witness which he recognized as that of Booth.)

Q. State whether or not the man Booth had frequent interviews with Atzeroth at the Pennsylvania House? A. He had; Atzeroth would generally sit in the sitting room, and Boo h would walk into the hall and then out again, followed by Atzeroth; Booth seldom entered the room; they had interviews in front of my house, and they would o ten walk off as far as the livery stable, where their conversation would take place.

Q. Did you at any time hear the prisoner Atzeroth speak of expecting to have plenty of gold soon? I so, state what you heard. A. He and some other young men whom he met came into my house. He had been drinking, and said, "Greenawalt, I am pretty near broke, though I have friends enough to give me as much money as will keep me ell my life, I am going away out of these days, but I will return with as much go d as will keep me all my lifetime."

Q. When was it he made that declaration? A. I think it was about the fir t f April. (He came to my house, I think, on the 13th of March last.

Q. State how long before the assassination he left your house. A. I think it was on the previous Wednesday morning.

Q. Had he any baggage with him? A. No sir.

Q. State when you next saw him? A. I next saw

TRIAL OF THE ASSASSINS AT WASHINGTON. 61

him on Saturday morning, the 15th of April, between two and three o'clock.

Q. Did he come into your house, and ask for a room at that hour? A. I had just come into the house, and gone to my room, when a servant came to get change for a five dollar bill, and told me there was a man by the name of Atzeroth down stairs who wanted lodging; I went down, and found Atzeroth and another man there.

Q. Did the two men take a room together? A. Yes sir; Atzeroth asked for his old room: I told him it was occupied, and that he would have to room with the other gentleman, whom I requested to go to his room with the servant; Atzeroth was going to follow him, and I said "Atzeroth, you have not registered;" he said, "Do you want my name?" and appeared to hesitate; he finally went back and registered his name.

Q. Will you describe the appearance of the man who was with him? A. He was a man about five feet seven and a half or eight inches in height, and about one hundred and ninety pounds weight; of a dark, weather-beaten complexion, and dressed poorly, his pants being worn through.

Q. Had he the appearance of a laboring man? A. Yes sir.

Q. Could you express an opinion as to whether the clothing worn by him were such as he probably ordinarily wore, or were assumed by him as a disguise? A. I guess they were more of a disguise; he had on a broadcloth coat which had been much worn; his whole appearance was shabby.

Q. What name did he give? A. I believe it was Sam Thomas.

Q. What became of him? A. He got up, I believe, about five o'clock the next morning, and left the house; a lady stopping at the house desired to leave in the 6:15 train, and I gave orders to a servant to that effect; she left before I got up, and as she was going out of the door this man Thomas went out and asked the way to the railroad; he had no baggage.

Q. Did Atzeroth remain? A. He left shortly afterwards, making towards Sixth street westwardly.

Q. How long afterwards? A. When the servant was returning he met Atzeroth and said to him, "Atzeroth, what brings you out so early in the morning?" "Well," said he, "I have business."

Q. Had he paid his bill? A. No sir; I did not see him again.

Q. Do you recognize him among these prisoners? A. I do.

Q. Did you observe any thing unusual in the conduct of these men when they first came? A. No sir; the man Thomas stared at me somewhat; he kept a close eye upon me.

Q. Did they have any conversation in your presence? A. No sir.

Q. Which of them asked for a room? A. Thomas asked for a room for himself; as I came in Atzeroth was lying on a settee and Thomas standing at the counter.

Q. Do you know the prisoner O'Laughlin? A. No sir.

Q. Did Thomas make any remark to you? A. All he said to me was that he was a poor writer.

Q. Were either of the parties armed? A. I did not notice; I heard it said that Atzeroth had a knife.

Q. Had Atzeroth on any previous occasion hesitated to enter his name on the register? A. No, sir.

Q. Did you ever see him armed? A. In March, I think, it must have been, I saw him have a revolver, which he had just bought; he came in there and made the remark that he had just bought it; I told him I wished I had known that he was going to buy such an article, as I had a small one which I would have sold to him.

Q. Do you think you would recognize the revolver which was in his possession? A. I think I would. A revolver was then exhibited to the witness which he described as being somewhat similar to the one shown him by Atzeroth, though he could not say that it was the same one.

Cross-examined by Mr. Dosler:—Q. State on what day before the 14th of April Atzeroth left your house? A. It was on the 12th I think.

Q. How long did he stay at your house on that occasion? A. From the 18th of March until the 12th of April; during that time he was away but once, when he stayed out one night; he told me he had gone to the country with a man by the name of Bailey.

Q. What were the arms which you have stated that you saw in the possession of Atzeroth? A. A large revolver, something similar to that one; other persons say that he had a knife, but I never saw him with one.

In reply to several other questions the witness stated that he did not remember having made or having heard any remark preliminary to that of Atzeroth with respect to his expectation of having gold or silver enough to keep him all his life: the man Thomas, who came to the hotel on the morning of the 15th with Atzeroth, did not seem to be intimate with the prisoner, though he judged them to be acquaintances; Atzeroth did not refuse to put his name on the register, nor did he say that he would not like to do it; he did not seem sleepy or in liquor.

The witness having been asked if he could identify the man Thomas from among the prisoners at the bar, pointed out the prisoner Spangler, as having some resemblance to that person. Thomas, however, had a moustache which the prisoner had not, and his hair was longer and his complexion darker. The witness stated that he did not see Atzeroth and his companion enter the house, and therefore could not tell whether they entered together.

Cross-examined by Mr. Ewing.—Q. What induced you to suppose that they came in together? A. My servant told me so.

Q. What kind of a moustache had the man whom you say the prisoner resembles? A. It was black; he had whiskers in front, and wore a dark, slouch hat.

By Judge Advocate.—Q. I understand you to say you are certain that you did not see the prisoner, O'Laughlin, at your house? A. I did not; I do not know the man.

Q. Did the hair or moustache of the man Thomas appear to be dyed? A. No sir.

Q. Did Atzeroth object to this stranger coming into his room? A. No sir.

Q. He simply assented to it when you told him there was no other room? A. Yes sir; I told him he would have to go with the man Thomas.

By the Court.—Q. Do you know whether they got up at the same time in the morning? A. I do not.

Q. Did they occupy the same bed? A. No sir.

Q. What day did Atzeroth leave your house before the murder? A. On Wednesday, I think it was; he said to me then, "Greenawalt, I owe you a couple of days' board; would it make any difference to you whether I pay you now or when I come back;" he added that it would be more convenient for him to pay when he came back; he allowed he was going to Montgomery county.

Q. Do you know the prisoner with the black moustache (O'Laughlin)? A. I do not.

Q. Do you recognize the face of the man Thomas among those of the prisoners at the bar? A. I cannot positively.

Testimony of John F. Coyle.

Q. Are you one of the proprietors of the *National Intelligencer*? A. Yes sir.

Q. State to the Court whether you were acquainted with J. Wilkes Booth during his life time? A. I knew him.

Q. Did you know him intimately? A. Not at all.

Q. J. Wilkes Booth, before he died, made this statement; that on the night before the assassination of the President, he wrote a long article and left it with one of the editors of the *National Intelligencer*, in which he fully set forth his reasons for his crime; will you state whether such a paper was received? A. I never heard of any such paper.

Q. Are you quite certain that no such paper was ever received at the office? A. Not that I ever heard of.

Testimony of Hezekiah Metts.

By Judge Holt.—Q. Where do you reside? A. In Montgomery county, Maryland.

Q. State whether you ever met the prisoner, Atzeroth, and if so, where and under what circumstances? A. I recognize the prisoner at the bar; on the Sunday after the death of Mr. Lincoln he was at my house and ate his dinner there; he was just from Washington and was inquiring about the news; some conversation took place about General Grant having been shot and we understood that he had been shot in the cars; he then said that "if the man that was to have followed him, had followed him, it would have been done;" I so understood him.

Q. Did he speak of the assassination of the President? A. Not that I recollect; I have no recollection of anything further.

Q. How far is your residence from Washington? A. About twenty-two miles.

Q. Did he represent himself as having come from Washington? A. Yes sir.

Q. Did he speak at all of the assassination which had just occurred here? A. I don't recollect; the conversation turned on General Grant.

Q. Did you make any inquiry after he made that statement? A. No, not at the time; we talked about the matter after he left.

Q. Did his manner seem excited? A. I could not say that it was.

Q. Where did he say he was going? A. He did not say.

Q. By what name did he call himself? A. He passed in the neighborhood under the name of Andrew Atwood.

Cross-examined by Mr. Doster.—Q. What is your business? A. Farming.

Q. How long had you known Atzeroth before the visit you have spoken of? A. I think it is between two and three years since I first got acquainted with him in that neighborhood; I merely knew him by sight; I do not recollect that I ever saw him but once before the Sunday he came there.

Q. You say he went by the name of Andrew Atwood around that vicinity? A. Yes sir, that is the name I knew him by.

Q. At what time of the day did Atzeroth arrive, and how long did he stay? A. He came, I suppose, between

10 and 11 o'clock; I suppose he stayed some two or three hours.
Q. Did he recognize you as an old acquaintance? A. He knew me.
Q. Did you speak about the murder? A. I do not recollect saying anything about the assassination.
Q. Was anybody else present and talking with you when he made the remark about somebody following General Grant? A. Yes, sir, there were a couple of young men; we were all in the room together; I was about three yards from Atzeroth when he made the remark.
Q. Was not this the answer—"that a man must have followed General Grant to kill him?" A. No, sir, it was not spoken in that way; it was, that if the man who was to have followed him had done so, General Grant would have been killed.
In reply to a question by the Court the witness stated that the young men present at the time of the prisoner's remark, given above, were brothers by the name of Leamon, who resided in the neighborhood.

Testimony of Sergeant G. W. Gemmell.

By Judge Holt.—Q. Do you recognize the prisoner Atzeroth as a man whom you ever saw before? A. Yes sir.
The witness then detailed the circumstances attending the prisoner's arrest, which occurred on the 19th; at the time of his arrest he denied that his name was Atwood, and gave another.
Q. Did the prisoner ask why you arrested him? A. No sir.
Q. He made no inquiry? A. No sir; I asked him just before he left Germantown, whether he had left Washington recently; he told me he had not; then I asked him whether he had not something to do with the murder and he said he had not.
Q. Did he persist in denying his name? A. He said that he had not given a fictitious name.
Q. At what time did you ask the question as to whether he was connected with the assassination? A. It was between seven and eight o'clock, as I was going to leave Germantown.
Q. You arrested him about four o'clock, and up to seven or eight o'clock he made no inquiry as to the cause of his arrest? A. No sir.
During the cross-examination the witness stated that he proceeded in quest of Atzeroth, in pursuance of orders from Captain Townsend, to find a man by the name of Atwood; witness could not state positively that the name just given by the prisoner was not Atzeroth; was certain that the prisoner stated that he had not come from Washington.

Re-examination of John Fletcher.

By the Judge Advocate—Q. Since leaving here have you visited the stable at the corner of Seventeenth and I streets, and examined the horse in regard to which you testified? A. Yes sir.
Q. Where did you find the animal? A. I found him in the middle of the Head-quarters stable, Seventeenth and I streets, in the first stall.
Q. Did you examine him and recognize him as the horse spoken of in your testimony as having been taken from your stable by Atzeroth? A. Yes sir; he was blind in the right eye.

Testimony of Thomas L. Gardner.

By the Judge-Advocate.—Q. Have you or not any knowledge of a dark bay, one-eyed horse, now in General Augur's stables, at Seventeenth and I streets, Washington? A. Yes sir.
Q. When did you last see the animal? A. I saw him on the 8th of this month.
Q. Have you any knowledge of the horse having been sold by your father, and if so, to whom? A. He was sold by my uncle, George Gardner, to a man by the name of Booth.
Q. When? A. Some time in the latter part of November last, I think.
Q. Do you mean J. Wilkes Booth? A. I do not know the first name.
Q. How near is your uncle's residence to that of Dr. Mudd? A. Not over a quarter of a mile away.
Q. Do you know whether Booth purchased the animal on the recommendation of the prisoner, Dr. Mudd? A. Yes sir.
Q. Did he come here alone or with others? A. He came there with the prisoner, Dr. Samuel Mudd.
Q. Describe the horse. A. He is a dark bay horse, and is blind in the right eye.
By the Court.—Q. Were you at your uncle's when Booth and Mudd came to buy the horse? A. Yes sir.
Q. Did they come in a carriage or on horseback? A. I think they were on horseback.
Q. Did they both leave together? A. Yes sir.
Q. Did Dr. Mudd take any part in the purchase or evince any interest in the matter? A. Not that I am aware of.
Cross-examined by Mr. Stone.—Q. Where did Booth take the horse? A. At his request I took the horse, next morning, to Montgomery's stable in Bryantown.
Q. Did Booth say what kind of a horse he wanted? A. He said something about wanting a horse for a buggy, with which to travel over the lower part of Maryland to look at the land. My uncle told him he would sell him a young mare, and Booth said that a mare would not suit him. He then showed him a horse, and Booth said finally that that horse would suit him. He said he only wanted a horse for one year.
Q. On what day of the week was this? A. I think it was on Monday.
Q. Did you see Booth at church on the previous day? A. No sir.
By the Court.—Q. Was Booth in the habit of staying at Dr. Mudd's when he was in the neighborhood? A. I do not know that he was ever in the neighborhood before; it was the first and the last time that I ever saw Booth.
By Mr. Stone.—Q. Did you ever hear of his being in the neighborhood? A. I think I did hear of his being in the neighborhood of Bryantown before that, but never since.

Testimony of Lieutenant John J. Toffey.

By Judge Holt.—Q. Have you any knowledge of a dark bay horse, blind of one eye, now at General Augur's stables in this city, corner of Seventeenth and I streets?
In reply, witness stated that on the night of the 14th of April, about half-past 12 o'clock he was going to the hospital where he was stationed, when he saw a horse standing near Camp Barry, about three quarters of a mile east of the Capitol. He took charge of the animal, and in compliance with orders finally delivered it to other hands, at General Augur's head-quarters, having taken his saddle off the horse. The horse was a large brown animal, blind of one eye.
A saddle was exhibited to the witness which he identified as the one taken off the horse by himself. He further testified that when he first saw the horse it was a little lame.
The Court then adjourned to meet to-morrow morning at 10 o'clock.

WASHINGTON, May 18.—The Court, after the evidence taken on Wednesday had been read, proceeded to the examination of witnesses.

Testimony of A. R. Reeve.

By the Judge Advocate.—Q. State where you reside, A. At Brooklyn, New York.
Q. In what business were you engaged in March last? A. In the telegraph business.
Q. Look at this despatch, and state what you know in regard to it. A. It was handed to me at the St. Nicholas Hotel by J. Wilkes Booth, to be sent to Washington.
Q. Will you read it? The witness read as follows:—
"New York, March 23, 1865.—To —— Weischman, Esq., No. 541 H street, Washington, D. C.—Tell John to telegraph the number and street at once. J. Booth."
Q. That was J. Wilkes Booth? A. It was.
Q. Was it sent on the day of its date? A. It was sent on the 23d or March to this city.
Cross-examined by Mr. Aiken.—Q. How do you identify that telegram? A. I remember that he signed the name of "J. Booth," instead of J. Wilkes Booth, which was his full name.
Q. Were any remarks made to you by the man who gave you that despatch at the time of his giving it to you? A. No sir; I was busy at the time, but in sending it I noticed that the middle name was left out.
Q. Are you in the habit of keeping all despatches sent? A. Yes sir.
By Judge Holt.—Q. Is this the original despatch? A. Yes sir.
By Mr. Aiken.—Q. What sort of a looking person gave you that despatch? A. If I saw his likeness I could tell.

Re-Examination of Lewis Weischman.

By Judge Holt.—Q. Look at that telegram and state whether you received it on the day of its date. A. I cannot say that I received it on the 23d of March, but I received a telegram of the exact nature of this one.
Q. Who is the person referred to there as John? A. John Surratt was frequently called John.
Q. Did you not deliver the message to him? A. I delivered the message to him the same day.
Q. What did he say? A. I questioned him as to what was meant by the number and street; he replied to me Don't be so —— inquisitive.
Q. See whether this is the telegram you delivered? A. It is.
The witness, by request of the Judge Advocate, then read the telegram, which was a copy of the one given above.
Q. Did you know the handwriting of Booth? A. I

TRIAL OF THE ASSASSINS AT WASHINGTON.

have seen his handwriting, and could recognize his autograph.

The witness was here shown the original telegram, purporting to have been written by Booth, and said, that is his handwriting.

Q. State whether, on or about the 4th of March last, you had an interview in your room with John Wilkes Booth, John Surratt and Payne, the prisoner at the bar? A. I will state that as near as I can recollect it was after the 4th of March, and the second time that Payne visited the house; when I returned from my office one day at half-past four o'clock and went to my room, I rang the bell for Dan, the negro servant, and in reply to an inquiry which I addressed to him he told me that John had ridden out at about half-past two o'clock in the afternoon, with six others, on horseback; on going down stairs I found Mrs. Surratt weeping bitterly and asked her what was the matter; she said to me, "go down and make the best of your dinner, John has gone away;" about half-past six o'clock John Surratt came home and was very much intoxicated; in fact he rushed frantically into the room; he had one of Sharp's small six-barrel revolvers in his hand; I said "John, why are you so much excited?" he replied, "I will shoot any man who comes into this room; my hopes are gone and my prospects blighted; I want something to do; can you get me a clerkship?" The prisoner, Payne, came into the room, and about fifteen minutes afterwards Booth came into the room, and was so much excited that he walked frantically around the room several times without noticing me; he had a whip in his hand; the three then went up stairs into the second story,and they must have remained there together about twenty minutes; subsequently I asked Surratt where he had left Payne; he said Payne had gone to Baltimore; I asked him where Booth had gone; he said to New York; some two weeks afterwards Surratt, when passing the post office, inquired for a letter under the name of James Sturdy, and I asked him why a letter was sent to him under a false name; he said he had particular reasons for it; this must have been two weeks after this affair, before the 20th of March; the letter was signed Wood, and the writer stated that he was at the Revere House in New York; that he was looking for something to do, but would probably go to some boarding-house in Grand street; I think West Grand street; this was the whole substance of the letter.

Q. Are you familiar with Booth's handwriting or simply with his autograph? A. I have seen his autograph at the hotel and have also seen his autograph at the house.

Q. Here is a note signed R. E. Watson-will you look at it and see whether that is Booth's handwriting? A. No sir, I would not recognize that as Booth's handwriting.

Q. Was there any remark made in their excited conversation on the occasion of which you have spoken as to where they had all been riding? A. No sir, they were not guarded; Payne made no remark at all; the only remarks made were those excited remarks by Surratt.

Q. Surratt had been riding, you say, and Booth had a whip in his hand? A. Yes sir.

Q. He appeared to have been with them also? A. Yes sir, he was much excited.

Cross-examined by Mr. Aiken.—Q. What time in the day did you meet Mr. Floyd on his way to Washington? A. It must have been about ten o'clock in the morning.

Q. Did you hear any of the conversation that passed between him and Mrs. Surratt at that time? A. No sir; I leaned back in my buggy, and Mrs. Surratt leaned sideways and whispered some words in Mr. Floyd's ear.

Q. Did she afterwards say anything to you as to what the conversation was about? A. No sir; the only conversation that I heard at that time was between her and Mrs. Ott; she was talking about Mr. Howell.

By Mr. Johnson.—Q. Was that at the same time? A. No sir; it was after the conversation between Floyd and herself.

Q. Was it on the same spot? A. No sir.

By Mr. Ewing.—Q. Do you recollect when it was that Booth played "Pescara," in the *Apostate*? A. Yes sir; he played it that night; that must have been about the 24th of March.

Q. Was it not the day before or the day after their return from the ride that he played in the "Apostate?" A. That I cannot say; it must have been at or the 4th of March; this man Payne was stopping at the house at the time, and when he came to the house he made some excuse to Mrs. Surratt, saying he would like to have been there before the 4th of March, but could not get there; by that circumstance I recollect that it was after the 4th of March; whether it was before or after the day that Booth played "Pescara" I can't say.

Q. Did you go to see that play? A. Yes sir. Booth sent complimentary tickets, at least gave a pass to Surratt for two, and he asked Surratt whether he thought I would go; Surratt said he thought not; when Surratt asked me I did go; the pass was a written one, and the doorkeeper at first refused us admission.

Q. State whether the affair of the ride was before or after Booth played in the *Apostate?* A. To the best of my recollection it was before.

Q. How long before? A. Well, as near as I can recollect, about two weeks before.

Q. You cannot state positively whether it was before or after the play in the *Apostate?* A. I would not like to state positively.

By Mr. Eakin.—Q. How did you learn anything with reference to the antecedents of Mrs. Slater? A. Through Mrs. Surratt herself.

Q. What did Mrs. Surratt tell you? A. Mrs. Surratt stated to me that she came to the house in company with this man Howe; that she was a North Carolinian, I believe; that she spoke French, and that she was a blockade runner or bearer of despatches.

Q. Where were you at the time Mrs. Surratt told you this? A. I was in the house, in the kitchen, or at least in the dining-room.

Q. Are you certain beyond all doubt that Mrs. Surratt ever told you that Mrs. Slater was a blockade runner? A. Yes sir.

Q. Had you before that time ever seen Mrs. Slater at the house of Mrs. Surratt? A. I myself saw her only once; I learned she had been to the house twice.

Q. Never mind what you learned; you saw her only once? A. Only once.

Q. How long was she there? A. Only one night.

Q. Did you have any conversation with her yourself? A. She drove us to the door in a buggy, the bell rang, and Mrs. Surratt told me to go out and take her trunk; there was a young man in the buggy with her; that was all the conversation I had with her; she had her mask down, one of those short masks that ladies wear.

On being interrogated by the Court as to the meaning of the word mask, the witness said that he intended to signify a veil of the ordinary description.

Q. Was any one besides yourself present on the occasion of this conversation? A. Not that I remember.

Q. On what day was that? A. It was some time in February; I do not remember the precise day.

Q. Did you hear anything said about Mrs. Slater afterwards? A. No sir.

Q. What was Mrs. Surratt's exact language in giving you this information? A. She said that this woman was from North Carolina, and that if she got North, there would be no danger for her, because, being French, she could immediately apply to the French Consul; that was about the only language I can remember.

By Mr. Doster.—Q. When John Surratt returned to the house in a state of excitement did he tell you the occasion of his excitement? A. No sir; he showed me his pistol and said that he would shoot any man who came into the room; I said, "John, why are you so excited, why don't you settle down like a sensible young man?" He said, "my hopes are gone, my prospects blighted, can you get me a clerkship?" Those were his precise words; I looked at him and thought he was foolish.

Q. You remarked that Mrs. Surratt was weeping bitterly; did she state the cause of her grief? A. She merely said go down and make the best you can of your dinner; that John had gone away; John, when he returned, said to me that he had on three pairs of drawers; I thought from that he was going to take a long ride.

By Mr. Eakin.—Q. By whom were you called upon first to give your testimony in this case? A. I was called by the War Department.

Q. By what member of the War Department? A. I was called on by Judge Burnett.

Q. Were you arrested? A. I surrendered myself up on Saturday morning, at eight o'clock, to Superintendent Richards, of the Metropolitan Police force; I stated to him what I knew of these men, Payne, Harold and Booth, visiting Mrs. Surratt's; I stated also what I knew of John Surratt.

Q. What was your object in doing this? A. My object was to assist the Government.

Q. Were any threats ever made to you by any officer of the Government, if you did not give this information? A. Not at all.

Q. Were any inducements held out to you by any officer of the Government? A. Not at all; I read in the papers that morning a description of the assassin of Secretary Seward; he was described as a man who wore a long grey coat; I had seen Atzeroth wearing a long grey coat; I went down to Tenth street, and met a gentleman, to whom I communicated my suspicions, and then went and delivered myself up to Superintendent Richards, of the Metropolitan Police force, and told him where this man Payne had been stopping, and also Atzeroth and Harold; I was then sent to General Augur's office; after leaving that place, I met a man who kept a stable at Thirteenth and E streets, who stated that a man had been to his place to hire a horse; he described the man as being of small stature, having black eyebrows and a kind of a smile on his face; he said the name was Harold; I then went with officer McDevitt to Harold's house, and procured photographs of him-self and Booth; officer McDevitt procured a photograph of Surratt; I related what I knew of Harold's habit of riding through Maryland, and that he had many acquaintances there, and that the assassins wou'd pr bably take their course through Maryland.

Q. Did y u ever say previous to your surrendering yourself and going to the office of Colonel Burnett, that you were fearful of an arrest? A. I myself had a great deal of fear; being in this house where these people were, I knew that I would be brought into public notice.

Q. I am not asking what you had to fear; but what you said?

Judge Bingham—You had better allow him to answer in his own way. A. As far as concerned my cognizance of anything wrong, I had no fears at all; when I surrendered myself to the Government I surrendered myself i.e. use I thought it to be my duty; it was hard for me to do so, situated as I was with respect to Mrs. Surratt and family; but it was my duty, and as such I have since regarded it.

Q. Did you at any time during the year 1863 board at a hotel called the Reynolds House? A. I did sir.

Q. Did you become acquainted there with a gentleman who went by the name of St. Marieon? A. I will state that in 1863 I met him at Marieon in Maryland at a villa, so called Langowan; he was introduced to me by a clergyman and was at that time teaching school; he spoke French, English and Italian fluently and his manners were very fascinating; he said then he had come from Montreal, and that he had been unfortunate in this country, having lost some five or six thousand dollars, the proceeds of a farm formerly owned by him in Canada; he stated also that he came to New York, embarked in a vessel to go to South America, and that the vessel was captured and he was thrown into Fort McHenry, from which place he was released through the agency of the French Consul; the witness added that the person to whom he referred, becoming destitute of means, took a situation on a farm; that he (the witness) subsequently met him, and finally promised to do all he could for him; two weeks after returning to Washington he was called upon by St. Marieon.

Judge Bingham then stated that there was no necessity for any further explanation.

Q. Did you pay his board at the Reynolds House, or become responsible for it?

Judge B ngham—I object to the question as being a matter of no consequence whether the witness did or did not.

Q. Did he state to you at any time that there was no aristocracy at the N rth, and he wished to go South?

Judge Bingham—I object to that also, as it is no matter whether he did or did not.

Q. Did he say to you that if he could not get to the South in any other way he would join a Federal regiment and desert?

Judge Bingham—I object to that, too, he is not a witness here.

Q. Do you know whether Mr. Reynolds reported any of h s "St. Marieon's" treasonable talk or language at that time to the War Department?

Judge Bingham—I object to that, too; I would like to know what t at is introduced for.

Mr. Eakin—It is introduced for the purpose of showing that the witness on the stand was in sympathy with the Confederates and Rebels, and that he assisted this man to get away to the South. I will have something else to prove afterwards.

The President of the Court—The time for our usual recess has arrived; the Court will now take a recess until two o'clock.

A rece s was accordingly taken.

Upon the res embling of the Court, the question propounded by Mr. Eakin was again put, and Judge Bingham said I at on immaterial matters that were not in evidence, an I should not be admitted in this manner. Of what concern was it what Reynolds reported. If the gentleman proposed to ask the witness whether he himself was guilty of any treasonable practices, no body would object to it. The objection was then sustained.

Mr. Eakin—In as much as the Judge Advocate has informed us that I e will not object to any questions that may be asked the witness with respect to his own conduct, I will address a few interrogatories to that effect.

Q. Did you give notice to St. Marieon that he would probably be arrested by the Government? A. No sir; I had no time to give such notice; St. Marieon rose one morning early and left; he afterwards enlisted in a Delaware regiment, and was taken prisoner and lodged in Castle Thunder.

Q. Are you a Clerk in the War Department? A. I have been.

Q. Did you, while a Clerk in the War Department, agree to communicate to any of the prisoners at the bar any information you might obtain from that Department? A. No sir.

Q. Are you acquainted with Mr. Howell? A. I have met him at Mrs. Surratt's house.

Q. What was Howell's first name? A. When he was at the house he gave the name of Spencer; he refused to give me his right name at the house; I afterwards learned from John Surratt that his name was Augustus Howell.

Q. Were you intimate with him? A. I was intro-

duced to him; I never had any conversation with him; on the contrary, I said to Captain Gleason, of the War Department, "Captain, there is a blockade-runner at our house, shall I give him up?" I agitated the question for three days, but I thought it might be the only time that the man might be there, and I let him go.

Q. Did you ever have any conversation with Howell in relation to going South yourself? A. I told him that I would like to go South; that I had been a student of divinity, and would like to be in Richmond for the purpose of continuing my studies.

Q. Did he offer to make any arrangements in Richmond with a view to getting you a place there? A. No sir.

By Mr. Clampitt.—Q. Was it your desire to go to Richmond for the purpose of continuing your theological studies? A. Yes sir.

Q. For what reason? (Objected to.)

By Mr. Eakin.—Q. While you were in the War Department did this man, Howell, teach you a cipher? A. Yes sir; he showed me an alphabet.

Q. What was the purpose of his teaching you the cipher? A. He stated no particular purpose.

Q. Was it not for the purpose of corresponding with you from Richmond? A. No sir; he made no arrangement for corresponding; the cipher alphabet was in my box, and no doubt was found there; I once wrote a poem of Longfellow's in t his cipher, and that is the only use I made of it; I showed the poem written in that cipher to Mr. Cruikshank, of the War Department.

Q. Is that all the use you ever made of the cipher? A. Yes sir; I never had a word of correspondence with Howell, and never saw him the second t me until I saw him in prison.

Q. Was any objections ever made by any of these prisoners at the bar to your b ing present at their conversations? A. Not any, that I heard, but they always withdrew themselves; when Surratt was in the parlor he would converse with me for about five minutes on general topics, and he would then give Booth a nudge, or Booth would give him a nudge, and they would go and sit up stairs for two or three hours; I never had a word of private conversation with them which I would not like the world to hear.

Q. Did Howell give you the key to that cipher? A. He showed me the cipher or alphabet and how to use it.

Q. He taught you it, did he not? A. I made no use of it whatever, except on that particular occasion, when I showed it to Mr. Cruikshank.

Q. That was not an answer to my question; he taught you the cipher, did he not? A. Well, yes, sir.

Q. Now, according to the best of your recollection, how soon was it after his return from Richmond? A. He had returned from New York, and he did not tell me when he had returned from Richmond, because it was the first and only time I ever saw the man in my life; he was well acquainted with Mrs. Surratt, and his nickname around the house was Spencer; he had been at the house a day or day and a half before I met him.

Q. Did he tell you that was the cipher used in Richmond? A. No sir.

Q. You stated that the prisoners were free and unreserved in their conversation while in your presence? A. They spoke in my presence on general topics, and so om they never spoke to me of their private business.

Q. Do we understand you as stating to the Court that in all your conversations with them you never learned of any intended treasonable act r conspiracy of theirs? A. I never did; I would have been the last man in the world to have suspected John Surratt, my schoolmate and companion, of the murder of the President of the United States.

Q. You state that your suspicions were aroused at one time by something you saw at Mrs. Surratt's? A. My suspicions were aroused by John Surratt, and by this man Payne and Booth coming to the house; my suspicions were again aroused by their frequent private conversations by seeing Payne and Surratt with bowle-knives, and by finding a moustache in my room.

Q. Yoursuspicions were not aroused, then, by the act of Surratt Laving on three pair of drawers? A. I thought he was going to take a long ride in the country, and perhaps he was going South.

Q. Then, your suspicions were aroused on all these different occasions, and you find no reason to believe that there was something in the wind that was improper, did you communicate your suspicions to the War Department? A. My suspicions were not of a fixed or definite character; I did not know what they intended to do; I made a confidante of Captain Gleason, of the War Dep rtment, and I told him that Booth was a secret sy m abizer; I mentioned snatches of conversation I had heard, and said to him, "Captain, what do you think of this all?" we even talked over what they might possibly be at; whether they could be bearers of despatches for blockade-runners; at one time I saw in the papers the capture of President Lincoln freely discussed, and I said to him, 'Captain, do you think any purty would attempt to capture the President?" He laughed and hooted at the idea.

Q. You did, then, fear of a proposition of that kind? A. I did not hear, but it was freely discussed in the papers; if you will refer to the *Tribune* of March 19th,

TRIAL OF THE ASSASSINS AT WASHINGTON.

you will see it mentioned; it was merely a casual remark that I made; the a suspicions arose in my mind after this horseback ride; I remarked to Captain Gleason that Surratt had come back, and told him that what they had been after had failed.

Q. How came you to connect the matter of the capture of the President, of which you read in the newspaper, with any of these parties?

T.e que tien was objected to by Judge Bingham as being wholly immaterial or irrelevant. The objection was sustained.

Q. Were you on intimate personal relations with the prisoners at the bar? A. Not in imate relations: I met them merely because they boarded at Mrs. Surratt's house: I met Atzeroth and went to the theatre with him; I l oked upon him, as did every one in the house, as a good-hearted countryman.

Q. But you were a schoolmate with John Surratt?
A. John had been my companion for seven years.

Q. Did you still profess to be a friend of his when you gave the information that you did to the War Department? A. I was his friend, but when my suspicions as to the danger of the Government were aroused, I preferred the Government to John Surratt; I did not know what he was contemplating; he said he was going to engage in cotton speculations and in the oil business.

Q. You did not know what he was contemplating; why then did you forfeit your friendship to him? A. I never forfeited my friendship; he forfeited his friendship to me.

Q. How so: by engaging in cotton speculations? A. No sir; by placing me in the position in which I am now: I think of the two I was more a friend to him than he was to me.

By Mr. Ewing.—Q. You spoke of reading a publication in the *Tribune*, of March 19th, referring to a plot to capture the President? A. Yes sir.

Can you not, by connecting that circumstance with the ride which these parties had in the country, fix more definitely the t me of that ride—whether before or after the date of that publication? A. I think it was after it; I would also state that I saw in the Washington *Republican* a statement concerning a contemplated assassination of President Lincoln, and Surratt once made a remark to me that if he succeeded in his cotton speculation his country would lose him forever, and his name would go down to posterity forever green.

Q. You think, then, that this occasion, when they appeared to have come in from a ride in the country, was after March 19th? A. Yes sir.

Q. Was your remark to Captain Gleason, respecting the probable capture of the President, made after the ride? A. Yes sir; I said to Capt. Gleason that Surratt's mysterious, incomprehensible business had failed, and I added, "Let us think over what it could have been;" we mentioned a variety of things, even the breaking open of the Old Capitol Prison; I would mention that after that ride, my suspicions were not so much aroused as before it, because neither Payne nor Atzeroth had been at the house since; the only one of them who visited was the man Booth.

Q. Have you ever seen the prisoner, Arnold? A. No sir.

Q. Did you first meet the prisoner, Dr. Samuel Mudd, on Seventh street, opposite the Odd Fellows' Hall? A. I did.

The witness further testified that Mrs. Surratt lived in the house on H street, next to the corner of Sixth, and that the point on Seventh street at which he met Dr. Mudd, was not on a direct route from the Pennsylvania House or the National Hotel to Mrs. Surratt's.

Re-Examination of John Greenawalt.

By the Judge Advocate.—Q. In describing the poorly dressed man who called at your house with Atzeroth on the morning of the 15th of April, you said that his hair was black, but omitted to state the color of his beard and moustache; state it now? A. Their color was dark.

Testimony of James Walker (Colored).

By the Judge Advocate.—Q. State whether or not on the 14th of April last you were living at the Pennsylvania House in this city and your business there. A. I was living there; I was twelve months there on the 6th of April last; my business was to make fires, carry water, &c.

Q. State whether or not you ever saw the prisoner Atzeroth at that house, and under what circumstances? A. He came there about 2 o'clock on the morning of the 15th of April, and left between 5 and 6 o'clock in the morning.

Q. Did he come there on foot, or on horseback? A. The first time he came on horseback, and I held the horse for him at the door.

Q. What hour was that? A. It was between 12 and 1 o'clock, I believe.

Q. What did he do while you were holding his horse? A. He went into the bar; I do not know what he done there; he came out again, and asked me to get him a piece of switch, which I did, when he rode off.

Q. Did you notice whether he had arms with him? A. I did not notice what he had; I did not see anything.

Q. When he came back at two o'clock was he on foot or on horseback? A. On foot; I was laying down and rose and let him in.

Q. Did he have a room? A. He desired to go to No. 52. I t 'ld him it was taken up; he stopped at No. 53.

Q. At what hour did he leave on that morning? A. Between five and six o'clock.

Q. Where did you see him at that hour? A. I went for a hack for a lady who was going in the 6:15 train, and when I was returning I overtook him as he was walking along slowly; he made no remark to me.

Q. Did you see another man who stopped there that night? A. He left in the morning about four or five minutes before Atzeroth, having stopped in the same room; he had no baggage.

Q. Do you remember his appearance? A. When he came in it was dark, the gas being pretty low; he seemed to have on dark clothes, and wore a slouched hat; he went to his room immediately, having paid for it in advance.

Q. Will you look at the prisoners at the bar and see if any of them resemble this man? A. I cannot say sir.

The cross-examination of this witness elicited no new points of interest. He testified that the horse used by Atzeroth on the night in question, was apparently a small light bay horse; he had seen Atzeroth have a belt containing a pistol and knife some four or five days before the assassination, but could not identify the weapons. He did not see any weapons on Atzeroth on the 14th or the morning of the 15th. Atzeroth had no conversation with the man by whom he was accompanied at the time.

Testimony of William Clendenin.

By Judge Holt.—Q. Look at that knife (the knife supposed to have been thrown away by Atzeroth on the night of the assassination) and say if you ever had it in your hand before? A. Yes. On passing down F street on the morning after the assassination on the south side of the street, between Eighth and Ninth, I saw a colored man pick up something from the gutter about ten feet from me; as I came up I asked him what it was and he gave the knife to me; a lady spoke to me from the third story window, and saw the knife in the gutter and sent the colored man down to get it; I took it and gave it to the Chief of Police; this was on the Saturday morning of the assassination.

Cross-examined by Mr. Doster—Q. What time in the morning? About 6 o'clock.

Q. Whereabouts precisely on F street was it? A. In front of the rear's house; it lay as if it had been thrown under the carriage step.

Testimony of J. S. McPhail.

By Judge Holt.—Q. State whether or not you had a conversation with Atzeroth in prison in which he said that on the night of the assassination of the President, he had thrown his knife away in the streets of Washington.

Question objected to by Mr. Doster, on the ground that the confession of the witness was under duress.

Q. Under what circumstances was the statement made to you? A. I received information that he desired to see me, and I went to see him accordingly; I found him in a cell in prison in irons.

Mr. Doster argued that the condition of the prisoner was such as to intimidate him, and to make his confession under such circumstances was improper to be given as evidence, and cited many authorities to sustain his objections.

The witness stated that he was Provost Marshal-General of the State of Maryland, which fact Atzeroth knew. Witness further stated that a brother-in-law of Atzeroth was on his force and a brother was tem porarily on his force also.

Both of them repeatedly desired the witness to see Atzeroth, and he went there with the permission of the Secretary of War simply at their instance. The prisoner was in irons, but had no cover over his face or head. The objection of the Counsel was sustained by the Court.

Witness then answered the question asked him in the affirmative.

Cross examined by Mr. Doster—Q. That was all he said? A. I did not say that. I answered the question, Yes.

Q. Did he describe the knife, or name the place where he threw it away? A. He said he threw it away just above the Kearndon House, which is on the corner of Ninth and F streets.

Q. Did he also say where his pistol was? A. He stated that it was at Matthews & Co.'s, Georgetown, in possession of a young man named Caldwell.

Q. Did he state how he got it there? A. He said he went there and borrowed $10 on the pistol, on Saturday morning, April 15th.

Q. Did the prisoner mention to you a certain coat containing a pistol and bowie knife, and exchanging it in the Kirkwood House, and if so did he state who it belonged to? A. He stated that the coat at the hotel belonged to Harold.

Mr. C. Stone, counsel for Harold, in a very loud voice exclaimed, "I object to that testimony." (Laughter.)

Testimony of Lieutenant W. R. Keen.

By Judge Holt.—Q. Did you pass the night of the 14th of April at the Pennsylvania House, in this city? A. I did.

Q. Did you see Atzeroth at the house that night? A. I did.

Q. Under what circumstances did you see him? A. I came into the hotel about 4 o'clock on Saturday morning; he was in bed when I arrived in my room; I asked him whether he had heard of the murder of the President, he said yes, and remarked what an awful thing it was; after that I went to bed, and when I awoke, about 7 o'clock, he was gone.

Q. Did you see his arms? A. No there; when he occupied room No. 51, I saw him have a knife and a revolver.

Q. How long before the assassination? A. I think it was the Sunday before, or the Sunday a week; I would not be positive; the bowie knife had a sheath. (A knife was shown to witness.) I could not swear that was the knife; but it was a knife about that size.

Q. State under what circumstances you saw the arms? A. He went out and left the knife on the bed; I took it and put it under my pillow; when he came in he asked, "Luke, did you see my knife;" he said he wanted that, and remarked, "if one fails I will have the other;" I handed it to him and he went out.

Q. Did he have a pistol? A. Yes, he always carried that around his waist.

Cross-examined by Mr. Doster.—Q. Did you know the prisoner, Atzeroth, before you met him at the Pennsylvania House? A. Yes sir.

Q. Did you speak about the assassination of the President immediately on going into the room that morning? A. No; he was in bed when I came right opposite, and it was five or ten minutes before I spoke to him.

Q. Did he say anything more than that it was an awful thing? A. I believe that is all.

Q. Was he undressed? A. He was in bed; I do not know whether he was undressed or not.

Q. You mention the prisoner calling you Luke, were you on intimate terms with him? A. Yes; that was the only name I ever heard him call me.

Q. Did you see him after this affair? A. No sir.

Q. When he said that if this failed the other would not, what else did he say? A. I do not know; this was a week or ten days before the assassination.

Q. At the time you heard the words had you been drinking with the prisoner? A. Yes, we had two or three drinks while we were lying in bed.

Q. Were these remarks made after these drinks? A. Yes.

Q. What kinds of drinks were these? A. Whisky cocktails, I believe.

Q. Do you remember anything else that was said in that interview? A. No; that was about all.

Testimony of Washington Briscoe.

By Judge Holt.—Q. On the night of the 14th April did you see the prisoner, Atzeroth, and if so, at what time? A. I did see him; he got into the car at Sixth street, and rode towards the Navy Yard; it was between half-past eleven and twelve o'clock.

Q. What did he say? A. He did not recognize me at all; after a while I asked him if he had heard of the news; he said he had; he then asked me to let him sleep in the store with me.

Q. Where was your store? A. Down at the Navy Yard; I told him I could not let him sleep there.

Q. What was his manner? A. He seemed to be excited.

Q. Did he urge you, or seem to be very anxious to sleep with you? A. Yes; he asked me three times.

Q. What became of him? A. He rode down as far as I did; got out when I did, and asked me again; the gentleman with me did not invite him to stop, and of course I had no right to do so.

Q. How long had you known him? A. Some seven or eight years.

Q. Did he then express his determination to go anywhere else? A. He said he was going back to what was formerly the "Kimmel" House, now the "Pennsylvania" House, in C street.

Cross-examined by Mr. Doster.—Q. Did you notice the precise time when you met Atzeroth that evening? A. No, but I think it was about half-past eleven or twelve o'clock.

Q. What time was it when he left you that evening, as near as you can tell? A. Near twelve o'clock; he stopped at the corner of J and Garrison streets, near the Navy Yard to wait until a car came back.

Q. What was his manner; did he appear to be distressed? A. I judged from his manner that he was a little excited.

Q. Had he been drinking? A. I hardly know; I did not notice particularly.

Testimony of Rev. Dr. W. H. Ryder.

Examined by Judge Holt.—Q. State your residence and profession. A. I reside in Chicago, and am a clergyman.

Q. State whether you recently made a visit into Richmond, and at what time? A. I left Chicago on the 8th of April, and arrived in Richmond on the 14th, where I remained till the 21st.

Q. While there did you find in the Capitol the archives of the so-called Confederate States, and it so, in what condition? A. I did; they were pretty generally confused, and scattered about on the floor.

Q. Did you, in common with others, pick up papers from the floor? A. Yes.

Q. State whether the paper you now hold in your hand was picked up in the Capitol at Richmond under the circumstances you mention? A. Yes; I picked it up either in the building or immediately about the building, or it was handed to me by some one who picked it up in the rubbish about the room; there were one or two persons with me; they were stooping down, and when they found anything of importance they would pick it up and preserve it; in some instances the orderly who was in attendance would hand me something, and I would put it in my pocket; having thus collected quite a number of things, they were thrown into a common receptacle and put into a box and forwarded to Chicago; this was one of the papers found.

The paper referred to was read by the Judge Advocate, as follows:—

"RICHMOND, February 11, 1865.—His Excellency Jefferson Davis, President C. S. A.:—When Senator Johnson, of Missouri, and myself waited upon you, some days since, in relation to the project of annoying and harrassing the enemy by means of burning their shipping, towns, etc., etc., there were several remarks made by you upon the subject that I was not fully prepared to answer, but which, upon subsequent conference with parties proposing the enterprise, I find cannot apply as objections to the scheme. First, the combustible material consists of several preparations, and not one alone, and can be used without exposing the party using them to the least danger of detection whatever. The preparations are not in the hands of Mr. Daniel, but are in the hands of Professor McCulloch, and are known but to him and one other party, as I understand.

"Second. There is no necessity for sending persons in the military service into the enemy's country, but the work may be done by agents, and in most cases by persons ignorant of the facts, and, therefore, innocent agents. I have seen enough of the effects that can be produced to say to you that in most cases without any danger to the parties engaged, and in others but very slight, that;—First, We can first burn every vessel that leaves a foreign port for the United States. Second, We can burn every transport that leaves the harbor of New York, or other Northern ports, with supplies for the armies of the enemy in the South. Third, Burn every transport and gun-boat on the Mississippi River, as well as devastate the country of the enemy and fill his people with terror and consternation.

"I am not a one of this opinion, but many other gentlemen are as fully and thoroughly impressed with the conviction as I am. I believe we have the means at our command, if promptly appropriated and energetically applied to demonstrate the Northern people in a very short time. For the purpose of satisfying your mind upon the subject I respectfully but earnestly request, that you will have an interview with General Harris, formerly a member of Congress from Missouri, who, I think, is able, by conclusive proofs, to convince you that what I have suggested is perfectly feasible and practicable.

"The deep interest I feel for the success of our cause in this struggle, and the conviction of the importance of availing ourselves of every element of defense, must be my excuse in writing you and requesting you to invite General Harris to see you. If you should see proper to do so, please signify to me the time when it will be convenient for you to see him.

"I am, respectfully, your obedient servant,
"W. S. O'LAHM."

On the back of the letter are two indorsements, the first being "Hon. W. S. O'Lahm, Richmond, February 12, 1865, in relation to plans and means of burning the enemy's shipping, &c. Preparations are in the hands of Professor McCulloch, and are known to only one party. He asks the President to have an interview with General Harris, formerly M. C. from Missouri, on the subject." The other is "The Secretary of State, at his convenience, will please see General Harris, and learn what plan he has for overcoming the difficulty heretofore experienced. J. D. 20th February, 1865. Received February 17, 1865."

Testimony of John Potts.

Examined by Judge Holt.—Q. State your occupation. A. I am Chief Clerk of the War Department, and have been so for twenty years.

Q. Are you perfectly familiar with the hand-writing of Jefferson Davis? A. I am.

Q. Look on the indorsements signed J. D., and see if it is in his hand-writing. A. In my belief it is.

Testimony of Nathan Rice.

Examined by Judge Holt.—Q. State if you are acquainted with the hand-writing of Jefferson Davis. A. I am; while he was Secretary of War I had to sign requisitions, and of course his hand-writing came before me every day.

Q. Look at the letter just read, and see if the indorsement is in the hand-writing of Jefferson Davis. A. I should think it was.

Q. You had ample opportunity of becoming acquainted with his handwriting? A. Yes; I would generally have from ten to twenty-five signatures before me every day, sometimes signed in my presence.

Testimony of General Joshua T. Owen.

Examined by Judge Holt.—Q. Do you know Professor McCulloh? A. I have known a gentleman who has been designated as Professor McCulloh, I suppose, for twenty years; he was Professor of Chemistry at Princeton College and Professor of Mathematics at Jefferson College, in Pennsylvania, where I graduated, about 1839 or 1840: if my recollection serves me right he was an Assayer at the Mint in Philadelphia.

Q. Do you know where he has been during the Rebellion? A. He has been in Richmond in the service of the Confederates; I may say his father was one of the Comptrollers in Washington; his name was Hugh; the same name as the present Secretary of the Treasury.

Q. Did he have some distinction as a chemist? A. Yes, he was perhaps more distinguished as a chemist than any other way.

Q. Was it in that capacity that he was employed in the Confederate service, as you understand? A. I do not know.

General Hunter here remarked, during his expedition up the valley he received a letter written by McCulloh, in which he stated that he had been only a Captain during the whole war, and that he was anxious for promotion.

The Judge Advocate-General remarked the letter itself would be desirable to go on record as a part of the history of the transaction.

General Hunter said he had given the letter to a brother-in-law, at Princeton, and that he would send for it.

Testimony of Judge Abram B. Olin.

Examined by Judge Holt.—Q. State whether or not on the morning of the 15th of April you visited Ford's Theatre and inspected what is known as the President's box? A. I was engaged on the 15th in taking the depositions of several witnesses; on Sunday, the 16th, I visited the theatre.

Q. State the examination which you made and the condition in which you found the President's box, doors, etc.? A. The first incident to which my attention was called was the incision in the wall prepared to receive a brace, the other end of which was to rest on the hand of the door; the brace itself was not there; I refer to the door across the passage leading to the box; it crosses it at an angle with the wall, and a brace fitting against the wall and pressing against the door would fasten the door very securely; I looked for the remains of the plastering that had been cut from the wall in making the incision, but as far as I could discern, they had all been removed; it was said to me that the pistol was discharged through the panel of the door; the entrance to this passage is somewhat dark; I procured a light and examined very carefully the hole through the door; I discovered at once that that hole had been made by some small instruments first, and cut out by some sharp instrument like a penknife; I thought I remarked the evidence of a sharp knife used in clearing out every obstacle to looking through the door; I then discovered that the clasp which fastened the first door for the box was made with a movable partition, to be used as one or two boxes, and therefore with two doors; I saw that the upper screw holding the clasp had been loosened in such a way that when the door was locked, by putting my forefinger against it, I could open the door; I desired to ascertain the exact position of the President's chair and for that purpose procured Miss Harris to accompany me, having understood she was in the box on that occasion; she located the chair as nearly as she recollected it where it was placed on the evening, and I seating myself in the chair, and closing that door, a person could place his eye near the hole, and the range would be about midway from the base of the crown. I directed my inquiries to ascertain the precise time of the occurrence, as there was some uncertainty as to whether the attack on Mr. Seward and the assassination of the President was by one or more persons.

Q. Did you see the bar that had been placed against the door, or had it been removed? A. It had been removed by some one; you could see the indentation in the panel of the door where the brace had been put in very well; it was quite perceptible where the brace had been; a brace fixed in the wall and placed against the panel of the door would have been very difficult to remove from the outside; I don't think it could have been removed without breaking the door, and, in fact, the more pressure that was made on the door the more secure it would be.

Q. Did the hole bear evidence of having been recently made? A. Yes; it was a freshly cut hole, as fresh apparently as if it had been made that instant.

Q. Can you describe the chair in which the President sat? A. It was a large, high-back chair, an arm-chair, standing on castors; I thought I could discern where his head rested, and although the covering itself was red, the marks of several drops of blood could be seen.

Cross-examined by Mr. Doster.—Q. Will you state whether the civil courts of this District are supposed to sit by consent of and to carry out the will of Lieut.

General Grant? A. I really do not know of any one who supposes that; at least he has given me no information on the subject.

A pause of a minute or two here occurred, during which the members of the Court conversed with each other in a low tone.

Mr. Doster said, "As there seems to be considerable objection to the question, I desire to state why it was asked;"—

The President of the Court said no objection was made to the question, and it has been answered, and no explanation is therefore necessary.

Re-Examination of Major Rathbone.

By Judge Holt.—Q. Did you go to the outside door after the shot had been fired in the President's box and examine how it was closed? A. I did, for the purpose of calling medical aid.

Q. In what condition did you find it? A. I found the door barred, so that people who were knocking on the outside could not get in.

Q. Did you make an attempt to remove the bar? A. I did remove it with difficulty.

Q. Was that after you had received a stab from the assassin? A. It was.

Q. Is that (bar exhibited to witness) blood on the bar from your arm? A. I am not able to say, but my wound was bleeding freely at the time.

Q. In what condition did you find the bar? A. It appeared to be resting against the moulding of the door, and I think it could not have been loosened out by any one passing from the outside.

Q. Did you notice the chair in which the President sat in particular? A. I did not, except that it was a large easy chair, covered with damask cloth.

Q. Do you not know whether it had rockers or not? A. My impression is that it had.

Q. Is that the bar the door was closed with? A. I am not able to say whether it is or not; my impression is that it was a different piece of wood.

Testimony of Isaac Jaquett.

By Judge Holt.—Q. Did you find that bar in Ford's Theatre, and if so, under what circumstances and when? A. After we had carried the President out I went to the box with several others; this bar was lying on the door inside the first door going to the box; I took it up and stood about there for some time, and took it home with me.

Q. There has been a piece sawed off, do you know anything in reference to that? A. Yes; there was an officer stopping at the house where I was boarding who wanted a piece of the bar to take away with him, and it was sawed off, but he did not finally take it away.

Q. Are there spots of blood upon it? A. Yes, they were fresh at that time.

Re-Examination of Joe Lemmons (Colored.)

By Judge Holt.—Q. Did you see persons engaged in decorating the President's box on the afternoon of the day of the murder? A. Yes; Mr. Harry Ford and another gentleman, I do not know his name exactly, were up there fixing it; Mr. Ford told me to go over to his room and get a rocking-chair, bring it down and put it in the President's box; I done so; I carried the chair into the President's box, set it down and went away; that is all I know.

Q. Had it been there before? A. Not this season.

Q. Was the back of his chair you brought down, high or low? A. A high-backed, cushioned chair.

Q. Did you see the prisoner Edward Spangler on the occasion? A. There was no one in there but Harry Ford and this other gentleman, who had been fixing it and started to come down.

Q. Was Spangler on the stage that evening? A. Yes; he was obliged to be there all the time; no worked there altogether, the same as I did; he had nothing to call him away, except when he went to his boarding house; he was not there on the stage when the chair was carried into the box.

Cross-examination by Mr. Ewing.—Q. You did not see Mr. Spangler on the stage, did you? A. No; I did not notice him particularly; I had been there so long I hardly ever noticed gentlemen so particularly

Q. And you do not know but what he might have had something to call him away just at that time? A. No sir, I do not.

Q. Who was this other gentleman in the box with Harry Ford? A. I may be mistaken, but I think his name is Buckingham.

Q. Was he employed about the theatre? A. He stayed there at night for to take tickets; he was a doorkeeper in front of the house; I think he was helping Harry Ford to fix the private box.

Q. At what hour in the evening? A. A little after 3 o'clock; I should think it might have been later or sooner; I had been out in the city taking bills around; I was about going on the fly; I took my meals wherever I could, and when he called me, I put down my meal and got the chair.

Q. Did you see Spangler as you went to the box at all? A. No; not when I went to the box nor when I came away.

Q. Describe the chair? A. There is no chair here like it; it was one of those high-backed chairs, with a high red cushion on it, covered with satin; the last season, when they got it, it was in the private box, but Mr. Ford told me take it out of the box and carry it up to his room.

Q. Was the furniture there manufactured for the box, and was it of the same character as the chair? A. Yes; a sofa and some other chairs; it was not my business the looking in this place, and I never noticed only when I was sent; the sofa was covered, I think, with the same material; I do not know whether the furniture was bought as the property of the stage or the private box.

By Judge Holt.—Q. Did you take a large chair out of this box at the time you put this one in? A. No sir.

Re-Examination of John J. Toffey.

By Judge Holt.—Q. Since you were examined yesterday state whether you have been to a stable, and the horse of which you weres peaking? A. Yes; I found him on the corner of Seventeenth and I streets.

Q. Did you recognize him as the horse you took up with the saddle and bridle under the circumstances you mentioned in your testimony? A. Yes sir.

By the Court—Q. Is there anything peculiar about that horse of which you were speaking? A. Yes; I found him on the corner of Seventeenth and I streets.

Q. Did y u recognize him as the horse you took up with the saddle and bridle under the circumstances you mentioned in your testimony? A. Yes sir.

By the Court.—Q. Is there anything peculiar about that horse which enables you to recognize him? A. Yes; his being blind in the right eye.

Testimony of William Eaton.

Examined by Judge Holt.—Q. State whether or not, after the assassination of the President, you went to the room of J. Wilkes Booth, at the National Hotel, and opened his trunk? A. I d d go there that same even ng under the authority of the Provost Marshal.

Q. What d d you do on arriving there? A. I found J. Wilkes Booth's room; I was shown to it by the book-keeper; I took charge of what things were in his trunk; the papers were taken to the Provost Marshal's office, and handed over to Lieut. Terry; I placed them in his hands.

Testimony of Lieutenant Terry.

By Judge Holt.—Q. State whether you are attached to the office of the Provost Marshal of this city. A. Yes, to Colonel Ingraham's office.

Q. State whether or not, after the assassination, the witness Eaton placed in your hands certain papers which he represented to have been taken from the trunk of J. Wilkes Booth. A. He did.

Q. State whether the letter you hold in your hands was one of these papers? A. Yes sir; the envelope was addressed to "J. Wilkes Booth, Esq., National Hotel, Washington, D. C.," and postmarked seemingly "Baltimore, Maryland, March 30th." The letter was read by Colonel Burnett to the Court, as follows:—

HOOKSTOWN, Baltimore Co., March 21, 1865.

DEAR JOHN:—Was business as important that you could not remain in Baltimore till I saw you? I came in as soon as I could, and found you had gone to Washington. I called, also, to see Mike, but learned from his mother he had gone out with you and had not returned. I concluded, therefore, he had gone with you. How me nsiderate you have been. When I left you, you stat d we would not meet for a month or so; therefore I made application for employment, an answer to which I shall receive during the week. I told my parents I had ceased with you. Can I then, under existing circumstances, come as you request? You know full well the Government suspicions something is going on the re; therefore the undertaking is becoming more complicated. Why not, for the present, desist, for various reasons, which if you took into you can readily see, without my making any mention thereof. You nor any one can censure me for my present course. You have been its cause, for how can I now come after telling them I had left you? Suspicion rests upon me now from my whole family, and even parties in the country, will be compelled to leave home anyhow, and how soon I care not. No, not one was more in for the enterprise than myself, and to-day would be there, had you not done as you have; by this I mean the manner of proceeding. I am, as you well know, in need; I am, you may say, in rags; whereas, to-day I ought to be well clothed. I do not feel right, stalking about without means, and from appearances a beggar. I feel my dependence, but even this was forgotten, for I was one with you. Times more propitious will arrive; you do not act rashly or in haste. I would prefer your first way. Go and see how it will be taken in R——d. And ere long I shall be better prepared to again a sist you. I dislike writing; would sooner verbally make known my views; yet, you now waiting, causes me thus to proceed. Do not in anger peruse this. Weigh all I have said; and, as a rational man and a friend, you cannot censure nor upbraid my conduct. I sincerely trust this, nor aught else that should or may occur, will ever obliterate our former friendship. Write me to Baltimore, as I expect to be in about Wednesday or Thursday; or, if you can possibly come on, I will truly meet you in Baltimore, at B corner.

"I subscribe myself your friend, "SAM."

Testimony of William McPhaill.

Q. Are you acquainted with the handwriting of the prisoner, Samuel Arnold? A. I am.

Q. Will you look at this letter and say if it is in his hat dwriting? A. Yes sir.

By Mr. Coxe.—Q. How did you become acquainted with his handwriting? stat) that first. A. He once placed in my hand a written statement.

Q. What instrument did he place in your hands? A. A confession.

Q. When did he write it? A. On the 19th of April.

Q. Where? A. In the back room of Marshal McPhail's office.

Q. Where is that? A. On west Fayette street, near Holliday, in Baltimore; the paper was handed to me, and by me to the Marshal; of its arrival in Washington I did not know anything, only I was informed of its having been h nded to t.e Secretary of War.

Q. And that was a paper purporting to be a statement of all that he knew of this affair? A. Yes sir.

Testimony of Marshal McPhail.

Q. State whether you are acquainted with the handwriting of the prisoner, Samuel Arnold? A. Only by receiving a letter from him, which was handed me by his father, and dated the 12th, at Fortress Monroe. The letter being then shown, the witness said, " Yes, this looks like it; this is the letter."

Q. Whose handwr ting is that indorsement on the back? A. I should think it was Mr. Arnold's.

Q. Have you looked at the body of the letter? A. No sir.

Q. You looked at the handwriting? A. No sir.

Q. Do you think it is his? A. I do, sir.

Testimony of Littleton Newman.

Q. Are you acquainted with the handwriting of the prisoner Arnold? A. No sir.

Q. Do you know him? A. Yes sir.

Q. Will you state whether or not some time last fall you were present when he received a letter in which money was inclosed; if the money was exhibited to you, and what was the character of this letter? A. On the 9th or 12th of September there was a letter brought to him; there was in the s me twenty or fi ty dollars, I don t recoll ect wh ch; I remarked he was thick, or had money and having read the letter, he handed it over to me and I read some half dozen lines, but I did not understand it; it was very ambiguous in its language, and I asked him what it meant; he said it was something big, and I would soon see in the papers, or something to that effect.

Testimony of Ethan J. Horner.

Q. Will you state whether or not some days after the assassination of the President, you arrested the prisoner Samuel Arnold? A. On the morning of the 17th of April last, Mr. Allen and myself arrested him at Fortress Monroe.

Q. Did you find any arms in his possession? A. Yes sir; we took them in the room at the back of the store in which he slept; we searched his person and a carpet-bag and got a pistol; he said he had another pistol and a knife also at his father's place near the Hookstown road.

Q. What kind of a pistol was that you found? A. A Colt's pistol.

Q. Was it like that; (showing the witness a pistol)? A. No sir; not like that; but he said he left a pistol like that at his father's.

By Mr. Ewing.—Didn't he say he left a knife and a pistol at Hookstown, and what else did he say to you? A. He made a verbal statement to us at Fortress Monroe; there was a letter given us by his father to give to him when we arrested him, and after we handed him the letter and he had read it I asked him it he was going to give us the statement, and he gave us one, together with the names of certain men connected with the abduction, or rather with the kidnapping of Abraham Lincoln.

Mr. Cox here rose and objected to any confession made by the prisoner that would or might tend to evidence against any other of the accused.

Mr. Ewing and Mr. Cox had a lengthy argument, which finally resulted in a ruling by the Court, admitting as evidence the statement of the witness of the whole conversation that took place at the time referred to.

The witness then continued, and said the prisoner had stated to him that about two weeks previous to his going to Fortress Monroe he was at a meeting, held at the Lichten House; I asked him who attended the meeting, and he gave me the names.

Here the witness took out a paper and read therefrom, J. W. Booth, M. O'Laughlin, G. W. At eroth, John Surratt, and a man with an alias of Moseby, and a small man whose name I couldn't recollect.

Q. So say whether he was present at the meeting himself? A. Yes sir; I asked him if he corresponded with Booth; he said first that he did not; then I mentioned to him a letter published in the Sunday Mercury, where there was given a statement of a letter found in J. Wilkes Booth's trunk, and I mentioned to him that the letter was mailed at Hookstown and signed "Sam;" when he said that he had written that letter, and that evening we brought him to Baltimore; I asked him if Wilkes Booth was acquainted any in St. Mary's county or Charles county, and he said he had letters of introduction to Dr. Mudd and Dr. Queer; I asked who he got them from, and he said he did not know; we proceeded to Baltimore and I left him in the office of the Provost Marshal.

Q. Di t he not state to you any description of what took place at the meeting? A. Yes; I recollect his saying that Booth not angry at him because he said if the thing was not done that week he would withdraw, and that Booth then said he ought to be shot, and he replied it took two to play at that game.

Q. Did he not say t. you that he then withdrew from the arrangement, and accepted a position with John W. Walton, at Fortress Monroe? A. Yes sir.

Q. Did he state the exact date when that meeting was held at Washington? A. He may have done so but I cannot recollect it.

Q. Did he tell you that he had seen Booth since that night? A. I d n't recollect whether he said he had seen Booth since that evening, but he said he would not have any connection with things if it was not done during that week, and that Booth said he would be justified in shooting him if he should withdraw.

Cross-examined by Mr. Ewing.—Did he not state to you that he d.d afterwards withdraw? A. He may have said so, but I don't recollect.

Q. He said to you then that after that time he had had nothing further to do with the conspiracy? A. Yes, he said that.

Q. Did he say where he went then? A. He went to Fortress Monroe and accepted the position under Walton.

Q. Did he say what time he accepted it? A. The 1st day of April or the last day of March, I am not certain which.

Q. Did he not say this interview was at Gautier's, instead of the Lichten House? A. I may be mistaken, but I think he said the Lichten House: I knew he said it was in Louisiana avenue, between Sixth and Fourand-a-half streets.

Q. Did he say anything as to what had been the purpose of the parties a. ter the time he withdrew? A. He said the purpose of the party when he was a member of it, was to abduct the heads of the Government, so as to force the North to have an exchange of prisoners, or something to that effect; I asked him, also, what his part was to be in the conspiracy, and I think he said that he was to catch the President when he was thrown from the box of the theatre.

With t.e exception of O'Laughlin and Mrs. Surratt, all the prisoners jo ned in the laugh which the Idea of Arnold catching Mr. Lincoln in his arms naturally induced.

Q. Did he say anything as to his writing a letter to Booth, or as to Bo ath's importuning him to continue in the plot? A. There was a good deal of talking, and I don't recollect all that was said.

Q. Don't you recollect h.s saying that Booth went to his father's house twice after that, in order to get him to go on with the conspiracy? A. No sir; I do not recollect that.

Q. Did he say anything as to whom the arms belonged? A. I asked him where he got the arms, and he said Booth got the arms for the whole party.

Q. Didn't he say Booth told him when he left the conspiracy to sell the arms? A. Yes sir.

Q. To what arms was he then alluding? did you understand him as re'erring to the arms at his father's house, to the one pistol? A. Booth told him to sell the arms.

Q. Did you understand him to mean that the pistol was part of the arms that he had at his father's house, the same arms? A. Yes sir.

By Mr. Cox.—Did he state to you that that was the first and only meeting he ever attended? A. No sir; it was the first meeting, from what he told me.

Q. Did he tell you that the meeting came to the conclusion that the plot was impracticable? A. He said he did.

Q. Did he tell you that they did? Didn't he say that the scheme fell through because they all concluded it impracticable? A. He only said that he, individually, considered it so.

By Judge Holt.—Q. Did I understand you to say that the meeting itself had determined to abandon the attack on the President? A. No sir; only himself.

Q. State whether you found a rope in his carpet bag at Fortress Monroe. A. I don't recollect any.

Q. Did he not tell you what the date of the meeting was? A. He may have, but I don't recollect; it was a week or two before he went to Fortress Monroe; he might have said three weeks.

By Mr. Aiken.—Q. Was the name of Mrs. Surratt mentioned to you by Arnold? A. No sir, not to my recollection.

By Mr. Ewing.—Q. Did you examine his carpet bag at Fortress Monroe? A. Yes sir.

Q. You found no rope there? A. I don't recollect say.

Q. Did he not say to you that Booth had a letter of introduction to Mr. Queen or Dr. Mudd? A. No sir, I understood him to say and Dr. Mudd.

Q. Which Dr. Mudd? A. There is only one, I think, in Charles county.

Q. Did he speak of Mr. Queen or Dr. Mudd? A. Dr. Queen and Dr. Mudd.

Testimony of Mr. Thomas.

Q. State whether or not you are acquainted with the prisoner at the bar, Dr. Mudd? A. I am, sir.

Q. State whether or not some weeks since, before the assassination of the President, you saw him and had a conversation with him. A. Yes sir.

Q. Where did it occur? A. At Mr. Downey's.

Q. In that conversation did he speak of the President of the United States? A. He said that the President of the United States was an Abolitionist, and that the whole Cabinet were such, and that the South would not be subjugated under Abolition doctrine: he said the whole Cabinet would be killed within six or seven weeks and every Union man in Baltimore; he made a remark to me that I was no be ter than they were.

Q. Was he silent in his manner? A. He was not much excited.

Q. Did you have any conversation with him about politics? A. I made the remark that the war would soon be over; that South Carolina and Richmond were taken, and we would soon have peace; then he went on stating that the South never would be subjugated; that the President and Cabinet were all Abolitionists and would be killed, and every Union man in the State of Maryland.

Cross-examination by Mr. Stone.—Q. How far is your place from Dr. Mudd's? A. About a mile and a half.

Q. Did you see him frequently? A. Not very.

Q. Was Mr. Downey present when you had this conversation? A. I believe he was out, sir.

Q. How long did he remain out? A. I am not able to say precisely.

Q. Did you have any conversation with Dr. Mudd before Mr. Downey left the room? A. I believe I had.

Q. He left while you were conversing? A. Yes sir.

Q. How did that conversation commence? A. It commenced about the war. I said the war would soon be over, and that I was glad to see it.

Q. Had you been discussing the question of exempting persons from military service? A. No sir.

Q. Nothing was said about that? A. Not a word.

Q. When did this conversation occur? A. Sometime in March; in the latter part of March.

Q. What was said after Downey's return? A. I asked him, as he had taken the oath of allegiance, whether he considered it binding; he said he was a loyal man, but he didn't consider the oath binding.

Q. Had you been at Downey's any other time during the year? A. That was the only time sir.

Q. How long did you remain there that day? A. Half o r three-quarters of an hour, perhaps.

Q. Was not Dr. Mudd's manner jocose? A. No sir.

Q. Did he seem to be in earnest? A. It is impossible for me to say whether he was in earnest or not.

Q. Did it leave any serious impression upon your mind? A. No sir, I didn't suppose such a thing could come to pass; I went home and repeated what he said, and we all laughed at it; I thought that the man had more sense than to use such an expression.

Q. Did Mudd look as if he really believed it himself? A. When he first said it I couldn't think that he meant it, but after the President was killed, and Booth had been at his house, I thought that he meant it.

Q. Did he tell you how the President and the Cabinet were to be killed? A. No sir.

Q. If you had supposed that there was any conspiracy would you not have given the information to the authorities? A. I did.

Q. Who to? A. To everybody I saw.

Q. Can you name any one you told it to? A. Yes sir; I told it t o my brothers, I told it to Watson, I told it to many persons in Woodville, I told it to old Peter Wood.

Q. But did you give any information to any one in authority? A. I wrote to Colonel Holland about it, the Provost Marshal of the Fifth Congressional District in Maryland.

Q. When? A. One week af.er he said it.

Q. Did you get an answer? A. No sir, and I came to the conclusion that the Colonel never received my letter.

Q. You are sure the conversation you have detailed is all that occurred? A. Yes sir.

Q. Who left first? A. We left about the same time.

Q. Did you go together? A. No; I went home, and he went to his house, I guess.

Q. When Mr. Downey returned didn't Dr. Mudd say to him that you had been calling the Rebel army our army? A. No sir nothing of the sort.

Q. Did you mention this conversation to your brother before the assassination? A. Yes sir.

Q. To which of your brothers? A. To Dr. John C. Thomas.

Q. Did you mention it to Mr. Watson before the assassination? A. Yes sir.

Q. What is his full name? A. Lemuel Watson.

Q. You spoke of Mr. Wood; was it Peter Wood, Sr.? A. Yes, the old man, sir.

Q. Did you mention it to him before or after the assassination? A. After, sir.

TRIAL OF THE ASSASSINS AT WASHINGTON.

Q. Mr. Downey didn't seem to think anything of this talk of Dr. Mudds? A. I told you he was not there at the time, sir, and when I mentioned it to him he said he was glad he did not hear anything about it.

Testimony of John Hopp.

Q. Look at that paper, and state if you have seen it before. Here the witness read the following telegram: "To M. O'Laughlin, No. 57 N. Exeter street, Baltimore, Md:—Don't you fear to neglect your business. You had better come at once. J. BOOTH."
Q. State whether you are a telegraphic operator in this city? A. I am a clerk in the office.
Q. State whether this despatch was sent at the time of its date? A. Yes sir; it was, but the paper should be 1865, and not 1864; that's one of the old printed forms.
Q. Do you know the handwriting of John Wilkes Booth? A. Yes sir; I saw him write that.
Cross-examined by Mr. Cox.—Q. "Don't you fear to neglect your business; you had better come at once." Can you tell me whether this is a question or a command?
Objected to, and the question was waived.

Testimony of E. C. Stewart.

Q. State whether you are a telegraphic operator in this city? A. Yes sir, at the Metropolitan Hotel.
Q. Look at this despatch and state whether you have any knowledge of its having been sent? A. Yes, I sent it myself. The witness reads:—
"March 27th, 1864, M. O'Laughlin, No. 59 Exeter street, Baltimore, Md. Get word to Sam. and come in with or without him on Wednesday morning. We sell that day sure. Don't fail. J. Wilkes Booth."
Q. Is this last March or last March a year ago? A. Last March; that is one of the old forms.
Q. Did you know this man? A. No sir.
Here a photograph of John Wilkes Booth was shown to the witness, who, on seeing it, said:—"That's the man that sent it."
Cross-examined by Mr. Cox.—Q. You know it was sent in March, 1865? A. Yes sir.
Q. It is dated 1864? A. That's one of the old forms; but I remember it was sent this year.
Q. Is that your indorsement on it? A. Yes sir.
Q. How long have you been an operator at the Metropolitan Hotel? A. About ten months.
By Judge Holt.—Q. You were not there in March, 1864? A. No sir.
The examination of this witness being concluded, the Court adjourned till 10 o'clock to-morrow morning.

WASHINGTON, May 19.—The witnesses for the defense were to-day dismissed until Monday. About twenty have thus far been summoned. The United States have probably thirty more witnesses to examine, and as the effort will be made to conclude the testimony for the prosecution to-morrow, the trial will probably be closed next week.

Testimony of Colonel J. H. Taylor.

By Judge Holt.—Q. State whether you are connected with the Provost Marshal's office at Washington? A. No sir; I am on duty at the head-quarters of the Department at Washington.
Q. Look at that paper, marked No. 7, and state whether you ever before had it in your hands, and from whom you received it? (The paper referred to was one taken from the trunk of J. Wilkes Booth, and in regard to which the witness, Lieutenant Tyrrell, testified that it was written in the cipher of the Confederate States.) A. I have had it in my hands; I received it from Lieutenant Tyrrell, an officer on duty in the Provost Marshal's office, on the night of the 14th of April; I gave it to Colonel Wells on the 15th.
Q. You received it from Lieutenant Tyrrell as one of the papers found in the trunk of J. Wilkes Booth? A. Yes sir; for which I had sent him.

Testimony of Charles Rosch.

By Judge Advocate Holt.—Q. Do you recognize the prisoner, Edward Spangler? A. I do not know him personally; I was not present at his arrest.
Q. Did you go to his house after his arrest? A. Yes sir.
Q. What did you find there? A. A carpet bag, in which was a piece of rope, which I measured afterwards and found to be eighty-one feet in length; the twist appeared to have been taken out of it; there was nothing else in the carpet bag except some blank paper and a dirty shirt collar.
Q. Where was that carpet bag with the rope left? A. At the house where Spangler took his meals, on the N. W. corner of Seventh and H street.
Q. When was it left? A. That I do not know.
Q. Who were with you when you took the rope? A. Two of the military of the Provost Marshal's force; I do not know their names.
Q. You did not see Spangler himself there? A. I did not; I was to go with the other officers to secure the papers, and we missed him; consequently I was not there when he was arrested.
Q. Had the carpet bag been opened? A. No sir; we made out to open it with some keys we found.

Cross-examined by Mr. Ewing.—Q. Where is the house at which you found the carpet bag? A. It is situated on the northwest corner of Seventh street and H street.
Q. Who gave it to you? A. We took it when we found it belonged to Spangler.
Q. Who was there? A. A man who was commonly called "Jake," who worked at the theatre in company with Spangler; this man told me that was Spangler's carpet bag, and that was all that Spangler had at the house.
Q. What persons were living or staying in the house. Did you see? A. There were a couple of persons, boarders, I presume, I did not know any of the parties.
Q. In what room did you find the carpet bag? A. In a bed room up stairs.
Q. In what part of the house? A. As near as I can judge, it was on the south side of the house; that is, the room faced the south.
Q. Describe the room? A. It was right near where Jake kept his trunk.
The Commission reassembled at two o'clock, after the usual recess.

Testimony of Chas. H. Rosch, Continued.

Q. Look at that coil of rope and state whether or not it is the same which you found in Spangler's carpet bag? A. (Looking at the rope.) I believe and am satisfied that it is.
Q. What did you do with the monkey wrench? A. I found no monkey wrench; I would here beg leave of the Court to correct so much of the testimony as refers to the locality which I stated; upon reflection I am convinced that the house was on the northeast corner of Seventh and H streets; the room was on the second floor.
Q. What was the number of the room. A. There was no number.

Testimony of Wm. Eaton, (Continued.)

Q. State to the Court whether you arrested the prisoner, Edward Spangler, and on what day? A. I arrested him; I do not recollect the day; it was the week after the assassination.
Q. Where did you arrest him? A. In a house on Seventh street, near the Patent Office; it must have been on the southeast corner of Seventh street and H.
Q. Do you know whose house it was? A. I do not.
Q. Did you find any weapons in his possession? A. No sir, I did not search him.
Q. Was it his boarding-house? A. I think it was.
Q. Who was with him? A. There were some ladies in the house.

Testimony of William Wallace.

By the Judge Advocate.—Q. State whether or not some time after the assassination of the President you arrested the prisoner, O'Laughlin? A. I did; on the 17th of April.
Q. Where? A. At the house of a family named Bailey, in High street, Baltimore.
Q. Was that his boarding house? A. I think not; I think his boarding house, or the house where he stopped, was that of his brother-in-law, No. 57 Exeter street.
Q. Did you ask him why he was there instead of his boarding house? A. I did; he said that when he arrived in town on Saturday he was told that the officers had been looking for him; and that he went away to the house of a friend of his, where he stopped on Saturday or Sunday night.
Q. Did he ask you what you had arrested him for? A. He seemed to understand what it was for.
Q. Did he ask you at all in regard to the cause? A. Nothing that occurs to my mind at present.
Q. Did he speak of the assassination of the President at all? A. He spoke of it as being a very bad affair.
Q. Did you find any arms in his possession? A. No sir; we searched him and found none whatever.
Cross-examined by Mr. Fox.—Q. Did the brother-in-law of the prisoner send for the prisoner or go with you to arrest him?
Judge Bingham objected to the question.
Mr. Cox stated that the object was to show that the brother-in-law of the prisoner went after him voluntarily.
Judge Bingham replied that the question was not properly a portion of the cross-examination, but was altogether new matter. What the prisoner said to his brother-in-law had not been offered in evidence, and, in addition to that, it had been shown that the prisoner had resolved not to be taken at home, and was going to change his boarding-house.
Mr. Cox.—The object of the prosecution, I presume, is to show that the purpose of the prisoner in changing his lodgings was to avoid arrest, the witness having testified that the prisoner was found elsewhere. I desire to ask him whether he found the prisoner at the instance of his (the prisoner's) brother-in-law.
The objection was overruled, the Commission deciding that the question should be answered.
A. The prisoner's brother-in-law, Mr. Mallsby, I am well acquainted with; he was recommended to me on Sunday evening as being a good Union man, as one to whom I could place confidence; he knew I was looking for Mr. O'Laughlin; I told him I wished him to assist me; he said that anything he could do to assist

LEWIS C. PAYNE.　　　DAVID C. HAROLD.

THE SCENE OF THE GREAT TRAGEDY.

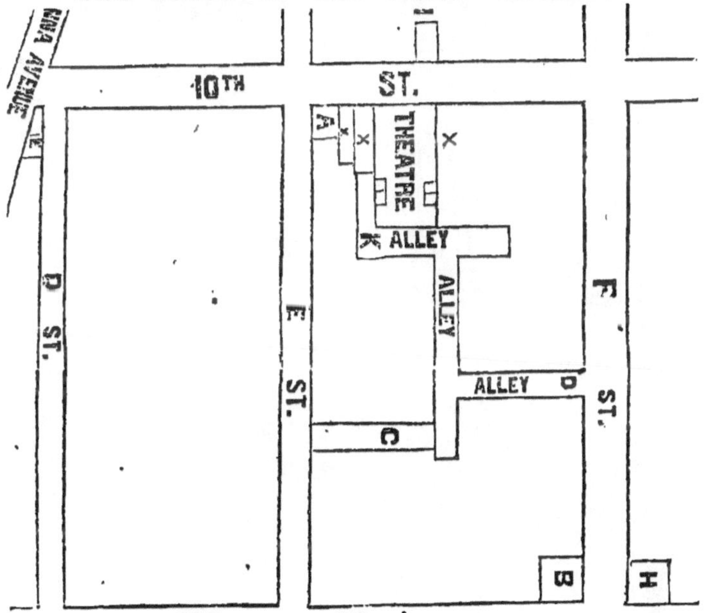

A—Public School.　B—Herndon House, (Hotel).
C—The only vacant lot communicating with alley
D—The only alley outlet to F street.
E—Bank (formerly Savings Bank).
X—Restaurants.　G—Newspaper Office.
H—Model House.
I—House taken to after the act.
K—The alley by which the murderer escaped.

(5)

TRIAL OF THE ASSASSINS AT WASHINGTON. 71

me he would do; that if he could get any information concerning the prisoner he would impart it to me; that on Sunday evening or Monday morning he came to me and told me that he thought if I went with him we could find O'Laughlin; I then went with him and arrested the prisoner.

Q. Did the prisoner say anything about having received any information as to whether the detectives had been at his house? A. I think he said that when he got to his house on Saturday afternoon he heard that they had been there.

Q. Did he protest his innocence of the crime? A. He said he knew nothing whatever about it.

Q. D'd he say he could show his innocence by the persons with whom he had been in company? A. He said he could account for his whereabouts all the time that he was in Washington, through parties who were there with him.

Q. Did he say he left home after being advised that detectives were there after him? A. I do not remember that he said so.

Testimony of James Gifford.

By the Judge Advocate.—Q. State whether you have been connected with Ford's Theatre in this city, and in what capacity? A. I have been in the capacity of builder.

Q. You were the carpenter of the building? A. Yes sir.

Q. Did you occupy that position on the 14th and 15th of April last? A. Yes sir.

Q. Did you observe the President's box on that day? A. No sir; I was not in it.

Q. Do you recollect having seen any one in it? A. Well, I saw Mr. Harry Clay Ford in it at one time, and Mr. Reybold.

Q. Any one else? A. No sir.

Q. Did you observe a large rocking chair which was in the President's box on the day of the 14th? A. I did not notice it on the 14th.

Q. When did you see it? A. I saw it on the following Sunday in the box.

Q. Do you know when it was placed in the box, and by whom? A. I do not.

Q. Do you know whether it was ever there before? A. I do not think it has been there before during this season; I saw it last season.

Q. Do you know who took it away? A. No sir.

Q. Do you know whether the stage scenes remain now as they were on the morning of the assassination The witness' reply was somewhat inaudible at the reporter's desk, but he was understood to say that with the exception of a slight disarrangement which had been made by order of the Secretary of War in order to secure a view of the stage, the scenes were in the same position as on the morning of the assassination.

Q. Have you examined the wall in the President's box? A. Yes sir.

Q. When did you examine it? A. I think it was on Monday morning after the assassination when I first saw it.

Q. You had not seen it before? A. No sir.

Q. When had you been in the box last? A. I cannot state positively; I judge it was within a week.

Q. Do you think that if the mortice had been there, you would have observed it? A. Yes sir, I should think so.

Q. Had it the appearance of having been very recently made? A. It looked so to me.

Q. By what instrument would you suppose it to have been made? A. I should think it was made by a knife.

Q. Would it not require a good while to make it with a knife? It is quite a large mortice? A. It would require a man some fifteen minutes, I should judge.

Q. If the three doors of the place were all closed it would have been entirely dark there, would it not? A. Yes sir.

Q. Do you not think that one or more of those doors must have been opened when this mortice was made? A. It might have been so; some light would have been required, I should think.

Q. Would not such an operation, made with an open door, be likely to attract the attention of persons connected with the theatre? A. If a knife were used it would not; if a chisel or hammer were used, they would create sounds.

Q. What were the duties of the prisoner, Spangler? A. He worked on the stage, made scenery, fixed up the stage &c.

Q. Was the decoration of this box within the line of his duties? A. No sir; there was a gentleman there by the name of Reybold, who was an upholsterer, whose duty it was to decorate the box, but he had a stiff neck, so he told me afterwards; when I asked him if I did not see him in the box he said, yes, but I did not decorate it.

Q. Where were you at the moment of the assassination of the President? A. I was standing about ten feet from the centre of the big lamp, just at the edge of the platform.

Q. On the stage? A. No sir; in front of the house, outside; I came out to the front of the house after having been in three or four minutes.

Q. You allude to the front part of the theatre? A. Yes sir.

Q. Had you been behind the scenes? A. Yes sir.

Q. How long before? A. About twenty minutes before.

Q. While there did you see the prisoner, Spangler? A. Yes sir.

Q. What was he doing? A. He was on the left hand side; I came out before the curtain and went up; he was willing to transact his business, which was scene shifting.

Q. Was it not usual for the passage way which leads to the back door to be kept entirely free of obstructions while a piece was being played? A. The outside passage was always kept free; the entrances were more or less filled with chairs and tables, though that depended on what was being played; sometimes, as in pieces where a large number of seats were used, the passages became jammed up.

Q. Do you know who made the mortice on the bar which was found there? A. I do not.

Cross-examined by Mr. Ewing.—A paper, which purported to be a plan of the interior of the theatre, was shown to the witness, with the request that he should state whether it was correctly drawn. The witness pointed out that it was deficient in several particulars.

Q. State whether the passage-way across the stage to the outer door, was ordinarily obstructed during the play? A. Only by people when there was a large company on the stage, there were never any chairs, tables or scenery in the way.

Q. Was it not necessary to keep the passage-way clear in order to allow the actors and actresses to pass without obstruction from the dressing room to the stage? A. Yes sir.

Q. How is the back door, the small one, usually left? A. It is usually left open after the performance is over.

Q. Do you mean that it is swinging open or merely unlocked? A. Left unlocked; the only door that is left open is the door leading to the side of the house.

Q. State what position Mr. Spangler occupied during the performance. A. His business was on the left hand side of the stage, the right hand from the audience.

Q. Was that on the side of the President's box? A. Yes.

Q. State at what times during the performance you were on the stage that night? A. I was on the stage until the curtain went up, when it was lowered I came around on the stage to see that everything was right.

Q. State at what times during the evening when you came on the stage between the acts you saw Mr. Spangler? A. I could not state the time exactly, I judge that the last time I saw him was about half-past nine o'clock.

Q. State whether you saw him each time? A. Yes sir, each time.

Q. He was your subordinate, was he not? A. Yes sir.

Q. State where you were during that play when you were not on the stage? A. I was in the front of the house; I walked down to H street and Tenth to look at a big lamp which I had put up there; during the performance of the first act I walked up to the corner of Tenth street and F, and took a glass of ale, during the second act and during the third act I did not leave the house at all.

Q. You were then in front of the theatre part of the time between the second and third act? A. I was on the stage between the acts.

Q. Where were you during the performance of the second act? A. To the best of my knowledge I was then in the front.

Q. All the time? A. Not all the time.

Q. How much of the time? A. Well I do not know; I walked in and stayed, may be, five or ten minutes and walked out.

Q. State whether or not you saw the prisoner, Spangler, at any time during that play, in front of the theatre? A. I did not; I do not think he could have been in front of the theatre without my knowing it, because the scene would have gone wrong if he had left the stage.

Q. Did you ever see Spangler wear a moustache? A. No sir; he never wore one since I knew him.

Q. Do you know how he was dressed that evening? A. No sir; I did not take any notice of him.

Q. How was he dressed ordinarily? A. About the same as he is now.

Q. Was not the *American Cousin* a play in which the scenes were shifted a good deal? A. They were what we call plain scenes; there was not much shifting; I believe there were some five or six scenes in each act.

Q. Then Spangler's presence there would have been indispensable to the performance? A. Yes sir; if he had not been there the scenes would not have gone on.

Q. Did you hear Booth call Spangler that night? A. No sir.

Q. What had Spangler to do with Booth? A. Nothing, that I know of; Booth was rather friendly, and everybody about the house was friendly with him; he had a winning way about him that would make every person like him; he was a good natured, jovial kind of man.

Q. Was he not very much in the habit of frequenting the theatre? A. I would see him there for a week, then he would go off and I would not see him for a couple of weeks.

Q. Did he not have access to the theatre as one of the employees would have? A. Yes sir.

Q. He had access by the back entrance at any time? A. Yes sir, at any time when the employees might go in.
Q. Day and night? A. At any time when the house was not locked up.
Q. Was not Spangler a sort of a drudge for Booth? A. He appeared so; he used to go down and help fix Booth's horses; I have seen him myself once or twice fixing up the horse.
Q. Was that hole in the wall cut into the brick? A. No sir, I believe not; to the best of my knowledge it was cut in only an inch.
Q. And it could have been done with a pen-knife? A. Yes sir; I think it might have been done with a pen-knife.
The witness was here shown the stick or bar found in the President's box, which, however, he failed to identify in any manner.
Q. How long would it have taken with an ordinary pocket knife to cut the hole in the wall of which you have spoken? A. I suppose that a man intent upon mischief, would have done it in ten or fifteen minutes; after the face of the plaster was once broken it could be accomplished very easily.
Q. I believe you stated that you did not know how the lock in the door of the President's box came to be loose? A. I do not know.
Q. When did you first hear that the President was coming to the theatre? A. I heard it between 11 and 12 o'clock on that day.
Q. Do you know whether he was invited to the theatre? A. I do not.

Testimony of Mrs. Martha Murray.

By Judge Holt.—Q. Look at the prisoners at the bar and see if you can recognize any of them? A. I have not seen any of them, unless it is that gentleman (pointing to Payne, who was directed to stand up); he has the same appearance of a man I saw.
Q. Was he the person of whom you speak a boarder at your house? A. Yes sir.
Q. Under what name did he pass? A. I did not hear any name; when Mr McDevitt came to the house afterwards I showed him the name on the book which I thought was entered when he came there, and Mr. McDevitt cut the name out of the book; I cannot remember what the name was.
Q. How long did he remain there? A. He came on Friday and left on Friday, two weeks afterwards.
Q. You keep the Herndon House, do you not? A. My husband does.
Q. Was the Friday on which he left the 14th of April last? A. Yes, the day the President was killed.
Q. What time in the day did he leave? A. About 4 o'clock; we had dinner at half-past 4; this gentleman said he was going away, and wanted to settle his bill, and wished dinner before the regular dinner hour; I gave orders to have an early dinner given him; I never saw anything further concerning him.
Q. Did he come to your house as an invalid? A. No; he said he came from the cars about 11 or 12 o'clock.
Q. Did he come alone, or with others? A. He came alone.
Q. Was he visited by others while there? A. I expect he was.
Q. Would you be able to recognize any person who visited him? Look at the prisoners. A. I do not see any one I could recognize; I never noticed any one, but one evening when at the supper table this gentleman came in; I had finished my supper, and got up, and did not pay any further attention; I left them sitting at the table.
Q. Had any one spoken to you for a room for this man before he came? A. No, not to my knowledge; some gentlemen have spoken to me for rooms, but I do not recollect any one speaking for this man.
Q. Do you remember whether John H. Surratt called at your house? A. I do not know him; I never heard of him in this circumstance.
Cross-examined by Mr. Doster.—Q. State to the Court the location of the Herndon House. A. It is on the corner opposite the Patent Office.

Testimony of Wm. R. Wells (Colored.)

By Judge Holt.—Q. State whether or not on the 14th of April last you were living in the house of Mr. Seward, Secretary of State, and if so in what capacity? A. I was in the capacity of a waiter.
Q. Look at the prisoners at the bar, and see if you recognize either of them. A. Yes, I recognize that man (pointing to Payne.)
Q. Did he attempt to come into the house of Mr. Seward on the night of the 14th of April? A. He did.
Q. State the circumstances connected with his entrance into the house. A. When he came he rang the bell and I went to the door, and then man came in; he had a little package in his hand, and said it was medicine from Dr. Verdi; he said he was sent by Dr. Verdi with particular directions how he was to take the medicine, and he said he must go up; I told him he could not go up; he then repeated the words over a good while, telling me he must go up, "must see him, must see him." I told him he could not go up, that it was against my orders; that if he would give me the medicine I would tell him how to take it if he would leave me the directions; he said that would not do,

and I started to go up, and finding he would go up I started past him and went up the stairs before him. I asked him to excuse me; I thought perhaps he would say that I refused to let him come up. I thought perhaps he might be sent by Dr. Verdi, and that he would tell Mr. Seward that I tried to stop him; he said, "All right," I noticed that his step was very heavy, and I asked him not to walk so heavy, he would disturb Mr. Seward; he met Mr. Frederick Seward on the steps outside the door, and had some conversation with him in the hall.
Q. If you heard that conversation state it? A. He said to Mr. Fred. Seward that he wanted to see Mr. Seward; Mr. Fred. Seward told him that he could not see his father; that his father was asleep at that time, to give him the medicine and he would take it to his father; that would not do; he said he must see him, he must see him; Mr. Fred. said, "you cannot see him, you cannot see him;" he kept on saying he must see him; Mr. Fred. says, "I am the proprietor here, I am Mr. Seward's son; if you cannot leave it with me you cannot leave it all;" he had a little more talk, and still holding the little package in his hand; Mr. Fred. would not let him see him any way; he started towards the steps as if to go down, and I started to go down before him; I had gone about three steps, and turned around, saying "do not walk so heavy;" by the time I had turned round he jumped back and struck Mr. Frederick Seward, and by the time I had turned clear around, Mr. Frederick Seward had fallen, and thrown up his hands, then I ran down stairs and called "murder." I went to the front door and cried murder; I then ran down to General Augur's head-quarters at the corner; I saw no guard there, and ran back; by that time three soldiers had come out of the building and followed me; I had got about half way back to the house when I saw the man run out and get on his horse; he had on a light overcoat, and no hat, but he had on a hat when he came into the house; I had not seen the horse at all before I halloed to the soldiers "there he is getting on his horse;" he got on his horse and started off, and I followed him as far as the corner of I and Fifteen-and-a-half streets; between on Vermont avenue, and I lost sight of him there.
Q. Did you see with what he struck Mr. Fred. Seward? A. I did not exactly see whatever it was; it appeared to be round and wound with velvet; I took it to be a knife afterwards.
Q. How many times did he strike him? A. I saw him raise his hand twice; I did not wait to see how many times he hit him; he hit him twice, and then I ran down stairs.
Q. Did this man say anything as he struck him? A. When he jumped back again he just said to him, "You," and hit him over the head; that is all I heard him say.
Q. Was Dr. Verdi Mr. Seward's family physician? A. He was.
Q. Did Payne advise you in talking to you? A. No, he did not say much to me; he only kept saying "Must see him," and walking very slowly forward all the time.
Q. Had you ever seen this man before, that you know of? A. No; never that I know of.
Q. When you came out did you observe any person about the door or pavement? A. No sir; no one at all.
Q. You did not observe his horse? A. I did not see any horse at all.
Q. How far from him were you at any time after he mounted his horse? A. I might have been as far as from here to that door, about twenty feet.
Q. Did you see the color of the horse? A. He appeared a bay horse, very stout; he did not appear to be a very hardy horse, and did not appear to be going very fast till he got to I street, and then he got away from me altogether.
Cross-examined by Mr. Doster.—Q. How old are you? A. I don't know exactly; I reckon between thirteen and twenty.
Q. How long had you been at Mr. Seward's? A. Three months.
Q. Have you ever been to school? A. Yes, four or five years.
Q. Where precisely was this man standing when you had this conversation with him? A. He was just inside the door; I had closed the door.
Q. Did he give you the package of medicine at any time? A. He did not hand it to me.
Q. You say he talked rough to you? A. He did not talk rough; he had a very fine voice when he came in.
Q. You say you recognize that man as the prisoner at the bar; state what there is about the man that resembles the man you saw that night? A. I noticed his hair, his pantaloons and his boots; that night he was talking to Mr. Fred. Seward nearly five minutes; he had on very heavy boots, black pants, light overcoat and a brown hat; his face was very red at the time he came in; he had very coarse black hair.
Q. Have you seen the same boots on this man? A. Yes, the night they captured him.
Q. Have you seen the same clothes on him? A. I have seen the same pantaloons; he had on black pantaloons.
Q. And would you infer from the fact that he wore black pants that it was the same man? A. No, I know his face.

TRIAL OF THE ASSASSINS AT WASHINGTON. 73

Q. What points about his face besides his hair did you notice? A. I noticed when he talked no kind of raised the corner of his lip and showed a wrinkle in his jaw, as though his teeth were very tight; I knew him the moment I saw him.

Q. Did he talk when you recognized him the first time? A. He did not talk then, but I noticed the raising of his lip that I had seen when he was talking with me.

Q. When have you seen the prisoner before since the night of the assassination? A. I saw him on the 17th at General Augur's head-quarters.

Q. How did you happen to go there to see him? A. They sent for me to the house; Mr. Webster and another gentleman came for me.

Q. What did they say to you? A. He sent a man up to the room where I was, and asked me to get up; I asked him what they wanted; it was in the night, about two or three o'clock; he said Mr. Webster wanted me; I had been getting up every night since the thing happened, and I asked him to ask Mr. Webster to come up to my room; I was tired of getting up at night; when I got up and saw Mr. Webster, he told me he wanted me to go down to General Augur's; I went down there; there was a light, very bright, in the hall at the time; they asked me how light it was at Mr. Seward's that night; I told them it was not light in our hall, that the burner did not give but very little light; they asked me what kind of a looking man the one was who came to see Mr. Seward; I told them he had black hair, thin lips, a fine voice, very tall and broad across the shoulders; there were about twenty or thirty gentlemen in there; they brought in one man and asked me if he was the one, and then brought in another; neither looked like him, and I told them no; they then opened the middle door, and this man came walking in; at the door the light was turned up very bright; as soon as I saw him, I put my finger right on his face, and said, " I know him, that was the man."

Q. Did either of the two men they showed you before look like the man? A. No, one had moustaches, the other whiskers.

Q. Were they as tall as this man? A. No, they were short; they did'nt look at all like this man.

Q. Had you at that time heard of any reward for the apprehension of the supposed assassin of Mr. Seward? A. Yes, I had heard of a reward for the different ones, but I had not heard of a reward offered for this one, and have not yet; I saw a bill posted up the next morning from General Augur's head-quarters, offering a reward, but not for this man.

Q. Did any one offer you money before for this man's apprehension? A. No sir.

Q. Did anybody threaten you? A. No sir.

Q. When the prisoner struck Mr. Seward and you went down stairs, did you find any soldiers there? A. No; the passage was free; the door was closed; I went down, opened the door, and kept on down to the corner.

Q. What kind of a pace had the horse when he rode away? A. It seemed as if he went very slow at first, for I kept up with him till he got to I street; then he went off at a rapid rate.

Testimony of Sergt. George F. Robinson.

By Judge Holt.—Q. State whether or not, on the night of the 14th of April last, you were at the residence of Wm. H. Seward, Secretary of State? A. I was.

Q. In what capacity there? A. In attendance as nurse upon Mr. Seward.

Q. Look at the prisoners here and see if you recognize either of them as having been at that house that evening? A. I see one of them who looks like him; the one in his shirt (pointing to Payne).

Q. State the circumstances attending the encounter between the person of whom you speak and Mr. Seward? A. The first I saw of him I heard a scuffling in the hall; I opened the door to see what the trouble was; as I opened the door he stood close up to it; as soon as it was opened wide enough he struck me and knocked me partially down and then rushed up to the bed of Mr. Seward, struck him and maimed him; as soon as I could get on my feet I endeavored to haul him off the bed and he turned on me; in the scuffle there was a man come into the room who clutched him; between the two of us we got him to the door, or by the door, when he clinched his hand around my neck, knocked me down, broke away from the other man and rushed down stairs.

Q. What did he strike you with? A. He struck me with his fist the last time; the first time with a knife.

Q. Did he stab you, and if so, where? A. Yes, here (pointing to about the centre of his forehead).

Q. Did he say anything when he struck you? A. He did not that I heard.

Q. Did he pass immediately to the bed of Mr. Seward when he first knocked you down? A. He did.

Q. Did you see him strike Mr. Seward? A. I did.

Q. With the same weapon he struck you with? A. Yes.

Q. How often? A. I saw him cut twice.

Q. Did he seem to be cutting at his head or where? A. He struck beyond the head and neck the first time; then he struck him in the neck.

Q. Describe how he held the knife? A. He held it in this way (raising the hand which held the knife, pointing downwards).

Q. Did it seem to be a large knife? A. It did.

Q. Did he say anything at all after stabbing him? A. Not that I heard.

Q. Did you observe the wound that had been inflicted? A. I did.

Q. Look at this knife and see if it is the same one held in his hand? A. It was about the length of that. It looked as though it might not be as wide as that, but I only saw it in motion.

Q. Describe the character of the wounds inflicted on Mr. Seward? A. There was one cutting his face down on the left side, and another one cutting his neck below. I think they were both made by the same blow. He was sitting partially up in bed at the time, his head reclining so that the same blow might have made both. The other cut was on the opposite side of the neck. There were three wounds in all. It was all bloody when I saw it. I do not know but there may have been more.

Q. Was Mr. Seward in his bed at the time? A. He was.

Q. From what cause? A. He had been thrown from his carriage.

Q. Were his limbs broken? A. I was told that one of his arms was broken and his jaw fractured.

Q. While striking him did Mr. Seward get out of his bed or remain in bed? A. He remained and received the stabs in bed.

Q. Did he during the struggle roll from the bed or remain in bed? A. He rolled out after we had left the bed; when I came back I found he was lying on the floor.

Q. You say that this man, during the whole of this bloody work, made no remark at all; that he said nothing? A. I did not hear him make any remark.

Q. When he came out of the room had Frederick Seward risen from the floor, or was he still lying? A. I did not see Mr. Frederick Seward around at all.

Q. Where was he when this man came out? A. The first I saw of Mr. Frederick he was in the room standing up; he had come inside the door.

Q. You say he knocked you down when he came into the room; what did he strike you with? A. I suppose with a knife; he struck me the last time with his fist; he and his arm around my neck and let go and struck me.

Q. Did he immediately go down stairs? A. He did.

Q. Did you see his encounter with Major Seward? A. I did not see that.

Q. After he left was any thing picked up which he left behind? A. There was, a revolver and his hat.

Q. Look at this revolver and see if you recognize it as the one he left? A. I should judge it was; I did not notice this in it (pointing to the rammer).

Q. I understand the Mr. Seward you speak of to be the Secretary of State, and the house you speak of to be in Washington city? A. Yes sir.

Q. Do you recognize this as the hat that was picked up?

A light-brown felt slouch hat was shown. General Wallace requested that the hat produced might be tried on Payne. It was handed to Payne's guard, who placed it on his head to the evident amusement of Payne himself.

"General Wallace said, "Does it fit loosely?" The guard replied, "No, it fits tight."

Mr. Doster, (Payne's counsel), "It is too small for him, I should say," (laughter.)

Testimony of Major A. H. Seward.

Examined by Judge Holt.—Q. State whether you are the son of Wm. H. Seward, Secretary of State? A. I am his son.

Q. Were you or not at his house on the night of the 14th of April last? A. I was.

Q. Will you state whether or not that night any one of the prisoners at the bar made his appearance at that house? A. Yes, I saw this large man who has no coat on (Payne).

Q. State the circumstances attending your meeting with him that evening? A. I retired to bed about 7 o'clock on the night of the 14th, with the understanding that I would be called at 11 o'clock, to set up with my father; I very shortly fell asleep, and so remained until wakened by the screams of my sister; I jumped out of bed and ran into my father's room in my shirt and drawers; the gas in the room had been shut down rather low, and I saw what appeared to be two men, one trying to hold the other; my first impression was that my father had become delirious, and that the nurse was trying to hold him. I went up and took hold of him, but saw at once from his size and the struggle that it was not my father; it then struck me that the nurse had become delirious and was striking about the room at random; knowing the delicate state of my father's health, I endeavored to shove the person I had hold of to the door, with the intention of putting him out of his room; while I was pushing him he struck me five or six times over the head with whatever he had in his left hand; I supposed it at the time to be a bottle or a decanter he had seized from the table; during this time he repeated with an intensely strong voice "I am mad, I am mad;" on reaching the hall he gave a sudden turn and breaking away from me, disappeared down stairs; while in the vicinity of the door of my father's room, as I was pushing him out, when he came opposite the light in the hall it shone on him, and I saw him distinctly; I saw that he was a very large man, with dark straight hair, smooth face and no beard; I noticed the expression of his countenance; I then went into my room and got my pistol which had to be taken out from the bottom of my carpet bag; I then went down stairs, intending to shoot the person if he attempted to return; while standing at the door the servant boy came back and said the man had ridden off on horseback; I then realized for the first time that the man was an assassin who had entered the house for the purpose of murdering my father!

Q. Did you then return to your father's room? A. I suppose it was five minutes before I got back; there was quite a crowd collected at the door; I sent for a doctor, and made arrangements to keep the crowd out; it may not have been three minutes.

Q. State whether you examined the number and character of the wounds given your father and brother, Mr. Fred. W. Seward? A. No, I did not examine them that night; I was beaten very badly myself; I found when I got up stairs again; after my father's wounds had been dressed and after my arm had been bandaged, I went in and saw my father; he had one very large gash on his right cheek, besides a cut on his throat, on the right side, and one under his left arm; I did not examine my brother's wounds; I did not know that night how badly he was hurt; the next day he was insensible and so remained, and it was four or five days before I saw what his wounds were.

Q. What did you then discover? A. There were two wounds about here (pointing to the left side of the head, over the ear); after the piece of the skull had been taken out it left the brain exposed.

Q. Had he received any stab at all from the knife? A. I never saw anything of my brother during the whole time.

Q. Did the wound indicate that a knife had been used? A. I thought myself it was done by a knife, but the surgeon seemed to think it was done by the hammer of the pistol; it was such a wound as I would have supposed might have been done with a knife.

Q. Did you see a pistol picked up in that room? A. I did not; I know there was one picked up.

Q. Did you see any article of clothing? A. Yes, a hat.

Q. Would you recognize it? (producing a hat). A. Yes, I am quite certain that is the hat; I saw the hat after it had been picked up and put in a bureau drawer; it was taken out and shown to me the next day; I did not see it that night.

Q. And you say you supposed it to have been the nurse? A. Yes; I had no idea who the man was until he was out of the house.

Q. You say that you were struck with a knife? A. The surgeons think it was with a knife I was struck; I supposed at the time it was with a bottle or a decanter; that the nurse had become delirious and was striking at random.

Q. Do you feel entirely satisfied that the person at the bar is the same man? A. I do.

Cross-examined by Mr. Doster.—Q. Be good enough to state whether this is the first time you have seen the prisoner since he was taken? A. No; I saw him on board the monitor the day after he was taken.

Q. Did you identify him then? A. Yes.

Q. Please state the circumstances. A. He was brought up on the monitor; I took hold of him the same way I did in the room, and looked up in his face; he had the same features, with his size, his proportions, his swarthy face, and no beard that I noticed, and when he was made to repeat the words, "I am mad, I am mad," I recognized the same voice, varying only in intensity.

Testimony of Richard C. Morgan.

Examined by Judge Holt.—Q. State whether or not on the 17th or 18th of April last, you were in the service of the Government, and if so, in what capacity? A. I am in the service of the War Department, acting under the orders of Colonel Olcott.

Q. State whether on one or both of these days, you had possession of the house of the prisoner, Mrs. Surratt? A. Yes.

Q. State where that house is? A. No. 548 H street, city of Washington.

Q. State whether or not you took possession of the house, and what occurred there? A. About twenty minutes past 11 o'clock on the evening of the 17th of April, in company with other officers, I went to the house of Mrs. Surratt for the purpose of seizing the papers that might be found, and of arresting the inmates of the house; after we had been at the house about ten minutes, and Major Smith, Captain Wennerskerch, and some other officers, had arrested the inmates of the house, who were in the parlor all ready to come out, I had sent an officer for a carriage to take them away, when I heard a knock and a ring at the door at the same time; Captain Wennerskerch and myself went to the door and opened it; the prisoner, Payne, came in; he had a pickaxe in his hand; he had on a grey coat and black pants, a hat made out of the sleeves of a shirt, I judged; as soon as he

came in and immediately closed the door, he said, "I guess I am mistaken," said I, "who do you want to see?" He replied, "Mrs. Surratt;" said I, "you are right, walk in." He took a seat. I said, "what did you come here for, this time of night?" he said he came to dig a gutter; that Mrs. Surratt had sent for him; I asked him when and, he said in the morning; I asked him where he last worked, and he said somewhere on Ninth street; I asked him where he boarded, he said he had no boarding house, that he was a poor man, and earned his living with the pickaxe in his hand; I asked him how much he made a day, he said nothing at all sometimes, sometimes one dollar, and sometimes one dollar and fifty cents; "have you any money?" "Not a cent." I asked him why he came at this time of night? he said he came to see where it was to be dug, so that he could commence early in the morning; I said, have you had no previous acquaintance with Mrs. Surratt? he said, No; I said, why did she select you for this work? he replied, that she knew he was working in that neighborhood; that he was a poor man, and she came to him; I asked him how old he was, and he said about twenty; I asked him where he was from; he said from Fauquier county, Va.; previous to this he had pulled out an oath of allegiance, handed it to me and said, that will show you who I am; I contained the name of Louis Payne, Fauquier county, Va.; I asked him if he was from the South; he said he was; I asked him when he left there; he said two months ago, in February; I asked him why he left; he said that he had to leave or go into the army; that he preferred to earn his living with the pickaxe; I asked him if he could read; he said no; I asked him if he could write; he said he could manage to write his own name.

Q. Is that the pick-axe he had on his shoulder (producing the jack)? A. Yes; I then told him he would have to go to the Provost Marshal and explain; he moved a little at that, and did not answer; the carriage had arrived to take up the women; they were sent off, and Payne was also taken away in charge of officers; Major Smith, Captain Wennerskerch, and myself remained to search for papers; we did not leave till 3 o'clock the next morning.

Q. Did Mrs. Surratt leave the house before Payne came, or afterwards? A. They were preparing to leave and were in the parlor; Mrs. Surratt was directed to get the bonnets and shawls of the others, so that there should be no communication with each other; she did so and they were just ready to go and had started to go when we opened the door; I think they passed out as Payne came in.

Q. Then she did not see him before she left? A. Yes, she must have seen him as she passed on; I heard no conversation in regard to it.

Q. State what papers you found there? A. I found several paper and photographs.

Q. Did you find three photographs of J. Wilkes Booth? A. No; the next morning I was shown a photograph of J. Wilkes Booth, taken from her house, found behind a picture; we found photographs of Jeff. Davis, Alex. H. Stephens and of Beauregard; we also found a card picture with this upon it, "Thus will it ever be with traitors—the mighty sic semper tyrannis."

Q. Will you give the name of the man who found the photograph of Booth? A. I think it was Lieutenant Dempsey.

Q. Were you or not afterwards at the Provost Marshal's office? A. About three o'clock in the morning I was there; Mrs. Surratt had been there and had been taken to the Old Capitol Prison before my arrival.

Q. Did you hear Mrs. Surratt say anything in regard to the prisoner at any time? A. No.

Cross-examination by Mr. Aiken.—Q. Have you not been in the habit of seeing exhibited about the city in shop windows the photograph of J. Wilkes Booth? A. I never saw one of them before the assassination of the President.

Q. Have you not seen photographs of Jeff. Davis and other prominent leaders of the Rebellion exhibited in shop windows? A. I never had one of them in my hands until I found them at this house.

Q. Do you not know that they have been so exhibited? A. I have not seen any since the Rebellion.

Q. Were not those photographs of which you speak found in a traveling sack? A. No, I am positive of that.

Q. Were any of the photographs found in that bag? A. No, they were found in portfolios and on the mantelpiece.

Q. State if Mrs. Surratt made any remarks in regard to Payne. A. As she passed out it now comes to my recollection that she made some remark to Major Smith, but I did not hear what it was.

Q. Did you examine the traveling bag which was taken from the house? A. No sir, I took the traveling bag but did not examine it; we had no key to open it.

Q. Did you examine it after you left the house? were not the photographs of Jeff. Davis and A. H. Stephens found in that bag? A. No, I saw it opened at the Provost Marshal's office, and it contained nothing.

Testimony of Major Smith.

By Judge Holt.—Q. State whether you were in Mrs. Surratt's house on the night of her arrest? A. Yes, I

was in charge of the party who took possession of the house.
Q. Did you see Mrs. Surratt after the arrest of the prisoner Payne? A. Yes.
Q. Did you make any inquiry of her in regard to him? A. After questioning Payne in regard to his occupation, and as to what business he had at the house that night, he said he was a laborer and that he came there to dig a gutter at the request of Mrs. Surratt; I stepped to the door of the parlor and said "Mrs. Surratt, will you step here for a moment;" Mrs. Surratt came there, and said, 1, "Do you know this man?" she said, raising her right hand. "Before God I do not know this man, and have never seen him." I then placed Payne under arrest, considering him a suspicious character, and that I should send him to General Augur's headquarters for examination.
Q. Was he standing in full view of her when she made this remark? A. Yes.
Q. You refer to Mrs. Surratt, the prisoner at the bar? (Mrs. Surratt raised her veil.) A. Yes.
Cross-examined by Mr. Aiken.—Q. Did you examine a bag taken from Mrs. Surratt's house? A. I found a bag there, but did not see it examined.
Q. Did you find any photographs there? A. I did, a number of them.
Q. Of what persons? A. Various persons; it is impossible to tell who they were.
Q. Did you find a photograph in that house of Jeff. Davis or Alexander H. Stevens? A. I do not remember.
Q. Are you aware or not that it is a common thing for photographers and keepers of book shops to advertise and sell photographs of the leaders of the Rebellion? A. I am not; I have not given such matters my attention.
Q. Have you not seen such things? A. I cannot say that I have.
Q. Have you not seen these photographs in the possession of persons supposed to be loyal? A. Yes, a great many, but only those who obtained them since the trial.
Q. Are you not aware that it is a common thing for the photographs of eminent actors to be published and scattered broadcast over the land? A. I am, of different actors.
Q. State distinctly where these photographs were found? A. They were found in Mrs. Surratt's house; some of them were found in a photographic album lying on the mantelpiece in the front parlor; there were pictures of different people, with whom I had no acquaintance at all.
Q. What was transpiring in the house at the time Mrs. Surratt made the assertion you speak of in regard to her knowledge of Payne? A. The man Payne had just come in at the front door; I was questioning him at the time in regard to what his profession was, if he had any, and what business he had at that house at that time of night?
Q. How was Payne dressed that night? A. He had on a grey coat, black pants, and a rather fine pair of boots; he had on his head what seemed to be a grey worsted shirt sleeve, which was hanging over one side.
Q. Were his pantaloons tucked into his boots? A. They were rolled up over the top of one leg only
Q. He did not strike you at the time as being a gentleman from his appearance, did he? A. Not particularly so.
Q. His appearance was not in any wise genteel, was it? A. Not at all.
Q. Are you of the opinion that any one would recognize a person in that garb, as the same person he had seen before dressed as a gentleman? A. I certainly am. (A dirty grey worsted knit shirt sleeve was here produced, and identified by witness as the one Payne wore on his head the night of his arrest.)
Q. What remark did you make to Mrs. Surratt as you were leaving the house? A. I made none.
Q. Did you say anything to her about being ready? A. I said nothing at all; I said get ready.
Q. What was her attitude at that time? A. She was seated at a chair in the front parlor.
Q. Was she not kneeling? A. She was not.
Q. Who was present at the time of the asseveration she made that she did not know Payne? A. Captain Wernle and Kirsch, subordinates in the Department.
Q. Was that all the remark she made to your about Payne? A. That was all the remark she made in my hearing.
Q. Mrs. Surratt did not attempt to evade the question you asked her, did she? A. No, her answer was direct.
Q. Was it light in her hall at the time? A. Yes, very light; the gas was turned on full head.
Q. Did Mrs. Surratt express any surprise or deep feeling at her arrest? A. No sir; she did not ask even for what she was arrested; she expressed no surprise or feeling at all.
Q. How many persons were arrested together? A. Mrs. Surratt, Miss Surratt, Miss Fitzpatrick, and Miss Jenkins.
Q. Was there no inquiry made of you as to the cause of the arrest? A. None whatever; when I came there I went up the steps and rang the bell; Mrs. Surratt opened the window and said "Is that you, Kirby?" the reply was that it was not Kirby, but open the door; she opened the door; I came into the hall and said "Are you Mrs. Surratt?" she replied "I am;" "the widow of John H. Surratt?" I added, "and the mother of John H. Surratt, Jr.?" she replied "I am;" I said "I have come to arrest you, and am in your house and take you to General Augur's for examination;" (a large grey dirty sack coat was produced and identified by witness as worn by Payne the night of his arrest.)
Q. How do you know that coat to be the one Payne had on? A. By the way any one would recognize such an article, from memory.
Q. What marks about it do you recognize? A. The color and general look of the coat.
Q. Are you sure the coat he had on was not what is called Confederate grey? A. I am very sure, as I said before, this is the coat.
Q. Then are you certain it was not a Confederate grey coat Payne had on when you arrested him? A. I have said I am certain this is the coat.
Q. Will you answer my question? A. I have already testified on that point, and I do not know whether I am called upon to testify three or four times.
Another coat, smaller, cleaner and a brighter grey, was produced.
Witness.—That is the coat, sir; I recognize it by the buttons; that was all that was wanting in the other coat; it was hard in the light in which I was standing to tell.
By Mr. Aiken.—Q. If you should see a gentleman dressed in black with a white neckcloth presenting himself as a Baptist preacher, and two months after you were to see this same man dressed as you have described Payne to be with a dirty shirt sleeve on his head, a nickname in his hand and his pantaloons stuffed into his boots, presenting himself as a laborer, do you think you would immediately recognize him as the same person? A. If I was very familiar with his countenance I should.
Q. You could recollect that, but you could not recollect a coat you had only seen a short time before, nor distinguish it from another so different in appearance as the coats. A. It is very hard to remember, as any one may well know, the color of a coat seen in the night time.

Testimony of Surgeon-General Barnes.

Examined by Judge Holt.—Q. State whether or not on the night of the 14th of April last you were called to see Mr. Seward, Secretary of State, and if so, in what condition you found him? A. On the night of the 14th of April, within a few minutes of 11 o'clock, I found the Secretary wounded in three places, and Mr. Frederick Seward insensible, and very badly wounded in the head; the rest of the family I did not see, as I was occupied with them.
Q. Describe the wounds of each of the gentlemen? A. Mr. Seward was wounded by a gash in the right cheek, passing through the angle of the jaw; by a stab in the right side of the neck, passing into the large muscle, and by a stab on the left side of the neck, passing into the body of the same muscle. Frederick Seward was suffering from a fracture of the cranium in two places; he was bleeding profusely, almost pulseless, and unable to articulate.
Q. How did the wound seem to have been inflicted on the head? A. By some blunt instrument, such as the butt of a pistol, a bludgeon, or something of the kind.
Q. What was the condition of Mr. Seward, Secretary of State, before that time? A. He was progressing very favorably; he was recovering from a shock received ten days previously, and was getting along very well; his right arm had been broken close to the shoulder, and his jaw fractured; but his most serious injury on the first occasion was from the concussion.
Q. Do you know whether a pistol was picked up in the chamber of Mr. Seward that night? A. Not while I was there, and I have never seen the pistol.
Q. Were the wounds of Mr. Seward very dangerous in their character? A. Very dangerous and he is still suffering from them.

Testimony of Thomas Price.

Q. State to the Court whether or not on the 14th of April you picked up somewhere in the vicinity of this city a coat. A. Not on the 14th, I did on Sunday the 16th.
Q. Where? A. On a piece of woods, between Bunker Hill and Fort Saratoga.
Q. Would you recognize that coat again? A. Yes sir; I think I would.
Here two coats were handed to the witness, one of dark home-spun Confederate grey, the other of a checked cream color, somewhat akin to the shade so often affected by gamblers.
Q. Look at these two coats and see if either is the one you picked up? A. This is the coat (holding up the lighter-colored one).
Q. Did you discover any traces of blood on the sleeve? A. Yes sir.
Q. Show it to the Court? A. (Holding out the sleeve partly turned inside out) There sir.
Q. How far from the city is the piece of woods where you picked it up? A. About three miles.

Q. Was it on the other side of the Eastern branch? A. On the east side of the Eastern branch, I should think, sir.
Q. On any road? A. there is a road runs from one road to another through this piece of woods, and on the eastern side of this road I found this coat.
Q. Did I understand you to say that blood was upon it when you found it? A. Yes sir; that's how I recognize it.

Cross-examined by Mr. Doster.—Q. When did you find that coat; state the exact time? A. Sometime about 2 o'clock on the 10th of April.
Q. Lying in the road? A. There is a kind of a path; I should think it a road for drawing wood; the grass had grown over it, and on a turn that was in the road I found the coat.
Q. What direction is that from Washington City? A. There is a valley runs in the direction of Harwood Hospital, and this strip of woods lies in that valley.
Q. It is northeast, then? A. Yes sir.
Q. I understand the branch to run east from Washington—was it east of that. on the other side of the branch? A. No, on this side.

Re-examination of Mr. Rosch.

Q. Were you present when the prisoner, Payne, was searched? A. Yes sir.
Q. Look at these articles and say whether all or any of them were found upon his person? (The witness identified the articles shown him, consisting of a pocket comb, a needle case, a tooth and hair brush and other articles.) Yes sir; they were handed by the prisoner to Mr. Simpson, and Mr. Simpson handed them to me.
Q. That big man there is Payne? A. Yes sir, that's the man.
Q. All these articles were taken from the person of the prisoner? A. Yes sir.
Q. Do you recognize these boots? A. Yes sir, as those he had on when pulled off in my presence. I noticed his socks were exceedingly clean, and tied up in something like Highland fashion.

Testimony of S. A. Clark.

Q. Look at these boots, and state if you discover any name written therein? A. I had these boots yesterday, and could discover writing in them. It had nearly disappeared from the effect of the acid with which I brought it out.
Q. What was it? A. It appeared to be J. W. Booth.
Q. Was it perfectly distinct? A. No sir, the J. W. was distinct, but the rest was obscure when I first received it; it was merely a black mark; the writing was covered, and I found it was one coat of ink covered over another, and I took off one coat of the ink.
Q. You say the J. W. was distinct; was the rest so obscure as to leave much doubt? A. Very little doubt, but I can't speak positively of a thing in itself obscure.
Q. What is your business? A. Printing and engraving in the Treasury department.

Cross-examined by Mr. Doster.—You state you had some doubts as to the name being Booth? A. I had doubts as to the B or B, the lower part of the B being less visible than the other.
Q. What process did you use? A. I took off the upper coat with oxalic acid.
Q. How did you separate the upper and lower coats? A. By using water as fast as the upper coat disappeared under the acid
Q. How was it made clear? A. At the moment the outer coat disappears the inner one begins to show.
Q. Did you have any idea what was the purpose in giving the boots to you? A. No sir.
Q. Who gave them to you? A. Mr. Fields, Assistant Secretary of the Treasury.
Q. Did he tell you who the boot was supposed to belong to? A. Yes sir.
Q. And who had worn them? A. Yes sir; Mr. Payne.
Q. You had then an impression that it was your duty to discover some name upon them? A. I expected to find the name of Payne, but I followed out the letters until I discovered "th" at the end.
Q. Is it possible to restore that name by any means? A. By none that I know.
Q. But do you think that, take it altogether, there is a reasonable doubt that it was the name of J. Wilkes Booth? A. I entertain very little doubt about it, though I can't swear positively to such a thing.

Testimony of Mr. Jordan.

Q. State whether or not you are associated with Mr. Clark in the examination of the name upon that boot, and if so, describe the process and the result? A. I was only requested to look at it after it had undergone what chemical action it was subjected to; I looked at the marks, and came to the conclusion that the name written there was J. W. Booth.
Q. Did you examine it through a glass? A. Yes sir.
Cross-examined by Mr. Doster.—Q. Did you know who the boot came from? A. No sir; the Assistant Secretary called me, and said I have something curious to show you.
Q. What day was that? A. Yesterday.
Q. Was the name distinctly legible? A. I don't think it was; a part of the name was quite distinct.
Q. What part of it? A. The first letter was quite distinct, the middle letter not so much so, and the third initial still less distinct, yet quite as clear in its character.
Q. Were the letters after the B dim? A. No sir; I don't mean to say they were distinct, but sufficiently so to indicate what it was.
Q. Now I will ask you what you thought that name was? A. I said I thought it was the name of a very distinguished individual.
Q. Are the gentlemen of the Treasury Department in the habit of receiving boots in connection with criminal trials? (The laughter that followed this question prevented the answer being heard at the Reporter's desk, and we are obliged to leave the public uninformed as to the habits of the Treasury in this particular.)
Q. Did you come to the conclusion as to what the name was before you knew whose the boot was supposed to be? A. Yes sir.

Testimony of Mr. Marsh.

Q. Look at that boot and state whether you made an examination of it to ascertain what name was written there? A. It was shown to me by Mr. Fields, the Assistant Secretary of the Treasury; I examined it and thought I could make out at first the letters A. J. or L. then A. W. and th, as the last letters; then I thought I made out a B. as a capital; that is all I could make out on a first examination; then I thought I could make out the letters reading letters; I was not satisfied about them, but about the B. and th I was.
Q. Did you examine it through a glass? A. No sir.
Q. In regard to those letters you mention, you have no doubt at all? A. No sir.
Q. In the intervening space was there room for one or two letters? A. For two or three, but that would depend on how they were written; it was about half an inch.

Re-examination of William H. Wells, (Colored.)

The proceedings of the Court were here delayed by an order from Judge Holt to remove the letters from the hands of Payne, in order that he might put on both the coats already spoken of in this record. When Payne was unlettered he rose, and there was a hush through the court, and every eye was directed towards him and mingled expressions of admiration and abhorrence could be distinctly heard; abhorrence at his real or supposed crime and admiration for his fine physical development. His face slightly flushed and his lips curled. An involuntary smile revealed the dimples in his cheeks to which the colored boy had alluded in his previous testimony. He first put on the coat of Confederate grey and over it drew the longer cream colored one. The hat was then handed to him and he put it on, and turning towards the young negro, bent his dark blue eye searchingly upon him.

Judge Holt then said to the boy—Do you recognize him now? A. Yes sir; but he had a white collar on, and looked quite nice, and he had one corner of that hat over one eye, turned down like; I tell you his eyes looked pretty fiery; here the boy shook his head as he added, "Oh, he knows me well enough;" in spite of the solemn importance of the words, the homely positiveness of the boy evoked a laugh, to which Payne himself replied by a renewal of his old smile.

Re-examination of Mr. Robinson.

While this witness was being looked for the Judge Advocate-General said, I wish this witness also to see the prisoner in his present dress, that he may give his opinion as to whether it is the same man or not. Having taken the stand Mr. Robinson said he is more like the man than he was before; I should think that he is, but yet I am not sure about it.
Q. You didn't state precisely the hour when this stabbing occurred, in your previous examination? A. It was not far from 10 o'clock.
Q. Was it before or after 10? A. I think it might be after.
Q. Do you know whether the pistol that was picked up there was loaded or not? A. It was loaded.
Q. Did you examine it? A. Yes sir.
Mr. Doster here asked that Miss Murray be recalled, to which the Court consented, in order that she might have an opportunity of seeing Payne with the coat and hat on. It was found, however, that Miss Murray had left the Court-room.

Testimony of Jacob Ritterspack.

Q. State whether you know Spangler, the prisoner at the bar? A. Yes sir.
Q. Where did he board? A. Where I did, on the corner of Seventh and G streets.
Q. Who arrested him? A. I do not know.
Q. What is the name of the house? A. It has no name, and there is no number to it.
Q. Who owns it? A. Mr. Ford.
Q. Who lives in that house? A. Mrs. Scott.
Q. Were you present when he was arrested? A. No sir.
Q. Who occupied the room with him? A. He never slept there; he just got his meals in the house.
Q. Had he a room in the house? A. No sir.
Q. Did you see the rope that was taken there? A. No sir; I only know he had a valise there; he used to keep

it there, but the detectives came and asked if he had anything there, and I said, nothing but the valise.
Q. You knew it was Spangler's? A. Yes sir.
Q. When did he take it there? A. I don't know.
Q. When did you give it to the detectives? A. On Monday, the 17th of April.
Q. Ain't you commonly called "Jake" about the theatre? A. Yes sir.

Testimony of Capt. W. M. Wannerskerch.

Q. State whether or not on the 16th of April you were at the house of the prisoner, Mrs. Surratt, in this city. A. No sir; I was there on the night of the 17th.
Q. Were you present when she and Payne met? A. I was present.
Q. Did you or did you not hear Major Smith address any remark to her, or make any inquiry of her in regard to Payne? A. He asked her if she knew Payne.
Q. Was she in the presence of Payne? A. She saw him.
Q. What did she say? A. She held up her hands in that position, and said, "So help me God, I never saw him before, and I know nothing of him."
Q. Do you recognize Payne then as the man? A. That is the man yonder.
Q. And is that woman there Mrs. Surratt? A. I cannot see her face.
Assistant Judge Advocate Bringham then requested that Mrs. Surratt be asked to unveil her face, which had the very natural effect of attracting to it the gaze of every spectator in the house; but, like Payne, she met the glance of the witness unmoved, and when he replied, " Yes sir, that's Mrs. Surratt," coolly and slowly replaced her veil before her face.
Cross-examined by Mr. Aiken.—Did you make any search of the premises while there? A. I did.
Q. What did you find? A. I found a number of photographs, papers, bullet moulds, and some percussion caps.
Q. In which room did you find the percussion caps? A. In Mrs. Surratt's room, on the lower floor, and I also found there the bullet mould.
Q. Were the caps lying loose about in the room? A. They were in one of the bureau drawers, and the bullet mould was on the top of the wardrobe.
Q. Was this room on the first floor? A. It was the back parlor on the first floor.
Q. What was the photograph you found there? A. There were a number found there, but I don't know whose likenesses they were.
Q. Did you find any of Davis or Stephens there, or any of the Rebel leaders? A. Yes, but not exactly photographs; they were lithographs, cartes de visite in the same style as photographs.
Q. Are you aware that dealers expose these for sale throughout the country? A. I have seen them in Baltimore eighteen months ago, but they were prohibited to be sold by the Commanding General at that time.
Q. Have you not seen photographs of the leaders of the Rebellion in the hands of persons known to be loyal? A. Not frequently.
Q. Well did you ever see them? A. Perhaps I did.
Q. Have you ever seen photographs of Booth in the hands of loyal men? A. Only in the hands of those who took an interest in having him arrested.
Q. Is it not a common thing for photographs of eminent actors to be exposed for sale? A. I think it is.
Q. Whereabouts were you when Mrs. Surratt made that observation? A. She was standing in the parlor near the hall door.
Q. What remark did you make to her when you were ready to take her from the house? A. The remark was made by Major Smith; he had sent for a cab, and when he said he was ready to take her away, she requested him to wait a while, and she knelt and prayed a little; she knelt down, but whether she prayed or not I can't say.
Q. How was Payne dressed when he came in? A. He was dressed in a dark coat, and pants that seemed to be black; he had a close fitting head dress, apparently a shirt sleeve, or the lower part of a pair of drawers, closely fitting around his head, and hanging down on the side six or seven inches.
Q. Is that the article? A. It looks very much like it; he was full of mud to his knees.
Q. D) you think you could recognize the coat he had on if you should see it now? A. Yes.
Q. Do you recognize it now? is that the coat? A. I think it was longer and darker.
Payne's hat was then placed upon his head, and his overcoat removed, and then the witness said, "That's the coat, and that's the way he had the head dress on."
Q. Are you sure you recognize the man? A. Yes sir; that is the man.
Q. Do you think if you should see a person dressed in genteel dark clothes, with a white cravat about his neck, looking like a Baptist Minister, and then see him three weeks after that covered with a shirt sleeve on his head and his pants thrust into his boots, you could recognize him as the same? A. I declare I don't know how a Baptist Minister does look.
Q. You think you would recognize a person in such a change of garb in a dim gas light? A. If I were asked to look at him and identify him I think I would; the

prisoner had taken no particular pains to disguise himself; his face looked as it is now, and I would recognize him if he put another coat on and covered himself with mud.
Q. Was there another remark made to you by Mrs. Surratt, with reference to Payne? A. No sir; even the one mentioned was not made to me.
Q. Did you see a black bag there? A. Yes sir, I have seen it; it was not opened in my presence; we had no means of opening it, and we had it sent to the Provost Marshal's office to be opened there.
Q. Of your own knowledge do you know anything that was in it? A. No sir.
By Judge Holt.—You found the bullet moulds on the top of the wardrobe in Mrs. Surratt's room? A. Yes sir.
Q. When Mrs. Surratt looked at Payne was there light enough for her to see him? A. Where he stood, that place was not only lighted by the hall light, but also by the light from the parlors.
By Mr. Aiken.—Q. Have you ever had any percussion caps in your possession? A. Yes sir.
Q. Have you ever had any bullet-moulds? A. I don't think I ever had.
Q. Isn't it a common thing for people to keep them in these times? A. I don't know.

Testimony of Lieut. G. W. Dempsey.

Q. Did you ever see this picture before? (The picture was a colored miniature representing three female figures, generally styled Spring, Summer and Autumn.) A. I saw that picture in the house of Mrs. Surratt, in the back parlor.
Q. Did you examine it? A. I did.
Q. What did you find underneath, between the picture and the back? A. A likeness of J. Wilkes Booth, a side-face view.
Q. Is that it? A. That is the same face, but the picture I found was a side view.
Objected to, but objection not sustained.
Cross-examined by Mr. Aiken.—Q. Have you ever been in the habit of seeing pictures of Booth, or the leaders of the Rebellion exposed? A. I was a prisoner in the South fifteen months, and saw many of the leaders of the Rebellion personally and in pictures.
Q. I mean in the loyal States? A. Very few, sir, except in newspapers.
Q. In loyal newspapers? A. Once, I think, a picture of Davis, as the former secretary of War, in one of the Sunday papers in New York.
Q. Have you not seen pictures of eminent actors exposed for sale? A. I am not a theatrical character and can't say that I have never noticed it, but I have seen pictures of Forrest and Macready.

Re-examination of Wm. W. Reichman.

Q. Look at the prisoner, Payne, and state whether you ever saw him dressed up with that coat on before. A. Yes sir, when he last came to the house.
Q. When he remained three days? A. Yes sir.
Q. State whether you ever saw that vest before. A. Yes sir; he also had a pair of boots.
Q. State whether he wore a white cravat, or not. A. He wore a black cravat.
Q. Did you ever know him to wear a white cravat? A. No sir; I never did.
Cross-examined by Mr. Doster.—Q. All this happened when you were giving information to the War Department, and on intimate terms with Mrs. Surratt and her family? A. I was on intimate terms for a time; it was on this occasion that Payne went to the theatre with Surratt to see the play of Jane Shore; I indicated my suspicions to Gleason at the time, and the very morning after that the horsehack ride took place.
Q. I was asking you to fix the date, that's all. A. It was about the 14th of March; he came to the house on the evening of the 13th and remained there the 14th, 15th and 16th; on the 18th he went to the theatre; it was when Forrest played there four nights in that week.
By Mr. Cox.—Q. So you fix the 16th as the date of that horseback ride? Yes sir; to the best of my recollection.

Testimony of Colonel H. H. Wells.

Q. State to the Court whether you had Payne in your custody on the 19th of April. A. Yes sir.
Q. State whether you took his clothes off. A. Yes; I took his coat, pants, vest and all off of him, on board the monitor.
Q. State whether he had a white shirt on. A. Yes sir, and an undershirt minus one sleeve; there is a very distinct mark by which they can be recognized; when I described to him his struggle with Mr. Seward I said, "I shall find the blood here," and I found it on the coat sleeve and also on the shirt sleeve.
Q. The white shirt? A. Yes sir. (Here the witness took the shirt, and said, there it is, pointing to the blood stains.) I called his attention to it and said, what do you say now? and he leaned against the side of the boat and said, nothing; I also took from him the boots that have been shown in court, and asked him where he got them; he said in Baltimore and that I should wear them three months; I called his attention to the raised head apparent from their being so little worn, and as at them to the Treasury Department to see if it was possible to ascertain what the time was.

Cross-examination by Mr. Doster.—Q. You saw the blood on the coat? A. Yes, on the sleeve.
Q. On the outside? A. No, on the inside, on the lining of the left arm.
Q. Did you threaten the prisoner at any time? A. No, sir.
Q. Did you not tell him he was a liar? A. I think I did tell him so several times; I called his attention to the blood on the coat and asked him how the blood came there, and he said he did not know how it came there.
Q. How did you know it was blood? A. Because I saw it.

Testimony of Miss Blise (Colored.)

Q. State where you live. A. At Bryantown.
Q. Do you know Dr. Mudd? A. Yes sir.
Q. How far does he live from Bryantown? A. Four miles.
Q. State whether or not, on the day after the President was murdered, you saw him riding into Bryantown. A. Yes sir.
Q. At what hour? A. It was in the evening, on a dark foggy day; I couldn't see the sun; it might be later than three or four o'clock.
Q. Was he alone? A. There was a gentleman with him when he passed; they were on horseback.
Q. How far from town do you live? A. Not more than half a mile; they went past my place.
Q. How long before Dr. Mudd returned? A. In a short time.
Q. How long after that before you went into town yours-d? A. Not more than eight or ten minutes.
Q. Did you find any soldiers? A. Yes sir.
Q. Did you hear the murder spoken of then? A. Yes sir.
Q. Was the other man with him? A. No sir.
Q. Did you ever hear who shot the President? A. No sir; I did not; I only heard that he was shot, from persons talking.
Cross-examined by Mr. Stone.—Q. If he had come the same road with Dr Mudd would you not have seen him? A. I was not there all the time.
Q. How long did Dr. Mudd stay in town? A. I didn't think he stayed more than a quarter of an hour.
Q. Can you tell whether the man with Dr. Mudd was an old man or a young man? A. I could not say.
Q. What sort of a horse had he? A. He appeared to be a bay horse.
Q. Had the soldiers been passing down there that day? A. I didn't see any till I went down town.

WASHINGTON, May 20.

The first witness examined to-day was Assistant Secretary of War Dana, as follows:—

Testimony of Mr. C. A. Dana.

Q. State what position you occupy in the Government. A. I am Assistant Secretary of War.
Q. Look at the instrument before you, and state if you have ever seen it before. A. I took it out of the office of Mr. Benjamin, the Rebel Secretary of State, in Richmond; I arrived in Richmond on Wednesday the 6th, and went into his office, where this was found, and brought it away with me, or rather, I sent it to Major Eckert, of the War Department; I saw it was the key to an official cipher; there were many papers and things lying around there, and as this seemed to be interesting, I took it away.
Q. Did you find it in a trunk? A. No sir; Benjamin's office consisted of a series of three or four rooms (I think four), Benjamin's personal office being the innermost of all; this was in the room next to his, occupied by his confidential secretary or assistant; most of the articles had been taken away; the record had been taken away, but I found several interesting documents, this amongst them.
By the Court.—Q. I should like to know the object of the instrument. A. It is a key to a cipher, by which certain letters of the alphabet can be used for other letters, and by using these pointers such a cipher can be translated or plain writing turned into cipher by interpretation.
Note.—The machine is about a foot long and eight inches high, and consists of a cylinder of wood, which has a paper envelope encircled with letters. This cylinder revolves in pivot holes at each end, and a bar across the top contains wooden indices pointing down to the letters.

Testimony of Major Eckert.

Q. Look at that cipher, and state if it was found in the trunk of J. Wilkes Booth; compare it with this other cipher of which Assistant Secretary Dana has just spoken, and state whether or not they are the same. A. They are the same, sir.

Q. You are somewhat familiar, are you not, with these things? A. Yes sir.
Q. You have no doubt as to these being the same? A. None at all, sir.
Q. State whether or not cipher despatches have from time to time fallen into the hands of the War Department, and been referred to you for examination. A. They have, sir.
Q. State whether they were the same cipher as this. A. Some of them were, sir; they were worked on the same principle.
Q. I speak now of the despatches of the 13th and 19th of October last; have you them now in your possession? A. I have, sir.
Q. These are the translations? Yes sir.
Q. Have you the originals? A. No sir; I have copies.
Q. State whether they are written in the same cipher of which you have spoken. A. I think they are; they may be different in the key word, but the principle is the same.
Q. Have you translated them? A. The clerks have.
Q. Were they worked out without any knowledge of this instrument at the time? A. Yes sir.
Q. Are these translations of those despatches? A. Yes sir.
The following were then read:—
OCTOBER 13.—We again urge the immense necessity of our gaining immediate advantages; strain every nerve for victory. We now look upon the re-election of Lincoln in November as almost certain, and we need to whip his hirelings to prevent it. Besides, with Lincoln re-elected, and his armies victorious, we need not hope even for recognition, much less the help mentioned in our last. Holcombe will explain this. Those figures of the Yankee armies are correct to a unit. Our friend shall be immediately set to work as you direct.
OCTOBER, 19, 1864.—Your letter of the 13th instant is at hand. There is yet time enough to colonize many voters before November. A blow will shortly be stricken here; it is not quite time. General Longstreet is to attack Sheridan without delay, and then move North as far as practicable toward unprotected points. This will be made instead of the movement before mentioned. He will endeavor to assist the Republicans in collecting their ballots. Be watchful and assist him.
Q. State whether the original was sent to its address. A. Yes sir.
Q. From what direction did the cipher of the 13th come? A. It came from Canada, and went to Richmond.
Q. From what direction did the cipher of the 19th come? A. It came from Richmond and went to Canada.

Testimony of General Hamilton.

Q. State whether you are familiar with the handwriting of H. S. Oldham. A. Yes sir; as familiar as I am with that of any man living.
Q. State whether that (handing him a paper) is in his handwriting or not. A. Yes sir.
The following is the paper handed to the witness:—
RICHMOND, Feb. 11, 1865.—His Excellency Jefferson Davis, President Confederate States of America:—When Senator Johnson and myself waited upon you, some days since, in relation to the project of annoying and harrassing the enemy by means of burning their shipping, towns, etc., etc., there were several remarks made by you upon the subject that I was not fully prepared to answer, but which, upon subsequent conference with the parties proposing the enterprise, I find cannot apply as objections to the scheme.
First. The combustible material consists of several preparations, and not one alone, and can be used without exposing the party using them to the least danger of detection whatever. The preparations are not in the hands of Mr. Daniel, but are in the hands of Professor McCullough, and are known but to him and one other party, as I understand it.
Second. There is no necessity for sending persons in the military service into the enemy's country; but the work may be done by agents, and in most cases by persons ignorant of the facts, and therefore innocent agents.
I have seen enough of the effects that can be produced to satisfy me that in most cases, without any danger to the parties engaged, and in others but very slight, we can:—1. Burn every vessel that leaves a foreign port for the United States. 2. We can burn every transport that leaves the harbor of New York or other Northern ports with supplies for the armies of the enemy in the South. 3 Burn every transport and gun-boat on the Mississippi River, as well as devastate the country and fill his people with terror and consternation.
I am not alone in this opinion, but many other gentlemen are as fully and thoroughly impressed with the conviction as I am. I believe we have the means at our command, if promptly appropriated and energetically applied, to demoralize the Northern people in a very short time. For the purpose of satisfying your mind on the subject, I respectfully but earnestly request that you will have an interview with General Harris, formerly a member of Congress from Missouri, who, I think, is able, by conclusive proofs, to convince

TRIAL OF THE ASSASSINS AT WASHINGTON. 79

you that what I have suggested is perfectly feasible and practicable.

The deep interest I feel for the success of our cause in this struggle, with the conviction of the importance of availing ourselves of every element of defense, must be my excuse for writing you and requesting you to invite General Harris to see you. If you should see proper to do so, please signify the time when it will be convenient for you to see him.

I am, respectfully, your obedient servant,
W. S. OLDHAM.

On the back of the letter are the two indorsements, the first being "Hon. W. S. Oldham, Richmond. February 12, 1865."

Q. State whether or not at the time of writing it he was a member of the Senate of the so-called Confederate States from Texas? A. I was present when he was elected by the Rebel Legislature of Texas to a seat in the Senate of the so-called Confederacy; since then I know it as a matter of public history; I have seen many speeches, resolutions, and bills introduced by him into that Senate, and published in the public prints.

Q. You are a citizen of Texas, formerly a member of Congress from there? A. Yes sir.

Q. Do you know the McCullogh mentioned in that letter? A. No sir.

Testimony of Surgeon-General Barnes.

Q. State to the Court whether or not you made an examination of the body of Booth after his death? A. Yes sir.

Q. Describe to the Court the scar which is alleged to have been on the neck and the general appearance of the body? A. On the left side of the neck there was a scar, occasioned by an operation performed by Dr. May for the removal of a tumor; it looked like the scar from a burn rather than an incision.

Q. How near the ear was it? A. Three inches below the ear.

Testimony of Frank Bloice.

Q. Where do you live? A. In Charles county.
Q. In the town or country? A. In the country, sir.
Q. How far from Bryantown? A. About half a mile.
Q. Were you there on the Saturday after the murder? A. I was there on Saturday evening, about four o'clock; as near as I can come to the time it was between three and four.
Q. Did you see Dr. Mudd there? A. Yes sir.
Q. What time do you think, that was? A. Between three and four, sir.
Q. Where did you see him? A. He came into a store while I was there.
Q. State whether the soldiers had arrived from Washington then? A. I don't know, sir, whether they had or not.
Q. Were you around about the town? A. I was in the store when he came in; I did not take much notice.
Q. What time did you leave the store? A. About just before night.
Q. When did he start? A. I didn't see him when he started; I did'nt take much notice of him.
By the Court.— Was the report of the President's assassination in Bryantown at that time? A. I don't know sir.
Q. Did you hear it? A. No sir, I didn't hear until the roads were guarded; that was a little before night.
Q. You heard it before you left Bryantown? A. Oh, yes sir.

Testimony of J. H. Ward.

Q. State where you live? A. Near Bryantown, Charles county.
Q. State whether you were there on the afternoon of the day following the murder of the President? A. I was; I live in the suburbs of the village; I went so soon as I finished my dinner, and arrived there about one o'clock; and so soon as I arrived I observed the military were in town with Lieutenant Murray, and perceived a great excitement, not only with the military, but with the people, and I imagined they were going to search the houses; as my wife was alone I went home lest she should be alarmed; a nigger came soon afterwards and said—Objected to.
Witness.—I must explain the facts because I know but little; I left him and went to the village; Lieutenant Dana had put the village under martial law, and the people were excited about getting home.
Q. Did you see Dr. Mudd? A. I can't say, the excitement was so great; I can't say I saw the Dr.
Q. What is your opinion, to the best of your recollection, about your having seen Dr. Mudd? A. I would not like to say positively, but it occurs to me from faint memory that he was there; the excitement has been so great ever since that time that I cannot say positively.
Q. You say the military were there and the people were much excited, and you returned home; how long did you remain at home? A. About three-quarters of an hour.
Q. Did you then hear of the assassination of the President? A. Yes, sir.
Q. Did you hear who the assassin was? A. Yes, sir. Booth; some gave him the name of Boose.

Q. Did you hear it everywhere spoken of? A. Yes, sir, at Bryantown I did.
Q. What time do you suppose you heard it? A. It was, I t ink, between one and two o'clock; it was a cloudy day, and I never paid any particular attention, but I think it was one and two o'clock.
Q. What time did you leave Bryantown? A. I could not give you the precise time; it was between two and three o'clock that I left the second time; it was then I found the military, and in a few minutes they told me that the President had been assassinated, and I came back.
Q. You say some said it was Booth and some said it was Boose that was spoken by some soldiers with whom the English language was not conversant? A. They would call him Borth, Booths and Boose; those who could speak audibly said it was Booth; those who had an amalgamation of the languages said it was Booths.
Q. Where were you when you first heard the President was assassinated? A. At home; I wanted to tell you it was through the authority of the darkey.
Q. Who was the darkey? A. Charles Bloice, the brother of the fellow whose testimony has just been taken.
Q. Did you ask him who assassinated the President? A. I have no knowledge of asking him, and I think he never told me.
Q. In what direction from the centre of the town do you live? A. I live in the eastern direction, principally in the suburbs.
Q. On the road between Pine Town and Dr. Mudd? A. I live close to the road leading to Bryantown.
Q. My question is do you live near or on the road between Bryantown and Dr. Mudd's? A. No sir.
Q. Is it your impression that you saw Dr. Mudd in the town? A. My impression is it it be Dr. Mudd that I saw, I saw him get on his horse; but I could not swear that it was Dr. Mudd.
Q. Did you see the face of this person? A. No sir not that I know of; but I could tell him by a side or a back view.
Q. How close were you to him? A. About ten or twenty yards, standing on the porch of the store.
Q. You are only able to swear to a faint impression? A. Yes, sir.
Q. What was the color of the horse this man was going to? A. I don't know.
Q. Do you know the horse Dr. Mudd usually rides? A. I have seen him on a great many horses, and there was a great many horses connected there; I have seen him ride a bay horse.
Q. Did you see Dr. Mudd when you first went into town? A. I think not.
Q. Was it immediately on your arrival on the second time? A. Yes, sir.
Q. Were you personally acquainted with Dr. Mudd? A. I have been for two years and five months, before that I had no personal acquaintance with him.

Testimony of Lieutenant Dana.

Q. State whether or not, on the day following the President's assassination, you were in pursuit of the assassins at Bryantown? A. Yes sir.
Q. State what hour you arrived there on that day? A. I sent an advance guard of four men, they arrived there twenty minutes or half an hour before I did; I arrived there very near one o'clock that afternoon, Saturday afternoon.
Q. State whether, on your arrival, the news of the assassination was spread all around there? A. Yes sir.
Q. Was any person mentioned as the assassin? A. J. Wilkes Booth? A. Yes sir, and some of the citizens asked me if I knew for certain it was he; as early as a quarter past – o'clock it was known that the President was assassinated and who the assassin was.
Q. Are you acquainted at all with the prisoner at the bar, Dr. Mudd? A. No sir.
Q. Have you any knowledge whether you met him on that occasion? A. No sir.

Testimony of Robert Nelson (Colored).

Q. Do you live in Washington? A. Yes sir; I did live in Virginia.
Q. Look at that knife, and state whether you found it in the street, and if so, when and where? A. It looks like the one I found opposite to Secretary Seward's.
Q. When did you find it there? A. The Saturday morning after the Secretary was stabbed.
Q. Did you find it on the pavement or in the middle of the street? A. In the middle of the street.
Q. Who did you give it to? A. Dr. Wilson.
Cross-examination.—Q. You say it was the same one? A. I said it was one like it.
Q. It was not in a sheath? A. No, it was not in a sheath at all.
Q. Was it in the street or the gutter? A. It was in the middle of the street.
Q. Right in front of the door? A. Yes sir.
Q. What time of day was it? A. Early in the morning; I was going to market; it was about five or six, I think.

Testimony of Dr. Wilson.

Q. Doctor, look at that knife and state whether or not it is the knife you received from any one? A. This

is the knife I received from the colored boy, just come from the stand, on Saturday, about ten o'clock in the day.
Q. On the 13th of April? A. Yes sir.
Q. Where did he give it to you? A. In the library of Mr. Seward; in the Seward library; he brought it in the door and handed it to me.

Testimony of Colonel J. B. Stewart.

Q. State to the Court whether or not you were at Ford's Theatre on the night of the assassination. A. Yes sir. I was.
Q. Did you see the assassin jump from the box? A. I did, at about 10 o'clock; I was sitting in the front chair near the orchestra, on the right hand side; there are two aisles to the orchestra, and my side was on the corner, on the left hand, right under and bringing me immediately next to the music stand; at the report of the pistol I was startled; I was speaking to my sister, my head being turned to the left; I glanced back to the stage; an exclamation was made and a man leaped from the President's box, lighting on the stage. He came down with his back slightly towards the audience, but as he was rising his face came fully in view; I rose and attempted to leap on the stage; I made two or three steps on the railing to the right after alighting from where I sat and keeping my attention on the man who had alighted upon the stage and who had jumped from the President's box; when I reached the stage, on looking to the left I perceived he had disappeared on the left hand egress: I exclaimed "stop that man," and then went past the length of the stage, and turning to the right, was at a distance of twenty feet from the door; but the door was slammed to. I ran and got to the door very quick, but on coming to the door I swung it the wrong way, but I remedied that and passed out; as I approached the door after I had last said, stop that man, some one said he has gone on a horse, and I heard the tramping of a horse; when I got out the door, I perceived a man mounting a horse; he was at that instant barely mounted; the moon was just beginning to rise, and I could see him better; the horse was moving as though prematurely spurred in mounting; I ran in the direction in which the horse was heading, at about eight or ten feet from the head of the horse, and the rider brought him around to the right again; the horse's feet were rattling violently on the stones; I crossed in the same direction, and was now on the right hand side of the horse, but he was gaining on me when about two-thirds of the way out of the alley he brought the horse forward and swept to the left of F street; I commanded him to stop; it all occupied but two seconds.
Q. You found the door closed; did you see anybody about the door? A. I did.
Q. One or more persons? A. I passed several in the passage, one or two men, perhaps five persons altogether; but near the door, on the right hand side, I passed a person standing, who seemed in the act of turning; I noticed everything; my mind is impressed with all that occurred, and I saw a person there who didn't seem to be moving about.
Q. Look at the prisoners and see if you recognize the man. A. I see but one face that would recall him to my mind.
Q. Which one? A. That one.
By the Court.—Stand up, Spangler. Witness.—That one looks more like the man than any other there.
Q. Describe his appearance.
Mr. Stewart here placed himself in an attitude, in order to show the Court the position in which he had seen the man, which was a three-fourths view.
Witness.—I didn't observe so far as to have a clear impression of his visage; he was turning from the door towards me.
Cross-examination.—Q. Was it the passage way between the scene and the green-room, about two and a half feet in width, through which Booth ran? A. I don't know where the green-room is; I never was there, but if I had a plan of the building I could point it out.
Assistant Judge Advocate Burnett then handed to Mr. Stewart a plan of the theatre by which he explained the route taken by Booth and by himself, and on which he marked the spot where he had seen the man alluded to in the latter part of his examination in chief.
Q. When you got out of the door the person was just rising into his saddle? A. He was in his saddle leaning forward; his left foot apparently was in the stirrup; he was leaning to the left the horse was leaving the walk in a sort of motion making apparently a circle; he was sufficiently mounted to go with the horse without being unbalanced; he was getting the horse under control for a forward movement.
Q. You could not say then that he had just got into the saddle? A. He was balancing himself in the saddle; I would form no opinion from his position and the motion of his horse that the moment he got his foot into the stirrup he started the horse, who having the rein drawn on one side more than the other did not at once make a straightforward movement.
By Judge Holt.—Q. I understand you to say that all the persons you met with in the passage as you approached exhibited great excitement, except this particular man? A. Every person that came under my notice in the brief space of not over two or three seconds as I ran through the stage toward the door were greatly agitated, and seemed literally bewildered, except the person near the door, who did not seem to be under the same excitement.
By Mr. Ewing.—Q. How long did it take you after entering that passage to get to the door? A. I can hardly time myself; I was running as hard as I could, and was only obstructed by passing these persons; it seemed to me about as quick as you would count one, two, three, four, five, from the report of the pistol until I reached the door; I knew the discharge of the pistol was either by accident or design, and that it was by design was solved by the man jumping on the stage; my impression was when he came from the President's box that the President had been assassinated; I was so much under that impression that though I had not heard a word after the person on the horse had gone off, I informed the people in the alley there that the person who went off on that horse had shot the President.
Q. You say you saw only the profile of this person in the passage? A. The profile and full face as he passed round.
By Judge Holt.—Q. Did you recognize Booth when you saw him on the stage? A. Oh, yes after I went out and returned I took my family home, and immediately ran down the street towards the house of Secretary Stanton, but finding persons had been there, I turned and went rapidly back to the police station; found Captain Richards, Superintendent of Police; gave him my name and what information I had, and said to him I thought I knew who it was; I had known Booth before by sight; some two years before; I was introduced to him one evening at the Metropolitan Hotel; then I had seen him on the stage, but I noticed him more during the past winter at the hotel; I was two evenings with some ladies at a hop at the National Hotel, and noticed this gentleman leisurely moving about the parlor; every person except the one I have mentioned, seemed to be perfectly bewildered on the stage; I felt very much vexed at his getting away.
By the Court.—How long was it after you heard the door slam until you saw this man balancing himself in the saddle? A. Not more than while I was making two steps.
Q. Are you satisfied that the door was closed by some other person than the one who went out of the door? A. I could not possibly be satisfied of that; there was nothing to preclude the possibility that the door was closed by Booth himself.
Q. Are you satisfied that the person you saw inside the door was in a position, had he been so disposed, to have interrupted the exit of Booth? A. Beyond a doubt he was.
Q. From his manner, he was cool enough to have done it? A. He showed no agitation like she other people did.
By Mr. Ewing.—Q. Were not the other persons you have spoken of also in a position to have interrupted the exit of Booth? A. O yes, at least at the moment I saw them every person I met could have obstructed my motion, except one person, who was three or five feet off to the right; that was the person I described who seemed to be passing off.
Q. Then the person you speak of nearest the door was in no better position to have obstructed the passage of Booth than any of the others, so far as you know? A. None whatever.
By the Court.—Q. Could this man nearest the door have opened it and gone out before you went out? A. Yes, the door was immediately within the control of the person who stood there.
By Mr. Ewing.—Q. Do you know whether any person on the stage, or in the passage as you went out, knew that the assassination had been committed? A. I cannot say that; they acted very much like people astounded at something that had just occurred.

Testimony of Robert A. Campbell.

Examined by Judge Holt.—Q. State where you reside? A. Montreal, Canada.
Q. Are you or not connected with the Ontario Bank of that city? A. I am, as first teller.
Q. Look upon that account, and state whether or not it is a correct abstract from the books of that bank? A. It is; I examined it before I came away.
Q. What is it? A. It is the account of Jacob Thompson with the Ontario Bank, Montreal.
Q. State on what day the account commences? A. The account commences May 30th, 1864; prior to that however, he left sterling exchange, drawn on the Rebel agents at Liverpool or London for collection; as soon as agents advised us of the bills being paid, the proceeds were placed to his credit; the first advices we had was May 30, and two thousand pounds sterling was the amount.
Q. State when the account closed? A. The account closed April 31, 1865.
Q. State the aggregate amount of credit and the aggregate amount drawn? A. The aggregate amount of credit was $649,873,323 there is now a balance due him of about $1733.
Q. Has he drawn lately to any considerable extent?

A. He has drawn $300,000 very nearly since March 1; he bought at one time $100,000 in sterling exchange.
Q. State the amount drawn out between the 1st and 19th of April? A. The first entry in April is on the 4th, a very small check of $100; there is a deposit receipt under date of 6th of April, of $18,000 which was to be paid when presented; on the 8th of April he purchased 441 pounds sterling exchange, and also 4000 pounds sterling on the same date; on the 24th of March he purchased $100,000 sterling.
Q. You know Jacob Thompson personally? A. Yes, I know him.
Q. State whether or not since the 14th of April last he has left Montreal? A. He has; I heard him say myself he was going away, and I know he has not been seen in the bank lately; one of the last transactions was a check given to a hotel keeper for, as I supposed, board; he said he was going overland to Halifax, *en route* to Europe.
Q. Can you fix the date of that? A. I could not; since then he has disappeared from Montreal.
Q. How long was this before navigation opened? A. I think about two weeks; I know I thought it strange he was going overland, when by waiting two weeks he could have taken a steamer.
Q. He was known and recognized as the agent of the Confederate States? A. His account was simply with Jacob Thompson; we did not know what he was; by newspaper report he was the financial agent of the Rebels; we knew that he bought Southern sterling exchange bills on their agents in the old country; a part of the time he resided in Upper Canada, and a part of the time in Montreal.
Q. Have you known him to be connected with other money transactions with other banks in Canada? A. Oh, yes; I knew of one transaction of fifty thousand with Niagara District Bank, at St. Catharines; that was a check drawn to the order of Mr. C. C. Clay, and deposited by him in Niagara District Bank; that bank sent it to us, and we put it to their credit; the date of that was August 16th, 1864.
Q. Did you know J. Wilkes Booth, the actor? A. I did; I had one or two transactions with him.
Q. How often did you see him in Canada? A. I could not say, I may have seen him a dozen times; I remember distinctly seeing him there.
Q. Did he have a small account at your bank? A. Yes he has still to his credit four hundred and odd dollars.
Q. Have you any knowledge how that credit arose? A. It was from a deposit that did not go through my hands, but through the hands of another receiving teller. The memorandum says check drawn on Merchants' Bank by Davis, 225 and ten twenty-dollar bills.
Q. Who was Davis, the person referred to as drawing the check? A. He was a broker in Montreal, and I am not sure whether he was introduced by Davis, or by T. C. Martin from the States, somewhere from Richmond or Baltimore; when Booth came into the bank he purchased a bill of exchange for sixty-one pounds and some odd shillings; he said he was going to run the blockade; he asked whether in case he should be captured his captors could make use of the exchange; I said no, not unless he indorsed the bill; he then said he would take three hundred dollars' worth, for which I think be paid American gold; these are the only two transactions he had with us.
Q. Look at these bills of exchange taken from the body of Booth, and say whether these are the ones you refer to. A. They are Ontario Bank bills; there is no doubt about that.
Q. State whether or not these drafts were intended for use in the States or for general disbursement? A. We can never tell that; we never ask our customers any questions; checks are generally made payable to bearer, but in certain instances the word "bearer" is scored out and "order" put over; Mr. Thompson, besides these sterling exchange transactions, has bought from us several times United States currency (greenbacks).
Q. In large sums? A. He bought on August 25th fifteen thousand dollars in greenbacks; July 14th, thirteen thousand one hundred and twenty-four dollars; that was the amount in gold; I could not say what was the amount in greenbacks; at that time I think exchange was about fifty-five.
Q. Did any of these transactions occur during the past spring? A. On the 14th of March he bought one thousand dollars at 44½, for which he paid five hundred and fifty-three dollars in gold; he bought several drafts in New York.
The Judge Advocate-General stated that there was only one other witness he desired to examine to-day. He was a very important witness; but for the same reasons stated in another instance, it was not desirable that his examination should be public.
The Court was thereupon cleared, and the remainder of its deliberations for the day were in secret session.

WASHINGTON, May 22.—The Court, after the reading of the evidence of Saturday, proceeded to take the testimony of Miss Honora Fitzpatrick, as follows:—

By Judge Bingham.—Q. State where you resided during the month of March last. A. I resided at the house of Mrs. Surratt, the lady who is at the bar.
Q. State whether during the time of your residence at her house last winter you saw John H. Surratt and other men in company with him there. A. I saw John Surratt.
Q. What other men came during the time you stayed there last winter? A. I saw John Wilkes Booth, and I saw two of the prisoners at the bar.
Which two? A. I saw Mr. Atzeroth and Mr. Wood (pointing to Payne).
Q. Did you know him by any other name? A. I did not know him by any other name.
Q. How often did you see this Wood at the house? A. I never saw him there except twice.
Q. When was that? A. I do not know exactly about the time; I saw him there once, I think, in March.
Q. How often did you see Atzeroth there? A. He did not stay at the house at any time.
Q. Did you see him there several times? A. He was there a short time.
Q. Did you understand whether he stayed there over night once? A. He did.
Q. Look at the other prisoners at the bar, and say if you have seen any one of them at Mrs. Surratt's house; have you seen the one standing in the corner (Harold)? A. I do not know; I never saw the man.
Q. State whether you, in company with John Surratt and this man Wood, visited Ford's Theatre one night in March last? A. Yes.
Q. Did you occupy a box in that theatre? A. Yes.
Q. Which box there did you occupy? A. I do not know; I did not pay any attention on which side it was.
Q. Was it the upper or lower box? A. I think it was the upper.
Q. State whether John Wilkes Booth came into that box that night while you, Wood and Surratt were in there? A. Yes.
Q. What lady accompanied you? A. Miss Deane.
Q. When did you leave Mrs. Surratt's house? A. I went to Baltimore on the six o'clock train, the day after we were at the theatre.
Q. How long were you absent? A. I was absent about a week.
By the Court.—Q. Do you recollect whether, on entering the theatre, you turned to the right or left to go to the box you occupied? A. I do not recollect which side.
The hour of one having arrived the Court took the usual recess for an hour.
After the recess, the Court took the

Testimony of Captain Dougherty.

Q. State whether or not you had command of a detachment of cavalry sent in pursuit of the assassin of the President, J. W. Booth. A. I had.
Q. The circumstances of the capture have been fully detailed by other witnesses; I will ask what part, if any, you took in the capture of Harold, and if any, state all he said on that occasion. A. There was considerable parley in reference to the arms he was supposed to have while he remained in Garrett's barn; we had a good deal of conversation with Booth about his coming out; Booth at first denied there was anybody else in the barn; finally he said "Captain there is a man here who wants to surrender awful bad;" Baker, one of the detectives, who was there, said to me "tell him to band out his arms and come out;" I repeated the direction to him, Harold, who was by the door, said, "I have no arms;" Baker said, "We know exactly what you've got;" I remarked to Baker, "You'd better let them come out;" Baker said, "Wait till Conger comes;" I said "No," and addressing the man at the door, said, "Open that door and I will take that man out myself;" the door was partially opened; Harold put out his hands, and I took hold of them and pulled him out; I put my revolver under my arm and turned him around to see if he had any arms; he had none; I asked him if he had any papers; he said "Nothing but this," pulling out a piece of map from his pocket; I took him back a short distance from the door, and just at that time the shot was fired and the door thrown open; I dragged him into the barn where Booth had fallen on the ground; the soldiers and detectives who were there came in and brought Booth out; I took charge of Harold; when I had brought him outside again he said, "Let me go, I will not leave, I will not go away;" said I, "No sir;" said he, "Who has been shot in the barn?" said I, "You know who it is;" he said "I do not;" he told me his name was Boyd; said I, "His name is Booth, and you know it;" he said, "No, he did not;" I had him tied by his hands to a tree about two yards from where Booth had been carried to the verandah of the house and kept him there until we were ready to return; Booth, in the meantime, died; I sewed him up in a blanket, having previously sent some cavalrymen for a doctor; I got a negro who lives about half a mile from there, with a wagon, put the body on board, and started for Belle Plain, where a boat was waiting.
Q. Where did Harold say he had met with this man? A. He told me he met him about seven miles from

Washington, by accident; I think he said between 11 and 12 o'clock on the night of the murder.
Q. Did he persist in saying he did not know Booth at all? A. He first said he did not know him, that he, Booth, said his name was Boyd.
Q. Did he state where they went after they had met in Maryland? A. He told me that they went to Matthias Point and crossed there.
Q. Did he mention the houses they stopped at on the way? A. Not to my knowledge; the house of Dr. Stewart was mentioned; whether he said so or not, I do not distinctly recollect.
Cross-examined by Mr. Stone.—Q. Did you hear Booth say anything about Harold's innocence? A. Booth said that he was the only guilty man, or words to that effect.
Q. Harold made no resistance at all? A. While coming home he said his feet were sore, and that he could not walk; I mounted him on a horse and tied him.
By Mr. Campbell.—Q. Did not Booth remark that this man was innocent? Was not this his expression? A. It was to that effect; I cannot swear that they were the exact words he used.

Testimony of Wm. E. Cleaver.

By Judge Holt.—Q. State your residence and occupation. A. I keep a livery stable on Sixth street in this city.
Q. State whether or not J. Wilkes Booth at any time kept a horse or horses in your stable. A. He did in January last.
Q. Can you describe any of the animals he kept there? A. Yes; a one-eyed bay horse was there about one month.
Q. Why was he taken away? A. He sold the horse on the 30th of January to Samuel Arnold, one of the prisoners at the bar.
Q. Did you see the horse afterwards? A. I saw the horse a day or two afterwards, when Arnold paid for the livery and took him away.
Q. Do you know anything about the terms or circumstances of the sale? A. I only know that Booth told me that he had sold the horse to Arnold, and that Arnold came a few days afterwards and paid the livery.
Q. Have you seen the horse since that time? A. I have not.
Q. Did you see Booth and John H. Surratt go out of your stable, riding or otherwise? A. Yes; John H. Surratt would occasionally hire a horse to go out to evening parties.
Q. With whom generally? A. With Booth; Booth gave directions to let Surratt use his horse any time he desired.
Q. Did you ever see the prisoner, Atzeroth, with Booth? A. Yes, I have seen him there with horses.
Q. With whom was Atzeroth generally in company at the stable? A. I never saw him with anybody; he was generally alone.
Q. Did you see him there frequently? A. No sir; I never saw him there but once.
By Mr. Ewing.—Q. Did you ever see Arnold after he took the horse away early in February? A. I did not.

Re-examination of J. L. McPhail.

By Judge Holt.—Q. State whether the prisoner O'Laughlin has been in the Rebel service. A. He has.
Q. How long was he in the military service of the so-called Confederate States? A. About one year; I think it was after the battle at Antietam, or South Mountain, he came in and gave himself up; that was in the year 1863, I believe; I examined the records of the Provost Marshal's office before I came out this morning, and found an oath of allegiance signed by Michael O'Laughlin, and myself and others, and concluded he was the prisoner at the bar of that name; the date is June 16th, 1863; I will state that O'Laughlin sent for me to correct what he thought was an error; he then stated that he did report at Martinsburg and took the oath of allegiance; I have here the oath, dated Baltimore, June 16th, 1863, signed Michael O'Laughlin.
Cross-examined by Mr. Cox.—Q. Does it appear by this oath that it was taken at Baltimore?—A. The oath so reads.
Q. An the prisoner stated that he gave himself up at Martinsburg? A. He told me he came into our lines at Martinsburg and there took the oath.
Q. Then may you not have been mistaken about the oath having been taken at Baltimore? A. If he had come into our lines at Martinsburg, and taken the oath there, when he came into Baltimore he would have reported. It is customary for parties who have taken the oath elsewhere, coming into the city, to report when they arrive.
Q. Do you know his handwriting? A. I have seen recently quite a number of documents which I believe to be in his handwriting.
Q. But you never saw him write? A. I believe not.
Q. Have you heard him acknowledge any of the letters you speak of to be his own? A. I have seen letters I believe he has acknowledged to be his own, but I have had no conversation with him about them.

By the Court.—Do you know anything about the prisoner Harold prior to his connection with this affair? A. Only from his own declaration.
Q. Do you know that his family reside in Baltimore? A. I do; they have resided there within my recollection, I suppose, for thirty years.

Examination of Dr. Verdi.

By Judge Holt.—Q. State whether or not on the night of the assassination of the President you were called to the house of Mr. Seward. A. I was; one of the servants came for me.
Q. At what hour? A. I do not recollect; perhaps a little before eleven on Friday night.
Q. State in what condition you found the persons at that house you were called to see. A. I found Mr. Hansell, a messenger of the State Department, lying on a bed, wounded by a cut in the side some two and a half inches deep.
Q. Did you see other persons in the house of Mr. Seward at the time? A. I saw every one of them.
Q. State who they were and describe their wounds. A. Mr. Wm. H. Seward, Frederick Seward, Major Seward, Robinson and Hansell.
Q. They were all wounded? A. Yes; I had seen Secretary Seward about nine o'clock that evening in his room; when I saw him next he was in his bed, covered with blood, blood all around him, and blood in the bed; Mrs. Seward, Miss Fanny Seward and his man Robinson were in the room.
Cross-examined by Mr. Doster.—Q. Did you see Mr. Frederick Seward on that occasion? A. Yes.
Q. State whether he was sensible or insensible. A. He had difficulty in articulating; he wanted to say something but could not express himself; he knew me perfectly well; he had a smile of recognition on his lips, as I was looking at his wound on the forehead he was evidently impressed that the severe one was on the back part of his head; he commenced moving his lips and pointing his finger there; I examined his wound and found his skull broken; I said, Do you want to know whether your skull is broken or not, and he assented; he remained sensible for half an hour and then went into a sleep; he woke up in about twenty minutes, when he was put to bed, and was very soon insensible.
Q. Did you also give the information, after examining the elder Seward, whether the wounds were mortal or not? A. Yes, when I came into the room where he was, I found terror in the expression of all his family, they evidently supposing his wounds were mortal; I examined him, and immediately reported to the family that, his wounds were not mortal, upon which Mr. Seward stretched out his hands, manifesting evident satisfaction.
Q. How long was it before Dr. Barnes made his appearance? A. Probably twenty minutes.
Q. Was, or was not Mr. Seward at the time of this attack in a critical condition? A. No sir; he had improved very much from his former injury, when his jaw was broken.
Q. State what the effect of these wounds were upon Mr. Seward in reference to his form or condition. A. The effect was to debilitate him and to make it still more difficult for him to rally.
Q. Have you not at some time before this trial stated that the wounds received by Mr. Seward had a tendency to aid in his recovering from the former injury? A. No sir; I have heard that such an opinion was expressed, but I do not know by whom; that was not my opinion.

Re-examination of John Borrow, alias "Peanuts."

By Judge Bingham.—Q. State whether or not you were working at Ford's Theatre in January last. A. Yes sir, I was.
Q. State if you know the stable in the rear of the theatre occupied by Booth's horses and carriage. A. Yes sir.
Q. Who fitted it up? A. The prisoner, Spangler, and a man by the name of Jones.
Q. Did he do that in January last, and before Booth put his horses in there? A. Yes sir.
Q. What did he do in the stable? A. It was raised up a little behind and stalls put in; a carriage room was also prepared.
Q. Was Booth there at the time he was doing it? A. He was there sometimes.
Cross-examined by Mr. Ewing.—Q. Did Booth occupy that stable with a buggy and horses from that time on? A. Yes; first he had a horse and saddle there; then he sold that horse and got a horse and buggy.
By Judge Bingham.—Q. When was that buggy sold? A. On the Wednesday before the President was murdered.
Q. Who sold it? A. Ned Spangler, the prisoner.
By Mr. Ewing.—Q. Do you know who he sold it to? A. He took it down to the bazaar, where they sell horses and carriages and he could not get what he wanted, and so he sold it to a man who keeps a livery stable.
Q. Did you go with Spangler to take it down? A. Yes sir.
Q. Did not Booth and Gifford tell Spangler on Monday to take it to the bazaar to sell? A. Yes; on the

TRIAL OF THE ASSASSINS AT WASHINGTON. 83

Monday before it was sold they told him to, and I went out and cleaned it off.

Testimony of James Maddox.

By Judge Bingham.—Q. Were you employed at Ford's Theatre last winter? A. I was.
Q. State who rented the stable for Booth in which he kept his horses up to the time of the President's murder. A. I did.
Q. When did you rent the stable? A. I think in December last.
Q. From whom? A. From Mrs. Davis.
Q. For whom? A. For Booth.
Q. Who paid the rent, and how was it paid? A. I paid it monthly.
Q. Who furnished the money? A. Booth.
Q. Were you present at the decoration of the box on Friday afternoon, the 14th of April last, occupied by the President? A. I was there at the time.
Q. Do you know who decorated it? A. I saw Harry Ford decorating it.
Q. Did you see anybody else? A. I do not remember any body else; there may have been others there.
Q. Do you know who brought the rocking-chair in which the President sat, to the box that day? A. I do not; I saw the colored man, Joe Semms, with it on his head that afternoon, coming down from Mr. Ford's room.
Q. You did not see who put it into the box? A. No sir.
Q. Have you ever seen that chair in the box before? A. Not this season; the first time the President came there we put it in; that was in 1863.
Q. And you do not know of its being there before for two years? A. No sir.
Q. Were you in the box that day? A. No sir; I have not. been in that box since 1863.
Cross-examined by Mr. Ewing.—Q. What has been your business at Ford's Theatre? A. Property man.
Q. Did your business require you to be on the stage while the performances were going on? A. Yes, when there was anything to do.
Q. What is your position on the stage? A. It is to see that the properties are put on right, and to give to the actors the property required to be used in the play.
Q. What part of the stage did you occupy? A. My room is on the stage, and I have no special position.
Q. Do you know the passage-way by which Booth escaped? A. I was shown the passage-way; I did not see him escape.
Q. State whether it is customary, during the performance, to have, that passage-way clear or obstructed. A. It is generally clear; I have never seen it blocked; when we are playing a heavy piece we generally have to run flats in there pretty well, but it is generally clear.
Q. Is the *American Cousin* a heavy piece? A. No sir.
Q. During the play of the *American Cousin* would the passage through which Booth made his exit properly be clear? A. Yes; it would properly be clear.
Q. Where was the prisoner Spangler's position? A. On the left-hand side of the stage; the side of the President's box; he always has been on that side since I have been in the theatre.
Q. Did you see Spangler that night? A. Yes sir.
Q. State at what time you saw him during the performance. A. I saw him pretty nearly every scene; if he had not been there I should certainly have missed him; I do not recollect seeing him away from his position at all; he may have been away, but if he had been when a scene changed some other person would have had to run his flat; every person would have been inquiring where he was.
Q. If he had been away for what length of time? A. If he had missed one scene they would have all known it; one scene sometimes lasts two minutes.
Q. In the third act in the *American Cousin* are not the scenes shifted frequently? A. Yes, there are seven scenes in that act, as Miss Keene plays it.
Q. Would it have been practicable for Spangler to have been absent during the performance of that act for five minutes without his absence being noticed? A. Yes sir.
Q. Would it have been for ten minutes? A. Yes, at particular times his absence for five minutes would have been noticed; during the second act the scene does not change for about half an hour; at one time during the third act the scenes are pretty rapid.
Q. Were you at the front of the theatre during that play? A. In the second act I was in the box office.
Q. Were you on the pavement? A. I went out the alley way, and had to go on to the pavement in getting into the office.
Q. Did you see Spangler there? A. No sir; I did not
Q. Have you ever seen Spangler wear a moustache? A. No; not since I have known him, and I have known him two years next month.
Q. Where were you at the moment the President was assassinated? A. At the first entrance leading to the left hand box.
Q. Did you see Spangler there shortly before? A. Yes sir; I think I did; I saw him in his proper position as I crossed the stage after the second scene of third act was on.
Q. How long was that before the President was assassinated? A. I think about three or four minutes; I will not state positively; it could not have been long.

Q. When you heard the pistol fired did you see Booth spring on to the stage? A. I did not; I saw him first, when he had nearly passed off the stage.
Q. Did you run after him? A. I heard them calling for water, and I went to my room for that.
Q. Did you see Spangler after that? A. I did not until the next morning, as I recollect.
Q. Did you hear Booth that night when he rode up to the theatre call for Spangler? A. No sir, I did not.
By Judge Bingham.—Q. Do you know whether that box was kept locked except when it was occupied or being decorated? A. I do not know.
Q. Do you know whether any of the other boxes were occupied that night? A. I do not think any of them were.
Q. Do you not know that they were not? A. I could not state positively whether they were or not; I did not take any notice except as to the President's box.
By Mr. Ewing.—Q. When did you first hear that the President was to come to the Theatre that night? A. About twelve o'clock that day.
Q. Who told you? A. Harry Ford.
Q. Do you know whether the President was invited to be present that night? A. I do not; a young man employed at the President's house told me that night that he had been down there, that morning to engage the box.

Testimony of Lieutenant R. Bartley.

By Judge Holt.—Q. State whether you have been in the military service, and if so in what position. A. I have been in the Signal Corps of the Army since August, 1863.
Q. State whether you have been a prisoner of war, and if so at what time. A. I was a prisoner at Richmond during a portion of the year 1864.
Q. At what prison? A. A part of the time at Libby, while I was in Richmond, and in other prisons at other times.
Q. State whether or not, during that time, you had occasion to observe that the Libby Prison had been mined by the Confederate Authorities, with a view of exploding it if the city was captured by Federal troops. A. When we were first taken to Libby we were informed, when taken into the hall, that the place had been mined; on the next morning we were taken into a dungeon in the cellar part of the building; in going to the dungeon we had to go round a place of fresh dirt in the centre of the cellar; the guards would not allow any person to pass over or near it; on inquiry why we were told there was a torpedo buried there; that remained there while we were in the dungeon, and some time after we had been taken up stairs.
Q. Did you have an opportunity to examine the torpedo? A. No, it was not opened while we were in the dungeon, we learned from officers who had charge that a torpedo was there.
Q. From the appearance of the ground and the place dug out, would you have supposed it to be a large or a small torpedo? A. The excavation apparently, from the fresh dirt dug out and put back again, was perhaps six feet in diameter.
Q. Was that already under the prison? A. Yes sir, directly under the centre of the prison.
Q. Did they explain to you the object for which it had been placed there? A. Yes; different persons, in conversation, told us the prison had been mined, on account of the raid near the city, under the command of Dahlgren; they said if the raid succeeded, and the prisoners were in danger of being liberated, they would blow us up.

Testimony of Colonel R. P. Treat.

By Judge Holt.—Q. State your position in the service. A. I am Chief Commissary of the Army of the Ohio, on General Schofield's staff.
Q. Have you been on duty recently in North Carolina? A. I have.
Q. State whether or not the army with which you were connected there captured several boxes said to contain the archives of the so-called Confederate States. A. Yes, they were surrendered by General Joe Johnston to General Schofield at Charlotte, North Carolina.
Q. State under what circumstances they were delivered to you by General Johnston. A. I think a letter was sent from Johnston, at Charlotte, to General Schofield, at Raleigh, stating that he had in his possession, at Charlotte, the archives of the War Department of the Confederate States of America, and that he was ready to deliver them to General Schofield on his sending an officer to receive them; the following day an officer of Schofield's staff went for them and brought them to Raleigh; from that point they were sent to Washington, and came in my charge.
Q. To whom did you deliver them here? A. To Major T. D. Ecker, of the War Department.
Q. Were those boxes labeled so as to designate the contents of each? A. Most of them were.

Testimony of Major T. D. Eckert.

By Judge Holt.—Q. State whether or not you received and examined certain boxes purporting to contain the archives of the War Department of the so-called Confederate states of America. A. I did receive them yesterday morning, and they have been opened by my direction, and to a certain extent have undergone examination by Mr. F. H. Hall.

Testimony of F. H. Hall.

By Judge Holt.—Q. State whether or not you have opened certain boxes delivered to you by Major Eckert as containing the archives of the so-called Confederate States of America. A. I have.
Q. Look at that paper and state whether it was found in one of those boxes. A. Yes, I recognize it as one of the papers found.
The paper referred to was read to the Court by Col. Burnett, and is as follows:—

MONTGOMERY, WHITE SULPHUR SPRINGS, Va.
To His Excellency the President of the Confederate States of America.—Dear Sir:—I have been thinking for some time I would make this communication to you, but have been debarred from doing so on account of ill health. I now offer you my services, and if you will favor me in my designs, I will proceed as soon as my health will permit, to rid my country of some of her deadliest enemies, by striking at the very heart's blood of those who seek to enchain her in slavery. I consider nothing dishonorable having such a tendency. All I want of you is to favor me by granting the necessary papers, etc., to travel on while within the jurisdiction of this Government. I am perfectly familiar with the North, and feel confident that I can execute anything I undertake. I have just returned now from within their lines. I am a lieutenant in General Duke's command. I was on a raid last June in Kentucky, under General John H. Morgan. I and all my command, except two or three commissioned officers, were taken prisoners, but finding a good opportunity while being taken to prison, I made my escape from them in the garb of a citizen. I attempted to pass out through the mountains, but finding that impossible, narrowly escaping two or three times being retaken, I directed my course North, and South through the Canadas for the assistance of Colonel J. P. Holcombe. I succeeded in making my way round through the blockade; but having taken the yellow fever at Bermuda, I have been rendered unfit for service since my arrival. I was reared up in the State of Alabama, and educated at its University. Both the Secretary of War and his Assistant, Judge Campbell, are personally acquainted with my father, Wm. J. Alston, of the Fifth Congressional District of Alabama, having served in the time of the old Congress in the years 1849, 1850 and 1851. If I do anything for you I shall expect your full confidence in return. If you give this I can render you and my country very important service. Let me hear from you soon. I am anxious to be doing something, and having no command at present, all or nearly all being in garrison, I desire that you favor me in this a short time. I would like to have a personal interview with you in order to perfect arrangements before starting.
I am, very respectfully, your obedient servant,
Lieutenant W. ALLSTON.
(Address me at these Springs, in hospital.)
On the above letter were the following indorsements.—
1. Brief of letter without signature.
2. Respectfully referred by direction of the President to the Honorable Secretary of War.
(Signed) BURTON W. HARRISON,
Private Secretary.
Received Nov. 29th, 1864, Record Book A. G. O. Dec. 8th, 1864, third A. G., for attention. By order J. A. Campbell, A. S. W.
By Mr. Aiken.—Q. From which box did you obtain that letter? A. From the box marked "Adjutant General's office, letters received from July to December, 1864."

Re-examination of William E. Cleves.

Q. State to the Court whether you have examined the horse you were from here sent to see. A. Yes sir.
Q. In what stable? A. At General Augur's headquarters.
Q. Is it the same horse that Arnold bought from Booth? A. Yes sir.
Q. You don't know what payment was made on the horse? A. I do not sir.
Cross-examined by Mr. Ewing.—Q. How do you know Arnold bought the horse from Booth? A. Only as Booth told me; it was credited to him next morning.
By Mr. Doster.—Q. Did you ever see that horse in the possession of Atzeroth? A. No sir.
The Judge Advocate-General stated that no more witnesses on behalf of the Government were present, and that unless the counsel for the accused were prepared to commence their defense, he would ask for an adjournment of the Court for the day.
Mr. Aiken remarked that the counsel for the accused preferred that the Government should close its evidence before commencing the defense.
After some conversation among the members of the Court, as to the practicability of accomplishing any business during the following two days, on account of the great review, the Court adjourned until to-morrow (Tuesday), at ten o'clock A. M.

WASHINGTON, May 23.—The Court met at half-past ten o'clock.
Mr. Cox called attention to an error in the record.
On Monday Marshal McPhail presented the form of the oath of allegiance, and judged it bore the signature of Mr. O'Laughlin, but the witness had not sufficient knowledge of the handwriting to swear to it positively, therefore it was not received as evidence, and was ruled out by the Judge-Advocate. He (Mr. Cox) did not, as stated, ask for the reading, but objected to it. He knew of no other way to correct the testimony than to ask that it be excluded from the evidence.
The Judge Advocate-General said that that was right, and so the request of Mr. Cox was complied with.

Testimony of Voltaire Randall.

Knew the prisoner Arnold; he examined the prisoner's carpet-bag, and found in it some papers, letters, clothing, a revolver and cartridges.
By Judge Advocate Holt.—Q. Will you look at this revolver? (The revolver was handed to the witness.)
A. This is the same revolver; I made a minute examination at the time; I examined it on the morning of the 17th of April, at Fortress Monroe; the pistol was loaded, and is loaded at this time.
The Court ordered the pistol to be discharged.
By Mr. Ewing.—It was at the store of John W. Wharton, a short distance from the fort.
The witness stated, in reply to Judge Advocate Holt, that the number of the pistol is 104,857.
General Howe remarked that the pistol was a Colt's navy revolver.

Testimony of Major Marsh.

Served in the military service as an officer in one of the Maryland regiments from 1861 until the 31st of August, 1864; he occupied the position of Lieutenant-Colonel; when he left the service he was a prisoner of war, and confined in the Libby Prison from the 15th of June until the 21st of March, 1864.
By Judge Advocate Holt—Q. State under what circumstances you were confined, the number of prisoners, and the treatment you received from the Rebel Government. A. I was captured three and a half miles from Winchester, on the Martinsburg road; I was in General Milroy's command, and was captured by General Ewell's corps, and taken to Winchester, where I was detained for two weeks on account of ill health; I was somewhat sick, on account of excess of duty and exposure; at the expiration of two weeks, my health having improved, I was compelled to march to Staunton; I was treated kindly on the road by the officers of the escort; when I arrived at Libby Prison the rations were small but tolerably fair at first; a half a loaf of bread was given to each man, with four ounces of meat, and several spoonsful of rice; after we had been there four months the meat, as a regular thing, was stopped, and we received it only occasionally; the prison authorities then deprived us of wheat bread, and gave us what they called corn bread; it was of a coarse character; I have known the prisoners to be without meat three or four weeks at a time; in addition to the miserable corn bread, a few potatoes were occasionally distributed, of the very worst character; this continued for some time, when the officers held a meeting with regard to the bad treatment which they had received; a letter was sent to Colonel Ould by General Streight, who was chairman of the meeting, complaining of the bad treatment, and asking for improvement; to this Colonel Ould replied, "The treatment was good enough, and better than the Rebel prisoners received at Fort Delaware and other places." Ould was the Rebel Commissioner of Exchange.
The witness continued:—"After I had been in Libby Prison five months I was taken sick with dropsy, for want of proper nourishment, and sent to the hospital; while there I saw men brought in from Belle Isle; their condition was horrible in the extreme; I was satisfied that they were in a starving condition; out of forty at least eight or twelve died the first night; I asked the surgeon in charge of the hospital, who was very kind to us at first, what was the matter with these men? he replied their condition was owing to want of proper treatment and nourishment and neglect; I had been there about two weeks when two of our officers made their escape; Major Turner, in charge of the prisoners, was passionate and insulting whenever he chose to speak; he took it into his head to remove us back from the hospital to Libby Prison; the room to which we were removed was wet with the washing of it out; some of the sick were in a dying condition, and were compelled to remain there twenty-four hours without cots or a morsel to eat, as a punishment because the two officers escaped; the treatment, I repeat, was very harsh; Colonel Fowler spoke to Major Turner with regard to the bad treatment, when the latter replied, "It is too ——— good for you Yankees."
The opportunity I had for seeing the bad treatment was when men were brought to the hospital; they were emaciated for want of food; when food was

TRIAL OF THE ASSASSINS AT WASHINGTON.

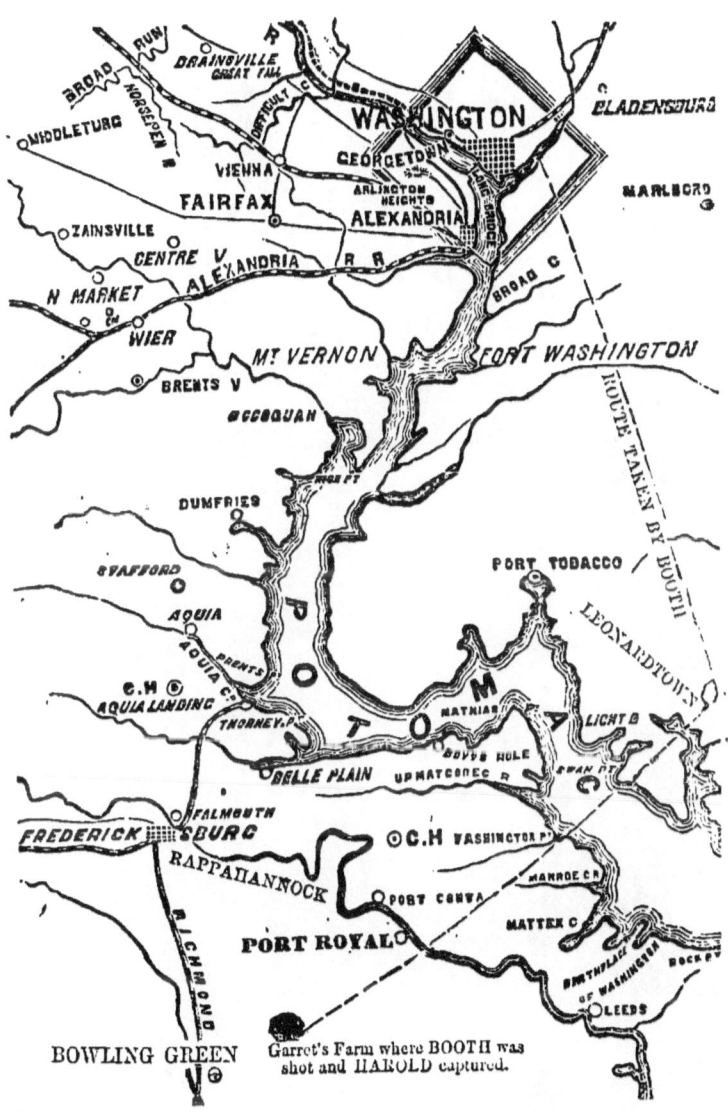

DEATH SCENE OF THE ASSASSIN.
Map showing where Booth was killed and Harold captured.

brought within their reach they were eager to get it, and they would gr: sp at it.
Q. Was there any pretense that this treatment was the result of necessity, or that they had not food enough? A. All the reply I could get was that it was a matter of retaliation, and that their prisoners were treated worse than ours.
Q. What proportion did the food bear to a ration, or for the comfortable support of life? was it one-half or one quarter? A. A man could possibly live on what was first given, although not a full ration; a man could not possibly live on it all the time; what was called corn bread appeared to be meal and bran mixed, and baked in a tough condition; for days we lived on that and water alone.

Examination of Captain Emory.

Was in the military service, and was captured at Winchester on the 15th of June, 1863, and exchanged on the 4th of May, 1864. He stated substantially the same as the preceding witness in respect to the food and bad treatment received by the Union prisoners. The money belonging to the prisoners was taken away from them, and, therefore, they could not buy food. The bearing of the Rebel keeper of the prison was very rude. He always abused the prisoners. When the latter were brought to the hospital their condition was awful, from the result, as it was generally understood, of starvation. After the battle of Chickamauga fifteen or sixteen of these sick prisoners were tied on a cart, to keep them from falling off, although there were ambulances near by not in use; they were tied like sacks of grain. The witness said he had to lie on the floor for a long time, and had not yet recovered his strength. The Committee of the Rebel senate knew of their horrible treatment, but did not notice them on their visit. On one occasion he told the men he wanted some medicine. Turner said he had none to give him, and added, "The treatment is good enough for Yankees." An Inspector of the prison, named Turner, said the object of the treatment was to kill the prisoners, adding, "It is good enough for you. You had no business to come here. If I had command I would hang all of you."

Testimony of Benj. Swearer.

By Judge Advocate Holt—Q. State to the Court whether you have been in the military service of the United States. I have; I was color sergeant in the regiment to which I belong.
Q. State whether or not you were a prisoner of war at any time. A. I was; I was captured on the 18th of October, 1863.
Q. State how long after your capture you continued a prisoner of war, and at what point you were confined. A. Five months and seven days; I was confined at Belle Isle.
Q. What number of prisoners were confined with you? A. When I left there were about thirteen thousand there.
Q. Were they kept in buildings, or simply on the naked sand? A. On the naked sand of the island.
Q. In what season of the year? A. In winter.
Q. Were they provided with any shelter? A. Some were.
Q. What proportion of them? A. I judge about one-half.
Q. What kind of treatment did you receive? A. We had about half enough food to live on.
Q. Of what did the rations consist? A. There were twenty-five pounds of meat served up for one hundred men, and a big share of that was bone; some corn bread was browned up with it.
Q. What opportunities had you for cooking it? A. It was cooked for us.
Q. What was the effect of this system of starvation upon the health of the men? A. It was very marked; the men had nothing else to live on, and I have seen men on that island starved to death ; more than that, the bodies of those who died were allowed to lie for eight or nine days in the trenches without being buried; they would not allow us to bury them; they laid there, to the best of my knowledge, from seven to nine days.
Q. Was that the subject of remonstrance on your part? A. I judge it was; I spoke to the lieutenant in charge of the prisoners on the island, and he told me he had nothing to do with it; that he had his orders from Major Turner.
Q You say that they positively refused you permission to bury the dead? A. Yes sir; I asked as a personal favor to be allowed to bury the dead, but was refused.
Q. Did the men die in large numbers? A. I helped to carry out from ten to fifteen and twenty a day; more than that, I saw men shot down without the slightest cause or provocation.
Q. State whether the death of these men was caused mainly by starvation. A. It was.
Q. Was any proposition made by the prisoners to the Rebel authorities to support themselves, if they should be allowed to secure provisions? A. I think there was; I cannot say for certain, but there was a large number who volunteered to work in order to get something

numbers of the men volunteered to work at building a machine shop there.
Q. You say that one-half of these prisoners, in the dead of winter, laid out at night on the open sand, without any shelter from the weather or any fuel to warm them? A. Yes sir; I laid there for three months without any shelter; my ordinary weight is about one hundred and seventy pounds, but when I came home I weighed only about one hundred and twenty-three; I do not think I would have lived had I staid there a month longer.

Testimony of Wm. Ball.

By Judge Advocate Holt.—Q. How long have you been in the military service of the United States? A. I enlisted in 1862.
Q. When were you captured by the enemy? A. On the 11th of May, 1864.
Q. How long were you a prisoner? A. About eleven months and twenty-two days.
Q. State where you were confined. A. At Andersonville, Ga.
Q. How many prisoners of war were there at the time of your confinement? A. I think that altogether there were in the neighborhood of thirty-two thousand.
Q. State what treatment they received from the Rebel authorities while you were there. A. The treatment was very poor indeed; they had no shelter whatever, but were compelled to live in a swamp; their blankets, hats, cups, their clothing in general, and their money, were taken from them.
Q. You say they were compelled to live in a swamp? A. Yes sir; the encampment was in a swamp.
Q. Had it any shelter? A. No shelter whatever.
Q. State whether there was woodland in that vicinity. A. Yes sir; there was splendid pine wood around there, any quantity of it.
Q. State the character of the rations served out. A. Well, sir, every morning when the wagon came around, there would be served to each man half a pint of corn meal, two ounces of bacon, and a half-spoonful of salt; this was all the rations for twenty-four hours.
Q. What was the character of the bacon? A. Well, it was alive.
Q. Was it rancid and rotten? A. Yes sir; once in a while we would get hold of a good piece, but not very often.
Q. What was the effect of this treatment on the prisoners? A. It was very hurtful, and killed them off; the largest number of deaths in any one day, so far as my recollection goes, was one hundred and thirty-three.
Q. Was it not understood there that most of these deaths were occasioned by starvation? A. It was.
Q. Was any remonstrance addressed to the Rebel authorities in regard to these things? A. I do not think there was.
Q. Did you hear any statement on that subject from the enemy? A. Yes sir.
Q. What did they say? A. They said they did not care a —— whether the Yankees died or not.
Q. Do you remember whether a man by the name of Howell Cobb, formerly Secretary of the Treasury of the United States, visited Andersonville? A. I do; he made a speech there. I think, some time in February.
Q. Do you remember the tone of that speech, or what he said in reference to the prisoners? A. He made some very bitter remarks; I do not recollect the exact terms.
Q. Were they in support of the policy which had been pursued in the treatment of prisoners, or otherwise? A. He said that was the best they could do for them, meaning the prisoners; that if the authorities looked after them a little more no doubt they would fare better; he only said a few words, and did not seem to care much about the prisoners.
Q. You say the men died at the rate of 100 to 150 a day? A. I think that the day on which the largest number of deaths occurred was the 11th of September, when 133 of the prisoners died.
Q. You say they were in the open sun; was the heat very great? A. It was very intense indeed.
Q. How was the water? A. We were obliged to drink water which had been made filthy in consequence of the garbage thrown in the creek above.
Q. Did you regard that as accidental or the work of design? A. I do not know positively; the Rebels always threw their filth and waste matter into the creek above, and the men got up a remonstrance, the reply to which was that they did not care a —— for the Yankees.
Q. How was the treatment in the prison; were many of the men shot? A. Yes sir; when I first went there in June, as many as six or eight a day were shot dead.
Q. Did it appear to you that they were shot in wantonness? A. If a man got half a foot over the dead line, or near it, he was shot; it was said that they got a thirty days' furlough for shooting a Yankee.
Q. Do you remember whether Howell Cobb referred in his speech to the Rebel emissaries at the North who were engaged in the work of firing Northern cities? A. He made some remark about a plan to burn and plunder the North; I cannot tell what were the words used.
Q. What was the treatment of prisoners who were

TRIAL OF THE ASSASSINS AT WASHINGTON.

sick in the hospitals? A. It was very poor indeed they got pitch-pine pills for the diarrhœa, pitch-pine pills for the scurvy, and pitch-pine pills for everything else; they did not get any regular medicine.

Q. Of what were these pitch-pine pills composed? A. Of a little pitch-pine, the stuff that runs out of the trees there, and a little vinegar; once in a while the patients would get a little medicine, or something, like it.

Q. Was any of the money taken from the prisoners returned to them? A. Not a cent.

Q. What was your experience in regard to the taking of your clothes and money? A. When I was first captured they took my shoes off, and I walked barefoot to Gordonsville; they then took from me my blanket and clothes, and for nine months I had nothing on but a pair of drawers and a shirt; I laid there on the open ground for nine months without a bit of shelter.

Q. Was that the common experience? A. Yes sir; there were thousands there in the same fix; the corpse of a man who died in the morning could not be approached by night within twenty feet, and pitch-forks had to be used to carry the body off to the trenches.

By the Court.—Q. Did you hear any reasons given for depriving the prisoners of their clothing? A. It was because they needed it for their own use; I would state here that clothing was sent there by our Government, and the Rebel Captain in charge over the prisoners took it himself, and this Captain was in command of the interior of the prison; Colonel Gibbs commanded the post.

Q. Was the quality of the provisions served out to you such that a man would not eat unless he was in a starving condition? A. Yes sir; I would not think of such a thing now, but a man in danger of starvation might eat them.

Q. Do you think it possible to sustain life for any great length of time on such food? A. I do not think a man could do it a great while; up to the day I left, which was the 24th of March, 16,725 men had died there; that was the number taken from the books by myself.

By Judge Holt.—Q. What proportion of those deaths, in your judgment and the judgment of other prisoners, occurred from starvation and in consequence of this treatment of which you speak? A. I have no doubt over one-half; the food which they received was the cause of their sickness, and after they got sick they did not receive any better food.

By the Court.—Q. Was there any medical treatment given to those suffering prisoners? A. Very little; indeed nothing of any benefit.

Testimony of E. W. Ross.

By Judge Advocate Holt.—Q. State whether or not you have been in the service of the Rebel Government. A. I never was in the army; I was a clerk at Libby Prison.

Q. Were you a clerk there in the month of March, 1864? A. Yes sir, about that time General Kilpatrick was making a raid in the vicinity of Richmond.

Q. State what knowledge, if any, you had of Libby Prison having at that time been mined by the Confederate authorities. A. I never saw the powder, but I saw the place where they said the powder was buried I was away one night about that time, and when I came back in the morning one of the colored men at the prison told me that some powder had been put into the building; when I went to roll call one of the officers asked me whether the powder was there, and I told him I did not know certainly, I saw the fuse in the office.

Q. Did you ever see the place where the powder was buried? A. Yes sir, frequently; two sentinels were placed over it to keep persons from approaching the place.

Q. Was the fuse kept in the office? A. Yes sir; Major Turner had it in charge; it was an eight-second fuse.

Q. Did he state to you that the powder was there? A. Yes sir, and also said that this fuse was to set it off.

Q. In what event was this explosion to take place? A. In case the raiders got into the city they would set it off.

Q. And blow up the prison and the prisoners? A. That must have been their intention.

Q. How long did that powder remain there? A. In May they took it out secretly.

Q. Do you know whether the fact of its removal was kept a secret from the prisoners themselves? A. I do not.

By the Court.—Q. Did you understand by whose authority the powder was put there? A. It was done while Winder was Secretary of War.

Q. State whether or not Major Turner, the keeper of the prison, did not seem to be acting under the authority of the War Department? A. He never told me that he was acting under any orders in the matter, or even that the powder was there.

Q. Was he not a subordinate of the War Department? A. Yes sir.

Testimony of John La Touche.

By Judge Holt.—Q. State whether or not you have been in the service of the Rebels? A. Yes sir; I was in the Confederate States Army.

Q. State whether or not you were on duty at Libby Prison in March, 1864? A. I had been detailed there and was on duty at that place at that time.

Q. State what knowledge you have, if any, concerning the mining of Libby Prison about that time by the Confederate authorities? A. Major Turner, the keeper of the prison, told me one day that he was going to see General Winder about a guard; I believe we had no relief that day; when he returned he told me that Gen. Winder himself had been to see the Secretary of War, and that they were going to put powder in the building; in the evening of the same day the powder came there; it was in twenty-five pound kegs, which were contained in boxes, and altogether amounted to, I suppose, one hundred pounds; a hole was dug in the centre of the middle basement, and the powder was put down therein; the ground was then covered over with gravel; I took one of the sentries from the outside of the building and placed him over this powder, so that no accident might occur; the next day Major Turner showed us the fuse in the office; it was a long fuse, and was made of gutta percha; the powder remained there until, I think, some time in May, when the prisoners were all removed from the prison; General Winder then sent a note to the office, with directions to take up the powder as secretly as possible; I do not remember the exact word.

Q. State whether you heard in what event this powder was to be set off? A. I did not hear at that time; I heard him say afterwards that in case of the raiders coming into Richmond he would blow up the place.

Q. Meaning the prison building and the prisoners in it? A. I suppose so.

Testimony of George N. McGee.

By Judge Advocate Holt.—Q. State whether you know the prisoner at the bar, Samuel Arnold? A. I do.

Q. State whether or not he has been in the military service of the Rebels?

Mr. Ewing.—I object. The ground of my objection is that Arnold is here on trial for having been engaged in a conspiracy to do certain things, and that it is not competent for the Government to show, it such be the fact, that before he entered into this conspiracy he was in the military service of the Confederate States. He is not on trial for having been in the military service of the Confederate States; he is not on trial for having taken the oath of allegiance and broken it, for they may see fit to follow this up by a statement of that kind, as has been done in the case of O'Laughlin. He is on trial for an offense defined clearly in the charge and specifications, and it is not competent, it seems to me clearly not competent, to attempt to aggravate the offense with which he is charged, and of which they seek to prove him guilty, by showing that he has been unfaithful to the Government in other respects and at other times, and it is introduced and can be introduced for no other purpose than that of aggravating his alleged acts in connection with the conspiracy. That course of testimony would be in effect at owing the prosecution to introduce testimony as to the previous character of the accused, and that is a right that is reserved to the accused always, and is never allowed to the prosecution. More than that, it would allow the prosecution to do what the accused is not allowed to do on his own behalf in the point of character, that is, to introduce specific acts, from which his character may be inferred.

Judge Advocate Holt.—I will make only a single remark. I think the testimony in this case has proven what I believe to be sufficiently demonstrative, how kindred to each other are the crimes of treason against the nation and the assassination of its Chief Magistrate. The one seems to be a necessary consequence of, as it certainly is a logical sequence from the other. The murder of the President of the United States, as alleged and shown, was, pre-eminently, a political assassination. Disloyalty to the Government was its guide, its only inspiration. When, therefore, we shall show, on the part of the accused, acts of intense disloyalty, the bearing of arms in the field against that Government, we show the presence of an animus towards that Government which relieves this accusation of much if not all improbability. This course of proof is constantly resorted to in other Courts. I do not regard it as in the slightest degree a departure from the usages of the profession. In the administration of courts of justice, the purpose is to show that the prisoner, in his mind and in his course of life, was prepared for the commission of this crime; that the tendencies of his life, so evidenced by open and overt acts, points to this crime; if not as a natural certainty, as a most probable result. It is in this view and with that object that the testimony is offered.

Assistant Judge Advocate Bingham referred to Roscoe's "Criminal Evidence," page 85 or 87, as authority for the rule of law that when the intent with which an act is done is initial, other acts of the prisoner not initial, to prove the intent, may be given in evidence. It was alleged in the charge and specifications that the prisoner Arnold, with others, engaged in a conspiracy to murder the President of the United States, and others, with intent to aid the Rebellion against the United States. The object here now was to establish that intent thus put in issue by proving that the prisoner himself was part of the Rebellion.

Mr. Ewing said that he would defer speaking upon

the general principle involved, and content himself with a reference to authorities in support of his position. He accordingly referred to several authorities on the subject, from only one of which we quote as follows:—"Evidence will not be admitted on the part of the prosecution to show the bad character of the accused unless he has called witnesses in support of his character, and even then the prosecutor cannot examine us to particular acts."

The objection was then overruled, and the following answer to the question was given by the witness:—A. I could not say positively.

Q. What knowledge have you on the subject? A. I have seen the prisoner in the uniform of the Rebel military service.

Q. Was it the uniform of a private soldier or of an officer? A. A private soldier.

Q. At what time was this? A. I cannot tell; I think it was in 1862.

By Mr. Ewing.—Q. At what time did you see the prisoner dressed in Rebel uniform? A. I think it was in 1861; I cannot say positively.

Testimony of John L. Caldwell.

By Assistant Judge Advocate Burnett.—Q. Where do you reside? A. At Georgetown.

Q. State where you were on the morning of the assassination? A. At Mathews & Company's grocery store, in Georgetown.

Q. State whether you saw at that time any of the prisoners at the bar, and which one. A. I saw that one, Atzerott, at about 8 o'clock; he came into the store; I asked him how he was, and so on; he told me he was going into the country, and asked me whether I did not want to buy his watch; I said no; I had no use for one; he then asked me to lend him ten dollars; I told him I had not the money to spare; he then took out his revolver, and said lend me ten dollars and take this as security; I will come back next week and return you the money; I thought the revolver was good enough security, so I loaned him the money.

A revolver was shown to the witness, which he recognized as the one referred to. It was loaded when he received it, but had the appearance of having been fired once.

Testimony of Mary Simms (Colored.)

By Assistant Judge Advocate Bingham.—Q. State whether you know any of the prisoners. A. I know that one, Dr. Samuel Mudd.

Q. State whether you were his slave, and lived with him. A. I was his slave, and lived with him four years; I left him about a month before last Christmas; I was free then.

Q. When you lived with the prisoner did you hear him say anything about President Lincoln? A. I heard him say when he (President Lincoln) came in here he stole in in the night, dressed in women's clothes; that they laid in wait for him, and that if they had caught him they would have killed him.

Q. State who visited him. A. A man by the name of Surratt visited him; also, a man named Walker Bowie.

Q. Who called this man Surratt? A. Dr. Sam. Mudd and Dr. sam. Mudd's wife called him Surratt.

Q. State the appearance of this man Surratt. A. He was young looking, rather slim, neither very tall nor short; his hair was rather light, at least not black.

Q. State where he slept when at Dr. Mudd's house. A. All of his men slept in the woods.

Q. State how many were with him when they slept in the woods. A. There was Captain White, from Tennessee; Benjamin Gwin, Andrew Gwin and George Gwin.

Q. How did they get victuals to eat while they were in the woods? A. When Dr. Mudd went in the house with the men to get his meals he put us out at the door to watch if anybody came along; then at other times he would send me with victuals down, and then stand behind a tree to watch when the Rebels would come out and get them.

Q. Did you ever see Surratt in the house with Mudd at any other time than when he was eating? A. Yes sir; when they wanted to talk they always went apart by themselves.

Q. Where did they go to? A. Upstairs in a room.

Q. State how you knew that the men whocame there were Rebels. A. They would often bring letters from Virginia.

Q. To whom did they bring the letters? A. To Dr. Sam Mudd.

Q. State whether he would give them letters to take back. A. Yes sir; and clothes and socks.

Q. What sort of clothing were these men dressed in? A. Some of them whom they called officers and soldiers would have epaulettes on their shoulders, and were dressed in grey coats and grey pants, trimmed with yellow.

Q. Did you hear Dr. Samuel Mudd say anything about sending anybody to Richmond? A. I heard him say something about sending my brother to Richmond; when he bought my brother he said he would have something for him to do in Richmond.

Q. What did he say he would have for him to do? A. To build batteries.

Q. Was your brother his slave? A. Yes sir.

The cross-examination of this witness, which was conducted by Mr. Ewing, did not elicit any point of general interest.

In regard to the prisoner, Mudd's remark that President Lincoln would have been killed, if caught, the witness testified that the remark was made four years ago. The man Walter Bowie was not only one of the visitors who slept in the house; the others remaining in the woods. Surratt among them, on beds made upon bed clothes procured at Mudd's house; Surratt frequently took dinner at the house, but was not seen by more than one other servant; he commenced coming last winter.

Testimony of Eleazer Eglin.

By Judge Holt.—Q. Do you recognize the prisoner, Dr. Samuel A. Mudd? A. I do.

Q. Were you his slave? A. Yes sir; I left him in August, 1863.

Q. State whether he said anything to you about sending you to Richmond.

Mr. Ewing objected to the question on the ground that it was irrelevant.

Judge Advocate Holt said the object of the question was to show disloyalty on the part of the accused.

The objection was overruled and the question repeated.

A. He told me that when I got so that I could travel he would have a place for me in Richmond.

Q. When was that? A. In June, 1863.

Q. State if you saw any men about Dr. Mudd's house when you were there, if so, where they staid? A. I saw some men there, and some of them staid in the woods in the daytime.

Q. Where did they get their victuals? A. I do not know.

Q. Did you see any victuals being taken to them? A. I saw victuals going that way often enough; I saw my sister, Mary Simms, taking them.

Q. How were these men dressed? A. Some in grey, and some in black clothes.

Q. Who was present besides yourself when Dr. Mudd said he was going to send you to Richmond? A. No person.

Testimony of Sylvester Eglin.

By Judge Holt.—Q. Did you live with Dr. Samuel A. Mudd? A. I lived with his father, about a quarter of a mile off.

Q. State whether you heard him say that he was going to send anybody to Richmond. A. I heard him say that he was going to send Eleazer, and me, and several others, to Richmond.

Q. To whom was he talking at the time? A. To Jerry Dyer and Walter Bowie.

Q. Where did the conversation take place? A. Down by my old master's gate, in the oats field, where the horses were kept.

Testimony of L. Washington (Colored.)

By Judge Bingham.—Q. Do you know the prisoner, Dr. Samuel A. Mudd? A. I do.

Q. Were you his slave? A. Yes.

Q. When did you leave his house? A. This October coming two years.

Q. State if while you lived with Dr. Mudd, you heard him say anything about President Lincoln. A. I heard him say he would not keep his seat long; I heard him say that some time summer before last.

Q. Was anybody talking with him at that time? A. There was a heap of gentlemen in the house; I do not know who they were.

Q. How were they dressed, and where did they sleep? A. Some had on grey clothes, some little short jackets, with a peak behind; sometimes they slept in the house, sometimes down in the pines, not very far from the spring.

Q. State how they got their victuals. A. Sometimes Dr. Mudd would carry it; sometimes the girl (Mary Simms); I did not stay about the house, but I happened to be there one day as they were setting down to dinner; Dr. Mudd set the children to watch while they were at dinner; the children said they were coming, and these men jumped up from the table and ran out the side door.

Q. Did you hear Dr. Mudd say anything about sending any one to Richmond? A. Yes; he said to one of the men, one day, that he would send him to Richmond.

Cross-examined by Mr. Ewing.—Q. How many times did you notice these men in the woods? A. They were there for a week or more, and I saw them seven or eight times; they all then went away together to the night.

Q. Do you know their names? A. I think one was Andrew Gwynne; I do not know the names of the others.

Q. Were they ever there at any other time than that week? I did not see them at any other time.

Q. What other person saw them there? A. The woman, Mary Simms, who was on here just now, saw them; her and another woman were in the room; I don't know any white person who saw them, except Dr. Mudd and his wife.

Q. Did dr. Mudd see them? A. I do not know.

Q. Did any of the field hands or any of the neighbors see them? A. I do not know of any.

Q. Where were the horses of these men kept? A. They kept their horses in the stable; sometimes Milo and sometimes Henry Ham.
Q. What time in the summer was it you saw them there? A. I think it was about August.

Testimony of Milo Simms (Colored.)

Examined by Judge Bingham.—Q. State whether you lived with the prisoner, Dr. Samuel A. Mudd. A. Yes, I was his slave; I left his house the Friday before last Christmas.
Q. State if at any time while you stayed at Dr. Mudd's house you saw any men there. A. I saw two or three there last summer.
Q. Where did these men stay? A. Sometimes in the house, and then down by the spring among the bushes; they slept down among the bushes.
Q. Did you see the bed down there? A. Yes; it was fixed under a pine tree, with a blanket, and rails at the head.
Q. Where did they get their victuals? A. From Dr. Mudd's; sometimes my sister carried it to them; sometimes they carried it their selves.
Q. When your sister carried it where was it put? A. Down by the spring.
Q. Who took it away? A. Sometimes John Surratt, sometimes one of the others.
Q. How did you know John Surratt? A. I heard them call him at the house.
Q. What kind of a looking man was he? A. He had light hair and whiskers and was a slim man.
Q. When there were men in the house was anything said by Dr. Mudd about watching? A. He set some children to watch who was coming; if any one was coming they were to tell him.
Q. Do you know whether anything was said about any one coming while these men were in the house? A. I do not.
Q. How were they dressed? A. They had on grey clothes with brass buttons.
Q. State if you heard any talk between Gen. Gardner and Dr. Mudd about Mr. Lincoln. A. Yes; I heard Mr. Gardner say "Lincoln was — son of a —, and ought to have been killed long ago;" Dr. Mudd said, "yes, that was much after his mind;" that was some time last fall.

Cross-examined by Mr. Stone.—Q. Did you work in the house or in the field? A. In the field, but sometimes when I was at the house I took the horses.
Q. How old are you? A. I reckon about fourteen years.
Q. Would you know John H. Surratt if you were to see him? A. I don't know as I would now.
Q. Who pointed him out to you? A. Dr. Mudd would say, "take Mr. Surratt's horse and carry him out to the stable and feed him."
Q. How often did you see him? A. Two or three times.
Q. How many came with him? A. Two or three.
Q. Where was it that you heard this talk between Mudd and Gardner? A. At Beantown.
Q. How far is Beantown from your house? A. About three miles; I went up with him after some liquor last summer.
Q. Was there anybody else there besides Mr. Gardner and Dr. Mudd? A. There were some men in there but I did'nt know them.
Q. Was not Andrew Gwynn there with Surratt? A. Not as I know of; I saw him at Dr. Mudd's father's house; I never saw Andrew Gwynn at Dr. Mudd's house.
Q. Who was with Andrew Gwynn? A. Jenny Dyer.
Q. When was the last time you saw John Surratt at Dr. Mudd's? A. Last winter.
Q. Did he stay all night? A. Yes.

Testimony of Wm. Marshall, (Colored.)

By Judge Bingham.—Q. State whether you were the slave of and lived with Dr. Samuel A. Mudd. A. I married near him.
Q. Do you know Ben. Gardner, one of his neighbors? A. Yes, Ben. Gardner was my wife's master.
Q. State if you heard any conversation between Gardner and Dr. Mudd about the battles on the Rappahannock. A. Yes; I heard Mr. Gardner say to Dr. Mudd, "Sam., we give them — you with the Rappahannock." The Doctor said "Yes we did." Gardner said that "Old Stonewall was the best of the Generals;" Doctor said, "Yes, he was quite a smart man;" Gardner said that "Lee had gone round up into Maryland; that he was going to cross the river at the Point of Rocks, remember that, and he would not be surprised if they were there now;" he said that "in a short time he would take the Capita , and Washington, and have Old Lincoln turned up in the house;" Dr. Mudd said "He would not be surprised."
Q. State whether Dr. Mudd made any objection. A. He did not.

Testimony of Rachel Spencer (Colored).

By Judge Bingham.—Q. State whether you were a slave of the prisoner, Dr. Mudd. A. I was; I left him in January last.
Q. While you were at Dr. Mudd's house did you see men come there at times? A. Yes, at the time men were passing through there last summer, some five or six came there.

Q. What sort of a dress did they wear? A. A black or blue; they slept in the pines, about twenty yards from the house, near the spring.
Q. Where did they get their victuals while they were there? A. At the house, and sometimes Dr. Sam took their victuals to them.
Q. When they would come into the house, did he say anything to any of the servants or boys about what they were to do? A. I was in the kitchen; they said they had to go to the door and watch.
Q. Did you hear the names of any of the men who called at Dr. Mudd's house? A. Yes; Andrew Gwynn and Walter Bowie.
Q. Did you see a young man among those who visited them? A. Yes; he slept in the pines, too, when they were there last summer.
Q. Describe his appearance. A. He was not very tall; he was fair looking and slender.
Q. Do you remember his being there more than once last summer? A. I do not.
Q. Do you remember hearing Dr. Mudd say anything about Richmond? A. I heard him tell one of his men he would send him to Richmond.

Cross-examined by Mr. Stone—Q. You say you saw them there in the summer; was it the first of the summer or the last? A. I do not know; it was warm weather; they all came together and went together; I believe they staid at the spring about a week.
Q. Where were their horses? A. In the stable.
Q. Was Mr. Best living there that year? A. Yes; to the best of my knowledge he came there the winter before.
Q. Do you know whether Mr. Albion Brooke was living there at the time these men were there. A. Yes he was.
Q. Did Mr. Best and Mr. Brooke also see these people? A. Yes sir.

By Mr. Bingham.—Q. Do you know whether Albion Brooke ever saw them or not, or did you merely suppose he did? A. He saw them.
Q. Did he tell you he saw them or how did you know it? A. He used to go with them; they were all together.
Q. Do you know whether Mr. Best ever saw them or not? A. I am not positive whether he did or not.

The Judge Advocate-General here stated that, reserving the right to introduce further testimony on the general subject of the Conspiracy, the prosecution would here close.

TESTIMONY FOR THE DEFENSE.

Mr. Aiken stated that by agreement amongst the counsel for the defense they would first introduce testimony in behalf of Mrs. Surratt. They would proceed as far as practicable this afternoon but would not consider the testimony closed in respect to any one until all the testimony for the defense was in.

Testimony of Father Wiggat.

By Mr. Aiken.—Q. State your residence in this city, and your occupation. A. My residence is Gonzaga College, in this city, in F street, between Ninth and Tenth; I am a clergyman.
Q. Are you acquainted with the prisoner, Mary E. Surratt? A. I am and have been for ten or eleven years.
Q. Has that acquaintance been of an intimate character? A. I knew her very well.
Q. Are you acquainted with her general reputation? A. I have always heard every one speak very highly of her as a lady and a Christian.
Q. In all that acquaintance has anything ever come to your knowledge that would indicate an unchristian character on her part? A. No, never.
Q. Are you acquainted with Lewis J. Weichman? A. Only very slightly; I saw him a few times; I am not well acquainted with him.
Q. State whether, from your knowledge, he has ever been a student of divinity.
Question objected to by Mr. Bingham, on the ground that the purpose of the question was to impeach the character of Weichman. He could not be contradicted in respect to entirely immaterial matter.
Mr. Aiken replied that the intention was to impeach Weichman's testimony in this and many other particulars, and as the foundation had been laid in the cross-examination the question was a proper one.
The objection was sustained by the Court.
Q. Was there in the city of Richmond a Catholic Theological Institute?
Question objected to by Mr. Bingham, for the same reason as last question, and objection sustained by the Court.
Q. In your acquaintance with Mrs. Surratt have you ever known of a defective eyesight on her part? A. No, not particularly.

Cross-examined by Judge Holt—Q. You say you know the character of the prisoner, Mrs. Surratt, for Christianity is good; have you any personal knowledge of her character for loyalty? A. No; my intercourse with her has never extended to political affairs.
Q. You have had intercourse with her as her pastor during the Rebellion, have you not? A. I am not her pastor.

TRIAL OF THE ASSASSINS AT WASHINGTON.

Q. How often have you been in the habit of seeing her during the Rebellion? A. Sometimes not for six months, sometimes six weeks and sometimes as often as once a week.

Q. Have you had free conversation with her? A. My conversation would only be for a few minutes, and then of a general character.

Q. Have you ever since the Rebellion heard her utter one loyal sentiment? A. I do not remember.

Q. Can you state whether it is not notorious among those who know anything of her, that she is intensely disloyal? A. I do not remember that this thing was ever talked about at all till since this last affair happened.

Testimony of Father Boyle.

By Mr. Aiken.—Q. State your residence in this city and occupation? A. My residence is at St. Peter's Church; I am a Catholic priest.

Q. Are you acquainted with the prisoner, Mary E. Surratt? A. I have some acquaintance with her; I made her acquaintance some eight or nine years ago; I have merely met her casually some three or four times since then.

Q. Do you know anything of her general reputation? A. I have always heard her spoken of as an estimable lady; I never heard a word said to her disadvantage.

Q. In all your acquaintance with her, did you ever hear her utter a disloyal sentiment? A. I never did.

Cross-examined by Judge Holt.—Q. Have you ever heard her utter a loyal sentiment? A. I never heard much of her sentiments at all; I saw her so little, and at such long intervals, that I could not undertake to say what her general character for loyalty is.

Testimony of Father Stonestreet.

By Mr. Aiken.—Q. State your residence and occupation. A. I reside at present in Washington ; I am pastor of St. Aloysius church.

Q. Are you acquainted with the prisoner, Mary E. Surratt? A. I am.

Q. How long have you been acquainted with her? A. I first met her more than twenty years ago in Alexandria; after that I did not see her for ten years, and since then only in transit as I was passing.

Q. Have you seen within the past two years been more intimate with her? A. I have scarcely seen her.

Q. Do you know her general reputation as a Christian and a lady? A. I have always looked upon her as a proper, Christian lady.

Q. Have you in all your intercourse with her ever heard her utter a disloyal sentiment? A. Never; but there was no question of the kind at the time I knew her.

Cross-examined by Judge Holt.—Q. State whether you have probably seen her since the beginning of the Rebellion? A. I do not remember whatever of her character for loyalty except what I have seen in the papers.

Testimony of Mrs. Eliza Hollahan.

By Mr. Aiken.—Q. Are you acquainted with the prisoner, Mrs. Surratt? A. I boarded with Mrs. Surratt from the 7th of February until the 10th of April.

Q. Are you acquainted with the prisoner, Payne? A. I never saw him as Payne; I saw the man pointed out as Payne at her house twice; he called himself Wood.

Q. When did he first come to Mrs. Surratt's house? A. I saw him first there in February, and the second time during the month of March.

Q. State under what circumstances he came to Mrs. Surratt's house, and how he introduced himself. A. Indeed I do not know anything about it; I went into the parlor and was introduced to him as Mr. Wood; I never changed a word with him at all.

Q. Did he represent himself a Baptist preacher? A. I asked Miss Ann Surratt who he was; she said he was a Baptist minister; I said I did not think he would convert many souls. (Laughter.)

Q. At that time, how long did he remain at Mrs. Surratt's house? A. I never saw him but one night.

Q. Did Mrs. Surratt keep a boarding house? A. I do not think she did; only my family and another young lady boarded there.

Q. Was she in the habit of giving people rooms in her house? A. I do not know anything about it; I never saw Mrs. Surratt until I went to board with her; I never heard of her.

Q. How long did Payne stay there when he came in March? A. I do not know; two or three days, I think.

Q. When was the last time you saw him at Mrs. Surratt's house? A. It was some time in March; I do not know the exact day; I thought he was a friend of theirs and never asked any questions about him; I think it was about the middle of the month; it was after the inauguration of the President I know.

Q. Have you ever seen the prisoner, Atzerott, at that house? A. I have, though I never heard his name there.

Q. When was that? A. I do not know; I saw him come in at times; the ladies called him "Port Tobacco."

Q. Was any objection made on the part of any of the family to his being there? A. I heard Mrs. Surratt say that she objected to Atzerott; that she would not board him; I heard her say at the table that she would rather he would not come there at all.

Q. Have you been intimate with Mrs. Surratt? A. I cannot say that I was intimate; I liked her very much; she was a very kind lady to board with.

Q. Did you have frequent conversations with her? A. Not very.

Q. Were you acquainted with J. Wilkes Booth? A. I have seen him at Mrs. Surratt's; I met him once in the parlor.

Q. Did he come frequently to Mrs. Surratt's house? A. I never saw him there but three or four times, and never met him but once.

Q. Did he spend most of the time when he came there in company with Mrs. Surratt? A. I think he did; he would ask for John Surratt, and if he was not there he would inquire for Mrs. Surratt.

Q. Have you learned anything while boarding with Mrs. Surratt of her defective eyesight. A. I never saw her read or sew after candle light.

Q. Have you been in the habit of attending church with Mrs. Surratt? A. Yes; during Lent we went to church very often together.

Q. Was she during that time constant in her religious duties? A. I believe so.

Q. When was the last time you saw her son, John H. Surratt, at her house? A. Some time in March.

Q. Have you seen him in the city since that time? A. I have not.

Cross-examined by Judge Holt.—Q. You say you never saw Mrs. Surratt sew or read after dark; have you not often met her in the parlor at gas-light? A. Yes.

Q. Did she ever have any difficulty in recognizing you or anybody she was acquainted with in the parlor by gaslight? A. No sir.

Testimony of Miss Honora Fitzpatrick.

By Mr. Aiken.—Q. When did you commence boarding with Mrs. Surratt? A. The 6th of October last.

Q. How long did you board there? A. Until the time I was arrested, after the assassination.

Q. When did you first meet at Mrs. Surratt's house the prisoner Payne? A. I do not know what month; I met him during the winter; I first saw him at breakfast.

Q. How many times did you meet him? A. I only saw him there twice.

Q. When was the last time? A. In March.

Q. How long did he stay at that time? A. I do not know; I started to Baltimore the next morning after he came.

Q. How long did you stay in Baltimore? A. A week.

Q. Was Payne gone when you returned? A. Yes.

Q. Do you know the prisoner, Atzeroth? A. I do.

Q. When did he first come to Mrs. Surratt's? A. I do not know the day of the month.

Q. How long did he stay there? A. Only a short time.

Q. Can you state under what circumstances he left? A. I do not know under what circumstances; I believe Mrs. Surratt sent him away.

Q. Are you aware of his getting drunk in the house and making disturbance? A. I am not; I heard he had bottles up there, but I didn't know anything about his getting drunk.

Q. What room did you occupy in the house? A. I slept in the same room with Mrs. Surratt and her daughter, Anna.

Q. Was there a photograph of Booth in that room? A. Yes sir.

Q. Was it yours? A. No.

Q. Have you ever seen that picture, "Night and Morning?" A. Yes.

Q. Was that yours? A. No; that belonged to Mrs. Surratt's daughter.

Q. Do you know anything about Booth's picture being placed behind that? A. No.

Q. Did you own many of the photographs in the house? A. Not many; I owned some in the albums.

Q. Were there photographs of Union Generals in the house? A. I saw one of McClellan, I think.

Q. Did you, while you were in the house, know anything of defective eyesight on the part of Mrs. Surratt? A. I know she could not read or sew at night, on account of her eyesight.

Q. Are you acquainted with Louis J. Weichmann? A. Yes.

Q. Was he treated in the house like a friend? A. He was treated more like a son.

Q. When did you last see Booth there? A. The Monday before the assassination.

Q. When did you last see John Surratt? A. The night that he left the house, two weeks before the assassination.

Q. Did you see him anywhere in the city during those two weeks? A. No.

Q. Did you ever buy any photographs of Booth or give one to Miss Anna Surratt? A. I bought one, and she bought one herself.

Q. Have you ever known Mrs. Surratt to be unable to recognize persons of her acquaintance in the street? A. I remember of her passing Mrs. Kirby in the street once, without recognizing her; she did not see her at all.

Q. Was Mrs. Kirby on the same side of the street with her? A. Yes sir.

Cross-examined by Judge Holt.—Q. Did you ever

know Mrs. Surratt to have any difficulty in recognizing her friends in the parlor by gaslight; did she always recognize you? A. She did.
Q. You speak of owning some of these 'photographs' did you own the photographs of Stephens, Davis and Beauregard? A. No sir, they did not belong to me.

Testimony of George H. Calvert.

George H. Calvert was next called as a witness for the defense, and questioned in reference to a letter written by him to Mrs. Surratt on the 12th of April last, but the letter itself not being in court, his examination was postponed until the letter could be produced.

Testimony of B. F. Gwynn.

By Mr. Aiken.—Q. Where do you reside? A. In Prince Georges county, Maryland, near Surrattsville.
Q. Are you acquainted with the prisoner, Mrs. Surratt? A. Yes; I have been acquainted with her seven or eight years.
Q. Were you present at her house in Surrattsville in April last? A. I was, the day the murder of the President; I came from Marlboro', and met her there; while I was passing in the carriage Mrs. Surratt said she wanted to see me, and I stopped to see her.
Q. Have you been in the habit of transacting business for her? A. Yes, I have transacted some business for her; I sold some land for her.
Q. Did you transact any business for her that day? A. Yes she gave a letter to me to give to Mr. Northe.
Q. Were you present at the house when Mr. Floyd returned? A. No sir.
Q. Are you acquainted with John M. Floyd? A. I am.
Q. Did you meet him that day? A. I did, at Marlboro'.
Q. What time in the afternoon of the 14th did you see him? A. At about four or four and a half I parted with him at the road; I did not see him afterwards.
Q. What was his condition at the time? A. He had been drinking right smartly.
Q. Did he seem to be considerably intoxicated? A. I could hardly tell that; he acted like a man who had been drinking some.
Q. Had you a personal knowledge of Mr. Northe's buying land of Mrs. Surratt? A. I had of his buying land of her husband.
Q. Did you know personally that she was there that day on that business? A. Not except by the letter.
Q. Was Mr. Floyd present at the time Mrs. Surratt handed you that letter? A. No sir.
Q. Did you see him again that afternoon? A. I did not.
Cross-examined by Judge Holt.—Q. Did you have any conversation with Mr. Floyd that afternoon? A. Yes, I think I did see him three or four times that day at Marlboro'.
Q. I mean at home? A. I did not see him after he got home.
By the Court.—Q. How far is it where you parted with him on the road to Surrattsville? A. About five miles.
Mr. Aiken.—Q. You received the letter? A. Yes, and read it; the direction on the outside was, to read it and deliver it to Mr. Northe.

Testimony of Captain Geo. Cottingham.

By Mr. Aiken.—Q. What is your business? A. Special officer in Major O'Beirne's Board of Enrollment.
Q. Were you engaged in making any arrests of parties after the assassination? A. I was.
Q. Did you arrest John M. Floyd? A. No sir; my partner, who was with me, arrested him.
Q. Did you see him after he was arrested? A. I did; he was put into my care at the Post Office at Surrattsville.
Q. What information did Floyd give you at that time? A. He denied knowing anything about it and for two days continued to deny it. I finally told him that I was satisfied he knew about it; that he had it on his mind and the sooner he got rid of it the better. He said, "Oh! my God, if I should make a confession they would murder me," said I, "who would murder you?" He said these parties in the conspiracy, I told him that if he was going to free himself by letting these parties get out of it, that was his business, not mine; I then put him in the guardhouse; he seemed to be much excited; the Lieutenant went to Washington for reinforcements; Mr. Floyd then stated to me that Mrs. surratt had come down to h's place on Friday, between four and five o'clock; that she told him to have the firearms ready; that two men would call for them at twelve o'clock; that two men did call that Harold dismounted from his horse and went into Mrs. Surratt's or rather Floyd's tavern, and said "I have something to tell you;" that Harold then told him to get those firearms; that the firearms were brought down and Harold took one; tha' Booth's carbine was carried to him, whether by Harold or Floyd I do not remember; but that Booth said he could not carry a carbine, it was as much as he could do to carry himself; that his leg was broken; that Booth said "We have murdered the President," and that Harold said "We have picked off Seward;" I asked Floyd why he did not state these facts in the first place and not allow these parties to escape; that he at least could have spoken about the firearms being in the house.
Q. What information did he give you about firearms A. I was in the house when he came in from Bryantown and commenced crying out and hammering, "Oh, Mrs. Surratt, that vile woman, she has ruined me;" I said to him, "You stated there were two carbines, and that Booth could not carry his; where is that carbine?" he told me it was up stairs, that Mrs. Surratt had some bags over it; I went up, but could not find it; I told them I would cut up the house before I would go away without it; with that he told the hired man to get an axe; I did not go into the room where he went until I heard three knocks on the wall, and I then went in, and after about the seventh blow I saw the carbine; it had been suspended by a string above the plastering; the string seemed to have broken and it had fallen down.
Q. How did you find the carbine where he told you it was? A. No; I hunted for it but could not find it.
Q. During these two days, when Mr. Floyd was denying all knowledge of these parties, did he mention the name of Mrs. Surratt? A. Not while he was denying it; after he confessed he mentioned her name.
Q. Who was present besides yourself at the time Mr. Floyd made this statement to you? A. Nobody that I know except that Mr. Jenkins, a brother of Mrs. Surratt, was up in the room when I said I knew that Mr. Floyd was guilty and that my mind was made up; I knew that he was in the conspiracy; there had been blockade-runners arrested at his house; his house was a head-quarters for Rebels and blockade-runners during Floyd's occupation of it.
Q. Did he ever make any further statement? A. Yes sir.
Q. What was that statement?
Question objected to by Mr. Bingham, and objection sustained by the Court.
Q. Do you recollect positively that Mr. Lloyd used the words "fire-arms?" A. I do.
Q. Did he tell you Mrs. Surratt bought them there? A. No; I think he said Johnny Surratt brought them there.
Q. When did Mr. Floyd state that Mrs. Surratt made that remark about the fire-arms? A. It was on Friday, between four and five o'clock.
Q. Did he have the appearance at that time of being very much frightened? A. Oh no, he was not afraid; everything he said was voluntary; I advised him when I sent him down to Colonel Welles to make a clean breast of it.
Q. What day of the week did he make this confession to you? A. I think it was on Tuesday or Wednesday; I will not be positive; my business was to prepare the way for other officers over me.
Q. Did he say anything at that time about Mrs. Surratt getting him into difficulty? A. Yes he did; he cried and threw his hands over his wife's neck and howled for his prayer book; Mr. Floyd's wife and Mrs. Offut were there and heard all the conversation in that room; I told them to turn me up.
Cross-examined by Judge Holt.—State whether at the time Mr. Floyd mentioned the reasons why he had concealed his knowledge of this matter? A. He said he was afraid of parties there; he was afraid if he made this confession they would murder him.
Q. Who did you understand him to refer to? A. To these engaged in this conspiracy.
Q. What was the precise language he used in reference to Mrs. Surratt? A. It was "Mrs. Surratt, that vile woman, she has ruined me; I am to be shot; I am to be shot!" he meant by that, I suppose, that his guilt was so great there was no hope for him.

Re-examination of R. J. Early.

(Former witness for the prosecution, but now summoned for the defense).—Q. You stated in your last examination that you came down to Baltimore on Thursday afternoon in company with O'Laughlin, Captain Henderson and Mr. Murphy; will you state in what train you came? A. On the half-past three o'clock train I believe.
Q. At what time did you reach Washington? A. At the usual time; I believe it takes two hours?
Q. Did you come on the Accommodation train? A. I don't know what train it was; I think it reached here about half-past five o'clock.
Q. Now I wish you would state, sir, where you and O'Laughlin went to when you left the cars, and every place you were present with him? A. After leaving the cars we made our way to the avenue to Lichaus or Pullman's hotel; I think we went inside there and came out again; Henderson went into a barber's shop to get shaved; O'Laughlin then asked me to go with him to the National Hotel; when we got there he went to the desk, telling me to wait, and he would detain me only a few minutes; I went as far as the door; he left me standing there, and came back again in three to five minutes, and after that we went back to Lichau's, and thence up the avenue.
Q. Did you take any supper there? A. No sir; we went as far as Eleventh street, and turned back and went to Welcker's dinner saloon, over Wall and Stevenson's, I think.
Q. Did you take supper there? A. Yes sir.

Q. How long did that last? A. I guess about three-quarters of an hour.
Q. What time did you leave there? A. About eight o'clock or half-past seven. I should say; after coming out of there we returned to Rullman's Hotel, and proceeded as far as the corner of Third street, where O'Laughlin and Murphy he left me and Henderson, saying they were going to see Mr. Hoffman, a sick man, and would see us on the corner again; they returned, accompanied by Daniel Lockran, and after that the five of us started up the Avenue to see the illumination; Mr. Lockran wanted us to go as far as the Treasury, as far as the public reservation, above Seventh street, when one complained of sore feet, and would go no further; we returned down the other side of the reservation, when Murphy and Henderson said they had to leave; that was getting on to nine o'clock, and we went into the Canterbury Music Hall just as they were finishing the first piece; we remained there till about ten o'clock, and then went to the Metropolitan Hotel, and from there went to Rullman's Hotel; we reached there about a quarter or half-past ten o'clock.
Q. Was O'Laughlin with you all that time? A. He was sir.
Q. How late did you remain there? A. About one hour sir.
Q. Did anybody join you there? A. Mr. Gillett was passing there with a lady at the time, and stopped and spoke to O'Laughlin, I believe; we left there then and the others joined us, and we went down the avenue as far as Second street. I believe: Mr. O'Laughlin was acquainted at a saloon on the corner of B and Second streets, where there was a dance or something going on, and took us over there; one of the party bought tickets, and we went into the ball; we stayed there about an hour, and came out and went up the avenue again, and went into the Metropolitan, and remained there till after one o'clock; we then went out for five minutes, came back and went to bed.
Q. Was O'Laughlin with you all that night. A. Yes sir.
Q. Do you know where Secretary Stanton's house is? A. No sir.
Q. Do you know where Willard's Hotel is? A. Yes sir.
Q. Now Stanton's house is more than six squares north of Willard's; I will ask you whether O'Laughlin could have been there between nine and eleven o'clock? A. No sir. (Objected to).
Q. Now sir, you stated that on Friday you woke him at the hotel, and that he was with you most of Friday? A. Yes sir.
Q. Will you explain again where he was till bed time on Friday night? A. I was only with him from nightfall; he was at the hotel from supper till the time he went out with Mr. Fuller.
Q. Where did you have supper? A. At Welker's, sir, at the same place.
Q. When did you go there? A. At about 8 o'clock.
Q. How long did you stay there? A. I suppose three quarters of an hour.
Q. You said you was there when the procession passed of Navy Yard men? A. Yes sir.
Q. Where did you go from there? A. We returned to Rullman's.
Q. How long did he stay there? A. I can't say exactly; I recollect distinctly his going with Fuller, but I don't recollect for certain whether it was before or after the procession passed.
Q. Do you know how he was dressed on Friday evening? A. Yes sir; he had a coat similar—it was just like a frock coat behind.
Q. Look at that coat (pointing to the prisoner); is that the same? A. Yes sir.
Q. Is that the same pants? A. Yes sir.
Q. Did you make them? A. Yes sir.
Q. What sort of a vest had he? A. It was of the same material as the pantaloons.
Q. What color? A. Well, a sort of plaid, only it is striped up and down, a kind of purple and green.

Cross-examination by Judge Holt.—Q. State whether or not you were under the influence of liquor that night. A. Well, yes, towards ten o'clock.
Q. How often did you drink before ten o'clock? A. I could not say how many times I drank; we drank pretty considerable.
Q. Eight times; ten times? A. I think we might have drank as often as that, but it was mostly ale; I never saw O'Laughlin drink any liquor.
Q. You were not separated from him at all on Friday evening? A. Not till the time he went out of the house.
Q. What time was that? A. Ten o'clock, or a little after.
Q. When did you see him again? A. On Saturday morning.
Q. Where did he leave you? A. At 10 o'clock on Friday night, at Rullman's Hotel.
Q. Where is that? A. Between Third and Four-and-a-half street, the second d.or from the *Globe* office.
Q. Did he go out then? A. Yes sir; with Mr. Fuller.
By the Court.—Q. How long were you at the dining table on Thursday? A. From three-quarters of an hour to an hour; we had to stay there until the dinners were got ready for the four of us.

Q. Was there considerable wine drank there that afternoon? A. No sir, we had no wine.
By Mr. Cox.—Q. Do you recollect what time it was when you left the Canterbury, on Thursday night? A. It was after the dance by some young ladies.
Q. Did I understand you to say O'Loughlin never drinks whisky? A. I seldom if ever saw him drink any.
Q. Did you ever see him drink? A. Only twice, I believe.
Q. Have you known him long? A. For the last five years, and for the last ten months more especially.

Testimony of Mr. Murphy.

Q. Where did you reside? A. In Baltimore, sir.
Q. Did you come to Washington on Thursday, April 13th. A. Yes sir.
Q. In what company? A. With O'Laughlin, Henderson and Early.
Q. Who proposed the trip? A. Henderson.
Q. What time did you get to Washington? A. About five o'clock.
Q. Will you state all that took place all that evening? A. We came from the depot down to Rullman's, and there took a drink or two; we started from there and went to the Metropolitan, and went to several places; we t ok supper at Walker's about eight o'clock; it might have been about half-past seven.
Q. How long were you occupied there? A. It might have been about half an hour.
Q. Did supper have to be prepared? A. Yes sir.
Q. After you left there where did you go? A. We went to Rullman's again, and there we met Dan Lockran; we then went to see the illuminations, and stopped on the corner of Ninth street and the avenue, and after stopping there some time we started, and went to the Canterbury, leaving them at ten o'clock to go to Rullman's; it was about a quarter past ten when we got there; we then went to Platz's, and said there about an hour and a half, and that brought us to half-past eleven or twelve o'clock; we then started for Riddles, on the corner of D and Second street, and staid there till half-past twelve or one o'clock, and then came back to the corner of Sixth street and the Avenue; and went from there to the corner of Tenth and the Avenue, where we staid a while.
Q. What was going on there? A. It was an all-night house, and we went in to get some refreshments.
Q. What time did you get back to the Metropolitan? A. About two or half-past two ; we went across the way to get a drink, and I think that brought us to half-past two o'clock, and then we went to bed.
Q. Did I understand you to say that O'Laughlin was with you all that time? A. Yes sir, all that day ; oh! he went with Early and left us about five minutes and went to the National Hotel; that was while Henderson was getting shaved; I didn't go but waited until they came back.
Q. Do you know where Secretary Stanton's house is? A. Yes sir.
Q. State whether O'Laughlin was there that night. A. No nearer than the corner of Ninth and Pennsylvania avenue.
Q. Did you see him on Friday? A. I was all day with him up to eight o'clock at night, when the three of them left me to go to supper.
Q. You did not go to supper then? A. No sir.
Q. Did you see him on Saturday? A. Yes sir, I was with him from nine o'clock until we went to the depot, got our tickets, and went to Baltimore?
Q. Were you at Rullman's Hotel when the news of the President's assassination reached there? A. No sir.
Q. During this trip what was his manner—did he appear excited? A. No sir; I never saw him in better spirits in all my life than he was then.
Q. I will ask you whether it was the plan of your party to go back to Baltimore on Friday afternoon? A. Yes sir, it was our intention to go, but we stayed at the intercession of Mr. Henderson, who wanted to see a lady.
So the whole party went up on Saturday? A. I did not go till Sunday morning.

Testimony of Mr. O. Lockran.

Q. Do you reside in this city? A. Yes sir.
Q. Do you know the accused? A. Yes sir.
Q. How long have you known him? A. About 18 or 20 months.
Q. Did you see him on Thursday, the 13th of April? A. Yes sir.
Q. At what hour? A. At about a quarter after seven.
Q. Where? A. On the steps of Rullman's Hotel, Pennsylvania avenue.
Q. Who was with him? A. Henderson, Edward Murphy, Barney Early and O'Laughlin were the whole party.
Q. Did you join that party? A. No sir; I went home to supper; I joined them about 8 o'clock; O'Laughlin and Murphy came to my boarding-house and we went by Adams' Express office; they had left Henderson and Early on Pennsylvania avenue.
Q. At that time where did you go? A. To Rullman's Hotel, and from there to corner Pennsylvania avenue and Ninth street; when we got there I should judge it was about 9 o'clock.

TRIAL OF THE ASSASSINS AT WASHINGTON.

Q. Did you look at your watch? A. Yes sir; some one said it was too late to go to the Treasury, and I looked at my watch and found it was nine o'clock, and went to the corner of Seventh and Louisiana avenue, and from there to the Canterbury.
Q. At what time did you go in there? A. At about half-past nine, I suppose.
Q. How long did you stay? A. Till ten or a quarter after.
Q. Where did you go from there? A. To the Metropolitan.
Q. And from there? A. To Rullman's Hotel.
Q. What time did you reach there? A. Probably at half-past ten o'clock.
Q. I will ask you whether the accused was with you from the time you joined them till the time you went to Rullman's Hotel? A. Yes sir.
Q. Do you know where Secretary Stanton's house is? A. No sir.
Q. Do you know where Franklin Square is? A. Yes sir.
Q. Could the accused have been there during that time? A. No sir.
Q. Did anybody join you at Rullman's Hotel? A. Yes sir; Mr. Rolette.
Q. How late were you with them? A. Till after twelve o'clock.
Q. Was O'Laughlin with you all that time? A. Yes sir.
Q. Did you sleep in the same house with them? A. No sir.
Q. Did you see them next day? A. No sir.
Q. Were you with them the next evening? A. Yes sir; between seven and eight o'clock, at the Metropolitan Hotel.
Q. Were you with them any time during the evening? A. Yes; till half-past nine or a quarter past.
Q. Did they go to Walker's when you were there? A. Not that I am aware of; I heard them speak of going to supper; I don't know whether they did or not.
Q. Did you see them any more after that? A. No sir; not that night.
Q. Did you notice the dress of O'Laughlin? A. He had on plaid pants and vest and a black coat.
Q. Look at the dress he has now. A. That looks like the pants but he had a vest on.
Q. What sort of a hat did he have? A. I think he had a black slouched hat on.
By the Court.—Q. What part of the Canterbury playhouse did you enter? A. We went into the fifty-cent place first, then Captain Henderson went to get his change corrected and they said they would give him tickets for the orchestra chairs, which was seventy-five cents apiece; so we moved from the place where we were first and went into the other seats just behind the orchestra.
Q. Did you all sit together? A. Two of us sat together, and the rest right behind us.
Q. You saw the whole party all the time you were in the house? A. Yes sir.
Q. None left till all left? A. We all left together.
Q. What was O'Laughlin's manner, did he seem excited? A. He appeared very lively and made the remark that they had come from Baltimore to see the illumination and have a good time.
Q. Was he intoxicated? A. I don't think he was; he was lively and merry-like.

Testimony of Mr. Rolette.

Q. What is your business? A. I am solicitor for a New York cracker bakery.
Q. Do you know the accused? A. Yes sir.
Q. How long have you known him? A. In the neighborhood of two years.
Q. Did you see him on the evening of the 13th of April? A. Yes sir, between ten and half-past ten o'clock I had been to the Capitol with a lady, and when I passed back I saw him on the steps of Rullman's Hotel.
Q. State whether you joined that party afterwards. A. Yes sir.
Q. How long were you with them that evening? A. Till about 12 o'clock.
Q. Did you see him the next day? A. Yes sir; on Friday morning, and I was with the whole party on Friday night until between eleven and twelve o'clock.
Q. Where were you when you received the news of the President's assassination? A. At Rullman's Hotel.
Q. Was O'Laughlin there? A. Yes sir.
Q. Do you know anything of his going away from the hotel that night? A. He and Fuller went out some time after the news was received of the President being killed.
Q. Did you notice his behavior when he heard the news of the President's assassination? A. I did not, sir.
Q. Do you know how he was dressed? A. He had on a pair of scotch plaid pants and vest.

Testimony of Mr. Purdy.

Q. Do you reside in the city? A. I do.
Q. What is your business? A. I am Superintendent of Rullman's Hotel.
Q. Do you know the accused? A. Yes sir.
Q. Did you see him on Thursday, the 13th of April?

A. I saw him with Mr. Rolette, Mr. Murphy and Mr. Early.
Q. Where were they? A. At my restaurant.
Q. At what hour? A. About half-past ten o'clock.
Q. How long did they stay? A. Till about twelve.
Q. Were they there all that time? A. I don't know; I was all round in the kitchen and other places; I closed about twelve o'clock.
Q. Were they there when you closed? A. Yes sir.
Q. Was O'Laughlin with them? A. Yes sir.
Q. You know him well? A. I have known him about three months.
Q. Did you see them on Friday night? A. Yes sir.
Q. At the same place? A. Yes sir.
Q. Were you there when the news of the assassination reached you? A. Yes sir.
Q. Did you communicate it to them? A. I told them that a Cavalry Sergeant told me the President was assassinated, and that Booth was the one who did it; he seemed surprised, and said he had been in Booth's company, and people might think he had something to do with it.
Q. What time did he leave there that night? A. Near one o'clock.
Q. Did the entire party go then? A. Yes sir.
By the Court.—Q. You say you have known him about three months; has he been much about the city? A. He would be down two or three times a week; sometimes I wouldn't see him for two or three weeks.
Q. Did he always stay at your house? A. Yes sir.
By Mr. Cox.—Q. Look at his dress, and say whether it is the same he wore that night. A. I think it is; I didn't pay much attention to his dress.

Testimony of Mr. Fuller.

Q. Do you reside in the city? A. Yes sir.
Q. Do you know the accused? A. Yes sir.
Q. How long have you known him? A. Between twelve and fourteen years.
Q. Did you see him on either Thursday or Friday, the 13th and 14th of April? A. I saw him on Friday, the 14th.
Q. Where? A. At Rullman's.
Q. What time of day? A. Between seven and eight o'clock in the evening.
Q. Did you see him any later? A. Yes sir; between ten and eleven.
Q. How near ten? A. I can't say exactly; it was between ten and eleven.
Q. Did you receive the news of the President's assassination that night? A. Yes sir.
Q. Do you know where he was between eight and ten o'clock? A. I do not, sir.
Q. What was his conduct when he heard the news of the President's assassination? A. He looked sorry.
Q. Did he show any fright? A. No sir.
Q. Did he say anything about Booth? A. No sir.
Cross-examination by Judge Holt.—Q. Did he go home with you? A. Yes sir; he used to often go home with me.
Q. Did you invite him to go down with you? A. I did sir.
By Mr. Cox.—Q. Did he ever reside in Washington? A. Yes sir.
Q. Is his brother in business here? A. Yes sir.

Re-examination of Captain Coldingham.

Q. State again the precise language that Mr. Floyd used in his confession with reference to Mrs. Surratt.
The question was objected to and withdrawn.
Q. I will ask the witness if he did not make a different statement to me with reference to Mr. Floyd's confession?
This question was also objected to, but after some discussion the objection was withdrawn by the Judge-Advocate-General, and the witness answered as follows:
A. I should like to relate the whole conversation between Mr. Aiken at the Metropolitan Hotel; I think it was Sunday evening; he asked me to take a drink, and I took a drink with him; he said I am going to have you as a witness in this case; he told me to sit on the sofa, but I said I would go outside; the first question he put to me was was I a Catholic; I told him no then he said Mr. Floyd had made a confession to me about Mrs. Surratt and said, will you state to me what that confession was: I said I decline that, but I will answer any question you put to me; he wanted to pick it out of me, and I didn't think I was bound to tell him.
Q. Did I ask you if Mr. Floyd said anything in reference to firearms? A. You asked me if Floyd had made a confession to me, and I said yes, and you said what was it and I declined answering, but I said I would answer any question you would ask.
Q. What did you tell me this afternoon? A. I told you a lie; you were trying to pick out of me, and I told you that you might call me into Court, and I would state what I had told you, a lie, and now state that I did do it.

Testimony of Mr. Morton.

Q. Did you see O'Laughlin in Baltimore on Sunday night? A. Yes sir.
Q. Do you know whether he had been informed that

an officer had been in search of him? A. That is what he told me.
Q. Did he say he was going to give himself up? A. Yes sir; he said he would on Monday morning.

Testimony of George B. Woods.

Q. Where do you reside? A. In Boston, sir.
Q. Have you been in the habit of seeing the photographs of leaders of the Rebellion exposed for sale there? A. Yes sir.
Q. Freely exposed? A. Yes sir; photographs of all celebrities.
Q. Have you seen them in the possession of persons supposed to be loyal? A. Yes sir.
The Court then adjourned until 10 o'clock to-morrow morning.

WASHINGTON, May 26.—The Court room was to-day again crowded with spectators of both sexes, the largest portion of them being unable to find seats. The main attraction is the appearance of the prisoners.
After the reading of the testimony taken yesterday, Mr. Aiken, the counsel for Mrs. Surratt, made an application for the recall of Mr. Van Steinaker as a witness for cross-examination, stating that since his examination material facts had come to the knowledge of Mrs. Surratt, which would enable the counsel to contradict the witness. He did not desire to call Steinaker as a witness for the defense.
Judge Advocate-General Holt said that the witness had been examined and discharged without objection by counsel. If the latter desired him for the defense the Government would make an effort to find him, but he declined to recall him as a witness for the prosecution.

Re-examination of B. F. Gwynn.

By Mr. Aiken.—Q. Did you carry a letter for Mrs. Surratt for Mr. Nothey on the 14th of April last, and if so is this the letter you carried? A. It is; I read the letter at the time, by her direction.
The counsel then placed in evidence the following letter:—
"SURRATTSVILLE, Md., April 14, 1865.—Mr. John Nothey,—Sir:—I have this day received a letter from Mr Calvert, intimating that either you or your friend have represented to him that I am not willing to settle with you for the land. You know that I am ready, and have been waiting for you for the last two years, and now, if you do not come within the next ten days, I will settle with Mr. Calvert and bring suit against you immediately. Mr. Calvert will give you a deed on receiving payment, (Signed) M. E. SURRATT, Administratrix of J. M. Surratt."

Testimony of Father Lanahan.

By Mr. Aiken.—Q. State your residence and occupation. A. My residence is at Charles county, near Beantown; I am a Catholic priest.
Q. Are you acquainted with the prisoner Mrs. Surratt? A. I have been acquainted with her about thirteen years, and intimately for nine years.
Q. Do you know her general reputation as a Christian woman? A. Yes; she is, in my estimation, a very good Christian woman.
Mr. Bingham—We do not want your estimation, but her general reputation.
Witness—Her character stands in the neighborhood where she lived as a good Christian woman.
Q. Has she been attentive to her Christian duties? A. I could not say exactly, because she does not belong to my congregation.
Q. Have you ever heard her express any disloyal sentiment? A. Never.
Q. Do you know personally anything as to defective eyesight on her part? A. I do not.
Q. Has she never, in your presence, been unable to recognize friends a short distance from her? A. I do not remember; I could not swear to that.
Cross-examined by Judge Holt.—Q. Have you had conversation with her since the Rebellion in regard to the affairs of the country? A. I have.
Q. Have you ever heard her express a loyal sentiment? A. I do not remember that I have.
Q. Is not her reputation that of a disloyal woman? A. I think not; she never expressed that sentiment to me; I may have heard her general reputation for loyalty or disloyalty spoken of, but I do not remember it.

Testimony of Rev. Father Young.

Q. State your residence and occupation. A. Residence at Dominick's Church, Washington; I am a Catholic priest.
Q. Are you acquainted with the prisoner, Mrs. Surratt? A. I have known her I think about eight or ten years; I cannot say that my acquaintance has been of an intimate character: I had a congregation in the part of the country where she lived, and in passing by her house about once a month I have occasionally called for about half an hour.

Q. Are you acquainted with her general reputation as a Christian lady? A. I am; so far as I have heard it spoken of, it has been with the greatest praise; I never heard anything whatever unfavorable to her character, but on the contrary everything highly favorable.
Q. In all your intercourse with her have you ever heard her express a disloyal sentiment? A. I do not recollect of ever hearing her speak on that question at all.
Q. Have you personal knowledge of any defective eyesight on her part? A. I cannot say that I have; I never heard of her having weak eyes.
Q. You have never been present when she was unable to recognize her friends at a little distance? A. Not that I remember.

Testimony of George H. Calvert.

Q. By Mr. Aiken.—State whether on or about the 13th of April last you addressed a letter to Mrs. Surratt, and if so, whether this is the letter? A. I did; this is the letter.
The counsel for the accused then produced the following letter, which was read.
"RIVERSDALE, April 12, 1865—Mrs. M. E. Surratt—Dear Madam:—During a late visit to the lower portion of the county I ascertained of the willingness of Mr. Nothey to settle with you, and desire to call your attention to the fact in urging the settlement of Mr. claim of my late father's estate. However unpleasant, I must insist upon closing up this matter, as it is imperative in an early settlement of the estate, which is necessary. You will, therefore, please inform me, at your earliest convenience, as to how and when you will be able to pay the balance remaining due on the land purchased by your late husband.
"Yours, respectfully,
"(Signed) GEORGE H. CALVERT, Jr."
Q. Were you at Surrattsville on the 14th of April? A. I was not.

Testimony of W. L. Hoyle.

By Mr. Aiken—Q. Are you acquainted with Mrs. Surratt, the prisoner at the bar? A. I have a store acquaintance.
Q. Are you acquainted with her general character? A. I know nothing of her, except as a store acquaintance; I have never conversed with her, except in the store.
Q. Have you heard Mrs. Surratt express any disloyal sentiment in your presence? A. I have not, either loyal or disloyal; I have had no political conversations with her.
Q. Are you acquainted with John H. Surratt? A. I knew him by sight.
Q. When did you see him last in this city? A. The latter part of February, or first of March, just prior to the draft.
Q. Describe his personal appearance. A. He is tall; rather of light complexion, delicate looking, and between twenty and twenty-three years of age; I think about six feet in height: I cannot say whether he wore a goatee or moustache; my impression is he did not.
Cross examined by Judge Bingham—Q. Do you know he was over five feet nine inches in height? A. Not positively.

Testimony of P. H. Manisby.

By Mr. Cox.—Q. State your residence and occupation. A. Residence, Baltimore; occupation, clerk to Eaton Bros. & Co.
Q. Are you related to the accused, Michael O'Laughlin? A. I am his brother-in-law.
Q. State when Michael O'Laughlin came to Baltimore from the South? A. I think it was in August 1862.
Q. State what his occupation has been from that time till the present? A. He came home somewhat sick and remained for about a month; he then went with his brother, who was in Washington in the produce and feed business; he remained with him until the fall of 1863, when his brother removed from Washington, having left his house there as a branch of his Baltimore business, and Michael attended to his business for him in Washington up to the 4th of March of this year; that is, there are evidences that Michael had the collection and receiving of orders from customers, the goods being supplied from Baltimore.
Q. Did this arrangement with his brother require him to be in Washington? A. I could not say positively how frequently he was here. He was here off and on for the period from that time, as his brother gave up business here until this last transaction on the 14th of April.
Q. Did you know J. Wilkes Booth? A. Yes, intimately. Mrs. Booth owns the property right opposite our house. Michael and William were schoolmates of John Wilkes Booth. They attended the school of A. M. Smith, not very far from the house.
Q. How long has his intimacy with them continued? A. To my positive knowledge it has been almost twelve years.
Q. Where was Michael's home in Baltimore? A. He lived with me, No. 67 North Exeter street.
Q. Can you state where he was in the month of April to the 13th? A. From the 18th of March until he came

down to Washington on the 13th of April he was with me.

Q. Can you speak with certainty about his being at home that time or part of it? A. He arrived home a.ter the assassination, on Saturday evening; I saw him about seven o'clock; the officers had then been to the house in search of him, and when I informed him of that fact, he told me—

Mr. Bingham.—You need not state what he said to you; declarations of the prisoner cannot be adduced in his defense

Mr. Cox stated that evidence had been adduced by the prosecution to prove that the prisoner was fleeing from arrest, and it was legitimate to meet that on the part of the defense, by showing that instead of fleeing he voluntarily surrendered himself.

Judge Holt remarked, that if the witness was cautioned not to repeat the declarations of the prisoner, he might go on to state the facts in connection with the arrest.

Q. Did the prisoner protest his innocence?

Question objected to by Judge Bingham. If the Government had called for any part of the declarations of the prisoner, his counsel would be entitled to draw them all out, but as that had not been done the question was inadmissable

Objection sustained by the Court.

Q. State whether or not, on Monday morning, the defendant author zed you to procure an officer to take him into custody? A. He did.

Mr. Bingham.—I objected to that; but as the witness has answered the question notwithstanding my objection, let it go.

Q. How long have you known the accused, O'Laughlin? A. For about twelve years.

Q. State what is his disposition and character? A. As a boy he was always very timid; from my observation of twelve years—

Mr. Bingham.—You need not state what you believe, the Court can draw its own conclusions.

Witness.—I have always regarded him as a very amiable boy. I do not remember ever having seen him in a passion in my life. On political questions he has never been violent. I have never heard him express any opinions on the issues of the day, except in a very moderate way.

Q. I want you to state the facts in regard to the alleged arrest. A. On Monday morning, in consequence of what Mitchell had said to Mr.—

Mr. Bingham.—I object to that.

After discussion, by the consent of Judge Holt, the following question was put:—

Q. State whether you surrendered the accused into custody of the officers by the authority of the accused himself. A. I did, by his authority, certainly.

The hour of 1 having arrived, the Court took a recess until 2.

After the recess the examination of Maulsby was continued.

Q. Did you take an officer to the house where the prisoner, O'Laughlin, was? A. With the permission of the Court, I would be glad to state the circumstances surrounding the case.

Judge Holt.—You may state them, but you must not repeat what the prisoner said.

Witness.—I was proceeding to state that I had seen the accused on Saturday afternoon, and an arrangement was then made, as I then supposed, for Sunday morning; on Saturday evening, at seven o'clock, I met Roberts and Early; they had just then returned from Washington; it is difficult to make out a connected narrative without stating the remarks of the prisoner; I saw Mr. Wallace for the first time on Sunday morning; he came to the house in search of Michael; other officers were with him at the time; on Monday morning I was sent for by Michael; I went off in a hack, and called for Wallace; I called at Carmichael's office; Wallace, did not know Michael's whereabouts at the time, but as the feeling was very high at the time, I thought these precautions were necessary; we then went to Mrs. Bailey's house, where he was stopping; I went in by myself, and Michael came out with me and gave himself up to the officer; there was nothing said from that time until he reached the Marshal's office.

Q. I think you have stated that Michael came home on Saturday evening. I ask you if he then informed you where he could be found if wanted. A. He did.

Mr. Bingham objected to the question, and asked that the answer might not be recorded.

The objection was sustained by the Court.

Q. You state that you knew Booth intimately. State whether he was a man of pleasing address?

Question objected to by Mr. Bingham.

Mr. Cox stated that it was the desire of the counsel for all the accused that some evidence should be introduced as to the character of J. Wilkes Booth, for the reason that if any of the accused should be found guilty, while the character of Booth would not affect their guilt or innocence, yet if it was found that Booth was a man of pleasing address, calculated to influence and control the minds of young men with whom he associated, that would be a mitigating circumstance.

Judge Holt said it would not mitigate the assassination by proving that Booth was a man of pleasing address. The objection was sustained by the Court.

By the Court.—Q .You have stated what has been the occupation of O'Laughlin since August, 1862 what was his occupation previous to that? A. He was in the Rebel service from 1861 to 1862.

Testimony for the prosecution resumed.

Testimony of Lewis W. Chamberlain.

By Judge Holt.—Q. State where you reside? A. In Richmond, Va.

Q. State whether you have been on duty there in the War Department of the Confederate States? A. Yes sir.

Q. In what capacity? A. As clerk in the War Office chiefly.

Q. State whether or not, while acting as clerk, you became acquainted with the handwriting of John A. Campbell, Assistant Secretary of War, and late Judge of the Supreme Court of the United States, and also with that of Harrison, Private Secretary of Jefferson Davis? A. Yes sir,

Q. Look at these indorsements on the letter (published some days ago) of Lieutenant Alston, proposing to proceed to the North and "strike at the hearts' blood of the deadliest enemies of the South," and see whether they are respectively in the handwriting of J. A. Campbell, Assistant Secretary of War, and of Burton C. Harrison. A. Yes sir.

Q. Was this Harrison private secretary to Jefferson Davis? A. He was so reported and recognized at the War Department.

Q. Look at that paper, and see if the marks on it are the ordinary official marks. A. It has the mark on it of the Secretary of War; also of General Cooper, Adjutant-General and Inspector-General. It seems to have been referred from the office of the Secretary of War to the Adjutant-General's office, where it was directed to be filed.

Q. Do I understand you to say that the John A. Campbell of whom you speak was formerly on the bench of the Supreme Court of the United States? A. He was so reported to have been.

Testimony of Henry Finegan.

Examined by Judge Holt.—Q. State where you reside. A. In Boston, Mass.

Q. State whether or not you have been in the military service of the country during this Rebellion? A. I have, as a commissioned officer.

Q. State if in the month of February last you were in Montreal, Canada? A. I was and remained there eleven days.

Q. Did you while there make the acquaintance of George N. Sanders, Wm. Cleary and others of that city? A. I did not make their acquaintance personally; I knew them very well by sight; I saw them at the St. Lawrence Hall, and various other public places in Montreal.

Q. Did you see Jacob Thompson or Beverly Tucker there? A. Not to my knowledge.

Q. State whether on one occasion, in' the month of February, you heard a conversation between George N. Sanders and Wm. Cleary, and if so, state what was said and where it occurred. A. I did; the conversation I heard took place at St. Lawrence in the event; it I am not certain whether it was on the 14th or 15th of February; I was sitting in a chair as George N. Sanders and William Cleary walked in at the door; they stopped about ten feet from me; I heard Cleary say, "I suppose they are getting ready for the inauguration of Lincoln next month;" Sanders said, "Yes, but if the boys only have luck, Lincoln will not trouble them much longer;" Cleary said, "Is everything well?" Sanders replied, "Oh ! yes; Booth is bossing the job."

Q. You saw these men frequently? A. Yes, I knew Sanders by description there the first time I saw him, and inquired concerning him of the clerks.

Cross-examined by Mr. Aiken.—Q. When did you leave the service of the Government? A. In September, 1863.

Q. Where did you reside before you enlisted in the service? A. In Boston, Mass.

Q. Where were you born? A. In Ireland.

Q. Did you not reside at the South before you went to Montreal? A. No sir.

Q. You say you were never introduced to any of those parties? A. Not to Sanders or Cleary; I was introduced to men who claimed to have escaped from prisons in the North.

Q. What time in the evening did this conversation at St. Lawrence Hall occur? A. I thing about six o'clock.

Q. You say you were about ten feet from them, Were they conversing in a loud or low tone? A. In a low tone, I thought.

Q. Where they standing close together? A. Yes sir.

Q. Did you ever see Clay there? A. No; not to my knowledge.

Q. Did you ever see Cleary? A. I did.

Q. Did you see Sanders? A. I did.

Q. Why is it you recollect these two and not the others? A. Because I saw them talking.

Q. How did you know it was them if you were never introduced to them? A. I knew them by sight several days before; I saw them testify in court in the St. Albans raiders case.

Q. What kind of a looking man was Cleary? A. He

is a man of medium size, of sandy complexion, sandy hair, and carries his neck a little on one side.
Q. Describe Sanders. A. Sanders is a rather low, short and thick-set, curly hair, moustache and goatee, sprinkled with grey, and a very burly form.
Q. Did you hear anything more about the job mentioned in that conversation? A. No sir.
Q. And did you not learn what the job was? A. I did not.
Q. When did you leave Montreal? A. On the 17th of February.
Q. When did you first give this information to any one? A. I spoke of it to two or three parties some time ago.
Q. Did you communicate it to the Government? A. Not then.
Q. Did you consider it of any importance at that time? A. No sir; I considered it at the time as a piece of braggadocia.
Q. When did you first communicate it to the Government? A. A few days ago.
Q. Did you ever see John H. Surratt in Canada? A. I do not know him.

Testimony of Charles Dawson.

By Judge Holt.—Q. Are you acquainted with the handwriting of J. Wilkes Booth? A. With his signature I am.
Q. Look at this card, (Booth's card sent up to President Johnson, at the Kirkwood House,) and see if it is his signature? A. It undoubtedly is.

Testimony of Charles Sweeney.

By Judge Holt.—Q. State where you reside. A. In New York city.
Q. Have you been in the army during the present war? A. I have.
Q. Have you been a prisoner? A. Yes; the first time I was in Libby two months; the second time I was put on Belle Isle, in Richmond, and then they took me to Andersonville, Georgia.
Q. How long did you stay there? A. They kept me about six months before they moved me to Savannah.
Q. State how you were treated in those prisons. A. At Belle Isle a man was allowed to have half a pound of bread a day, and soup, with a little rice and bread scattered in it, and occasionally a little piece of meat; when we went to the hospital we had a little better bread and meat, but there was not much of it; when I first went to Andersonville we got a pretty good quantity of rations; we had all we wanted of corn meal, but the bacon was very strong; they then commenced to cut down our rations, and they got to be very short, but still we made out to live the best we could; then we went down to Savannah; but I ain't done with Andersonville yet; they used to tell the guard that whenever a man got over his dead line to shoot him, and for every man shot they would give a furlough of forty days, and whenever a man got even his hand over the dead line they would shoot him down as if he were a dog; at one time we were digging a tunnel, and one thing or another in the camp, trying to make our escape, and a cripple, a man with one leg, told on us; he ran outside the dead line once and the guard protected him, but Captain Burch told the guard that if he did not shoot that man he would shoot him, so the guard had to shoot him; I had a brother at Andersonville, who was very sick and dying for eight days; there was nothing he could eat; the corn meal and beef was not fit for a dog to eat; I tried to get some money to buy something to feed him, but the guard said, "Let him starve to death;" then I went to the Doctor, and asked him to go and see my brother in the tent, who was dying, but he said "no, let him d-e;" before he died he said to me, "my dear brother, never take an oath of allegiance to their Government, but stick to your own Government;" I said I would, and have done it; I tried two or three times to make my escape, but was recaptured; the first time they brought and gagged me for six hours; it was so cold that I could hardly talk when I got up; the next time I thought I would escape and make my way to General Stoneman, who was on a raid, but they caught me and took me back to Captain Winder, who had me put in the stocks; the sun was so hot that in the next day I got sick, and could eat nothing for six days, and pretty nearly died; but please God I have a little life in me yet. Do you want to hear anything about General Cobb? (Laughter.) He made a speech down there, and told the people of Georgia that the graveyard there was big enough to hold all those in the stockade, and that they intended to starve them all to death. Somebody in the crowd said if he could catch "Old Abe" he would hang him, and Cobb said if he could catch him he would do the same thing.

Testimony of James Young.

By Judge Holt.—Q. Have you been in the military service of the United States during this Rebellion? A. I have.
Q. Have you been a prisoner of war during that time. If so, how long and in what prison were you confined? A. I was for nine months at Andersonville, and at other times at Florence and Charleston, S. C.
Q. State the treatment you and other prisoners of war received at the hands of the Confederate authorities? A. At Andersonville, rations of a very inferior quality of corn bread and bacon were furnished they were very badly cooked; the quantity would usually be a piece of bread four inches long, three wide and two thick, and we would get about two or three ounces of pork.
Q. What was the effect of these rations upon the health of the prisoners? A. It was very injurious; they died in large numbers.
Q. What was the average number of deaths during your stay there? A. The report for August I understood was 3044.
Q. Were you in the open sun or under shelter? A. In the open sun.
Q. What was the temperature of the atmosphere? A. It was extremely hot in the day and cool at night.
Q. What was the character of the water they gave you? A. The water was very poor; it was saturated with the filth and garbage of the cook-houses before it came into the grounds.
Q. Was the character of the ground marshy? A. Yes; the creek ran through the centre of it.
Q. How far was it from Woodland? A. It appears that there was no woodland all around—in fact the stockade was made from wood taken out of it.
Q. Was there higher ground around also? A. Some higher.
Q. Were you there during the cold weather? A. No; I was at Florence during the cold weather.
Q. What were the declarations made by the keepers of the prison when complaints were made; did you hear what was said by them? A. I never heard anything at Andersonville, but at Florence I heard some pretty hard threats; they threatened to starve us because our army had made a raid through their country, and had destroyed food.
Q. Did you receive the same treatment at Florence as at Andersonville? A. Worse.
Q. Was the amount of food given sufficient to sustain life for any long time? A. No it was not; men who were without any extra means, money, trinkets or watches, with which to purchase extra food, ran down upon it until they died; I had some money and bought some extra provisions, and so kept my health tolerably good; the allowance I drew for ten days was two pounds of meal; the three weeks I was at Charleston we were used very well, except that they shot down our men on any excuse.
Q. Did this often occur? A. Yes.
Q. Did it seem to be encouraged by the officers? A. It did seem to be.
Q. Did you know of any man being rebuked or punished for having shot one our men? A. No, never; the general report in camp was that every guard was allowed thirty day's furlough for every man he shot; this was at Andersonville.
By the Court.—Who was the officer in command at Charleston, when you were there in prison? A. I cannot tell; I did not know.

Testimony of John S. Young.

By Judge Holt. Q. Where do you reside? A. In New York.
Q. State whether you knew Robert Kennedy, who was hung in New York some time since. A. I did.
Q. When was he hung? A. I think on the 25th of March last.
Q. State whether or not before his execution he made a confession, which was afterwards published in the papers of the country? A. He did.
Q. Have you that confession with you? A. I have.
Q. Did he make it to you? A. He signed a statement in my presence, but not the confession.
Q. To whom was the confession made? A. It was made, I believe, to Colonel Martin Burke, on duty at Fort Lafayette.
The Judge Advocate-General said there was a mistake in summoning this witness, that he supposed the confession was made to him; he would, however, read the confession to the Court and let it be placed on record. The confession, as published in the papers, was then read.

TESTIMONY FOR THE DEFENSE RESUMED.

Testimony of James H. Nothy.

By Mr. Aiken.—Q. Where do you reside. A. About fifteen miles down in Prince George county.
Q. State whether or not you purchased some land from Mrs. Surratt. A. I did; seventy-five acres, some years ago.
Q. Did Mr. Gwynn bring you a letter on the 14th of April last? A. He did.
Q. Who was that letter from? A. From Mrs. Surratt.
Q. Have you been in the habit of meeting Mrs. Surratt at Surrattsville? A. Only that one time; she sent for me to come there; I owed her part of the purchase money, and she wanted it settled; this letter was sent out on Friday; I did not see her that day at all.

Testimony of Dr. John C. Thomas.

By Mr. Stone.—Where do you reside? A. A. Woodville, Prince George county.
Q. What is your occupation? A. I am a physician

TRIAL OF THE ASSASSINS AT WASHINGTON.

Q. How long have you been practicing? A. Nineteen years.
Q. State whether you are a brother of the D. Thomas who has been examined here as a witness. A. I am.
Q. State whether your brother made any communication to you on the subject of a conversation with Dr. Mudd in relation to the assassination of the President? A. The conversation that passed was at my house on Sunday morning, he came there to Woodville, to church; I asked him the news; he was just from Bryantown the day before, and he was full of news; he was speaking of the arrest of Dr. Mudd, the finding of a boot at his house, &c.; during the conversation he repeated a remark that Dr. Mudd had made some weeks before.
Q. State whether he had ever mentioned that conversation to you before that time? A. No; never before that time.
Q. And this was after the assassination and after the arrest of Dr. Mudd? A. Yes; the soldiers were at Bryantown, and Dr. Mudd had been arrested, as I understood; I had not heard anything of the boot before; my brother made an error as to the date, and I think he is satisfied of it.
Q. I understand you, then, to say that was the first time you ever heard your brother speak of that conversation, and that he did not speak of it before the assassination? A. He did not; that was the first time he mentioned it.
Q. State whether you have or not attended your brother professionally sometimes. A. I have in some serious attacks; he had a very serious paralysis attack with paralysis of body; he was for some time laboring under considerable nervous depression, and was mentally affected by it, so that his mind was not exactly right for a long time.
Q. State whether your brother's mind is now sound at all times? A. I am under the impression that it is not at all times.
Q. When his mind is not in its proper state, is he not credulous, very talkative and unreliable? A. He is credulous and very talkative; very apt to tell everything he hears, and believes everything he hears; I do not pretend to say he would tell things he did not hear.
Q. State whether, when his mind is not in a proper condition, his memory and reason are not both somewhat affected, and memory also, when these attacks come on, but when he is in the enjoyment of good health he seems to be rational; he has not had an attack now for some time, and his health has been better.
Cross-examined by Judge Bingham.—Q. State whether you know on what Sunday it was that your brother made that statement in regard to Dr. Mudd; was it not Easter Sunday immediately following the assassination? A. I expect it was Easter Sunday; I think it was somewhere about that time.
Q. Now state what that conversation was in respect to the President, Cabinet and Union men of Maryland being assassinated within thirty days. A. He said that Dr. Mudd said Lincoln and the whole Cabinet would be killed in a few weeks, and that he as well as the other Union men in Maryland would be killed; Mr. Wood was present at that time.
Q. You are certain that in the same conversation he spoke of the boot being found in Dr. Mudd's house? A. Yes sir.
By the Court.—Q. On the day of this conversation are you certain your brother was in his right mind? A. He seemed to be.
Q. He was not much excited? A. No, not at all.
Q. Do you think he was capable of telling the truth on that day? A. Yes.
Q. From your knowledge of your brother's character for truth and veracity, of his mental condition, did you have any doubt in your mind that Dr. Mudd had said what he reported to you? A. I thought probably my brother was jesting at the time, and I observed that if such was not the fact, he ought not to state it; he said it was certainly true, that he had made that statement to him in Bryantown; I supposed he had told it as he heard it.

Testimony of Samuel McAllister.

By Mr. Stone.—Q. Where do you reside? A. In Washington.
Q. How long have you resided in Washington? A. Since the 24 day of December last.
Q. What is your occupation? A. I am clerk in Pennsylvania House, Washington.
Q. Have you the register of that house with you? A. I have, (producing the register.)
Q. State whether the name of Dr. S. A. Mudd appears on that register as having been entered in the month of January, 1865. A. I have examined the month carefully, and the name does not appear.
Q. Do you know the accused, Dr. Samuel A. Mudd? A. I do not; he may have stopped at the house, and if he did his name is on the register, as we do not allow any person to stop at the house without registering.
Q. Turn to the 23d of December last and state whether you find the name of Mudd? A. Yes sir; the name is here, Samuel A. Mudd.
Q. State whether you find the name of another than named Mudd on that day? A. Yes sir; J. T. Mudd.

Q. What is the rule of the house in regard to guests registering their names?
Assistant Judge Advocate Bingham objected to the question. The objection was overruled.
A. All persons stopping at the hotel are required to register their names: often persons come in and take meals; they do not register their names, but no person stops in the house over night without being required to register.
By Assistant Judge Advocate Bingham.—Q. Do you know who slept in the room with Atzeroth on the night of the assassination? A. No sir; I was in bed at the time Atzeroth came.
Q. You do not know whether Dr. S. A. Mudd was in the house or not in the month of January? A. No sir, his name is not on the register.
By the Court.—Do you know whether Dr. Mudd might have been in the house under an assumed name? A. I could not tell anything about that.
Q. Are you acquainted with the person registered as Mudd? No sir.

Testimony of Jos. T. Mudd.

By Mr. Ewing.—Q. State whether you are acquainted with the prisoner, Dr. Samuel A. Mudd? A. I am.
Q. Where do you reside? A. In the Fourth Election District of Charles county, about a mile and a half from the house of Dr. Samuel A. Mudd.
Q. State whether you came with the accused to Washington last winter, and if you did, give the particulars of your visit. A. I came with him to Washington on the 23d of December last; I recollect the date from the fact that we returned home on Christmas eve, which was the 24th.
When we got to Washington we left our horses down by the Navy Yard, and walked up to Pennsylvania avenue; it was in the evening; we went to the Pennsylvania House and registered our names, I think for lodgings; however, as we had not been to dinner, we concluded that we wanted something better than an ordinary supper, so we went to a restaurant on the avenue, known as the Walker Restaurant; we ordered supper, and remained there possibly an hour; after leaving there, we walked into Brown's Hotel, where we stayed about half an hour; we then went into the National Hotel; there was a tremendous crowd in there, and we got separated; I recognized an acquaintance in the crowd, and got into conversation with him; after that I came out of that place, and went along the avenue, stopping in several clothing stores, for the purpose of looking at some clothing which I intended to purchase next morning; I then walked up to the Pennsylvania House, and very soon after I arrived Dr. Mudd came very soon after we went to bed; in the morning, after breakfast, we went to the store of a man by the name of McGregor, I think, and purchased a cooking stove; we were together after that once or twice during the morning; I had clothing to buy, and some little purchases to make, which I attended to; I saw the prisoner during the morning repeatedly; every five or ten minutes I would be with him; about one o'clock we left the avenue, and came down to the Navy Yard, got our horses, and between two and three o'clock sent home; we came and returned together.
Q. Were you in the Pennsylvania House when the prisoner rejoined you, after your separation from him at the National? A. I was sitting near the fire-place in the front room as you enter, near the office where the register is kept; Dr. Mudd, when I first saw him came through the folding door into this room from the other room.
Q. Was any one with him as he entered? A. I think not; there might have been but I saw none.
Q. You say you were not separated from him the next morning more than five or ten minutes at a time? A. I think not; after the purchase of the stove he had some shoes and some little things to buy and we separated, but I saw him frequently; once, I think, he was coming from the Bank of Washington, where he had some little business.
Q. Do you know by whom the articles bought by him were taken to his house?
Judge Bingham objected to this question as being of no consequence.
Mr. Ewing said he thought it a matter of much consequence. The prosecution had proved by one witness a meeting between Booth and Mudd here in Washington, and the defense expected to be able to show conclusively that if there was any such meeting it must have been at this visit; therefore the necessity of showing that the accused came here on business unconnected with Booth; that the meeting with Booth had been put in evidence as a part of the conspiracy, and the defense had a right to show by the acts of the accused that he came to Washington on a purely legitimate business visit.
Judge Bingham replied that the interview alleged to have taken place in Washington, between Mudd and Booth, was in another month from that here designated, and the attempt to show the purchase of certain articles, and everything connected with their transportation to the house of the prisoner, would, if allowed, result in throwing no additional light whatever on the subject. The objection was not sustained and the question was repeated. A. I took home a portion of his purchases myself; the stove was to have been

TRIAL OF THE ASSASSINS AT WASHINGTON. 97

taken home by a Mr. Lucas, who was then in market with his wagon; I went twice with Dr. Mudd and twice by myself; Mr. Lucas said that if he sold out his load of poultry he would take the stove down, and if he did not he would not be able to take it down that trip.

Q. Are you well acquainted with Dr. Samuel Mudd? A. I am; I have known him from early youth.

Q. Do you know his general character in the neighborhood in which he resides for peace, order and good citizenship? A. It is exemplary; I think I never heard anything to the contrary; he is of an amiable disposition, a good citizen and a good neighbor, besides being honest and correct.

Q. Do you know his character in the neighborhood as a master of his slaves? A. I do; I have lived close by him all my life, and believe him to be humane and kind; I never thought his niggers done a great deal of work, but have always considered that they were treated very humanely.

Q. Do you know of Booth's having been in that country? A. I do; I saw him at church; that is, I saw a stranger there, and I asked who he was, and was told it was Booth, a great tragedian; from the description given of him, and the photograph, I am satisfied it was the same man; that was in the latter part of November or early in December.

Q. Do you know on what business Booth was in that country? A. Only from the common talk, what I heard others say.

Q. What was the common talk?

Judge Bingham objected to the question.

Mr. Ewing said that he knew it was the object of the Government to give the accused here liberal opportunities of presenting their defense, and he did not think the Judge Advocate intended, by drawing tightly the rules of evidence, to shut out evidence which might fairly go to relieve the accused of the accusations against them. It was better not only for them but for the Government whose majesty had been violated that there should be great liberality in allowing the accused to present whatever evidence they might offer. The defense wished to show that Booth was in the country ostensibly according to the common understanding of the neighborhood, for the purpose of investing in lands. This was introduced as explanatory of his meeting with Dr. Mudd, whose family, as the defense expected to show, were large landholders and anxious to dispose of their lands.

Judge Advocate Holt stated that he was in favor of allowing the accused to indulge in the utmost latitude of inquiry, and that when he fell short of maintaining that spirit he would be obliged if the Court would do it for him. In this instance, however, a mere idle rumor in regard to which a cross-examination could not be made, was not, in his opinion, properly admissible. The objection was sustained, and the question was not put.

Cross-examined by Judge Holt.—Q. Do you know the reputation of the prisoner, Dr. Mudd, for loyalty to the Government of the United States? A. I really do not so far as my own knowledge goes; I have never known of any disloyal act of his.

Q. Have you ever heard any disloyal sentiment expressed by him? A. No sir; I have heard him express sentiments in opposition to the policy of the Administration.

Q. Do you know that he has been opposed to the action of the Government of the United States in its endeavors to suppress this Rebellion, and that his opposition to it has been open and undisguised? A. No sir; I do not know that.

Q. Do you know that he has constantly held that the State of Maryland had been false to her duty in not going with the other States in Rebellion against the Government? A. I have never heard him say so.

Q. Have you not from time to time seen Confederate officers about his house? A. Never sir.

Q. You spoke of his amiability towards his servants, did you ever hear of his shooting any of them? A. I have heard of it.

Q. Have you any doubts of its truth? A. No sir.

By Mr. Ewing.—Q. State what you heard about his shooting his slave. A. I heard that his servant was obstreperous; that he ordered his servant to do something which he not only refused to do, but started to go away; Dr. Mudd had his gun with him, and he thought he would shoot him to frighten him; I heard him say so myself; he shot him somewhere in the calf of the leg.

Q. Was it with a shot-gun? A. Yes sir.

Q. Did you ever hear anything of the servant having attacked him with a curry-comb? A. I do not think I ever heard that; I heard but little about the matter.

Q. Did you hear that his servant's leg was broken by the shot? A. No sir; I heard it was a flesh wound.

Q. You speak of having heard him express himself in opposition to the policy of the Administration; did he express himself with any violence? A. No sir, I never knew him to make use of any expression in gentlemen's company which could not be admissible in ladies' society.

Q. Did he ever talk much in opposition to the Administration? A. I never heard him talk a great deal in opposition to the Administration except with reference to the emancipation policy.

Testimony of Francis Lucas.

By Mr. Ewing.—Q. Where do you live and what occupation were you engaged in last December? A. I live in Charles county, near Bryantown, Md., and was and have been a huckster for several years.

Q. State whether there was any arrangement made between you and Dr. Mudd as to carrying some articles from this city down home for him last December? A. On Christmas eve Dr. Mudd came to me in market and asked me to take a stove home for him; he came to me several times, and I promised to do it if I could.

Testimony of John C. Thompson.

By Mr. Stone.—Q. Where did you reside last Fall? A. At Dr. Queen's, in Charles county.

Q. Did you know Wilkes Booth? A. I had a slight acquaintance with a man bearing that name.

Q. State how that acquaintance commenced? A. I was introduced to a man styling himself Booth; I do not know whether the name was Wilkes Booth or not, by Dr. Queen, my brother-in-law; I think that was in October or November last.

Q. Was this introduction given to you by Dr. Queen at his house? A. Yes sir; Booth came there, I think, on a Saturday night.

Q. Had any of the family there known him previously? A. I think I can say with certainty that none of the family ever heard of him before.

Q. State how he got admission there? A. Dr. Queen's son, Joseph Queen, brought him there from Bryantown.

Q. Where is Dr. Queen now, and what is his condition? A. He is at his place, in Charles county; he is a very old man, being seventy-four years of age, bedridden and infirm.

Q. Did this man Booth bring any letters of introduction to Dr. Queen? A. I think he brought a letter from somebody in Montreal if I am not mistaken it was from a man by the name of Martin.

Q. Did you see the letter? A. I hardly glanced over the letter, and paid very little attention to it; as well as I remember, it was simply a letter of introduction to Dr. Queen, saying that this man Booth wanted to see the country.

Q. State whether you were present at the first conversation between Dr. Samuel A. Mudd and this man Booth? A. On Sunday morning, this man Booth, Dr. Queen and myself went to the church at Bryantown and I introduced Booth to Dr. Mudd.

Q. State what was Booth's ostensible object in visiting the country? A. It was for the purpose of purchasing land; that I am confident of, as for so stated to me; he asked me the price of land in that section, and I told him as well as I knew that the land varied in price from five to fifty dollars per acre, according to the quality and situation and the improvements upon the land.

Q. Did he make any inquiries of you as to who had land for sale? A. Yes; I think I told him I did not know who had land for sale, but that Mr. Henry Mudd, the father of the accused, was a large property holder, and he (Booth) might purchase land from him.

Q. Did he make any inquiry as to distances from the river? A. As well as I remember he did make inquiries of me about the roads in Charles county, but I was not informed in regard to roads there; the only road of which I had any knowledge was the road from Washington, known as the Stage Road, leading down to Bryantown, he asked me in regard to the roads leading to the Potomac River; I told him I was not conversant with these roads; that I knew them as far as Allen's Fresh and Newport, but no further.

Q. Did Booth make any inquiries as to the purchase of horses in the neighborhood? A. I think he did; I think he asked me if there were any horses in the neighborhood for sale; I told him I did not know; that the Government had been purchasing horses.

Q. State whether the meeting of Booth, Dr. Queen and yourself with Dr. Mudd at church was casual. A. It was simply accidental.

Q. Where did you meet Booth? A. In the church yard in front of the church door, where the male portion of the congregation are in the habit of assembling just previous to Divine service; I happened to see Dr. Mudd there with various other gentlemen, and I introduced him to the others present; I had no idea as to what the man's business there was further than that he was a purchaser of lands; I think he told me the night before he had made a speculation or was a shareholder in an enterprise in Western Pennsylvania somewhere, and, as far as I remember, told me he had made a good deal of money out of these operations.

Q. Did Booth stay at Dr. Queen's house during that visit? A. I think he stayed there that night and the next day.

Q. Did you ever see Booth again? A. I think I saw him again about the middle of December following; he came to Dr. Queen's a second time and stayed all night, and left very early the next morning; I did not see him after that.

Cross-examined by Assistant Judge Advocate Burnett.—Q. How near do you live to Dr. Mudd? A. I think the distance is about seven or eight miles.

Q. Is your acquaintance with Dr. Samuel A. Mudd

and his affairs of a very intimate character? A. I am not intimately acquainted with him; I know him personally.
Q. You say that Booth spoke of purchasing lands. A. Yes sir; I told him that Mr. Henry Mudd, the father of the accused, was an extensive land holder, and he would probably be able to purchase lands from him.
Q. He did not in that conversation say anything to you about purchasing land from Dr. Samuel Mudd? A. No sir.
Q. Do you know whether Dr. Samuel Mudd owns any land there? A. I am not positive as to that.
By Mr. Stone.—Q. Who lives nearest to this city, Dr. Queen or Dr. Mudd? A. I think Dr. Mudd lives the nearest.
By the Court.—Q. Did you see the name attached to the letter of which you have spoken? A. Yes sir; I think the name was Martin; I do not know the christian name.
Q. You have never heard of the man whose name was signed to that letter? A. I did not.
Q. Did Booth, to your knowledge, ever buy any land in Maryland on the strength of that letter of introduction? A. Not to my knowledge.
The Court adjourned till to-morrow morning.

WASHINGTON, May 27.—After the evidence taken yesterday had been read, the following witnesses were to-day called for the prosecution:—

Testimony of George F. Edmonds.

By Judge Advocate Holt.—Q. What is your profession? A. Counsellor at Law.
Q. State whether or not in the trial which recently occurred in Canada of certain offenders, known as the St. Albans raiders, you appeared as counsel for the Government of the United States. A. I had charge of the matter for the Government of the United States.
Q. State whether in the performance of your professional duties there, you made the acquaintance of Jacob Thompson, William C. Cleary, Clement C. Clay, George N. Sanders, and others of that clique? A. In the sense in which the term is generally understood, I did not; I knew these persons by their being pointed out to me daily; I did not have the honor, if it may be called, of their acquaintance.
Q. Were the defendants in court? A. They were.
Q. Were they engaged as officers of the Confederate Government in defending these raiders? A. They seemed to exercise the functions, and recognized each other accordingly.
Q. Mention the persons whom you met there, and who were so recognized. A. I do not think I saw Mr. Thompson more than once; I saw C. C. Clay during the early part of the proceedings almost daily, and Mr. Sanders during the whole of the period; Mr. Cleary, whom you mentioned, I saw to know at a later period, when he was examined as a witness on the part of the defendant.
Q. Did he represent in his testimony on that trial, that those persons were engaged in the Confederate service, and that his raid was made under authority of the Confederate Government? He so represented, and did all those persons, and they stood upon that defense.
Q. Will you look at this paper and state whether or not you have seen the original of the document? A. I have seen the original.
Q. Was it or was it not given in evidence on the trial to which you refer? A. It was given in evidence on the trial on the part of the defendants.
Q. Given in evidence by them as a general document? A. It was.
Q. Is that a correct copy? A. I cannot swear that it is an exact copy, but I examined the original very carefully, and I am able to swear that it is a substantial copy, and I have no doubt it is a literal copy.
The paper was then given in evidence, and was read, as follows:—

CONFEDERATE STATES OF AMERICA, WAR DEPARTMENT, RICHMOND, Va., June 16, 1864.—To Lieutenant Bennett H. Young—Lieutenant:—You have been appointed, temporarily, First Lieutenant in the Provisional army for special service. You will proceed without delay to the British Provinces, where you will report to Messrs. Thompson & Clay for instructions. You will, under their directions, collect such confederate soldiers who have escaped from the enemy, not exceeding twenty in number, as you may deem suitable for the purpose, and will execute such enterprises as may be entrusted to you. You will take care to commit no violation of the local law, and to obey implicitly their instructions. You and your men will receive from these gentlemen transportation and the customary rations and clothing, or the commutation therefor.
(Signed) JAMES A. SEDDON, Secretary of War.

Q. Was the Young referred to in that connection one of the St. Albans raiders? A. I do not know that I can answer that question literally; he produced that document and protested to be the person.
Q. He was on trial as such? A. He was on trial as such, and produced that document as his authority for the acts he had committed.

The testimony of the witness having been concluded, Judge Advocate Holt stated that since closing the case on the part of the Government so far as concerned the individual prisoners, he had discovered an important witness, before unknown to him, whose examination he desired should now be made.

Mr. Ewing inquired as to which of the prisoners the proposed testimony was likely to affect?

Judge Holt replied that it referred directly to the case of Atzeroth.

Mr. Doster said that he had not opened the defense for Atzeroth, and, therefore, would not object to the reception of the testimony.

The witness was then called and testified as follows:—

Testimony of Colonel William R. Nevins.

By Judge Advocate Holt.—Q. Where do you reside? A. In New York.
Q. State whether or not you were in this city in the month of April last, and if so, on what day? A. I was here on the 12th of April; I think I recollect the day from the fact that a pass which I received from the War Department bears that date.
Q. Where did you stop in this city? A. At the Kirkwood House.
Q. Look at the prisoners at the bar and see whether you recognize either of them as a person whom you met in that house on that day? A. That one there (pointing to Atzeroth), I think he is the man.
Q. State under what circumstances you met him, and what he said to you? A. He had on a coat darker than that; as I was coming out he asked me if I knew where the Vice President's room was, and I told him that the Vice President was then at dinner; there was no one there then except him and me.
Q. Did he ask where the room of Vice President Johnson was? A. Yes sir that was his first question; I did not know the number of the Vice President's room, but I knew it was on the right hand side next the parlor; however, I said to him, "the Vice President is eating his dinner."
Q. Did you then part with him, or where did he go? A. I passed on.
Q. Did you leave him standing there, or did he go away? A. Well, he looked in the dining room; I do not know whether he went in or not.
Q. You say you pointed out the room to him? A. Yes, sir.
Q. Was the room in view from where you pointed it out? A. Yes sir; it was on the passage as you go into the dining room, and between that and the steps as you go down to the dining room is where this man met me.
Cross-examined by Mr. Doster.—Q. What time of day was this? A. I think it was between four and five o'clock; there was no other person at dinner but the Vice President himself; I was going away at the time, and was in a great hurry.
Q. Whereabouts in the building did this conversation take place? A. In the passage leading into the dining-room.
Q. Did the prisoner look into the dining-room? A. From the passage you cannot look into it, but by going down a few steps you can see in.
Q. I understood you to say that he looked into the dining-room? A. I pointed to the Vice President, Mr. Johnson, who was sitting at the far end with a yellow-looking man standing behind him.
Q. What length of time was occupied in this conversation? A. I do not suppose over three minutes.
Q. Have you seen the prisoner since that time until you saw him to-day? A. No sir.
Q. Describe the dress and appearance of the prisoner? A. I was in a hurry when I met the prisoner, and am therefore unable to give a very minute description of his dress; it was dark; he had on a low-crowned black hat, but it is his countenance by which I now recognize him.
Q. State to the Court your age. A. I was born on February 22d, 1803.
By Judge Advocate Holt.—Q. State whether or not in coming into the presence of the prisoner, Atzeroth, this morning, you recognized him at once, without his being pointed out to you. A. I recognized him without his being pointed out to me.
Q. No indication as to the person was made to you? A. No sir.

Testimony of Bettie Washington, (Colored).

By Mr. Stone.—Q. State where you reside. A. I live at Dr. Samuel Mudd's; have been living there since the Monday after Christmas.
Q. Were you a slave before the Emancipation Proclamation was issued? A. Yes, sir.

[In reply to a series of questions propounded to her, the witness then testified in substance that she had not been absent from the house of the prisoner, Dr. Samuel Mudd, for a single night since she first took up her abode with him until she came to Washing-

TRIAL OF THE ASSASSINS AT WASHINGTON.

THE ARSENAL BUILDING, WASHINGTON, D.C., WHERE THE ASSASSINS AND CONSPIRATORS WERE TRIED.

ton; that during that time the prisoner had been absent from home on three separate occasions; first at Mr. George Henry Gardner's party, where he staid late in the evening; second, at Giesboro', where he went to buy some horses; and third, to Washington, from which place he returned on the day after his leaving home.

Q. Did you see the men called Harold and Booth? A. I saw only one of them, the small one; I was standing at the kitchen window, and just got a glimpse of him as he was going in the direction of the swamp.

Q. How long after you saw him did you see Dr. Mudd? A. I did not see Dr. Mudd with the man; I saw Dr. Mudd about three or four minutes afterwards at the front door.

A photograph of Booth was here exhibited to the witness, but she failed to identify the likeness as that of any one she had ever seen.

During a brief cross-examination, conducted by Assistant Judge Advocate Bingham, the witness testified that an interval of about a week or two took place between the prisoner's departure from home, and that his brother accompanied him on these occasions.

Re-examination of Jeremiah T. Mudd.

By Mr. Ewing.—Q. Are you acquainted with the handwriting of the accused, Samuel A. Mudd? A. Yes sir.

Q. State whether you see his handwriting on that page (exhibiting to witness the register of the Pennsylvania Hotel at Washington, on the page headed Friday, December 23, 1864)? A. I do.

Q. Do you know at what hotel in Washington the prisoner was in the habit of stopping? A. I do not.

Q. Are you acquainted with Daniel G. Thomas, who has been a witness for the prosecution? A. I am.

Q. Do you know his reputation in the neighborhood in which he lives for truth and veracity? A. I do; it is bad.

Q. From your knowledge of his reputation for truth would you believe him under oath? A. I do not think I could; it has been my impression that—

Judge Bingham.—You need not state your impressions.

Mr. Ewing—Proceed with your answer.

A. I have just stated that I did not think I could.

Cross-examined by Assistant Judge Advocate Bingham.—Q. Do you base his general reputation upon your personal knowledge and acquaintance with him? A. Yes sir, and upon what I generally heard spoken by others.

Q. What do you say that you generally heard spoken by others in regard to his reputation for truth? A. That it was pretty bad.

Q. How many people did you ever hear speak of his general reputation for truth before the taking of this testimony the other day? A. I heard several speak of it.

Q. How many, ten? A. I think so; I will not say positively; I am speaking now from what I have heard generally.

Q. Can you name the ten? A. I really do not know.

Q. Can you name half of the ten? A. I think I can; I might name a dozen.

Q. Well, who are they? A. I might name Dr. George Mudd for one.

Q. When did you hear Dr. George Mudd speak on the subject? I heard him speak of it as late as two years ago.

Q. What did he say of the general character of the witness for truth? A. That it was bad; that he did not believe his general character for truth was good.

Q. How did he come to say that? A. It was in connection with some matters that occurred about the time of stationing Colonel Birney down there.

Q. You did not understand that Thomas was opposed to Colonel Birney? A. Not at all; I simply mention that as being about the time.

Q. State all the circumstances in that connection? A. It was about the fact of Thomas having a man named Payne arrested there—for what I do not know; the man who was arrested had a brother in the Rebel army, and some of his brother's friends came to his house.

Q. Then the arrest was made on the charge of entertaining Rebel soldiers? A. Yes sir; I presume it was.

Q. Was that the only man whom you overheard assail this man's character for truth? A. I believe there were others.

Q. Who were the others? A. I do not know that I can name them.

Q. If you cannot name two men who ever assailed his character for truth, how can you come to the conclusion that his general reputation for truth is bad? A. Well, I heard a number say so.

By the Court.—Q. What relation are you to the prisoner? A. My father and his father were cousins.

Q. Have you been intimate with him? A. Moderately so; we met frequently, as I live in his neighborhood.

By Mr. Stone.—Q. Have you been in the habit of serving on the juries in the county where you live? A. I have, frequently.

Q. State whether Mr. Thomas has not frequently been a witness in court when you were present? A. I do not recollect of his having been a witness in court.

By Judge Bingham.—Q. Have you heard any one assert that Mr. Thomas ever swore falsely in court? A. No, sir.

Q. Are you aware of the fact that he has been a supporter of the Government and has acted as an official for the Government since the Rebellion broke out? A. Yes, sir.

Q. Are you aware of another fact, that a very considerable portion of the people in St. Charles county are reputed somewhat disloyal and a good deal favorable to this Rebellion? A. I am aware that several young men from our section have gone into the Rebel army.

Q. Yes; and many of those left behind have been making a good deal of clamor; have they not acted against the Government, and in favor of the Rebellion? A. Not to any great extent.

Q. That is the general report, is it not? A. Well; yes sir.

Q. Are not the men who have spoken against this man Thomas of that class who bear the general reputation of being against the Government? A. I really do not know.

Q. Have you any knowledge of Rebels being fed and concealed in that neighborhood by the residents there? A. I have not; I have seen men in Bryantown passing and repassing who I was told were Rebels; as to their being fed or concealed in my immediate neighborhood I have no knowledge.

By Mr. Ewing.—Q. You have spoken of Dr. George Mudd as one of the men who said that he regarded the reputation of Thomas for veracity as bad; state whether Dr George Mudd is a Rebel sympathizer or not. A. I regard him as having been, throughout this war, as strong a Union man as any in the United States; I never heard him express the slightest sympathy with the Rebellion.

Q. What is his reputation for loyalty? A. I think there would be very little difficulty in establishing the fact of its being very good; he is so regarded universally.

By Judge Bingham.—Q. Did you ever hear Dr. Geo. Mudd say anything against the Rebellion? A. Very often.

By Mr. Stone.—Q. Did Mr. Daniel Thomas hold any position under the Government? A. He said that he was a detective.

Q. Do you know such to be the fact from any other source than himself? A. I do not.

Q. Under whose orders did he claim to have been acting? A. I think under Colonel Holland, the Provost Marshal of our district.

Re-examination of Benjamin F. Gwynn.

By Mr. Ewing—Q. State whether last summer, in company with Captain White, from Tennessee, Captain Perry, Lieutenant Perry, Andrew Gwynn, George Gwynn, or either of them, you were about Dr. Samuel A. Mudd's house for a number of days. A. I never saw any of these parties except Andrew Gwynn and George Gwynn, and have not been in Dr. Mudd's house since about the 1st of November, 1861, nor nearer to it than the church since the 6th of November, 1861.

Q. State what occurred in 1861, when you were in the neighborhood of Dr. M dd's house. A. I was with my brother, Andrew J. Gwynn, and Jerry Dyer; about that time General Sickles came over into Maryland, arresting everybody; I was threatened with arrest, and left the neighborhood to avoid it; I went down to Charles county and stayed with my friends there, as everybody else was doing; there was a good deal of running around about that time.

Mr. Ewing—Go on and tell all about it.

Assistant Judge Advocate Bingham objected to the witness being allowed to state anything further on this point, as it was not in issue what was done in 1861.

Mr. Ewing said the prosecution had shown by four or five witnesses that a party, of whom the witness on the stand was one, had been collected in the pine woods in the neighborhood of Dr. Mudd's house, having their meals brought to them by his servants; and had also attempted to show that these persons were in the Confederate service, and that Dr. Mudd was guilty of treason in attempting to secrete them. If the defense showed that this was not done last year, it would not be a complete refutation of the testimony, because it may be alleged to have been done previously. The defense wished to show that this concealment was the concealment of a much smaller party than was stated, and of men who were not in the Confederate service, and also that it occurred at another time from that stated. To deny the accused this opportunity would be to withhold a most legitimate line of defense, and to refuse to allow him to refute the whole mass of loose testimony of ignorant servants (ignorant as to dates), would be most unjust.

Judge Bingham contended that there was no color of excuse for the attempt to introduce testimony in regard to the year 1861. The reason why the objection was not made sooner was because the prosecution had been unable to perceive the purpose of the counsel for the defense in following such a course. It was proper for them to swear this witness as to his whereabouts, so as to contradict the testimony of Mary Simms, who had sworn to having seen him last summer. To go further than that was not legitimate. If this course was persisted in, and every witness called in regard to 1861 was to swear deliberately and maliciously false, there would be no power in the court to punish them for perjury, for the simple reason that there was no issue before the Court, either in the evidence adduced or in the charges and specifications which would authorize any inquiry about it.

The objection was sustained.

The Commission then took a recess until 2 o'clock, at which time the body reassembled.

Re-examination of Benjamin F. Gwynn. Continued.

By Mr. Ewing.—Q. State where the party of whom you have spoken as being in the pines got their meals and slept. A. They slept in the barn, near the spring, on bedding furnished from Dr. Mudd's, and were furnished with meals by Dr. Mudd; we remained there about four or five days.

Q. State the circumstances of your being there and what occurred. A. As I said before, I went down there and stayed around the neighborhood, part of the time at Dr. Mudd's house and part of the time elsewhere; he gave us something to eat, and some bed clothing.

Q. Were you and the party with you in his house during the time you were there? A. Yes sir, almost every day, I think.

Q. Where were your horses? A. At the stable, I think; I do not know who attended to them.

Q. Do you know where John H. Surratt was at that time? A. I think he was at college.

Q. Do you know whether there were any charges against you and the party that were there? A. I came up to Washington about the first of November, and gave myself up, having got tired of staying away; they administered to me the oath, and I then went home; I think they said there had not been any charges against me.

Q. What induced the party to go to the pines to sleep? A. To avoid arrest, I did.

Q. What reason had you for supposing you would be arrested? A. Almost everybody in our neighborhood was being arrested, and I understood I would be, too; so I went down there.

Q. Have you seen Surratt in Charles county since? A. I have not; I wish to state here that it was not in November I slept in the pines, it was in August.

Q. You spoke of Andrew J. Gwynn being there with you; will you state where he has been since? A. He has been South.

Q. What relation do you bear to him? A. He is my brother; he lives in Prince George's county, some eight miles from my house.

Q. Did you hear of Andrew J. Gwynn being in that section since 1861? A. I heard he was there some time during last winter, I think.

Q. What time in 1861 did he go South? A. In August.

Cross-examined by Judge Advocate Holt.—Q. You spoke of the universality of arrests in 1861; did you understand that they were confined to persons suspected of disloyalty and disloyal practices? A. They were, generally; there were several volunteer companies there whose members were arrested.

Q. Were those companies organized for the defense of the United States. A. They were commissioned by Governor Hicks.

Q. On what grounds did you suppose you would be arrested? A. I was a captain of a company down there.

Q. Organized for what purpose? A. It was called a home guard, and was raised for the purpose of protecting the neighbors; at that time there was a good deal of disaffection among the blacks; it was thought to be a proper time for raising companies through the country; I therefore petitioned Governor Hicks, and he gave me a commission.

Q. Was it not understood they were organized to stand by the State in any disloyal position she might take against the Government of the United States? A. Yes sir, I so understood it; they arrested several members of my company, and, as I understood there was a warrant for my arrest, I left.

Q. You slept in the pines for the sole purpose of escaping arrest? A. Yes sir.

Q. Dr. Mudd, I suppose, concurred fully in your sentiment and the sentiments which pervaded the local organizations? A. I do not know what his sentiments were at the time.

By Mr. Ewing.—Q. When was this company, of which you were captain, organized? A. I think in the fall of 1860 or winter of 1861.

Q. Before or after the election of Mr. Lincoln? A. I do not know; I think we commence to organize our company before that, but were not fully organized until after that time.

Q. How far was the locality of this organization from Dr. Mudd's place? A. About ten miles.

Q. Do you know whether Dr. Mudd was a member of any of these volunteer companies? A. I think he was a member of a company gotten up in Bryantown.

Q. Are you sure of that? A. I do not know positively; I think so.

Testimony of Jerry Dyer.

Examined by Mr. Ewing.—Q. State where you live. A. I live in Baltimore.

Q. State where you lived prior to that. A. In Charles county.

Q. Do you know the prisoner, Dr. Samuel A. Mudd? A. Yes sir.

Q. How far from the house of Dr. Mudd? A. About a mile and a half in a direct line.

Q. When did you leave your residence in Charles county? A. In May, two years ago.

Q. State how long before you went to Baltimore you had lived in Charles county. A. I was raised there.

Q. State whether you knew Sylvester Eglan, who has been on the witness stand. A. I do not know him by that name; he was called Eli; he is a little boy, a servant of the father of Dr. Mudd;

Q. Do you know his brother Frank? A. Yes.

Q. Do you know Dick Gardner or Luke Gardner? A. Not by that name; I knew Dick and Luke Washington, who, I presume, are the ones you mean.

Q. State whether in August, 1863, at the house of the accused, Dr. Mudd, under an oak tree, when you was in conversation with Walter Bowie and the accused, the accused said he would send Sylvester Eglan and his brother Frank, and others of his servants, to Richmond. A. I never had any such conversation with him in my life, and in August I was not in the county; I went to Baltimore the first day of August, and remained until October, when hearing that some of my hands had left the farm, I went down to see about everying on the farm; about thirty or forty hands left the neighborhood about that time.

Q. And you never, at that or any other time, heard him threaten to send any of his servants to Richmond? A. Never; I heard, when I got down in the county, that such a report had been started there by a certain man in the neighborhood; I never heard Dr. Mudd say any such thing.

Q. Did you ever meet Dr. Mudd in company with Walter Bowie? A. Not that I know of.

Q. Can you say that you never met Dr. Mudd in company with Walter Bowie at the house of Dr. Mudd's father? A. I am satisfied I never did; I recollect about two years ago, in the fall of 1862 or spring of 1863, when some one rode into the lane, I turned and asked who that was coming; he said:—"That is Walter Bowie; I wonder what he wants here?" and turned and went into the house; he stayed about for some minutes, and then went away; I don't recollect whether Dr. Mudd was there or not; my impression is he was not.

Q. Do you know Andrew Gwynn? A. Very well.

Q. Do you know where he has been since 1861? A. He has been in the Rebel army.

Q. Have you ever seen him since 1861? A. I have not.

Q. Did you meet him with Surratt and Dr. Blanford at the house of Dr. Mudd? A. Never; I never saw Surratt there in my life; the only time I saw him at all was coming into Bryantown some two or three years ago.

Q. Do you know whether or not any of Surratt's family were in Bryantown then? A. He had a sister there at school.

Q. Did you last year see Surratt drive up to the house of Dr. Mudd's father, and take his horse out of the buggy? A. I did not.

Q. Are you acquainted with the witness Miles Simms? A. Yes, I know him; he used to live with Dr. Mudd.

Q. Do you know Rachel Spencer, Elving Washington, Elge Eglan, and Mary Simms? A. Yes.

Q. State whether any of them were servants of Dr. Mudd in 1861. A. I think they all were; I know I bought the woman Elvina about 1860 or 1861.

Q. State whether you were at Dr. Mudd's house, or in the neighborhood, with Ben Gro run, in the summer of 1861? A. I was in September, 1861.

Q. How long were you at the house? A. We were in the neighborhood about a week.

Q. What were you doing? A. We were knocking about in the bushes and pines; there was a report that everybody was to be arrested; they were arresting a great many men in that neighborhood; Mr. Gwynn came down and said they had been to the house to arrest us; I also received notice that I was to be arrested; I came to Dr. Mudd's and stayed about there, sleeping in the pines where his house and mine several nights; we were two nights very near his spring.

Q. Where did you get your bed clothing? A. At Dr. Mudd's house.

Q. Where did you get your meals? A. When we were near his house Dr. Mudd brought the meals in; a part of the time we were on the opposite side of the swamp; while we were on this side we were about two hundred yards from his (Dr. Mudd's) house; he would sometimes bring down a basket, with bread, meat, whisky, &c., and the girl (Mary Semmes) sometimes brought coffee.

Q. Who took care of the horses of the party? A. I believe the horses were let at Dr. Mudd's stable, and suppose the boy Milo took care of them; he was about there.

Q. State how the parties were dressed? A. They had on citizen's clothes.

Q. Who composed the party? A. Ben, Gwynn, Andrew Gwynn and myself.

TRIAL OF THE ASSASSINS AT WASHINGTON. 101

Q. Were apples and peaches ripe about that time?
A. It was about peach season.
Q. Do you know whether a watch was kept at Dr. Mudd's house when you were there? A. I recollect telling the children to keep a lookout and let no know.
Q. Do you know whether Albion Brooks was about the house at that time? A. I think he was not living there, but he often came across there.
Q. Do you know whether there was any warrant for your arrest on any charges against you? A. I do not; there was a general stampede of people, and a great excitement in that whole community.
Q. Do you know Daniel S. Thomas, one of the witnesses for the prosecution? A. I have known him quite intimately since he was a boy; I have seen much of him for the last two or three years.
Q. Are you acquainted with the reputation in which he is held in the community in which he lives for veracity? A. I only know from public rumor; there are very few who have any confidence in him.
Q. From your knowledge of his reputation for veracity would you believe him under oath? A. I would not.
Q. Are you acquainted with the accused, Dr. Mudd?
A. Yes; I have known him from a boy.
Q. What is his general reputation for order and good citizenship. A. I have never heard the slightest thing against him; he has always been regarded as a good citizen, as a man of peace; I have never known him have any difficulty, but have always regarded him as a peaceable, quiet citizen.
Q. What is his reputation as a master over his servants? A. I have always considered him a very kind, humane master; I have not known anything to the contrary, with the single exception of his shooting that boy.
Cross-examination by Judge Holt.—Q. You say you would not believe Mr. Thomas under oath; have you ever heard him charged with having sworn falsely on any occasion? A. I do not know as I have.
Q. He is rather a talking, noisy man in the neighborhood, is he? A. Yes.
Q. He talks a great deal about the Union, and a great deal against the Rebellion, don't he? A. I believe he does.
Q. He has a reputation of being intensely loyal to the Government, has he? A. I think he has; I believe he is considered loyal
Q. Have you been loyal during the Rebellion? A. I do not know that I have been guilty of any act against the Government.
Q. I speak of your sentiments; have you during this Rebellion desired the Government to succeed in putting it down? A. I never wanted two Governments.
Q. The question is a direct and plain one, I desire you to answer? A. I can only answer that by saying I never wanted this Government broken up; I would rather have seen one Government.
Q. Will you please answer the question directly; yes or no? A. I hardly understand your question; I think I have desired the Government to succeed.
Q. You say you have committed no overt act of disloyalty? A. Not that I am aware of.
Q. Have you ever spoken kindly of the Government and encouragingly to your loyal neighbors and friends?
A. I certainly have; I have endeavored to dissuade young men from going into the Southern army.
Q. Were you or not the member of a loyal organization the object of which was to stand by the State of Maryland in the event of her taking ground against the Government of the United States A. I belonged to a military organization.
Q. You state that you were at Dr. Mudd's in 1861; did you not suppose at that time that this organization of which you were a member was regarded as disloyal to the Government? A. I hardly know how to answer the question; circumstances have changed so since then; at that time everything was confusion and excitement, and I can hardly answer the question.
Q. Have you any knowledge of the existence of a treasonable organization in this country known as "the Knights of the Golden Circle" or "Sons of Liberty?" A. I have not except what I have seen in the papers.
Q. At the time when you were a member of this organization, in the summer of 1861, was not the subject of the Legislature of Maryland passing an ordinance of secession discussed among you? A. Not to my knowledge; I may have heard such a thing spoken of, but I do not know that it was discussed to any extent.
Q. Can you mention the names of any persons who have been most decided in expressing the opinion you have stated in regard to Mr. Thomas' character for truth? A. It has been the talk of almost every man in that whole country.
Q. Have you ever heard of a man of known loyalty (an ardent supporter of the Government) speak of Mr Thomas as a man not to be believed under oath? A. I do not know as I have.
By the Court.—Q. Did not you rejoice at the success of the Rebels in the first battle of Bull Run? A. I do not know as I did particularly.
Q. Did you generally? A. I do not know as I did.
Q. On which side were your sympathies at that time? A. I suppose with the Rebels at that time; I judge so; I do not know.
Q. When Richmond was taken on which side were your sympathies? A. With the United States Government; I wanted them to take Richmond and the war to stop.
Q. What time did your sympathies undergo a change and what produced that change? A. I do not know; the only thing I objected to was the emancipation of the slaves; that I thought was wrong.
By Judge Burnett.—Q. How about the draft? A. I joined a club.
Q. To save yourself from being drafted? A. Yes.
Q. What did you say about the draft being enforced?
A. Not a word that I know of.
By Mr. Ewing.—Q. Was the understanding of which you have spoken as to the character of the witness, Thomas, for truth in his neighborhood during the war or before? A. I spoke of him from his reputation for years back; five or six years, probably.
Q. Was what you have heard based on an estimate of his veracity chiefly then or since the war? A. I do not know; he has not borne a very good reputation since he was a boy, I have heard him spoken of as a man who would talk a great deal and tell stories.
By Mr. Stone.—Q. What is your business in Baltimore? A. I am doing a commission business, selling tobacco, &c.

Testimony of Dr. Wm. T. Bowman.

By Mr. Stone.—Q. Where do you reside? A. Bryantown, Charles county.
Q. Did you know J. Wilkes Booth? A. I did; I first saw him, I believe, at church, in Bryantown; I was told that his name was Booth, and a few days afterwards I saw him again at Bryantown.
Q. Do you know what was ostensibly his visit to that part of the country? A. When I saw him again at Bryantown he asked me if I knew any person who had land to sell; I told him I had some; I would dispose of; he asked where it was, and I pointed out the place; he then asked me about the price, and I told him there were two tracts, one of 180 acres, another belonging to the estate, and told him the price; he then asked me if I had any horses to sell; I said I had several horses for sale, he said he would come down and look at them.
Q. Did you know of Dr. Mudd's land being for sale before you came down there? A. I heard him say last summer that he could not get hands to work his farm, and that he believed he would sell and go into the mercantile business at Benedict, a place east of Bryantown, on the Pawtuxent River.
Q. Do you know whether prior to that time Dr. Mudd was in a treaty with any other one about the sale of his land? A. I think he was.
Q. Do you know whether Booth inquired of any one else about land in that neighborhood? A. I do not.
Q. What is the distance from Bryantown to the Pawtuxent River at the nearest point? A. About ten miles.
Q. What is the distance from Bryantown to the nearest point on the Potomac? A. I think Matthias Point is the nearest crossing, about five miles distant.
Q. How far does Dr. Mudd live from the Pawtuxent line? A. About eight or nine miles;

Testimony of George Booles (Colored.)

Q. Where do you live? A. With Dr Samuel Mudd.
Q. At which of his places? A. At the place near Bryantown.
Q. How far is that place from John McPherson's?
A. About half a mile.
Q. State whether you saw the doctor on Easter Saturday evening. A. Yes sir.
Q. Where? A. Just below my house, coming from Bryantown.
Q. Does the main road from Bryantown to the swamp lead by your house? A. Yes sir.
Q. To go to Bryantown from Mudd's you can either go up the swamp or by your place? A. You can go the plantation path or the road, either one.
Q. Did Dr. Mudd, coming from Bryantown, pass through your place? A. Yes sir.
Q. Was there any one with him? A. No sir; no one.
Q. Are there any woods between you and McPherson's? A. Only a few bushes and briars in the swamp.
Q. Where had you been that evening? A. On the swamp, with my hogs; as I came, I met Dr. Mudd coming from Bryantown; he kept on with his business and I kept on with mine; it was between three and four o'clock.
Q. Did you see no one pass up either road? A. No sir.
Q. Is there any road that turns out between your house and McPherson's? A. No, only the path that goes to McPherson's house.
Q. Did you see anybody on horseback or standing there? A. No sir.
Q. Did you go near enough to see them if there had been any one? A. Yes, I should have seen them as I passed across the main road.
Q. Did you pass quite near the little swamp? A. Yes sir.
Q. How was the Doctor riding? A. At his usual gait.

Q. Was that Dr. Mudd's usual route when he went to Bryantown? A. Yes; he always passed through that way.
Q. You are attending to that place for old Dr. Mudd, are you not? A. Yes sir.
Q. Did Dr. Mudd stop? A. Yes sir; and he spoke to me; he asked me w..ere I had been, and I told him.
Cross-examination.—Q. You told him you had been in the swamp? A. Yes sir.
Q. Did he ask you if you had seen anybody there? A. No sir.
Q. How far was he from Bryantown? A. About one mile.
Q. What sort of a horse was he riding? A. The bay filley.
Q. Is it his horse? A. Yes sir.
Q. Had you seen it before? A. Yes sir; I knew it well.
Q. 'Th.s was on the by road? A. Yes sir.
Q. Did he say anything about Bryantown at all? A. Not one word sir.
Q. Yo.i could not see all over the swamp? A. No sir.
Q. A man might have been there off his horse and you not see him at all. A. Yes sir.

Testimony of Mary Jane Semmes.

Q. Where did you reside last year? A. With Dr. Samuel Mudd.
Q. Did you reside there the whole year? A. Yes, except when I went visiting at my sister's; I never stayed over two or three weeks at a time.
Q. Do you know Captain B. Gwynn? A. I have a slight acquaintance with him.
Q. Do you know him when you see him? A. Yes sir.
Q. Do you know Andrew Gwynn and Geo. Gywan? A. Yes sir.
Q. Do you know John Surratt? A. Yes sir; I have seen him once.
Q. Were any of the parties whom I have mentioned at Dr. Mudd's last year? A. I never saw them.
Q. None of th m? A. Not one.
Q. Do you know of anyone staying in the woods and being fed from the house? A. There never was any one there that I ever heard of.
Q. What time of year was it that you paid these visits to your sister? A. In March last; March twelve months I staid three or four weeks.
Q. You were at Dr. Mudd's during the spring season and fall? A. Yes sir.

Testimony of A. S. Howell.

Q. Of what State are you a resident? A. Of Virginia; I was formerly of Maryland.
Q. Are you acquainted with Mrs. Surratt? A. Yes sir.
Q. When did you first make her acquaintance? A. About a year and a half ago sir.
Q. State to the Court if you were present with Mrs. Surratt and her father at Surrattsville? A. No sir.
Q. Did she, at any time that evening, hand you a newspaper to read for her? A. Yes sir, I think she did.
Q. Did you learn the fact at that time that she could not read by candle light? A. No s r, I think not.
Q. But she did hand you the paper to read for her? A. Yes sir.
Q. Have you been to her house in this city? A. Yes sir.
Q. At what date? A. On the 20th of February.
Q. What time did you go there; was it in the day or evening? A. After dark; possibly about eight o'clock.
Q. Was the gas lit in the hall? A. Yes sir.
Q. Was Mrs. Surratt able to recognize you then? A. Not till I made myself known to her.
Q. How many times did you speak to her before she recognized you? A. I don't remember exactly.
Q. Did you tell her who you were? A. Yes sir.
Q. Are you acquainted with Lewis Weichman? A. Yes sir.
Q. How long did you remain at Mrs. Surratt's? A. I was there two days.
Q. What was your object in going there? A. On a visit as much as anything else, I had no business there in particular.
Q. What was your reason for not going to a hotel? A. I knew them, and thought I would spend the time better there than at a hotel.
Q. Were you short of money at that time? A. Yes sir.
Q. Had you sufficient means to pay your expenses at a hotel? A. I don't think I had, s.r.
Q. After you made the acquaintance of Mr. Welchman did you show him any cipher? A. I showed him how to make one, then he made it himself.
Q. Was it s mple or complicated? A. I could tell the cipher if I saw it.
Assistant Judge Advocate Bingham then said—Show him the cipher on the record. It is number three or four.
Q. Was it like that or similar to it? A. It was like this but this is not the one, I think.
Q. Did Welchman give you any information with regard to the prisoners we at that time had on hand?
Objected to and the question waived.
Q. Did you have any communication with Mr. Welchman with regard to his going South? A. Yes sir, I had.
Q. State what it was and what he said? A. He said he would like to go south.

Q. What reason did he give for wishing to go South? A. He did not give any particular reason.
Q. Did he say anything in connection with his going South about h s symp.thies?
Objected to and the question was withdrawn.
Q. Did you have any conversation wi h Weichman with regard to getting him a place in Richmond? A. He asked if I thought he could get a place there as clerk; I told him it was doubt ul, because the wounded soldiers had the preference there, by order of the War Department.
Q. State whether he stated to you what his sympathies were. (Objected to, but the objection was withdrawn). A. We were talking matters over, and he said that he intended to go South and wanted to go with me, and I said if t at was the case he h i better go then, as I didn't know when I should er ss the river again; he said he was not ready to go just then he to d me he a sympathies were with the South; and that the South, he though t, would ultimately succe d.
Q. Did he say that he had done all he could do for the Southern Government? A. I believe he d d.
Q. Did he say he was always a friend to the South? A. He did.
Assistant Judge Advocate Bingham stated that he objected to all this. He might be overruled, but in th s court or out side of it he would object to any such proceedings, and stated that in his opinion it was a mere burlesque on justice.
The Commission sustained the opinion of the Assistant Judge Advocate.
Q. While at Mrs. Surratt's did you learn of any treasonable plot or enterprise in existence? A. I did not sir.
Q. Did Surratt ever g ve a des.atch, verbal or written, to take to Richm nd? A. No sir.
Q. Did Welchman give you a full return of the number of prisoners? A. Yes sir, he stated to me the number that the United States Government had, and the number they had over what the Confederate Government had; I doubted it, but he said he had the books in his own office to look at.
Cross-examination.—Q. Where do you reside? A. In King George's county, Virginia.
Q. How long have you resided there? A. About two years off and on.
Q. Where d.d you reside in Maryland? A. Before the war in Prince George's county.
Q. Does your family reside here? A. Yes sir.
Q. When did you first make the acquaintance of Mrs. Surratt, and her family? A. A year and a half ago.
Q. Where? A. Down in the country, at their hotel.
Q. Was she living there then? A. Yes sir.
Q. You know John Surratt? A. Yes sir.
Q. Did he accompany you to Richmond? A. Never sir.
Q. What has been your occupation for the last year and a half? (This question was o jected to, and the objection was overruled). A. I have had no particular occupation since I ve been out of the army.
Q. What army? A. The Confederate army.
Q. What portion of the army did you serve in? A. In the First Maryland Artillery till July, 1862; I then left the service.
Q. Were you mustered out? A. I was discharged on account of disability.
Q. What have you been doing since that? A. I have not been employed in any particular business.
Q. What have you been doing? A. No.hing.
Q. Haven't you been making trips to Richmond? A. I've been there sir.
Q. How frequently? A. Some time once in two or three months; I've been there twice since the first of April, twelve mon hs a o.
Q. And those two times were when? A. In December last and in February.
Q. Did you go alone in December? A. There might have been some gentlemen with me.
Q. Where did you cross the line of the blockade? A. In Westmore.and county.
Q. Well, in February, who accompanied you? A. Half a dozen persons.
Q. Who were they? A. Persons from the neighborhood.
Q. Any from Washington? A. No. sir.
Q. What was your business there in December? A. No more than to see my friends, and buy some drafts.
Q. Did you buy any drafts? A. I think I did.
Q. Drafts on whom?
[The witness here objected to answer that question, on the ground that he did not wish to cr.minate others.]
Q. Were they persons in Washington? A. No, sir.
Q. Who were they drawn on? A. On some of my friends in Maryland.
Q. What part of Maryland? A. In Prince George's county.
Q. Were any of those drafts drawn on any of the accused? A. No, sir.
Q. That was in December? A. Yes sir.
Q. What was your business there in February? A. To see my friends.
Q. Did you carry any despatch? A. No; never in my life.
Q. Did you take any notes, or bring any back? A. No sir.
Q. Did you bring back any drafts? A. Yes sir.

TRIAL OF THE ASSASSINS AT WASHINGTON. 103

Q. From whom? A. From friends of mine in the army.
Q. How far did you carry despatches? A. I never carried any.
Q. You are acquainted with the Surratts? A. Yes sir.
Q. How often have you visited them; how often did you go to Richmond after you became acquainted with them? A. About half a dozen times.
Q. You say Weichman asked you to get him a place in Richmond? A. He didn't ask me to get him a place, he asked me if I thought that he could get a place.
Q. How did you come to talk about things in Richmond? A. I suppose he understood I was there from my conversation.
Q. Where was this? A. In his room.
Q. At Mrs. Surratt's? A. Yes sir.
Q. Was there any other pers n present? A. No sir.
Q. Did you ever talk with Surratt about being at Richmond? A. I might.
Q. Did you or did you not? A. I disremember; I can't say positively.
Q. Weichman knew you had been there? A. Yes sir.
Q. I would ask you whether this has not been your business for the last year and a half? A. No sir.
Q. Have you any other occupation; do you do anything else for a support? A. Why, I've been speculating a little in Virginia.
Q. Where? A. In King Georges county.
Q. Were you not known by your friends as a blockade runner? A. I don't know.
Q. What name did you go by besides the name you have given here? A. They sometimes called me Spencer.
Q. Well, is that your name? A. My name is A. S. Howell.
Q. What is the S. for? A. Spencer.
Q. Why did you not give it when asked for it under oath? A. Well, I wasn't particular; I thought A. S. Howell was enough.
Q. Is Spencer your name? A. It is one of my names; some of my friends call me Spencer.
Q. Was it given you in your infancy? A. I don't know.
Q. Give to the Court your full name. A. A. of Howell.
Q. Is that your full name. or only the initials of your name? W at is your name in full? A. I seldom use "S" in my name; my proper name is A. S. Howell.
Q. When running the blockade, what name did you go by? A. By the name of Howell.
Q. When were you arrested? A. In March.
Q. How recently had you then come from Richmond? A. I had not been in Richmond for three weeks.
Q. That was in March? A. Yes sir.
Q. Do you remember the time in March? A. I think it was about the 20th or 21st.
Q. When you went to Richmond, in February, do you remember who accompanied you? A. I remember one man by the name of Surratt.
Q. Did any person from this city accompany you? A. No sir.
Q. Any from Maryland? A. No sir; they were all from Virginia.
Q. This cipher, where did you get it? A. I've been acquainted with it some seven years.
Q. Where did you learn it? A. In a magician's book.
Q. What did you use it for? A. I had no use for it.
Q. What did you carry it for? A. I did not carry it; I could make it in twenty minutes.
Q. Did you ever teach it to John Surratt? A. No sir.
Q. Did you ever meet, at Surratt's house, Mrs. Slader? A. I never met her at Surratt's house; I met her here in Washington.
Q. When? A. In February.
Q. A out what date? A. The 20th or 2d.
Q. Did you have any conversation with her? A. Yes sir.
Q. Did she accompany you to Richmond? A. Partly.
Q. Did she ever come back with you? A. I met her accidentally in Westmoreland county.
Q. Do you know the object of her visit to the Confederacy? A. No sir; I saw her first in Westmoreland county, Va.
Q. When was that? A. In February last.
Q. Did you meet her at Surratt's house? A. Not till after I had met with her on the Potomac.
Q. When did you see her on the Potomac? A. About the first of February.
Q. Did you come here together? A. No sir.
Q. Where did she go to? A. New York city.
Q. Did you accompany her any distance? A. Only across the river.
Q. You met her again at Mrs. Surratt's house? A. Yes sir.
Q. Did she go in? A. No sir; she stayed in the buggy.
Q. Who was with her? A. A young man.
Q. Who was he? A. John Surratt.
Q. Did she afterwards come to the house? A. No sir.
Q. How long did you stay at Surratt's? A. Two days or two days and a half.
Q. Did you have any conversation about your Richmond trip? A. Not particularly as I know of; I had a talk with Weichman, and told them I had been to Richmond, but they already had heard it.
Q. They knew you had been in Richmond? A. They knew I was from Richmond sometime previous.
Q. Did you have any conversation with Mrs. Surratt about the matter? A. I don't know sir.
Q. Did you meet Mrs. Slader in Richmond? A. Yes sir.
Q. When? A. Last February.
Q. After which she was with John H. Surratt? A. Yes sir.
Q. She went directly with Surratt? A. I don't know sir.
Q. You don't know whether she was with him on the 2d of March? A. No sir.
Q. Do you know what her business was in Richmond? A. No sir; I didn't inquire.
Q. You only know that soon after you saw her at Mrs. Surratt's, you saw her at Richmond? A. ——.
Q. What other of your friends d d you meet at Mrs. Surratt's? A. I don't know that I met any.
Q. Did you meet Atzeroth there? A. I think Atzeroth was there.
Q. Do you know whom he came to see? A. I do not sir.
Q. Did you see this man Wood or Payne there? A. No sir.
Q. How many of the prisoners have you seen there? A. I think I have seen two.
Q. What two? A. Atzeroth and Dr. Mudd.
Q. Where did you see Dr. Mudd? A. At Bryantown.
Q. Tell us where your acquaintance first commenced with Dr. Mudd? A. I have known him a long while, but I have not lately seen him.
Q. Did you bring any drafts on him? A. No sir.
Q. Or messages to him? A. No sir.
Q. Were you ever at his house? A. Yes sir.
Q. When? A. Over a year ago.
Q. When coming from or going to Richmond? A. I was not coming from Richmond, and had not been there.
Q. How soon after did you go? I don't know.
Q. How long did you stay with Dr. Mudd? A. Only an hour or two.
Q. Did you take dinner with him? A. No sir.
Q. Now who was it that drew these drafts, and upon whom were they drawn, and what was their amount? A. I bought one from Mrs. Mary Surratt on her brother.
Q. To what amount? A. Two hundred dollars.
Q. Who else? A. I bought one from a young man.
Q. On whom? A. On his mother.
Q. For how much? A. Twenty-five dollars.
Q. State what drafts you received that you collected? A. None of any amount, except one on a man named Janner, which I got money on to pay those parties for the drafts.
Q. Do you recollect what you paid for the two hundred dollar drafts? A. I think I paid eight hundred dollars in Confederate money for one hundred.
Q. What drafts did you bring to this city? A. I never brought any.
Q. What drafts did you bring to Baltimore? A. None sir.
Q. What drafts to St. Charles county? A. I never brought any.
Q. Have you any of those drafts here? A. I have none with me.
Q. What did you do with them? A. I left them down in the country.
Q. Where? A. At my sister's.
Q. What is her name? A. Mrs. Langley.
Q. And she has all with her that are uncollected? A. I think so.
Q. Have you ever taken the oath of allegiance to the United States Government? A. No sir, I never have. By Mr. Ewing.—Q. I wish to ask you whether you ever s w Dr. Mudd about Bryantown? A. Yes sir, I have been about Bryantown a good deal before the war; was raised in the county.
Q. You have seen Mudd there before the war? A. Oh, yes sir.
Q. Were you ever at Mudd's house at any other time since the war? A. I don't think I have been sir.
By Colonel Burnett.—Q. You say this conversation took place up stairs, between you and Weichman, and in his room? A. Yes sir, a portion of it.
Q. Was any other person present? A. I don't think there was.
Q. How come you to remember that conversation and not be able to remember the conversation with Mrs. Surratt, or anybody else in the house? A. Well sir, it just came to my mind by the question being so pointed.
Q. Did you know that he belonged to any company for the defense of Washington, and that he had a quarrel with one of the family on account of his Union sentiments? A. I never heard a word about it, sir.
Q. You didn't know that one of the lad es struck him in the quarrel, because he wore blue so diers' pants? A. No sir, I never saw him wear blue soldiers' pants.
Q. Don't you know that he was turning you over to pick out of you about your visits to Richmond? Don't you know he tried to find out what your objects were? A. If he did he didn't succeed (Laughter).

Q. I rather think he did; didn't you know he belonged to a military company here for the defense of Washington? A. No sir.
By Mr. Aiken.—Q. Did Weichman, in that conversation, or not, state that he had done all he could for the South? A. Yes sir; but I can't recollect the exact words.
The Court here adjourned to ten o'clock on Monday morning.

WASHINGTON, May 29.—After the reading of the previous day's record Mr. Clampitt, on behalf of the counsel for Mrs. Surratt, read a paper as follows:—

Mary E. Surratt, one of the accused, in asking for the recall of Henry Von Steinaker, a witness for the prosecution, through her counsel, that in regard to the said Steinaker she proposes to prove that, shortly after the breaking out of the war, he was a member of General Blenker's Staff, serving in the capacity of a topographical engineer officer; that while under sentence of death at or near Cumberland, for attempting to desert to the enemy, that on or about the month of May, 1862, he made a second attempt to desert, with better success, and entered the lines of General Imboden's command, of the so-called Confederate States, in or about the month of May, 1862, scattered between Winchester and Romney, Va., and that most of the time from that date till May, 1863, he was employed as a draughtsman by Major-General J. E. B. Stuart, of the so-called Confederate army, that in May, 1863 the said Steinaker voluntarily joined Company K. of the Second Virginia Infantry, as a private, and drew pay, bounty, clothing and the usual allowances of a private soldier, and that he was detailed as an assistant to Captain Oscar Hericks, an engineer officer of the staff of Major-General Edward Johnson, of the so-called Confederate States Army, and remained with him during the Pennsylvania campaign of 1863, he took no company until he arrived near Chancellorsville, where he fell in with Assistant Surgeon McQueen, of the so-called Confederate States Army, and two other gentlemen in said service; that he never ranked in said service as an engineer officer, or received the pay of one; that he was frequently in the guard-house for shooting or threatening to shoot negro-fatigued with piloting United States troops near Mine Run, Va., and other serious charges; that he stole moneys which were placed in his charge; that he stole a horse from Lieutenant David M. Cockerill, of the Second Virginia Infantry, and was tried by court martial for the same and found guilty, and that soon after the spring campaign of 1863, he stole some clothing near the north of Richmond, and escaped to Winchester, Virginia, representing himself as being in charge of the dead body of Major Henry K. Douglas, Assistant Adjutant-General on General Johnson's staff, who is now present before this Court, alive and well; that he never saw J. Wilkes Booth, the actor, in Virginia, or at the camp at any time of the Second Virginia Regiment of Infantry, and that no such meeting of Confederate officers as he speaks of in his testimony ever took place, where the plans for the assassination of President Lincoln were discussed.

By her counsel, (Signed)
REVERDY JOHNSON,
FRED. A. AIKEN,
J. W. CLAMPITT.

Judge Advocate Holt said that he was not informed where the witness was, but he was perfectly willing that he should be recalled if found.

General Wallace inquired whether the Judge Advocate had ever declined or refused to issue the proper summons for the reappearance of the witness?

Judge Advocate Holt said that he had not, but on the contrary, had signified his desire to secure his attendance.

General Wallace said that he made the inquiry for the purpose, if the Judge Advocate had never refused to summon the witness, of objecting to putting such a paper as that upon the record.

Mr. Clampitt called attention to the fact that no allegation had been made that the prosecution had refused to call the witness.

General Hunter said that the decision of the Court last week was that if the defense desired Von Steinaker recalled every effort should be made to recall him.

Mr. Aiken replied that the defense then stated that they did not wish him called as a witness for the defense. When upon the stand he was not cross-examined, for the reason that the defense knew nothing about him.

General Hunter inquired if anything was known of Von Steinaker's whereabouts.

Mr. Aiken said that all that was known of him was, he was brought here after his having been released from Fort Delaware, and he had now gone, no one knew where.

Judge Advocate Holt asked by whom the paper just presented had been signed.

Mr. Aiken said it had been signed by the counsel for Mrs. Surratt and would have been carried by Major-General Edward Johnson, formerly of the Confederate army, who was present as a witness, and by members of his staff.

General Wallace.—I would like to know for which one of the prisoners that paper is considered necessary.

Mr. Aiken.—For Mrs. Surratt; and it has a bearing in a degree upon all of them.

General Wallace.—Will the gentleman please state the connection of that paper with Mrs. Surratt's case?

Mr. Aiken.—The connection, as we understand it, is simply this:—We wish to prove that Mr. Booth was not in Virginia at the time stated by Von Steinaker; that no such meeting of Confederate officers, as he alleges, took place; that no plans for the assassination of President Lincoln were discussed. I think the language used by the witness was that one of the officers told him Lincoln must "go up the spout;" that so far as they were concerned, the officers in the camp of the Second Virginia Regiment were not aware of any such plan; that they did not see Mr. Booth in that camp, and that if any such plan to assassinate the President did exist, Mrs. Surratt had no connection with it, and knew nothing about it.

Judge Advocate Holt said, it is not necessary to recall the witness to prove that.

Mr. Aiken.—We propose to call the witnesses here as to whether they would believe Von Steinaker on his oath.

Judge Advocate Holt said that he was willing to acquiesce in the application, but he wished the Court to consider whether a paper such as the one which had been read, so stringently damatory in its character, should be allowed to go upon the records, when really it was the basis of no application which has not been considered and granted.

General Wallace.—I for my part wish to say now that I understand, distinctly, and hold in very supreme contempt, such practices as that. It is very discreditable to the parties concerned, to the attorney, and if permitted, in my judgment, will be discreditable to the Court.

Mr. Clampitt.—May it please the Court, I do not desire standing in a position that would be doing anything that would redect upon the counsel in the degree that a member of the Court has spoken, but I understand my position. May it please the Court, as one of the counsel for Mrs. Surratt, we are here standing within the portals of this constituted temple of justice, and here for the purpose of defending the very citadel of life, and we feel it to be our duty to use every exertion in our power, consistent with forms that obtain before a court, to impeach and destroy the testimony of any witness whose testimony can properly be impeached, and we do it for the purpose, if possible, of shielding the accused. It is, at the same time our bounden duty, under obligation that we owe to our client, that we should spread before the Court the character of the witnesses on the part of the prosecution who has made this explanation. I hope it will be satisfactory to the Court.

General Wallace.—It is not satisfactory to me for the reason that he has in no instance been denied the privilege which he has sought by that paper.

General Howe.—Neither has he shown any connection of the paper with the case of his client.

Mr. Aiken.—The Judge Advocate has stated that if Von Steinaker could be readily found he had no objection to his recall. There seems to be a misunderstanding, however, in regard to our asking for that. We did not propose to summon him as our own witness, but we have presented this paper in accordance with a strictly legal form.

General Wallace.—Yes, we understand that.

A vote was then taken by the Commission upon the question of allowing the paper to be entered upon its records, and the result of the vote was announced to be that the paper should not be entered.

The witness above referred to by the defense not being present the Commission proceeded as follows:—

Testimony of Mr. Davis.

Q. Where do you reside? A. At Dr. Samuel Mudd's.
Q. How long have you resided there? A. Since the 9th of January last.
Q. What has been your employment there? A. Working on the farm.
Q. Have you been there constantly since you first went there on the 9th of January? A. I have; I was absent from the plantation only one night.
Q. Do you remember what night that was? A. No sir, I don't really know; it was in the month of January.
Q. State how often Dr. Mudd has been absent from home from the time you went there up to his arrest, and the circumstances attending his absence? A. He has been away from home only three nights; the first time he went to Mr. George Henry Gardner's party, taking his family with him, and returning the next morning; that was in January, on the 26th; the second time he came to Washington with Mr. Lowellyn Gardner, with whom he also returned; that was on the 23d of March; I am enabled to recollect the day by the fact that while he was away the barn blew down; the third time he came to Washington.

Q. Do you know John H. Surratt or John Wilkes Booth? A. I do not.
Q. State whether you were or were not ill while at Dr. Mudd's, and for how long? A. I was very ill for better than three weeks. I was taken ill in February, and my sickness lasted until March.
Q. State whether Dr. Mudd attended you during your sickness? A. He did.
Q. State whether you did or did not see Dr. Mudd every day during all the time you were at his house? A. I saw him every day during the time I was there, except on the three occasions that he was away.
Q. State whether during the time you were there, you ever heard the names of John H. Surratt, John Wilkes Booth, or David E. Harold mentioned in the family? A. I did not.
Q. Were you at home on the Saturday before Easter, the 15th of April? A. I was.
Q. Do you know anything of two men being there that day? A. I saw two horses there; I heard that two men were there.
Q. Do you know at what time that evening they left? A. B'tween three and four o'clock.
Q. Were you out as usual working that day? A. I was.
Q. Did you see either of the men? A. I did not.
Q. Where were you on the Friday after the assassination of the President? A. I was on the farm, at work.
Q. State whether you went for Dr. Mudd? A. I did.
Q. Where was he? A. He was at his father's.
Q. What did you tell Dr Mudd?
Assistant Judge Advocate Bingham.—You need not state what you told him.
The question was waived.
Q. Some soldiers were at the house and you went for him? A. Yes sir.
Q. He came home with you? A. Yes sir; he came as far as the barn, and then went on ahead of me, and I went to work.
Q. When you went after Dr. Mudd what did you tell him? A. I told him there were some soldiers at the house who wanted to see him.
Q. Was there anything said between you about a cart? A. No sir.
Q. Did you ever hear Dr. Mudd, dur'ng the time you were with him, express any disloyal sentiment? A. I did not.
By Mr. Ewing.— On the day after the President's assassination did you take breakfast with the family? A. No sir, I did not take either breakfast or dinner with the family that day; I was out attending the horses.
Q. What did you understand about certain parties having been in the house? A. Nothing more than that two men were there; one with a broken leg.
Cross-examined by Judge Bingham.— Q. How do you know that Dr. Mudd went to George Henry Gardner's? A. I saw him going there.
Q. How far was it? A. Not over a quarter of a mile.
Q. Where were you? A. I was home at the time.
Q. His horse's head was that way? A. No sir; he walked.
Q. That is all you know about that? A. Yes sir.
Q. You say you did not see two men there on Saturday? A. No sir, I did not.
Q. How do you know that they had left the house on Saturday? A. Because their horses were gone when I returned to the house at four o'clock in the afternoon.
Q. How did you know that the men were gone? A. I thought so.
Q. You did not know it? A. No sir.

Testimony of Juliann Bloís (Colored).

By Mr. Ewing—Q. State whether you formerly lived at the house of Dr. Samuel A. Mudd. A. I did.
Q. When did you go there to live and how long did you stay? A. I went there on Christmas before last Christmas.
Q. Did you ever know of any Confederate officers or soldiers being about Dr. Mudd's house? A. No sir.
Q. Did you ever see Andrew Gwynn, Ben Gwynn or this man—exhibiting to witness a portrait of Surratt—at that house? A. I did not.
Q. Did you ever hear the names of Ben Gwynn, Andrew Gwynn or Surratt mentioned in the house while you were there? A. No sir.
Q. State what sort of a master Dr. Samuel A. Mudd was. A. He treated me very well, as also all that were around him; he was very kind to us all; I lived with him a year, and he never spoke a cross word to me that I know of.
Q. Did you ever know of his whipping Mary Simms? A. No sir, he never struck her that I knew of.
Q. Do you know w'.at Mary Simms left the house for? A. On one Sunday evening Mrs. Mudd told her not to go away, but she would go; the next morning she (Mrs. Mudd) struck her with a little switch; I do not think she hurt her, as the switch was a small one.
Q. Did Dr. Samuel Mudd never whipped her at all? A. No sir; I never heard of him striking her.
Q. What is the general reputation of Mary Simms among the colored people around there? A. She is not a great truth-teller sir, because she has told lies on me.
Q. Do you know what the colored folks around there generally think of her? A. Well, they generally think she is a liar.
Q. Do you know what the colored folks there think of Mylov Simms as a truth-teller? A. They thought the same of him as of Mary; if he got angry with you he would tell a lie on you for the sake of satisfaction.
Q. That was the general opinion about him? A. Yes sir.
Q. Did you ever hear Dr Samuel Mudd talk about the government of Mr. Lincoln? A. I never did.
Q. You left there two days before last Christmas; do you know anything about Dr. Samuel Mudd going away on that day? A. Dr. Samuel Mudd said he told me he was going to Washington to buy a cooking stove.
Q. Where have you lived since you left Dr. Samuel Mudd's? A. With Mr. Wall, in Bryantown.
The Commission then took a recess until two o'clock at which time the body reassembled.

Testimony of Dr. George D. Mudd.

By Mr. Ewing.—Q. State your residence and business. A. I am a practitioner of medicine in the village of Bryantown, Charles county, Md.
Q. State whether you know the prisoner, Samuel A. Mudd, and what relation, if any, exists between you. A. I know him; his father and my father were first cousins; he was a student under me some years ago in the study of medicine.
Q. State whether you know his reputation in the neighborhood in which he lives—for peace, order and good citizenship. A. I know of no one whose reputation is better in that regard; it is very good.
Q. State what is his reputation as a master. A. I have always considered him a humane man towards his fellow man, whether servant or otherwise; he always clothed and fed his servants well, and treated them kindly, so far as I knew.
Q. State whether or not you saw Dr. Mudd on the Sunday a'ter the assassination of the President. A. Yes sir; I saw him at church; he overtook me after that on my way home to Bryantown, and I rode with him as far as his house.
Q. State whether he said anything to you about any persons having been at his house.
Judge Advocate Holt objected to the question on the ground that the Government had not offered the declarations of the prisoners in evidence.
Mr. Ewing said that he proposed to show by the witness, who was a man of unique standing and active loyalty, that the prisoner had informed him that on Saturday morning there were two suspicious persons at his house and had desired the witness, if he thought it advisable, to notify the military authorities of the fact of their being at his house, but not to tell it at large about them lest the parties and their friends might assassinate him (the prisoner) for the disclosure. This was a part of the very substance of those actions of the prisoner by which it was sought to implicate him, and was connected with acts of the preceding and subsequent days which the prosecution had shown. This statement was virtually an act, and was done during the time of that alleged silence on his part, which had been urged as a means of implicating him as an accessory before and after the fact in this murder. If the fact that he had been silent was to be urged against him, was not the fact of his breaking that silence to be introduced in his behalf? Moreover, the statement was made at a time when the prisoner could not have known that any suspicions were directed against him. In support of his position Mr. Ewing read from "Russell on Crimes," vol. ii, p.758, and other authorities.
Judge Advocate Holt remarked that when partial declarations were given in evidence the accused had a right to insist that the whole should be given. In the present instance the prosecution had not offered declarations of the prisoner. The ground upon which it was sought to introduce them, was that they were part of the transaction itself. But the transaction at the time these declarations were made had been completed; it had closed the day before it consisted of the fact of the prisoner having concealed and entertained these men and sent them on their way rejoicing, and that transaction on which the prisoner was now arraigned by the Government was complete at 4 o'clock on Saturday afternoon. It was now proposed to introduce a declaration on the part of the prisoner made twenty-four hours afterwards—after he had had time to review his conduct. It was not competent to declare the motives by which his previous acts were governed, because there was no means of reaching these motives, or of introducing any testimony in regard to them.
Mr. Ewing replied the transaction was not wholly closed. The charge here was one of concealment, not only of the persons of those men while they were in the house, but a concealment of the fact that they had been in the house. Of our witnesses who testified that they went to Dr. Mudd's house on Saturday, two stated that Dr. Mudd denied that the men had been at his house, and the accused now desired to show that he did give information to the Government on Sunday, through the witness on this stand, that the men were at his house. The objection of the Judge Advocate was sustained, and the question was not put.

TRIAL OF THE ASSASSINS AT WASHINGTON.

Q. State whether you communicated to the military authorities, in Bryantown, the fact of any suspicious persons having been at the house of Dr. Samuel A. Mudd on Saturday? A. I did.

Q. State to whom you communicated? A. I communicated, I think, to Lieutenant Dana, who was the principal in command of the military there at that time.

Q. When did you communicate it to him? A. I think it was on Monday morning.

Q. What statement d d you make to him? A. I stated to him that Dr. Mudd had informed me that two suspicious persons were a his house ; that they came there a little before day-break on Saturday morning, and that one o. them had a broken leg which he bandaged; that they were laboring under some degree of excitement; more so he thought than should have been caused by a broken leg; that these parties had said they came from Bryantown, and were inquiring the way to Parson Wilmer's; that whilst there one of them called for a razor and shaved himself, thereby altering his appearance; that he (Dr. Mudd) improvised a crutch or crutches for the man with the broken leg, and that they went the direction of Parson Wilmer's, I think; that is about the whole of what I told the Lieutenant.

Q. Of whom did you get t is information? A. Of the prisoner, Dr. Samuel A. Mudd.

Q. What time on Monday did you make the communication? A. I think Monday morning.

Q. By whose authority did you make the communication? A. The mentioning of that matter to me, or any other matter bearing on the assassination, particularly such an assassination as the country and the world now mourn, was my warrant and authority from him and everybody else who knew me.

Q. At the time he imparted this information to you, was anything said about communicating to the military authorities? A. When I left him I told him I would mention the matter to the authorities and see what could be made of it; he told me he would be glad if I would, but he could make such an arrangement he would much prefer that he should be sent for, and that he would give every information in his power relative; that it became a matter of publicity he feared for his life, on account of guerrillas that might be infesting the neighborhood.

Q. Did you say to what authorities you would mention it? A. To the military authorities at Bryantown.

Q. Did you make any other communication to any other military authorities of the fact stated by Dr. Mudd? A. Yes sir; I was sent for, I think, on Tuesday afternoon, by your detectives, who asked me to go up into a room with them, where they questioned me very particularly relative to t is affair; I stated to them what I have already stated here, and upon my inability to answer such questions as they propounded, they ordered a carriage and asked me to direct wm to Dr. Samuel Mudd's house; I told them I would do it, and that I would go with them; they seemed to prefer that, and I did go with them.

Q. State what happened when you went there. A. Dr. Mudd was not at the house; the detective went in-side while I remained at the door; I saw him coming and told him as he entered the house that the detectives had come there to ascertain the particulars relative to that matter about which he had spoken to me; that I had made the statement to the military author-ties which he had made to me on Sunday, and that they were making special inquiry in reference to it; I had already said to these gentlemen (the detectives) th t I was confident that the Doctor would state to matter just as I stated to them, and left the room and did not re-enter it during their examination of him.

Q. Name the officers that went with you. A. One was named Lloyd, another Gallaghan, and the others were Lieutenant Lovett and a Mr. Williams.

Q. State whether any inquiry was made by any of them, a ter the conference with Dr. Mudd, with re. erence to the route. A. When we got in the wagon, or, I think, just before getting in, they asked me if I would show them the way to Parson Wilmer's; it was then near nightfall, and I told them I would certainly do so if necessary; I then turned and asked Dr. Mudd, who was standing outside the door, what was the best route to take to Parson Wilmer's, and he gave me the information; before we got to the main road to Bryantown these gentlemen conclud d, in consequence of my stating to them that another road was preferable, to take that other road.

Q. State whether or not anything was said by either of those gentlemen about Dr. Mudd having denied that the two men were at his house.

Assistant Judge Advocate Bingham objected to the question, when it was withdrawn.

Q. State whether you were in Bryantown on Saturday at the time of the reception of the news of the President's assassination. A. I was there when the news came, and remained all evening; I did not leave the village.

Q. What did you hear as to the person or persons implicated in the assassination? A. Lieutenant Dana on whom I called for information, told me that the party who attempted the assassination of Secretary Seward was named Boyle, and claimed him to be the same who had previously assassinated Captain Wat kins, of Anne Arundel county, Maryland, and that the party who assassinated the President was supposed to be a man by the name of Booth, and that he thought the assassins had not yet got out of Washington.

Q. Was Boyle known in that region of country? A. Yes sir; he had been about there, but not for three or four weeks, or later than two or three days after the assassination of Captain Watkins.

Q. What was his character as known there; was he known as a desperado and guerrilla? A. He was; his character was very bad.

Q. State whether you were at church on Sunday, and what was known there about the assassination of the President. A. I was at church on Sunday; it was known that the President of the United States was assassinated, and the matter was talked of.

Q. Was it, or was it not known that Booth had not crossed the river? A. No one to my knowledge, supposed that he had crossed the river at that time.

Q. Did you have any conversation with Dr. Samuel A. Mudd at the church, or hear his conversation as to what he knew of the assassination? A. No sir; I heard him—

Judge Bingham objected to allowing the witness to state what he had heard the prisoner say.

The objection was sustained and the question was not put.

Q. At the time you speak of having made a communication to the officers was anything said to them by you about Dr. Mudd having gone with one of the parties to a marriage, and it so state what? A. I told them so and that is a part I forgot to mention, that Dr. Samuel Mudd did go to ascertain to see if he could get a carriage to take them away from the house; that he went to his father's and down below there; that he went with the younger of the two men but failed to get a carriage and they le t his house on horseback.

Q. Did you tell them anything as to how the man's leg was broken? A. Yes, I think I told them that one bone of his leg was broken.

Q. Did you tell them anything as to how it was said to have occurred? A. Yes, from the fall of a horse.

Q. State the distance of the church at which you saw Dr. Sam. Mudd, the Sunday after the assassination, at Bryantown. A. I would suppose it to be about six and a half miles from Dr. Sam. Mudd's house.

Q. Did you give them any description of the persons of these two men, and if so, what? A. I do not think I gave them any.

Q. State whether you are acquainted with D. J. Thomas, one of the witnesses for the prosecution. A. I know him.

Q. Are you acquainted with the reputation in which he is held, where he is known, for veracity? A. His reputation for veracity has always been very bad since I have known him.

Q. How long has that been ? A. Since he was a boy.

Q. Could you state what his reputation for veracity was he ore the war? A. I do not think it was any better than since the war.

Q. From your knowledge of his character tor veracity, would you believe him under oath? A. If there were a motive to misstate facts, I would not.

Q. Do you know anything pro essionally of his mental c. ndition? A. I have considered him an insane man.

Q. State how and from what cause. A. I have seen him manifest such an abnormal condition of mind as to relieve him from re ponsibility for a crime in a Criminal Court; he is not always as insane; there seemed to have been a regularness in his mani estations of Insanity sometimes; I have met him when there was not much more disordered condition of mind than eccentricity would imply; I would state that in approaching the question of insanity I feel a great d.fidence and distrust, although it belongs to no pro ession more than in me; I feel as if I should be perplexed when the great master minds of the country, who have studied and understand thoroughly all forms of medical and legal jurisprudence as I apprehend gentlemen of the Court to be, and particularly the Judge Advocate, are to be my interrogators on the subject of insanity.

Q. Is his reputation for veracity based upon the fact of his insanity alone? A. I cann t say that it is; I think it probable that his veracity is worse when insane manifestations are prominent.

Q. Is his reputation for veracity good during times when his mental condition appears to be best? A. I never so estimated it.

Cross-examined by Judge Bingham.—Q. Be good enough to te.l the Court what works you have read on insanity. A. I have read a great many works upon insanity and medical jurisprudence.

Q. What work on medical jurisprudence have you read? A. Taylor's, and others on physiology and insanity.

Q. Do any of these works tell how crazy a man has to be to make him unable to tell the truth. A. I do not know as they do especially.

Q. Do you wish to state here to-day that Daniel Thomas is so crazy that he does not know how to tell the truth? A. No sir; I mean to say there seems to be a mental and moral insanity.

Q. You say that at times he is more insane, mentally and morally, than he is at other times; now, when he is less crazy is he more likely to tell the truth? A. I

OF THE ASSASSINS AT WASHINGTON. 107

d to tell extravagant stories
ly.
wear that he is so crazy that
to tell the truth when he is
A. I am not.
was his condition of mind
ny before this Court? A. I
h of him of late.
ty? A. I look upon moral
which persons are particu-
te in vario s ways.
ental insanity? A. When a
iminating and appreciating

)aniel Thomas that he was
plain matters when he was
I do not know that I did; I
why I considered him in-

is the form of insanity under
rs? A. There is no specific
pt at times a peculiar excite-
cciute matters and things as
t dementia; it is not mono-
aberration of mind; there is
which exacerbates and re-
r that it has any particular
rticular form of insanity.
i of insanity would lead him
he never had? A. I have
'mind when I do not doubt
him to labor under most de-
lucinations. Q. You have
ngs he never heard? A. Yes,

ntertained the opinion that
d mind? A. I went to a pri-
orhood w1.en Thomas was a
nothing very eccentric and
he was different from other
musement, in the way of re-
ates seven or eight years ago,
nat; an insane condition of
itself in him; so that the
of every one in the neighbor-
was crazy.
an opinion to any one that
I mind previous to this? A.
; before the war.
he has ever been objected
urt of justice? A. I do not,
n him to be a witness before
one occasion I did.
bjected to on a ground of in-

tion of Dr. Sam Mudd for
From my association with
r him as sympathizing with

him harbor Rebels or dis-
; I have never known him
o act; I have generally con-
d as very temperate in his
ous relative to the war; his
tter of discussion was the
lon, which he maintained; he
poken very temperately, and
is epithets against the heads
as much more temperate on
than many other citizens of
and Southern Maryland.
local organizations in the
our neighborhood. Will you
ject and how they were re-
organization at Port Tobacco
w.ich, I think, was treason-
vas for the purpose of quelling
ghborhood, and it may have
Dr. Samuel Mudd for some
' Richmond and surrender
as taking a very handsome
downfall of the Rebellion; I
an oath to him last year, and
d with the respect and reve-
the oath, making a decided
to whom I administered the
far as I know he has obeyed
h.
hen did you administer the
f I remember rightly, it was
eople was taken relative to
mend the constitution of the
e or July of last year.
n official capacity? A. I was
o Judges as Chief Judge of
f the regular Judge. I think
to some two hundred that

has he spoken of the down-
sure? A. I think from and
oath, if not before.

onel Martin Burke.

le whether or not you knew
I had charge of him.

Q. Look at that paper and see if it is a confession
made by him, A. It is,
Q. State whether it is the confession of Kennedy,
made in your presence, and if so, how long before his
execution. A. It was made in my presence; I do not
know how long before his execution; I think a day or
two.
The confession referred to was read to the Court by
Col. Burnett stating that this Kennedy's object in pour-
ing phosphorus on the floor at Barnum's Museum was
not to burn it, knowing from experiment that it would
not set the boards on fire, but to perpetrate a huge
joke; and that the object in attempting to burn the
hotels was to retaliate for the devastation perpetrated
by Sheridan in the valley; not to turn women and
children, but to show the people of the North that the
desolations of war were not to be confined to the South
alone.

Testimony of H. B. Carter.

By Judge Holt.—Q. Where do you reside? A. In
New Hampshire.
Q. State whether or not you were in Montreal last
fall. A. Yes sir,
Q. At what hotel? A. St Lawrence Hotel.
Q. State whether or not you met George N. Sanders
and Jacob Thompson, Dr. Blackburn, J. Wilkes
Booth, or any of them. A. I saw George N. Sanders,
J. Wilkes Booth, Beverly Tucker, Dr. Blackburn and
others whose names I do not now recollect; I saw
Thompson at Niagara Falls on the 17th of June.
Q. How long were you at this hotel? A. From the
9th or 10th of September until about the 1st of February.
Q. State whether you observed the persons you have
named in intimate association during that time. A.
They were; all the Southerners who boarded there
were intimate with each other, and had little to do
with any one not sympathizing with them.
Q. Did you know J. W. Booth before you went there?
A. I did.
Q. Did you observe him in intimate association with
George N. Sanders and others? A. I did.
Q. Look at the prisoners at the bar, and see whether
you recognize any of them as persons you met in Canada. A. I could not swear that I ever met any of
them there.
Do you remember to have heard the name of John
Surratt spoken of in this circle of men? A. I do not
know that I do.
Q. Do you remember having heard the name of
Payne? A. I saw a man by the name of Payne every
morning, but there is no man I see here I would call
by that name; I think the man I saw was of the name
of John; he was one of Payne's brothers; there were
two of them who were arrested in connection with
the St. Albans' raiders, but they were discharged; I do
not think I have ever seen this man.
Q. Was Dr. Blackburn there the greatest part of the
time? A. I think he was there when the Donegal
Hotel closed, about the 20th of October.
Q. State whether he seemed to be associated with J.
W. Booth and the others you have mentioned. A. He
was; but whether he came there before Booth or not I
could not say. He was one of that clique of men who
con'cderated together.
Cross-examination by Samuel Foster—Q. You say
you were acquainted with persons by the name of
Payne, neither of which is the prisoner at the bar. I
ask you whether you knew where they came from, or
anything about them? A. Only from what I heard
from general reputation; I heard these were a party
who originally came from Kentucky; that they had
been in the counterfeiting business.
Q. What time was it that you saw these men? A.
John Payne, who boards there, came to the house
every day, and was still there when I came away.
Q. Did you see, about the time that you saw these
Paynes, a man by the name of Montgomery? A. I
saw no man by that name that I know of,
Q. Did you ever see the Paynes there in company
with a man named Cleary? A. I have John Payne; I
could not say I have the other.
Q. Did you ever see either of them in company with
C. C. Clay? A. I never saw Clay but very little; I have
seen them in company with Sanders, Tucker and
Blackburn every day.
By Judge Holt.—Q. Could you name any other Rebels
in Montreal who constituted a part of this c.rcle you
have named? A. I could mention General Carroll, of
Memphis, B. Wood, a man about thirty-five years
old, a gentleman by the name of Clark, and an old
gentleman from Florida who wore a queue; I think his
name was Westcott.
Q. Do you remember a man from Indiana by name
of Dodge? A. I do not recollect him now.
Q. Or a man by the name of Walker? A. No sir; I
know many men I met every day but I do not know
their names. They rather gave me the cold shoulder
after they found my sympathies were with the North,
and had very little to say to me.
By Mr. Aiken.—Q. Do you recollect Dr. Morrill
there? A. No, not by that name; I might remember
him were I to see his photograph.
Q. Did C. C. Clay have a room at the St. Lawrence
Hotel? A. I could not say.
Q. Did you see Payne go to the rooms of any of
these persons? A. I once saw him coming out of

TRIAL OF THE ASSASSINS AT WASHINGTON.

Sanders' room: I never saw him going in or coming out of any of the others.

Q. And you are sure he hears no resemblance to the prisoner at the bar? A. Very little; he was an older man; I should not think of his being any relation to the man; there is no resemblance that I discover.

Testimony of Godfrey J. Hyams.

By Judge Holt.—Q. Where have you resided during the last year? A. At Toronto, Canada.

Q. State whether or not, while there, you made the acquaintance of Dr. Blackburn. A. Yes sir I did, about the middle of December, 1863; I knew him previous to that by sight, but I never had any conversation with him; I have known him since that time.

Q. Did you know him as in the Confederate service? A. I did not know he was in the Confederate service; I knew he was doing work for the Confederates.

Q. State what arrangements, if any, this Dr. Blackburn made with you for the purpose of introducing the yellow fever into the United States; give all the particulars of your arrangements; what was done under it. A. I was introduced to Dr. Blackburn by the Rev. Stewart Robinson at Queen's Hotel, Toronto; Dr. Blackburn was about to take South some soldiers who had escaped from Northern prisons; I asked him if he was going South himself; he asked me if I wanted to go South and serve the Confederacy; I said I did; he then told me to come up stairs, that he wanted to speak to me; I went up stairs with him into a private room; he offered his hand to me as a Freemason in friendship and said he would never deceive me; that he wanted to place confidence in me for an expedition; he asked me if I would like to go on an expedition; I told him I did not care if I did; he said I would make an independent fortune by it—at least one hundred thousand dollars—and more glory than General Lee; that I could do more for the Southern Confederacy than if I had taken one hundred thousand soldiers to reinforce General Lee; I considered after a time, and told him I would go; he then told me he wanted me to take a certain quantity of clothing—he did not say how much (coats, shirts and underclothing)—into the States, and dispose of them at auction: he wanted me to take them into Washington City, into Norfolk, and as far South as I could go where the General Government held possession; he wanted me to sell them on a hot day or night; it did not matter what money I got for the clothes, I was just to dispose of them for what I could get.

Q. What did he tell you you were to receive for your services? A. He said one hundred thousand dollars; he said I should have sixty thousand dollars as soon as I reported back to Canada, and that if the things succeeded I could make one hundred thousand times as much.

Q. Where were you to get possession of the clothes? A. I was in Toronto to go on with my legitimate business, and if I left I was to inform Dr. Stuart Robinson where I was, and he was to telegraph or write to me somewhere about the month of January, 1864; I went on with my work until, I think, the 4th of January, 1864; on Saturday night I had been out to take a pair of boots home to a customer of mine when I returned my wife had a letter in her hand from Dr. Robinson, which he had just called and left there: I called on Dr. Robinson and asked him what I was to do; Robinson said he did not know anything about it; he did not wish it necessary to commit any overt act against the United States Government; that I had better take only enough money to carry me down to Montreal; I had a letter to Mr. Plauchier, who gave me directions to proceed to Halifax, where I was to meet Dr. Blackburn: the letter was dated May 10th, 1864; from Havana I went down to Halifax; Dr. Blackburn arrived there about the twelfth of July from Havana; he sent down to the hotel where I was staying and I went to see him; he told me that he had clothing there which had been smuggled off, and in accordance with his directions took an express wagon belonging to the hotel down to the steamboat landing and got there eight trunks and a valise ; he directed me to take the things to my hotel and put them in a private room, which I did, and notified Dr. Blackburn; he asked me if I would take the valise into the States and send it by express accompanied with a letter as a present to President Lincoln; I objected, and the valise was taken to his hotel; he ordered me to scratch the marks off the trunks; they had Spanish marks on them; he told me a man would go with me the next morning to make arrangements with one or two vessels going to Boston to smuggle the trunks through; I went down as directed, and made application to Captain McGregor; I do not remember the name of the vessel; the one who went with me had a consultation with Captain McGregor; I do not know what he said, but Captain McGregor refused to take the trouble; we next went to the barque Halifax, Captain J. O'Brien; the officer who was with me said I had some goods I wanted to take to my friends, and presents—silk and satin dresses, &c., and that he wanted to make an arrangement to smuggle them into Boston; the captain said he had a private consultation; when they came out he consented to take them on the Halifax, and smuggle them in; he took them on board his vessel that day, on arriving at Boston it was five days before we got an opportunity of getting them off, but he succeeded at last in doing it, and expressed them through to Philadelphia; from there I brought them to Baltimore, and brought five trunks here to Washington; four of them I gave to a man representing himself as a sutler, from Boston, by the name of Myers; I understood at the time he was a sutler in Sigel's army; he said he had found some goods that he was to take to Newbern, North Carolina; my instructions were to make a market for the goods, and I turned them over to him; Dr. Blackburn told me at the time that he would have about $100,000 worth of goods got together that summer to be disposed of.

Q. What did he state to you was his object, if any, in disposing of these goods? A. To destroy the army, and anybody in the country.

Q. Did he state that these goods had been carefully injected with yellow fever? A. Yes sir.

Q. Did he explain to you the process by which he had infected them? A. He did not; he told me there were other parties engaged in it, he did not say who they were, who were about injecting other goods with small-pox, yellow fever, and so on.

Q. Did you understand that the goods in this valise, intended to be sent as a present to President Lincoln, had also been carefully injected with yellow fever? A. I understood him it had been injected with yellow fever and small-pox; I declined to take them.

Q. Did you ever learn from him whether he had ever met that valise to the President? A. No, I did not; I have heard it was sent to him.

Q. What disposition of this trunk and clothes did you make in Washington? A. I turned them over to W. L. Wall & Co., commission merchants; I requested an advance on them; they gave me an advance of $100, and I went back to Canada.

Q. Do you remember the date of that transaction? A. I think it was about the 12th of August, it is it was the largest of the five trunks; it had two watches in it, and was known as "big No. 2;" my orders were to be sure and have the trunk sold in Washington.

Q. Did you send any of the others further South or yet there? A. I turned them over to the sutler, who put them in a steamboat for Norfolk; I applied to General Butler for a pass to go through myself, but the reply was that the army was about to move, and that no persons would be allowed a pass not connected with it.

Q. State what occurred on your return to Canada. A. I went through to Hamilton without stopping; there I had to wait for the cars, and was met by Mr. Holcomb and C. C. Clay; they both shook hands with me, greeted me heartily, and congratulated me on my safe return and on my making a fortune; they told me I should be a gentleman for the future; I telegraphed to Dr. Blackburn, who was then staying at Montreal, as Mr. Holcomb had told me, that I had returned; the next night between 11 and 12 o'clock; Dr. Blackburn came up and knocked at the door; I was in bed, but looked out of the window and saw Dr. Blackburn; he told me to come down and open the door; that I was like all other rascals after doing something wrong, a raid the devil was after me; he was accompanied by James H. Young; he asked how I disposed of the goods, and I told him he had sold it was all right if "big No. 2" had been disposed of; that that would kill at sixty yards' distance; I then told him that everything had gone wrong in my business there since I had been away, and that I needed some money; he said he would go to Col. Thompson and make arrangements to draw on him for any money I desired; he said the British authorities had solicited his attention to the yellow fever raging at Bermuda; that he was going on there, and, as soon as he came back, he would see me; I went to see Jacob Thompson on the next morning; he said that I was glad that I had been there and made arrangements to pay me one hundred dollars when the goods had been disposed of according to his directions: I told him I needed the money; he said:—"I will give you fifty dollars now, but it is against Dr. Blackburn's request; when you show me that you have sold the goods I will pay the balance; I gave him a receipt for fifty dollars on account of Dr. Blackburn; this was the 11th or 12th of August; the next day I wrote a letter to Mr. Wall, here, saying I had gone to Canada and he sold the goods, and asked him to remit to me the proceeds at Toronto; when I got the letter of William L. Wall I took it to Colonel Thompson; he said he was satisfied with it, and gave me a check for fifty dollars on the Ontario Bank of Montreal; I gave him a receipt for fifty dollars on account of S. P. Blackburn.

Q. State whether or not Jacob Thompson, in all your connection with him, seemed to have a perfect knowledge of the character of the goods you were selling? A. Yes, sir.

Q. Did you mention to him the large sum that had been promised to you by Dr. Blackburn? A. I did, and he said the Confederate Government had appropriated $200,000 for that purpose.

Q. How did he excuse himself for not giving you more? A. When Dr. Blackburn returned from Bermuda, I wrote to Montreal and told him I wanted money; he made no reply; I then sent down to R. H. Young; subsequently I met Dr. Blackburn, who said I had written him very hard letters, abusing him, and that he had not any money to give; he got into his car-

TRIAL OF THE ASSASSINS AT WASHINGTON. 109

place and drove off, and never gave me any satisfaction, or paid me anything more.
Q. State under what name you passed when in Washington. A. J. M. Harris.
Q. Where did you stop in this city? A. At the National Hotel, and I brought the goods there.
Q. Can you give the precise date? A. I think it was the 8th of August, 1864.
Q. In what name did you write this letter to Dr. Blackburn? A. In my own name.
Q. In what name did you write to Mrs. Hall? A. In the name of J. W. Harris, the same as I had registered myself at the hotel.
Q. Can you state whether C. C. Clay and Professor Holcomb, when you met on your return, in their conversation with you, seemed always perfectly to understand the business you were engaged in? A. Yes; after I returned back to Canada I met Clay, Holcomb, Preston, Beverly Tucker, Dr. Blackburn, and several other gentlemen at the Clifton House, Niagara Falls.
Q. They then had a knowledge of your enterprise? A. Yes sir.
Q. And they complimented you upon your success? A. Holcomb and Clay d d.
Q. How do you know they had this knowledge? Was there a conversation between them that left no doubt on your mind as to the fact? A. In the conversation at the Clifton House I stated that I intended to return that night to Toronto; Dr. Blackburn had no money; he told me that he would go to H lcombe, who had Confederate funds; he said that Holcombe was going to stay there, and when he returned he would get money from him or Thompson for the expedition; that he had to get it from one of them; I understood from that time that they knew all about it; I never spoke to them directly about it at all; I took it for granted, when they congratulated me on my safe return at Hamilton, they must have known all about it.
Q. You speak of Stuart Robinson, a divine, of Louisville, Kentucky; who introduced you to Dr. Blackburn. Did he seem to have a knowledge of the business you were engaged in? A. Not from me; I don't know what knowledge he had from Dr. Blackburn. He said he did not know the nature of the business I was going on, and that he did not want to commit any overt act. All I know is that Dr. Robinson took good care of me all the time I was there that time until Dr. Blackburn wrote for me. He did not give me any money. I borrowed $10 to come down to Montreal from Mr. Preston. I went down to Montreal and saw Mr. Slaughter, who was to furnish me with funds to take me to Hali ax. He said he was short of funds, that he had lost several hundred dollars by the failure of a bank. He gave me $45 and said I had better go to Holcombe at the Donegana House. I saw Mr. Holcombe and told him I was short of funds and wanted $40. He said I had better take $50, but I replied saying I did not want it.
The Judge Advocate asked the counsel for the defense whether they desired to cross-examine the witness.
Mr. Aiken replied that before the witness was discharged he desired to know whether it was the purpose of the Judge Advocate to make use of the testimony in the summing up against any of the prisoners.
Judge Holt replied that it was expected that reference would be made to all this testimony in summing up, but that the object of this testimony was to connect the Rebellion with this crime.

Testimony of Wm. L. Wall.

By Judge Holt.—Q. Are you a merchant in this city? A. I am an auction and commission merchant.
Q. State whether, last summer, you received on consignment from a person representing himself as J. W. Harris, certain trunks and goods? A. While I was out of town last August, my book-keeper received from a party named Harris, a lot of shirts and coats, which he desired to be sold at auction the next morning; the book-keeper said he would sell them; he asked for an advance on them, and $100 per trunk was the amount advanced, and the goods were sold the next morning; I did not see them at all.

Testimony of A. Brenner.

By Judge Holt.—Q. Were you employed last summer in the service of Mr. Wall, commission merchant in this city? A. Yes sir.
Q. State whether in the month of August a man representing himself as J. W. Harris sent to the store of Mr. Wall certain packages of goods for sale. A. A man calling himself Harris brought a package of goods to the store for sale; I thought him a suffer returning home, and I advanced him one hundred dollars upon them and sold them the next day; he said there were twelve dozen shirts, but there turned out to be more; I rendered an account of the sales to him at Toronto, Canada, with the balance of his money, in accordance with a letter received from him directing it, which I have here; it is dated at Toronto, September 1st, 1864, and he states that he had written to me previously in respect to five trunks, containing one hundred and fifty woolen shirts and twenty-five coats, but had received no response, and asked me to send him a check on New York for the proceeds.

Q. Do you remember anything about the marks which were on the o d trunks? A. No sir; I remember the shirts were thrown promiscuously into the trunks; I sorted them out into packages of a dozen and sold them.
Q. Do you remember whether any trunk was marked No. 2? A. We marked them in selling them.
By the Court.—Did it seem to be new c othing? A. I thought when I first opened the trunk it was not, and had doubts about its being a safe investment, but on looking farther I saw it was new; it appeared to be crammed down into the trunk.
Q. What amount d d the shirts bring? A. I see by the account sales which I have here that the whole amount was $1,4290.

Testimony of Thos. L. Gardner.

Q. State whether or not you came up in company with Dr. Mudd to Washington last spring. A. I did, sir.
Q. State the date of the visit. A The 23d day of March, I think, sir.
Q. State what t me you left home to come up. A. On the 23d, in the morning, after the usual break fast time.
Q. State the purpose of the vi-it. A. We came up to attend a sale of Government horses, which was to take place on Friday, but we heard it was to take place on Tuesday, and so were disappointed.
Q. Go on and state where you and Dr. Mudd were during that visit. A. We left our horses at Martins, walked across the street, came down the avenue, and went to a carriage factory; we then went to a livery-stable, where he looked at some second-hand wagons, and then went over on the island to Mr. Clark's, and remained there till about dark, till the store was about to close up; Dr. Mudd and myself walked around to Dr. Herring's, where we remained some two or three hours, and then returned to Mr. Clark's, where we remained all night; the next morning we took leave of Clark, and went into the Capitol to look at the paintings; we then went and took the street car, and went up to Martin's and got our horses, and after dinner we left and returned home.
Q. S ate wh slept with Dr. Mudd. A. Dr. Mudd and myself slept together; there was but one bed in the room, and we occupied that.
Q. State whether you and Dr. Mudd were separated during the visit. A. No, sir; not at all; I am confident that at no time were we out of one another's sight from our leaving Martin's until we started back.
Q. Did you not see anything of Booth during that visit? A. No, sir.
Q. Did you go into the National Hotel? A. No, sir; I think we stopped talking in front of the National Hotel looking at some Rebel prisoners passing, but we did not go in.
Q. Do you recollect the contest during the Congressional election in your district in which Calvert was the Union candidate and Harris was the Secession or opposing candidate? A. Yes sir, Harris ran as a Peace candidate.
Q. Do you know which one Dr. Mudd supported? Objected to.
Q. Do you know on what ticket Calvert was running? A. As an unconditional Union candidate.
Q. Do you know which Dr. Mudd supported? Objected to.
Cross-examined by Colonel Burnett.—Q. Did you say that Mr. Calvert was running as a better U on candidate than Mr. Harris at that electio ? A. Yes sir.
Q. Was not Mr. Harland a candidate? A. I don't know.
Q. Were the o her two peace candidates both of them? A. I don't know.

Testimony of Mr. Downing.

Q. State where you live. A. In Charles county, near Mount Pleasant.
Q. State whether you are acquainted with Dr. Samuel Mudd. A. I am very well acquainted with him.
Q. Are you a quainted with Mr. Thomas who testified here? A. Yes sir, I was raised with b th of them.
Q. State whether or not Dr. Mudd and Mr. Thomas met at your house last spring. A. Yes sir, between the 1st and 15th they both met at my hou e.
Q. Did they meet at any other time this Spring at your house? A. No sir.
Q. Did they come together? A. Yes sir; Mr. Thomas came two or three hours be ore Dr. Mudd.
Q. How long did Dr. Mudd stay there? A. About half an hour; I don't think he staid over half an hour.
Q. Were you present all the time Dr. Mudd was there? A. Yes sir; I never left the room.
Q. State whether or not, in that convesation at that time, Dr. Mudd sa d that Pres dent Lincoln was an Abolitionist; that all the Cabinet were such, and that the South could n t be subjugated by Abolition doctrine, and that the President and Cabinet would a l be killed in six or seven weeks. A. There were no such words spoken in the house, to my knowledge; I stopped there all the time; he came there to see me to collect a little doctor's bill, and stopped there about half an hour; as I walked out, Dr. Mudd rose and followed me out; I went directly home; Mr. Thomas stayed with me an hour afterwards.
Q. Could Dr. Mudd have had any conversation with Mr. Thomas without you hearing it? A. No sir; even

if they had whispered I could have heard it, I was so close to both of them.
Q. Was any part of the statement I have recited to you made by Dr. Mudd on that occasion? A. Not to my knowledge.
Q. Do you think you would have noticed it if it had been? A. I should certainly.
Q. State whether or not, two or three weeks after that occasion, you met Mr. Thomas on the road between your house and his, and whether he said to you that at your house Dr. Mudd had said that the President and the Cabinet and every Union man in the State of Maryland would be killed? A. He never said such a word; I never heard a word of that kind.
Q. Neither before nor after the assassination? A. No sir, neither.
Q. On that occasion did Dr. Mudd say that he did not consider the oath of allegiance worth a chew of tobacco? A. Not that I recollect; there never was a word of it spoken.
Q. What was the conversation about? A. Daniel Thomas was saying to Dr, Mudd that he was appointed a de ecteve, and then referred to others; to Dyer and to Dr. George Mudd, and, perhaps, to one Hawkins; to being detective as well as he could, but didn't pretend to catch anybody himself; it was his duty, he said, to go to their houses, but he said he never would catch any body.
Cross-examined.—Q. Were they talking during the whole half hour? A. Yes; they were detailing a lot of foolish things.
Q. What did Dr. Mudd say? A. I had no conversation with them.
Q. What did Dr. Mudd say to Thomas? A. He said that he was a jack.
Q. What did he call him a jack for? A. Thomas said he was appointed a Deputy Provost Marshal, and Dr. Mudd said, "I am a better educated m..n than you are, and I am not fit for that office," and then they talked, and Mudd called him a jack; I didn't like that, for I don't suffer jacks to come into my house.
Q. How long were you gone before Dr. Mudd went out? A. Not two seconds.
By Mr. Ewing.—Q. Did I understand you to say that you were not out of the room during that interview? A. Yes, sir; I was sitting about one yard from your it was cold weather; we had not wood enough on the fire, and we all sat close to it.
Q. You heard all the conversation? A. Yes, sir; every word that was spoken.

Testimony of H. L. Mudd, Jr.

Q. Where do you live? A. Near Bryantown.
Q. How far from the accused? A. Three-quarters of a mile.
Q. Did you last winter or spring, in company with Dr. Mudd, come up to the neighborhood of Washington? A. Yes sir.
Q. State where you both went? A. We left home on the 10th of April and stopped about twelve miles from Washington. We went to Giesboro' to buy horses and stayed there till 10 o'clock. We didn't find any horses that suited us as they were nearly all diseased. I made a proposition to go down to Martin's near the bridge and get some dinner, and we went and took dinner there.
Q. Where did you go then? A. Directly home.
Q. State whether you were separated from Dr. Mudd during that visit. A. Not during that visit; we were all the time together.
Q. State whether you crossed the eastern branch. A. No sir.
Q. Did you go on to Washington? A. No sir.
Q. State whether you saw anything of John Wilkes Booth during that visit. A. No sir, I did not.
Q. Do you know anything about any other visits Dr. Mudd made to Washington? A. Yes sir, on the 23d or 24th day of December and on the 2d day of March he was there.
Q. Who came with him the first time? A. Jerry Dyer.
Q. Who came with him the second time? A. Mr. Gardner.
Q. State whether you know anything, except of those two visits, from the 1st of January to the present time. A. I saw him three or four times a week, sometimes at church, and sometimes at home; I never saw him anywhere else.
Q. How long have you been living within three-quarters of a mi.e of Mudd's place? A. All my life.
Q. Did you live there last year? A. No sir; I was at college, but I came home on the 27th day of June.
Q. Have you been here ever since? A. Yes sir; ever since.
Q. Do you know of any part of the Confederate soldiers being about your brother's house since the 29th day of July, 1864? A. I do not sir.
Q. Did you hear or see John Surratt at your brother's house? A. Never, sir.
Q. State to the Court whether or not your father is a land owner in the county. A. Yes sir.

Q. How large? (Objected to by Assistant Judge Advocate Bingham.)
Q. How large a farm is it that your father has? A. Between four and five hundred acres.
By Colonel Burnett.—Q. Do you mean that he owns it? A. Father gave it to him; he never had any deed for it; he is simply there as a tenant; my father owns it.
Q. Don't you know that Dr. Mudd does not own a foot of land of any kind? A. I do not, sir.
By Mr. Ewing.—The Witness—I have always understood that the farm was set apart for him by his father; it is known as his farm.
Q. Do you know of your brother having sold and received the proceeds of any land belonging to your father? A. Yes sir; the land on which Mr. Forey now lives he bought from my father; the house was burnt down and my brother sold the farm.
Q. Who held the title? A. My father sir.

Testimony of Mr. Hardy.

I live in Charles county, two miles and a half above Bryantown; I dined at the house of Dr. Mudd's father one week after the assassination; a messenger came for him to go to his own house and I went with him; we met Lieutenant Lovett in Dr. Mudd's yard; Dr. Mu ld introduced Lieutenant Lovett to me, and he then walked into the house, and Dr, Mudd told Lieutenant Lovett that the boot was in the house, and asked him if he wanted it; I think he mentioned it after we got into the house; no inquiry had been made before in my hearing.
Q. Was anything said about where it was found? A. Mrs. Mudd said she found it in dusting the room under the bed.
Cross examination.—I don't know what remark was made about searching the house.
By Mr. Ewing.—Q. Who gave the boot to the officer? A. Dr. Mudd himself.
Q. What time of day was it? A. Between 12 and 1 o'clock; we had d nner at Dr. Mudd's father s; I d dn't see the messenger; I think it was Mr. Davis' child ran in and said Mr. Davis was in the yard and wished to see Dr. Mudd.

Testimony of Dr. Blandford.

Q. Where do you live? A. In Prince George county, about twenty miles from the city.
Q. State whether or not, during last spring or winter, you accompanied Dr. Mudd toward Washington. A. I did, on the 11th of April, to Giesboro', to attend a sale of Government horses there.
Q. State who was in company with him. A. His brother; we arrived at the sale about five in the hour, and I remained there with him till twelve o'clock, examining horses; they were of an inferior quality; and he made no purchases during my stay there; at about half-past twelve o'clock I left him and made an engagement to meet him again; I went to Washington and got back to Martin's at about half-past two o'clock, and found Dr. Mudd there.
Q. When you started for Washington you left his brother with him at Giesboro'. A. Yes sir.
Q. Did you find him there when you returned? A Yes sir.
Q. State where Martin's is. A. On the forks of the road, not more than one hundred yards from the bridge; one road leads to the right, and the other is the stage road leading into the country.
Q. That is on the other side of the Eastern Branch? A. Yes sir.
Q. Have you any knowledge of Dr. Mudd offering to sell his farm? A. I think he said he would like to sell it.
Q. When did you hear him speak of that? A. For several years back.
Q. What place did he refer to? A. The place that he lived in; I heard him speak of it in the last eighteen months several times.
Q. How long did you stay at Giesboro' together? A. Till eight or nine o'clock.

Testimony of Mr. Martin.

I am acquainted with both Dr. Samuel Mudd and Henry L. Mudd, and also with Dr. Blandford; I saw them on the 23d of March, and also, I think, on the 4th of April last; both Dr. Samuel and Henry L. Budd were at my house for one or two hours; Dr. Blandford joined them between three and four o'clock.
Q. Was Dr Mudd there afterwards, between that time and the assassination? A. No sir; neither w_s Henry L. Mudd nor Dr. Blandford.

Testimony of Mr. Montgomery.

I am acquainted with the prisoner, Dr. Samuel Mudd; in last December he made an arrangement with me for bringing a share to Washington; I reckon it was on the 23d or that month, in the morning.
The Court then adjourned till ten o'clock to-morrow morning.

TRIAL OF THE ASSASSINS AT WASHINGTON. 111

WASHINGTON, May 30.—Visitors of both sexes continue to crowd the court room almost to suffocation. At the trial Messrs. D. Hubbard, John F. Roberts and Charles E. Follows, of Col. Baker's Detective Force, are in attendance, enforcing order and courteously attending to their appropriate duties.

The record of the previous day having been read, the prosecution proceeded to call three witnesses, the remaining being for the defense. Their testimony was as follows:—

Testimony of Lewis F. Bates.

By Judge Advocate Holt.—Q. State where you reside. A. In Charlotte, N. C.
Q. How long have you resided there? A. Little over four years.
Q. In what business have you been engaged there during the past year? A. I have been engaged as Superintendent of the Southern Express Company for the State of North Carolina.
Q. State whether or not you saw Jefferson Davis recently at Charlotte, N. C., and under what circumstances. A. He stopped at my house on the 19th of April last.
Q. Did he make an address to the people on that occasion? A. He did, on the steps of my house.
Q. State whether or not, in the course of that address, or towards the close of it, a telegram was received by him announcing the assassination of the President of the United States. A. It was.
Q. From whom? A. From John C. Breckinridge.
Q. Did he or did he not read that telegram to the crowd? A. He did.
Q. Look at this (exhibiting to witness a telegram), and see whether it is the same despatch? A. I should say that it was.
The despatch was then read, as follows:—
GREENSBORO, April 19, 1865.—His Excellency President Davis:—President Lincoln was assassinated in the theatre in Washington, on the night of the 14th inst. Seward's house was entered on the same night and he was repeatedly stabbed, and is probably mortally wounded.
(Signed)   JOHN C. BRECKINRIDGE.
Q. State what Jefferson Davis said after reading this despatch to the crowd. Endeavor to recollect his precise language. A. At the conclusion of his speech to the people he read this despatch aloud and made this remark:—"If it were to be done it were better that it were done well."
Q. You are sure these are the words? A. These are the words.
Q. State whether or not, in a day or two afterwards, Jefferson Davis, John C. Breckinridge and others, were present in your house at Charlotte? A. They were.
Q. And the assassination of the President was the subject of conversation? A. A day or two afterwards that was the subject of their conversation.
Q. Can you remember what John C. Breckenridge said? A. In speaking of the assassination of President Lincoln he remarked to Davis that he regretted it very much; that it was unfortunate for the people of the South at that time; Davis replied, "Well, General, I don't know; if it were to be done at all, it were better it were well done; and if the same were done to Andrew Johnson, the beast, and to Secretary Stanton, the job would then be complete."
Q. You feel confident that you recollect the words? A. These are the words used.
Q. State whether or not the regret which John C. Breckenridge expressed at the assassination was because of its criminality, or simply because it was unfortunate for the people of the South at that time? A. I drew that conclusion.
Q. Was there any remark made as to the criminality of the act? A. No sir, he simply remarked that he regretted it as being unfortunate for the South.
Q. Of what State are you a native? A. Of Massachusetts.

Testimony of J. C. Courtney.

Q. Where do you reside? A. At Charlotte, N. C.
Q. In what business were you engaged there? A. In the telegraph business in connection with the Southern Express Company.
Q. Look at the telegraph despatch of which Mr. Bates has just spoken, and state whether or not it passed over the wires at the date indicated? A. Yes sir; that is a true copy. (A copy of the message telegraphed on the 19th of April last, to Jefferson Davis, was shown to witness.)
Q. From what point? A. From Greensboro', signed by John C. Breckinridge.
Q. This despatch was sent from the office to Jefferson Davis at Charlotte? A. When the message was received he was en route to Charlotte; it was delivered to him at Mr. Bates' house, in Charlotte.

Judge Advocate Holt then stated that inasmuch as the counsel for the prisoner, Spangler, had not as yet opened the case for the defense, he desired to call another witness for the prosecution in regard to that prisoner.

No objections being made, the following witness was called:—

Testimony of Jacob Ritterspach.

By Ass't stant Judge Advocate Bingham.—Q. State whether you were a carpenter at Ford's theatre down the 14th of April last? A. I was.
Q. Were you present on the night of the 14th when the President was shot? A. I was.
Q. Which box in the theatre did the President occupy that night? A. It was on the left hand side of the stage, the right hand side as you come in from the front.
Q. When the shot was fired did you hear anybody cry "Stop that man?" A. I did.
Q. State where you were and what you did when you heard the cry "Stop that man?" A. I was standing on the stage, about the centre, behind the scenes, when somebody cried out, "The President is shot!" Then I saw a man running across the stage towards the back-door; he had a knife in his hand; I run to the last entrance, and as I came up to him, he grabbed for me, and struck at me with his knife; I jumped back; he then ran out and slammed the door shut; then I went to open the door, and I thought it was kind of fast; I could not get it open very readily; at that time somebody cried out, "Which way?" and I answered "This way." Then I got out, but the man had got on his horse and gone down the alley; I then came in and met Spangler.
Q. What Spangler? A. Edward Spangler, the prisoner, and he kind of slapped me on the mouth with his open hand, and said, "Don't say which way he went." I asked him what he meant by slapping me in the mouth, and he said, "For God's sake, shut up!" that was all he said.
Q. When you went out that door had anybody else besides the man with the knife gone out before you? A. I did not see anybody.
Q. Did anybody go out after you? A. Yes, but I do not know who it was.
Q. Did you leave the door open when you ran out? A. Yes sir.
Q. What was your business on the stage? A. My business was to shove the wings.
Q. State what sort of a man, if any, went out after you. A. I thought he was a tall, pretty stout man.
Q. Do you know him? A. No sir, I did not notice him particularly.
Q. When you came back into the theatre was the door open or shut? A. It was open.
Cross-examined by Mr. Ewing.—Q. State where you were standing when you heard the pistol fire. A. In the centre of the stage.
Q. Where was Spangler then? A. He was about in the same place, just about where we shoved off the scenes; he was standing there, and seemed to look pale.
Q. You are certain you both stood there when the pistol was fired? A. Yes sir.
Q. Did you know that the pistol had been fired immediately after it happened? A. Not right away; I did not know what had happened until I heard somebody halloo "Stop that man; the President is shot."
Q. When you came back whereabouts was Spangler? A. In the same place where I left him.
Q. Was there a crowd there? A. The actors were there and some strangers; there were some women standing there belonging to the theatre; I do not know their names?
Q. Do you not know one of them? A. I do not know any of their names, not having been acquainted with them; I had been there only four weeks.
Q. Did any one of them take any part in that play that night? A. Yes sir, some of them did.
Q. What parts did they take? A. I do not know what parts, but one they used to call Jennie.
Q. How close was she to you when Spangler struck you? A. About three or four feet.
Q. She heard Spangler state the words you have given? A. I do not know.
Q. He said it loud enough for her to hear? A. Not so very loud.
Q. He said it in the usual tone? A. Yes sir, he looked scared and kind of crying.
Q. Did you hear the people crying "burn the theatre?" A. No sir; I just heard them hallooing "hang him, shoot him," that was all I heard.
Q. You mentioned what Spangler did and said to you to several persons since then? A. Yes sir; I do not know, I think I told some detectives that came there.
Q. Did you tell either of the Messrs. Ford? A. No sir; I told Gifford.
Q. What did you tell Gifford that Spangler said? A. I told him Spangler said I should not say which way he ran.
Q. When did you tell Gifford? A. The same week, I think that I was released from Carrol prison, the week before last.
Q. Do you not know what they called the detective whom you told? A. No sir; he had black whiskers and a very heavy moustache, and weighed about 140 pounds.
Q. Can you recollect anybody else to whom you told it? A. I might have said something about it at the table in the house where I boarded.
Q. Did you see Booth open the door? A. Yes sir.
Q. Did you see him shut it? A. No sir.
Q. How close to you was this big man who ran out after you? A. He might have been five or six yards

from me when I heard him or somebody else halloo out "which way!" I have not seen that man since.
Q. How long was it before you came back to where Spangler was standing? A. It might have been two or three minutes.
Q. And he was crying? A. He looked so; he seemed scared.
Q. What did you say to him before he spoke to you as you have stated? A. I did not say anything.
Q. Were you at supper with Spangler on the night before the assassination? A. Yes sir; we boarded together.
Robert Martin, a witness for the defense, being called, stated that he was mistaken in that portion of his testimony of yesterday referring to the visit of the prisoner, Dr. Samuel A. Mudd, to his house on the 4th of April. It was Jerret Mudd, not the prisoner, who visited him, and the date was 11th instead of 4th of April. The witness further stated that the prisoner, in company with Jerrett Mudd, called on him while he was in market in Washington on the 23th of December last, and that he saw the prisoner again on the 23d of March, in company with Mr. Lewellyn, the occasion of these gentlemen stopping over night at his house, and that he did not recollect seeing him on any other occasion.

Jerry Dyer, a witness for the defense, being recalled, stated that he had never gone into Virginia. He intended to say that he had not crossed the Potomac since 1861, but did get to Richmond, Virginia, at that time with the party who had been sleeping in the pines.
By Assistant Judge Advocate Bingham—Q. Who were the parties whom you accompanied to Richmond at the time of which you speak? A. Ben. Gwynn and Andrew Gwynn.
Q. That was after the Rebellion commenced? A. Yes sir.
Q. Did you see Jefferson Davis while you were in Richmond? A. I did, but I never spoke to him in my life; I remained in Richmond only about a week, and did not meet with any of the officers of the Rebel organization there except Taylor, to whom I went to get a pass.
Q. What business took you to Richmond? A. I went there to avoid arrest.
Q. You preferred to fall into the hands of the enemy? A. I regretted very much the necessity of going there.
Q. To what pines do you refer in your testimony? A. To the pines about Dr. Mudd's house.
Q. Did you sleep in the pines at night? A. Yes sir.
Q. Who fed you? A. Dr. Samuel A. Mudd.
Mr. Ewing objected to a further examination of this witness, as all these facts had already been stated by him in his examination in chief.
General Hunter inquired whether the witness had not sworn that he was a loyal man and had been such from the beginning of the Rebellion?
Judge Bingham replied that he so understood.
Q. Did you not belong to an association hostile to the Government of the United States? A. I belonged to a cavalry company.
Q. Was it not the purpose of that organization to stand by the state of Maryland in any position she might take, loyal or disloyal? A. That I do not know.
Q. Did you not publicly proclaim yourself in favor of the secession of Maryland? A. Not that I am aware of; I may have done it.
By Mr. Ewing.—Q. State whether when you went to Virginia you entered into the Confederate service. A. I did not; I did not go for that purpose.
Q. State whether when you returned you took the oath of allegiance. A. I did.
Q. State whether you have done any act to aid or encourage the Rebellion since taking the oath? A. I have not, that I am aware of.
By Mr. Bingham.—Q. When did you take this oath of allegiance? A. In 1861; I am not positive as to that; I know it was a short time after I returned.
Q. Who administered the oath of allegiance? A. One of the lieutenants or captains; I think, down at General Hooker's camp.

Testimony of Marcellus Gardner,

By Mr. Ewing.—Q. State whether you know the prisoner, Dr. Samuel A. Mudd. A. I do.
Q. State whether he has ever said anything to you about offering his land for sale, and, if so, when? A. I have heard him, on several occasions, during the past two years, state that he wanted to sell out.
Q. Were you at the church in the neighborhood on the Sunday after the assassination? A. Yes sir.
Q. Was the fact of the assassination of the President then known and talked about at the church? A. Yes sir; I think it was generally known.
Q. State whether the name of the assassin was generally known. A. I think not.
Q. Did you see Dr. Mudd there? A. Yes sir.
Q. State whether you heard Dr. Mudd say anything as to how he regarded the assassination.
Assistant Judge Advocate Bingham objected to the question.
Mr. Ewing said that he had again brought this question before the Court for the purpose of calling their attention specially to the character of the declaration which he expected to prove, that Dr. Mudd spoke of the assassination as an atrocious and revolting crime,

and a terrible calamity to the country; and that he spoke of it generally among his neighbors at the church in that way. The prisoner was charged with a concealment of the fact of those two men being at his house, which was a concealment extending over Sunday, and his declarations showing his feelings with reference to the crime during the time he was alleged to have been acting accessory to it were admissable.
The objection of the Judge Advocate was sustained, and the question was not put.
Mr. Ewing then stated that he had no further examination of the witness to make.

Testimony of Jos. N. Saylor.

By Mr. Stone.—Q. Where do you reside? A. In the Eighth Election District of Prince Georges county, Maryland.
Q. State whether you know the general reputation of Daniel G. Thomas for truth and veracity. A. I know his general reputation in that respect pretty well, both from report and observation; it is bad.
Q. From his general character for truth and veracity would you believe him on his oath? A. From my own knowledge of him I would not.
Q. How long have you known Thomas? A. Since he was a small boy.
Q. Did you know his general character for truth and veracity before this war? A. I have known him all the time; I never heard him spoken of well at any time; his reputation is that he never tells the truth when a lie will answer his purpose.
Cross-examined by Judge Holt.—Q. Did you ever know of Mr. Thomas speaking falsely when under oath? A. I never knew him to be sworn.
Q. Did you ever hear it charged upon him that he swore falsely? A. I do not know that I ever did.
Q. The reputation of which you speak is, that he talks idly, extravagantly and unreliably, but that reputation does not extend to any statements which he would make while under oath. A. I never heard that he had been charged with swearing false y.
Q. Is he not reported to be an honest and loyal man in his neighborhood? A. Well, he is sometimes one thing, and sometimes another, just as the prospects of either side vary.
Q. Have you been loyal yourself since the Rebellion? A. I have.
Q. Have you constantly desired that the Government should succeed in suppressing the Rebellion? A. Always.
In reply to some further questions, the witness said that his ground for suspecting the loyalty of Mr. Thomas at particular times, were based upon what that person had told others; that personally he was very friendly with Mr. Thomas, their residences being near each other; that he had never had any private or political differences with that gentleman, and that the reputation of Dr. George Mudd, as a loyal man and a supporter of the Government, was universal in that neighborhood.

Testimony of Wm. A. Mudd.

By Mr. Stone.—Q. Do you know Dr. S. A. Mudd? A. I do.
Q. How far do you live from him? A. About a mile and a half.
Q. State whether at any time last year you saw a Captain White, from Tennessee, or a Lieutenant Perry, at or about Dr. Samuel Mudd's premises. A. I never did.
Q. Did you see Andrew or Ben Gwynn or George Gwynn about his premises at any time last year? A. No sir; I have not seen Andrew Gwynn since he left for the South; Mr. George Gwynn I have seen at our church several times since he returned.
Q. Did you see any person staying out in the woods, about Dr. Mudd's, during last year? A. I did not; I never saw a man there that I had heard of as having been South, except one; I recollect seeing Mr. Ben Gwynn at the Doctor's; I rode up, and ascertained from him that he was scouting, or something of that kind; that has been quite three years ago; it may have been in the first year of the war; it was the time I understood they were after him.

Testimony of Francis S. Walsh.

By Mr. Stone.—Q. Where do you reside? A. I have lived in this city since 1837; I am a druggist.
Q. Do you know the prisoner Harold? A. Yes, I have known him ever since he was a boy. I have known him intimately since October, 1863.
Q. Has he been in your employ. A. He was for nine months, as a clerk.
Q. State as near as you can his character? A. He lived in my house; I knew nothing objectionable in his character. He was like most young men light and trifling in some things, but in his moral character I saw nothing to find fault with. He was temperate in his habits and regular in his hours.
Q. State whether he was or was not in his general character more of a boy than a man? A. I think so.
Q. State whether or not he was easily influenced or persuaded by any one around him? A. I should think he was more easily than boys or young men of his age; he was boyish in many respects.
By Judge Holt.—Q. What do you suppose to be his age? A. About twenty-two years.

TRIAL OF THE ASSASSINS AT WASHINGTON.

Interior View of the Court Room Occupied by the Military Commission.

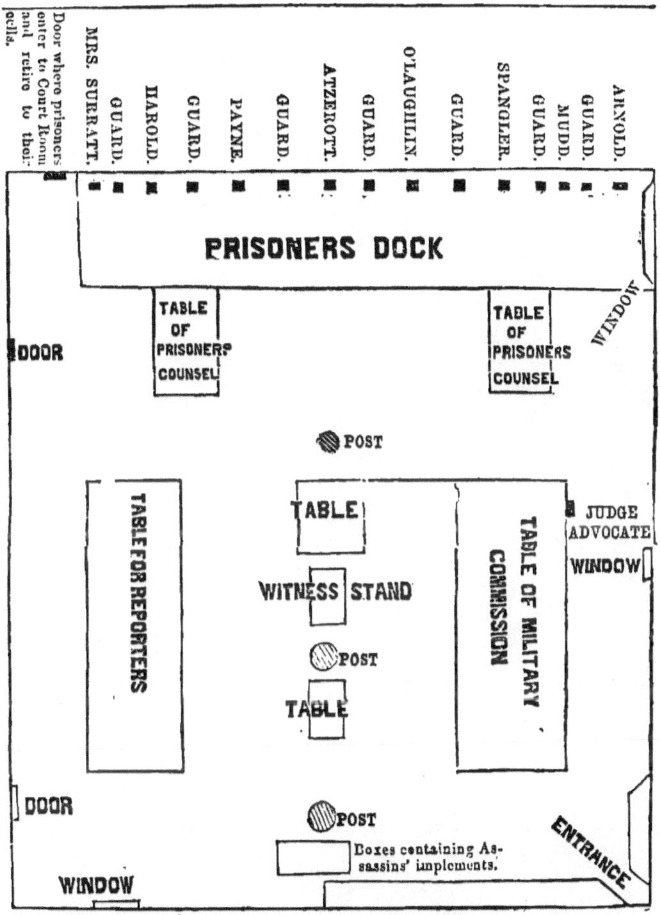

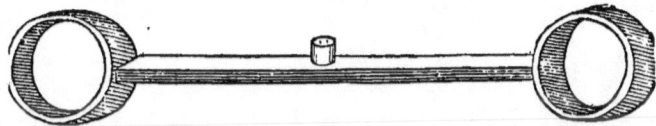

THE PRISONERS' MANACLES.

The above is a correct drawing of the manacles used in confining the arms of the prisoners. The wristlets are attached to an iron bar, about twelve inches in length, which prevents the wearer from joining his hands, as in the old-fashioned shackle, where the clasps are connected by chain links, thus effectually preventing the culprit from unfastening or breaking them.

Testimony of James Nokes.

By Mr. Stone.—Q. Where do you reside? A. I have lived at the Navy Yard in this city since 1827.
Q. Do you know the prisoner Harold? A. I have known him from his birth, about twenty-two years, I believe.
Q. Have you seen a good deal of him? A. I have been intimate in his family for about eighteen or nineteen years.
Q. How large a family? A. Seven or eight; he was the only son.
Q. State what is his general character for boyishness; whether he was easily persuaded or led away. A. I have always looked upon him as a light, trifling boy, of very little reliability.
Q. Is he or is he not easily persuaded by any one around him? A. I should think he was.
Q. More so than the generality of young men of his age? A. Yes sir, I am certain of that.
Q. Would he be especially liable to be led away by any one of fascinating address? A. I have never heard him enter into any argument with any one; all his conversation that I have heard has been of a light and trifling character.

Testimony of William H. Kielott.

By Mr. Stone.—Q. Where do you reside? A. I have lived in this city for fifteen years.
Q. State whether you know the prisoner, Harold, well? A. I do.
Q. Have you known him all the time? A. Yes; for nearly thirteen years.
Q. State whether you saw him during the month of February last? A. I think I did.
Q. How often? A. I could not say how often; I was at home; I live next door to his father's, and have occasionally seen him in the yard, morning and afternoon; I suppose I saw him nearly every day.
Q. State whether or not he is of a trifling character, and easily persuaded. A. I believe he is; I saw him very often in boys' company; I should think he was more of a boy than a man; he never associated with men at all.

Testimony of Emma Harold.

By Mr. Stone.—Q. State whether you are the sister of the prisoner, David E. Harold. A. I am.
Q. State whether he was at home on the 15th of February last? A. Yes; I remember it from the fact of sending a valentine to him, which he received on the 15th.
Q. Had you any talk with him in relation to that valentine on the 15th? A. No; but my sister had.
Q. State what was the next date you can fix on which he was at home? A. The 19th; I remember that date by the fact that I brought a pitcher of water up stairs; he met me in the hall, and wanted I should give it to him; he tried to take it away from me; I held on to it, and it spilled over; that was the Sunday morning after St. Valentine's day.
Q. And you do not remember his being at home between these times? A. He was at home, but I cannot fix the day.

Testimony of Gen. Edward Johnston.

The Rebel Major-General Edward Johnston was here called to the stand.
Gen. Howe.—Before this witness is sworn I wish to submit a motion to the Court. I will state the facts upon which I base the motion. It is well known, as it is to a great many officers of the army, that the person now on the stand, Edward Johnston, was educated at the National Military Academy, at Government expense, and that since that time, for years, he has held a commission in the army of the United States. It is well known in the army that it is a condition precedent to resigning a commission that an officer should take an oath of allegiance and fidelity to the Government. In 1861 it became my duty as an officer to free from a Rebel party of which this man was a member. That party struck down and killed loyal men who were in the service of the Government; since that time it is notorious to all the officers of the army that the man now here introduced as a witness has openly borne arms against the United States, except when he has been a prisoner in the hands of the Government; I understand that it is proposed he shall testify before this Court; he comes here as a witness, with his hands red with the blood of his loyal countrymen, shot by him or by his assistants, in violation of his solemn oath as a man and as an officer; I submit, therefore, to this Court whether he does not stand in the eye of the law as an incompetent witness; I regard the offering as a witness of a man standing in open violation of the obligations of an oath administered to him as an officer as an insult to the Court, and an outrage upon the administration of justice; I move that this man, Edward Johnston, be ejected from the Court as an incompetent witness.
General Ekin—I rose to second the motion. I am glad that this question has now been presented to the Court. I regard this man as clearly incompetent as a witness. In my judgment, of all the men in this country, for those who have been educated by the Government, nourished by the Government, protected by the Government, and who have joined the enemies of the Government, to come into a Court of justice, and especially before a military commission of a character such as that here assembled, is the height of impertinence, and I trust the resolution which has been presented will be adopted by this commission without hesitation.
Mr. Aiken—Before the Commission decides upon the motion of Gen. Howe it is proper for me to say that I was not aware of the fact that because a person had borne arms against the Government it would disqualify and render him incompetent as a witness. Therefore, I could not, of course, have intended any insult in introducing Gen. Johnston as a witness. It will also be recollected that at least one witness who has borne arms against the Government was introduced here by the Judge Advocate without objection of any member of the Court.
General Kautz—Q. Does this person appear here as a volunteer witness?
Mr. Aiken—He does not.
The Judge Advocate-General—I feel bound to say, that as a rule of law, before a witness be rendered so infamous as to become absolutely incompetent to testify he must be convicted by judicial proceeding, and the record of that proceeding must be produced as the basis of his incompetency; without that condition any evidence of his guilt only applies to his credibility. This court can discredit him as far as they please upon that ground, but I do not think the law would authorize the Court to declare this witness incompetent, however unworthy he may be of credibility.
General Lew Wallace—I hope, for the sake of the character of this investigation, and for the sake of public justice, not for that of the person introduced as a witness, but for that of the prisoners at the bar, now on trial, the officer making the motion will withdraw it.
General Howe—Upon the statement of the Judge Advocate-General that this person is not technically an incompetent witness, I withdraw the motion.
By Mr. Aiken—Q. What is your present status as a prisoner of war? A. I am a United States prisoner of war, captured at Nashville, now confined at Fort Warren, in Boston harbor.
Q. Were you or were you not an officer in the so-called Confederate service, and, if so, of what rank? A. I was a Brigadier-General in the Confederate States army from the year 1873 up to the date of my capture.
Q. Did you have a higher rank than that? A. I did.
Q. Are you acquainted with Henry Steinacker? A. I am acquainted with a man who went by that name and who represented himself to me as Henry Von Steinecker.
Q. Was he a member of your staff? A. He was not.
Q. Did he rank as an engineer officer, and receive pay as such? A. He did not rank as an officer, neither as an engineer, staff, or line officer; he was a private.
Q. To what regiment and company did he belong? A. He belonged to the Stonewall Brigade, Second Virginia Infantry, I think; I am not positive on that point; I do not remember the company.
Q. Was the Second Virginia Infantry attached to your division? A. It was part of the Stonewall Brigade, and that was one of the brigades of my division.
Q. State to the Court how, when, and under what circumstances Von Steinacker presented himself to you. A. In the month of May, 1863, a man accosted me in Richmond, in Capitol Square, by my name and the rank I bore in the United States Army, as Major Johnston; he told me he had served under me—
Judge Bingham—What has that to do with it? there has been no inquiry made as to his services under you—
Witness—Well, he met me in Richmond and applied for a position in the Engineer Corps, stating that he had served under me previously; that he was a Prussian by birth, and an engineer by education, and he would like to get in the Engineer Corps in our service.
Judge Bingham—You need not tell what he said.
Witness—He applied to get into our service; I had no such position to give, and declined giving it, and he left me; he called again and made a second application for the position; I told him I could not give it to him; I was then ordered off to Fredericksburg, and in about a week this man appeared there again, and made application for a position either in the Engineer Corps or on my staff; I told him I could not give him a position in either, but that if he would enlist as a private, from his representations of himself as an engineer and a draughtsman, I would put him on duty in the Engineer Corps as a private; on these conditions he enlisted as a private in the Stonewall Brigade, Second Virginia Infantry, and I assigned him to special duty at headquarters; he was to act as draughtsman and assist my engineer officer, and he so continued to act till I was told he had left.
Q. Was he subjected to court-martial at that time?
Question objected to by Judge Bingham, on the ground that records of courts-martial must be produced, and he did not think there were any courts down in Virginia in these days that could try at all.
Mr. Aiken stated that, as under the circumstances the records of the court could not be produced, parole evidence could be admitted, and he presumed the question was not seriously objected to.

TRIAL OF THE ASSASSINS AT WASHINGTON.

The objection was sustained by the Court.

Q. Where in Virginia was your encampment after the battle of Gettysburg? A. Near Orange Court House.

Q. Do you know or not of a meeting of the officers of that brigade at the camp of the Second Virginia Regiment? A. I know nothing of it, and never heard anything of the kind.

Q. Did you ever learn the fact that a secret meeting was held there at that time? A. I never heard of any such secret meeting.

Q. Did you ever at any meeting of the officers of your division hear plans discussed for the assassination of the President of the United States? A. I never heard any plans discussed in any meeting of t. e officers, nor did I ever hear the assassination of the President alluded to by any individuals in my division.

Q. Are you acquainted with J. Wilkes Booth, the actor? A. I am not; I never saw him.

Q. Look at that picture (Booth's) and see if you ever saw the man? A. Never, to my knowledge; I did not know, in fact, there was such a man until after the assassination of President Lincoln.

Q. Have you a personal knowledge of the fact of Lieutenant David Cockerill losing a horse?

Judge Bingham—I object. We do not propose the question of horse stealing here, it is not in the issue.

Mr. Aiken—The charge was made in the paper presented that Von Steinacker had been guilty of horse stealing, and I understood we were to be permitted to prove any allegations in that paper.

Colonel Burnett—Anything that is legitimate and competent to be proved. We did not go further.

The objection was sustained by the Court.

Q. Did you ever learn anything while at the South of a secret association by the name of 'The Knights of the Golden Circle," or "Sons of Liberty?" A. I never belonged to any such association myself, and never knew any one who was reputed to belong to them, and never knew anything of them.

Q. While in Richmond have you heard it freely spoken of in the street and among your acquaintances that the assassination of the President of the United States was a desirable result to be accomplished? A. I never heard it spoken of as a desirable object to be accomplished; in fact, as I said before, I never heard any officer or person allude to the assassination of the President as desirable, to the best of my recollection.

Q. Was Von Steinacker a member of Gen. Blenker's staff? A. Not that I know of; he told me that he was.

Q. Did he state to you that he was a deserter from our service? A. He stated to me that he had deserted or attempted to desert, and was apprehended.

Cross-examined by Judge Bingham.—Q. Have you ever been in the service of the United States? A. I have.

Q. Were you educated at the United States Military Academy? A. Yes sir.

Q. How long had you been in the army of the United States? A. I graduated in 1858.

Q. And had been in our army down to the breaking out of the Rebellion? A. Yes sir.

Q. What was your rank in the army at that time? A. Captain and Brevet Major of the Sixth United States Infantry.

Q. State how you got out of the service of the United States. A. I tendered my resignation, which was accepted.

Q. Tendered it to whom? A. To the Adjutant General of the United States; I tendered it in May, 1861; it was not accepted for three or four weeks; I received the acceptance of my resignation in June following.

Q. Did you then enter into the Rebel service. A. I went to my home in Virginia, where I remained a few weeks; I then entered the Confederate States' service, and have been in it ever since.

Q. What was the final rank held by you in that army? A. Major-General.

Q. Were you a Major-General in 1865? A. I was for a part of 1865; I think my rank as Major-General commenced in February of that year.

Testimony of Mrs. Mary E. Jenkins.

Examined by Mr. Stone.—Q. State whether you know David E. Harold. A. Yes, I know him.

Q. Can you state whether he was or was not in Washington on the 18th of last February? A. He was at my house on the 18th and received my rent; I have his receipt to show.

Testimony of Mrs. Potts.

Examined by Mr. Stone—Q. State whether you know one of the accused, David E. Harold. A. Yes.

Q. State to the Court whether he was or was not in Washington on the 20th of February last. A. I cannot state whether he was or was not; he came to my house on the 19th, and I told him I would send the money to the house, which I did; I did not see him the next day; he used to come to my house, and when I would not be prepared to see him I would tell him I would send the money to his house; his receipt was dated the 20th of February.

Testimony of the Rebel Major H. K. Douglass.

Examined by Mr. Aiken.—Q. State to the Court whether you ever held a commission in the so-called Confederate service? A. I have, several; my last commission was that of Major and A. A. G.; I served as such on the staff of six general officers, and among others on that of Major-General Edward Johnston.

Q. Are you acquainted with Henry Von Steinacker? A. I know a man by the name of Von Steinacker; I do not know what his first name is.

Q. Was he or not a private in your service; and if so, in what regiment? A. He was in the Second Virginia Infantry, Stonewall Brigade.

Q. Did he receive the pay, bounty and allowances of a private? A. I don't know.

Q. Do you recollect, after the return of your army from Gettysburg, where it was encamped. A. I was wounded at Gettysburg, and left in the hands of the enemy; I was a prisoner for nine months.

Q. When you returned to camp did you meet Von Steinacker again? A. I do not remember seeing him again. I got a letter from him immediately after I returned to camp.

Q. Do you know of any secret meetings ever being held in your camp, at which the assassination of President Lincoln was discussed? A. No I do not.

Q. Were you acquainted with J. Wilkes Booth, the actor? A. No.

By the Court.—Q. Were you ever in the United States service? A. I was not; with the permission of the Court I would like to make a statement. General Howe, "I object to the *prisoner* making any statement." General Foster, "I hope the witness will be allowed to make his statement." The President, "If no further objection is made the witness will proceed with his statement.

Witness, "I just wish to say to the Court, understanding that evidence has been given by which implication has been cast on the 'Stonewall' Brigade," that as a man who has held positions in that brigade as private, and line and staff officer, I think their integrity as men, equal to their reputation for gallantry as soldiers, would forbid them to be employed as night assassins of President Lincoln. In their behalf I only wish to say that I do not believe they knew anything about or in the least sympathized in any such unrighteous or unsoldierly action."

Testimony of Oscar Henricks.

Examined by Mr. Aiken—Q. Have you been in the service of the so-called Confederate States. A. I have as engineer officer at one time on the staff of General Edward Johnston, and at others that of different General officers.

Q. State whether you are acquainted with Henry Von Steinacker? A. I am.

Q. When and under what circumstances did that commence? A. He was detailed by me as draughtsman immediately after General Johnston took command.

Q. Was he employed as such? A. I employed him as such.

Q. Did he ever have the rank or pay of an Engineer officer? A. He did not.

Q. Are you acquainted with J. Wilkes Booth, the actor? A. I am not.

Q. Did you ever see a person calling himself by that name in camp? A. No sir.

Q. Do you know of any secret meetings of officers ever taking place in your camp, at which the assassination of President Lincoln was discussed? A. None ever did take place.

Q. Did you ever learn the fact that Von Steinacker was a member of General Blenker's Staff?

Question objected to by Judge Bingham, and withdrawn.

Q. Did you ever learn the fact of his deserting the service of the United States?

Question, objected to by Judge Bingham, and withdrawn.

Q. Do you know that fact? A. I do not, only from his statements and acknowledgments on several occasions to me.

Q. Have you ever heard of or been cognizant of a secret treasonable society, for the purpose of the assassination of the President of the United States? A. I am not cognizant of any, nor have I ever heard of any.

Q. Were any members of your staff or yourself members of an organization known as Knights of the Golden Circle or Sons of Liberty. A. So far as I am concerned I never have been, nor do I know of any of the others having been.

Q. Have you heard declarations made in Richmond to the effect that President Lincoln ought to be assassinated? A. I have not.

Testimony of Thomas C. Nott.

Examined by Mr. Aiken—Q. Where do you reside and what is your occupation? A. I reside in Prince George county, and have been tending bar at Mrs. Surratt's place for Mr. Floyd.

Q. Did you see Mr. Floyd on the 14th of last April? A. Yes sir, I saw him in the morning of that day, and also just before sunset.

Q. What was his condition at that time? A. He was pretty tight when I saw him; he was going around to the kitchen in a buggy; he had been to Marlboro', and was carrying round there some fish and oysters; I did not see him when he came back, and the next I saw of him he was fixing a buggy Mrs. Surratt was in.

Q. Had he been for weeks before drinking a good deal? A. Yes, he had been tight pretty nearly every day and night too.

Q. Did he really have the appearance of an insane man? A. He did at times.

Cross-examined by Judge Bingham.—Q. Did you see him tie the buggy of Mrs. Surratt? A. With assistance he did; I do not know whether Mr. Floyd, Mr. Weichman or Captain Gwynn tied it; they were all there; I was not present at the buggy; I saw them fixing it, and that is all I saw; I was across the street, returning from the stable.

Q. And do you know how tight a man is by looking across the street? A. No; I was with him after that, nearly all night.

By Mr. Clampitt.—Q. Do or do you not know whether Mr. Floyd attended Court at Marlboro' that day? A. He did.

Q. Where did you first see him that afternoon? A. Driving around the kitchen; he came round to the front of the house while Mrs. Surratt was there.

Q. Did you hear any conversation that took place between Mr. Floyd and Mrs. Surratt? A. I did not.

Q. How close were you to the buggy? A. Probably fifteen or twenty yards off.

By Judge Bingham.—Q. What Captain Gwynn was that who was at Mrs. Surratt's buggy? A. Captain Ben. Gwynn.

Q. Upon reflection do you not recollect that he had gone he ore Mrs. Surratt came? A. I do not recollect anything of the kind.

Testimony of J. Z. Jenkins.

Examined by Mr. Aiken.—Q. Where do you reside? A. In Prince George county.

Q. Were you or were you not at Surrattsville on the 14th of April last? A. I was.

Q. Are you acquainted with Lewis J. Weichman? A. Yes.

Q. Were you at Surrattsville at the time he drove up to the house with Mrs. Surratt? A. Yes.

Q. Did Mrs. Surratt or not at that time show you a letter? A. She did, from George Calvert.

Q. Did she show you any other papers? A. She showed two judgments obtained by Charles B. Calvert in the Circuit Court of our county, against Mr. Surratt.

Q. Do you know, of your own knowledge, whether that business brought Mrs. Surratt to Surrattsville that day? A. I only know she showed me this letter and judgments.

Q. Did you transact any business for Mrs. Surratt that afternoon? A. I made the interest due on the judgments.

Q. Did she express to you during her entire stay at Surrattsville that day any wish or desire to see John M. Floyd? A. She did not.

Q. Were you at the place when Mr. Floyd drove up? A. Yes.

Q. What was his condition at that time? A. He was very much intoxicated.

Q. Was Mrs. Surratt upon the point of going away when Floyd drove up? A. Yes: she had been ready to start for some time before Floyd drove up; she had business with Captain Gwynn, and when he came she went back and stopped.

Q. At what time did you leave? A. About sundown, I judge.

Q. Have you, during the last year or two, been on terms of intimacy with Mrs. Surratt? A. Yes sir.

Q. Have you, in all your intercourse with her, heard her breathe a word of disloyalty to the Government? A. Not to my knowledge.

Q. Have you at any time ever heard her make any remark or remarks showing her to have a knowledge of any plan or conspiracy to assassinate the President, or any member of the Government? A. No sir.

Q. Have you ever heard her mention at any time any plan for the capture of the President? A. I have not.

Q. Have you been frequently at the house of Mrs. Surratt when Union troops were passing? A. Yes sir.

Q. From your personal knowledge of the transactions that occurred there and there, can you state whether or not she was in the habit of giving them milk, tea, and such other nourishment as she had in the house? A. Yes, frequently.

Q. Was she in the habit of receiving pay for it? A. Sometimes she did and sometimes she did not.

Q. Do you recollect on or about the time of a large number of horses escaping from Giesboro' whether or not any of them were taken up and kept on her premises? A. Some of them, I disremember how many.

Q. Were these horses fed and kept by her or not? A. Yes.

Q. Were they all given up? A. Every one.

Q. Do you know whether she took a receipt for them? A. She received a receipt, but never got any pay.

Q. Can you state whether you ever knew Mrs. Surratt to commit any overt act of any description against the Government? A. I never did.

Q. Was it not Mrs. Surratt's constant habit to express warm sympathy for the sick and wounded of our army? A. I do not remember ever hearing her say anything about that.

Q. Do you know of a defective eyesight on her part? A. I have been present when she would be unable to read or sew by gaslight; this has been the fact for several years.

Q. Do you recollect on any occasion of her failing to recognize immediately friends who were near her? A. I do not recollect any.

Q. Do you not recollect that on one occasion Mrs. Surratt gave the last ham she had to Union soldiers? A. I do not.

Q. Do you know of a person by the name of A. S. Howell? A. Yes, I have seen him; he stopped at the hotel, I think twice.

By Mr. Clampitt.—Q. Did you or not, meet Mrs. Surratt on the Tuesday preceding the assassination? A. I can't say on Tuesday; it was a few days before.

Q. When you met her did not you ask for the news, and did not she state in reply that our army had captured General Lee's army?

The question was objected to by Colonel Burnett, as irrelevant.

Mr. Clampitt said he desired to show that the prisoner at that time, exhibited a loyal feeling in the matter.

Colonel Burnett replied that the only legitimate means of proving loyalty were to prove her reputation for and acts of loyalty; these could not be proved by her declarations.

Mr. Clampitt replied that as the Government had endeavored to prove the disloyalty of the accused, he thought it was competent to prove her loyalty, but he would nevertheless vary his question, and ask the witness what was the reputation of Mrs. Surratt for loyalty? A. Very good.

Q. You have never heard her express any disloyal sentiment? A. No sir.

Cross-examined by Colonel Burnett.

Q. What relation are you to the prisoner, Mrs. Surratt? A. She is my sister.

Q. Where did you reside while she was living at Surrattsville? A. About a mile and a half this side, and I have been residing there since.

Q. Are you now under arrest? A. I am. I was arrested and brought here last Thursday week.

Q. Where were you on the evening of the day previous to your arrest? A. At Lloyd's Hotel.

Q. Did you meet at that place Mr. Coltenback? A. Yes.

Q. Did you have any conversation with him at that time in reference to this trial? A. Yes, sir, we were talking about the trial.

Q. Did you meet a man by the name of Cottingham there? A. Yes, I went there with him.

Q. At the time you met Coltenback, what was said about the trial in reference to the witnesses summoned against Mrs. Surratt? A. I think I told him I would look at the paper and see.

Q. Anything else? A. Not that I know of; I might have told him that my sister found his family.

Q. What relevancy had that to the conversation? A. I disremember how the conversation commenced.

Q. Did you at that time and place say to Mr. Coltenback that if he, or any one like him, undertook to testify against your sister, you would see that they were got out of the way? A. I did not say anything of the kind.

Q. Did you say you would send any man to hell who testified against your sister? A. I did not.

Q. Did you use any threats against him if he appeared as a witness against your sister? A. No, nothing like that.

Q. State what you did say on that subject? A. I told him I understood he was a witness, and he was to be a strong witness against my sister, and I told him he ought to be as she had raised his family.

Q. Did you call him a liar? A. I disremember.

Q. Was there any quarrel exhibited in that conversation? A. I did not mean it if there was.

Q. Did you have any talk about John Surratt having returned from Richmond? A. Not to my knowledge.

Q. Did you talk about John H. Surratt's going to Richmond or mention anything about a paper showed you that he had been to Richmond? A. No, I never mentioned John Surratt's name.

Q. Did you see the letter found by Mr. Collenbach in the bar? A. I did not.

Q. How did you learn that Mr. Collenbach was to be a witness? A. He told me himself.

Q. When did you come in front of a witness? A. I think about ten o'clock: I went in with Mr. Cottingham.

Q. Did you or did you not use any threat against Mr. Collenbach? A. Not to my knowledge.

Q. Wouldn't you know it if you had? A. I think I ought to; I do not think I did use any, only in reference to the public press; I told him I would look at his statement.

Q. And if you found in the public press that he had testified against your sister what did you say? A. I do not recollect.

Q. On the evening of the 14th, when you saw Mr. Floyd and Mrs. Surratt and Gwynn, how long had you been at Floyd's house? A. I judge it was about two

o'clock when I got there, and I stayed till about sundown, or a little after.
Q. How many persons did you see there during that time? A. I suppose from ten to fifteen.
Q. Did Gwynn leave before Mrs. Surratt did? A. I think he did.
Q. Do you recollect whether he saw Mrs. Surratt on that occasion or not? A. He did see her in the parlor; I went in at the door as he spoke to her.
Q. Who was in there? A. Mr. Weichman, I think.
Q. Did you see Gwynn come out? A. I do not recollect that I did see him when he left the house and went home.
Q. Did you hear the conversation between him and Mrs. Surratt? A. No, I did not go into the parlor while they were conversing.
Q. You have been asked here as to Mrs. Surratt's loyalty? What has been your attitude towards the Government during this war? A. Perfectly loyal, I think.
Q. How did you stand when the question of the secession of Maryland was under discussion? A. I spent $500 to hold her in the Union, and everybody in that neighborhood will testify.
Q. Have you never taken part in any way against the Government during the entire war? A. Never by act, word, aid or sympathy with the Rebels.
By Mr. Aiken—Q. State if you know for what you are under arrest? A. I do not.
Q. State if you had any conversation with Mr. Cottingham about a $20000 reward? A. Our Commissioners had offered $1000 reward to any party who would give information on the subject of the assassination; he claimed it for the arrest of John M. Floyd, and asked me if I would see the Commissioners and ascertain whether he would get it or not.
Q. When you stated to Collenback that he ought to be a stirring witness against your sister, because she had brought up his children, did you mean it, or did you speak ironically? A. I did not mean it at all.
Q. Is it a fact that Mrs. Surratt did rear that family? A. Partially so.

Testimony of Anna E. Surratt.

Q. State your full name. A. Anna E. Surratt.
Q. Are you under arrest at the present time? A. Yes sir.
Q. When were you arrested? A. On the 17th of April.
Q. Are you acquainted with Atzeroth? A. I have met him several times.
Q. Where? A. At our house in Washington city.
Q. When did he first come there? A. Sometime after Christmas; I think it was in February.
Q. How long did he remain there then? A. He did not stay over night, to my knowledge; he used to call sometimes now and then.
Q. Can you state from your own knowledge whether or not Atzeroth was given to understand that he was not wanted at the house? A. Yes, sir; mamma said she did not care to have strangers there, but we treated him with politeness, as we did every one who came to the house.
Q. Do you or do you not know of frequent instances in which Mrs. Surratt failed to recognize her friends? A. Yes sir.
Q. Is she able to read or sew by gaslight? A. No sir.
Q. Have you not often plagued her about wearing spectacles? A. I told her she was too young-looking to get spectacles yet, and she said she could not see to read or sew without them of dark mornings; she could read some, but she seldom sewed on a dark day.
Q. Do you know Lewis J. Weichman? A. Yes.
Q. Was he a boarder at your mother's house? A. Yes sir.
Q. How was he treated there? A. Too kindly.
Q. Was it or not your mother's habit to sit up and wait for him when he was out late? A. Yes; just as she would wait for my brother; Weichman engaged a room for Atzeroth; when he came Weichman and he used to make private signs to each other.
Q. Did you refer to Atzeroth or Payne? A. To Atzeroth.
Q. At what time did Payne first come to your house? A. He came one night after dark, and left early the next morning.
Q. How long was that before the assassination? A. It was after Christmas, not very long after.
Q. How many times did he come there? A. He stayed one night when he first came and we did not see him again for some weeks; it was Weichman who went to the door, and it was Weichman who brought Payne in there; I went down stairs and told mamma he was there, and she said she did not understand and did not like strangers coming to the house, but to treat him politely as she had been in the habit of treating every one who came; he called two or three times after that.
Q. Did he ask for accommodations for the night? A. Yes sir; and he said he would leave the next morning, and I believe he did.
Q. Were you acquainted with Booth? A. Yes sir, I have met him.
Q. When was he last at your house? A. On the Monday before the assassination.
Q. Did your mother go to Surrattsville about that time? Yes sir; on Friday, the day of the assassination.
Q. Do you know whether or not the carriage was at

the door ready to go when Booth came? A. Yes, I think he came and found her about to go: she had been speaking about going a day or two before or that on a matter of business, and she said she was obliged to go.
Q. How long did Booth remain? A. Not over a few minutes: he never stayed long when he came.
Q. Do you recognize that picture as ever belonging to you? (The picture known in this record as "Spring, Summer, and Autumn" was shown to the witness.) A. Yes sir, it was mine; it was given to me by Mr. Weichman.
Q. Was there any other picture in this frame? A. I put one of Booth's behind it. I went to a gallery with Miss Ward, and while we were there we saw some of Booth's, and as we know him; we got some of them, but my brother told me that he would take them away from me and so had them.
Q. Do you recollect any photographs of Davis and Stephens? A. Yes sir, and General Lee and General Beauregard and a few others; I don't remember them all.
Q. Where did you get them? A. Father gave them to me before his death, and I prized them very highly on his account.
Q. Did you have no photographs of Union Generals? A. Yes sir; of General McClellan, General Grant and Joe Hooker.
Q. Do you recollect the last time you saw your brother? A. Yes sir.
Q. How long was that before the assassination? A. On the Monday before it was two weeks.
Q. Have you seen him since? A. No sir.
Q. Was he and your brother on friendly terms? A. I never asked him; he used to call to see him sometimes; one day I know he said Booth was crazy, and he wished he would not come there.
Q. Where was your brother in 1861? A. At college.
Q. What college? A. St. Charles College.
Q. Was he a student there at that time? A. Yes sir; but not of divinity.
Q. How long was your brother at that college? A. For three years; but he spent his vacations at home in August.
Q. Miss Surratt, did you at your mother's house, at any time, on any occasion, ever hear a word breathed as to any plot, or plan, or conspiracy in existence to assassinate the President of the United States? A. No sir.
Q. Did you ever hear any remarks made with reference to the assassination of any member of the Government? A. No sir.
Q. Did you ever hear it discussed by any member of the family to capture the President of the United States? A. No sir, I did not; where is mamma?
By Mr. Ewing—Q. What year did your brother leave college? A. In 1861 or 1862; the year my father died; (sotto voce) where is mamma?
Q. What year were you in school at Bryantown? A. From 1854 to 1861; the 16th of July was the day I left.
Q. Did you ever see Dr. Mudd at your mother's house at Washington? A. No sir.
The girl here kept nervously glancing towards the dock, and tapping the stand with her foot impatiently. The counsel, Mr. Ewing, with an evident desire to keep her occupied till the usher came to lead her through the crowd to the witness room, said to her:—Is Surratt's wife on the road between Washington and Bryantown?
By this time the usher had arrived, and the Court told her that she could go. As she arose she answered the question in the affirmative, adding, in a quick, sharp voice, "Where is mamma?"
Mr. Aiken came forward, and, telling her that she would soon see her mamma, led her on into the anteroom adjoining court.
As Miss Surratt was leaving the stand a member of the Court handed her a small white pocket handkerchief, which she had dropped; she snatched it from him quickly and rudely, without a word of thanks. On cross-examination was had of this witness, and when, with reportorial curiosity, we asked the reasons why, the most technical and dry of the judges advocate simply told us it would have been cruel, the girl having a greater load of sorrow upon her than she could bear.

Testimony of Lemons.

Q. State whether you know Atzeroth. A. I do sir.
Q. How long have you known him? A. Since he was a boy.
Q. Were you at the house of Hezekiah Mentz on the Sunday after the assassination? A. I was sir.
Q. Did you see the prisoner there? A. Yes sir.
Q. Did you have any conversation with him. A. Yes sir.
Q. State what the conversation was. A. I met Atzeroth at Mentz's between 11 and 12 o'clock on the Sabbath after this affair had occurred, and when first I approached Mr. Atzeroth I said, are you the man that killed Abe Lincoln? and says he, yes; and then we both laughed; we was joking; well, says I, Andrew, I want to know the truth, is it so that the President is killed? there was a great excitement in the neighborhood and I wanted to know; he said, it is so, and that he died on Saturday at 3 o'clock; I went on to ask him

if it was so about the Seward's; about the old man having his throat cut; he said yes; that Seward was stabbed, or rather cut at, but not killed; I asked him whether it was correct about Mr. Grant; he said he did'nt know whether it was so or not, and we went to dinner, and at the dinner table my brother asked him if Mr. Grant was killed, and he said he did'nt suppose he was, and said if it had been done it was probably by some man who got into the same train or car that he did; I was not in his company over a half an hour.
Q. Did you hear him say that if the man who was to follow Grant had followed him he would have been killed? A. No, he said if Mr. Grant was to have been killed it must have been by a man who got into the same car or into the same train of the two.
Q. Was or was not the prisoner during that day very much excited? A. Well, he was confused or appeared so at the dinner table, and there was something between the young lady and him that he had been paying his attentions to.
Q. Was he paying his addresses to the daughter of Mr. Mentz? A. Yes sir, he had been.
Q. Was she or not throwing him the cold shoulder that day? A. Yes sir, it appeared so.
Q. And he was down in the mouth about it, was he? A. Yes sir.
Q. Were you with the prisoner all the time he was speaking with Mentz that day? A. No sir.
Q. He could not at the dinner table make any remark without your hearing? A. No sir.
By Colonel Burnett.—Q. Did you have any other talk with Atzeroth that day? A. No sir.
Q. Didn't you walk down with him to the stable? A. No sir, that was my brother.

Testimony of Mr. Lemons, (Brother of the Foregoing Witness.)

Q. Do you know Atzeroth? A. Yes sir.
Q. How long have you known him? A. Some eighteen months or two years.
Q. Were you at the house of Mr. Mentz on the Sunday after the assassination? A. Yes sir.
Q. Did you have any conversation with the prisoner then? A. I asked him about Mr. Grant, Mr. General Grant, and asked him if it was so or not; he said he did'nt suppose it was, and then he said, if it is so some one must have got into the same train of cars he did; when me and him were in the yard, after that, he said, what a lot of trouble I see; I said, what have you to trouble you? he said, more than I shall ever get shed of; that was about all that he said.

Testimony of Mr. McAlister.

Q. Do you know Atzeroth? A. Yes sir.
Q. How many years have you known him? A. Only since March last.
Q. State whether or not, on the 14th day of March, he called at your house and took a drink. A. Yes sir; about ten o'clock; I don't know the exact time.
Q. Did you notice whether he was excited or not? A. I did not.
Q. What do you know about his being a coward or a brave man? A. I have heard men say that he would not resent an insult.

Testimony of W. W. Brisco.

Q. How long have you known Atzeroth? A. Six or seven years, at Port Tobacco.
Q. What is his reputation for bravery? A. He was always considered a man of not much courage.

Testimony of James Keller.

Q. State whether you are the proprietor of the livery stable on E street, near the corner of Eighth. A. Yes sir, one of them.
Q. State whether or not you let Atzeroth have a horse on the 14th of April, out of your stable? A. Yes, a small bay mare, fourteen and a half hands high; he got the horse about half-past three o'clock.
Q. Did the prisoner write his name on the slate? A. He did, sir, but my partner rubbed off the contents of the slate a few days after.
Q. Did he write it in a small or large hand? A. In a tolerable hand.
Q. Did he hesitate to put his name down? A. No sir.
Q. Did you require any reference? A. Yes sir.
Q. Did he give you any? A. Yes sir.
Q. Who did he give you? A. A number of persons in Maryland, and some at Port Tobacco.
Q. Any names in Washington? A. Yes sir.
Q. Who? A. John Cook was one.
Q. Where does Mr. Cook live? A. Right opposite me.
Q. Did you go there and inquire after Atzeroth? A. Yes sir.
Q. When was that horse returned? A. I can't say; I did not stay till he returned.
Q. Did he pay for the horse? A. Yes sir; he paid me five dollars.

Testimony of Samuel Smith.

Q. Are you stable-boy at Keller's stable? A. Yes sir.
Q. Did you ever see the prisoner before? A. No sir.

Q. Were you in the stables on the night of the 14th of April? A. Yes sir.
Q. Did the bay mare come in that night? A. Yes sir.
Q. What time? A. To the best of my knowledge, eleven o'clock; we have a clock there, but it isn't going.
Q. What condition was the mare in? A. Pretty much as she was when she went out.
Q. Did she look as if she had been ridden hard? A. No sir.
Q. Was there no foam on her? A. No sir. (Mr. McAllister was here recalled, and having testified that he had seen a pistol and a dirk knife in the possession of Atzeroth, and that he had kept the same for him one day, he was shown the knife and pistol said to have been found in the alleged coat of Atzeroth, but declares himself unable to positively identify either. The pistol he knew was not the same.)

Testimony of Miss Harold.

Q. Are you the prisoner's sister? A. I am, sir.
The witness was then shown the coat and the handkerchief found in the coat alleged to have been taken from Atzeroth's room, but she could not identify either as the property of her brother.

Testimony of Captain F. Monroe.

Q. State whether you had custody of the prisoners at the bar subsequent to their arrest. A. Yes sir.
Q. Where? A. On board the monitors.
Mr. Donner then desired to hand into court a written request from the prisoner Atzeroth that his confession to Captain F. Monroe be admitted.
Counsel stated that he was aware that he had no legal right to insist upon this and that he merely made a question for the liberality of the Court to decide.
Judge Holt then remarked:—"I think it is greatly to be deplored that counsel will urge such matters on this Court as they know and admit to be contrary to law."
The Court then decided that the confession should not be received, and Captain F. Monroe was, therefore, dismissed from the stand.
Charles Sullivan, ex-Governor Farwell, and others, were then called on the part of the defense; but they not being present, the Court adjourned till ten o'clock to-morrow morning.

WASHINGTON, May 31.—Before the Court to-day, the following evidence was elicited:—

Testimony of Hartman Richler.

By Mr. Doster.—Q. State your residence. A. I reside in Montgomery county, Maryland.
Q. Are you a cousin of the prisoner Atzeroth? A. I am.
Q. State whether the prisoner came to your house subsequent to the assassination of the President. A. He came there on Sunday evening.
Q. Give the particulars of his visit. A. I met him as I was on my way to the Church; he remained in my house from Sunday evening until Thursday morning, about 3 or 4 o'clock, and during that time he did not make any attempt to hide himself, but walked about and worked in the garden a little.
Q. Did you notice anything peculiar about his appearance when you first met him? A. No sir: he looked the same as he always did when he came to see me.
Q. Were you present at his arrest? A. When he was arrested in the house I was down stairs, and he was up stairs.
Q. Did he hesitate to go when they arrested him? A. He was very willing to go.
Q. Do you know whether he was in possession of a large quantity of money? A. I do not.
Q. Do you know anything about his reputation for courage? A. No sir.
Q. Did the prisoner have on an overcoat when he came to your house? A. When we arrested him in the morning he had on the same coat as he has now; it was a kind of grey overcoat.
Mr. Doster then stated to the Court that all of the witnesses summoned in the case of Atzeroth were not present, and that he could not proceed in the order he desired until they were present. He intended to set up the plea of insanity, and had sent for friends and relatives of the prisoner, who were to be brought several thousand miles distant, who had not arrived.
The defense then proceeded with the cases of the other prisoners.

Testimony of William S. Arnold.

By Mr. Ewing.—Q. What relation are you to the prisoner, Samuel Arnold? A. I am his brother.
Q. Where do you reside? A. At Hookstown, Montgomery county, Md.

TRIAL OF THE ASSASSINS AT WASHINGTON.

Q. State what you know, if anything, as to the whereabouts of the prisoner from the 20th of March last to the 1st of April? A. From the 21st of March until Saturday, the 25th, he remained in the country; he then went to Baltimore, and returned on the 20th, going again to Baltimore on the 28th or 29th; on the afternoon of the 1st of April he started for Fortress Monroe; while in Baltimore he stayed at his father's house, and I saw him at home almost all the time I was there.

On the cross-examination of the witness, which was conducted by Assistant Judge Advocate Burnett, he stated that the only means by which he knew that the prisoner came to Hookstown on the 21st, was the fact that he had purchased some farming utensils on that day, and made an entry of the purchase in a book which he kept at home. The pistol delivered to the witness by the prisoner on the 1st of April was loaded at the time. The prisoner had fired the loads out and reloaded it while in the country.

Testimony of Frank Arnold.

By Mr. Ewing.—This witness, in answer to a series of questions, testified that he was a brother of the prisoner, Samuel Arnold; that he lived in Baltimore county, and occasionally in the city, at his father's house; that the prisoner slept with him on the nights of the 30th and 31st of March; and that, having received a letter from a Mr. Wharton, at Fortress Monroe, to which gentleman he had made application for a situation, he started to go to the Fortress on Saturday afternoon, April 1st, about 4½ o'clock.

Testimony of Jacob Smith.

By Mr. Ewing.—The substance of the testimony of this witness may be summed up as follows:—He resides at Hookstown, Maryland, about half a mile from the residence of Wm. S. Arnold, brother of the prisoner, Samuel Arnold; saw the prisoner nearly every day between the 20th and 22d of March, and about the 1st of April, sometimes three or four times a day; occasionally at the house of his brother, and again while he would be crossing witness' farm.

Cross-examined by Assistant Judge Advocate Burnett.—I was not sure as to the day on which the prisoner came to Hookstown, having no means of ascertaining positively; he may have stayed until the 30th, or left before then.

Testimony of John T. Ford.

By Mr. Ewing.—Q. State where you reside. A. In the city of Baltimore.
Q. State whether or not you are the proprietor of Ford's Theatre, in the city of Washington. A. I am.
Q. Are you acquainted with the prisoner, Edward Spangler? A. I am.
Q. How long has he been in your employ? A. I think from three to four years, at intervals, over two years continuously.
Q. State whether you were in or about the theatre or in this city at the time of the assassination of the President. A. I was in the city of Richmond on the day of the assassination; I arrived there about two o'clock on that day.
Q. Were you acquainted with John Wilkes Booth? A. I have known him since early childhood, since he was ten or eleven years of age, and intimately for six or seven years.
Q. State whether you have ever heard Booth speak of Chester, and if so, in what connection?
Assistant Judge Advocate Bingham objected to the question, and it was not pressed.
Q. State whether Booth ever applied to you to employ Chester, who has been a witness for the prosecution, in your theatre?
Assistant Judge Advocate Bingham objected to the question.
Mr. Ewing stated that the object of the inquiry was not to attack Chester, but rather to corroborate his assertions, and to show that at the same time that Booth was endeavoring to induce Chester to join a conspiracy for the capture of the President, he was also endeavoring to induce Mr. Ford to employ Chester, in order that when once in the theatre he (Booth) might use the man as an instrument. This would go to kill the case of several of the prisoners at the bar, particularly that of Arnold, who, in his confession, stated that the plan was the capture of the President; and also the case of the prisoner Spangler, by showing that Booth was not able to get in the theatre any instrument to assist him in his purpose.

Assistant Judge Advocate Bingham stated that a party who conspired to commit a crime might approach the most upright man in the land with whom, before his criminality was known, he might be on terms of intimacy. It was then the misfortune of such a man, not his crime, to be approached in that way, but it did not follow because Booth approached this man Chester, that he (Booth), either living or dead, was armed with the power of coming into a court of justice and proving what he said to that third person.

The objection was then sustained, and the question was not put.
Q. State what were the duties of the accused on the stage. A. The accused, Spangler, was employed as a stage hand, not as the stage carpenter; he was a laborer, and his duties were to assist in getting the scenery into place, and removing it from the grooves, as the necessities of a play required; those were his duties at night; during the day he was to assist in doing the rough carpenter work incidental to certain plays.
Q. State whether his duties were such as to require his presence upon the stage during the whole of the play. A. Strictly, no sir; his absence for a moment might impair the success of the play, and cause dissatisfaction among the audience; it is very important for the success of a play that the changing of the scenery should be attended to promptly from the rising to the falling of the curtain; there were intervals, it is true, but the prisoner could not judge exactly how long a scene might last.
Q. State whether his constant presence during the second scene of the third act of the American Cousin would be necessary. A. It would, unless he was accurately informed of the duration of that scene; it is rather a long scene; longer, perhaps, than any other of that act.
Q. How is it with the first scene? A. It is quick, but a few moments; the other eight or ten minutes.
Q. How is it with the second act? A. The duration of a scene, I would say, depends in a great degree upon the activity of the parties engaged in it; I hardly think there was an interval of more than five or eight minutes between those scenes.
Q. Therefore the constant presence of Spangler upon the stage would have been necessary? A. It would.
Q. What were his duties in the intervals between the scenes? A. To be prepared for the next change; to be ready with his scene and to remain at his post of duty, as an emergency often arises during the performance of an act requiring extra service on his part.
Q. State who had the regulation and control of the passage-way through which Booth escaped. A. The stage manager directs and the stage carpenter executes the work belonging to that part of the theatre, and the entire stage.
Q. State the names of those persons. A. John B. Wright was the stage manager, and James J. Gifford the stage carpenter.
Q. Was the prisoner (Spangler) charged with the duty of keeping the passage-way in order? A. It was no duty of his, unless specially assigned to him by the stage carpenter.
Q. State whether that passage-way is usually obstructed in any way. A. It should never be obstructed; my positive orders were to keep it clear and in the best order; it is a passage-way used by parties coming from the dressing-room and green-room, and in a play like that of the American Cousin, in which the ladies were in full dress, it was absolutely necessary for a proper performance that there should be no obstruction there.
Q. Do you know whether, as a matter of fact, that passage-way was kept clear by the stage manager? A. The stage manager was a very exact man in all those details; I have always found it clear, unless in the performance of some spectacular play, when at times it would be partly encumbered.
Q. State whether you ever knew Spangler to wear a moustache. A. I never did.

The witness was further examined, and the following testimony elicited:—The prisoner seemed to entertain a great admiration for Booth, who was a peculiarly fascinating man, and who seemed to exercise a control over the minds and actions of his inferiors; he excelled in gymnastic exercises, and his leap from the President's box to the stage was not one which required any rehearsal; he had often introduced a similar leap into the witch scene of Macbeth; since the latter part of September last, during the entire theatrical season, Booth frequently visited the theatre, and had his letters directed there; the prisoner (Spangler) had lived in Baltimore, and considered that place his home, usually spending his summer months in the neighborhood of that city, engaged in fishing and crabbing.

The rope found in Spangler's carpet bag was here shown to the witness, who testified that in his opinion it might have been used by the prisoner in catching crabs, though experienced crabbers used a much longer rope. He had seen such a rope used by amateurs. In regard to his visit to Richmond, the witness testified that his object in making the visit was to see an uncle, a very aged man, and a mother-in-law, who resided there. He had not heard of the assassination of the President until the Sunday evening following, while on his return.

Cross-examined by Judge Advocate Holt.—Could not say positively whether the private boxes in the theatre were ordinarily kept locked; Mr. Gifford, the stage carpenter, had control of such matters, and the keys of the boxes were kept by Mr. James O'Brien, the chief usher. The authorized parties having tickets for sale for those boxes on the day of the assassination were witness' brothers, James R. and Harry Clay Ford. The play of the American Cousin, when first introduced, was an exceedingly popular play, but of late years had drawn only fair audiences. From the characters of the two men, and their relations to each other, witness believed Booth to have been capable of exercising a great influence, either for good or evil, over the prisoner (Spangler).

The Court then took a recess till two o'clock, at which time the body reassembled.

Re-examination of Mr. Ferguson.

By Mr. Ewing.—Q. State whether directly after the assassination of the President you saw Mr. Stewart get upon the stage. A. I am not acquainted wit Mr. Stewart; after Booth passed off I saw a large man, in light clothes, with a moustache, jump upon the stage; a moment afterwards Miss Harris called for water in the box; this large man, whoever he was, turned around and looked towards the box; some one halloed, catch him; Miss Laura Keene ra'sed her hands and said; We have caught him, or, We will catch him; I then saw this man run out; it was probably two or three minutes after Booth run out before he jumped upon the stage.
Q. Had you seen anybody else run out before him? A. No one but this man Hawk.
Q. If any one had gone out before would you have seen him? A. I think so; I thought it was very singular that no one got on to the stage.
Cross-examined by Judge Bingham.—Q. On which side of the dress circle were you? A. On the right side; on the same side with the President's box.
Q. How near did you sit to the private boxes on that side? A. I went close to them, so near that I could not see what was passing below distinctly; I saw Laura Keene when she ran in.

Re-examination of Mr. Best.

By Mr. Ewing.—Q. State your business in Washington. A. I am manager of Grover's Theatre.
Q. State whether you were in the habit of seeing John Wilkes Booth during the last season, before the assassination of the President, and if so whether he made any inquiry of you with regard to the President attending the theatre? A. I have seen him about there frequently, and he made such an inquiry the day before the assassination; he came into the office some time during the afternoon of Thursday, and interrupted me and the prompter of the theatre in reading the manuscript; he seated himself in a chair and entered into a conversation upon the subject of the illumination; there was to be a general illumination of the city on Thursday; he asked me if I intended to illuminate; I told him I did to a certain extent, but my green illumination would be on the next night, in anniversary of the fall of Sumter; he asked me if I was going to invite the President; I think my reply was "yes, and that reminds me I must send that invitation;" I had had it in mind for several days to invite the Presidential party to attend on the night of the 14th.
Q. Did you invit'e the President? A. I sent Mrs. Lincoln an invitation; my notes were generally addressed to her as the best means of accomplishing the object.
Q. Was there anything marked in Booth's manner of making the inquiry? A. His manner struck me as rather peculiar; he must have observed that we were busy, and it was not usual to come in and disturb us; he pushed the matter so far that I got up, laid the manuscript away, and entered into conversation.
Q. State whether or not it is customary in theatres to keep the passage-way between the scenes and the green-room and dressing-room clear. A. Yes; its should be a point with the stage carpenter to keep the stage clear and the scenes put away; it depends somewhat upon how much room there is.
Q. Would you consider three feet a wide or a narrow passage? A. I should consider it rather narrow, but there are no two theatres alike in that respect; it would be more necessary to keep the passage clear if it was narrow than if it was wide, of course.
Q. Would you consider a leap from the second tier of boxes in Ford's Theatre to the stage an extraordinary or difficult one? A. From my present recollection I should say not very difficult.
Q. State what boxes the President was in the habit of occupying when he attended Grover's Theatre.
Question objected to by Judge Bingham as irrelevant.
Mr. Ewing stated that the object was to show that it was easier to escape from Ford's Theatre than Grover's, as the reason why Ford's was selected by Booth for the accomplishment of his purpose.
The objection was sustained by the Court.

Testimony of H. A. James.

By Mr. Ewing.—Q. State whether you were at Ford's Theatre when the President was assassinated. A. I was.
Q. State the position of Piersoff and Edward Spangler at the time it occurred, if you know what they were. A. I was standing on the stage ready to draw a flat, and Spangler was standing right opposite to me on the stage at the time I heard the shot fired off.
Q. From the position you were in could you see the President's box? A. I could not; neither could Spangler; he was standing behind the scenes; he was on the same side with the President's box, and I was on the opposite side.
Q. When the shot was fired did you see what he did? A. I did not; I didn't notice whether he removed away or remained.
Q. What did you do yourself? A. I really do not know what I did; I was excited at the time; I did not go anywhere; I was standing there behind the curtain.

Q. Which was nearer the door out of which Booth ran, you or Spangler? A. I think I was nearest the door, though there was very little difference.
Q. Did you see anybody near Spangler at the time? A. I did not.
Q. Had you seen him previously during the play? A. I had; every time the scene was to be changed I saw him at his post; I did not notice him at any other time.
Q. What was the condition of the passage-way at that time? A. It was clear; it was the business of Spangler and myself to keep it clear; perhaps more Spangler's business than mine.
Q. Do you know whether Spangler saw the President when he entered? A. Yes; I was standing opposite him; I heard the applause, and Spangler applauded, with them, both with his hands and feet; he seemed as pleased as anybody to see the President come in.

Testimony of F. H. Dooley.

By Mr. Doster—Q. State your business in this city. A. I keep a drug store on Seventh street, near the avenue.
Q. Examine these articles, both brush and liquorice, taken from Atzeroth, and see if your trade mark is upon either of the articles. A. It is not.

Testimony of H. L. Mudd.

By Mr. Ewing—Q. In your cross-examination day before yesterday, you stated that your brother, Dr. Samuel Mudd, was a tenant of your father; I wish you to sta'e what you mean by that? A. I was rather confused at the time, and do not know exactly what I meant; I suppose that to be a tenant a man must pay some rent; my brother never paid any rent nor any part of the proceeds of the farm.
Q. How do you know that? A. I know it very well; I kept all my father's accounts; the farm was always treated as my brother's.
Cross-examined by Colonel Burnside—Q. Did not the farm belong to your father? A. I considered that it belonged to my brother.
Q. Has he any title to it? A. No; my father has the title, but my brother has his word that it belongs to him.
Q. Has he any title to it? A. No; my father has the title, but my brother has his word that it belongs to him.

Examination of Dr. Davis.

By Mr. Stone.—Q. Where do you reside? A. In this city, near the Navy Yard.
Q. Have you ever been in the army? A. I was in the Quartermaster's Department on General Wood's staff during the Mexican war.
Q. Do you know the prisoner, Harold? A. I have known him from early youth; part of the time I lived next door to him, though for the last several years I have lived four or five squares from him.
Q. State what is his character. A. I do not know that I can state it in any better terms than that he is a boy; I consider that all his life there has been very little of the man about him; from my knowledge of him I should say that nature has not endowed him with as much intelligence as people generally have; I know his family well; I have always known them; I suppose he is about 22 years old.
Cross-examined by Judge Bingham.—Q. Do you think that Harold has intellect enough to know that it is a great crime to commit murder? A. He undoubtedly knows the difference between right and wrong.

Testimony of Henry Clay Ford.

By Mr. Ewing.—Q. What business were you engaged in immediately preceding the 14th of April last? A. I was treasurer of Ford's Theatre.
Q. When was it first known there that the President was coming to the theatre that night? A. It was known to me about half-past eleven o'clock; I had been to breakfast and came back, and then learned that the President had engaged a box.
Q. State whether J. Wilkes Booth was at the theatre after that on that day, and if so, at what time? A. He was there at twelve o'clock; about half an hour after I returned.
Q. State whether or not the fact that the President was coming to the theatre that night was communicated to Booth. A. I do not know; I did not tell him.
Q. Did you see anything of Booth afterwards that day? A. Not until evening.
Q. Did you see him when you were going to the theatre that day? A. No; I saw him coming down the street, I think, as I stood in the door of the theatre; he commenced talking to some parties there; one of them went to the office and brought out a letter, which he sat down and read with the steps of the office; this was about twelve o'clock, and he stayed, I should think, about half an hour.
Q. State what you know about the preparations of the theatre for the reception of the President that night? A. When I got to the theatre my brother told me the President was to be there that night; it was Mr. Raybold's business to see about the decorations of the box, but he took neura'gia in his face that day, and I fixed it up; I found two flags which I looped up and placed in position, then another flag came down from the Treasury Department, and I attended to the putting the new flag in the centre; I had a part of the furniture changed; a sofa and high-backed chair brought

from the stage, and a rocking chair brought from my sleeping-room. up stairs.

Q. Did you receive any suggestions from anybody as to the preparation of the box? A. Only from Mr. Raybold and from the gentleman who brought the third flag down there.

Q. What had Spangler to do with the decoration of the box? A. He took out the partition between the two boxes, leaving them both in one.

Q. Was it usual to remove the partition on such occasions? A. Yes, we always removed it when the President came there.

Q. How many times had the President been at your theatre during the winter and spring? A. I suppose about six times.

Q. How did Spangler come to go to the box? A. I suppose Mr. Raybold sent him.

Q. Was Spangler in the box during the time you were there decorating it? A. No, he was at work on the stage at that time; I called for a hamuner and nails, which he handed up to me.

Q. Do you know whether he was apprised of the fact that the President was to come there that evening? A. He knew the President was coming, for he took out the partition.

Q. Do you know whether there was any penknife used in the preparation of the President's box? A. I used a penknife in cutting a string by which the picture was tied; I forgot it and left it there.

Q. Had the picture been there before? A. No.

Q. Why was this chair brought from your sleeping room to the President's box? A. For nothing more than to put it with the other furniture; it was a part of the same set of furniture which was originally placed in the reception room; but the ushers were in the habit of lounging in it, and I took it into my room.

Q. Do you know whether Booth was in the habit of engaging any boxes at your theatre? A. Yes sir.

Q. What box is it that he was in the habit of engaging? A. The one he always engaged was number 7, which was part of the box occupied by the President nearest the audience.

Q. How often did he occupy that box during the season? A. He procured a box tour or five times; I do not know whether he ever occupied it or not.

Q. Do you know whether Booth's spur caught in one of the flags as he leaped from the box? A. I did hear that it caught in the blue flag in the centre; I do not know it.

Q. Who put that flag there? A. I did; it was the one obtained from the Treasury building.

Q. Was there anything special or unusual in the arrangement of that box? A. The picture had never been placed in front of the box before; we mostly used smaller flags, but as General Grant was to come with the President that night, we borrowed those flags from the Treasury Department.

Q. State where you were during the performance of the American Cousin, prior to the assassination. A. In the ticket office.

Q. Were you not on the pavement, in front, at all during the performance. A. I suppose I must have passed in and out two or three times.

Q. Did you see anything of the prisoner, Edward Spangler during that time? A. No sir.

Cross-examined by Judge Bingham.—Q. Do you know the fact that the other boxes in the theatre were or were not occupied that night? A. None were occupied, I think; I could tell by looking at the books.

Q. Do not you remember boxes being applied for and the answer being given that they were all taken? A. None were applied for to me.

Q. Did not you sell all the tickets? A. No; there were four of us.

Q. Do you not know that Booth occupied the other boxes? A. No sir; from my information he did not.

Q. Or anybody else for him? A. No applications of any kind were made to me for them; there may have been applications made that I know nothing about.

Q. State whether there were any mortices in the wall behind the President's Box when you was up there decorating it. A. There were not.

Q. You know there was one when the President was murdered; do you know it? A. I have heard so; I have not been in the box since.

Q. Was there a bar there for the purpose of fastening the entrance to the door that afternoon? A. I saw none.

Q. Was there any such contrivance there before that day? A. I never knew of any; I know there was not.

Q. Was there a hole bored through the first door that opened into the President's box before that day? A. I don't know of there being any there.

Q. Were the screws to the locks of the doors of the President's box drawn before that day? A. Not to my knowledge; I do not know.

Q. Will you swear that they were not drawn when you decorated the box that day? A. It was not drawn in my presence nor to my knowledge; if it had been done I did not notice it.

By Mr. Aiken.—Q. When you first saw Booth in the theatre that day how long did he remain? A. I suppose half an hour; I went into the office and when I came out he was gone.

Q. Was the letter Booth had a long or short one? A. It was very long: it was either four or eight pages, I am not certain which.

Q. Had it been published at the time Booth left the theatre that the President would be there that night? A. When I came into the theatre that morning my brother told me that he would write a little notice and put it into the evening papers that the President was to be there.

Q. When could any one have had a knowledge of the fact, unless they came to the theatre? A. Not unless my brother told them.

Q. In what direction did Booth go after he left the theatre? A. I do not know.

Q. Did he seem to be in a hurry to complete the conversation and get away from the theatre? A. No sir.

Q. When he learned the fact that the President would he there that evening, did you notice any particular change in his manner or conversation? A. No sir; he sat down on the steps, opened his letter, and occasionally would look up and laugh.

Q. Do you recollect the name of the messenger from the White House? No sir, I do not.

Q. Did this conversation with Booth take place in the theatre? A. No; but on the sidewalk in front of the gallery steps.

Q. Where was he when he read the letter? A. He sat in the main entrance door of the theatre.

Q. When he came there, got the letter, and went away? A. There was some young men talking with him; I recollect Mr. Gifford. Mr. Evans and Mr. Guerlin.

Q. Is Mr. Evans an attache of the theatre? A. Yes, an actor there.

By Mr. Ewing.—Q. Do you think if there had been a hole in the wall in the little passage between the President's box and the wall, four or five inches one way, and two inches the other, could you have noticed it? A. If the door had been opened against the wall it would have brought it behind, and I would not have noticed it; if the door had been closed, I certainly would have noticed it.

Q. Is not that passage pretty dark even when the door is open? A. Yes.

Q. Did you observe the side of the wall? A. I did not take particular notice of it.

Q. If there had been an augur hole through the partition with the President's box would you have been likely to notice it? A. I do not think I should.

Q. Did you ever see the prisoner Arnold about the Theatre? No, I do not know him at all.

By the Court.—Q. Do you not know that the intended visit of the President was published in the morning papers? A. It was not.

Q. Do you state in a drinking saloon, near Ford's Theatre, that the President was to be there? A. No sir.

Q. Was it announced that General Grant was to attend the theatre in company with the President? A. It was.

Testimony of Wm. Withers, Jr.

By Mr. Ewing.—Q. In your previous examination you were unable to state definitely whether the door leading out of the passage where Booth went was shut or not, can you state now? A. Yes, the door was shut.

Q. Do you recollect that fact distinctly? A. Yes after he knocked me down, as I stated in my former testimony, he made a plunge for the door, which was shut, but he opened it very easily, rushed out and pulled the door after him.

Q. Were you at the theatre that day at twelve o'clock? A. I cannot recollect; I think I had a rehearsal that day at ten o'clock; there was no music in the American Cousin requiring it; but I think we had a rehearsal of the song I composed.

Q. Did you see Booth or not during that day? A. I did not.

Testimony of James R. Ford.

By Mr. Ewing.—Q. What business were you engaged in about the time of the assassination of the President? A. I was business manager at Ford's Theatre.

Q. State whether you were apprised that the President intended to visit the theatre that night? A. At about half-past ten o'clock that day the young man from the President's house, who usually came on such errands, came on that occasion; I do not know his name; he seemed to be a runner; he had been to the theatre half a dozen times for boxes previously.

Q. Had the President been previously invited for that night? A. No sir.

Q. State whether on that day, and if so, how soon after you received that information it was communicated to J. Wilkes Booth? A. I saw him about half-past 12 o'clock, some two hours after I had received the information, on the corner of Tenth and E streets. He was going up towards Eleventh street. I do not know whether he had been at the theatre.

Q. Had you any knowledge of the President's intention of visiting the theatre that night previous the return to receiving this message? A. No sir.

Q. Did you have anything to do with the decoration of the box the President was to occupy? A. Nothing whatever.

Q. Did you procure anything to decorate it with or not? A. I procured a flag from the Treasury Department

ment; I could not obtain the one I wanted; a 30-foot flag.
Q. State whether or not, on any occasion, you had a conversation with Booth as to his purchase of lands, and if so, where?
Question objected to by Judge Bingham, as irrelevant and immaterial.
Mr. Ewing stated that in the testimony of the witness Weichman a conversation at the National Hotel, between Booth and the prisoner, Mudd, was introduced as a circumstance showing Mudd's connection with the conspiracy. The purpose of this evidence was to show that, if that conversation ever occurred, it proved nothing, inasmuch as conversations on the part of Booth with various parties in reference to the purchase of land in the lower part of Maryland, were very frequent.
The objection was sustained by the Court.
Q. Do you know of a visit made by Booth into Charles co'nty last fall? A. I don't know except from what he told me.
Mr. Bingham.—You need not state what he told you.
Mr Ewing insisted on the question being answered in full.
Col. Burnett.—Have you answered that question?
Witness.—I say I have never known him to go there.
Q. Have you ever heard him say what his purpose was in any visit he may have made to Charles county last fall?
Question objected to by Judge Bingham and objection sustained.
By Mr. Cox.—Q. Did you send notice of the President's intended visit to the Star that afternoon? A. I did of his intention and of that of General Grant; I sent it about twelve o'clock.
Q. In whose handwriting was it? A. In mine; I wrote it.
Q. About what time did the first edition containing that notice appear? A. About two o'clock, I think.
Q. Had you sent it before you met Booth coming up the street with that letter? A. Yes.
Q. Did you have any conversation with Booth that day? A. No, I merely spoke to him.
By Mr. Aiken—Q. Do you know John H. Surratt. A. No, sir.
Q. Did you see any of that description (picture of Surratt shown) about there that day? A. I don't know any such person.
Q. Do you know the actor, McCullough, and if so, do you know what time he left the city. A. I know him; he left I believe when Forrest did, which I believe was the first of January; he played an engagement with him.
Q. Did McCullough return to this city in company with Forrest, on the first of March? A. He did, on Forrest's last engagement; I do not know what time that was.
Q. Was it before the 1st of April? A. I think so.
Q. Do you know of your own knowledge whether McCullough had left the city before the 1st of April? A. I do not; I have no means of knowing when he left; I could ascertain from the books of the theatre when Forrest left.
Cross-examined by Colonel Burnett.—Q. Where were you when you wrote that notice for the Star? A. I was in the ticket office; no one was present.
Q. Had you had any conversation with any one about sending that notice? A. I asked Mr. Phillips, the actor, to write me a notice, and he said he would do so, writing the regular advertisement.
Q. Did you speak to any one else? A. I spoke to my younger brother about the propriety of writing it; I did not speak to any one else.
Q. Had you seen Booth prior to writing that notice? A. No sir.
Q. How did you send it away? I sent one to the Star and carried the other to the office of the Republican myself.

Testimony of J. Boney.

Q. Where were you on the night of the 14th of April? A. At Ford's Theatre.
Q. What was your business there? A. I was playing what is called "responsible utility."
Q. State whether you knew anything of Booth's having rode up to the alley door and called for Spangler? A. He called for me first; I don't know whether he came on a horse or not, but he told me to ask Spangler to come and hold his horse; I didn't see the horse; I was on the opposite side, and I said "Booth wants you to hold his horse;" he went; Booth came inside, and said he, "can I go across the stage;" said I, "no, the dairy scene is on;" Spangler then called me, and told me to call "Pea Nut John," to hold the horse, saying that Gifford was away and the responsibility of the scene was all on him.
Q. Did you see Spangler any more that evening? A. I did three or four times.
Q. Where? A. On the stage.
Q. Was he in his proper position? A. Yes sir.
Q. Did you see him about the time the shot was fired? A. About two minutes.
Q. Where was he then? A. On the same side of the President's box.
Q. Did you see him after the shot was fired? A. I saw him five or six minutes after.

Q. Where was he then? A. On the stage with a crowd of people.
Q. What was he doing there? A. I took no notice of him at all.
Q. Did you see Booth as he left? A. I saw him as he made his exit at the first left hand entrance; he had a long double-edged knife that looked like a new one.
Q. Did you see anybody follow him? A. I did not see any man get on the stage until he had made his exit.
Q. How long after did you see a man get on the stage? A. Two or three seconds.
Q. Who got on the stage first after Booth? A. A tall, stout gentleman with grey clothes; I think he had a moustache.
Q. What did he do? A. He made his exit the same way that Booth did.

Testimony of J. J. Gifford.

Q. Did you know anything of a horse and buggy belonging to Booth being sold a week or so before the assassination? A. I heard Booth tell Spangler to send the horse and buggy to Tattersall's and sell it, one week before the assassination.
Q. Do you know Mr. Jacob Witherspough? A. I knew a man who worked in the theatre by that name; he was there two or three weeks.
Q. State whether or not, since he was released from Carroll Hall, or just previous to his release, he told you at the prison of the assassination of the President, not to say which way he went, meaning Booth; and did he say that Spangler hit him on the face with the back of h's hand? A. No sir; he said he had been down and had not told a lie knew and wanted to know it he could make another statement; I told him certainly, and that he ought to be very particular and state the whole truth.
Q. State whether you know anything of the accused, Spangler, being in the custom of crabbing and other fishing. A. Yes, I know he would go on Saturday night and stay till Sunday morning; I have never seen him fishing myself.
Q. State whether his rope could be used for that purpose. A. Yes sir; but they tie another small line out of the end.

Testimony of Dr. McKinn.

Q. Where do you reside? A. In Washington, in the eastern part of the city.
Q. Do you know Harold? A. yes sir.
Q. How long have you known him? A. I don't know when I have not known him for the last two years; I have known him very well for the last six years.
Q. State his character. A. He was a light, unreliable, trivial boy, and is in mind about eleven years of age; I never would allow him to put up a prescription of mine, if I could go elsewhere, believing that he would tamper with it if he thought he could play a joke upon anybody by it.
The Court here adjourned until ten o'clock on Friday morning.

WASHINGTON, June 2.—After the reading of the record, the examination of witnesses for the defense was resumed.

Testimony of Charles Bulger.

By Mr. Ewing.—The substance of the testimony of this witness was as follows:—Witness knew the prisoner, Edward Spangler, having boarded at a house at which the prisoner boarded for five or six months; after the assassination the accused remained at the house for several days.

Testimony of John Gunther.

By Mr. Ewing.—The testimony of this witness was substantially the same as that of the previous witness. He testified to having boarded for several years at the house at which the prisoner stopped for six or seven months, and was certain of having seen him about the boarding house some two or three days after the assassination. Witness never saw him wear a moustache.
Cross-examined by Judge Advocate Bingham.—Saw the prisoner generally in the morning or evening; the accused did not sleep at the boarding-house.

Testimony of Thomas J. Reybold.

By Mr. Ewing.—Q. State how long you have been in Washington, and what has been your occupation here? A. I have not lived permanently in Washington, only since the last Monday of December one year ago, at which time I came to Washington for Mr. Ford; I was employed at that gentleman's theatre to take charge of the house; to see to the front of the house, and purchase everything that was to be purchased for the house; any repairs to the house were done through my orders; that was my business there; in the absence of either of the Messrs. Ford, I went in the box-office and sold the tickets.
Q. State whether you know anything as to any of the locks of the private boxes being broken, and if so, what you know. A. I think it was during Mrs. Bowers' engagement, in March, about the 7th, when being one

day at dinner, Mr. Merrick, of the National Hotel, asked me to reserve some seats for him that evening, three. I think, in the orchestra; I did so; Mr. Merrick had not arrived by the end of the first act, and as it was customary for all reserved seats not occupied at the end of the first act to be taken by other persons present wanting seats, those seats were taken shortly after that; Mr. Merrick, accompanied by his wife, Mr. Martin and several ladies came in and I was in ormed of their arrival, and asked what I had done with the seats reserved for them, and I went to see about them, and found that the usher had filled them; I then took them up stairs to Box 6, which was locked and could not be entered; I then crossed to Box No 7 and 8, generally termed the President's Box, which were also locked; I endeavoured to force it open by applying my shoulder to the door, but failing in that I used my foot and succeeded in kicking it open.

Q. State whether that or led into the box which the President occupied at the time of the assassination? A. It did, by request; when the President occupied the box we would take the partition out, and the two boxes would then be occupied as one.

Q. When the two boxes are thrown into one by which door do you enter the President's box? A. The door of Box 8.

Q. Do you know whether that was the door that was used on the night of the assassination? A. Yes sir, it was; the other one could not be used.

Q. Do you know whether the lock that was burst open was afterwards repaired? A. I do not; I never examined it afterwards; I suppose it was my place to have reported the fact, and though I frequently passed into the box afterwards I never thought of having the lock fixed.

Q. To whom would you have reported for repairs? A. To Mr. Gifford.

Q. But you made no report to him of it? A. No sir, I never said anything about it; I never thought it worth while to mention it.

Q. State whether you have any knowledge of Booth occupying either of those two boxes shortly before the assassination? A. I cannot say positively that he did; it was about two weeks, I think, prior to the 14th that Mr. Booth engaged private box No. 4, and in the evening of that day came again to the office while I was sitting in the vestibule, and asked for an exchange of the box for box No. 7, one of the Presidential boxes, and the one in which a hole was found to have been bored he occupied that night, either Box No. 7 or 8, I cannot swear positively which box.

Q. State whether there were any box tickets sold at the theatre up to the time of the opening. A. To the best of my knowledge there was not; I said none; I was not in the office all the time that day; I was there during the afternoon, and also in the morning, when the tickets were obtained for the President by his messenger; I do not know positively whether there were any sold, or whether there were any applications for any.

Q. State at what hour the President engaged those seats? A. Between 10 and 11 o'clock in the forenoon.

Q. Had he been previously invited? A. Not to my knowledge.

Q. Did you see the messenger? A. I did, and was talking to him.

Q. State whether you saw anything of Booth that morning after the President had engaged the box? A. I cannot say whether it was after or before that time; I saw him that morning; he got a letter from the office that morning; he generally came there every morning, his letters were directed to Mr. Ford's box in the Post Office and were brought to the theatre every morning.

Q. Did Booth get more than one letter that morning? A. Not to my knowledge.

Q. State if you know any reason why the rocking chair in which the President is said to have sat that night should have been in the position in which it was? A. The position in which it was then was the same in which I had placed it myself on two other occasions when the President occupied that box, and the reason was that it placed in any other position the rockers would be in the way; the removal of the partition left a triangular corner to the left of the balustrade of the box, and the rockers went into the corner and were out of the way; that was the only reason why I put it there.

Q. When was that? A. During last winter a year ago.

Q. It had not been used in the box during this last reason up to that time? A. The sofa had been used; it had not.

Q. State what you saw of Spangler, if anything, after the assassination. A. I do not recollect seeing him after that; I only knew that he was arrested in the house on the following Saturday morning.

Q. Was he not about the theatre after that morning? A. I cannot say; in accordance with my usual custom I went to Baltimore on that Saturday night to visit my family, who resided there.

Q. Was the theatre closed until your return? A. It was; I returned on Monday morning.

Q. Examine that rope (exhibiting rope found in the carpet bag of the prisoner Spangler) and state whether you know of any such rope being used about the theatre, and whether, from its flexibility, you would judge that it had been used? A. From its appearance I know that it has been used; if it had not it would be lighter in color; it is like the ropes that are generally used in the flies for drawing up the scenes; what is called a border rope.

Cross-examined by Assistant Judge Advocate Bingham.—Q. You say that kind of a rope was used in the theatre in fixing up the flies? A. The wings; or, at least, the borders.

Q. If the rope had been used in the theatre it would have belonged there, would it not? A. Yes sir.

Q. The proper place would not be a carpet-sack half a mile away? A. No sir, I do not think it would.

Q. Mr. Spangler would not supply the theatre with a rope at his own expense? A. It is not my opinion that he did.

Q. The rope that he used, which you have described, is a permanent fixture, is it not? A. Sometimes we use a great many of these ropes, and then take them down and they lay up in the loft until we need them again.

Q. Was it the inner or the outer door of the box that you forced open? A. It was the inner door.

Q. Is Box 8 the one nearest the stage? A. It is.

Q. Could you, by direct force, have burst open the door of the box, the keeper of which was fastened by screws, so as to have drawn the keeper without splitting the wood? A. I might have started the keeper; it would have been according to the length of the screws.

Q. Is not the facing of that door of pine? A. Yes sir; as far as I can judge.

Q. Is it your opinion that the keeper of the lock could have been burst off by force without splitting the wood? A. I think so; it might have been so.

Q. When were you in the box last? A. The morning after the assassination.

Q. When before the assassination? A. About five minutes that afternoon.

Q. Did you see either a mortice in the wall or a piece of wood to fasten the door? A. No sir.

Q. Did you see a mortice there the morning after the assassination? A. No sir; my attention was not called to it.

Q. State what you know, if anything, about the rocking chair in which the President sat being placed in the box? A. I do not know who put it there, but I know who was ordered to put it there; I was in the box only about five minutes, when I assisted in fixing the flags; it was then in the corner of Box 7, and sitting in the position in which the chair was then placed, the President would have his back to the audience, and his side partially toward the stage.

By Mr. Ewing.—Q. Was it after Booth played "Pescara" that he occupied that box? A. I could not tell that; he ordered the box on two occasions, but on one occasion did not use it for he told me in the evening that he would not be able to use that box, as some ladies stopping at the National Hotel had disappointed him.

Q. How long was it before the assassination that he used it? A. About two weeks.

By the Court.—Q. Do you know of what material that rope is made? A. I think it is a Manilla rope.

By Judge Advocate Holt.—Do you or not know that the color of a rope does not depend on its age or its use? A. I know that water will make the color of a rope darker, but its color, so far as my knowledge extends, does depend upon its use.

Testimony of Henry E. Merrick.

By Mr. Ewing.—Q. State your business? A. I am clerk of the National Hotel.

Q. State whether or not some time before the assassination of the President you went to Ford's Theatre and Mr. Reybold showed you to a box? A. Yes sir, it was on the evening of the 7th of March; I had my wife and other ladies with me, and we were shown to a box on the right hand side as you pass down the dress circle; it was the box nearest the entrance; I do not know the number.

Q. Are you certain that it was the box furthest from the stage? A. Yes sir.

Q. Do you know any thing about the door being forced open? A. The door was forced open by Mr. Reybold, who was unable to find the key; the keeper, I think was forced off; at least, the screw that held the upper part of the keeper came out and it whirled around and hung by the lower screw; we then entered the box and remained there during the play.

Q. Do you know when John McCullough, the actor, was last at the National Hotel? A. Our books show that he left there on the 26th of March; he paid his bill on that day, and since then I have not seen him.

Q. Was he in the habit of stopping at your hotel? A. No sir; I have never known him to stop at any other hotel.

Q. Was he there on the 2d of April? A. Not to my knowledge.

Cross-examined by Assistant Judge Advocate Bingham.—Q. Many persons come into your hotel to visit guests of the house and go away again without your knowing it, do they not? A. They might call there on their friends.

Q. On the night of which you have spoken as the occasion of your visit to the theatre you entered the first

box that you came to in passing down the dress circle?
A. Yes?.
Q. The box next the stage you did not enter at all?
A. I did not; we entered the first box.

Testimony of James Lamb.

By Mr. Ewing.—Q. State where and in what capacity you were employed at the time of the assassination of the President. A. At Mr. Ford's theatre, where I have been employed for the last two seasons, over a year, in the capacity of scene painter.
Q. Examine that rope (exhibiting to witness the rope found in Spangler's possession), and state whether you have seen any ropes like that used in the theatre. A. I have; but all ropes of this description bear some similarity; ropes like that are used in the theatre for suspending borders that hang across the tops of the scenes; they are called border ropes.
Q. What is the length of ropes used for that purpose in the theatre? A. Not less than eighty (80) feet; they are used for raising and lowering the borders; these borders are long strips of canvas, which are painted to represent interiors and exteriors; sometimes, when it is necessary to alter them, they are lowered upon the stage for the purpose of being repainted; the ropes used are about the length of this one.
Q. Examine it carefully, and state whether it has the appearance of having been used. A. It has the appearance of having been chafed, and a new rope would be a little stiffer, it strikes me.
Q. Does it look as if it had been used as a border rope? A. I cannot say that there is anything about it that would lead me to form an opinion on that point; it is the same kind of a rope that is used for that purpose, but if it had been so used, I think there would do a knot here; one end appears to have been cut; there were about forty or fifty such ropes employed about the theatre.

By Assistant Judge Advocate Bingham.—Q. Were you acquainted with John Wilkes Booth? A. I knew him by sight; I never spoke a word to him.
By the Court.—Q. Of what material is that rope? A. I should say it was hemp.
By Mr. Ewing.—Q. Have you any reason to believe, from an examination of the rope, that it was not used as a border rope? A. No sir.
Q. Did you see anything of the prisoner, Edward Spangler, after the assassination? A. I saw him on Saturday, the day after the President was assassinated; I was in the theatre loitering about from ten o'clock until the military took possession of the building; my feelings were excited, and I remained on the spot the whole day, and saw Spangler several times during the day.
Q. Where did you see the prisoner, and who were with him? A. I saw him on the stage; there were several others there; Maddox, a man by the name of Jake, Mr. Gifford, Mr. Wright, and Mr. Carland.
Q. Who were with Spangler? A. There was no companionship particularly; they all seemed to be loitering about.
Q. What time in the day was that? A. About twelve or one o'clock; I did not see Spangler since until I saw him this morning.

Testimony of William R. Smith.

By Mr. Ewing.—Q. State your residence and business. A. I live in Washington, and am Superintendent of the Botanic Gardens.
Q. Were you in Ford's Theatre at the time of the assassination? A. I was.
Q. Did you see Booth pass off the stage? A. I did.
Q. Did you see Mr. Stewart get on the stage? A. Mr. Stewart was about the first that got on the stage; it is my impression that Booth was off the stage before Mr. Stewart got on it; I saw Stewart turn around and look up at the box in which the President had been murdered; I did not watch him any further.
Q. You think that Booth got off the stage before any one got on it? A. Yes sir.

Re-Examination of Jacob Ritterspaugh.

By Mr. Ewing.—Q. When you were examined for the prosecution you spoke of Spangler having slapped you in the face after your return from following Booth, and of his saying:—"Shut up, don't say which way he went?" A. Yes sir.
Q. Did you make the same statement the next day when you were in the theatre to Mr. Lamb, and on the night of the assassination to Mr. Carland when he aroused you from sleep? A. Yes sir; Mr. Carland, when he awakened me, asked me what Ned said to me, and I told him that Ned had slapped me in the mouth and said:—"Don't say which way he went."
Q. Were you not on the stage on the afternoon of the day of the assassination? A. Yes sir.
Q. State what you and Spangler saw. A. I saw a man in the dress circle smoking a segar, and I asked Spangler who he was; he said he did not know; I then said we ought to tell him to go out, and Spangler said he had a right there; I resumed my work and sat awhile looked around again, and saw the man sitting in a private box, on the right-hand side of the stage; after that the man went out.
Q. Was the man near enough to hear what Spangler said? A. Yes sir.

By Assistant Judge Advocate Bingham.—Q. Do you know what man that was? A. No sir.
By Mr. Ewing.—Q. What time in the evening was that? A. About six o'clock in the evening of the day on which the President was assassinated, and just before we went to supper.
By Assistant Judge Advocate Bingham.—Q. Where did you say that man was? A. In a private box, one of the lower boxes in the dress circle on the right hand side of the stage.

Testimony of Louis J. Carland.

By Mr. Ewing.—Q. State whether you are acquainted with Jacob Ritterspaugh? A. I am.
Q. State whether you saw him in Mr. Gifford's room on the night of the assassination after it had taken place, and what did Ritterspaugh say on that occasion? A. He was asleep, and on my awakening him he appeared frightened and thought I was Mr. Booth; I asked him where Spangler was, and he said he did not know, that when he last saw Spangler he was standing behind the scenes just after Booth ran out the back part of the theatre, and that he said to Spangler, "that was Mr. Booth," Spangler slapped him in the mouth and said, "you don't know who it was; it might have been Booth, and it might have been somebody else."
Q. Did Ritterspaugh tell you that Spangler slapped him in the face and said, Don't say which way he went? A. No sir.
Q. Did he tell you anything to that effect? A. No sir.
Q. Are you sure that he did not say it to you? A. I am certain.
Q. Where was Spangler when you first saw him after the assassination? A. In the theatre on the stage; I was in his company till Sunday night, when I went to the Hermann House, and he went to sleep in the theatre; I suppose he left to go there to sleep.
Q. Where was he during Saturday and Sunday? A. On the Saturday night after the murder he was going to sleep in the theatre as usual, but there was some talk about burning the theatre, and, being a heavy sleeper, he was afraid to sleep there, so he came to my room and I let him sleep there all night; on Sunday morning I went to church, and met him again in the street near the theatre; we walked around that afternoon and parted in the evening.
Q. Do you know whether or not, during those two days you were with Spangler, he had much money? A. He had very little change.
Q. State whether Booth often frequented the theatre and stayed about there a great deal, and on what terms was he with the employees? A. On very intimate terms; he seemed to become familiar with people on a short acquaintance.
The rope found in Spangler's carpet-bag was exhibited to the witness, when he stated that it resembled one used by Mr. Spangler and Mr. Ritterspaugh, about two weeks before the murder, to carry up some lumber to the fourth story of the theatre. He thought it had the appearance of having been used and of having lain out of doors.

Cross-examined by Assistant Judge Advocate Bingham.—Q. Spangler usually slept in the theatre? A. Yes sir.
Q. He did not sleep there on the night of the murder? A. No sir.
Q. Did he sleep there on Sunday night? A. No sir.
Q. Where and at what time did you awaken Ritterspaugh? A. It was on the first floor, in what was called the manager's office, and at about twelve o'clock on the night of the murder I was alone at the time.
Q. To whom did you tell what Ritterspaugh said to you? A. To nobody but Wm. Withers, Jr.; I told him on the Sunday afternoon after the assassination.
By Mr. Ewing.—Q. Was Ritterspaugh fully awake when you had the conversation with him? A. Yes sir.

Testimony of James Lyon.

By Mr. Ewing.—Q. Are you acquainted with Jacob Ritterspaugh. A. Yes.
Q. Did you see him on the day after the President was killed? A. I did, on Saturday.
Q. Did he say anything to you about a conversation he had had with Spangler directly after the assassination? A. Yes; he was grumbling and saying it was well for Ned that he had not something in his hand at the time; witness asked why; said he, "Ned struck me last night a very hard blow, and said shut up," in a mocking tone, "you know nothing about it."
Q. In what connection did he say that happened? A. He said he was acquainted with Booth, and remarked to Spangler as Booth ran out, "I know who that was; that was Booth who ran out;" then Ned said "Shut up; be quiet; what do you know about it."
Q. When did he say that was? A. That was while the party, Booth or whoever it might be, was leaving the stage, that is, making his escape; then man Jake then rushed up and was making this explanation, "I know him; that was Booth;" Ned then turned around and struck him with the back of his hand and said, "shut up; you know nothing about it; what do you know about it; keep quiet."
Q. Did or did not Jacob Ritterspaugh say that Spangler said to him "do not say which way he went," or any words to that effect? A. He did not, I am sure,

Cross-examined by Judge Bingham.—Q. State now exactly what Jake said to you on that occasion. A. He said "I followed out the party and was close at his heels; I said to Spangler, I know him," or words to that effect.
Q. He said he was right at Booth's heels, did he? A. No, not that, he said he was nearly.
Q. Did not you say he followed the party close at his heels? A. Well, I say he did, and received a blow from Spangler and that shut him up.

Testimony of J. W. Bunker.

By Mr. Ewing.—Q. What is your occupation? A. I am clerk at the National Hotel in this city.
Q. State whether or not after the assassination of the President you found any articles in Booth's room at the hotel. A. I packed up Booth's luggage and had it removed to our baggage room on the day after the assassination.
Q. Did you find any carpenter's tools? A. I found a large-sized gimblet with an iron handle in his trunk; I took it and carried it to my room; I afterwards gave it to Mr Hall, who was attending to Ford's business.
Q. Do you know whether John McCullough, the actor, was in Washington on the 1st of April? A. I have examined our books thoroughly and find that the last time McCullough registered was on the 11th of March; he left the house on the 26th of that month; his name is not on our books after that date.
Q. Where was he in the habit of stopping when he came to Washington? A. He made his home at the National; I have never known of his stopping at any other place.
Q. Did you see him in the city after the 26th of March? A. I did not.

Testimony of Chas. B. Hall.

By Mr. Ewing.—Q. Where have you been living for the past two or three months, and what has been your occupation? A. I have been acting as clerk for Mr. Wharton a sutler at Fortress Monroe.
Q. Is his store inside the fortifications or outside? A. It is outside, at what is called Old Point.
Q. Are you acquainted with the prisoner, Arnold? A. I got acquainted with him at Mr. Wharton's store; he came there in the latter part of March or the 1st of April; I cannot fix the date; it was on a Sunday.
Q. State how long he r-mained there, and what his business was. A. He was assisting me at book-keeping; he stayed there two weeks and one day, I think.
Q. Did you see him there constantly at that time? A. No; I was engaged at another place part of the time; I saw him, however, every day.
Q. State whether or not, and if so, when, Arnold made any application for employment. A. He did; I think about the 1st of March some time.
Q. Do you know what became of Arnold's letter? A. Major Stevens has it.
Q. How many letters did he write applying for a position? A. I only saw one; that I answered myself.
Q. At what time was the answer written? A. I could not tell that; it was about a week before Arnold came; I wrote for him to come.
Q. Did you see Arnold every night during the time of his employment? A. Yes sir; he slept in Mr. Wharton's store every night.

Testimony of George Craig.

By Mr. Ewing.—Q. State where you live, and how you have been employed for the last four months. A. I have been at Old Point, and have been employed by Mr. Wharton as salesman.
Q. Have you seen the prisoner Samuel Arnold? A. I saw him at out the latter part of March or the first of April, on Sunday, for the first time.
Q. What boat did he come on? A. I cannot tell.
Q. How long did he remain there? A. About two weeks, to the best of my knowledge; he was a clerk in Mr. Wharton's establishment; chief clerk I believe.
Q. How often did you see him during his stay there? A. I saw him every day; I cannot say how many times a day.

Testimony of James Lusby.

By Mr. Stone.—I reside in Prince Georges county; I am not very much acquainted with John M. Floyd; I got acquainted with him since Christmas; I saw him in Marlboro' in April last; I do not know exactly the day; it was on Good Friday, on the day that Lincoln was killed.
Q. Did you see Mr. Floyd on the evening of that day at Surrattsville. A. I and him went that day from Marlboro'.
Q. What was Floyd's condition at that time? A. He was very drunk I thought; I reached Surrattsville about one minute and a half before he did; I drove up to the bar-room door; he went up to the front door.
Q. Did you see the prisoner, Mrs. Surratt, there that day? A. I saw her as she was starting out to go home.
Q. Was she all ready to go home at the time Floyd drove up? A. Yes, the buggy was there waiting for her, and she left about fifteen minutes afterwards.
Cross-examination by Judge Holt.—Q. You drove upon one side of the house and Floyd went round to the other side, didn't he? A. Yes; there was a front yard he went through; when I first came I went into the bar-room and got a drink.

Q. Did you see Mrs. Surratt when you first came? You didn't see her in the bar-room, did you? A. No.
Q. And you didn't see her when she first came up? A. No.
Q. You didn't see her until you got your drink? A. I d'sremember whether I got my drink when I first saw her or not.
Q. You say Floyd was drunk; how do you know that fact? A. I have seen him be fore.
Q. Did you see him drinking? A. Yes; and I took drinks with him.
Q. Which drank the most? A. I never measured mine.
Q. Were you as tight as he was? A. Not quite as tight.
Q. Were you after you had the additional drink? You had the advantage of taking that drink at Surrattsville, while Floyd went around to the kitchen. hadn't you? A. I don't know; I never tried to pass even with him; I did not say I was drunk; I don't know whether I was, though I had drank with him right smart that day.
By Judge Burnett.—Q. Do you live at Surrattsville? A. Not a tol-a and a half below.
Q. What has been your business for the past two or three years? A. I have been a farmer at the time; I have never be-n away from home further than Washington in my life.
Q. Was Floyd sober enough, wasn't he, to drive his own horse and to take his fish, &c. into the kitchen? A. He drove his own horse; I didn't see him go to the kitchen.
Did you see him fix Mrs. Surratt's buggy? A. No; I do not know anything about that.
Q. How long before he arrived at the house had you seen him? A. I came all along with him from Marlboro', sometimes in front and sometimes behind him.
Q. How far is it from Marlboro' to Surrattsville? A. About twelve miles; it is a last drive of about two and a half hours.
Q. Did you stop to get any drinks on the road? A. No.
Q. Then he was two and a half hours without getting any drinks before he came to Surrattsville? A. Yes sir.

Testimony of Matthew J. Pope.

By Mr. Doster.—Q. State where you live and what your business is. A. I live down at the Navy Yard, and keep a livery stable; I did keep a restaurant, but I do not now.
Q. State whether or not, on or about the 12th of April, the prisoner Atzerodt called at your place and wanted to sell a bay horse. A. There was a gentleman called at my stable, I don't know exactly the day, to sell a large bay horse, blind in one eye.
Q. How old did he seem to be? A. I don't know; I did not take any particular notice of his age, and I do not know that I examined him at all.
Q. Do you remember the person who brought the horse there. A. I do not know as I would remember him were I to see him again.
Q. Look at the prisoner Atzerodt and see if you recognize him as that person? A. I do not know. The features are nearly alike. If he was the one he is not nearly so stout a man as he was then, I did not take much notice of him. He asked me if I wanted to buy a horse, I told him I did not. It was some time in the afternoon; his horse stayed at the stable to rest for some two or three hours; he went to the restaurant and took a drink; he went away with a man by the name of John Barr; after a t me he came back, and the man who brought the horse then took him away.
Q. Don't you remember this man Barr was drunk at the time? A. He had been drinking a little; I do not know whether he was drunk or not; Mr. Barr was one of the mechanics at the Navy Yard; he carried on wheelwrighting.
Q. Was not this the very day of the illumination on the part of the mechanics? A. I do not know; I think it was several days before the assassination of the President, but I took very little notice.
Q. Have you or not found an umbrella left at your house by the prisoner? A. It was left by the man who brought the horse to the stable, at the same time he eft the horse.

Testimony of Miss Margaret Branson.

By Mr. Doster.—Q. Where do you live? A. I live in Baltimore, and first saw the prisoner Payne at Gettysburg. I do not remember the time, but it was immediately a ter the battle of Gettysburg. He was there as a volunteer nurse. He was in my ward and very kind to the sick and wounded. I don't know whether he was there as a nurse or not. I don't know if he was a soldier. He had on no uniform. As nearly as I can recollect he was dressed in blue pants with no coat and a dark slouch hat. He went by the name of Powell and by the name of Doctor.
Q. How long did you know him there? A. I do not know the time; I was there six weeks, and I do not know whether he was there the whole time or not.
Q. In the hospital, where he seemed to be attending to the sick and wounded, were the patients both Con-

federates and Union soldiers? A. Yes: I left the hospital the first week in September; I met Payne again some time that fall and winter; I do not remember when; I met h m at my own home; he remained there only a few hours; I had very little conversation with him.

Q. Did he state to you where he was going? Objected to by Judge Bingham on the ground that declarations of the prisoner could not be read in evidence.

Mr. Doster replied that he intended to set up the plea of insanity in the case of Payne, and that while the declaration of the prisoner would not be admissible to prove his innocence, yet to prove his insanity his declarations were acts, and therefore admissible.

Judge Bingham replied that the counsel had laid no grounds for this course of examination to prove insanity.

Mr. Doster said that the prosecution themselves had laid the ground by proving a series of acts of assassination which he should claim were the work of an insane man.

Judge Bingham remarked that he supposed it was, then, the theory of the counsel that a man might take a knife large enough to butcher an ox, rush past all the attendants in the house, wounding and maiming them, stab a sick man in his bed again and again, and escape punishment on the ground that the acts were too atrocious for a sane man to commit.

Mr. Doster replied that all the circumstances connected with the assassination bore upon themselves evidence of the work of an insane man. The prosecution had proved that the accused had entered the house by a stratagem very likely to be resorted to by an insane man without the slightest possible disguise, stopping for five minutes to talk to a negro on his way; after committing the deed making no attempt at concealment, leaving his pistol and hat there in the room and throwing away his knife deliberately where it could be found, in front of Mr. Seward's door, getting on his horse and riding away so deliberately that a man on foot could follow him for a square; then, instead of escaping as he could very well have done on b s horse, turning his horse loose, wa dering about the city, and finally going to the house of all others where he would be liable to be arrested. He claimed that the prosecution, in the proof of these acts, has laid abundant ground for the examination he was now making, and he called attention now to Payne's stolid manner in Court, so different from that of the other prisoners.

Mr. Clampitt said that he did not deny the right of the counsel to set up the plea of insanity or any other plea for his client, but he rose indignantly to protest against his bringing in the house of Mrs. Surratt, as a place where such a man would be most likely to be arrested; there was no evidence that the house of Mrs. Surratt was not a place he would be likely to go to for the purpose of hiding and screening himself from justice.

The objection was sustained by the Court.

Q. How long did he stay at your house? A. A few hours.
Q. Do you know where he went then? A. I do not.
Q. When did you see him the third time? A. In January of this year, at my own house.
Q. Describe how he was dressed at the time. A. In black clothing, citizens' dress.
Q. What did he represent himself to be? A. A refugee from Fauquier county, Virginia; he gave his name as Payne.
Q. How long did he stay at your house? A. I think six weeks and a few days; I do not remember the exact time.
Q. Do you remember about the date he came in January? A. I cannot; I think he left about the beginning of March.
Q. Did he ever see any company while here? A. Never to my knowledge.
Q. Did you ever see J. Wilkes Booth? A. No sir.
Q. Do you know whether Payne was ever called upon about that time by J. Wilkes Booth? A. No sir.
Q. Did he or not take a room in your mother's house? A. Yes.
Q. What were his habits? Was he quiet, or did he go out a good deal? A. He did not go out a great deal; he was remarkably quiet.
Q. In what way did his quietness show itself? A. He was a great deal in his room; be seemed to be reserved and I thought seemed to be depressed in spirits.
Q. Was he or not exceedingly taciturn? A. He was remarkable for not saying anything.
Q. Have you or not a library in your father's house? A. No; we have a good many old books; a good many medical ones.
Q. Do you know whether the prisoner can read? A. I do not.
Q. Did he or did he not give himself up to reading medical works while he was there? A. He did.
Q. Was not his taciturnity so remarkable as to be commented on by the rest of the boarders? A. I think not.
Q. Do you know whether the prisoner was at that time in possession of a great amount of money? A. I do not; he had enough to pay his board.
Q. Do you know how the prisoner happened to leave your house? A. We had a negro servant who was exceedingly impudent to him.

Judge Bingham.—You need not state what passed between the girl and that man.

Mr. Doster.—The witness is just to state that, Judge Bingham.—Why?
Mr. Doster.—It is for you to show why she should not.
Judge Bingham.—Well, let her answer it.
Witness.—He was arrested by the authorities and sent North to Philadelphia.

Cross-examined by Colonel Burnett.—Q. He was arrested as a Southern refugee, was he not, and made to take the oath of allegiance? A. I do not know what he was arrested for, as I never knew the reason why; he was taken to the Provost Marshal's office and was afterwards released and returned to the house.

Q. Do you know whether he came directly to Washington when he left in March? A. I do not.
Q. Did he make any acquaintance in Washington while he was boarding at your house? A. Not that I know of.
Q. Was he absent any time while he was at your house? A. Never but one night to my knowledge.
Q. How many persons boarded at your house? A. I do not know.
Q. Were there any other Southern refugees boarding at your house? A. None but him.

By Mr. Doster.—Q. Was or was not the prisoner, during the month of February, gone long enough to have made a journey to Canada and back again? A. Not to my knowledge.
Q. If he had been would you have known it? A. I certainly would. Q. In what hospital did you see him at Gettysburg? A. In the General Hospital; Dr. Chamberlain's.
Q. Who did the prisoner seem to be nursing, the Confederate or Union wounded? A. He attended to different ones in my ward, and I had both in my ward.
Q. Was your mother with you there? A. No.

Testimony of Margaret Knigane.

By Mr. Doster.—Q. State whether you are a servant in the house of Mr. Branson. A. Yes sir.
Q. Did you see the prisoner Payne there? A. Yes; he came there in January or February and stayed till about the middle of March.
Q. Do you remember at any time a controversy that Payne had with the negro girl there? A. Yes, he asked her to clean up his rooms there; she said she would not do it. He asked her why, she said she would not do it. He called her some names, and slapped her, and struck her.
Q. Did he not throw her on the ground, stamp on her body and try to kill her? A. Yes.
Q. Did he not strike her on the forehead? A. Yes.
Q. What did the negro girl do in consequence? A. She went to have him arrested.
Q. Did he or did he not say he would kill her? A. He did while he was striking her.

Testimony of Dr. Charles Nichols.

By Mr. Doster.—Q. Have I at any time given you any intimation of the answers I expect you to give before this Court? A. You have not.
Q. What is your official position and your profession? A. I am a doctor of medicine and Superintendent of Government Hospital for the Insane.
Q. How long have you occupied that position? A. Thirteen years.
Q. What class of persons do you treat in your asylum? A. Insane persons exclusively.
Q. Are they not persons who have been in the service of the Government exclusively? A. No; my patients include the insane of this district, and occasionally private patients from other portions of the country.
Q. Is or is not the great mass of persons you treat composed of soldiers and sailors? A. It is.
Q. Please define moral insanity? A. When the moral or perceptive faculties are affected, exclusively of disease of the brain, I call it moral insanity.
Q. What are some of the principal causes inducing moral insanity? A. My impression is that insanity is oftener caused by physical disease than by moral causes; the fact that insanity takes that form is apt to depend on the character of the individual becoming insane.
Q. Is active service in the field, among soldiers, at any time, the cause of moral insanity? A. It is not a frequent cause, but I have known of cases of moral insanity among soldiers.
Q. Has or has not insanity increased very much in the country during the present war? A. It has.
Q. Has it not increased much more proportionally than the increase of the army? A. It has.
Q. How is this increase accounted for? By the diseases, hardships and fatigues of the soldier's life, to which the men were not accustomed before going into the service, I think.
Q. Are young men who enlist more exposed to insanity than men who enlist in middle life? A. I am not sure that they are; my impression is that young men accommodate themselves to a change in their manner of life much more easily than men of middle age.
Q. What are some of the leading symptoms of moral

insanity? A. The cases are as different as the individuals affected. If a man, for instance, believes an act to be right which he did not believe to be right in health, and which people generally do not believe to be right, I would regard that as a symptom of moral insanity.

Q. Is depression of spirits at any time considered a symptom of insanity? A. It is.

Q. Is great taciturnity considered a symptom? A. It is a frequent symptom of insanity, though I can conceive how taciturnity could exist without insanity.

Q. Is disposition to commit suicide a symptom? A. It is.

Q. Is great cunning in making plans a concomitant of insanity? A. The insane frequently exhibit great cunning in their plans to effect their object.

Q. Is it or not possible for a madman to confederate with other madmen or insane men in their plans? A. It is not impossible but it is unfrequent.

Q. Do madmen ever confederate together in plans? A. Very seldom.

Q. Is or is not a morbid propensity to destroy a proof of insanity? A. Not a proof, but a very common attendant on insanity.

Q. Is it a symptom of insanity if any one apparently without provocation or cause commits a crime? A. I should regard it as giving rise to suspicion of insanity, but not a proof of it at all.

Q. Is or is not conduct different from the usual mode of the world, the best proof of insanity? A. I will answer that by saying that no single condition is a proof of insanity in every instance, but that an entire departure from the usual conduct of men could be regarded as strong ground to suspect the existence of insanity.

Q. Are not madmen remarkable for great cruelty? A. My impression is that madmen exhibit about the same disposition in that respect that men generally do.

Q. Do not madmen in committing a crime seem to act without pity? A. They frequently do.

Q. If one should try to murder a sick man in his bed, without ever having seen him before, would it be presumptive proof of insanity? A. It would give rise in my mind to a suspicion that the man was insane; I should not regard it as proof.

Q. If the same person should at the same time try to murder four other persons in the house, none of whom he had ever seen, would it not strengthen that suspicion? A. I think it would.

Q. If the same person, in the commission of the deed, were to stop for five minutes' conversation, and then walk away, deliberately leaving his hat and pistol behind, and then ride away so slowly that a man could follow him on foot, would not that further corroborate the suspicion of insanity? A. I think it would; it is a peculiarity of the insane that when they commit criminal acts that they make little or no attempts to conceal them; but this is not always the case.

Q. If the same person should cry out while stabbing one of the attendants, "I am mad! I am mad!" would it not be further ground for suspicion that he was insane? A. Such an exclamation would give grounds. In my mind, to a suspicion that the man was feigning insanity.

Q. What would be the ground for that suspicion? A. Because insane men rarely make such exclamations or similar ones; they very rarely excuse themselves for criminal acts on the ground that they are insane.

Q. Do not madmen sometimes say they are mad? A. They do sometimes; but it is not feigning with them.

Q. Do you not remember cases in your medical experience when madmen have told you they were mad? A. They frequently do it in this way:—An individual knows he is regarded as insane, and if taken to task for any improper act sometimes a man will excuse himself on the ground that he is insane, and therefore not responsible.

Q. If the same person I have mentioned should, although in possession of a sound horse, make no effort to escape, but abandon his horse and wander off into the woods, and come back to a house surrounded with soldiers, where he might expect to be arrested—would that not be an additional ground for suspicion of insanity? A. I should regard every act of a man who committed a crime indicating that he was indifferent to the consequence, as a ground for suspicion that he was insane.

Q. If this same person should return to this house I have spoken of with a piece of his drawers for his hat, seeing the house in possession of soldiers, would not that be additional proof of insanity. A. I can hardly see what bearing that would have on the question of insanity.

Q. I understand you to say that madmen seldom disguise themselves; the disguise in question consisted of a piece of drawers taken for a hat; I asked whether the disguise indicated the work of a sane or an insane man? A. It would depend upon circumstances; with insane men it is a common peculiarity that they dress themselves in a fantastic manner; for example, making head-dresses of pieces of odd garments; they do it apparently out of childish fancy for something fantastic to attract attention; I do not recollect the case of an insane person dressing himself in garments of that kind for the sake of disguising himself.

Q. If this same person, after his arrest, should express a strong desire to be hung and great indifference to life, would that be an additional ground for suspicion of insanity? A. I think it would.

Q. Would it be further ground of suspicion if he seemed totally indifferent during his trial, and laughed when he was identified, betraying a stolidity of manner entirely different from his associates? A. I think it would.

Q. State what physical sickness generally accompanies insanity. If any. A. I believe disease either functional or organic of the brain, always accompanies insanity; no other physical disease necessarily, or perhaps usually accompanies it.

Q. Is not long continued constipation one of the physical conditions accompanying insanity? A. Long continued constipation frequently precedes insanity, but is not very frequent among the actually insane?

Q. If this same person I have described had been suffering from constipation for four weeks, would that be an additional ground for insanity? A. I think some weight might be given to that circumstance.

Q. If the same person during his trial, and during his confinement, never spoke until spoken to at a time when all his companions were peevish and clamorous; if he never expressed a want when all others expressed many; if he continued the same expression of indifference while others were nervous and anxious, if he continued immovable except a certain wildness in the movement of his eyes, would it not be additional ground for believing him to be insane? A. I think it would.

Q. If this same man, after committing the crime, should, on being questioned as to the cause, say he remembered nothing distinctly but a struggle, with no desire to kill, would not that be additional ground for suspicion of insanity? A. I think it would.

Q. What are the qualities of mind or person most needed by a keeper to secure control over madmen? A. self-control.

Q. Are not madmen usually managed by persons of strong will and resolute character? A. Yes; I think they are.

Q. Are there not instances on record of madmen towards all others, and yet who towards their keepers are as docile and obedient as dogs towards their masters? A. Not that servile obedience which a dog exhibits towards his master; it is true that the insane are comparatively mild and obedient to certain persons, while they are more or less violent towards certain other persons.

Q. Would it not be possible for such a keeper, who could exercise such control over a madman, to direct him to commit a crime, and secure its commission? A. I should say it would be very difficult unless it was done in a few minutes after the plan was laid and the directions given.

Q. Is not the influence of some persons over madmen so great, that their will seems to take the place of the madman's? A. There is a great difference in the control different individuals have over insane persons, but I think it rare that the control reaches the extent you have described, or the extent, I may add, that is popularly supposed.

Q. Do you recognize or not a distinction between mania and delusion? A. A certain distinction, inasmuch as delusion may accompany any and every form of insanity, while the term mania applies to a particular form, which may or may not accompany delusion.

Q. I ask whether instances of insane delusion are not more frequent during civil war than any other forms of insanity? A. My impression is that they are not as frequent; insanity is of a more general character, so far as my experience goes during the war, among soldiers than it usually is.

Q. Does or does not constantly dwelling on the same subject lead to insane delusion? A. It frequently does.

Q. For instance, if a body of men who own slaves are constantly hearing speeches and sermons vindicating the divine right of slavery, and when the institution was not threatened at all should finally go to war for its support, would not that be an evidence that these men were deluded? A. I think it would; but it does not follow that the delusion is not what I would technically denominate an insane delusion arising from disease of the brain, and for which a man is irresponsible.

Q. If one of these same men should own slaves and believe in the origin of the institution, fight in its defense, and believe that he had also fought in defense of h s home and fi eside, should attempt to assassinate the men who were the leaders of those he believed were killing his friends, would not that give rise to the suspicion that he was laboring under a fanatical delusion?

The question was objected to by Colonel Burnett; if the counsel was about through with his examination, he would not object; otherwise he would object to the continuance of an examination entirely irrelevant and foreign to the issue.

Mr. Doster replied that he had about a dozen more questions to put; that he had sent for witnesses in Florida, who had not yet arrived, and his examination of Dr. Nichols was in anticipation of their testimony, and in order to obviate the necessity of recalling him as a witness.

TRIAL OF THE ASSASSINS AT WASHINGTON.

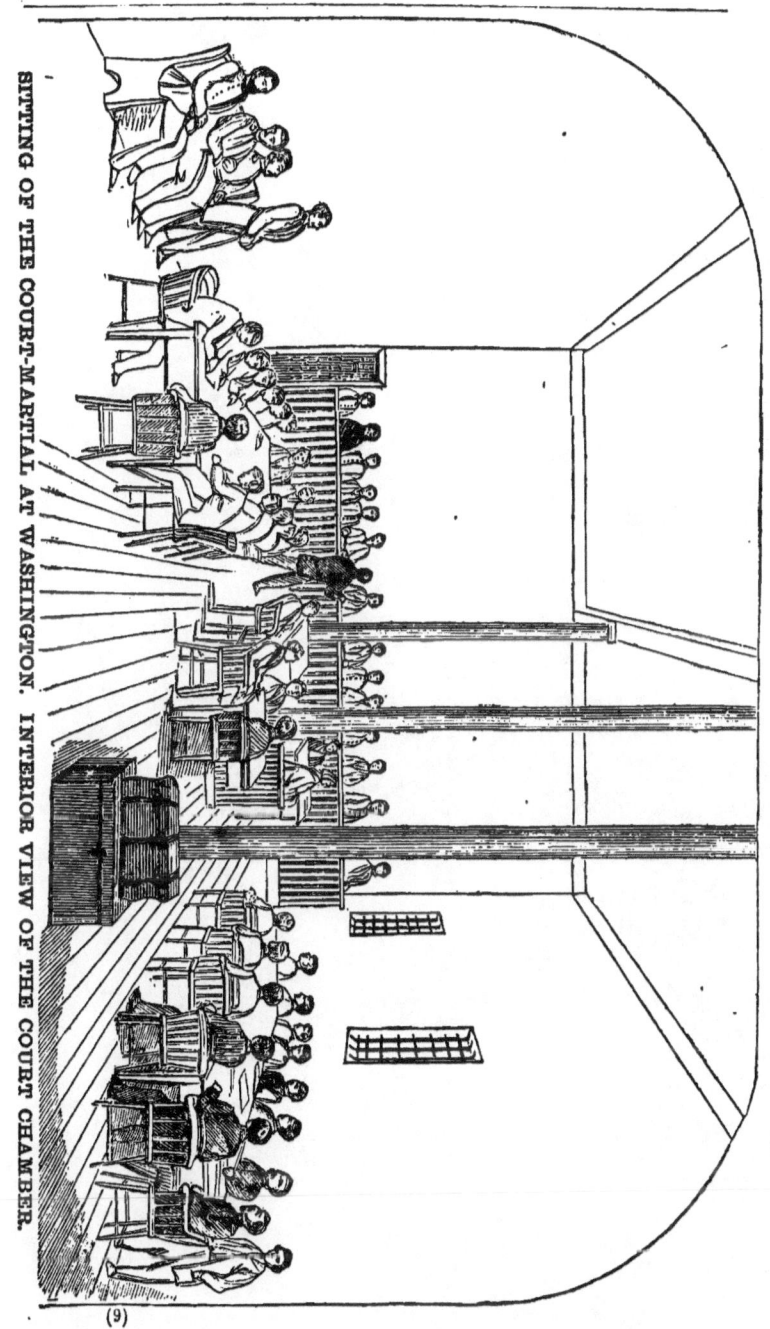

SITTING OF THE COURT-MARTIAL AT WASHINGTON. INTERIOR VIEW OF THE COURT CHAMBER.

The objection sustained by the Court.

Q. Is it your opinion that the person I have spoken of in committing the crime alleged under the circumstances was conscious that he was acting contrary to law, or whether he was laboring under any and what delusion?

Objected to by Judge Bingham, on the ground that the case put was one entirely hypothetical, and as such the witness was not qualified to answer it.

Mr. Doster replied that he had not the right to make the application to any particular case; that he had taken the question from the books he cited to sustain his position, "Wheaton on Criminal Law."

Colonel Burnett said that the counsel was proceeding in an examination based upon a hypothesis, having no application to any state of facts proved in this case, and there was no law found in any book that would uphold him in such a course. The Assistant Judge-Advocate had been instructed by their chief to allow the utmost liberality to counsel in the defense, but it was their duty to interpose when counsel were proceeding so far as to render the record absurd and contemptible.

Mr. Doster replied, that he believed the question was strictly legal, but knowing very well the result of the objection in this Court he would waive the question, and put it in this form:—

Q. Under this state of facts would, or would not, the inference of insanity result therefrom? A. If I may be allowed to make an explanatory answer, I will say that I have thus far given categorical answers to the questions put; I am, as a rule, very much opposed to giving opinions upon hypothetical cases for the best of reasons, as I conceive that I have now; I could give no definite opinion upon the facts implied, therefore, in the questions that have been submitted; every case of insanity is a case of itself and has to be examined with all the light that can be thrown on it, and it is impossible for me to give an opinion, therefore, upon a hypothetical case.

Testimony of Mr. Dawson.

Q. Are you a clerk in the National Hotel in this city? A. Yes sir.

Q. Look at that letter and see if it was ever received in the National Hotel? A. It was found among the initial letters, a couple of days before I was there; I noticed it and the initials struck me as rather peculiar.

Q. Do you know the exact date when it was read? A. No sir.

By Judge Advocate Bingham.—You opened it when you brought it to me; it was not opened before? A. No sir.

Mr. Pittman, at the request of the Court, then read the following letter:—

SOUTH BRANCH BRIDGE, April 6, 1865.—Friend Wilkes:—I received yours of March 12th, and reply as soon as practicable. I saw French Brad and others about the oil speculation. The subscription of the stock amounts to $8000, and I add $1000 myself, which is about all I can stand. Now, when you sink your well go deep enough. Don't fail. Everything depends on you and your helpers. If you can't get through on your trip after you strike ile, strike through Thornton's Gap and cross by Cacca pon, Romney, and down the branch, and I can keep you safe from all hardship for a year. I am clear of all surveillance, now that Infernal Purdy is beat. I hired that girl to charge him with an outrage, and reported him to old Kelly, which sent him in the shade, but he suspects too much now. Had he better be a fenced for good. I send th s up by Tom and if he don't get drunk you will get it by the 8th. At all events it can't be understood if lost. I can't half write. I have been drunk for two days. Don't write so much highfalutin the next time. No more, only Jake will be at Green's with the funds. Burn this. Truly yours,

(Signed) LOU.

Sue Guthrie sends much love.

(Mailed at Cumberland Md., May 8th. This letter, according to the post-mark, was mailed at Cumberland, Md., May 8th, although it is dated May 6th.)

Q. To whom besides Wilkes Booth, who stopped at your hotel, do the initials belong? A. As far as I remember, I don't know anybody else to my knowledge.

Testimony of Mr. Nott.

Q. I believe that you were the barkeeper or one of the attendants at the hotel at Surrattsville. A. Yes sir.

Q. How long was that your employment? From January, till I was arrested on the 14th of April; one time I was away a week, and sometimes I would be away a day or two.

Q. I desire to ask you what your attitude has been toward the Government since the war? A. I have never done anything against it.

Q. Or said anything against it? A. No sir.

Q. Nor against the Union party in Maryland? A. No sir.

Q. Do you know Mr. Smooth? A. Yes sir.

Q. What is his first name? A. Edward.

Q. Do you recollect having any conversation with him on the 14th of April? A. I do not, sir.

Q. Do you recollect his saying to you that it was supposed John H. Surratt was one of the murderers? A. No sir.

Q. Do you recollect telling him that Surratt was undoubtedly in New York? A. No sir; I may or I may not, but I do not recollect.

Q. Did you say to him that "John knows all about that matter, and that you could have told him all about it, and it would have occurred, six months ago?" A. No sir.

Q. Did you at that time tell him not to mention the conversation you had with him? A. No sir; I don't think I could have said such a thing.

Q. You have never been unfriendly to the Government? A. No sir.

Q. You have never taken sides with the Rebels?

By Major-General Hunter.—Q. Where were you at the time of the first battle of Bull Run? A. I have not had any particular home since the death of my wife; I think I was in Hill's place.

Q. Did you rejoice at the success of the Rebels? A. No sir, I guess I did not.

Q. Don't you know that you did? A. No sir, I know nothing of the kind.

Q. What Church do you belong to? A. The Catholic Church, when I belong to any at all.

Q. That'll do, sir; I have no more questions to ask you.

By Colonel Burnett—Q. How long since you belonged to that Church? A. Not for seven years, sir.

Q. You only occasionally belonged to the church, eh? Well, that's all.

Testimony of Mr. Reybold.

Q. Have you visited Ford's theatre since you were upon the stand? A. Yes sir, I have.

Q. Have you examined the keepers of the locks of boxes 7 and 8? A. Yes sir.

Q. State the condition in which you found them. A. Box 8 had been forced and the wood was split; box 7 was also forced, you could pull the screws in and out; box 8 the keeper is forced aside.

Q. State whether or not it was done by any instrument. A. I think not; it was done by force applied to the inside of the door.

Testimony of Mr. Plant.

Q. What is your residence and occupation? A. I am a dealer in furniture at present; my residence is No. 350 G. street, between Ninth and Tenth, Washington city.

Q. Have you ever been engaged at any time in cabinet work? A. For the last fourteen years, more or less.

Q. Have you visited Ford's Theatre to-day? A. I have.

Q. State whether you examined the keeper on the private boxes; and, if so, what boxes? A. Yes, I did, boxes 7 and 8, and to all appearance they had both been forced open; No. 7 I could pull the screws out and push them in with my thumb and fingers; in box 4, directly under, the keeper is gone entirely.

Q. State whether or not, according to your professional opinion, the keeper of boxes seven (7) and eight (8) were made loose by an instrument or by force applied from the outside. A. I should judge, sir, by force from the outside.

Q. State whether you noticed a hole in the wall in the passage which leads into the boxes. A. Yes sir.

Q. State whether it had the appearance of having been covered. A. Yes sir; it has been, but I could not say with what, there being no remnant left.

Q. Did you notice a hole in either of the doors of the boxes? Yes; in the door of box No. 7.

Q. What size? A. Not more than a quarter of an inch in diameter; it is larger on the outside than on the inside; a sort of wedge shaped.

A. Could you tell how that was made? A. I should judge with some instrument; one part felt as if it was made with a knife at the right hand side and the bottom of the hole, and another part looked as if made with a gimlet; one part feels rough, as if made by the withdrawing of the gimlet after the hole was bored.

Q. Do you think that a gimlet was used in making the hole? A. Yes sir, something of that sort, but it might have been done with a knife.

Testimony of William Smooth.

(Witness for the prosecution.)—Q. State where you reside. A. In Prince George county.

Q. How near Surrattsville? A. About one mile.

Q. Are you acquainted with a man named Jenkins, a brother of Mrs. Surratt? A. Yes sir; I know two of her brothers.

Q. Do you know the one who has testified in this case, J. B. Jenkins? A. Yes sir.

Q. State what position he has occupied towards this Government during the Rebellion. A. During the first year he was looked upon as a Union man; after that he was looked upon as a Secesh sympathizer.

Q. Do you know Mr. Nott? A. Yes sir.

Q. Did you have any conversation with him on the Saturday succeeding the murder? A. I had.

Q. State what it was. A. I met two young men connected with General Augur's head-quarters, and one of them told me Surratt was supposed to be the man who cut Mr. Seward, and I asked Mr. Nott if he could tell me where Surratt was; he said he reckoned he was in New York by that time; I asked him why that was, and he said, "My God, John Surratt knows all about this, and do you suppose he is going to stay in Washington and let them catch him; I could have told you this thing was going to happen six months ago;" then said he, "Keep that in your skin, for if you would mention it it would ruin me."

Q. What was Nott's attitude to the Government? A. I have heard him speak against the Government, and denounce the Administration in every manner and form, and heard him say that if the South didn't succeed he didn't want to live another day.

In a long cross-examination the witness simply repeated his testimony in chief.

Testimony of Mr. Roby.

Q. State where you reside. A. In Prince George county.
Q. How far from Surrattsville? A. Three or four hundred yards.
Q. Are you acquainted with J. C. Jenkins? A. Yes sir.
Q. How long have you known him. A. Since 1861.
Q. State to the Court whether you held any position under the Government. A. I was appointed an enrolling officer on the 12th of June, 1864.
Q. State to the Court what the reputation of Jenkins is or has been since 1861 with reference to loyalty. A. I never heard but one opinion, and that is that in 1861 he was looked upon as a Union man, and after that time as a sympathizer with the South.
Q. Has he been in the attitude of a talker against the Government? A. Yes sir, since 1862.

Cross-examination.—Q. Were you a member of Cowan's Company in 1861? A. No sir; I was a member of another company.
Q. You state that up to 1862 Jenkins was regarded as a Union man? A. Yes sir; I saw him once between the 9th of April, 1861, and the 19th of July; he was begging money for a Union man's family who had been killed; the next time I saw him was at my house, and he was then opposed to the nominees of the Union party.
Q. What have you heard of Jenkins since 1862? A. I have been living near Surrattsville since September, 1863, and have seen Jenkins nearly every day; he was then a talking against the Government, and at the election at which we voted for the new Constitution, he said he had been offered office under the "damn Government," but would not hold office under such a "God-damned Government."
Q. What Government? A. The Government of the United States.
Q. What do you mean by the Government? A. The laws, the Constitution, and the enforcement thereof.

The Court here adjourned till 10 o'clock to-morrow morning.

The Name of Payne Said to be Powell.

WASHINGTON, June 3.—After the reading of the record of yesterday the trial was proceeded with.

Testimony of Ex-Governor Farwell, of Wisconsin.

By Mr. Doster.—Q. State whether on the evening of the 14th of April last you went from Ford's Theatre to the room of Vice President Johnson. A. Between ten and half-past ten o'clock on that evening I went directly from the theatre to the Vice President's room.
Q. State whether you found the door of the room locked or open A. It was locked, I think; I am not certain.
Q. Did you find anybody apparently lying in wait about the room? A. I did not discover any one.
Q. If anybody had been lying in wait about the room would you have been able to see them? A. I did not look at anything but the door, and did not see any one at the door.
Q. What did you do after you got to the door? A. I rapped, but received no answer; I rapped again, and said in a loud voice, "Governor Johnson, if you are in the room I must see you."
Q. Did you enter the Vice President's room? A. I did, and remained there half an hour.
Q. While you were there was the room visited by any strangers? A. A number of persons came to the door; after I got inside I locked and bolted the door, and did not allow any person to come in without it was some one personally known to the Vice-President or myself; I also rang the bell for the servants.
Q. State whether you ever saw the prisoner Atzeroth before? A. Not to my knowledge.
Q. Do you take your meals at the Kirkwood House? A. I do.
Q. Have you not observed persons asking to see the Vice President while he would be taking his meals? A. No sir, only when, as I have been at the table, some gentleman would ask me casually whether the Vice-President was in.

Testimony of John B. Hubbard.

By Mr. Doster.—Q. State whether at times you are in charge of the prisoner, Payne? A. I am.
Q. Have you at any time during his confinement had any conversation with him? A. I have.
Q. State what was the substance of that conversation?
Assistant Judge Bingham objected to the question, on the ground that the declarations of the prisoner were not admissible.
Judge Advocate Holt stated that as a confession of the prisoner, it would not be admissible, but if merely designated to show his condition of mind, it might be considered.

The question was then answered, as follows:—
A. I was taking him out of the court room the other day when he wished they would make haste and hang him, that he was tired of life; and that he would rather be hanged than come back here.
Q. Did he ever have any conversation with you in reference to the subject of his constitution? A. Yes sir; about a week ago.
Q. What did he say? A. He said that he had been so ever since he had been here.
Q. What had been so? A. That he had been constipated.
Q. Have you any personal knowledge as to the truth of that? A. I have not.
Q. To whom did you tell what the prisoner said to you? A. To Colonels McCall and Dart.
By Assistant Judge Advocate Bingham.—Q. What else did the prisoner say to you? A. That was all he said.

Testimony of Colonel W. H. H. M'Call.

By Mr. Doster.—Q. Have you at any time had charge of the prisoner Payne? A. I have.
Q. Are you alone in charge of him? A. No sir; Colonel Frederick, Colonel Dart and myself have charge of him.
Q. How is the duty divided between you? A. We have each eight hours out of the twenty-four.
Q. Does your duty lead you to be cognizant of the conduct of the prisoner in his cell? A. Yes sir.
Q. Do you know anything with reference to the constipation of the prisoner? A. To the best of my knowledge, until last evening, he had no relief since the 28th of April.
Q. Have you ever had any conversation with the prisoner on the subject of his own death? A. No sir.

Testimony of John E. Roberts.

By Mr. Doster.—Q. Is it a part of your duty to take charge of the prisoner Payne? A. I have not had special charge of the prisoner; my duties are general.
Q. Have you at any time had a conversation with him? A. Yes sir.
Q. Have you ever spoken to him on the subject of his own death? A. On the day that Major Seward was examined here, and the prisoner was dressed in a coat and hat, as I was putting the irons on him again he told me that they were treating him pretty close and he wanted to die.
Q. Did he say that he was tired of life? A. I have told you all that he said.
Q. You never had any further conversation with him? A. Not at all not on the subject of death; words passed between us now and then on the stairway.
By Assistant Judge Advocate Bingham.—Q. Did he say that he was tired of life and he wanted to die? A. Yes sir.
Q. He coupled with that the remark that they were tracing him pretty close; in other words finding him out? A. Those were his words.

Testimony of Lieut. John W. Dempsey.

Q. State where you are on duty? A. At No. 541 H street, in command of the guard having charge of the house of Mrs. Surratt.
Q. State whether you were with the party that made an examination of the house at the time the house was searched? A. I was with the party that came to the house on the 14th or 20th of April; the house was searched before I sat; I was not in command of the guard that first went to the house.
[A photograph of J. Wilkes Booth was here shown to the witness, and identified by him as the one which he had found behind a picture of Morning and Evening. The back of the photograph bore the name of J. Wilkes Booth in pencil marks.]

Testimony of James R. O'Brien.

By Mr. Ewing—Q. State where you were employed on the 14th of April and for some months preceding that day. A. In the Quartermaster-General's office.
Q. Had you any engagement with Mr. Ford? A. Yes sir; I was usher at the theatre during the evening performances.
Q. Do you know anything as to the condition of the keepers of the locks of boxes 7 and 8? A. The keeper of box 8 was wrenched off or broken in some way; I do not know how; I was absent one evening at home sick, and I afterwards found it broken off.
Q. When did you notice that the keeper of the door of box 8 had been broken? A. I noticed it the first time afterwards that I went into the box; that was

TRIAL OF THE ASSASSINS AT WASHINGTON. 129

sometime before the assassination; I could not say how long before.

Q. Do you know whether the door could be fastened afterwards by locking? A. It might be locked, but I thought that if shoved it would come open; it would always shut tight, and I had no occasion to lock it.

Q. How was the keeper of the door of box 7. A. It appeared to be all right; I always locked that box.

Q. Which door was used when the Presidential party occupied the two boxes? A. The door of box 8.

Q. How was it generally left after the party entered? A. Always left open.

Q. Do you know whether the door leading into the passage which separates the two boxes from the wall had a lock upon it? A. No sir; it had no lock.

By Assistant Judge Advocate Bingham.—Q. The outer door had a latch, had it not? A. No sir; it was not fastened at all.

Q. Box eight is nearest the stage, is it not? A. Yes sir.

Testimony of Dr. Blanford.

By Mr. Ewing.—Q. State whether you are acquainted with the country along the routes from here to Surrattsville and Bryantown and through Surrattsville to Port Tobacco? A. As far as Bryantown and Port Tobacco I am acquainted with it, but not further.

Q. Are you acquainted with the locality of Dr. Mudd's house? A. I am. (A map of the locality referred to, showing the different roads leading from Washington to Bryantown and vicinity, was shown to the witness; also a plot drawn by himself, giving the different localities in the neighborhood of Dr. Samuel A. Mudd's house, both of which he testified were accurately drawn.)

The hour of one o'clock having arrived, the Commission took a recess, as usual, until two, at which hour the body reassembled.

Examination of Susan Stewart, (Colored).

By Mr. Ewing.—Q. State where you reside? A. At Mr. John Miller's, about a mile from Bryantown.

Q. How near do you live to the house of the colored man John Boose? A. Only a short distance.

Q. You both lived on the little cut-off road leading through the farm? A. Yes sir.

Q. State whether you know Dr. Samuel A. Mudd the prisoner. A. I do.

Q. State whether you saw him on the day after the President's assassination, and where? A. I saw Dr. Mudd on Easter Saturday between three and four o'clock in the evening; I saw him out by the corner of the barn near Mr. Murray's house, riding along slowly by himself.

Q. At the time you saw Dr. Mudd, could you see the main road from where you were standing? A. I did not take any notice of the main road; some one said "here comes a gentleman," and I went to the door and saw it was Dr. Mudd.

Q. How much of the main road could you see from where you were standing? A. About a quarter of a mile or more.

Q. Did you see anybody on the main road? A. I did not if there had been anybody with him I could easily have seen the person.

By Assistant Judge Advocate Bingham.—Q. This was on Easter Saturday afternoon? A. Yes sir.

Q. Dr. Mudd was coming apparently from Bryantown? A. Yes sir.

By Mr. Ewing.—Q. Did you see which way he was coming, whether he was coming from Bryantown or not? A. No sir.

Testimony of Primas Johnson (colored).

Q. Do you know the prisoner, Dr. Mudd? A. Yes sir.

Q. State when you saw him after the President's assassination? A. I saw him on the Saturday afternoon afterwards, about three or half-past three o'clock.

Q. Did you see him as he was going to Bryantown that day? A. Yes sir.

Q. Did you see anything of a man riding along with him as he was going to Bryantown? A. No sir; Master Sam. Mudd was by himself; there was a man went along after he had gone on.

Q. Did you see anything of that man who followed Master Sam. Mudd coming back? A. Yes sir; the same man that went in towards Bryantown came back by himself about an hour and a half, I reckon, before Master Sam, Mudd.

Q. Where is Mr. Bonse's house? A. I suppose it is a couple of miles this side of Bryantown, on the road between Bryantown and Dr. Sam. Mudd's.

Testimony of Charles Bloyce.

By Mr. Ewing—Q. Do you know the prisoner, Dr. Samuel A. Mudd? A. Yes sir.

Q. Were you about his house last year, and if so, how often? A. I went there on the 12th day after the Christmas before last, and was about the house every Saturday and Sunday, except between the 10th of April and the 20th of May, when I was hauling seine.

Q. Are you the husband of one of his servants, who has been here as a witness? A. Yes sir.

Q. Have you ever seen Ben. Gwynn or Andrew Gwinn? A. Yes sir, about four years ago, when the war first commenced, they passed along by Mr. Dyer's.

Q. Did you see either of them about Dr. Mudd's house last year? A. No sir.

Q. Did you see or hear anything of Watt Bowie, John H. Surratt, Capt. White, of Tennessee, Lieut. Perry, or J. Wilkes Booth? A. No sir.

Q. Neither saw nor heard of any of them about Dr. Mudd's house last year? A. No sir.

Q. Did you know of any Confederate officers or any men in uniform being about there last year? N. No, sir.

Q. Do you know Mary Simms? A. Yes sir.

Q. Do you know what the colored folks about there think of her as a truth-teller? A. The folks there said she was not much of a truth-teller; that she told such lies they could not believe her.

Q. What did they think about Mylo Simms? A. They thought the same about him; I used to think myself that he was a liar, because he used to tell me lies sometimes.

Q. What was Dr. Mudd's character as a master of his servants? A. I would call him a first-rate man; I never heard of him whipping or saying anything to them; they did pretty much as they pleased.

Q. Did you ever hear him threaten to send any of his servants to Richmond? A. No indeed, I never heard one of them say a word about it.

By Assistant Judge Advocate Bingham.—Q. Did you ever hear anything about his shooting any of his servants? A. I did hear that.

Q. You thought that was first-rate fun? A. I don't know about that. (Laughter.)

Testimony of Marcus P. Norton.

Colonel Burnett stated that in the discretion of the Court this witness had been called to give testimony bearing more or less directly upon the prisoners, Dr. Mudd, Atzeroth and O'Laughlin. It was the practice in Military Courts, even after the testimony had been closed on both sides, for the Court to call and examine further witnesses if in their judgment necessary. If, however, the counsel for the defense wish to interpose an objection, now was the proper time for them to do so.

Mr. Cox stated that he should object, for the reason that it had once been distinctly announced that all evidence on the part of the Government, except that strictly rebutting in its nature, was closed only so far as should relate to the general subject of the conspiracy, and not affecting directly the case of any one of the prisoners.

Mr. Ewing said that so far as he was concerned he was willing that any further evidence should be introduced, provided time was given for the defense to meet it.

Colonel Burnett replied that it was for that very purpose he had called the witness now.

The Court decided to receive the proposed evidence.

By Colonel Burnett—Q. Where do you reside? A. In the city of Troy, N. Y.

Q. State where you were during the latter part of the winter and beginning of this year. A. I was at the National Hotel, in this city, from about the 10th of January until the 10th or middle of March.

Q. While there did you become acquainted with J. Wilkes Booth? A. Not personally acquainted; I knew him by sight; I had seen him act several times in the theatre.

Q. While at the hotel state whether you saw any one with him? A. There are those that I recognize as having seen during that time in company with J. Wilkes Booth; rather, I should say I saw those two men with him. (Atzeroth and O'Laughlin).

Q. At what time? A. I do not remember the exact day; it was near to the inauguration of President Lincoln; Atzeroth I saw twice, and the other one I suppose four or five times.

Q. State whether at any time you accidentally overheard any conversation between Booth or either of these parties, and if so, what it was? A. I did with Atzeroth; I can't give the precise language, but the substance of it was that if the matter succeeded as well with Johnson as it did with Buchanan, they would get terribly sold.

Q. Did you hear any other conversation? A. There was something said that the testimony of witnesses would be of vital character that very little could be proved by them; Booth's statements I heard in the same conversation on the evening of either the 2d or 3d of March last; I did not know what was referred to.

Q. State now which of the other prisoners you have seen before, and under what circumstances. A. I saw that one (Dr. Mudd) once, while I was at the National Hotel; he came to my room on the morning of the 3d of March, entered hastily, and appeared to be somewhat excited; he said he had made a mistake, that he wanted to see Booth; I told him Booth's room was perhaps on the floor above; I did not know the number; from the apparently excited manner of his person entering my room I left my writing and went out into the hall and followed him; he went down stairs, and as he reached the story below he turned and looked at me.

Q. Did or did not you, when you first entered the room this morning, recognize the prisoner, Mudd, as the person you met on that occasion? A. I pointed him out to H. Jones this morning, the prisoner I now

see was the one, or it was a person exactly like him; I am satisfied he was the man.
Q. Did you ever see him afterwards? A. Not before to-day.
Q. State what circumstances enable you to fix the date. A. I fix it from the fact of its proximity to the inauguration; I think it was about ten or eleven o'clock on the morning before.
Q. Might it not have been in the previous month of February? A. I think the day I have named was the date.
Q. Are you as certain about that as you are of the identity of the prisoner? A. I am.
Cross-examined by Mr. Cox.—Q. Can you fix the date of the conversation O'Laughlin had with Booth? A. I cannot.
Q. Was any person in company with them while they were conversing? A. No, sir.
Q. Did you overhear anything said in any of these conversations? A. No, I was not near enough.
By Mr. Ewing.—Q. How do you fix the third of March as the day Dr. Mudd entered your room? A. Only from the fact of the inauguration; I did not make any memorandum of it, or charge my mind particularly with the date; I recollect the morning Dr. Mudd entered my room I had a motion pending in the Supreme Court of the United States for that day, and I was preparing my papers.
Q. When did you argue the motion? A. On that day.
Q. What was the motion? A. It was to dismiss a certain patent case from the Court for want of jurisdiction, in a case originating in the Northern District of New York.
Q. How was he dressed? A. That I could not say; his garments were black, and he had a hat in his hand; I do not know as I can give any name to the hat; it had a high crown.
Q. Can you describe any other article of dress? A. No, it was a hasty glance coming in and going out.
Q. Do you recognize the prisoner Mudd with as much certainty in your own mind as you do the others? A. In my own mind I have no doubt as to either of the three.
Q. Do you recognize any of the other prisoners at the bar? A. I do not know that I ever saw any of the others before.
By Mr. Doster.—Q. State if you can the precise date of the conversation between Atzeroth and Booth? A. I cannot; the place was in the office of the hotel and the time was early in the evening.
Q. How did you happen to hear them? A. I was sitting in a seat near them; in a hotel, we sometimes overhear parties, even when talking with others.
Q. "God-damn" ...lking in a loud or low tone of voice?
"Were they t..."...... ... and tone of voice.
A. They were not talking in a very lo...... ....nt him two or three feet.
Q. How near were you to them? A. With... cr three feet.
Q. Was the prisoner dressed then as he is now? A. I should think not; I did not take particular notice, however; I passed it as I do a thousand other things.
Q. You do not recognize him, then, by his dress? A. No; by his appearance; I do not know as he had so much of a scowl upon his face then as now.
Q. Was he as fleshy then as now? A. I could not say as to that; I did not take his dimensions as to his avoirdupois weight.
Q. You say you have not seen Atzeroth since then until to-day; about two months ago? A. About that.
Q. Have you repeated that conversation from that time until to-day? A. I spoke to Mr. King about it once.
Q. Are you in the habit of remembering conversations you overhear casually for two months? A. I remember some things a long time.
Q. Are you in the habit of remembering faces for that time? A. I do sometimes.
Q. And you can swear to that precise conversation? A. I have only undertaken to repeat the substance of it.
Q. Are you a lawyer? A. I am.
Q. And have you read the testimony in this case? A. Not generally at all; I have read the examination of two or three witnesses.
By Mr. Coxe.—Q. Were the conversations you saw between Booth and O'Laughlin in the public hall? A. They were; I heard none of them.
By the Court.—Q. What is the character of your eyesight? A. I am somewhat near-sighted; I always wear glasses.
Q. Do you have perfect confidence in recognizing people's countenances? A. I would at the distance I saw these men.
Q. What was the impression created by this man who came into your room that led you to follow him? A. It was his hasty entrance and hasty exit.
Q. Did he seem embarrassed or mistaken when he entered the room? A. He seemed somewhat excited, and apologized by saying he had made a mistake.
Q. Had you occupied that room previous to that day? A. I had been changed into that room perhaps ten days previously.

Cross-Examination of L. S. Roby.

By Mr. Ewing.—Q. State where you live. A. In Charles county, Maryland.
Q. Were you in Bryantown on the day after the assassination of the President? A. I was on the evening of that day; I arrived there at three o'clock, I guess.
Q. State what you heard about the assassination of the President. A. We heard before getting there of the fact, but I did not believe it; when we got near there, however, I found soldiers stationed along the road, and I inquired of them and they said it was a fact; I made inquiry as to who was the perpetrator; they said it was somebody who belonged to the theatre; they did not give the name, and spoke as though they did not know; I had conversation with several; there was a great deal of confusion, but before I left I heard it was Booth, from Dr. George Mudd.
Q. Were you about Bean's store during the time you was there? A. I passed it, but did not go in.
Q. State whether you are acquainted with D. J. Thomas, who has been a witness for the prosecution? A. I am.
Q. Do you know his reputation in the neighborhood in which he lives, for veracity? A. It is bad.
Q. From your knowledge of his reputation for veracity would you believe him under oath? A. I do not believe I would.
Cross-examined by Colonel Burnett.—Q. How near do you live to Mr. Thomas? A. Within four or five miles.
Q. How intimately have you known him for the last four or five years? A. I have known him quite intimately.
Q. State what your own attitude has been toward the Government since the Rebellion? A. It is my belief I have been a loyal citizen; I have done no overact in any shape or manner.
Q. Have you said anything against the Government or given any counsel or assistance to the Rebels? A. No; there are some acts of the Administration that I have not spoken pleasantly about; nothing else.
Q. Have you said anything against any of the specifications of the Government in seeking to put down this Rebellion? A. I do not think I have.
Q. Have you maintained the attitude of a friend of the Government or of a friend to the south during the Rebellion? A. Shortly after the war broke out I took an oath of fealty to the Government, and have strongly adhered to it, neither turning to the left nor to the right.
Q. What acts of the Administration have you talked against? A. Arbitrary arrests.
Q. Arbitrary arrests of Rebels? A. No, of citizens.
Q. Were they not Rebels? A. No, they professed to be loyal citizens; I do not recollect who they were.
Q. Do you recollect a man by the name of Joyle? A. I do.
Q. Do you know him as the man who murdered Captain Watkins? A. I have only seen him once since that time.
... .ll you not harbor him and feed him after the murder? A. ... No sir; he came to my house on the morning after the general election; I live not far from the road; he only stayed a short time; the only time I have seen him since the mur...der was once on the road.
By Mr. Ewing.—Q. In your statement in regard to the veracity of Mr. Thomas as a witness did you refer to his reputation before or since the war? A. All the time; he seems to be a kind of man who will imagine things that are not true, and get to believe they are facts, and stick to them all the time.
By Judge Bingham.—Q. You do not mean to say that he would tell what he did not believe to be true? A. No, but he would tell things not true, although he believed them himself to be true.

Testimony of E. D. R. Bean.

By Mr. Ewing.—Q. State your occupation? A. I am a merchant at Bryantown.
Q. State whether the prisoner, Dr. Mudd, made any purchases of you the day after the assassination of the President? A. I think I sold him some calico; I only remember the day from some circumstances that fixed it in my mind.
Q. State what you heard that day in Bryantown as to the assassination of the President? A. I heard that day that the President was assassinated; as I asked by whom, and I understood it to be a man of the name of Boyle, who was said to have murdered Captain Watkins.
Q. Did you on that day hear that it was Booth who assassinated the President? A. I cannot particularly say; my impression is that I did not on that day.
Q. Were there soldiers in and out of your store that day, and citizens? A. Yes, and that the subject of the assassination was the general topic of conversation.
Q. State whether you had any conversation with the prisoner, Dr. Mudd, about the assassination? A. The day I sold him the calico I had some discussion with him on that subject; I remarked to him it was bad news.
Judge Bingham—It is not competent for the witness to state that conversation.
Mr. Ewing said he was aware that similar questions had been overruled, but still, believing the question was a proper one, he desired to have it entered and the decision of the Court upon it.
The objection was sustained by the Court.
Q. It was the conversation you had with Dr. Mudd

that enabled you to fix the date when you sold the calico. Was it? A. Yes sir.
Cross-examined by Judge Bingham.—Q. When did you learn that Booth was the man who had murdered President Lincoln? A. Really I do not remember the day.
Q. Then you do not know that it was not on Easter Saturday, do you? A. I do not.
Q. Did you hear, at the same time, that the man who had murdered the President had been traced to within three miles of Bryantown? A. I do not know whether it was at the same time; I heard some time that he was traced to within three or three and a half miles of that place.
Q. Can you tell how you heard it? A. I do not know; it was in general conversation.
Q. Did you connect the sale of the calico with that fact, as well as the killing of the President by Booth? A. I did not; I think I did not hear of that fact.
Q. How do you know it was on Monday? A. I do not know.
Q. And you cannot positively state that it was not on Saturday? A. No sir.
By Mr. Ewing.—Q. But your impression is that you did not hear it on Saturday? A. My impression is that I did not.

Testimony of John R. Giles.

By Mr. Cox.—Q. Where do you reside? A. At Rollman's Hotel, Pennsylvania avenue, Washington.
Q. Do you know the accused, Michael O'Laughlin? A. Yes, I have known him personally for about four months.
Q. Did you see him on the Thursday before the assassination of the President? A. I saw him in the evening he was with a Mr. Murphy, with Lieutenant Henderson, Purdy and several others.
Q. Where was it? A. It was at our place, two doors from the Globe office; I saw him early in the evening, and then later, about ten o'clock, and they remained till after eleven o'clock.
Q. Did you join them when they went out? A. I did, and was with them till one o'clock.
Q. Did you see them on Friday evening, the evening of the assassination? A. I did; I was with them all the evening.
Q. Was O'Laughlin at your hotel at the time the news of the assassination of the President was received? A. Yes, he was; I should think it was about half-past nine or ten o'clock.
Q. Your house is owned by a man by the name of Lichau, is it not? A. Yes.
Q. Is it the house known as the Lichau House? A. No; the Lichau House is on Louisiana avenue, between Fifth and Sixth streets, near Canterbury Music Hall.
Cross-examined by Judge Bingham.—Q. You think the news of the President's murder came along about half-past nine or ten o'clock? A. I think so; I could not tell certainly; I did not look at the clock.

Re-Cross-Examination of Mr. Reed.

By Mr. Aiken.—Q. Are you acquainted with John H. Surratt? A. I know him by sight.
Q. State the time you saw him last. A. I saw him about half-past two o'clock on the day of the assassination, the 14th of April.
Q. Did you ever have any conversation with him? A. I cannot say that I have since; I was quite a boy; he has been merely a speaking acquaintance.
Q. Where were you when you saw him? A. I was standing on the stoop of Hunt & Goodwin's military store.
Q. State how his hair was cut. A. It was cut very singularly; it was rounded down, and fell on his coat collar behind.
Q. Did he have a moustache or whiskers? A. I do not know that he had; in fact, I did not look at his face, particularly, at all.
Q. Look at that picture of John H. Surratt, and see if you recognize it? A. It is very much like the clothing, but it is not the style of hair he had when I saw him.
By Judge Bingham.—Q. That is the picture of John H. Surratt, is it not? A. Yes, it is a fair picture of him, though his hair is not cut as it was when I saw him on the 14th of April.

Testimony of Miss Anna Ward.

By Mr. Aiken.—Q. State your residence. A. In Washington city.
Q. Are you acquainted with the prisoner, Mrs. Surratt? A. Yes, I have known her for seven or eight years.
Q. Have you ever known her on any occasion fail to recognize you or her friends when you have met her? A. She failed to recognize me once when I met her on the street; I had also failed to recognize her; she made an apology to me and I made the same apology to her.
Q. Are you near-sighted? A. I am; this was on Seventh street; Mrs. Surratt's daughter was with her, and called her attention to the fact that she had not spoken to me.
Q. Did you ever have occasion at any time to read for her? A. Yes, I gave her a letter to read; she returned it to me, and asked me to read it, saying she could not see to read by gas light.

Q. Do you recollect any other occasion when she failed to recognize persons? A. I do not know that I do.
Q. Did you receive a letter from John H. Surratt not long since? A. I did.
Q. Where is that letter? A. I gave it to his mother; I presume it has been destroyed.
Q. Please state to the Court, as well as you can recollect, all the circumstances of John H. Surratt's affair with you in engaging a room at the Herndon House. A. He called one afternoon and asked to see me.
Judge Bingham. You need not state that conversation.
Mr. Aiken. Very well, then, we turn the witness over to you. Perhaps you may want to make some inquiries yourself about that matter.
Cross-examined by Judge Bingham.—Q. Have you been in the habit of visiting often at Mrs. Surratt's? A. Occasionally, up to the day of the assassination; that was the last day I visited her.
Q. On all the occasions when you went to the house did she recognize you without difficulty? A. Yes; once or twice she opened the door for me; at other times I sent my name up.
Q. She was quick to recognize the voice, wasn't she? A. Yes.
Q. You are acquainted with John H. Surratt? A. Yes.
Q. Did you go with him or go alone to the Herndon House to obtain a room? A. I did not obtain a room, I simply went there to ascertain if there was a vacant room.
Q. When was that? A. I do not know; it was a long time ago.
Q. Was it probably the last of February or perhaps of March? A. It may have been.
Q. You went there to obtain a room for a delicate gentleman, did you not? A. I did not know what person.
Q. Have you met any of the prisoners at the bar? A. I can't see them well enough to answer; I do not think I have.
Q. Did you meet any strangers at Mrs. Surratt's house? A. I met Booth there, and I met two gentlemen who boarded there.
Q. You got a letter from John H. Surratt, postmarked Montreal, Canada East? A. Yes.
Q. When did you receive it? A. I received two from him; the first on the day of the assassination; I do not recollect the date of the second; there was a very short interval between them.
Q. You delivered both of these letters to Mrs. Surratt? A. I delivered one to her, and the other to her daughter Anna.
Q. Have you seen it since? A. No.
Q. Did you answer any letters received from him? A. Neither of these; he wrote me two letters at the same time, inclosing the letters for his mother; I answered those addressed to me.
Q. And all were about the time of the President's assassination? A. No; I do not recollect when: they were all after he left home, and I think very soon after the President's assassination.
Q. You haven't got any of them? A. No sir.
Q. Do you know where the letters to yourself have been destroyed? A. I do not; I left them with his mother, and have not inquired for them since.
Q. You asked for a room to rent at the Herndon House for a man? A. I did not; I simply asked for some rooms.
Q. Who was with you at that time? A. No one; I was alone, on my way to the Post Office.
By Mr. Aiken.—Q. Have you known Mrs. Surratt as a lady always attentive to her duties? A. I have.
Q. Do you know anything as to her general character? A. My knowledge of her has always been that of a Christian and a lady.
By the Court. Q. Do you attend the same church as Mrs. Surratt? A. I do, sir.

Testimony of Mr. Gessford.

By Mr. Ewing. Q. State in what business you were employed on the 14th of April last? A. I was ticket-seller at Ford's theatre.
Q. How long were you at the ticket office during the day or night? A. My business at the ticket office commenced about half-past six in the evening.
Q. State whether or not the private boxes, except those occupied by the party of the President, were applied for that evening? A. No sir.
Q. State whether or not any tickets to those boxes had been sold during the day? A. I think not.
No further witnesses for the defense being in attendance, Mr. Doster made application for a personal examination to be made of the prisoner Payne by Dr. Nichols, Superintendent of the Government Institution for the Insane, for the purpose of testing the sanity of the prisoner. The application was granted.
Mr. Doster also requested that the testimony for the defense be not considered as closed until George Powell, the father of Payne, and other witnesses, who had been summoned from Florida, who would testify in respect to Payne's antecedents and the tendency on the part of the family to insanity, should be present.

Judge Bingham. Then are we to regard that as an authentic statement that the prisoner's name is Powell?
Mr. Doster.—I have stated that his father's name is Powell, and I take it for granted the inference will be drawn that that is the name of the prisoner.
Colonel Burnett stated that a reasonable time would be allowed for the defense to meet the new evidence introduced by the Government to-day. Further than this he hoped there would be no postponement.
The President of the Court said that ample time had been allowed to obtain witnesses for the defense, and that the request of Mr. Doster would not be granted.
The Court then adjourned until Monday at 10 o'clock A. M.

The Suppressed Testimony.

The following testimony in secret session of the Court has been obligingly furnished for publication. That of Sanford Conover has heretofore been surreptitiously printed in a mutilated form, and hence the necessity of now publishing it entire.:—

Testimony of Richard Montgomery.

Richard Montgomery, a witness called for the prosecution, being duly sworn, testified as follows:—
By the Judge Advocate.—Q. Are you a citizen of New York? A. Yes sir.
Q. State whether or not you visited Canada in the summer of 1864. A. I did.
Q. How long did you remain there? A. I remained there, going back and forth, ever since, until within about a week and a half or two weeks' time.
Q. Did you or not know in Washington City, Jacob Thompson, formerly Secretary of the Interior, and Clement C. Clay, formerly of the United States Senate? A. I did.
Q. Will you state whether you met those persons in Canada and where? A. I met them in Canada. At Niagara Falls, at Toronto, at St. Catharine's, and at Montreal a number of times, and very frequently since the summer of 1864 up to this time.
Q. Did you or not meet George N. Sanders? A. I did.
Q. And a man by the name of J. P. Holcomb? A. Yes sir, Professor Holcomb.
Q. Can you name any other Rebel citizens of the United States in Canada, of note, that you met? A. Yes sir, I met Beverly Tucker, N. C. Cleary (I think those are the initials) and a great many others under fictitious names; there was another one by the name of Harrington; those are the ones that I principally had communication with; I met another one by the name of Clay, not Clement C. Clay; I met one Hicks up there also.
Q. Under how many different names did Jacob Thompson pass in Canada, do you know? A. It would be impossible for me to tell you; I know him under three or four, and others knew him under other names; his principal name was Carson.
Q. Do you know under what name Clement C. Clay passed? A. Yes sir; one of them was Hope; another, T. E. Lacy; I have forgotten the initials of his name as Hope; T. E. Lacy was the principal one; another one was Tracy.
Q. State any conversation you may have had with Jacob Thompson in Canada, in the summer of 1864, in regard to putting the President of the United States out of the way, or assassinating him. A. During a conversation in 1864, Jacob Thompson said to me that he had his friends (Confederates) all over the Northern States, who were ready and willing to go any length for the good of the cause of the South, and he could at any time have the tyrant Lincoln, and any others of his advisers that he chose, put out of his way; that he would but have to point out the man that he considered in his way and his friends, as he termed them, would put him out of it, and not let him know anything about it if necessary; and that they would not consider it a crime when done for the cause of the Confederacy.
Q. Did you or not see Thompson some time in the month of January, 1865, and where? A. That was in Canada, in Montreal.
Q. Will you state what he then said to you, if anything, in regard to a proposition which had been made to him to rid the world of the tyrant Lincoln? A. He said a proposition had been made to him to rid the world of the tyrant Lincoln, Stanton, Grant, and some others; that he knew the men who had made the proposition were bold, daring men, and able to execute anything that they would undertake without regard to the cost; that he, himself, was in favor of the proposition, but had determined to defer his answer until he had consulted his Government at Richmond, and that he was then only awaiting their approval; he said that he thought it would be a blessing to the people, both North and South, to have those men killed.
Q. This was in January? A. That was in January last.
Q. What time in the month was it? A. It was about the middle of the month: I saw him a number of times; I could not give the exact day of that conversation.
Q. Was it about that time that you saw Clement C. Clay, and had a conversation with him? A. No sir; in the summer of 1864, immediately after Mr. Thompson had told me what he was able to do, I repeated the conversation to Mr. Clay, and he said "that is so; we are all devoted to our cause, and ready to go any length, to do anything under the sun," was his expression, I remember, "to serve their cause."
Q. Look at those prisoners at the bar, and see if you recognize any of them as having been seen by you in Canada, and under what circumstances, A. I have seen that one without his coat, there (pointing to Lewis Payne, one of the accused;) I don't know his name.
Q. Will you state when, and under what circumstances you saw him? A. I have seen him a number of times in Canada; I saw him about the Falls in the summer of 1864, and I saw him again, I guess it was the last time and had some words with him, at the Queen's Hotel, at Toronto City, Canada West.
Q. State all that occurred at that time. A. I had had an interview of some time with Mr. Thompson; several others had sought an interview while I was closeted with him, and had been refused admittance; after I was through with Mr. Thompson, and in leaving the room, I saw this man, Payne, in the passage way, near his door; Mr. Clement C. Clay, Jr., was talking with him at the time; Mr. Clay stopped me and held my hands, finishing a conversation in an undertone with this man, and when he left me for a moment he said "wait for me, I will return;" he then went and spoke to some other gentlemen who were entering Mr. Thompson's door, and he came back and bid me good-bye, asking me where he could see me in half an hour, and I told him, and made an appointment to meet Mr. Clay; while Mr. Clay was away from me I spoke to this man, and asked him who he was; I commenced talking about some of the topics that were there, and he rather hesitated telling who he was; he (Payne) said, "Oh, I am a Canadian, giving me to understand that I was not to ask any more.
Q. Did you not ask Thompson or Clay who he was? A. Yes sir, I made some mention in regard to this man to Mr. Clay, in the interview I had with him about half an hour after I saw him standing in the passageway, and he said, "What did he say?" said I, "He said he was a Canadian;" and he said, "That is so, he is a Canadian," and laughed.
Q. Did he say he was one of their friends, or make any remark of that sort? A. He said, "We trust him."
Q. What was the idea conveyed by the term "Canadian" with his laugh? A. That was a very common expression among the friends of theirs that were in the habit of visiting the States, and gave me to understand that I was not to ask any more questions; that their intercourse was of a very confidential nature, and that their business was of a very confidential nature.
Q. Have you been to Canada since the assassination of the President? A. Yes sir.
Q. State whether you met any of these men of whom you have spoken on your return to Canada, and if so, what conversation you had with them there in regard to the assassination of the President? A. I met Beverly Tucker, a very few days after the assassination, three or four or five times?
Q. Where? A. At Montreal.
Q. What conversation had you? A. He said a great deal in conversation about the wrongs that the South had received from the hands of Mr. Lincoln, and that he deserved his death long ago; that it was a pity that he did not have it years ago, and that it was too bad the boys had not been allowed to act as they wanted to.
Q. Do you mean by the boys the men who were to assassinate him? A. Yes sir, the Confederate soldiers who were up there, who had been engaged in their raids; they used the expresssion "their boys" in regard to their soldiers and the men in their employ; it is common among them.
Q. Did you meet with Booth there? A. No sir, I never saw Mr. Booth in Canada.
Q. Did any of those men of whom you have spoken say that Booth was one of the men referred to by Jacob Thompson who was willing to assassinate the President? A. Yes sir; W. H. Cleary told me: I related to him the conversation I had had, or a portion of it, with Mr. Thompson in January, and he said that Booth was one of the parties to whom Thompson had reference.
Q. I'd he say in that connection anything further in regard to him? A. No sir; he said in regard to the assassination that it was too bad that the whole work had not been done.
Q. What did you understand by that expression, "the whole work?" A. I inferred that they intended to assassinate a greater number than they succeeded in trying to.
Q. Do you know what relation this man Cleary sustained to Thompson? A. Mr. Holcomb told me I would find Mr. Cleary to be the confidential, a sort of secretary to Mr. Thompson; Mr. Thompson told me he was posted upon all of his affairs, and that if I sought him at any time that he might be away I could state my business to Mr. Cleary, and it would be all the

TRIAL OF THE ASSASSINS AT WASHINGTON. 133

same; that I could have perfect confidence in him, that he was a very close-mouthed man.

Q. Did Cleary make any remark when speaking of his regret that the whole work had not been done; was any threat made to the effect that it would be yet done? A. Yes sir; he said they had better look out; we are not done yet, and remarked that they never would give up.

Q. What statement did Cleary make to you, if any, in regard to Booth's having visited Thompson? A. He said that he had been there twice in the winter; that he thought the last time was in December; he had also been there in the summer; he said he had been there before December; he thought that that was the last time.

Q. On your return to Canada did you learn from these parties that they supposed themselves to be suspected of the assassination, and were they taking any steps to conceal the evidence of their guilt? A. Oh yes sir; they knew a very few days after the assassination that they were suspected of it; Tucker and Cleary both said they were destroying their papers.

Q. Have you stated what Tucker said to you when you had an interview with him after you returned? A. He said it was too bad that they had not been allowed to not when they wanted to.

Q. (Submitting to witness a paper containing a secret cipher.) Will you look at this and state if you are familiar with the cipher used by the Confederate authorities? A. I am familiar with two of them; the paper containing the cipher was here offered in evidence.

Q. Do you recognize that as one of the ciphers in use among the Confederates? A. Yes sir.

Q. During your stay in Canada, were you or not in the service of the Government and seeking; to acquire for its use information in regard to the plans and purpose of the Rebels, who were known to be assembled there? A. I was.

Q. To e able you to do this, did you or not deem it proper and necessary that you should assume a different name from your real name, and that under which you now appear before this court? A. Yes sir, I did.

Q. What did you learn they were doing, if anything? A. They were destroying a great many papers; they also know that they were going to be indicted in Canada for violation of the neutrality laws a number of days before they were indicted.

Q. How did you learn they were destroying papers about that time? A. They told me.

Q. Which one of them? A. Each of them made mention of that.

Q. What name did you assume in your intercourse with them? A. I assumed as my proper name James Thompson, and then leading them to suppose that that was my right name, and that I wished to conceal it there, so as not to be identified by the Federal spies; I adopted other names at any hotel I might be stopping; I never registered Thompson on the book; I led them to suppose that I wished to conceal that name, but James Thompson was the name that they had supposed was my proper name.

Q. Your whole object in all this was simply to ascertain their plans against the Government of the United States? A. Yes sir; that was my whole object.

Q. Will you state how you became acquainted with this cipher which has just been shown you? A. I saw that cipher in Mr. Clay's house, the private house in which he was stopping in St. Catharines.

Q. When was that? A. That was in the summer of 1864.

Q. Have you not also been the bearer of despatches for these persons? A. Yes sir; I was intrusted with despatches to carry from Canada to Richmond.

Q. Did you carry them? A. I carried some to Gordonsville with instructions that I was to send them from there.

Q. Did you receive despatches in reply? A. Once I did.

Q. Were they carried back? A. Yes sir, they were carried back.

Q. Did you come through Washington; did you make them known to the Government? A. Yes sir; each time I delivered the despatches, always to the Government of the United States; I passed nothing that I took, except by their permission

Q. From whom were the despatches received at Gordonsville received? A. A gentleman who represented himself to me as being in their State Department, and sent with the answer by their Secretary of State.

Q. And you bore the despatches to whom; to Thompson or Clay? A. I bore it back to Mr. Thompson.

Q. All of these men, Thompson, Clay and Cleary, represented themselves as being in the service of the Confederate Government? A. Yes sir.

Q. When was it that you received that despatch at Gordonsville? A. It was in the fall, I believe; it was in October.

Q. Did you ever hear the subject of these raids from Canada upon our frontier, and of the burning of our cities spoken of among these conspirators? A. Yes sir, many times.

Q. By Thompson, Clay, Cleary, Tucker, Sanders, and those men? A. Yes sir; I know that Mr. Clay was one of the prime movers in the matter before the raids were started.

Q. You understood in your conversations with them that all these men fully approved of these enterprises? A. Yes sir, they received the direct indorsement of Mr. Clement C. Clay, Jr.; he represented himself to me as being a sort of representative of the War Department.

Q. Do you not consider that you enjoyed fully the confidence of those men, so that they freely communicated to you? A. I do; I do not think they would have intrusted those despatches to me unless they had the fullest confidence in me.

Q. Did they or not, at all times represent themselves as acting under the sanction of their Government at Richmond? A. They represented themselves as having full power to act without reference to them; they repeatedly told me, both Mr. Clay and Thompson, that they had full power to act by their Government in anything they deemed expedient, and for the benefit of their cause.

Q. Were you in Canada at the time the attempt was made to fire the city of New York? A. Yes sir.

Q. Was that the subject of much conversation among these people? A. I left Canada with the news two days before the attempt was made to bring it to the Department at Washington.

Q. That such a project was contemplated? A. Yes sir.

Q. You knew that it originated there and had the full sanction of these men? A. Yes sir.

Q. Do you mean to say the same in regard to the St. Albans raid? A. Yes sir; I did not know the point where that raid was to be made, but I told the Government at Washington that they were about to set out on a raid of that kind before the St. Albans raid; I also told them of the intended raid upon Buffalo and Rochester, and by that means prevented those raids.

Q. Captain Beale, who was subsequently hanged at New York, was known there as leading in this enterprise, was he not? A. I did not know him by that name.

Q. Was he spoken of among those men? A. I never heard him spoken of; they were in the habit of using their fictitious name in conversation with each other.

Q. You say that you do not know anything about Beale? A. No sir; I knew that the object of his mission was contemplated; I did not know who were to be the immediate executors of the plot; I knew of the plan at the time, and reported it.

Q. Did you hear the subject of the funds by which all these enterprises were carried on spoken of among these conspirators as to who had the funds, or the amount they had, or anything of that sort? A. Yes sir, in regard to the raiding Mr. City had funds.

Q. Did you ever hear the probable amount spoken of by any of them? A. No sir; he represented to me that he always had plenty of money to pay for anything that was worth paying for; he told me he had money, but I do not know in what bank in Montreal these Rebels keep their account and funds? A. No sir, I do not.

Q. You know that there was a Bank of Ontario in Montreal? A. Yes sir; I know that there is such a bank; I know that they deposited in several different banks; they transacted a good deal of business, in what I think is called the Niagara District Bank; it is almost opposite where Mr. Clay's residence was in St. Catharine's; during the summer they transacted a great deal of business at that bank.

Q. What seemed to be George N. Sanders' position there if he had a defined position? A. Mr. Clay told me that I had better not tell him the things that I was bent upon nor the things that they intrusted to me; that he was a very good man to do their dirty work; that is just what Mr. Clay told me.

Q. He was then doing their work, but it was dirty work? A. Mr. Clay said he associated with men that they could not associate with; that he was very useful in that way; a very useful man to them indeed.

Cross-examined by Mr. Aiken.—Q. Where are you from? A. New York city originally.

Q. What time in the year was it that you said Mr. Thompson told you a proposition had been made to him? A. In the early part of the year.

Q. In January? A. In January.

Q. You stated, I think, that immediately after that you saw Mr. Clay? A. No sir, I did not.

Q. When did you see Mr. Clay? A. Immediately after the conversation in the summer.

Q. The summer of 1864? A. Yes sir, in which he spoke of "Thompson" being able to put the President out of the way whenever he was ready.

Q. Did you ever hear anything in Canada of Mr. Surratt as being connected with the plot? A. I did not.

Q. Did you receive any pay from the Confederate Government for going to Gordonsville with despatches? A. I received for the services, to defray railroad expenses, the equivalent of one hundred and fifty dollars in greenbacks; it was not one hundred and fifty dollars in greenbacks; it was, I have forgotten the amount, in Canada money; gold was about 260 at the time; I have forgotten what it was; I received that and reported the fact of having received it to the War Department at

Washington, and applied it on my expense account as having been received from the Government.
Q. On your return with the Gordonsville despatches for the Rebels in Canada did you leave a copy of those despatches here? A. I handed the original despatches over to the authorities, and those of them that they selected to go ahead I carried on, and those they did not they retained.
By the Court.—Q. I want to ask an explanation of an answer you made, I understood you in your testimony to say that after the assassination of the President some of those who had been engaged in it had returned to Canada, and you said they expressed regret that they had not been allowed to proceed earlier?
A. You misunderstood me; I did not say that any of those who had been engaged in the attempt at assassination or in the assassination had returned to Canada.
Q. But those who directed it from Canada expressed regret that they had not been allowed to proceed sooner? A. One of the parties, the one who represented himself as being a commercial agent, Mr. Beverly Tucker, said that it was a pity that the boys had not been allowed to act when they first wanted to.
Q. Did you understand why they were prevented in not proceeding sooner? A. I did not; I inferred, though, from what I had heard from Mr. Thompson before, that he had detained them in order that he might choose a fitting opportunity.
Q. Your impression was that they were detained up to that time by Mr. Jacob Thompson? A. I inferred so because when he spoke of the matter to me in his conversation of January, 1865, he said he was in favor of the proposition that had been made to him to put the President, Mr. Stanton, General Grant, and others out of the way, but had deferred giving his answer until he had consulted his Government at Richmond, and was then only waiting their approval.
Q. Did you understand that he had received the answer, and given the direction following that? A. I never understood so; I never asked the question or received that reply.
Q. What was your impression? A. My impression was that he had received the answer; I inferred that he had received that approval, and that they had been detained waiting for that, from what Beverly Tucker said.
Q. I understood you to mention the name of Prof. Holcomb in connection with that of Sanders, Clay, and others. I would like to know how far you can identify him in these movements, plans, and operations of these men? A. I made a proposition to Mr. Clay to carry despatches for them, not to do their work, as a means of getting into their confidence. And Mr. Cleary told me before Mr. Holcomb that he had authority to sign his (Clay's) name by power of attorney, and his own, both of them being representatives of the Confederate States Government, as they called it.

Testimony of James B. Merritt.

James B. Merritt, a witness called for the prosecution, being duly sworn, testified as follows:—
By the Judge Advocate.—Q. Of what State are you a native? I do not know whether I am a native of New York or Canada, but have always hailed from New York.
Q. What is your profession? A. Physician.
Q. Have you been residing or not for some time in Canada and if so, in what part of Canada? A. I have been in Canada about a year or nearly a year, part of the time at Windsor, part of the time at North Dumfries, Waterloo county.
Q. Were you or not in the month of October or November last in Toronto, Canada? A. I was.
Q. State whether you met there a man by the name of Young. A. I met George Young there.
Q. Did Young profess to be from Kentucky? A. I believe that he did; I believe he was formerly of Morgan's command, Kentucky.
Q. Did you meet a man named Ford, also of Kentucky, a deserter? A. Yes sir.
Q. Did you meet a man named Graves, from Louisville? A. Yes sir.
Q. Did you have any conversation with Young in regard to public affairs of that time? A. Yes sir, some.
Q. Will you state what he said to you, if anything, in regard to some very important matters being on the tapis in the interest of the Rebellion? A. He asked me if I had seen Colonel Steele before I left Windsor.
Q. Who was Colonel Steele? A. Colonel Steele, I believe, is a Kentuckian; what his given name is I do not know.
Q. Was he a Rebel, in the Rebel service? A. He had been, as I understood, a Rebel, in the service.
Q. Proceed with what Young told you? A. He asked me if Colonel Steele had said anything to me in relation to the Presidential election. I told him that he had not. Then he said we have something on the tapis of much more importance than any raid that we have made or can make, or something of that character.
Q. Did he proceed to state what it was? A. I asked him what it was; he said it was determined that "old Abe" should never be inaugurated; if I understood right that was his expression; I asked him how he knew; he said he knew that he would not be inaugura

ted; they had plenty of friends, I think he said in Washington, and he spoke in relation to Mr. Lincoln, and used some ungentlemanly words; called him a —— old tyrant, or something like that.
Q. That was Young? A. Yes sir.
Q. Did you afterwards see Steele and Sanders together? A. Yes sir.
Q. You mean Geo. N. Sanders? A. I do; I was introduced to Geo. N. Sanders by Colonel Steele.
Q. Will you state what, if anything, was said in relation to the same matter by either of them on that occasion? A. I asked Colonel Steele what was going to be done, or how he liked the prospects of the Presidential election; Colonel Steele's expression was, "the old tyrant never will serve another term if he is elected;" Mr. Sanders said "he would have to keep himself very close if he did serve another term."
Q. Did Sanders say that at the same time that Steele said the —— old tyrant never should serve another term? A. Yes sir.
Q. Were you afterwards in Montreal, in the month of February last? A. I was.
Q. Did you or not hear among the Rebels there the subject of the assassination of the President freely spoken of? A. Yes sir.
Q. Did you or not hear mentioned the names of persons who were willing to assassinate him? A. I heard Mr. Sanders name over a number of persons that were ready and willing, as he said to engage in the undertaking to relieve the President, Vice President, Cabinet and some of the leading generals.
Q. What, if anything, did George N. Sanders say in relation to their having plenty of money to accomplish these assassinations? A. Mr. Sanders said that there was any amount of money to accomplish the purpose; I think that was the expression used.
Q. That was the assassination? A. Yes sir; he read a letter which he said he had received from the President of the Confederate States.
Q. Meaning Jeff. Davis? A. Yes sir, which letter justified him in making any arrangements that he could to accomplish the object.
Q. Was there not a meeting of those Rebels at that time in Montreal, where Sanders was, and where you were also? A. Yes sir.
Q. Was it at this meeting that Sanders read this letter from Jeff. Davis? A. Yes sir.
Q. Will you state some of the language of that letter, the strong language which he used, if the tyranny of Mr. Lincoln was submitted to? A. I do not know that I can use the exact language.
Q. The substance of it? A. The letter was in substance, that if the people in Canada and the Southerners in the State, were willing to submit to be governed by such a tyrant as Lincoln, he did not wish to recognize them as friends or associates, or something like that.
Q. And you say that in that letter he expressed his approbation of whatever measures they might take to accomplish this object? A. Yes sir.
Q. Was that letter read openly in this meeting by Sanders? A. Yes sir.
Q. After it was read was it or not handed to members of the meeting and read by them, one after another? A. Col. Steele read it, I think; Capt. Scott read it, and Young and Hill.
Q. These were all known as Rebels, were they not? A. I believe they were.
Q. Did they or not all acquiesce, after reading it, in the correctness with which Sanders had read it openly to the meeting? A. There was no remark made as to any misstatement of the letter by Sanders.
Q. As far as you could judge did it seem to be since that meeting that it was proper to have this object accomplished? A. I did not hear any objection raised.
Q. You said that was in the month of February; can you say at what time of the month that meeting was held? A. I should think it was somewhere about the middle of February.
Q. By whom were you invited to attend the meeting? A. Captain Scott invited me to attend the meeting.
Q. Was it on that occasion or on some other that Sanders named over the persons who were waiting to accomplish this assassination. A. At that time.
Q. Will you state whether among the persons thus named John Wilkes Booth was mentioned? A. Booth's name was mentioned; I do not remember that the John Wilkes was added to it.
Q. Did you see Booth yourself in Canada? A. Not then; I saw Booth in October, 1864.
Q. Can you recall now other names that were mentioned besides Booth's? A. Yes sir; George Harper was one, Charles Caldwell, one Randall and Harrison.
Q. Do you hear that person, Harrison, spoken of by any other name? Did you hear the name Surratt mentioned? A. I heard Surratt's name mentioned.
Q. Do you know whether it was the same person or not? A. I do not think it was.
Q. This name is John Harrison Surratt. A. Surratt's name was mentioned.
Q. Did you see the prisoner, Harold, in Canada, at that time? A. I say I saw Harold; I saw the one who was called Harrison, in Toronto.
Q. Would you recognize him? look at these prisoners, and see if you recognize him. A. After looking at the

prisoners, I should think that third one on the bench there was the man (pointing to Harold).
Q. He was spoken of as one who was ready to accomplish assassination? A. I understood Mr. Sanders to say he was ready to accomplish it, or assist in it; his name was mentioned in connection with others, by others; he went there by the name of Harrison.
Q. Look at the remainder of the prisoners and see if you recognize any of them. Do you remember having seen the prisoner Payne in Canada? A. I do not; I should not recognize as ever having met in Canada any except Harold.
Q. Did I understand you to say that in the conversation occurring between these Rebels and their friends there was no reserve at all in discussing the question of the assassination of the President and his Cabinet? A. I do not think you understood me correctly if you understood me that there was no reserve; there was not a great amount of reserve.
Q. It was discussed freely among themselves, then? A. Yes sir.
Q. Among the persons named was there not one who bore the nick-name, probably it was "Plug Tobacco" or "Port Tobacco?" A. "Plug Tobacco." I never saw him that I know of, but I heard the name.
Q. Was he in this list that Sanders spoke of? A. I am not positive whether Sanders used his name or not, but I think he did.
Q. Do you remember that Sanders, in speaking of Booth as one who was willing to assassinate the President and Cabinet, mentioned as among the reasons for it he was related to Beale, who had been recently hanged in New York? A. He said that Booth was heart and soul in this matter, and felt as much as any person could feel, for the reason that he was a cousin to Beale, who was hung in New York; whether he was a cousin or not, I do not know.
Q. What did he say, if anything, in regard to the assassination of the Vice President, now President, of the United States? A. He said that if they could dispose of Mr. Lincoln it would be an easy matter to dispose of Mr. Johnson, as he was, such a drunken sot it would be an easy matter to dispose of him in some of his drunken reveries.
Q. Did he say anything in regard to Mr. Seward, the Secretary of State? A. When he read the letter he spoke of Mr. Seward, and I inferred that that was partially the language of the letter; I think it was that if these parties, the President, the Vice President and Cabinet, or Mr. Seward, could be disposed of it would satisfy the people of the North that they (the Southerners) had friends in the North, and that a peace could be obtained on better terms than it could otherwise be obtained; that they, the Rebels, would endeavor to bring about a war between the United States and England, and that Mr. Seward, through his energy and sagacity, had thwarted all their efforts.
Q. That was suggested as one of the reasons for getting rid of him? A. Yes sir, for removing him.
Q. At a later period, say early in April, did you meet any of these parties? A. Yes sir.
Q. State who they were and what conversation occurred between you and them. A. I was in Toronto on Wednesday and Thursday, the 5th and 6th of April last, and in the evening of Wednesday I was on my way going to the theatre when I met Harper and Ford; they asked me to go with them and spend the evening, and I declined, as I was going to the theatre the next morning I was around by the Queen Hotel, and I saw Harper, Caldwell, Randall, Ford, and one Charles Hall.
Q. Did you see a man called Texas? A. Yes sir.
Q. State the conversation which occurred then between you? A. Harper said that they were going to the States, and they were going to kick up the damnedst row that had ever been heard of yet; there was some other conversation passed among us; I do not now remember what it was; nothing of any importance, till in the course of an hour or two afterwards I met Harper, and he said if I did not hear of the death of old Abe, or the Vice President, and of General Dix, in less than ten days, I might put him down as a damned fool; the 5th, as I find on looking at my visiting list, and this was on the 6th.
Q. Did Harper at the time, or not, speak of Booth and Surratt as being at Washington? A. I think that Booth's name was mentioned as being in Washington, but I do not remember Surratt's at that time.
Q. Was anything said in regard to their having friends in Washington? A. They said they had plenty of friends here, and that there were some fifteen or twenty going to Washington.
Q. Did you or not call afterwards and ascertain that Harper had in fact left on the 8th of April? A. On the Saturday afterwards I was at Galt; Harper's mother is living some four or five miles from Galt, between that and Paris; I ascertained then that he had been to the place where he had been stopping, and Caldwell, too, and had started for the States.
Q. After you had ascertained this information that they had left for Washington probably for the purpose of assassinating the President, what steps, if any, did you take in the matter? A. I went to a justice of the peace for the purpose of giving information to have them stopped; his name was Davison.
Q. State what occurred on your application? A.

When I gave the information, he said that the thing was too ridiculously absurd, or supremely absurd to take any notice of; it would only make me appear very foolish to give such information, and cause arrests to be made on those grounds, as it was so inconsistent that no person would believe it.
Q. And therefore did he or not decline issuing any process? A. He declined to issue process.
Q. Do you or not know at what time this man Harper returned from the States to Canada? A. I have no personal knowledge that he returned at all.
Q. What knowledge have you on the subject? A. I was in Galt on Friday again, and found there, from Mr. Ford, that he had been home on Thursday, and had started to go back to the States again; that was the Thursday after the assassination.
Q. Did you know while there one Colonel Ashley, a Rebel officer? A. I did not know that he was a Rebel officer; I knew that he was a Rebel sympathizer; he was a broker at Windsor, opposite Detroit.
Q. Did you ever see a letter from Jacob Thompson, formerly Secretary of the Interior, to him? A. Some time last fall, I cannot tell exactly what time, Colonel Ashley handed me a letter, which he said he had received from Jacob Thompson, asking him for funds for the benefit of the Rebels, to carry out their objects in Canada, and he asked me if I could not contribute; he read me the letter.
Q. What did you understand from him and from that letter to be those objects? A. My understanding was that the purpose was to raise means to pay the expenses of those who were unable to pay their own expenses, to go to the States and make raids; I so understood the meaning of the letter; I may have misinterpreted it.
Q. Did you have any conversation with Jacob Thompson or Clement C. Clay? A. I had a conversation with Mr. Clay.
Q. At what time? In February.
Q. State what it was. A. I spoke to him in Toronto about the letter that Mr. Sanders had exhibited in Montreal—the letter of Jefferson Davis.
Q. Did you state to him what that letter was? A. He seemed to understand the nature and character of the letter perfectly; I asked him what he thought about it, and he said he thought the end would justify the means; that was his expression.
Q. Justify the assassination? A. That the end would justify the means.
Q. You say that when you mentioned to him the letter from Jefferson Davis approving of this plan of assassination, he seemed to understand it perfectly? A. Yes sir, he seemed to understand it.
Q. You spoke of having heard the name Surratt; do you remember that he was at any time pointed out to you while you were in Canada? A. He was pointed out to me once.
Q. At what time was that and where? A. It was in February, and, I think, in Toronto.
Q. With whom was he there, did you observe? A. I did not see him with any one; he was walking on the other side of the street, and was pointed out to me as being Surratt, and I am inclined to think it was Scott, who pointed him out; and when he was pointed out Scott, Ford and myself were standing on the sidewalk.
Q. How often did you see Booth there? A. I saw Booth there two or three times.
Q. With whom did you generally see him associating? A. I do not know that I could tell; I sat at the table with him once at the St. Law rence; Sanders was at the same table, and Scott and Steele and myself.
Q. Did you see Sanders and Booth together? A. I do not know that I did any more than at the table; they were conversing with each other at the table; we all drank some wine at Mr. Sanders' expense.
Q. Was not Booth recognized by them all as their friend and as fully committed to any enterprise they were engaged in? A. I cannot answer that question, for I do not know.
Q. Did you hear what Sanders said of Booth? A. I know what was said in the meeting; outside of that I did not hear any person speak particularly in relation to Booth.
Q. Did you have personal acquaintance with Booth yourself? A. No sir; I had seen him a good many times on the stage, and knew him very well by sight.
Q. (Exhibiting to the witness the photograph of J. Wilkes Booth, exhibit No. 1.) Is that a correct representation of him? A. I should think that was the man.
Q. What is the full name of Harper, of whom you have spoken? A. George Harper.
Cross-examined by Mr. Stone.—Q. Did you see the man who was called Harrison, and whom you now think is Harold, more than once in Canada? A. I think I saw him two or three times.
Q. At what time did you see him? A. In February.
Q. What time is February? A. About the middle, or somewhere about the 13th or 20th of the month.
Q. Did you make his acquaintance? A. I did not.
Q. Do you remember who pointed him out to you? A. I think that it was a Mr. Brown, and Ford and Holt were together.
Q. Was it in a street? A. In a saloon.
Q. Night or day? A. In the evening.
Q. Did you notice him more particularly than the

generality of persons in the saloon? A. I noticed him a little more particularly on account of his name having been mentioned in connection with others at Montreal.
Q. Was this in Montreal? A. No, this was in Toronto.
Q. Was Booth in the saloon? No.
Q. After he was pointed out you saw him once or twice, and then he went by the name of Harrison, you say? A. It is my impression that he went by that name; I do not remember having heard the name of Harold mentioned at all.
Q. Did you see him after that at any time till now? A. No, sir, I did not.
Q. And you saw him to-day for the first time since that? A. Yes, sir.
Q. How was he dressed then, do you remember? A. I do not know that I do.
Q. I mean the general style of the dress; was he dressed well or not? A. I did not see anything about his dress that particularly attracted my attention.
Q. I do not mean the color of his clothes, but was he genteelly dressed? A. I should think he was comfortably dressed; some people's ideas of gentility differ from those of others.
The hour fixed by the rules for that purpose having arrived, the Commission took a recess till 12 o'clock P. M.
Court room, Washington, D. C., Friday, May 2, 1865, 2 o'clock P. M. James J. Murphy, Edward V. Murphy and Robert Congales were duly sworn by the Judge Advocate as reporters to the Commission in the presence of the Court.

Cross-Examination of James B. Merritt.

Continued by Mr. Aiken.—Q. Where were you born? A. I was born in Canada.
Q. Then you are a native of Canada? A. The first question asked me by the Judge Advocate, was what State are you a native of; my answer was that I could not tell; I can explain it in my people lived in Rome, Oneida county, New York; father and mother were in Canada visiting and taking care of some of their friends at the time I was born; the question was raised the first time I offered my vote whether I was a native of New York or Canada, and was undecided.
By the Judge Advocate.—Q. That was what you meant by your answer? A. Yes sir.
By Mr. Aiken.—What is your age? A. Nearly forty.
Q. How often did you visit Canada last summer and fall? A. I have been there all the time since May last, pretty much, with the exception of a few days in December, and at that time I occasionally went back and forth to Detroit.
Q. What was your business in Canada? A. Practicing medicine.
Q. When did you first meet any of the parties you have named in Canada? A. Some of them I met the first day I was there.
Q. You went in May? A. Yes sir, I went in May.
Q. Where were they? A. Ford was there in May.
Q. By whom were you introduced to those parties? A. Some of them introduced themselves.
Q. Were you introduced to any of them? A. Then I was introduced afterwards to some; Colonel Ashley introduced me to Mr. Clay.
Q. Was that the first introduction you had to these parties? A. That was the first introduction I had to Mr. Clay.
Q. To any of them? A. Oh, no! I think Colonel Ashley introduced me to two or three others; there, among the rest, was Captain Scott.
Q. How was it that you were on such confidential terms with these gentlemen? A. Because I was a good Southerner, and represented myself as such.
Q. Is that the reason why you were asked to contribute? A. Yes sir.
Q. On account of your known status there as a Southerner? A. They supposed I was a good Southerner, and I presume that was the reason Mr. Ashley asked me to contribute.
Q. You spoke of drinking wine with Mr. Sanders; was that before or after the meeting at which the letter was read to which you referred? A. That was after the interview we had in October, but before the meeting at which the letter of Davis was read.
Q. Where was that meeting held? A. In Mr. Sanders' room.
Q. Who invited you to be present at that meeting? A. Captain Scott.
Q. Is it possible that a portion of that letter has been misapprehended; I would like to have you state the main points in it again? A. Mr. Sanders read the letter aloud; I did not read the letter myself; I think that I stated that in the commencement; the purport of the letter was that Mr. Davis did not wish to recognize any persons as his friends who were willing to submit to be governed by Mr. Lincoln, conveying the sentiment the language might be varied a good deal, and that if the President and Vice-President, and some of the Cabinet, and the leading generals could be disposed of, it would justify the people of the North that they (the Rebels) had friends here.
Q. That was stated in the letter? A. That was stated in the letter; I think that was the meaning of the let-

ter; the phraseology I perhaps do not exactly remember.
Q. We want to know what was actually said in the letter. A. I say that that was the substance; I do not say that was the exact phraseology.
Q. Was there anything more in the letter? A. There was considerable; it was quite a lengthy letter.
Q. Did you make any expressions at the time in the meeting? A. No sir.
Q. Did you see the justice of the peace to whom you referred immediately after that meeting? A. No sir.
Q. How long was it afterwards? A. It was over a month.
Q. What time was the letter read? A. The letter was read in February, and I went on the 10th of April to see the justice of the peace.
Q. After the justice of the peace refused to accede to your request, what did you then do? A. I then called upon a judge of the Court of Assizes, made my statement to him, and he said I should have to go to the grand jury.
Q. What did you do then? A. I did not do anything; I went home.
Q. When did you first communicate to the Government this information that you have detailed here? A. I think it was two weeks ago to-day.
Q. Since the assassination of the President? A. Yes sir.
Q. What was your object in keeping this information so long to yourself? A. There was no authority to communicate it to.
Q. But as a good citizen you were bound to communicate it; why did you not do it? A. In the first place I was not here where I could communicate; I am a practicing physician in North Dumfries, Canada; it is some five hundred or six hundred miles from here.
Q. There is a post office at Dumfries? A. Yes sir; there is one.
Q. There is one at Toronto and one at Montreal? A. Yes sir.
Q. Is that the only reason that you have? A. No sir; I cannot assign any particular reasons why I did not communicate it, the Government, though, was in possession of the information without my communicating it, I understand.
Q. Was it not owing to the fact that you are a Southerner in your feelings and affiliations? A. No sir.
Q. Where were you when Mr. Surratt was pointed out to you, as you state? A. In Toronto, I think.
Q. At what time of the year was that? A. That was in February.
Q. In February, 1865? A. Yes, sir; last February.
Q. Did you have a good view of the gentleman? A. I saw him on the street.
Q. Were you on the same side of the street with him, or across? A. On the same side; he was pointed out coming towards me, and on the opposite side; he crossed on the same crossing, and passed down by me.
Q. What sort of a looking man was he? A. I never saw him; but he is a man. I should think, as tall as I am, nearly five feet six inches or seven or eight bones, rather slim, and he wore a moustache.
Q. What was the color of that moustache? A. Dark.
Q. What was the color of his hair? A. I did not notice his hair particularly; I noticed that he had a moustache.
Q. What was the color of his eyes? A. I do not know that I noticed.
Q. How was he dressed? A. Dressed in ordinary clothes, like any gentleman would be.
Q. Dark colored clothes? A. I should think they were, but I might be mistaken.
Q. Are you pretty positive that they were dark-colored clothes? A. I would not be positive that they were; I would not be positive that it was Surratt, either, because I do not know the man.
Q. What day of the month was that, as near as you can recollect? A. I should think it was somewhere in the neighborhood of the 20th, perhaps; it was after the middle, I should judge.
Q. Who was the American Consul at Toronto? A. I do not know; I do not know an American Consul in the province.
Q. Did you ever meet him? A. Not that I know of.
Q. There was one there?. A. I do not know that I ever met him.
Q. When you were drinking wine at Mr. Sanders' expense, and in convivial conversation with him, did he disclose to you freely any of the plans and purposes of the Southern men in Canada? A. Not at the table.
Q. Did he privately in his room? A. I had no conversation with Mr. Sanders, except what I had at those Interviews, in relation to any conduct of the Southerners in Canada; that was in his room at the time I was introduced to him by Clem. Steele.
Q. To go back again—under what circumstances was the gentleman whom you think was Surratt pointed out to you? A. I do not know that it was under any particular circumstances; a man by the name of Ford, who was present at the meeting held in Montreal, said:—"Doctor, that's Surratt."
Q. Was Surratt mentioned in the meeting? A. Surratt's name was.
Q. Were you talking with Ford at that time in regard

to any of the plans and purposes divulged in that meeting? A. Yes sir.
Q. Was that the occasion? A. That is how he happened to speak of this man.
Q. You think he was a man about five feet six inches high? A. Five feet six or eight inches, I should judge.
Q. Your impression is that he was dressed in dark clothes? A. I could not say what his clothes were; he might have been dressed in dark clothes, or dark grey, or grey; I could not now tell, for the life of me, what he was dressed in.
Q. You think he had a dark moustache? A. I think his moustache was dark; it was not red; at least I think it was not.
By the Judge Advocate.—Q. I understand you to say that the occasion of Surratt's being pointed out to you was because he was one of the men willing to accomplish this assassination of the President? A. He was one of the men spoken of by Mr. Sanders; Mr. Ford was present at the time Mr. Sanders mentioned it.
Q. How many were present at that meeting? A. I should think there were ten or fifteen.
Q. How many can you name? name as many as you can. Q. There was Mr. Sanders, Colonel Steele, Capt. Scott, George Harper, Caldwell, Ford, Kirk, Benedict, George Young and Byron Hill.
Q. Do you know whether this Harper was or was not from Richmond, Virginia? A. I believe that Harper and Caldwell were both residents of Richmond, Virginia; at least they represented themselves as such.
Q. Did they represent themselves as have been in the Rebel service? A. I believe they had been; I think they had been in the Rebel service; whether they were commissioned or private I cannot say.
Q. The Clay of whom you have spoken is Clement C. Clay, of Alabama, formerly of the United States Senate, is it not? A. Yes sir; C. C. Clay—a tall, slim man.
By Mr. Aiken.—Q. From what point did you communicate this information to the Government? A. In the War Department.
Q. Did you come directly here? A. Yes sir; I have in my pocket a letter from the Provost Marshal-General, stating that he had received a letter which proved to have been written by Squire Davison, giving information of my visit to him when I wished to have Harper and Caldwell arrested, and when, on the receipt of that letter, they sent to Canada for me; it you wish to see the letter I can produce it.
By the Judge Advocate.—Q. By whom was that letter written? A. By General Fry.
The Judge Advocate, without objection, offered the letter in evidence. It is as follows:—
"WAR DEPARTMENT, PROVOST MARSHAL-GENERAL'S BUREAU, WASHINGTON, D. C., April 29, 1865.—To Dr. J. B. Merrill, Agent, Canada West.—SIR: I have been informed that you possess information connected with a plot to assassinate the President of the United States and other prominent heads of this Government. The bearer has been sent to present this letter to you, and to accompany you to this city, if you will come. The Secretary of War authorizes me to pledge you protection and security, and to pay all expenses connected with your journey both ways, and, in addition, to promise a suitable reward if useful information is furnished.
Independent of these considerations, it is hoped that the cause of humanity and justice will induce you to act promptly in divulging anything you may know connected with the recent tragedy in this city, or with any other plots yet in preparation. The bearer is directed to pay all expenses connected with your trip.
"I am, &c., very respectfully,
"Your obedient servant,
"JAMES B. FRY,
"Provost Marshal-General."
The original of the foregoing is annexed to this record, and marked Exhibit No. 5.
By the Judge Advocate.—Q. It was under that letter you came? A. Yes sir.
By the Court.—Q. The witness in giving the reason for his admission to the meeting of the conspirators in Canada, said it was because he was a good Southern man, and then in giving a reason for not communicating this information to the Government, he said emphatically that he was not a good Southern man—how is that discrepancy explained? A. I said they admitted me because I was a good Southern man, and I said it in such a way that I thought it would be understood that I had made the impression on their minds that I was a good Southern man; God knows I am not a Southern man in sentiment, because I have taken the oath of allegiance too often.
By Mr. Aiken:—Where were you at the time Mr. Ashley asked you to contribute? A. In Windsor, opposite Detroit.
Q. You stated that you did not contribute anything at that time. A. I did not.
Q. Did you ever contribute anything for that specific purpose? A. No sir.
Q. Either in money, or services, or advice? A. No sir.
Q. When did you leave New York? A. Four or five or six years ago, more than that.

Q. When were you last in New York city? A. I have not been there, I think, since 1858 or 1859.
Q. Did you know anything of the plot to burn that city? A. I did.
Q. Did you communicate that to any one? A. I did.
Q. To whom? A. To Colonel Hill, of Detroit.
Q. How did you come to find out anything about it? A. I heard it talked of at Windsor.
Q. Did you communicate your knowledge before or after the attempt to burn that city? A. Before the attempt.
Q. Are you acquainted with Robert Burfall, of Toronto? A. No sir.
Q. Did you ever see him? A. Not that I know of.
Q. He is the Consul there. A. I do not know him.
Q. Who of the Southerners communicated to you their intentions to burn New York city at Windsor? A. Robert Drake, formerly of Morgan's command.
Q. Was he the only one? A. Another, of the name of Smith; I do not know Smith's first name, but they were both of Morgan's command, and they both had been to Chicago to attend the Presidential convention; they went there for the purpose of destroying the public peace and releasing the prisoners at Camp Douglas; at least they told me that was their object in going after they returned.
Q. After you had been thus made aware of the plot to burn the city of New York, and commit that depredation in Chicago, why did you continue your friendly relations with that class of men? A. For the purpose of giving information when I should find it of importance; another thing, my practice was mostly among that class of men; among Southerners; if you go to Canada you will find that nine-tenths of the people are rank Rebel sympathizers.
Q. Did you continue your friendly or confidential relations with them sister that? A. I did.
Q. By whom were you paid for communicating the information? A. I never have received a dollar; the Government did advance me money here the other day to pay my expenses; I have proof in my pocket, which I can show, if it is necessary, from the Provost Marshal at Detroit, that I furnished valuable information without any remuneration.
Q. Why after this, and you were continuing your relations with them, should they continue to think you a good Southerner? A. You must ask them; they can give you more information on that point than I can.
Q. Did you intentionally deceive them? A. My intention was to get all the information I could from them.
Q. At the same time pretending to be their friend? A. Yes sir.

Testimony of Sandford Conover.

Sandford Conover, a witness called for the prosecution, being duly sworn, testified as follows.—
By Judge Advocate Bingham.—Q. State your full name and present place of residence. A. Sandford Conover, Montreal, Canada.
Q. How long have you resided in Montreal? A. Since October last.
Q. State where you resided previous to going to Canada. A. I resided a short time in Baltimore.
Q. State whether you resided further South before that. A. Yes sir, at Richmond?
Q. State what you were doing at Richmond? A. I was a clerk in the War Department for a time.
Q. How long? A. Upwards of six months.
Q. Do you mean the War Department of the Confederate States Government, as it was called? A. Yes sir, in the Rebel War Department.
Q. Who was at that time Secretary of War for that organization? A. Mr. James A. Seddon.
Q. How did you come to be in the Rebel service? A. I was conscripted, and detailed for a clerkship; it was a cheap way of getting clerks.
Q. State to the Court whether when you were over in Canada you made the acquaintance of any of the persons connected with the Confederate organization, as it was called, Rebels from the Southern States. A. I did, and have been quite intimately associated with them.
Q. State the names of those with whom you were so acquainted in Canada. A. George N. Sanders, Jacob Thompson, Dr. Blackburn, Beverly Tucker, William C. Cleary, Lewis Castleman, the Rev. Mr. Cameron, Mr. Porterfield, Captain Magruder, and a number who are of less note.
Q. Did you know Clement C. Clay? A. I knew him; I may also include Generals Frost, of Missouri, and Carroll of Tennessee.
Q. Were you also acquainted with any persons who occasionally visited the persons named in Canada from the United States? A. I knew some.
Q. What were their names? A. I knew Mr. Surratt; I knew Booth.
Q. John Wilkes Booth? A. Yes sir.
Q. State whether you saw either of those persons last named in Canada since then once? A. I never saw Booth since then once; I saw Surratt on several successive days.
Q. With whom did you see them when there? A. I saw Surratt on a number of days in April last; I saw him in Jacob Thompson's rooms, and I also saw him

in company with George N. Sanders at two or three places.
Q. Did he pass by the name of John H. Surratt? A. Surratt; I am not positive about his first name; I have heard him called Jack, by some.
By Mr. Castleman.—Q. Describe the personal appearance of this Mr. Surratt? A. He is a man about five feet nine, ten or eleven inches, somewhere in that neighborhood I should judge; a spare man, light complexion and light hair.
Q. You say you saw him in Montreal in April last? A. Yes sir.
Q. About what time in April? A. It was within a week before the President's assassination; I think about the 6th or 7th of April; somewhere in that vicinity.
Q. In whose company was he at the time you saw him there? A. I saw him in Mr. Thompson's company and in Mr. Sanders'.
Q. You say you saw him in Mr. Thompson's room? A. I saw him in Mr. Thompson's room.
Q. State whether he gave any communication to Mr. Thompson in his room, in your presence, and what that communication was? A. There was a communication there at that time, from which it appeared that Mr. Surratt had brought despatches from Richmond to Mr. Thompson: these despatches were the subject of the conversation.
Q. From whom in Richmond were the despatches brought? A. From Mr. Benjamin; I think there was also a letter in cipher from Mr. Davis; I am not positive as to the latter, but there was a letter, whether it was in cipher or not.
Q. Do you mean Judah P. Benjamin, Secretary of State of the so-called Confederacy? A. Yes sir.
Q. You say the despatches were the subject of conversation; what did they say was the substance of the despatches, or about what did they purport to be? A. I had some conversation with Mr. Thompson previously on the subject of a plot to assassinate Mr. Lincoln and his Cabinet, of which I had informed the paper for which I was correspondent, and I had been invited to participate in that enterprise.
Q. By whom had you been so invited? A. By Mr. Thompson, and on this occasion he laid his hand on the papers or despatches there and said, "This makes the thing all right," referring to the assent of the Rebel authorities.
Q. Did they speak of the persons that the Rebel authorities had consented might be the victims of this plot? A. Yes sir; Mr. Lincoln, Mr. Johnson, the Secretary of War, the Secretary of State, and Judge Chase.
Q. Did they say anything about any of the Generals? A. And General Grant.
Q. In that conversation was anything said, and if so, what was said by Thompson and Surratt, or either of them, touching the effect the assassination of these officers named would have upon the people of the United States, and their power to elect a President? A. Mr. Thompson said on that occasion. I think, I am not so positive, that it was on that occasion, but he did say on the day before the interview of which I speak, that it would leave the Government entirely without a head; that there was no provision in the Constitution of the United States by which they could elect another President.
Q. If these men were put out of the way? A. If these men were removed.
Q. State whether any other member of the Cabinet was named in that connection touching the despatches and the approval from Richmond. A. No sir, no further than this; Mr. Welles was named, but Mr. Thompson said it was not worth while to kill him, he was of no consequence; that was the remark made at the time.
Q. You stated that there was a letter in cipher from Davis, as well as the despatches of Secretary Benjamin? A. Yes sir.
Q. Was the substance of the letter of Davis also spoken of? A. Only generally.
Q. In connection with the despatch? A. Yes.
Q. Was any other subject mentioned? A. Yes. If may be allowed I will state my first interview on that subject.
Q. When was your first interview with him on that subject? A. In February last.
Q. About what time in February?* A. In the early part of February.
Q. That was where? A. That was in Mr. Thompson's room in the St. Lawrence Hall Hotel.
Q. State if you please what was said at that time by Mr. Thompson on that subject, in your presence. A. I had called on Mr. Thompson to make some inquiry about a raid that had been contemplated on Ogdensburg, New York, which had failed because the United States Government had received some information of the intention of the Rebels, and were prepared for it; and I called to see what was to be done next, seeking items for my newspaper, and being supposed by Mr. Thompson to be a good Rebel; he said we would have to drop it for a time, but we would catch them asleep yet, and he observed "there is a better opportunity—a better chance to immortalize yourself and save your country;" I told him I was ready to do anything to save the country, and asked what was to be done; he said some of our boys are going to play a grand joke on

Abe and Andy, that was his expression; this led to explanations, when he informed me it was to kill them, or rather to remove them from office, to use his own expression; he said it was only removing them from office; that the killing of a tyrant was no murder.
Q. State whether anything was said at that time on the subject of commissions from the Rebel authorities in his hands blank. A. He had commissions and conferred one on Booth; I am not so positive whether he had conferred it on Booth or not, but he had one, either then or subsequently, that Booth had been commissioned, and that everybody engaged in the enterprise would be commissioned, and if it succeeded or failed, and they escaped to Canada, they could not be successfully claimed under the extradition treaty.
Q. State whether you have any personal knowledge of their holding these commissions in blank from the Confederate States. A. Yes sir; the commission conferred on Bennett H. Young, the St. Albans raider, was given to him in blank.
Q. By whom? A. It was a blank commission filled up and conferred by Mr. Clay.
Q. What name was attached to it as it came into their hands from the men from Richmond, if any? A. James A. Seddon, Secretary of War.
Q. State to the Court whether you saw the commission yourself. A. I did.
Q. At whose instance were you called to see it? A. Mr. Thompson.
Q. State whether you were asked to testify about the genuineness of Seddon's signature, you having been a clerk in the Department. A. I was.
Q. By whom were you asked? A. By Mr. Thompson and Mr. Abbott, the counsel in the case, and also by Sanders, and Young himself.
Q. State whether you did testify on the question of the genuineness of the signature of Seddon. A. I did.
Q. In that Court? A. I testified before Judge —— the signature was genuine.
Q. Are you acquainted and familiar with the handwriting of James A. Seddon, the Rebel Secretary of War? A. Yes sir.
Q. State now to the Court, upon your oath here, whether the signature to the blank commission you saw was his genuine signature or not. A. It was his genuine signature.
Q. You say you had a subsequent conversation with Thompson a ter the one you have spoken of, as early as February, before the time you met him with Surratt; what time in February was it that you had this subsequent conversation? A. I had conversations with him from day to day almost every day during the whole of February.
Q. On any one of these occasions did he offer you one of these commissions in the work of the assassination of the President? A. Nothing further than this, that he suggested that I might immortalize myself and save the country, and in that same connection said that Booth had been commissioned, and that every man who would engage in the enterprise would be.
Q. In their subsequent conversations state anything that was said about the extent to which this plot was to be carried, what language was used, &c. A. At another time I had a conversation with Mr. William C. Cleary, the day before or the day of the assassination.
Q. Where at? A. At St. Lawrence Hall; we were speaking of the rejoicings in the States over the surrender of Lee, and the capture of Richmond, and so on, and Cleary remarked that they would put the laugh on the other side of their mouths in a day or two. I think that was the day before the assassination took place.
Q. How did he say they would do it? A. There was nothing further than that said; it was known that I was in the secret of the conspiracy, and it was that we had reference to; it was talked about as commonly as we would speak of the weather.
Q. Did you have any conversation with Sanders about that time about it? A. One time before that I had a conversation with Sanders, and he asked me if I knew Booth very well; he expressed some apprehension that Booth would make a fizzle of it; that he was dissipated and reckless, and he was afraid the whole thing would prove a failure.
Q. What business were you engaged in in fact during your stay in Canada, while you were ostensibly a Rebel? A. I was a correspondent of the New York Tribune.
Q. State to the Court whether before the assassination of the President, you communicated to any person in the United States what information you had received about the intended raid on Ogdensburg, or the assassination of the President? A. I did to the New York Tribune, and they declined to publish it, because they had been accused of publishing sensation stories of that kind before, and they feared there might be nothing in it, and did not wish to be accused of publishing sensation stories.
Q. State whether you mean to be understood as saying that you communicated both the plot to make a raid on Ogdensburg, and the other in regard to the assassination of the President, or only one? A. Both.
Q. About how long before the President's assassination did you make the communication? A. I did it in March last, and also in February, I think; I gave

TRIAL OF THE ASSASSINS AT WASHINGTON.

them a paragraph on the subject before the 4th of March.
Q. In order that we may be certain about it, I ask you again, without indicating myself the date, about what time was it that you saw this Surratt, whom you have described in the room of Thompson in Montreal, as the bearer of despatches from Richmond? A. It was about the 7th or 8th of April last. I could not state it to a day. It was within four or five days preceding the assassination.
Q. State what was said by Surratt, if anything, indicating his connection with the plot. A. There was considerable conversation on the subject; I am unable to remember anything Surratt said in particular, but from the whole conversation I inferred that he was to take his part, whatever it might be.
Q. State whether the substance of his conversation was that he was one of the persons in the plot to execute the conspiracy on the President and his Cabinet. A. That was the understanding.
Q. Was that the substance of his conversation or not? A. That was the substance of the conversation.
Q. I should like to know whether anything was said in the several conversations you had with Thompson, Clay and Sanders about the use of money in this business or not? A. I do not think there was, but it was always well understood there was plenty of money when there was anything to be done; I do not think I ever heard anything said about money or compensation at all.
Q. When you say it was always understood, do you mean it was so stated in general terms, by these men, or not? A. I do not think there was anything said on the subject; there may have been but not in my presence; I think there was nothing said on the subject of money.
Q. Did Surratt state at that time, at what time he had left Richmond, or not? A. I do not remember that he did, but it was a few days before; I do not know whether he stated it or whether I understood it from Mr. Thompson, or how, but the understanding was that it was a very short time before; he was just from Richmond, as I understood it.
Cross-examined by Mr. Doster.—Q. Did you ever see the prisoners, Payne or Atzeroth, in Canada? A. No sir; I do not think I ever saw either of them anywhere (the prisoner, George A. Atzerodt, stood up for identification); no sir, I have no recollection of ever seeing him; I think not.
Q. You state that you had never seen the prisoner, Payne, in Canada? (Payne stood up for identification.) A. I have no recollection of it.
Cross-examined by Mr. Aiken.—Q. When did you leave Richmond to go North? A. In December, 1863.
Q. Did you go immediately to New York? A. Yes sir.
Q. Did you, in New York, make an arrangement to become the correspondent of the *Tribune?* A. No sir; I contributed articles which were published, and my arrangements were made in writing afterwards; the first article I contributed was from this city.
Q. Was the arrangement made in New York? A. No sir; it was made by letter.
Q. Where was it made? A. It was made in answer to my first communication; I enclosed the letter for publication to the editor of the New York *Tribune*, which was put out, and I was requested to continue my correspondence, and do so, and received compensation from time to time.
Q. What I want to get at is, where you were at the time you were engaged as a correspondent of the *Tribune;* were you in Washington at the time you made a regular connection with the *Tribune;* a correspondent. A. Yes sir.
Q. Then how soon did you go to Canada? A. I went to Canada last October.
Q. In addition to being a correspondent of the *Tribune* were you in the service and pay of our Government? A. No sir.
Q. Have you ever received compensation or pay from our Government for services rendered? A. Not one cent nor promise.
Q. Did you give out while in Canada, was it generally understood, that you were a correspondent of the *Tribune*. A. No, sir; it was understood that I was a Rebel.
Q. When you asked these gentlemen whom you have named, if they had items that would be fit for publication, what paper did they suppose you were in correspondence with? A. I never asked them for any items, they never supposed I was a correspondent for any paper.
Q. You said something about items for a paper. A. I was seeking items, but I did not ask for them; what I, however, learned in conversation, and learned from these parties, was because they supposed that I was a Rebel, and was in their confidence.
Q. Then they never had any means of knowing that you were a correspondent of the *Tribune?* A. No sir.
Q. Were you admitted freely to their meetings? A. Yes sir, quite so.
Y. And to their confidence, too? A. Yes sir, they may have had secrets that I am not aware of, but I certainly know of a great many of their matters that they intended to keep secret from the public.

Q. Was the disclosure of the intended raid on Ogdensburg published in the *Tribune?* A. I think it was; I contributed a letter with information of that kind in it.
Q. Did I understand you as stating to the Court that you also communicated to the *Tribune* something of the plot about the assassination? A. Yes sir; I wrote them on that subject.
Q. Did you communicate it to any one else? A. No one but to the *Tribune* and my own family.
Q. What was your idea in not communicating that important intelligence at once to the Government, instead of to the *Tribune?* A. I supposed that in giving it to the *Tribune* that it amounted to the same thing as giving it to the Government; I supposed that the relations between the editor and proprietors of the *Tribune* and the Government were such that they would lose no time in giving their information on the subject, and I did not choose to have the information go to the Government directly from me, in regard to this as in regard to some other secrets of the Rebels in Canada that I have exposed; I requested Mr. Gay, of the *Tribune*, to give information to the Government, and I believe he has formerly done so.
Q. You must have been aware, as a newspaper man, that if the fact was published in the newspapers, it would defeat the opportunity of capturing the parties? A. Certainly so, sir.
Q. How many times did you see Surratt in Canada? A. I saw him for three or four times in succession, I think in April last.
Q. In whose room did you meet him? A. I saw him in Mr. Jacob Thompson's room; I also saw him in Mr. Sanders' room once.
Q. Had you any conversation with him personally? A. I had.
Q. What did he say to you? A. Nothing more than speaking about Richmond, and asking him how it looked, and what changes there were in it.
Q. He never said anything to you personally himself about the intended assassination? A. No sir, only what was said in Mr. Thompson's room; I was introduced to him by Mr. Sanders; that was the first I had seen of him.
Q. Since you learned of the assassination, to whom did you communicate your previous knowledge of it? A. To the *Tribune* people?
Q. Did you go in Canada by the name of Sandford Conover? A. No sir.
Q. What name did you go by there? A. James Watson Wallace.
Q. Fix the precise date, if you can, when you met Mr. Surratt at Mr. Thompson's rooms? A. I could not say within two or three days; I think it might have been the 7th, or 8th, or 9th of April.
Q. On or about that time? A. Yes sir, it was near that time.
Q. Did you learn anything while in Canada of the attempt to fire the city of New York? A. Yes sir, I heard the matter discussed.
Q. Did you communicate that intelligence to any one? A. I knew nothing of it until after the attempt had been made.
Q. In representing yourself to those parties as being a good Rebel, and being in confidence, were you ever charged with the execution of any plot or project of theirs? A. No sir.
Q. You never received any pay from our Government, or from the so-called Confederate Government, since you have been in Canada? No sir; from no one, except the New York *Tribune.*
Q. Did you sign your name to the articles in the *Tribune* that were published? A. No sir.
Q. Gave no signature? A. No sir, none at all; it was not desirable to the publishers.
Cross-examined by Mr. Cox:—Q. Did you hear discussed among these individuals the project of the capture of the President and conveying him off to Richmond? A. Yes; I think I heard that talked of in February.
Q. Did you ever attend a meeting of all those persons—Thompson, Clay, and others? A. I have been with Messrs. Thompson, Sanders, Tucker, Cleary, and Gen. Carroll at the same time.
Q. Have you ever attended a meeting for the purpose of considering plans, of hearing among themselves any advices from Richmond? A. Not for the purpose of considering any plans.
Q. Were you present at any meeting in which a letter from Davis was read? A. No, not when it was read, those letters were all in cipher, and I merely heard the substance of them repeated.
Q. You spoke of Mr. Thompson's laying his hand upon some letter, and saying that made it all right? A. That referred to the despatches from Richmond, brought by Surratt.
Q. That was in April, was it not? A. Yes sir, it was in April; I had previously asked Mr. Thompson, when he first suggested that I should participate in this affair, if it would meet the approbation of the Government at Richmond; he said he thought it would, but he should know in a few days; that early in February.
Q. I thought I understood you to state that he said the authority was given in February? A. No, sir, in April, in Surratt's presence.

140 TRIAL OF THE ASSASSINS AT WASHINGTON.

Q. And he then referred to those papers as having furnished the assent? A. Yes, sir.
Q. The first statement in February, was that he was expecting despatches from Richmond, and expected them in a few days? A. Yes, to know whether the affair would receive the approbation of the Government or not.
Q. Did you understand that that communication in April was the first official approval that they had received from Richmond of the plan to assassinate the President. A. I understood that. It was not said that it was the first, but I knew no others.
Q. You understood that was the first? A. Yes sir; I inferred that.
By Mr. Aiken.—Q. In all your conferences and familiar interviews with those rebels in Canada did you ever he ir the name of Mary E. Surratt mentioned as a friend of theirs? A. I never did.
By Assistant Judge Advocate Bingham.—Q. Did you state in answer to one of the questions put to you on the examination anything about a remark, by Mr. Jacob Thompson, that it was not murder to kill a tyrant? A. Yes sir; he said that killing a tyrant in such a case was no murder, and he asked me at the same time if I had ever read the work entitled "Killing no Murder," a letter addressed by Colonel Titus to Oliver Cromwell.
Q. In what conversation was it that Jacob Thompson made use of that expression? A. That was in the conversation in February.
Q. Was it in that conversation he named the Cabinet officers and others that were to be victims of this conspiracy? A. Yes sir; it was at that time Mr. Hamlin was to have been included had the scheme been carried out before the fourth of March.
Q. Was he named especially? A. Yes sir, with the rest.
Q. Were the parties that you have enumerated named also in February? A. Yes sir.
Q. What members of the Cabinet? Q. The Secretary of War, the Secretary of State, General Grant, Judge Chase, the Vice President and President Lincoln.
Q. In April who else was named? A. The same persons, with the exception that Mr. Hamlin was omitted and Vice President Johnson put in his place.
By the Court.—Q. You have stated that you were a conscript in the Rebel service? in what State were you conscripted? A. South Carolina.
By Assistant Judge Advocate Bingham.—Q. Of what state are you a native? A. New York.
Q. Where were you residing when you were conscripted? A. Near Columbia, South Carolina.
By the Court.—How did you come from Richmond? A. I ran the blockade; I walked it most of the way; I rode in the cars to Hanover Junction, and from there walked.
Q. By way of the Potomac? A. I came up through Snickersville to Charlestown, Virginia, and from there to Harper's Ferry, and so on.
Q. As I understand you, you said you saw these blank commissions that were signed by Sedden, Secretary of War, to be given to the persons that were to be engaged in the assassination of the President and Cabinet? A. I saw commissions after they had been filled.
Q. In Canada? A. Yes, sir.
Q. Did you see how much of them was blank, when they came there from Richmond? A. They were all blank but the signatures.
Q. Was there no grades of rank in them? A. No sir, that was put on by the agents themselves; they conferred these commissions at pleasure.
Q. Did you understand that these commissions were to be given upon their engaging in this affair as sort of cover in case they were taken, or that they were to go into the army? A. It was a cover, so that in case they were detected they could obtain that they were Rebel soldiers, and would therefore claim to be treated as prisoners of war, and it was understood that they would be protected as such.
Q. These commissions, you say, were to be given to them as soon as they engaged in this enterprise? A.—
By Mr. Stone.—Q. Were these commissions to be conferred principally as a reward for carrying out this assassination project, or for any of these enterprises that were prosecuted on the borders? A. It was to enable the parties upon whom they were conferred to act officially as Rebel soldiers, and be protected as such in case they were detected.
Q. Could that apply to anything but raids on the borders; they could not expect an assassin to be protected by a commission? A. It was no murder, Mr. Thompson said.
Q. Did the giving these commissions have reference to the assassination, or embrace all enterprises on the border? A. It embraced the who's of them, but I think Booth was especially commissioned for this purpose; the commissions were all in blank; the commission of B. H. Young was a commission of the same sort, and was filled up and conferred by Mr. Clay; he never was in Richmond at all.
By Assistant Judge Advocate Bingham.—Q. I forgot to ask you what time it was you saw J. Wilkes Booth in Canada? A. I saw him in the latter part of October, I think.

Q. With whom was he? A. I saw him with Sanders at Mr. Thompson's, but more about the St. Lawrence Hotel; he was strutting about, dissipating, playing billiards, &c., &c.
By Mr. Cox.—Was it in February that Mr. Thompson said he had conferred one commission on Booth? A. It was in the early part of February, or it might have been the latter part of January.
By the Court.—Q. Did the same party that planned the assassination plan the burning of New York and other cities? A. I do not know anything further than that I have an opinion on the subject; I presume they did.
Q. Is it your belief that they did? A. Yes sir.
Q. This same party? A. I have heard them talk of some other enterprises of the same sort; some they have under consideration now; the same men planned the St. Albans raid.
Q. Were the commissions you speak of similar to those issued by the Government to army officers? A. They were merely signed by the Secretary of War and not by the President.
By Mr. Aiken.—Q. You referred to the same party, in speaking of the St. Albans raid; what party do you mean? A. Mr. Thompson and Sanders.
Q. You do not mean Surratt and Booth? A. No sir.
Q. Were these commissions signed by Jefferson Davis in blank? A. No sir; by James A. Sedden, Secretary of War.
By Associate Judge Advocate Bingham.—Q. Is it not the custom for the President to sign them also? A. They have not lived long enough to have a custom; on the trial of the St. Albans raiders General Carrol and a number of other officers of the Confederate army testified that the custom was that Rebel officers had their commissions signed only by the Secretary of War.
By the Court.—Q. Are you familiar with the cipher which they had in the Rebel War Department? A. No sir; I am not.
Q. You could not tell one if you should see it? A. I could not.
By Associate Judge Advocate Bingham.—Q. I am instructed to make an inquiry of you, in consequence of a question asked you by the Court; what conversation, if any, did you hear among those Rebel refugees in Canada about the burning of New York city and other Northern cities? A. There was a proposition before their council, their junta, to destroy the Croton Dam, by which the city of New York is supplied with water, and it was supposed it would not only damage the manufactures, but distress the people generally, everywhere; but Mr. Thompson remarked that they would have plenty of fires, and the whole city would soon be destroyed by a general conflagration, and without sending any Kennedy, or anybody else there, and if they had thought of this scheme before, they might have saved some necks.
Q. When did he say that? A. That was a few weeks ago.
Q. Who was present when he said that? A. Mr. Thompson, myself, Mr. Sanders, Mr. Castleman and General Carroll.
Q. Do you know of anything being said between those parties, or any others, of the same man you have named in regard to the description from Chicago last year. A. I heard a very great deal of talk about it, and know they had arms concealed there, and that they had a large number of men concealed away at Chicago; some eight hundred men there.
Q. Did Thompson and the others state for what purpose? A. Releasing the prisoners, it was understood.
Q. What prisoner? A. At Camp Douglas, I think they called it, or Camp Chase, or what ever camp it may have been in which they were confined.
Q. You mean Rebel prisoners? A. Yes sir; I think they called it Camp Douglas.
(The Commission then adjourned until Monday morning, May 22d, at 10 o'clock. Monday morning May 22d, Sanford Conover recalled for the prosecution.)
By the Judge Advocate.—Q. You have probably observed that, in some judicial proceedings which have recently taken place at Nassau, it has been made to appear that a certain Dr. Blackburn packed a number of trunks with cloths infected with the yellow fever for the purpose, through them, of introducing the pestilence into the city of New York; I wish you to state whether or not the Dr. Blackburn referred to in those proceedings, is or is not the same person to whom you referred in your testimony on Saturday as being in intimate association with Thompson, Clay, and others? A. It is the same person, but I never saw him with Clay.
Q. Will you state the persons whom you saw associating with this Dr. Blackburn, in Canada? A. Jacob Thompson, George N. Sanders, Lewis Sanders, son of George, ex-Governor Westcott, of Florida; Lewis Castleman, William C. Cleary.
Q. Was Clay among them? A. No sir, I never saw Clay with them; also, Mr. Porterfield, Captain Magruder, and a number of Rebels of lesser note.
Q. State whether or not this Dr. Blackburn was recognized there and known as an agent of the so-called Confederate States. A. Yes sir; he was said to be an agent, and represented himself as an agent.

TRIAL OF THE ASSASSINS AT WASHINGTON.

EDWARD SPANGLER. G. A. ATZEROTH.

SAMUEL ARNOLD. MICHAEL O'LAUGHLIN.

TRIAL OF THE ASSASSINS AT WASHINGTON. 141

Q. Just as Jacob Thompson was an agent? A. Yes; yes.

Q. Will you state whether or not you had any consultation among these men upon the subject of introducing the pestilence into the cities of the United States, and what was said, and when? A. In January last I know of Dr. Blackburn's employing a person to accompany him for that purpose.

Q. Name the party? A. Mr. John Cameron, for the purpose of taking charge of goods and bringing them to the cities of New York, Philadelphia and Washington, as I understood.

Q. You mean goods infected with yellow fever? A. Yes sir; I heard Dr. Blackburn say that about a year before that time he had endeavored to introduce the fever into New York, but, for some reason which I do not remember, failed; he went from Montreal about a year ago last January to Bermuda, or some of the West India Islands, for the express purpose of attending cases of yellow fever, collecting infected clothing, also, and forwarding it to New York, but for some reason the scheme failed.

Q. Did you learn on his return, in the course of that consultation, what he had done and what had interfered, if anything had, to lead to a failure of the enterprise? A. I have seen him, but not to speak to him since his return.

Q. Was Jacob Thompson present at these consultations? A. On one occasion I remember Jacob Thompson, and Mr. Clay, and I think also Lewis Sanders.

Q. Will you state whether or not they concurred in the enterprise of Dr. Blackburn introducing the pestilence in the manner indicated? A. Yes sir; they all favored it, and were all very much interested in it; at this time it was proposed to de-troy the Croton dam, and Dr. Blackburn proposed to poison the reservoir, and made a calculation of the amount of poisonous matter it would require to impregnate the water so far as to render an ordinary draught poisonous and deadly.

Q. Had he taken the measure of the aqueduct, so as to a certain what amount would be required? A. He had the capacity of the reservoirs, and the amount of water that was generally kept in them.

Q. Was the kind of poison which he proposed to use mentioned? A. Strychnine, arsenic and acids—prussic acid, and a number of others which I do not remember.

Q. Did he or not regard the scheme as a feasible one? A. Yes; Mr. Thompson, however, feared it would be impossible to collect so large a quantity of poisonous matter without exciting suspicion, and leading to the detection of the parties; but whether the scheme has been entirely abandoned or not I do not know; so far as the blowing up of the dam is concerned it has not been.

Q. Will you state whether or not Thompson fully approved of the enterprise, if practicable? A. Yes sir.

Q. Discussed it freely? A. Yes sir.

Q. Did the other persons whom you have named also discuss it and approve it? A. Mr. Lewis Sanders and Mr. Cleary, I remember very well, did.

Q. When was this matter discussed? A. In January last; I have heard it spoken of since.

Q. Among the same persons? A. With the exception of Dr. Blackburn.

Q. It was spoken of by a Mr. Montross? A. Patton, of Mississippi; also, a Rebel who had been a medical purveyor in the Rebel army.

Q. Where does the agent, John Cameron, of whom you speak as having been employed by Dr. Blackburn for this purpose, live? A. He has lived in Montreal; he declined to go, being fearful of taking the yellow fever and dying himself.

Q. Do you know whether a large compensation was offered him? A. Yes sir; to the extent of several thousand dollars, he told me.

Q. Did you understand whether this was to be paid by Jacob Thompson? A. I understood by Dr. Blackburn or by the agents; I think Mr. Thompson was the monied agent for all the other agents; I think they all drew on him or what money they received; I know that some of them did.

Q. You say that up to the time when you left Canada, or at the assassination of the President, you did not know whether this enterprise for poisoning the people of the city of New York had been abandoned or not by these conspirators? A. No sir, I did not know whether it had been abandoned; so far as the destruction of the dam is concerned that part of the scheme had not been abandoned.

Q. The only difficulty which Jacob Thompson suggested, I understood you, was that the collection of so large an amount of poison might attract attention to the operation? A. Yes sir; Mr. Thompson made a suggestion of that kind, but Mr. Pattin and others thought it could be managed in Europe.

Q. Pattin himself is a physician, is he not? A. Yes sir.

Q. State whether in connection with this enterprise for introducing pestilence to our cities you have heard mentioned the name of Harris as an agent in any way? A. I do not distinctly remember that I have; I think I have heard him mentioned, but I have never seen the person.

Q. Have you any recollection as to where he probably resided at that time? A. Toronto, I think.

Q. You have no knowledge of any part he actually performed, or undertook to perform? A. No sir; there were other parties in Montreal that Mr. Blackburn had also employed, or endeavored to employ, but I don't remember their names at the present time; I know the parties very well by sight when I see them; there were two medical students.

Q. Do you know whether any of these persons accompanied him when he went to Bermuda for the purpose of carrying out his plans? A. I do not know; I think one of them did; I have seen him since, however, I saw him with Dr. Blackburn two or three days before I left for New York.

Q. Did you not while in Canada make the acquaintance of Dr. Stuart Robinson, a Doctor of Divinity, who was a refugee from Kentucky? A. Yes sir; residing in Toronto; he has been editor of a paper in Kentucky, which I think has recently been suppressed.

Q. Was he or n it present at any of those conversations of which you have spoken? A. He has been present when some of their schemes were being discussed; I do not remember whether he was present when the yellow fever project was discussed or not, or whether it was when it was proposed to poison the Croton water but on one of those occasions he was present.

Q. Will you state whether on that occasion he approbated the scheme? A. He approved of it; he approved of anything; he said that anything that could be done under heaven, would be justifiable under the circumstances; that was his expression.

Q. He pronounced that is an exponent of divinity? A. Yes sir; he is related to the Breckenridges of Kentucky, I think.

Q. Is he not regarded as one of the most violent of all the traitors who have taken refuge in Canada? A. Yes sir.

Q. Have you seen John H. Surratt in Canada since the assassination of the President? A. Yes sir.

Q. On what day did you see him, do you remember? A. I think it was three or four days after the assassination.

Q. Where at? A. I saw him in the street with Mr. Porterfield.

Q. Who is Mr. Porterfield? A. Mr. Porterfield is a Southern gentleman made a British subject by a special act of the Canadian Parliament.

Q. He is from the South? A. Yes sir, he has been for some time a broker or banker there; he took charge of the St. Albans plunder from the Ontario Bank, when prematurely given up by Judge Coursol.

Q. He is one of the intimate associates of the Southern traitors? A. Very intimate with Thompson and Sanders.

By Mr. Aiken.—Q. At what time did you say you saw Surratt in Canada after the assassination? A. I think it might have been three or four days; it might have been a day more or less either way.

By the Court.—Q. Is the Captain Magruder you mention the same who was formerly in the United States Navy? A. Yes sir, a brother of General Magruder of the Rebel army.

Q. Can you state the full name of this Dr. Blackburn, and what State he is from? A. I do not know; I think he is from Mississippi, but I am not sure; I do not think I ever heard his full name.

Q. Was there only one Dr. Blackburn about there? A. That is all; it is the same party who was connected with the yellow fever project; there is no doubt about its being one and the same person.

By Judge Holt.—Q. Will you state your age, and where you were born and educated? A. I am twenty-eight years old; born in New York and educated there.

Q. I understood you to say the other day that you were conscripted and forced into the Rebel service? A. Yes sir.

Q. And you escaped on the first moment you had an opportunity? A. Yes sir; after being detailed as Clerk in the War Department.

Q. Will you state whether or not, throughout, you have not been, in your convictions and feelings, loyal to the Government of the United States? A. I have always been so.

Q. Have you or not personal knowledge that Jefferson Davis was the head of the so-called Confederate States and was called its President, and acted as such, controlling its armies and civil administration? A. It was a matter of public notoriety in the offices controlled by him, and I do saw him act as such.

Q. In the War Department, when you were detailed as an officer he was fully recognized as such? A. Yes sir.

Q. I am not sure whether you have stated precisely, if you have not done it I wish you would state who were present at the conversation which you had with Jacob Thompson early in April when he laid his hand on the despatches? A. Mr. Surratt, General Carroll I think, myself, and I think Mr. Castleman, and I believe there were one or two others in the room sitting further back.

Q. Can you state whether any of them participated in the conversation? A. General Carroll, of Tennessee, did. He was more anxious that Mr. Johnson should be killed than anybody else.
Q. Did he so express himself? A. He did; he said that if the —— prick-louse was not killed by somebody he would kill him himself.
Q. Did he refer by that expression to the then Vice President, Johnson? A. Yes sir, that was his expression.
Q. What did that expression mean? A. A word of contempt for a tailor; it is a tailor's louse; it is a word of contempt for a tailor—at least Webster so defines it; that was the sense in which Carroll used it.
Q. Was it not the sense of those present, as you gathered it from the conversation, that they regarded the enterprise of assassinating the President fully confirmed by the Rebel authorities at Richmond? A. That was distinctly said.
Q. Will you state whether or not you saw J. Wilkes Booth associating at any time with George N. Sanders? A. I never saw Booth except on one day and evening, and then he was strutting about the St. Lawrence Hall, as I have already said, and he was in conversation with Sanders and Thompson; I saw them talking with Booth, but I was not present at any conversation with either.
Q. Had J. Wilkes Booth, in Canada, in association with these men, any nickname, and, if so, what was it? A. I have heard him called "Pet."
Q. By whom? A. I do not distinctly remember; by several; I think by Thompson, and by Cleary I am sure.
Q. In that circle of men you have mentioned you found him so-called? A. Yes sir; I can speak positively as to Cleary, and think also Mr. Thompson.
Q. This Stuart Robinson, D. D., of whom you have spoken, is he not the editor of the journal called the *True Presbyterian*, in Kentucky? A. He was an editor, but the paper has been suppressed, by order of the Commanding General of that Department, I believe.
Q. You have heard so? A. I was told so.
Q. Were you in Canada at the time Kennedy was executed in New York for having fired the city? A. I was.
Q. Was his execution the subject of conversation among the men of whom you have spoken? A. Yes sir, a great deal.
Q. Will you state whether or not in those conversations, the crime for which he was executed, firing the city of New York, was recognized as having been performed by the authority of the Rebel Government? A. It was by the direction of Mr. Thompson.
Q. Did you learn that much from Mr. Thompson himself? A. Yes sir, I think I may say I learned it from Mr. Thompson, or at least by conversation in his presence.
Q. Kennedy was spoken of and recognized as an agent of the Rebel Government? A. Yes sir; Thompson said Kennedy deserved to be hanged, and he was devilish glad he had been hanged, because he was a stupid fellow and had managed things very badly.
Q. On the ground of his being a bungler? A. Yes sir.
By Mr. Aiken.—Did you ever meet more than one Surratt in Canada? A. No sir.
Q. Was Surratt introduced to you as coming from Mississippi? A. No sir.
Q. Was the place mentioned whence he came, A, I do not remember that it was, but I was left with the impression that Surratt was from Baltimore; I never heard that, and I do not know how I gained the impression, but I had an impression of that kind.
Q. Did you ever hear of any Surratts from Mississippi while you were there? A. No sir.
Q. Did you have a regular weekly salary from the *Tribune* or were you paid by the letter? A. I was paid by the letter.
Q. Where did you board in Montreal? A. I boarded in Craig street and in Monica street.
Q. You did not board at the St. Lawrence Hotel? A. No sir; all these parties I have named did not board there; some did: Mr. Sanders did not, and Mr. Tucker only part of the time.
Q. Where did Jacob Thompson board? A. At St. Lawrence Hall.

MONDAY'S PROCEEDINGS.

The record of the previous day having been read, the examination of witnesses was continued as follows:

Testimony of Rev. Wm. B. Evans.

By Judge Advocate Holt.—The testimony of this witness was to the effect that he was well acquainted with J. Seed Jenkins; knew his general reputation to be that of a disloyal man, though in 1861, and previous to that period he had pretended to be in favor of the Union; had known him to be open and out-spoken in his sympathy with the Rebellion: was slightly acquainted with the prisoner, Dr. Samuel A. Mudd; about the first or second of March, while coming to Washington, the prisoner passed witness coming in the same direction, and entered the city just before witness; did not see him accused in the city on that occasion; neither saw him return nor know where he stopped while in the city.

On the cross-examination of witness, conducted by Mr. Clampitt, the following evidence was adduced:—Have been acquainted with Mr. Jenkins about fifteen years; he pretended to be a Union man in 1861, but witness believed him to be a hypocrite; knew from his actions that he was opposed to the Government; those actions consisted in his betting that the South would succeed, and that the country would go to ruin; did not bear him use these expressions, but only heard from others that he had made use of them; did not know that he was a loyal man in 1863, or that he attempted to procure Union votes on the occasion of an election in Maryland; knew him to attempt to raise a disturbance at the polls in order to keep Union men from voting, in consequence of which he was arrested.

Testimony of T. B. Robey.

Townley B. Robey, on being examined by Judge Advocate Holt, testified substantially as follows:—
Have known J. Seed Jenkins for several years; from my personal knowledge of his uniform conduct and conversation I have known him to be one of the most disloyal men in the country, open and out-spoken in his hatred of the Government; heard him curse the President of the United States, and say that old Lincoln offered him an office, but he would not hold an office under such a damned Government.
Cross-examined by Mr. Clampitt.—Have known Mr. Jenkins for four or five years; knew him to be a Union man and a Know-nothing until he abandoned the Union party, which he did immediately upon losing a negro servant, which he had held as a slave; never heard of any attempt on his part to secure Union votes in Washington by inducing citizens of Maryland to return to their residences, though, on one occasion, in 1861, he hoisted a Union flag; never had any suit against Mr. Jenkins, but he had commenced a suit against Andrew B. Robey; witnessseen in consequence of his arrest for disorderly behavior on the occasion of an election in Maryland; the suit was for an alleged false imprisonment.

Testimony of John M. Thompson.

John M. Thompson, on being examined by Judge Advocate Holt, testified that he had known Mr. Jenkins for many years; that four years ago that gentleman was reported to be loyal, but that for the last two years and six months his reputation was the reverse of that, his alleged disloyalty being of an open and outspoken character; witness himself had been loyal to the Government throughout the Rebellion; witness lived in the family of Mrs. Surratt for two years, and from conversations of that lady, which were invariably against the Government, he believed her to be disloyal.
Cross-examined by Mr. Clampitt.—In 1861 and 1862 Mr. Jenkins was considered a Union man; in 1863 he was not; witness never knew of his coming to Washington at any time to procure the votes of Union citizens of that State who had moved here but had not lost their residences in Maryland; at one time Jenkins raised a Union flag, but that was in 1861, when he had the reputation of being a loyal man; witness had heard him say that he hated the Government, but had not heard him state any cause for his hate; in regard to the emancipation policy in the State of Maryland Jenkins said that it was all wrong; never heard him say that he was no good a Union man as there was in the State of Maryland, but that he was opposed to some of the acts of the Administration.
By Assistant Judge Advocate Burnett.—Q. Which side did he say he would fight for in case he was forced to fight? A. He said he would go for the South.
At the instance of Mr. Ewing, counsel for the prisoner, Dr. Samuel A. Mudd, who were not present at the opening of the Court, the following witness for the prosecution was recalled, and his cross-examination resumed:—
Re-cross-examination of Rev. W. B. Evans, Pastor of the Fifteenth Street New School Presbyterian Church (colored) of Washington, by Mr. Ewing.—I am acquainted with the prisoner, Dr. Samuel A. Mudd; I have seen him at the Catholic Church at Bryantown; it was in December, 1859, when I saw him there: was never introduced to the prisoner; saw him after that different times in Washington City; on the street and about the hotels; I think I met him once in the National Hotel; think I saw him last winter at the house, or going into the house of Mrs. Surratt; I could not say what time last winter I saw him, unless I referred to my journal; I never visited Mrs. Surratt's house; the house which I saw the prisoner enter was on H street, I think, between Ninth and Tenth or Eighth and Ninth streets; I suppose it was Mrs. Surratt's house; I asked a policeman. I believe, at the time, and also asked a lady standing on the pavement, whose house I was then indicating the one into which saw the prisoner enter, and was told it was Mrs. Surratt's house; I could not positively say whether it was or not; do not recollect exactly between what streets the house was situated, though I think it was between the Catholic office and the President's house; could not say whether it was a two or three-story house; do not collect whether it stood on a square on the pavement, or stood back; cannot say whether there was a portico

TRIAL OF THE ASSASSINS AT WASHINGTON. 143.

in front; the house was on the south side of H street; I was riding down the street at the time; going to see Rev. Mr. Butler, of the Lutheran Church; I did not see him on that day, but went to a prayer meeting at his church; saw Mrs. Ward there; could not name any others that I saw at the church; I could not name others whom I saw on that day, except Mrs. Sophia Brussy and Miss Pumphrey; I stopped at the houses of those ladies on other occasions during last Winter; when detained in the city over night, I would stop at the house of Mrs. Brussy, who is my s. I.e's aunt; I saw Dr. Mudd entering Mrs. Surratt's house; he was dressed in dark colored clothes and a soft felt hat; I have seen his father within three years on the road coming to this city; I mentioned the fact of my seeing Dr. Mudd, the prisoner, on the road to Washington, to my wife only; the fact of seeing him go into Mrs. Surratt's house I mentioned to my father-in-law; I ho'd a secret commission under the Government, and am a detective officer.

Examination of Miss Fanny Mudd.

By Mr. Ewing.—The prisoner is my brother. I am familiar with the whereabouts of the prisoner during a portion of the time, from the 1st to the 5th of March last. On the 1st, which was Ash Wednesday, my sister was taken sick; on the 2d my brother, the prisoner, called at the house and breakfasted with us; on the 3d he came to the house from his barn, where he had been stripping tobacco, at about eleven or twelve o'clock in the morning. He took dinner and stayed till two o'clock when he went away, but returned about four o'clock with some medicine for my sister. On the 4th of March he came to dinner, and on the 5th he visited us in the evening, in company with Dr. Blanford. I am able to recollect these dates from the fact that the 1st of March was Ash Wednesday, which, among Catholics, is a day of obligation to attend divine service. I am confident that the accused was not absent from home during the 1st and 5th of March. I have been in the habit during the last four years of visiting my brother's house frequently. I never heard of John H. Surratt being there. I heard of Booth being at the house once, that was about the 1st of last November. In 1861 there were three gentlemen who slept in the pines around my brother's house, Mr. Jerry Dyer, Andrew Gwynn and Ben. Gwynn.

Testimony of Mrs. Emily Mudd.

By Mr. Ewing.—Q. Where do you reside? A. In Charles county, Maryland, at the house of the father of the prisoner, Dr. Mudd.
Q. State what you know as to the whereabouts of Dr. Mudd between the 1st and 5th of March last? A. The 1st of March was Ash-Wednesday, and we went down to church; on the 2d of March, Dr. Mudd was summoned to his father's house, and reached here before breakfast, and remained to see his sister; on Friday, the 3d, he came over to dinner about 12 o'clock, and finding his sister much worse, he came over again in the evening to bring her some medicine; he came again on Saturday to dinner, and I think he was there to dinner on Sunday also.
Q. Do you know Andrew Gwynn? A. I do; I have not seen him since the fall of 1860; he was in the habit of visiting at Dr. Mudd's father's before that; I have not heard of him being at Dr. Mudd's house since 1861.
Q. Have you heard of Captain Perry, Lieutenant Perry, and John H. Surratt being there? A. I have not.
Q. Have you ever known Confederate officers or soldiers to be about Dr. Mudd's house? A. No sir, I have been there myself very frequently since 1861.
Q. State whether you saw Dr. Mudd, the prisoner, on his way home from towards Bryantown the day after the assassination of the President? A. Yes; I was standing at the window and saw him pass; there was no one with him.

Cross-examined by Judge Bingham.
Q. Where did you first see him on Saturday? A. He rode by the house towards Bryantown, I think between 1 and 3 o'clock, and when he came back I expect it was 4 o'clock.
Q. Do you know of your own knowledge that Dr. Samuel Mudd was at home on the 1st of March? A. I do not.
Q. And of your own knowledge do you know that he was at home until he came to see your sister the next day at noon? A. I do not.

Testimony of Charles Duell.

For the prosecution, by Judge Holt.—Q. Where do you reside? A. In Washington.
Q. Have you recently been in North Carolina? A. Yes, in Morehead City.
Q. State, while there, if you picked up a letter written in cipher? A. I did pick up the letter that I now see before me; I found it on the 2d of May, at the Government wharf, at Morehead City, floating in the water, and I subsequently deciphered it; it is addressed to J. W. Wise, and is as follows:

"WASHINGTON, April 13, 1865.—Dear John—I am happy to inform you that Pet has done his work well. He is safe, and old Abe is in hell. Now, sir, all eyes are upon you. You must bring Sherman. Grant is in the hands of old Gray ere this. Redshoes showed a lack of

nerve in Seward's case, but fell back in good order. Johnson must come. Old Crook his him in charge. Mind well that brothers' oath and you will have no difficulty. All will be safe and enjoy the trust of our leaders. We had a large meeting last night; All were bent on carrying out the programme to the letter. The rails are laid for safe exit. Old I——, always behind, lost the list at City Point. Now I say again, the lives of our brave officers and the life of the South depends upon the carrying this programme into effect. Number two will give you this. It is ordered no more letters shall be sent by mail. When you write sign no real name, and send by some of our friends who are coming home. We want you to write us how the news was received there. We receive great encouragement from all quarters. I hope there will be no getting weak in the knees. I was in Baltimore yesterday. Pet had not got there yet. Your folks are well and have heard from you. Don't lose your nerve.   O. B. No. 5.

Q. In what business were you engaged at the time? A. In drawing piles; I found this letter when I was at work.
Q. Do you know anything of the person the letter is addressed to? A. No; I know nothing about him, and could hear nothing of him.

Cross-examined by Mr. Aiken.—Q. You state that you deciphered that letter; did you know anything of the key to the cipher? A. A gentleman here told me he had seen it before; we found that the first letter was "W," and we supposed it was dated at Washington, and taking that as a key we tried the letter, but found it did not come out; we then took the date at Washington, and with that commenced making it out; I had no acquaintance with the cipher myself until I came to Washington.
Q. You state that you found the letter in the river; was it much blurred? A. It did not seem to have been in the water a long time, and was very little blurred.
Q. Was anybody with you at the time you picked the letter up? A. Yes sir; A. M. Ferguson.

Testimony of James Ferguson.

By Judge Holt.—Q. State whether you have recently been at Morehead City, N. C.? A. I left there a week ago Wednesday, in company with Mr. Duell.
Q. State whether or not you were present when a cipher letter floating in the water was picked up. A. Yes, I was the one who discovered the letter, and called the attention of Mr. Duell to it; he picked it up; this was on the 1st or 2d of May last.

Testimony of John S. Barr, for Defense.

By Mr. Doster.—Look at the prisoner, Atzeroth, and see if you know him. A. I do; all I know about him is that he came to my shop one evening, at the Navy Yard, and I went to Pope's restaurant with him; we had several drinks together, and he then took supper with me, and afterwards we went back to the restaurant and had more drinks, after which he took his horse and rode off; this was between the 10th and 13th of April.
Q. Do you not remember that it was on the 12th of April? A. It was somewhere about that time. I had some work done that day, which I have charged on my book here as on the 12th of April.

Testimony of Betty Washington, Col'd.

By Mr. Ewing.—State where Dr. Mudd was on the 1st of March last? A. He was down at the tobacco bed preparing it ready to sow; that was on Ash Wednesday; he staid there until about dinner, when Mr. Blandford came, and they went into dinner; it was raining that evening, and he staid in and I did not see him go out any more that evening.
Q. Where was he the next day? A. The next day, Thursday, he was cutting brush, and was there all day; I went out, too, and was loading the cart.
Q. Did you see anything of him on Friday, the 3d of March? A. On Friday he was stripping tobacco, took dinner at his father's and come back about night.
Q. Did you see him on Saturday, the 4th of March? A. He took breakfast at home; in the afternoon he went to the Post Office at Beantown, and came home about night.
Q. Did you see him on Sunday? A. He went to church and was at home at night.
Q. Do you know where he was on the last day of February? A. Yes; he was at work at the brush.
Q. While you were at work at Dr. Mudd's, did you ever hear or see John H. Surratt? A. Not there.
Q. Would you have noticed him if he had been there? A. If he had been there I would have known the name.
Q. Do you know Mary Semmes, and, if so, state what the colored people about there think of her as a truthteller? A. They all give her a bad name as a story-teller.

Cross-examined by Judge Holt.—Q. On the 2d of March Dr. Mudd took breakfast at home did he? A. Yes he took his breakfast at home, and he took his dinner and supper at home too that day.
By Mr. Ewing.—Are you certain he took breakfast at his house the day after Ash-Wednesday.
Question objected to by Judge Bingham, and objection sustained.

Testimony of Wm. P. Wood.

By Mr. Clampitt.—Q. State your official position. A. I am Superintendent of the Old Capitol Prison.

Q. State whether you are acquainted with A. Z. Jenkins, who was a witness in this case. A. I have known him five or six years rather intimately; he has always been an opponent of the Democracy; he was with the Know Nothings, and also one of the Union party when it was formed in 1861; he was considered one of the most reliable men in the district; in 1862 he refused to vote for Holland on the ground that he was under obligations to go for Calvert, who owned that section of the country, and he said he believed him to be a good Union man.

Q. State whether he did not labor and urge his friends to labor and expend his money freely to keep Maryland in the Union up to 1862? A. Yes.

Q. You say he went for Calvert in the election you speak of; did he not go against Harris? A. Yes, he did; Calvert was considered by some a Union man; Harris was considered a Democrat of the Secession school.

Q. Did not Mr. Jenkins remark that if Calvert did not run he would support Holland? A. He agreed to do that.

Q. Did not you receive certain information from Mr. Jenkins which you submitted to the War Department, and which finally, resulted in the capture of Booth? A. I received some information from Jenkins, which I forwarded to Judge Turner.

Q. Did you consider that as a loyal act? A. I was satisfied that he would give me the information if he had it, when I started out.

Q. Do you believe Mr. Jenkins to be a consistent loyal man? A. I do; I do not believe he is a friend of the Administration, on account of the negro question, but outside of that he is a loyal man.

Cross-examined by Judge Holt:—Q. Has not Mr. Jenkins been for some time past bitterly hostile to the Government; and if that is so, do you not consider that as disloyalty? A. I have had very little to do with him lately, and have not regarded him as sound as I did formerly; in the last election he voted for Harris, I believe, and associated with that sort of men.

Testimony of John Acton.

John Acton testified that he lived about a mile and a quarter from Bryantown, and that on the day of the assassination he saw Dr. Mudd going toward Bryantown, riding a grey horse; the was no one with him at the time he first saw him, but another man who was riding behind him overtook him, and they rode on together; in about three-quarters of an hour he saw that person riding back by himself.

The witness stated, on cross-examination, that he could not identify Harold, certainly, as the person he saw on that occasion. He looked very like him, but he did not notice particularly the man so much as he did the horse. The horse he rode was a bay. When he saw the person coming back he was going up the road, in the same way he had come down. This was about three miles from Bryantown.

Marion L. McPherson.

A witness, called by Mr. Ewing, testified that he lived about three-quarters of a mile from Bryantown, and he was at Bryantown on the day after the murder, from about two o'clock till four P. M. While there he heard that a man by the name of Boyd, who had killed Captain Watkins, had murdered the Secretary of State. He did not learn who had assassinated the President, although he made inquiry of citizens and soldiers while there. Was in Bean's store and heard the murder talked over. Saw Lieut. Dana there, and on Monday saw him sitting outside with Dr. George Mudd, with whom he was speaking. Knows the reputation of Dr. George R. Mudd to be that of a good Union man as any in the United States. The reputation of D. J. Thomas for veracity is bad.

John McPherson.

Called by Mr. Ewing, testified that he was at Bryantown on the day after the murder, from two until seven o'clock; heard much general conversation about the assassination, but did not hear till Monday that Booth was the assassin; saw Lieutenant Dana on Monday morning, in company with Dr. George Mudd; did not hear the conversation; the reputation of Daniel J. Thomas for veracity is bad; the reputation of the prisoner, Mudd, is that of an honorable man and good citizen.

Cross-examination.—Never heard he was charged with false swearing, and would not say that he would not believe him under oath.

John T. Langdon.

Called by Mr. Ewing, testified that he was at Bryantown on the day after the assassination of the President; heard much conversation on the subject, but did not hear till Monday who was charged with the murder.

Peter Trotter.

Examined by Mr. Ewing.—Lives in the village of Bryantown; was there the day after the murder and heard it talked of; asked some soldiers who did it, and they said it was done by Boyd, who murdered Captain Watkins; the reputation of D. J. Thomas for veracity is very bad; would not hold ve him under oath.

Cross-examined by Judge Holt.—Have always been loyal to the Government, and desired it to succeed in putting down the Rebellion; Mr. Thomas is very unpopular in the neighborhood; he never heard him speak in favor of the Rebellion; have never taken the oath of allegiance; called on a captain about three weeks ago, to take it, but he had no blanks; took the oath in Baltimore once to get my goods out; at that time my sympath es were with the Rebellion; have never been engaged in blockade-running; don't know whether I should believe Thomas if he were speaking in a court of justice against the Rebellion or not.

By Mr. Ewing.—Before the war Thomas' veracity bore the same reputation it has now; I have heard him talk at bad.y as some of the Rebels, but at the beginning of the war he had the reputation of being a loyal man.

By the Court.—Am a native of Scotland, and have never been naturalized here; have voted three times in this country, but not for the last two years; the first time I voted was in a Presidential election, and afterwards for local officers; do not think I voted upon the adoption of the amendment to the Constitution of Maryland; do not know why I didn't vote.

Testimony of Benjamin Gardiner.

Saw Dr. Mudd at church on the Monday after the assassination, and then saw him in conversation with his neighbor. That was about 100 o'clock in the morning.

Testimony of Thomas Davis.

Have lived at Dr. Mudd's house since the 9th of January; Dr. Mudd was at home on the 1st of March; he came to see witness, who was sick; it was Ash Wednesday, and he said he cou'd give me no meat; he came to see me on the 1st, 2d, 3d, 4th and 5th day of March twice a day; he came every day while I was sick, in the day time.

Mr. Ewing then offered in evidence the following telegram:

MONTREAL, June 2d, 1865.—I left Washington on Monday evening, March 20th, and have not been there since. You can have my testimony before the American Consul here, if required.

JOHN McCULLOUGH.

Testimony of John Davis.

Live in Prince George county, Maryland; Dr. Mudd was at home at 10 o'clock in the morning, on the 2d of March last; my son was sick; I went to see him and found Dr. Mudd there.

The Court then went into secret session, and finally adjourned until 10 A. M. to-morrow.

Tuesday's Proceedings.

WASHINGTON, June 6.—The reading of the previous day's record occupied the Commission until 1 o'clock, when the body took a recess until 2, at which hour they reassembled.

D. J. Middleton, Clerk of the United States Supreme Court, being examined by Mr. Ewing, testified that Marcus P. Norton, a witness who had been before the Court, argued a motion before the Supreme Court of the United States on the 3d day of March last. The object in calling this witness was to fix a certain day in regard to which Norton, a witness, had previously testified.

Mr. Ewing, counsel for the prisoner Dr. Samuel A. Mudd, then addressed the Court as follows:—By reason of information which I have received since the witness Daniel J. Thomas was last upon the stand, I ask the privilege of the Court to recall this witness for the purpose of further cro s-examination in regard to a single point. I wish to show that this witness, whose testimony is of vital importance in the case, gave that testimony from corrupt motives. I expect to show through five or s x of his neighbors that by his own declarations, made since he appeared upon the stand for the prosecution, he did it from the hope and expectation of a large reward. To be more precise, I expect to prove that he stated to Eli J. Watson, on the 1st of June, that he had testified here, and that Dr. Mudd would surely be convicted; that he asked Watson for a certificate of the fact that he was the first person who gave information which led to the arrest of the accused, and that he thus stated to Watson that if he could get such a certificate from him and others he would get a reward of twenty-five thousand dollars, because of the information leading to the arrest and because of the fact of conviction. I expect to show, further, that subsequent y, on the same day, in conversation at Wm. Watson's house, near Horsehead, with John it, Richards, Benj. J. Naylor, George Lynch, Lemuel Watson and Wm. Watson, he stated to them that he wished them to give him certificates as being the first person who gave information which led to the arrest of Dr. Mudd; that he ha't been present here and testified, and that Dr. Mudd would shortly be convicted, and that if they would give him the certificate he desired he would receive a reward of ten thousand dollars by reason of his efforts in the case. I wish to show further, that subsequently, upon a magistrate of the neighborhood, Mr. James W. Richards, riding up, Thomas, in the presence of these last named gentlemen, submitted to that gentleman the question as to whether, upon his getting these certificates, he would not be entitled to the reward of ten thousand dollars, in case Dr. Mudd should be convicted. It seems to me that if the witness stood before this Court fair on all the testimony which has preceded this evidence, it should justly go to diminish the weight of his testimony in the minds of the Court, by showing that he was testifying under the hope of a large reward; and in the light of the evidence that has been given that he manufactured a lie to procure the arrest and conviction of Dr. Mudd, being actuated by a mercenary motive.

Assistant Judge Advocate Burnett stated that the prosecution would interpose no objection to the evidence.

The following witness was then called:—

Re-cross-examination of D. J. Thomas.

By Mr. Ewing.—I was at Wm. Watson's, near Horsehead, on Thanksgiving day, the first of the present month, with John R. Richards, Benj. J. Naylor, Geo. Lynch, Lemuel Watson and Wm. Watson, when Jas. W. Richards, a magistrate, rode up; I did not say to Mr. James W. Richards that I had been asking the gentlemen present for a certificate as proof of the fact that I was the first person who gave information leading to the arrest of Dr. Samuel A. Mudd; neither did I say I had stated to them that Dr. Mudd would be convicted, or that if they gave such a certificate, and Dr. Mudd should be convicted, I would receive a reward of $10,000; I did not say to any of the persons in whose company I then was what I have just denied saying to Mr. Richards; I never expected a cent for what I might do in this case as a witness; I did not tell Richards that I was the person who gave the notice which led to the arrest of Dr. Mudd; I never told any one that I told the gentleman referred to that the expression in Washington City in regard to Mudd was that he would "go up;" I also asked their opinion as to whether I would be entitled to any portion of the reward in the event of Dr. Samuel Mudd being convicted, but never asked them for a certificate of the fact that I was first to give them information concerning Mudd; the other day I was telling John D. Moran and Daniel B. Moran about the conversation between Dr. Mudd and myself previous to Dr. Mudd's arrest, when John D. Moran said that I told him about that before; I had forgotten having told him; Moran said that I told him that before the issue, sination of the President, but I have no recollection of it; I never said to Eli J. Watson that I wanted him to certify that I gave the information which led to Dr. Mudd's arrest, or that I was entitled to the reward of twenty-five thousand dollars for giving that information.

Testimony of James A. Richards.

By Mr. Ewing.—I am acquainted with the witness, D. J. Thomas; was with him and others in the droveyard of William Watson, at Horsehead, Prince George county, on the 1st of the present month; he stated that he had called on William Watson and B. J. Naylor for a certificate that he was entitled to a portion of the reward offered for the arrest of Booth and his accomplices; that he had informed the officers of Dr. Mudd's arrest, and that if they would certify to that fact; he would be entitled to the reward; that if Dr. Mudd was convicted he would receive ten thousand dollars; the certificate he wanted was that he informed them concerning Dr. Mudd's arrest or of his having been arrested; he did not certify to having led to the arrest; the reputation of D. J. Thomas in the community where he lives is very bad; if I believed he had any prejudice or any money at stake, I would not believe him under oath; his reputation for veracity before the war was pretty much the same as it is now.

Cross-examined by Judge Bingham—The day this conversation took place at William Watson's was on Thursday; when I rode up Lemuel Watson remarked to me, " I am glad you have come; you are a justice of the peace; Daniel says he is entitled to so much reward, and I want you to say whether he is entitled to it;" I don't recollect what I said at the time to Thomas; he applied to Watson for a certificate that he had informed them of Dr. Mudd's arrest; that if he could get this certificate he could get a portion of the reward, or words equivalent; if he had said, " If you give me a certificate that I informed you of Dr. Mudd's arrest, he would be entitled to a reward," that would have been words equivalent; we told him we thought he was entitled to twenty thousand dollars; we meant it as a joke and told him so afterwards, but did not at the time; he replied that he did not want a certificate of me, or words to that effect; he told me he did not want me to swear to a lie for him to get twenty thousand dollars.

Q. Didn't you swear a little while ago that you had told him he had better take twenty thousand dollars? A. If I did I recall it: what I intended to say was, that I told him and Watson told him that he was entitled to twenty thousand dollars, but that was a joke; I did not know that he was entitled to anything, I have had no connection at all with the Rebellion, and have not sympathized with it; I have been all the time during the Rebellion in Charles and Prince George counties, keeping school.

By Mr. Ewing.—I have been a hearty supporter of all the measures of the Government to suppress the Rebellion; Mr. Thomas was not a hearty supporter of the Government in 1861; I met him on the way from school during that year, and he stated that he was going down to join the Southern army, and when Beauregard came over he was going to come back and hang a man. Thomas P. Smith; Thomas was not a loyal man at the beginning of the war.

Mr. Ewing at this point introduced in evidence the general order of the War Department of 20th April, 1865, offering one hundred thousand dollars reward for the arrest of Booth and his accomplices, and liberal rewards for information leading to the arrest of any of the parties.

Testimony of John F. Davis.

By Mr. Ewing.—I was at the house of Dr. Mudd, the prisoner, the Tuesday following the assassination of the President; I went to the field and informed him of the fact that Lieutenant Lovett and a party of soldiers had come to arrest him; I came up with him to the house, and was there met by George Mudd; he met Dr. Sam Mudd just at the end of the kitchen.

Q. State what Dr. George Mudd said to Dr. Sam. Mudd.

Judge Bingham—I object to that question.

Mr. Ewing (the witness having retired from the room) stated that his object was to rebut the testimony introduced by the prosecution, that Dr. Mudd denied that there had been any persons at his house on that morning. The defense had already proved in a roundabout way that the prisoner had informed Dr. George Mudd that two suspicious persons had been at his house on Saturday morning, and requested him to communicate the fact to the military authorities, which he had done, and he proposed to show by this witness that Dr. George Mudd now informed him that, having given information as he requested, the detective had come for the purpose of questioning him on this subject; and as Samuel Mudd, knowing the fact that information had already been communicated from him through Dr. George Mudd, of the visit to his house of two suspicious persons, it was unnatural to suppose that the prisoner would then, as stated by one of the witnesses for the prosecution, have denied that any persons had been at his house.

Judge Bingham said the purpose was to bring in the declaration of the third person to the accused, which was utterly incompetent.

The objection was sustained by the Court and the witness recalled.

Q. State whether Dr. Samuel Mudd betrayed any alarm when you informed him that the detectives had come to his house. A. None that I know of; he manifested no unwillingness to go to the house, and came right up there with me.

Testimony of L. S. Orme.

By Mr. Ewing.—I am acquainted with the witness, J. D. Thomas; I know his reputation in the community in which he lives for veracity; I never heard him tell any story in my life of any length that he did not tell a good many things not true; I do not know any man down there who would believe him in anything he would undertake to tell; I have known him since before he was grown; in any matter in which he was prejudiced, I would not believe him under oath, and would hardly believe him anyhow.

Cross-examined by Judge Holt.—I am loyal to the Government to the best of my ability; I have always wished that the Union might be sustained; I never wanted to see two Governments; I always thought the North would succeed, if either.

By Mr. Ewing.—Thomas was not a loyal man when the war commenced; he begged me once, in the fall of 1861, to go South with him; the first of the war he was looked upon as a great friend of the South, and a great help to them as far as his ability would go, which was not much.

Testimony of H. L. Mudd, Jr.

By Mr. Ewing.—I did not see my brother, Dr. Samuel Mudd, on the 1st day of March, but I think he stayed at home on the 2d of March I think he came to my father's house to see a sick s'ster; on the 3d of March he was sent for, also, at 10 o'clock, to go to my father, and took dinner with us about two o'clock; he came back again the same day, and brought some medicine; I went to his house again the same night, and brought some medicine over; on the 4th of March I also saw him; the distance from my father's house to the Navy Yard bridge, Washington, is between twenty-seven and thirty miles; I do not know that my brother, Dr. Mudd, ever owned a carriage of any description, and if he had I should have known it: my father does not own a buggy, or a rockaway, of any description; he owns a large double carriage, as large as any of the hacks you see in the city.

Testimony of Dr. J. H. Blandford.

By Mr. Ewing.—A. I saw Dr. Mudd at home on the 1st and 5th of March; on the 1st at his house, making a tobacco bed, and on the 5th at church; Dr. Mudd does not own a buggy, neither does his father a buggy or a rockaway, but owns a large family carriage.

Testimony of Dr. Allen.

By Mr. Ewing.—A. Dr. Mudd was at my house on the evening of the 23d of March last; he came in with H. A. Clark and a Mr. Gardiner (I do not know his first name) who lives out in Dr. Mudd's neighborhood; they came at near eight o'clock in the evening, and stayed till between twelve and one o'clock that night; there were several persons in there; I fixed the date at the 23d of March because I remember that on that day a tornado swept over the city, and a negro boy was killed; I had seen Dr. Mudd once before that time; I was introduced to him by Mr. Clark, I think in the early part of 1864; I had not seen him since that time, and these are the only two occasions I think I saw him.

Testimony of Dr. Clark.

By Mr. Ewing.—I saw Dr. Mudd, the prisoner, with Mr. James Gardiner and others at my house in the latter part of March; they came to my store between 6 and 7 o'clock, and went to my house to tea, and after tea went round to Dr. Allen's office, and remained until between 12 and 1 o'clock; there were some ten or a dozen persons there; Dr. Mudd remained at my house that night and left the next morning; after breakfast he and Gardiner went off together; they roomed together at my house that night; I have not seen him since till yesterday; I do not know J. Wilkes Booth, John H. Surratt, or Wm. Weichman, and did not see any of them at my house or Dr. Allen's that night; Dr. Mudd was not out of my sight from the time he came to the store that afternoon until he went to bed at my house that night; the only way I fix the date is by a storm that day in which a negro boy was killed; we were playing cards that evening at Dr. Allen's.

Two witnesses were called relative to the confession of the prisoner Arnold, while on the way from Fortress Monroe to Baltimore, but their examination was not continued further than putting preliminary questions.

Mr. Ewing stated that several important witnesses had been subpœnaed and would without doubt be present to-morrow, but that no further witnesses on behalf of the defense were now present.

Mr. Aiken remarked that there were two or three witnesses he desired to examine still in defense of Mrs. Surratt, but that if they did not appear before the witnesses for the other prisoners had all been examined, he would not ask for any delay but would be ready at any time to sum up in her defense.

The President of the Court notified counsel that, in accordance with the uniform practice of courts-martial they would be required to present their arguments in writing.

The Judge Advocate-General also stated, in order to guard counsel against unnecessary delay, that following the usual course in courts-martial, no opening would be made on the part of the Government. Arguments on behalf of the accused would be made, to which a reply would be made on behalf of the Government, and no further arguments allowed. Mr. Aiken and Mr. Ewing remarked that they would prefer that the Government should, in advance, indicate its own theory in respect to the accused. The Judge Advocate-General replied that their general course of examination would indicate that.

General Hunter stated that hereafter the hour of meeting of the Court would be eleven o'clock instead of ten.

The Court then adjourned.

WEDNESDAY'S PROCEEDINGS.

WASHINGTON, June 7.—The record of the previous day was read, and the Commission then went into secret session, and after a short time the doors were reopened. After considerable delay, in consequence of the non-attendance of witnesses, the testimony proceeded as follows:—

Re-Examination of Geo. Boose (Colored.)

By Mr. Ewing.—The day in regard to which I testified previously as the one on which I met the prisoner, Dr. Samuel A. Mudd, on a byroad, near my house, was Easter Saturday, the day after the assassination; from the point where I crossed the main road I could not see the whole of that by-road; if anybody had been traveling along the main road with Dr. Mudd, the person would have been very near me when I crossed the road.

By Assistant Judge Advocate Bingham.—Did not say that I saw Dr. Mudd when he turned off the main road, and not having seen him then could not say that there was no person with him.

Testimony of R. E. Skinner (Colored.)

By Mr. Ewing.—I live in Charles county, Maryland, and have been the slave of Mrs. Thomas, mother of Daniel J. Thomas, whom I have known for thirty years; his reputation as a truth-teller is bad, but I could not say that I would not believe him on his oath; have heard gentlemen say that they would not believe him on his oath; when the war broke out he was not a loyal man; since then he has been changeable.

By Assistant Judge Advocate Bingham.—Have not heard any one since the commencement of the present trial speak of Thomas as a man who could not be believed on oath; did not hear any gentleman say that he was not to be believed on oath in a court of justice.

There being no further witnesses present, Mr. Ewing stated that there remained to be called, in Mudd's case, thirteen witnesses, none of whom lived more than twenty-four miles from Washington. He presumed that the subpœnas of the witnesses had miscarried, as he was informed late last evening that a number of them had stated that they had not been subpœnaed.

Assistant Judge-Advocate Burnett said that the subpœnas in each case had been promptly issued and sent to General Augur's Head-quarters, with the direction of the Secretary of War that they be served forthwith.

The Commission then took a recess until two o'clock, at which hour the body reassembled.

Testimony of John W. Wharton.

By Mr. Ewing.—I live in Baltimore; am engaged at Fortress Monroe, on the outside of the fort; the prisoner, Samuel Arnold, was in my employment as a clerk from the 2d to the 17th of April, the day of his arrest; during that period I was absent only three days; the prisoner performed his duties regularly and faithfully during the time he was employed by me; I received a letter from the prisoner about the latter part of March, before he entered into my employ.

Q. Did he say anything in that letter in regard to his former occupation?

Assistant Judge-Advocate Bingham objected to the question as irrelevant. The objection was sustained.

Mr. Ewing then moved that the translation of the cipher letter alleged to have been found in the dock of Morehead city, North Carolina, be stricken from the record for the twofold reason that it bore upon its face no evidence that it was fictitious, and that upon the plainest rule of evidence it was wholly inadmissible, inasmuch as the letter was in cipher, and the handwriting had not been identified, and it had not been shown to have been addressed to, or been in the possession of anybody connected with or charged to have been connected with the conspiracy. The rule in regard to declarations in cases of conspiracy was that they might be admitted where they were declarations of one of the conspirators and that where they are the declarations of a conspirator they must accompany some act of the conspiracy.

Mr. Ewing read from Benaye, page 289, and stated further that the contents of the letter had not been shown to be declarations of any one of the conspirators, but were entirely unconnected with the subject under investigation, and were, therefore, inadmissible. The motion had not been made sooner by the speaker, owing to the fact that he was not in the court-room when the letter was prosecuted, and was not informed of its presentation until to-day. (The letter referred to has been published.)

Assistant Judge Advocate Bingham stated that it was alleged in the charge and specifications that this conspiracy was entered into by the parties named, and by others unknown. He cited instances in which the declarations of parties who were neither indicted nor on trial were admissible as far as those declarations had a bearing upon cases of conspiracy, and the principle was well settled that a letter written and never delivered was admissible on a trial of conspiracy. The letter in question would not probably affect the accused at the bar, but it should not be excluded from the Court on that account.

The speaker contended that a sufficient foundation had been laid to justify the introduction of the letter, as it had been shown that Booth plotted the assassination of the President, with the agents of the Rebellion in Canada, who weighed him out the price of blood; that it fell to the lot of one of the conspirators to go to Washington and to strike a murderous blow in aid of the Rebellion; that another was ordered to go to Newbern, N. C. and that this infernal letter was picked up in the vicinity of Newbern, and the fact that it was written by a conspirator was patent on its face. Had the letter been found in the pocket of Booth, who would say that it would not have been admissible in evidence against him, and against every one else conspiring with him in this bloody work?

After further argument, the commission decided not to sustain the motion of Mr. Ewing.

Testimony of Miss Minnie Pole.

By Mr. Ewing.—I am acquainted with the prisoner Arnold; saw him on the 20th of March, in an omnibus going to Hookstown, and the 27th at his uncle's, on the occasion of a party there; saw him again on the 28th at witness' house, near Hookstown.

Judge Advocate Holt stated that having learned that the defense would not call any further witnesses with a view to impeach the character of the witness for the prosecution, Lewis J. Weichman, he would now call several witnesses for the prosecution.

Testimony of John Ryan.

By Judge Advocate Holt.—Have been acquainted with Lewis J. Weichman for nearly a year, though not intimately, merely having occasional conversations with him as I met him on the street; his reputation for veracity and uprightness has always been good; from my knowledge of his character I would believe him under oath, or if not under oath; do not believe he would tell a falsehood; I recollect a conversation which took place between him and myself about the time of the evacuation of Richmond; my impression is that during the conversation he rejoiced at the prospect of a restoration of the Union; have no recollection that he ever expressed any other than loyal sentiments.

Cross-examined by Mr. Eakin.—Cannot remember any conversation with Weichman on political subjects prior to the evacuation of Richmond, other than that of which I have spoken; do not recollect ever having heard him express any other than Union sentiments; he never represented to me that his relation with the War Department was of a confidential nature; never heard anything said against his character for honesty and veracity.

Examination of Frank Stott.

By Judge Holt.—I have known Lewis J. Weichman about sixteen months; his reputation as an honest, truth-telling man is very good indeed, as far as I know it; we were both in the public service in the same office; he bore an excellent reputation for loyalty there; he was always outspoken and frank in his friendship for the Government, as far as I knew; he was connected with a military volunteer organization for the defense of Washington.

Cross-examined by Mr. Aiken.—I made my acquaintance with Mr. Weichman as a clerk in the War Department; my relations with him were not very intimate; I never heard of his being a detective in the War Department; the military organization of which I speak was composed exclusively of clerks in the Department; it was considered at the time the organization was formed equivalent to dismissal from office not to join it.

Testimony of James P. Young.

By Judge Holt.—I am clerk in General Meigs' office; I have known the witness Weichman since 1856; his reputation has been that of an honest, truth-telling man, without any reproach whatever; I was a college classmate with him in the Central High School of Philadelphia, in the summer of 1859; he remained in that college two or three years; I met him in Washington about eighteen months ago, and have since been very intimate with him; I have had many conversations with him on the subject of the country, and I regard him as an entirely loyal man; I may state that he was a member of the Union League; he has at all times been frank and unhesitating in his expressions of loyalty.

Cross-examined by Mr. Aiken.—The Central High School of Philadelphia is both a college and a school for boys; we entered Divisions H, G and F, which corresponds with the "freshmen class" in college; I never heard Weichman declare his intention to become a minister; I could not state whether or no his intention to join the military organization to which he belonged was an equivalent to his dismissal from office or not; I don't know when he joined the Union League; I am also a member, and I know that he is by unmistakable signs; Mr. Weichman gave the signs by which members know each other.

Q. What signs did he give you? A. He gave me signs which are peculiar to the Union League.

Q. What are these signs?

The question was objected to by Judge Bingham as wholly immaterial.

General Foster.—I object to the counsel taking up the time of the Court by asking any such questions.

Mr. Aiken.—My object is to show that the witness does not know that he is a member of the Union League, the only competent evidence being his signature to its Constitution. But I withdraw the question.

Testimony of P. T. Ransford.

P. T. Ransford was called, and gave the same testimony as the last two witnesses in respect to Weichman's loyalty.

Testimony of John T. Hollahan.

By Colonel Burnett.—I have resided in Washington all my life; commenced boarding at Mrs. Surratt's house, on H street, the first week in February, and continued till the Saturday night after the assassination; saw Atzerott there several times at meals, but did not know him by name; I saw Payne there once, at breakfast, under the name of Wood; Atzerott was with John Surratt and two or three friends, all together at the table; heard none but general conversation; did not know of Mrs. Surratt's defective eye-sight; I was always recognized by her; I have seen Booth there frequently in the parlor, with Mrs. Surratt and the young ladies; I never saw Harold at that house; I saw Mrs. Slater there; I was dressing myself one morning about half-past seven o'clock, and saw Mrs. Slater getting into an open carriage; Mrs. Surratt was on the pavement at the time, talking to this lady; I am not positive whether she gave this lady any assistance or not; this was about two weeks previous to the assassination; I saw John H. Surratt for the last time on the 3d of April; I didn't know then where he had returned from; I learned it after the assassination, from Weichman; the last time I saw John H. Surratt previous to the 3d of April he was getting into a buggy with this lady; he rapped in my room door about 10 o'clock on the night of the 3d of April, the day the news was received of the evacuation of Richmond; I gave him sixty dollars, in payment of forty in gold he exchanged with me; he said he wanted to go to New York, and could not get it discounted in time for the early train.

Cross-examined by Mr. Aiken.—I don't know who Atzerott came there to visit; I don't know anything of the displeasure of the family at Atzerott being there, except from what I have heard them say; they sometimes made fun of him, while he was there; I was not at the house often at night, and don't know whether Mrs. Surratt was able to read and sew by gas-light or not.

Q. Can you state whether Weichman gave himself up after the assassination, or whether he was arrested and taken to the police office.

Question objected to by Colonel Burnett as not legitimate to cross-examination.

Q. Did you accompany Weichman to Canada.

Question objected to by Colonel Burnett for the same reason as above.

Q. Who were the first parties who entered Mrs. Surratt's house the night after the assassination.

Colonel Burnett. You need not state that.

Q. State if you have any knowledge of John H. Surratt being in this city since the 3d of April? A. None.

Q. Did you see Weichman at three o'clock Saturday morning, April 15th? A. I did.

Q. Where was he?

Colonel Burnett—All this is outside a proper examination.

Mr. Aiken stated that the counsel for the defense had not objected to any testimony, legal or illegal, sought to be introduced by the Government, and they claimed the same liberality in introducing testimony tending to shield the accused from the crimes with which they were charged.

Colonel Burnett replied that the rebutting evidence, as to this point, was commenced by the Government upon the statement of the counsel for Mrs. Surratt that his evidence for impeaching the character of Weichman was closed; he denied that the Government had introduced any evidence not legal or legitimate.

Mr. Ewing said that with the consent of the Judge Advocate, he proposed to put some questions to this witness, as a witness for the defense.

Colonel Burnett assented, and the examination was continued by Mr. Ewing:

I knew a Mr. Jarboe; I do not know whether his name is Judson or not; I never saw him at Mrs. Surratt's house or heard of his being there; I never knew the prisoner, Dr. Mudd, to go there or heard of his being at the house.

Q. State whether Weichman gave himself up after the assassination of the President.

Question objected to by Colonel Burnett. Mr. Aiken had been excluded from asking the question because he had stated that he had close his evidence upon this point and he desired now to see whether the Court would allow the same list of questions to be turned over to the counsel for another prisoner and in no way affected by the testimony and put to the witness.

Mr. Ewing declared the reprimand as unnecessary and exceedingly out of place. It was not the business of the Court to know where he got his questions, and the Assistant Judge-Advocate had stepped beyond the proprieties of his position when he undertook to get that information. He would, however, state that the questions were written by himself originally and handed by him to Mr. Aiken, who was examining the witness.

Col. Burnett said that Mr. Ewing was only permitted to make the witness his own by his courtesy, and he now withdrew his consent.

Judge Holt remarked that the witness had been placed in the hands of Mr. Ewing as his own witness, and he doubted the right now to withdraw his consent.

Judge Bingham made the further objection of the incompetency of the testimony, till the foundation had been laid, of asking the question first of Mr. Weichman himself.

The objection was sustained by the Court.

Q. Did you go with Weichman to Canada and back? A. I did; he appeared to be a good deal excited; he was much excited the morning after the murder; the first persons who entered Mrs. Surratt's house on the Saturday after the murder were McDevitt, Clark and others, of the Metropolitan Police; it was about two o'clock in the morning; I think Weichman opened the door to let the men in; I did not see whether he was dressed or not; I took Weichman down myself to Superintendent Richardson the morning after; he did not express himself as wishing to be delivered up.

Testimony of Jas. McDevitt.

By Col. Burnett.—I went to Mrs. Surratt's house with other officers, about 2 o'clock the night after the murder; a lady put her head out of one of the upper windows and asked who was there; we asked if Mrs. Surratt lived there, and she said she did; Weichman then came down and opened the door; he appeared as if he had just gotten out of bed; he was in his shirt, pants and stockings; he went to Canada in my charge for the purpose of identifying John H. Surratt; he had abundant opportunity to escape while in Canada, and, in fact, I let him in Canada and returned to New York.

Cross-examined by Mr. Aiken.—Weichman did not make any confessions in regard to himself; when I left him in Montreal he was in company with officer Begley, but he could have escaped, for he went out once with a citizen of Montreal, accompanied by an officer, to identify some parties at St. Lawrence Hall.

Judge Bingham objected to the testimony as immaterial. Everybody knew that when Weichman was taken within a foreign jurisdiction he was free.

Witness.—I did not find John H. Surratt at St. Lawrence Hall; his name was registered on the 6th of April, and again on the 18th; he left the hotel the day we arrived in Canada, which was on the 20th of April; I got the first information that I would be likely to find Surratt in Montreal, and that is the reason why I took Weichman there; Mrs. Surratt stated to me when I called there that she had received a letter that day from John, dated in Canada; we were inquiring for the son; she said she had not seen him for two weeks, but had received a letter from him that day; I asked her where it was, she said, "somewhere about the house;" I could not find the letter; I didn't ask Mrs. Surratt to find it.

Testimony of J. Z. Jenkins.

By Colonel Burnett.—The witness detailed the particulars of assembling a party of Union men in the early part of the war, and watching a flag by night and a day to prevent secession sympathizers from hauling it down. The witness was, at that time, the only man of any means not a Democrat in his district. He made great efforts and expended money needed for his family in getting Union votes. He had always been a loyal man, and voted for Charles B. Calvert in 1 2 last in the last election voted for Harris Democrat, the first time in his life he had ever voted the Democratic ticket. He had not lost any property in consequence of the war, except his negroes, and never made any complaints of that.

Testimony of Andrew Collenback.

By Colonel Burnett.—I met J. Q. Jenkins on the night of the 17th of May, at Floyd's Hotel, in Surrattsville; he said he understood I had been telling lies on him, and if he found it to be the truth, he would give me the —— whipping I ever had; after that he said if I tested against him, or any one connected with him, he would give me a —— whipping; that was in the presence of Mr. Cottingham and Mr. Floyd; he did not mention Mrs. Surratt's name; I have known him about ten years, and never heard him express any disloyal sentiments; I did not consider him on that occasion very drunk; but he had been drinking.

Cross-examined by Mr. Aiken.—I did not take any son of mine to Alexandria and put him in the Rebel army; he went there by his own consent, and without mine; I did not place any restrictions in the way of his going; Mrs. Surratt has not given my family very much in the way of food and clothes; she has not been a friend any more than one neighbor would be to another; my son returned from the Rebel army about three weeks ago; I have been a Democrat in politics during the war; I do not recollect that I have often said I wished the south to succeed or expressed disloyal sentiments.

Testimony of Judson Jarbol.

By Mr. Ewing.—I live in Prince George county; I do not know of any other Judson Jarbol living in that county; I never saw the prisoner, Mr. Mudd, before his arrest, and did not know him last winter on H street, or any other time; I saw Mrs. Surratt in April; I had not seen her for three years before; I have not seen the Rev. Mr. Evans, who used to live in our neighborhood, for several years until recently; I met him some three weeks ago on the street; I was standing in the corner of Grand Seventh street, and he walked past me; he used to attend the Methodist church in my neighborhood.

Cross-examined by Judge Bingham.—I know John H. Surratt; have not met him very often; I met him on Seventh street some time early in March, at a restaurant opposite the Odd Fellows' Hall; several persons were with him; I cannot state who; I only just spoke to him; I did know J. Wilkes Booth; I know Harold; he was not with Surratt when I met him on Seventh street; I do not think I knew any of the other persons except Mrs. Surratt; I met her at the Carroll Prison I was unfortunately there myself; my daughter was in a room with her, and I went to the room to see my daughter; I did not talk to her about John or about Harold; I do not know that I got into any particular trouble with the Government; I was arrested on the road on the 15th of April; I do not know why; there is no charge against me that I know of; I would like to know if I am here as a witness or on trial.

Judge Bingham.—You have the right to decline on the ground that the answer will criminate you. I want to know whether you were not accused of offences against the Government in Maryland? A. I do not think I was; I do not know what I was arrested for; I have not heard of a soldier being killed lately down in my neighborhood; they asked me something about a man named Boyle, if I knew him, and if I had not harbored him; I told them I had not; they said he was charged with the murder of a man by the name of Watkins; I knew Doyle when he was a boy, but I have not seen him for four years; I do not know when the murder was committed; Captain Watkins lived a long ways from me; I do not think I have joined in any jollification in honor of Rebel victories; I could not expect the success of the Rebellion.

Mr. Ewing said this was a species of inquisition of a witness not often indulged in.

Judge Bingham stated that the witness must answer, unless on the ground that his answer would criminate himself. The examination was a proper one.

The witness resumed.—I hardly know what will criminate me here. (Laughter.)

Q. Is it your opinion that these Confederates down here are criminals at all? A. I do not know much about it.

Q. Have you not expressed an opinion that the Confederacy was all right? A. I do not think I have.

Q. Do you not think that way? A. I think a good many things.

Q. State whether you made an assault upon a man on election day, about four years ago, and what you did to him. A. Are you going to try me for that, because I have been tried for that twice. (Laughter.)

Q. State whether you attacked a man down there about four years ago, and killed him. A. There was a pretty smart attack made on me; I understand the man was killed, but I do not know who did it; I have answered these questions before, and I do not know whether I ought to answer them again; I could not tell whether somebody killed him or not.

Q. Did you have a hand in it? No answer.

Q. What was the man's name that was killed? No answer.

Mr. Ewing to witness.—If you have any statement you wish to make of the circumstances of the case you can make it.

Witness.—I do not know whether the Judge wants to know all the particulars about it or not. I have been tried by our Court and acquitted.

By Mr. Ewing.—Q. In what court were you tried? A. In our County Court.

Q. Were you, during last spring, winter or fall in any house on H street, in Washington? A. I do not think I was; I do not think I have any acquaintances living on H street; I do not know in what part of the city Mrs. Surratt lives; I never saw her house in my life, and do not know anything about her residence at all.

By Judge Bingham.—Q. You say you were tried in your county court; what were you tried for? A. I suppose I was tried for what you said a while ago; you said I killed a man; I was tried in that case.

Q. Were you tried for the murder of a Union man? A. I do not know whether he was a Union man or not.

Mr. Thompson and Dr. Danford were called by Mr. Aiken, and testified to the loyalty of the witness, J. Z. Jenkins.

Re-Examination of Miss Anna Surratt.

By Mr. Aiken.—Q. State whether you recognize that picture. (Picture containing the motto, "Thus will it ever be with tyrants. Virginia the mighty; Sic semper tyrannis.") A. Yes; it was given to me by a lady about two and a half years ago; I asked her for its use at first refused to give it to me; I put it in my portfolio, and it has lain there ever since; I have scarcely seen it.

By Mr. Ewing.—Q. How long have your family been living at the house they now occupy on H street, between Sixth and Seventh streets? A. Since the first of October last.

Q. Have they occupied any other house in Washington? A. No sir.

Q. Have you seen Judson Jarboe at your house? A. No; he never visited there and I never saw him there; I have seen him pass, when I was in the country, in a buggy, but have never spoken to him; I was not acquainted with him.

Q. Are you the only daughter of Mrs. Surratt? A. Yes, I am her only daughter.

Q. Did you ever see or hear of Dr. Samuel Mudd being at your house? A. No sir.

The Court then adjourned.

THURSDAY'S PROCEEDINGS.

WASHINGTON, June 8.—The record of the previous day was read.

Mr. Ewing, with the consent of the Judge Advocate, filed in evidence Order No. 26. dated February 22, 1865, defining the boundaries of the Military Department of Washington, together with a map, identified by a witness, Dr. Blandford, as correct, showing the roads and localities in the neighborhood of the house of the prisoner, Dr. Mudd.

Judge Advocate Holt filed in evidence, without objection, Order No. 141, certified by the Secretary of War, promulgating the proclamation of the President of the United States, and dated Sept. 24, 1862, suspending the writ of habeas corpus, and providing for the trial by military authority of all disloyal persons, and aiders and abettors of the Rebellion, &c. The Secretary of War certifies that the order is a true copy, and that the same is in full force and not revoked.

Mr. Aiken asked permission to offer in evidence, on the part of Mrs. Surratt, the following paper:—

ST. LAWRENCE HALL, MONTREAL, June 3, 1865.—I am an actor by profession, at present filling an engagement at Mr. Buckland's Theatre in this city; I arrived here on the 12th of May; I performed two engagements at Ford's Theatre in Washington during the past winter, the last one closing on Saturday evening, 25th of March; I left Washington on Sunday evening, 26th of March, and have not been there since; I have no recollection of meeting any person by the name of Weichman.
JOHN McCULLOUGH.

Sworn to and subscribed before me, at the United States Consulate General in Montreal, this third (3d) day of June, A. D. 1865. C. H. POWERS,
Vice Consul-General.

Judge Bingham objected to the reception of the paper on the ground that it was wholly immaterial whether Mr. McCullough ever met the witness Weichman or not. Weichman, when on the stand, had been asked by the other side whether he saw McCullough, and it was not competent now to attempt to impeach him on that issue, as it was not material whether he did or not see McCullough.

Mr. Eakin said the paper furnished a complete refutation of a statement made by Weichman, so far as concerned the fact of his having seen McCullough, and this was material in so far as it contradicted one item of the statement of that witness.

Judge Advocate Holt read from several authorities in support of the position assumed by the prosecution. The objection of the Judge Advocate was sustained and the paper ruled out.

Testimony of Colonel J. C. Holland.

By Mr. Ewing.—I am Provost Marshal for the Fifth Congressional District of Maryland; I am acquainted with Daniel J. Thomas; I did not at any time during last spring or winter receive a letter from him to the effect that Dr. S. A. Mudd had said to him that President Lincoln, his whole Cabinet and every Union man in the State of Maryland would be killed within six or seven weeks; I never received from Thomas any letter in which the name of Dr. Samuel A. Mudd was mentioned; I did receive a letter from him, dated February 9th, 1865 Mr. Thomas was what was called an independent detective, that is he was not commissioned under the Government, but by me specially to arrest deserters and drafted men who failed to report, for which his compensation was the reward allowed by law for such arrests; such commissions were given to all who applied for them.

By Assistant Judge Advocate Burnett.—The letter which I read from Thomas had some reference to Dr. Geo. Mudd, with whom I am acquainted.

The hour of one o'clock having arrived, the Commission took a recess until two o'clock, at which time the body reassembled.

Testimony of Alex. Brownre.

By Mr. Doster.—I live in Port Tobacco; I have known the prisoner Atzerodt for the last six or eight years; Atzerodt was at Port Tobacco several times during the spring; at one time, about the latter part of February, I was going to the country, and he went with me; I think on that occasion he had come from Bryantown, and was riding a sorrel horse; I never considered the prisoner a courageous man; he is generally known as being a coward; as an instance of his want of courage, I have seen him make pretty good time in getting out of the way when a pistol was fired during a melee or anything of that kind.

Testimony of John S. Baden.

By Mr. Ewing.—I live in Prince George county, Maryland. I am acquainted with Daniel J. Thomas. He is generally known as a very untruthful man. From my knowledge of his character I do not think I would believe him under oath.

Cross-examined by Judge Advocate Holt.—I never knew Thomas to swear falsely. I do not hold that because a man speaks an untruth he will necessarily swear falsely.

Mr. Ewing stated that there remained to be called eight witnesses in the case of Mudd, whom he desired to question, with a view to an impeachment of the witness Thomas, but they were not present. One of that witnesses was expected to testify in regard to the whereabouts of Mudd on the 2d of December last.

Mr. Doster stated that, in the case of Payne, he desired to call six additional witnesses, for the purpose of showing the antecedents of the prisoner, and the predisposition of his whole family to insanity. The process for subpœnas in the cases of these witnesses were filed at least ten days ago, and they should either now appear or some cause be shown for their continued absence. In the case of Atzerodt three witnesses not in attendance who did acknowledge to have been summoned.

Mr. Doster gave their names as follows:—Associate Justice Olin, of the District of Columbia, Marcus P. Norton and Henry Burden.

Judge Holt stated to the Commission that the witnesses named had failed to appear after having been duly summoned as stated by the counsel and suggested the propriety of using compulsory measures to secure their attendance.

Mr. Doster said that he did not wish to be understood as asking for the arrest of the witnesses; that he would hesitate long before asking for the arrest of a Judge of the Supreme Court.

Judge Holt remarked that those who administered the law ought certainly to show obedience to it. He had understood that Judge Olin had adjourned his Court to-day in consequence of the military review which was taking place in Washington, and if the Commission so ordered, he would take measures to compel the attendance of that gentleman before the body as soon as possible.

Mr. Doster said that the testimony proposed to be taken in Payne's case was very material, inasmuch as the question of insanity could not be passed upon by Dr. Mitchell, whom the Court had permitted to see the prisoner, until Payne's antecedents were proven, and this could not be done except by those absent witnesses.

Assistant Judge Advocate Burnett then prepared an order, which was indorsed by the commission, directing General Hartranft, Provost Marshal of the court-room, to arrest and bring before the court, the witnesses named above who had failed to obey the process.

Testimony of Francis R. Farrell,

(Called for the Government). Q. Where did you reside? A. In Charles county, Maryland, near Bryantown; I fell in with Dr. Mudd, the day following the assassination; he came to my house on Easter Saturday, between 4 and 5 o'clock; he came down the new road which leads to Bryantown, and went back the same way; my house and Dr. Mudd's are about half way from Bryantown.

Q. When Dr. Mudd was at your house was the assassination of the President the subject of conversation?

Mr. Ewing objected to the question on the ground that it was not rebutting evidence.

Judge Holt said he could offer it as an expression on the part of the prisoner, and on that ground alone.

The Court voted that the question should be answered.

The witness answered.—I was in my house when Mr. Hardy, who was at the yard gate with Dr. Mudd, halloed to me that the President was assassinated, and Seward and son injured; I asked the Doctor about it and he said it was so: I asked him who assassinated the President, and the Doctor replied a man named Booth; Mr. Hardy then asked him whether it was the Booth who was down here last fall; the Doctor said he did not know whether it was so or not, as there were three or four by the name of Booth; if that was the one he knew him; the Doctor said he was very sorry the thing had occurred.

Q. How long did Dr. Mudd remain at your house? A. Not more than fifteen minutes; he did not give the particulars of the assassination.

Cross-examined by Mr. Ewing.—Dr. Mudd said it was the worst thing which could have happened; it made it a great deal worse for the country than while the war was going on; Dr. Mudd seemed to be entirely in earnest; Dr. Mudd came to see Mr. Hardy about some rail timber, and Hardy told him where he could get some, but Dr. Mudd said it was too far to haul.

Testimony of Edward Frazer.

By Mr. Doster.—I have known the prisoner, Atzerodt, for about ten years; during the latter part of February or early in March last he was at Port Tobacco for a day or two; he may have stayed there longer than that; among those who know him he has the name of being a pretty good natured fellow, but lacking courage; I have known him on several occasions to act cowardly

Testimony of Lewis Harkins.

By Judge Advocate Holt.—Q. State where you reside? A. I reside in St. Louis, and have resided there for eight or nine years.

Q. You may remember that within the last year or two there have been extensive burnings of steamboats on Western and Southern waters. State to the Court any knowledge you may have concerning agents of the Confederate Government who were engaged in that business and who they were? A. A man by the name of Tucker was one, Minor Mayers was another.

Q. Is he a Missourian? A. Yes sir.

Q. Was he in the service of the Confederates? A. Yes sir; Thomas L. Clark was another; a man by the name of Barrett was another.

Q. They were all agents of the Confederate Government, so called? A. Yes sir.

Q. State in what business they were engaged. A. Burning steamboats on the Mississippi, Ohio and other rivers.

Q. Was the man Barrett of whom you speak a lawyer, or had he ever been a member of Congress? A. I could not say; I have heard him called Colonel Barrett.

Q. State how these men were associated together and what were their operations. A. Their operations consisted in burning steamboats carrying Government freight, boats that were used as army transports and some that were not so used.

Q. Do you know by means of what combustible materials these steamboats were burned? A. No sir; I suppose it was done by matches.

Q. Will you enumerate the boats that were burned by the operations of these parties? A. The steamboats *Imperial* and *Robert Campbell*, the steamer *Janiet D. Taylor* and others were burned at Louisville; there were boats burned at New Orleans; but I do not recollect their names.

Q. Were they large vessels? A. Some were large and some small; they were owned by private parties.

Q. Was there any loss of life connected with the destruction of those vessels? A. There was on the *Robert Campbell*.

Q. Were they burned in the stream or while lying near the shore? A. The *Robert Campbell* was burned in the stream while under way.

Q. Was it understood that the agent was on board, or that he had merely deposited combustible matter in the vessel? A. He was on board.

Q. Where was that vessel burned? A. At Milliken's Bend, twenty-five miles above Vicksburg.

Q. Was there considerable loss of life? A. Yes sir.

Q. State whether the plan of operations embraced the destruction of the Government hospitals and storehouses? A. It embraced anything pertaining to the army.

Q. Do you know anything of the burning of a hospital at Nashville? A. I do not; all that I know is that a certain man claimed compensation for it.

Q. Do you know the man who claimed compensation from the Confederate Government for that service? A. His name was Dillingham.

Q. What amount did he claim? A. He did not put any amount; he just put in a statement.

Q. To Richmond? A. Yes sir.

Q. At what time was that hospital burned? A. In June or July, 1864; the fire occurred at night; I did not hear of anybody being burned.

Q. State whether or not you have been at Richmond. A. I have.

Q. Did you while there have an interview with Jefferson Davis, the so-called President of the Confederacy, and Benjamin, the Secretary of State? A. I was in Richmond from the 24th to the 25th day of August, 1864, and then had an interview with the Secretary of War, Secretary of State and Jefferson Davis.

Q. State what occurred at that interview. A. Mr. Thomas L. Clark, Dillingham and myself went there in connection with boat burning, and put in claims to Mr. James A. Seddon, to whom I was introduced by Mr. Clark; Seddon said he had thrown up that business; that it was now in the hands of Mr. Benjamin; we went to Mr. Benjamin and presented our papers to him; he looked at the papers and asked me whether I was in St. Louis; I told him I was; he asked me whether I knew anything about the papers; I told him I did; that I believed they were right; he then asked Mr. Clark if he knew me to be right; Mr. Clark said that I had been represented to him by Mr. Magers as being "all right;" he told me to call again the next day with Mr. Clark and Mr. Dillingham; that he had shown the papers I had left to Jefferson Davis, and he wanted to know whether we would not take thirty thousand dollars and sign a receipt in full; we told him we would not do it; well, he said, then if Mr. Dillingham was to claim this thing at Louisville, he wanted a statement of that thing; we went back to the hotel and I wrote out a statement myself; it read that Mr. Dillingham had been hired by General Bishop Polk and sent to Louisville expressly to do that work.

Q. To burn the hospitals? A. Yes sir, and I signed Mr. Dillingham's name to it; that was given to Mr. Clark; Mr. Clark took it over to Mr. Benjamin, and made a settlement with him for fifty thousand dollars; thirty-five thousand dollars down in gold, and fifteen thousand on deposit, to be paid him four months afterwards, provided those claims proved correct; he gave us a draft on Columbia, S. C., for thirty-four thousand eight hundred dollars and two hundred dollars in gold, in Richmond; the draft we got cashed in Columbia and brought the money along with us.

Q. You received the gold on that, did you? A. Yes sir; while there Mr. Benjamin said that Mr. Davis wanted to see me; I went in, and Mr. Davis, Mr. Benjamin and myself sat there and talked; the conversation turned on a bridge between Nashville and Chattanooga; the long bridge they called it; Mr. Benjamin mentioned it first I believe; Mr. Davis asked me if I knew where it was; I told him I did, but I did not; I had never been there; he said he wanted to know what I thought about destroying that bridge; that they had been thinking about having it destroyed; I told him I did not know what to think about it; he said I had better study it over; I finally told him I thought it could be done, and Mr. Benjamin (I think it was Mr. Benjamin) made the remark that he would give four hundred thousand dollars if that bridge was destroyed, and wanted to know if I would not take charge of the matter; I told him I would not have anything to do with it unless the papers were taken away from those men down there, and that nobody should be allowed to come up any more; they said it should be done; then the conversation turned on the burning of steamboats; I told Mr. Davis that I did not think it was any use to burn steamboats, and he said no, he was going to have that stopped; I then told him that the best way to stop that, would be to take the papers away from those men he had there immediately; that there were men lying around the south whose papers would run out, and they would come back to get them renewed, and that it would not be done; he said that what I had suggested should be done; I saw the next day a published order revoking those papers.

Q. These papers were permits or authority to do this work, were they? A. Yes sir.

Q. He knew that you had received this pay for the work done? A. I presume he did; he knew that I had received the money.

Q. The statements you made out were statements of the service done and the amount claimed? A. Yes sir.

Q. What was the sum originally demanded? A. Fifty thousand dollars; he wanted to pay us at first thirty thousand in greenbacks.

Q. You expressed the opinion to Davis that no good was to be accomplished by burning those boats in that manner? A. I did.

Q. And he said he was going to abandon that policy? A. He did.

Q. He did not condemn what had been done? A. He did not condemn what had been done.

Q. He knew what had been done? A. He appeared to know.

Q. Did you come to any understanding about rates in regard to the destruction of the bridge? A. We came to an understanding that we were to receive four hundred thousand dollars for doing it; I asked Mr. Davis whether it made any difference as to where the work was done; he said it did not, that Illinois would do; that it would include anything pertaining to Quartermaster's stores for the army, and that it ought to be as near Sherman's base as possible; that Sherman was the man who was doing them more harm than any one else at that time.

Q. These men whom you have named Barrett, and others, were they in the Confederate service? A. Yes.

Q. Do you know where Minor Majers is now? A. I have every reason to believe that he was in Canada, and that he left there and went to Bermuda Hundred; that was the last I heard from him.

Q. Do you know whether all these men are members of any secret organization? A. They principally all belonged to a secret organization.

Q. What was the name of that organization? A. It goes by the name of the O. A. K. organization.

Q. The Order of American Knights? A. Yes sir.

Q. Will you say whether you were a member of the order?

No answer.

Q. You need not answer if by so doing you will criminate yourself.

The witness made no reply.

Q. You say you are not able to state decidedly the process by which these boats were burned. Were any combustibles besides matches used? A. I do not think there were.

Q. Do you remember the position which Barrett held in the association? A. I understood he held the position of Adjutant-General of the State of Illinois.

Q. The Adjutant-General of the O. A. K's.? A. I could not say whether of the O. A. K's. or of the Sons of Liberty.

Q. Do you know whether Magers and Barrett were in July last at Chicago? A. Mr. Magers left St. Louis either last June or July to go to Canada, and I presume he went then by way of Chicago.

By the Court.—Q. Was the steamer *Hiawatha* one of the number of those burned? A. She was.

TRIAL OF THE ASSASSINS AT WASHINGTON. 151

Q. Do you recollect the number of lives that were lost then? A. I do not.
Q. Do you recollect the number of lives lost on the *Imperial*? A. I do not think there were any lost on the *Imperial*.
Q. She was one of the finest and largest on the Western waters, was she not? A. She was.
Q. Are you a steamboat man? A. Yes sir.
Q. What steamboats have you been running on? A. I was on the *Von Phul* last, Captain Vaughn.

Testimony of John F. Hardy.

I am acquainted with the prisoner, Dr. Samuel A. Mudd; my residence is in the same neighborhood with that of the prisoner. On the day after the President's assassination I met him about two hundred yards from my house, when he said to me that there was terrible news; that the President had been killed, and that Mr Seward and his son had been assassinated by a man named Boyle. Booth's name was mentioned somehow, and he said that he did not know which of the brothers it was; that there were several. This conversation took place shortly after sundown of the 15th. He said nothing about the two men having been at his house. I had seen Booth at the church there last fall and asked his name, when I was told that it was Booth; and at the time of the conversation with the prisoner, I asked him when Booth's name was mentioned whether it was the same Booth who had been down there before, and he said he did not know.

Cross-examined by Mr. Ewing.—The conversation I have mentioned was commenced while the prisoner; he said he had got the news from Bryantown, where he had been; he seemed to feel all the sorrow he expressed in regard to the assassination; the object of the prisoner visiting me at the time was in regard to some rail timber; when I first saw Booth down there I think it was some time in November, and that it was about a month since when I saw him a second time; I did not see or hear of any one having been with the prisoner when I met him.

By Judge Bingham.—The prisoner did not tell me from whom he had received the news of the President's assassination, and nothing more than he had heard it from Bryantown.

Testimony of Eli M. Watson.

By Mr. Ewing.—I reside near Horsehead, Prince George county; I have been acquainted with Daniel J. Thomas since he was a boy; his reputation in the neighborhood in which he lived for veracity is bad; from my knowledge of his general reputation I would not believe him under oath; I saw Thomas in my field on the 1st day of June; he then told me that he was a witness against Dr. Mudd, and that Joshua S. Naylor had sworn to put down his oath, but that if his oath stood he would get a portion of the reward offered for Booth.

Cross-examined by Assistant Judge Advocate Bingham.—The conversation in the field was begun by Thomas; he said he was going around to summon people as to his character, and that he was going to have me summoned as one.

Cross-examination of Marcus P. Norton.

I saw Booth play in Washington, and in the city of New York, and also in Boston; I cannot tell how many times I saw him play; I cannot remember any particular fact connected with Booth's representations on the stage, because I never made any memoranda of such things, but frequently attended plays when away from home; was not personally acquainted with Booth; during my stay at the National Hotel I saw him in conversation with others besides the prisoner.

The cross-examination of this witness was continued further, but failed to bring out any new points.

Testimony of Henry Burden.

I live in Troy, and know the witness Norton who has just testified; his reputation for veracity is bad; I would not believe him on oath.

Cross-examined by Judge-Advocate Holt.—I have been interested in a patent concerning horse shoes; Mr. Norton was engaged as counsel on the opposite side; I cannot say that there was much ill-feeling occasioned by that controversy; it did not form any opinion of Mr. Norton's character because of that controversy; I was not acquainted with him at that time; my acquaintance with his character is based upon what I have known of him since; my relations with him have not been either of a particularly friendly or unfriendly character; when I declare to the Court that he is not to be believed on oath I am giving expression to the opinion of the mass of the people of Troy who know him; my opinion is arrived at from the testimony by which he was impeached.

The Court then adjourned.

WASHINGTON, June 9.—The reading of the previous day's record occupied until about 12 o'clock.

Testimony of Judge Abram B. Olin.

By Mr. Doster.—I have resided in Troy, New York, about twenty years; I know Marcus P. Norton, a lawyer, who resided there; I know his reputation for veracity to be bad; if his prejudices or passions were excited I would not believe him on oath.

Cross-examined by Judge Holt.—I never had any private relations with Mr. Norton; in stating an opinion of his character for veracity I am also giving expression to the opinion of the people of Troy; I have known him to be engaged in controversies concerning patents; I have known instances in which much feeling has been shown in such controversies; I knew Henry Burden, a citizen of Troy; Mr. Burden has had several suits and controversies with respect to inventions, in which suits Mr. Norton was interested as counsel; the conversations of a man of Mr. Burden's influence and position, with those of his friends, continued as they were, through a series of years, under the excitement of legal controversies, may to some extent afford an explanation of the repute in which Mr. Norton is held, among those who know him; though his reputation was questionable before, so far as the witness was aware.

Testimony of Miss Mary Mudd.

By Mr. Ewing.—I am a sister of the prisoner, Samuel A. Mudd; during the month of March last I saw him on the 2d, 3d, 4th, 5th, 6th and 7th; I remember the fact because on the 1st I was taken sick, and on each of those days he was at the house where I resided; about this time a colored woman in the neighborhood was taken sick, and he attended her up to the 3d of March; he frequently called at our house to inquire after my mother; on the 3d of March he came there; I know he came twice from the fact that the first time he came he had no medicine with him, and went to get it; my father is very feeble and not able to travel; he is confined to his bed; on the 23d of March, the prisoner, my brother, came to Washington, in company with Mr. Llewellyn Gardner; during January he went to any convening party at Mr. Henry Gardner's; he did not own a buggy of any description; I never knew him to wear a black hat; he usually wore a drab colored slouch hat; I have not known of Andrew Gwynn being about my brother's house since 1861; I have heard since that he was in the Confederate service; I know nothing of Confederate officers or soldiers having ever stopped at my brother's house; I saw Booth at the church in that neighborhood on one occasion, at which time he purchased a horse from Mr. Gardner; Booth was in Dr. Queen's pew at church when I saw him; I never saw him but once; in 1849, 1850 and 1851, my brother was at college; he was not at home on holidays; I know nothing of Booth's having been lodged at my brother's house.

Testimony of John L. Turner.

By Mr. Ewing.—I live in the lower part of Prince Georges county; I am acquainted with Daniel J. Thomas; his general reputation in the community in which he lives is not as good as it ought to be; the people do not think him a truthful man; I do not think I could believe him on oath; his reputation of Dr. Mudd as to loyalty has been very good during the whole war; I have always been loyal to the Government; I voted for Mr. McClellan at the last election, because he said he was as good a Union man as Mr. Lincoln; otherwise, I have always supported the Administration; I have been acquainted with the prisoner, Mudd, since he was a boy; I always considered him a loyal man, and I never knew or heard of his doing anything in support of the Rebellion.

Testimony of Polk Deakins.

By Mr. Ewing.—I live in Charles county, Maryland; have known Daniel J. Thomas, a witness for the prosecution, as long as I can remember; his reputation in the community is very bad; from my knowledge of his reputation for veracity, I would not believe him under oath, if he had any inducement to swear falsely; in 1861, I think it was, he told me he was going over to Virginia, and wanted me to go.

Cross-examined by Assistant Judge Advocate Bingham.—I was persuaded to go to Virginia, but did not go.

Several other witnesses were called whose testimony coincided with that already taken in impeaching the veracity of Daniel J. Thomas, and others, who have been called for the prosecution.

The witnesses also testified to the loyalty of Dr. George Mudd.

The usual recess of an hour was then taken, after which the following witnesses were called:—

Re-examination of Miss N. Fitzpatrick.

By Mr. Aiken.—I was present when Payne was arrested at Mrs. Surratt's house, but did not recognize him at the time, nor until the shirt sleeve was removed from his head at Gen. Augur's office; when Payne came to Mrs. Surratt's, before the assassination, he passed by the name of Wood; I have often threaded a needle in the daytime for Mrs. Surratt; I have known her eyesight to be poor.

By Mr. Ewing.—I know Judson Jarboe; I never saw him at Mrs. Surratt's, or heard of him being there; never knew of the prisoner, Dr. Mudd, being there.

152   TRIAL OF THE ASSASSINS AT WASHINGTON.

By Judge Advocate Burnett.—Mrs. Surratt, her daughter and myself were in the room with Payne at General Augur's office; Mrs. Surratt, in speaking of Payne, said that that was not John Surratt, but I never heard her say that she had never seen Payne; I did not hear what passed when Mrs. Surratt was called out into the hall of her house to see Payne on the night of the arrest; I only heard Mrs. Surratt say that he was not John Surratt, and that whoever called that ugly man her brother was no gentleman.

Testimony of Mrs. Nelson.

I am the sister of the prisoner, Harold; never heard him speak of the accused, Dr. Samuel Mudd; I never heard the name of Mudd mentioned in the family.

Testimony of Wm. J. Watson.

By Mr. Ewing.—I live in Prince George county; I am not very intimately acquainted with Daniel J. Thomas; saw him on the 1st of June, when he said that if Dr. Mudd was convicted on his testimony, it would be conclusive evidence that he (Thomas) had given information which led to the arrest of one of the conspirators; he asked me to give him a certificate that he was entitled to the reward of one thousand dollars.

By Assistant Judge Advocate Bingham.—I told Thomas I would not give him the certificate, and asked him whether, in his conscience, he believed himself entitled to the reward. I would believe Thomas on oath, though his reputation is not as good as that of others. His general reputation for truth is not good, but I think he lies more in self-praise than in any other manner.

By Mr. Ewing.—Mr. Thomas was represented not to be a loyal man in the beginning of the war. At the last Presidential election he electioneered for George B. McClellan.

Re-examination of John T. Ford.

By Mr. Ewing.—I have known the accused, Edward Spangler, nearly four years; his character for peace and kindness was well known, though he was disposed to drink at times, which would not make him vicious, but would unfit him for work; I never knew him to be involved in more than one quarrel while he was in my employ, and that was through drink; he was not a man who was likely to be intrusted with the confidence of others, not having much self-respect; I never heard him express a political sentiment.

A number of witnesses were then called, on the part of the prosecution, in regard to the character for veracity and integrity of Mr. L. F. Bates, a witness for the Government, who had testified that on the 19th of April last, Jefferson Davis stopped at his house in Charlotte, N. C.; that he there made a speech, during which he received a telegram from John C. Breckenridge, announcing the death of President Lincoln, when he made the remark, "If it were to be done, 'twere better it were well done," &c.

All of the witnesses testified that they had known Mr. Bates for years, and never knew or heard of his character being questioned.

Examination of Wm. Wheeler.

By Judge Advocate Holt.—I have been intimately acquainted with Marcus P. Norton from twelve to fifteen years; I knew him first at school, in Vermont, subsequently at Troy, N. Y., where he now resides; I reside, when at home, at Laansinburg, three miles above Troy, of which place I was formerly a resident; from my personal knowledge of his reputation for truth and integrity, it is good; I would have no hesitation in believing Mr. Norton under oath.

Cross-examined by Mr. Doster.—I have been living in Washington since the 15th of April last; I have heard of cases of attempted impeachment of Mr. Norton, but I know nothing about them, except by general remark, that they were failures; one or two such cases, I have understood, have essentially failed; when at school, which was from 1850 to 1853, Mr. Norton was an active, persevering scholar; my relations with him have never been of a particularly friendly character; he is engaged by first-class houses in Troy; I have not lived in Troy for fifteen or twenty years.

By Judge Advocate Burnett.—Mr. Norton has frequently visited the county in which I live; I have also frequently met him in Troy; I am well acquainted with the people there; about two years ago I was called on to give testimony in a case in which Mr. Norton was employed as counsel by a very reputable and wealthy firm.

Testimony of Silas H. Hodges.

I reside at present in Washington; hold the position of Examiner-in-Chief of the Patent Office; I have resided in Rutland, Vermont, for over twenty years; I have been intimately acquainted with Marcus P. Norton for eleven years; he is well known in the vicinity of Rutland; I never heard anything said against his reputation until within the last two or three years; anything that I have ever heard against his reputation has grown out of previous litigation, in which he was connected; outside of those cases, in which much angry feeling was exhibited, I never heard Mr. Norton's reputation questioned, and never heard of any attempt to impeach him before that litigation.

Mr. Ewing stated to the court, as a means of saving time, the following proposition had been agreed to by the Judge Advocate. The three witnesses named had been sent for but had not arrived, and the counsel had not seen them. The proposition was as follows:—"It is admitted by the prosecution that John F. Watson, John Richardson and Thomas B. Smith, loyal citizens, will testify that they are acquainted with the reputation of Daniel J. Thomas, where he lives, and that it is bad, and that from their knowledge of it they would not believe him on oath; and further, that John A. Richardson, above named, will testify that Daniel J. Thomas, a witness for the prosecution, made the statement on the 1st of June last, as sworn to by William Watson, before the court this day; and the prosecution agree that this statement he put on record and received and weighed by the court, as though the said witness had actually testified before it.

After some time spent in consultation with the counsel for the prisoner, Dr. Mudd, Judge Advocate Holt stated that being disposed to allow the accused at the bar the benefit of all the evidence that could be adduced in their favor, he had consented that the declarations of Mudd concerning two suspicious men at his house, previously ruled out by the Court, should be taken for what they were worth.

Re-examination of Benj. Gardner and Dr. George A. Mudd.

Benjamin Gardner and Dr. George A. Mudd being then recalled for the defense, testified that Dr. Mudd stated on the Sunday morning after the assassination, that "we ought immediately to raise a home guard and hunt up all suspicious persons passing through our section of country, and arrest them, unless they can show that they are actually traveling under proper authority, for there were two suspicious persons at my house yesterday morning."

To Dr. George A. Mudd the prisoner said, on Sunday morning that "he regretted the assassination, as it was a most damnable act;" he also narrated the particulars of the visit of two suspicious looking men to his house on the morning of the previous day, stating that they seemed to be laboring under some degree of excitement more so than would be supposed to accompany the mere breaking of the leg of one of the men; that they stated that they had come from Bryantown, and inquired the way to Parson Wilmers; that whilst there one of them called for a razor and shaved off either his whiskers or moustache; that he in company with the smaller of the two went down the road towards Bryantown in search of a vehicle to take them away from his house, and that they finally left his house on horseback, going in the direction of Parson Wilmer's; when about parting with each other he expressed requested the witness, Dr. George D. Mudd, to communicate the fact of the presence of these suspicious men to the military authorities at Bryantown, and that if called upon he would give every information in his power relative to the matter, but he did not desire it to be publicly known that he had divulged the visit of these men, for fear of being assassinated by the guerillas.

Re-examination of Hon C. A. Dana.

The Hon. C. A. Dana was then recalled for the prosecution, and identified certain letters as having been received by him when Assistant Secretary of War from Major-General Dix. One of these letters, bearing date November 17, 1864, was signed by General Dix, and was explanatory of the other, which has already been published; being the one found in a Third avenue railway car of New York city, and commencing as follows:—"St. Louis, October 21, 1864.—Dearest Husband. Why do you not come home? You left me for two days only, and you have now been away from home more than two weeks, and in that long time only wrote me one short note—a few cold words with a check for money, which I did not require," etc.

The witness stated, further, that upon receiving the letters in question he took them to President Lincoln, who looked at them without making any particular remark, as this was only one instance among many in which such communications had been received; the President, however, attached more importance to these communications than to others, as the witness subsequently found them in an envelope, which was marked, in the President's hand-writing. "assassination."

Mr. Ewing then stated to the Court that the Judge Advocate-General had agreed to admit that D. E. Monroe, a witness for the defense, who was still absent, would testify that he heard at the church which Dr. Mudd, the prisoner, attended on Sunday, April 16, from Mrs. Moore, who had just come from Bryantown, that it was Edwin Boo'h who was implicated in the assassination.

A discussion arose among the members of the Court as to the propriety of entering upon the record anything which was not sworn to as evidence.

After some time spent in this discussion the Court directed General Hartranft as Provost Marshal to send for and compel the attendance of D. E. Monroe, the absent witness.

The Court then adjourned.

WASHINGTON, July 10.—The record of the previous day was read, and the examination of witnesses continued as follows:—

Testimony of Daniel F. Morris.

By Mr. Ewing.—I live in Charles county, Maryland; on the Sunday after the assassination of the President I heard from Mr. Moore, who came from Bryantown that morning, that it was Edwin Booth who assassinated the President; know the reputation of the witness, Daniel J. Thomas, to be not very good; the people consider him untruthful, and would not believe him under oath in the community in which he lived; Mr. Thomas would not believe he believed an oath; in the efforts of the Government to suppress the Rebellion I have sympathized with the Government, but did not approve of the abolition of slavery.

The cross-examination of the witness developed no new facts.

Testimony of L. A. Gobright.

(Called for the defense.)—I am a journalistic agent and telegraph reporter for the Associated Press; I was at Ford's Theatre on the night of the assassination, having reached there five minutes to 11 o'clock; there was a difference of opinion among persons at the theatre as to whether Booth was the assassin or not; during the short time I remained there, I was not at that time satisfied that Booth was the assassin.

My Assistant Judge Advocate Bingham.—Q. But you became satisfied during the night that it was Booth, and telegraphed that fact? A. I did not so telegraph that night.

Q. You became satisfied, the next day, that Booth was the assassin? A. It was so announced the next morning in the official Bulletin.

The counsel for the prisoners, Mudd, Spangler and Arnold. Mr. Ewing, announced to the Court that the case had now been closed for the defense, so far as these prisoners were concerned.

Mr. Doster, on behalf of the prisoner Payne, stated that Dr. Nichols, who had been permitted to examine the question of the prisoner's alleged insanity, was not yet prepared to report; and that several witnesses who were expected to testify on that question, had not yet appeared, one of them being the prisoner's father, Rev. Mr. Powell, of Florida.

The President of the Court General Hunter, remarked that he had understood that Dr. Nichols could not give any report on the question of insanity until the prisoner's antecedents were shown, and that, therefore, the Court would be asked to wait for the prisoner's father, who lived in Florida.

Mr. Doster said that in the State of Maine it was customary, when a plea of insanity was introduced in behalf of the prisoner, to hand him over to a physician for a proper determination of the question. He thought it not more than just that on a trial for his life, the prisoner should have the benefit of whatever evidence could be adduced in his favor; that while it might cost the Court a delay of six or eight days in awaiting the arrival of the witness summoned from Florida, the absence of the testimony of that witness might cost the prisoner his life. He asked that the prisoner be permitted either to bring his friends here or to be allowed a regular scientific investigation of his case.

Judge Advocate Bingham stated that the prisoner's counsel had had forty days in which to procure the attendance of all witnesses, and that every application on the part of the defense for witnesses had been granted as soon as made.

Judge Advocate Holt then called several additional witnesses for the prosecution.

Examination of Henry G. Edson.

By Judge Advocate Holt.—I reside at St. Albans, Vermont; my profession is that of an attorney and counsellor at law; I was engaged as counsel during the judicial investigation which occurred in Canada in connection with what was known as the St. Albans raid; while at St. Johns, Canada, I heard George N. Sanders say, in speaking of the St. Albans raid, that he was ignorant of it before it occurred, but was then satisfied with it; that it was not the last of the kind that would occur, but that it would be followed up by the depleting of many other banks and the burning of many other towns on the frontier, and that many a "Yankee" (using a coarse and vulgar expression) would be killed; he said that there were organizations of men ready to burn and sack Buffalo and other places, and that the Yankees would soon see these plans fully executed; that any precautions made by the Government to prevent them would not prevent, though they might defer them; Sanders at that time was acting as counsel for the prisoners.

Testimony of John L. Ripple.

By Judge Advocate Holt.—I am a First Lieutenant of the Thirty-ninth Illinois Regiment, and entered the service as a private in 1861; was a prisoner of war, and was confined for six months at Andersonville, Ga.; while there I heard a Rebel officer, Quartermaster Huhn, state that if Abe Lincoln was re-elected he would not live to be inaugurated; that was before the Presidential election; he also stated that they had a party in the North who would attend to the President and Mr. Seward; I heard the Lieutenant in charge of the guard say that they had friends who would see that Lincoln was not reinaugurated; that was, I think, after the Presidential election; the character of the food furnished to the prisoners at Andersonville was poor, both in quantity and quality; the prisoners died in large numbers, and I have no doubt that in many cases the deaths of the prisoners were brought about by starvation and the horrible treatment to which they were subjected; I heard the Rebel officers say in answer to the remonstrances of the prisoners that the treatment was good enough for them; they should every one die; I heard a certain Captain Wilkes, who had charge of the prisoners, say that on the first of July the location of the place in which the prisoners were confined, and everything connected with it, seemed to look to the creation of disease, and the infliction on the part of the Confederate authorities of every possible suffering short of death; that Libby treatment was not so bad; packs of blood-hounds were kept lying around the camp at Andersonville.

There being no further witnesses present, Judge Advocate Holt gave notice that the Court could not wait much longer for the witnesses in the case of Payne, who had failed to appear.

The President of the Court stated that the Court would wait until Monday morning, at 11 o'clock, to hear the report of Dr. Nichols on the alleged insanity of Payne.

The Court then adjourned to the hour stated.

WASHINGTON, June 12.—The reading of the record of Saturday having been concluded, the following witnesses were examined:—

Testimony of Mrs. L. Grant.

By Mr. Doster.—I reside in Warrenton, Va.; I recognize the prisoner Payne as a man whom I saw on the road in front of my house, having three Union soldiers in his charge; an attempt was made to kill the prisoners, and the man called Powell (meaning Payne) tried to prevent it, and I heard him say that he was a gentleman and wished to be treated as such; that if they attempted to kill the man he had captured he would defend his prisoner at the peril of his life; one of the prisoners was killed, when the party left the road, and I did not see them afterwards; the affair occurred last Christmas.

Cross-examined by Judge Advocate Holt.—I was speaking of the affair to a citizen, and telling him this man tried to save the Union soldiers, when I was informed that his name was Powell; I had not seen him before, nor have I seen him since until to-day, but I am certain he is the man.

By the Court.—He was dressed as a Confederate, and I thought they called him lieutenant; there were the marks of an officer upon him; he looked more genteel than the common soldiers.

Testimony of John Grant.

By Mr. Doster.—I am the husband of the witness who has just left the stand; at the time the affray occurred in front of my house, about Christmas last, I was returning home and was within three hundred yards of my house, when the firing on the roads commenced; all I heard was that the prisoner at the bar, who went by the name of Powell, had tried to save the lives of two Union soldiers; the prisoner was not an officer, so far as I am aware.

Testimony of J. P. Patterson.

By Mr. Cox.—I am an ensign in the navy; I have known the prisoner, Michael O'Loughlin, about six years; on the afternoon of Thursday, the 13th of April, we came together from Baltimore to Washington, reaching here between five and six o'clock; we came up the avenue and stopped at Rullman's Hotel; I then went into a barber shop to get shaved, and the prisoner proceeded up the street, but rejoined me before I had been shaved; he was not out of my company at any other time that evening; I went up the avenue with him to look at the illumination, but did not go farther than Seventh street; we went to the Canterbury about nine o'clock, and stayed there about three-quarters of an hour, after which we returned to Rullman's Hotel, getting there between ten and eleven o'clock; we remained there about half an hour, and then went out again; the avenue was so crowded during the evening that it was almost impossible to get along; I can state positively that the prisoner was not near the house of the Secretary of War on Franklin Square at any time on Thursday evening; we retired between one and two o'clock on Friday morning; the prisoner was at his room when I called next morning; he was not with me on Friday afternoon; on Friday evening I met him at Rullman's Hotel; he was there with me until ten o'clock, and then went out in company with a man by the name of Fuller; that was after the assassination; we had arranged to return to Baltimore on Friday morning; and I proposed to stay until evening, which we did.

Cross-examined by Judge Advocate Holt.—It was impossible for the prisoner to have been at the house of the Secretary of War before ten or eleven o'clock on the evening of the 13th of April, as I did not part with him at any time; when he rejoined me at the barber shop, after leaving me on Thursday afternoon, he told me he had been to see Booth; that evening between 8 and 6 o'clock; the next morning he was to go to see Booth, and I called for him at the National Hotel, but he was not there; I then went to his room and saw him there; he said he had been to see Booth, but did not see him; that Booth was out; he did not state his object in endeavoring to see Booth.

By Mr. Cox.—He did not say anything about Booth owing him money; he merely said that he had been to see Booth on Friday morning; he told me he had not seen Booth.

By Judge Advocate Holt.—I had no particular reason for staying in town until Friday evening; I suggested to the party in whose company I was, O'Loughlin among the number, that we should remain until Friday evening; I had no special reasons for so doing; O'Loughlin did not make any suggestions of that kind; the arrangements for our visit to Washington we determined on Monday in Baltimore, Thursday being the day fixed; I suggested the day; the party done a great deal of drinking while in Washington; it would be impossible for me to say how many times we drank; I do not think it could have been more than ten; one of the party, Mr. Early, was not sober.

Testimony of H. R. Sweeney.

By Mr. Aiken.—I am acquainted with John M. Floyd; I met him on the 14th of April last at Marlboro, and rode with him a portion of the way from Marlboro towards his home; he seemed to be considerably under the influence of liquor; he drank, or attempted to drink on the road, at least to put the bottle to his lips; the bottle contained liquor.

Cross-examined by Judge Advocate Holt.—I drank with him; I could not tell who drank the most; both drank from the same bottle; he seemed to be considerably excited which I attributed to the influence of drink; he was alone in his buggy; I was on horseback; he was excited in conversation and general deportment; I do not think I was excited myself. I suppose he knew what he was doing, and where he was going at least; I thought he was able to take care of himself.

By Mr. Clampitt.—I have known J. Z. Jenkins, a brother of Mrs. Surratt, for sixteen years; I have heard it said of him that he was a zealous Union man; on one occasion a Union flag was raised within a hundred yards of the house in which I boarded, and there being a rumor that an attempt would be made to cut it down, Mr. Jenkins formed one of a party who stood guard around it all night; I heard that he came to Washington to get votes for the Union ticket in Maryland, but I do not know anything of that; I believe him to be to-day a consistently loyal man.

By Judge Advocate Holt.—I have never acted against the Government that I know of; I was strictly neutral in my conduct and feelings in regard to the Rebellion; I was perfectly indifferent as to whether the Rebellion failed or succeeded.

By the Court.—I parted with Mr. Floyd, on the occasion of which I have spoken, about six miles from Surrattsville; I did not take more than one drink out of the bottle from which Mr. Floyd drank.

Mr. Aiken, counsel for Mrs. Surratt, stated that when, on Friday last, he announced that he would not delay the court after the other counsel for the accused had closed their defence, he had not learned some important facts since communicated to him. On Friday afternoon last he visited Surrattsville and Marlborough, and while on that visit acquired some facts which he believed to be of material importance in the case of the accused, Mrs. Surratt. He therefore asked the privilege of introducing that testimony. The witnesses would probably be present to-morrow, and their examination might occupy not more than a couple of hours, and would not be likely to affect materially any rebutting testimony which the Government might have to offer.

Judge Advocate Holt stated that, inasmuch as some important testimony for the Government still remained to be taken, and the witnesses might not arrive to-day, but would be present to-morrow, there would be no loss of time. He was therefore disposed to grant the request of counsel.

Testimony of Assistant Adjutant-General E. D. Townsend.

By Judge Advocate Holt.—Q. State whether or not you are acquainted with G. J. Rains, a Brigadier-General in the Rebel military service. A. I was very well acquainted with G. J. Rains, who in 1861 resigned his commission as a Lieutenant-Colonel of the Fifth regular United States Infantry.

Q. Were you acquainted with his handwriting? A. Yes sir.

Q. Look at that indorsement and state whether you believe it to be in his handwriting (exhibiting a paper to witness). A. To the best of my knowledge and belief it is.

The paper referred to was given in evidence without objection; it is dated Richmond, December 16, 1864, and is addressed to Captain S. McDaniel, commanding torpedo company, signed by John Maxwell. It sets forth in substance that in obedience to the order of the person to whom it is addressed, and with the means and equipment furnished by him, the writer left Richmond on the 26th of July, 1864, for the line of the James River, to operate with the horological torpedo against the enemy's vessels navigating that river; the writer was accompanied by Mr. R. K. Dillard, whose services were engaged for the expedition; after sundry adventures the two men reached City Point before daybreak on the 9th of August last and the writer gives the result of his operations as follows:—Requesting my companion to remain behind about half a mile, I cautiously approached the wharf with my machine and powder, covered by a small box; finding the captain had come ashore from a barge then at the wharf, I seized the occasion to hurry forward with my box; being halted by one of the wharf sentinels I succeeded in passing him by representing that the captain had ordered me to convey the box on board; hailing a man from the barge I put the machine in motion and gave it in his charge. He carried it aboard, the magazine contained about twelve pounds of powder; rejoining my command we retired to a safe distance to witness the effect of our effort. In about an hour the explosion occurred. Its effect was communicated to another barge beyond the one operated upon, and also to a large wharf building containing the enemy's stores, which were totally destroyed. The scene was terrific, and the effect deafened my companion to an extent from which he has not recovered. My own person was severely shocked, but I am thankful to Providence that we have both escaped without lasting injury. We obtained and refer you to the inclosed slip from the enemy's newspapers, which afford their testimony of the terrible effects of this blow. The enemy estimate the loss of life at fifty-eight killed and one hundred and twenty-six wounded, but we have no reason to believe it greatly exceeded that. The pecuniary damage we heard estimated at four millions of dollars, but of course we can give you no exact account of its extent.

The writer then details the capture of the vessel Jane Duffield, by a party of which Acting Master W. H. Hinds, of the Confederate States Navy, and the writer were members; the capture occurred on the 17th of September last, in Warwick River; the party further stated that he was finally compelled to abandon these operations in consequence of the vigilant watch kept upon him and his coadjutors by our forces; the indorsements on the letter were by Z. McDaniels, Captain of the Confederate Army secret service, and G. J. Rains, Brigadier-General, Superintendent, that of the latter being to the effect that John Maxwell and R. K. Dillard were sent by Z. McDaniels into the enemy's line by the authority of the writer, for some such purpose, and that when the tremendous explosion occurred at City Point, on August 9th, the supposition was strong that it was done through their agency; a further indorsement was as follows:—

"Certified copy forwarded to War Department, June 3d, 1865.

"(Signed) J. KELLOG, A. A. G."

Assistant Judge Advocate Bingham, by permission of the Court, placed upon record certified copies of the journals of the Senate and House of Representatives of the Congress of the United States, showing that Abraham Lincoln and Hannibal Hamlin were elected President and Vice-President of the United States, for four years from the 4th day of March, 1861, and that Abraham Lincoln and Andrew Johnson were elected President and Vice-President of the United States, for four years from March 4th, 1865.

Assistant Adjutant-General E. D. Townsend, being recalled, testified that from and after the fourth day of March, 1861, until the fifteenth day of April, 1865, when he died, Abraham Lincoln acted as President of the United States; that for four years preceding the fourth of March, 1865, Hannibal Hamlin acted as Vice President of the United States, and that from the fourth of March, 1865, until the 15th of April, of the same year, the day of the death of Abraham Lincoln, Andrew Johnson acted as Vice President of the United States.

TRIAL OF THE ASSASSINS AT WASHINGTON.

PORTRAIT OF "JEFF. DAVIS," IN HIS WIFE'S CLOTHES.

TRIAL OF THE ASSASSINS AT WASHINGTON. 155

Mr. Doster stated that he had received a note from Assistant Surgeon Coddington of the Government hospital, informing him of the death of the wife of Dr. Nichols, and asked that Dr. Hall be substituted for that gentleman as the proper person to examine into the question of the alleged insanity of the prisoner, Payne.

The proposed substitution was accordingly made. The President of the Commission gave notice that the report of Dr. Hall would be expected to-morrow morning.

Re-examination of Rich. Montgomery.

By Judge Advocate Burnett.—Q. Examine that paper and state when and from whom you received it. A. I received that letter from C. C. Clay, Jr., on the evening of the 1st or 2d of November, 1864.
Q. State whether you saw Mr. Clay write any portion of that paper. A. Yes sir, a very considerable portion of it.
Q. You know that to be his handwriting? A. Yes sir; he wrote the letter in the house in which he was writing, on Clark street, I think that is the name, at Catharine's Canada.
Q. To whom did you deliver the paper? A. To Hon. C. A. Dana, Assistant Secretary of War.
(Exhibiting to witness a second paper). State whether that is a copy of the letter which was made by you for more convenience in reading? A. It is; that is a correct copy.
Q. There are certain blanks and omissions here; had you any instructions with reference to giving information as to what should be inserted? A. Yes s.r, I was instructed to deliver that letter to Mr. Benjamin, Secretary of State of the Confederate States, and to tell him that I was informed of the names to be in the blanks; there are several blanks.
Q. What was the reason for omitting the signature of this letter? A. That was for my safety principally, and so that it might not be used as evidence against the writer; both reasons were given to me by Mr. Clay?
Q. Do you know at what time Clement C. Clay left Canada? A. About the 1st of January, I think.

The letter was then read, bearing date St. Catharine's, C. W., Nov. 1, 1864, and addressed to Hon. J. P. Benjamin, Secretary of State, Richmond, Va. It gives a detailed account of the circumstances connected with the St. Albans raid, the writer stating that Lieutenant Bennett H. Young who led the raiders, was well known to him as one whose heart was with the South in their struggle, and that in this attempt to burn the town of St. Albans and rob the banks he acted according to the writer's instructions, and urging the Confederate Government to assume the responsibility in the premises.

The letter also speaks of a Captain Charles H. Cole, an escaped prisoner of war in the Rebel Forrest's command, who was captured on board the United States war steamer *Michigan*, on Lake Erie, while engaged in an attempt to capture the vessel and liberate the Rebel prisoners on Johnson's Island. The writer protests against Cole being treated as a spy, and gives various reasons why he should be regarded as a prisoner of war, and concludes with a statement that "all that a large portion of the Northern people, especially in the Northwest, want, in order to resist the oppression of the despotism at Washington, is a leader. They are ripe for resistance, and it may come soon after the Presidential election." The letter was not signed, the reason given being that no signature was necessary, as the messenger presenting it and the person to whom it was addressed could identify the author.

Messrs. Jacob Shaver and Willis Huniston, citizens of Troy, N. Y., being called for the prosecution, testified that they had been intimately acquainted with Marcus P. Norton; a witness in this case for the prosecution, for a number of years; that in the city of Troy, where he is well known, his reputation for veracity and integrity is very good; that they would believe him on oath or otherwise; that they knew him to be a lawyer in good practice, and that an attempt which had been made to impeach his character had proved unsuccessful.

Testimony of Horatio King.

By Judge Advocate Holt.—I live in Washington City; I have held the positions of Assistant Postmaster-General and Postmaster-General of the United States; I made the acquaintance while here of Marcus P. Norton, a lawyer, of Troy, N. Y.; I have known him quite intimately for eight or ten years; I have always regarded him as being scrupulously honest and from my knowledge of his character I would unhesitatingly believe him under oath.

By Mr. Doster.—I have never lived in Troy; I do not know what Mr. Norton's reputation is in that city; I have had some connection with him in a patent; I never heard any one in Washington speak otherwise than favorably of him; I never heard of any attempt to impeach his veracity.

By Judge Advocate Holt.—During March last I saw Mr. Norton in this city, and had frequent conversations with him; in one of these conversations he mentioned to me the circumstance of a person having abruptly entered his room in the National Hotel; I do not remember for whom he said the person inquired.

By Mr. Doster.—Q. Did you ever hear Mr. Norton say that he had overheard a conversation between Booth and the prisoner, Atzeroth, at the National Hotel. A. He made some allusion to it; I think it was about the 18th of May, which was, I think, the date of his letter.

Assistant Judge Advocate Burnett handed to the witness a letter, which was identified by him as one he had received from Mr. Norton, about the 17th of May, from which he read as follows:—

"I believe Johnson was poisoned on the evening of March 3d, or the morning of March last; I knew of something which took place at the National Hotel last winter, between Booth and strangers to me, which, since the death of our good President, have thrown me into alarm and suspicion, and about which I will talk with you when I see you."

Testimony of William H. Roherer.

William H. Roherer being called for the prosecution, testified to his knowledge of the handwriting of Clement C. Clay, of Alabama, and identified the letter given above as having been written by that person.

There being no further witnesses, the Court adjourned.

WASHINGTON, June 13.—Mr. Cox called the attention of the Court to the following item in the *Evening Star* of yesterday, copied from a Maryland newspaper:—

"A MYSTERIOUS LETTER.—On the 4th instant, two men named French and McAleer, of South Branch, Virginia, were arrested by Major Meyers, and brought to this city, and lodged in the guard-house, on the charge of writing a mysterious letter addressed to J. Wilkes Booth, and which was submitted in evidence before the assassination court at Washington. It turns out now that the letter was a fraud, perpetrated by a person named Purdy, who is said to be a Government Detective, and who, entertaining a bitter hatred towards the parties arrested, availed himself of this mode of wreaking revenge. French and McAleer have been released and Purdy has since been arrested and placed in close confinement, on the charge of committing the alleged fraud."—*Cumberland (Maryland) Union.*

Mr. Cox said if this letter was a fraud the defense ought to have the benefit of it. He had not been able to find it (the letter in question), but supposed it referred to the letter addressed to J. W. B., at the National Hotel.

Judge Bingham said it bore date April 6th, 1865. The matter should not go on record. If the parties want Purdy let him be brought here, but for the introducing newspaper paragraphs for which nobody was responsible. The letter referred to as a fraud bears evidence upon the face of it as having been written by one concerned in the murder of President Lincoln. Though it never reached the person to whom it was addressed, yet the writer was none the less guilty.

Judge Holt said the matter was now undergoing investigation, and there would certainly be no concealment made of the result. It should go on the record.

Mr. Ewing said a great deal looser papers than this had been placed on the record, and he instanced the letter found floating in the Roanoke at Morehead City, N. C.

The Court took a recess till two P. M., in order for a medical survey as to Payne's insanity.
At two P. M. the Commission reassembled.

Testimony of Dr. James Chall,

By Mr. Doster.—Witness testified that he had examined the prisoner, Payne; first, in regard to his physical condition, his eye had a p.rfect y natural look, except tant it had no intellectual expression, though capable of evincing a great deal of passion and feeling; the shape of his head was not symmetrical, the left side being much lower developed than the right; the pulse was about thirty six-above the natural average; in other respects, with the exception of a matter in regard to which the Court had been informed, his health seemed to be good; upon questioning him in regard to his memory, the prisoner answered all questions put to him willingly, but his mind appeared to be very inert; his intellect was of a very low order, and dull and feeble. Witness described to the prisoner a supposed case, in which a person had committed the crime with which he was charged, and asked him whether he thought a person who committed such an act would be justified, and he said he thought they would. Upon being his reason for this opinion, his answer amounted to this—that he thought in war a person was entitled to take. I. e.
Q. From your whole examination of the prisoner are you of the opinion that there are reasonable grounds for believing that he is insane? A. I should say that there were; it seems to me that no man who was perfectly sane could exhibit the same utter insensibility which the prisoner manifests; there was no attempt at deception; he answered my questions, so far as his mind would permit him, without any apparent intent to deceive or mislead me; I could not give

a positive opinion as to whether he was laboring under either mental or moral insanity.

By Judge-Advocate Holt.—Q. I understand you to say that what you have discovered as peculiar in the condition of Payne is not insanity, but extreme insensibility? A. I cannot discover any positive signs of mental insanity, but of a very feeble, inert mind; a deficiency rather than a derangement of mind; a very low order of intellect.

Q. From the whole examination you have made do you regard the prisoner, Payne, as sufficiently sane to be responsible for his acts? A. I have not altogether made up my mind upon that; I do not think that the single examination I have made would suffice to decide the question, but I believe that there is enough to warrant a suspicion that he may not be a perfectly sane and responsible man; I cannot give any positive opinion upon that point.

Q. The sub-stance then of your opinion is that there are grounds for suspicion, but you do not express any positive opinion. A. Yes sir; I do not express any opinion that he is either mentally or morally insane, but that there are grounds to justify a suspicion of his insanity; I attached some importance to his physical condition; it is generally known that persons insane have, with few exceptions, an unusual frequency of pulse; the prisoner's pulse was thirty-odd strokes above the ordinary standard.

Q. Was he laboring under any excitement? A. Not the least; he was perfectly calm; his memory was very slow, and at times it appeared very difficult for him to answer a simple question; he could not remember the maiden name of his mother.

Q. Do you think that was sincere or an affectation? A. I think it was sincere; his memory is very deficient.

Q. Did you ever before meet with a man who was known in the community as a sane and a responsible man who did not know the name of his mother? A. Yes, sir; I have known of persons who forgot their own names.

Q. Then you do not consider the forgetfulness of names an evidence of insanity? A. No, sir.

Mr. Doster asked that the witness be permitted to continue his examination into the alleged insanity of the prisoner.

The request was acceded to, and Dr. Stevens, Surgeon-General Barnes and Surgeon Morris were appointed by the Court to assist Dr. Hall in the examination.

Testimony of John T. Hoxten.

By Mr. Aiken.—I reside in Prince George county and have resided there about forty years; my residence is at Surrattsville; I have known the prisoner, Mrs. Surratt, for many years; her reputation among those who knew her there as a truthful, kind and good Christian lady is very good; I have frequently met her since the commencement of the war, but never had any conversation with her on political subjects.

Witness was acquainted with J. Z. Jenkins. His impression was that he was a good Union man. I am acquainted with the Rev. Wm. A. Evans; I know that he kept a store in the neighborhood in which I lived some ten years ago; I know nothing of his present reputation for truth and veracity.

By Mr. Clampitt.—Cannot say that Mr. Jenkins is now a consistent Union man; he was two years ago; the report in the neighborhood now is that he is not loyal; never knew him to commit any disloyal act.

Testimony of Wm. W. Hoxten.

By Mr. Aiken.—I reside near Surrattsville, and have known the prisoner, Mrs. Surratt, for about twelve years; she has always been looked upon in our neighborhood as a very good, kind, Christian lady, and a church-going woman; have met her frequently of late years, and never heard her express a disloyal sentiment; I knew J. Z. Jenkins at the commencement of the war; he was known as a very strong Union man, and bore that reputation until he lost his negroes; I never knew of his expressing any sentiments opposed to the Government.

Testimony of Henry Hawkins (Colored).

By Mr. Aiken.—I have lived at Surrattsville about eleven years; was formerly a slave of Mrs. Surratt; she always treated me kindly; remember that on one occasion some Government horses broke away from Giesboro' and came to Mrs. Surratt's stable, they were fed and taken care of at her expense; never heard any political expressions from Mrs. Surratt; she frequently fed Union soldiers passing her house, and gave them the best she had; do not think she took any pay for it; I sometimes heard that Mrs. Surratt could not see very well; have seen her wear spectacles.

Testimony of Rachael Semus, (Colored.)

I lived with Mrs. Surratt for six years; was hired by her; I never had any reason to complain of hard treatment while with her; she frequently had Union soldiers, and always tried to do the best she could for them, giving them the best in the house, and very often giving them all in the house; I recollect that one time she cut up the last ham for a party of Union soldiers; never knew her to take pay from the soldiers; have seen them come there and get refreshments and not pay; never knew her to say anything in favor of the South; knew her eyesight to be failing; have frequently threaded a needle for her.

Re-cross-examination of John M. Floyd.

By Mr. Aiken.—When the carbines were first brought to my house they were taken up stairs by John H. Surratt and myself, and put between the joists, where they remained until Mrs. Surratt called to give directions in regard to them, which was Friday, the 14th of April; in accordance with her directions I took them out from where they had been secreted, and kept them ready for whoever would call for them; that in all I also prepared two bottles of whiskey (a bottle was exhibited to the witness, which he stated to be like those used in his bar-room, but was not one of the two of which he had spoken).

The witness continued.—It was here Harold, not Booth, who said to me on the night of the murder:— "Floyd, make haste and get those things."

Re-examination of Mrs. Offutt.

By Mr. Aiken.—Saw Mr. Floyd on the evening of April 14th; he was very much under the influence of liquor, more so than I had seen him for some time past; for some four or five months he has drank freely; I did not hear the full confession of Floyd to Captain Cottingham, but heard some remarks; I did not hear him say "That vile woman, she has ruined me."

Mr. Aiken stated to the Court that when on the stand before, the witness had not recovered from a spell of sickness, and having previously taken laudanum, her mind was confused in giving her testimony, and that she now desired to correct a portion of that testimony. After consultation between the counsel for Mrs. Surratt and Assistant Judge Advocate Bingham the witness was directed to make any statement she desired. She then said, "when previously I was on the stand, I was asked if Mrs. Surratt handed me a package, and I said no; but she did hand me a package, and said she was requested to leave it there; that was between five and six o'clock.

The re-examination of the witness was then resumed as follows:—Witness had no knowledge of the contents of that package; saw something in Mr. Floyd's hands after he came in the house, when Mrs. Surratt told him he could not say that it was the package; saw him have the package after he came in, but not while he was coming in; never heard Mrs. Surratt utter any disloyal expressions; remember instances of defective eyesight on the part of Mrs. Surratt; on one occasion she told witness that her eyesight was failing very fast.

By Assistant Judge Advocate Bingham.—Witness stated before that Mrs. Surratt and John M. Floyd had a conversation outside the house on the afternoon of Mrs. Surratt's visit; did not see the package after it was brought in the house; do not know whether Mrs. Surratt did or did not hand a package to Mr. Floyd.

Re-Examination of Major Eckert.

By Assistant Judge Advocate Bingham.—Witness stated that the day on which General B. F. Butler was ordered to leave New York, after the last Presidential election, was the 11th of November, and that General Butler made application to be allowed to remain until the following Monday, the 19th of November, which application was granted.

Re-examination of Richard Montgomery.

By Assistant Judge Advocate Bingham.—Witness stated that the hour for the departure of the train which left Montreal, Canada, to connect with the through trains for Washington was three o'clock P. M.; that the distance between Montreal and Washington was usually traveled in thirty-six to thirty-eight hours; that a person leaving Montreal at three o'clock on the afternoon of the 12th of April would reach Washington before daylight on the morning of the 14th.

Cross-examined by Mr. Aiken.—A person leaving Montreal on the afternoon of the 12th would arrive in the city of New York, at the furthest, at eleven o'clock in the forenoon of the 14th; leaving New York at six or seven in the evening, one would arrive at Washington in ten or eleven hours.

Re-Cross-Examination of J. S. Debonay.

By Mr. Ewing.—At the time the pistol was fired on the evening of the assassination witness was on the stage of Ford's Theatre, leaning against the corridor scene, on the left-hand side; when I first saw the prisoner, Spangler, after the escape of Booth, he was shutting the scene back, so as to allow the people to get upon the stage; that was about a minute and a half after Booth ran across the stage, followed by Mr. Stewart; Spangler then ran to the green-room to get some water for the persons in the President's box; I saw Spangler go to the door when Booth called him, previous to the assassination; did not hear any conversation between Spangler and Booth; witness was on the pavement in front of the theatre about five minutes before the assassination; did not see Spangler there at any time; never knew Spangler to wear a heavy moustache.

John Pyle and Andrew Collenback were then called for the defense, the former sustaining the character of one of the witnesses for the defense, J. Z. Jenkins, and the latter testifying in regard to the remark made by Mr. John M. Floyd, that he had been innocently persunded into the matter, referring to the custody of the shooting-irons by Mrs. Surratt or Mrs. Surratt's family. The counsel for the prisoners, except in the case of the prisoner Payne, whose alleged insanity is yet to be reported upon, severally stated that their defense had closed.

There being no further witnesses present, the Commission adjourned till to-morrow at 12 o'clock M.

WASHINGTON, June 14.—The previous day's record was read, when the Commission took a recess until two o'clock, in order to allow an examination of the prisoner Payne by the commission appointed for that purpose.

The Commission reassembled at two o'clock, when Mr. Doster stated that he had closed the defense in the case of the prisoner Payne, and did not propose to call as witnesses the medical gentlemen who had been appointed to investigate the condition of Payne as to his insanity.

Judge Holt then stated that these gentlemen would be called for the Government.

Re-examination of Dr. James C. Hall.

By Judge Holt.—The witness had examined the prisoner, Payne, this morning, and was assisted by Drs. Norris and Porter, and, subsequently, Surgeon-General Barnes joined in the examination. The prisoner was asked almost the same questions that were put to him yesterday, for the purpose of ascertaining whether his answers would be similar; he answered with rather more promptness than before, and his answers were much the same.

Q. Are you now prepared to express an opinion whether or not, in your judgment, the prisoner is a sane and responsible man? A. I am now prepared to say there is no evidence of mental insanity; the prisoner's mind is feeble and uncultivated, but I cannot discover sufficient evidence of mental incapacity.

Cross-examined by Mr. Doster.—Q. What are you prepared to state as to his moral insanity? A. We asked him the question to-day whether he believed in a God; he said that he did, and that he was a just God; he also acknowledged to me that at one time he had been a member of the Baptist Church; I asked him the question whether he thought that the assassination of an enemy in time of war was justifiable and after some little hesitation he said he believed it was.

Testimony of Dr. Norris.

The witness, in company with Surgeon-General Barnes, and other medical gentlemen, made an examination this morning of the prisoner Payne, and arrived at the conclusion that he was a sane man. There was nothing in the prisoner's looks, speech, or conduct to indicate that he was of unsound mind; on the contrary, his reasoning faculties appeared to be good, as also his judgment.

Cross-examined by Mr. Doster.—I am not familiar with cases of insanity; I do not think the conduct of the prisoner during the examination could have been that of a madman; the prisoner might be a monomaniac, but if such was the case, the witness would probably have had his suspicions aroused, as such persons almost invariably, in conversation with strange persons, refer to the subject of their insanity.

Testimony of Surgeon-General Barnes.

By Judge Advocate Holt.—The prisoner, Payne, was examined by the witness and other medical gentlemen, but no evidence of insanity was discovered; the coherent manner in which he narrated his story of himself, giving the places at which he had been, and his occupation, and, more important than all, his reiteration of the statements made by him on yesterday, were proofs of his saneness.

Testimony of Dr. Porter.

By Judge-Advocate Holt.—Having been present this morning at the examination of the prisoner, Payne, the witness believed that he was a sane man. The prisoner had been under the witness' care since his confinement in the Arsenal, and from the inspections which he had made, witness arrived at the conclusion that he was a sane and responsible man.

The cross-examination of this witness was mainly with reference to what constituted mental or moral insanity, and was terminated by the President of the Court objecting to the course of examination as improper.

Assistant Judge-Advocate Bingham entered upon the record several papers, among which were a certified copy of the resolution of the Senate of the United States consenting to and ordering the appointment of William H. Seward as Secretary of State of the United States, and the qualification of Andrew Johnson, on the 18th of April, 1865, as President of the United States.

Judge Holt said that some additional testimony, relating exclusively to the general conspiracy and not affecting either of the prisoners particularly, would be offered on behalf of the Government. Having understood that one of the arguments for the defense had been fully prepared, he desired the Court to hear it, with the understanding that it should not preclude the offering of this testimony.

Mr. Aiken said it was the wish of the counsel that all the testimony which the Government had should be handed in before that argument was presented to the Court. It had been thought possible that Mr. Johnson himself would be present to-morrow to deliver the argument in person. If he was not present, Mr. Clampitt, by agreement among the counsel, would present the argument to the Court.

Judge Holt inquired as to which of the prisoners the argument was intended to apply.

Mr. Aiken said it was an argument relative to the jurisdiction of the Court which was prepared by Mr. Johnson and in which all the counsel concurred. It was intended for all the prisoners.

Assistant Judge Advocate Bingham said that Mr. Johnson was not counsel for all the prisoners.

General Wallace said that if the argument on the jurisdiction of the Court was ready it would not be improper for the Court to hear it, and in order to consider the question he moved that the Court be cleared.

The motion was agreed to. when the Court was cleared. After some time the doors were reopened, and it was announced that the Court had adjourned until Friday morning at 11 o'clock.

WASHINGTON, June 16.—Colonel Tompkins, member of the Court, was not present at the session of the Court to-day, on account of indisposition.

Testimony of Robert Purdy.

By Judge Advocate Holt.—The witness said he resided in Virginia, and had been in the Government service since 1861; a letter heretofore published, purporting to have been dated at South Branch Bridge Virginia, April 6th, 1865, addressed to "Friend Wilkes," and referring to certain oil speculations, and suggesting an escape by way of Thornton's Gap in case the party failed to get through on his trip after striking Ge, was shown to the witness, who stated that he had never seen it before; the witness testified that the allusions to Purdy contained in the letter had reference to himself; that the writer was known to him as a person by the name of Jonas McAleer, and that some of the allegations of the letter, especially that with reference to a difficulty with the girl spoken of, were untrue.

Cross-examined by Mr. Aiken.—South Branch Bridge is on a branch of the Potomac River, about twenty-two miles from Cumberland; letters are not usually mailed from South Branch Bridge, but from a little village known as Green Spring Run, just above it; there is no post office box at South Branch Bridge; there are no oil wells in that vicinity.

Testimony of D. S. Eastwood.

By Judge Advocate Holt.—I live in Montreal, Canada, and am assistant manager of the Montreal branch of the Ontario Bank; I am acquainted with Jacob Thompson, formerly Secretary of the Interior of the United States, and with the account which he kept in the Ontario Bank; the moneys deposited in that Bank to his credit accrued from the negotiation of bills of exchange drawn by the Secretary of the Treasury of the so-called Confederate States upon their agents at Liverpool.

Q. State whether or not in the course of the disbursements made by Jacob Thompson of the fund placed to his credit, this requisition was drawn on the bank. (Exhibiting to witness a paper, given below). A. It was, it is in my handwriting.

Q. Please read it to the Court. A. (Reading the paper.) Montreal, August 10, 1864. Wanted, from the Ontario Bank on New York, in favor of Benjamin Wood, Esq., for $25,000 current funds, $10,000, debit $15,000. The paper shows that the requisition was originally drawn in favor of Benjamin Wood, Esq., and that the name of D. S. Eastwood was substituted.

Q. State the exact condition of the paper. A. As it reads now it is a draft on New York, payable to the order of D. S. Eastwood, that is, myself.

Q. State how that change in the requisition occurred. A. The name of Benjamin Wood, as it appeared originally, was erased at Mr. Thompson's request, and my name as an officer of the bank was substituted.

Q. That is the original paper, is it not? A. It is.

Q. Now look at this bill of exchange, (exhibiting another paper to witness) and state whether it was drawn upon that requisition. A. It was.

By request of the Judge Advocate the witness then read the paper to the Court. It is dated Montreal, August 10, 1864, and is directed to the Cashier of the City Bank, New York, the wording being as follows:—"At three days sight please pay to the order of D. S. Eastwood, in current funds, twenty-five thousand dollars, value received, and charge the same to account of this branch." The indorsement on the bill directs the payment to be made to Hon. Benj. Wood, or order. Signed B. F. Wood.

Q. You state that the twenty-five thousand dollars for which this bill was drawn, is the same for which that requisition was made by Mr. Thompson in the name of Benj. Wood? A. It was.

Q. State whether or not the bill of exchange you have just read is the original one? A. It is.

Q. Where did you obtain it? A. I obtained it in New York, from the Cashier of the bank on which it was drawn.

Q. Does it bear the marks of having been paid? A. I am not acquainted with the usual marks of cancelling in New York, but I understood that it was paid.

The witness stated further that he was not acquainted with the Benjamin Wood referred to, but he supposed it to be the same who at the date of that transaction was a member of the Congress of the United States.

Cross-examined by Mr. Aiken,—I do not recollect of having ever cashed any drafts or checks in favor of either James Watson Wallace, Richard Montgomery, James B. Merritt or John Wilkes Booth. About the first of October last Booth purchased a bill on the bank of Montreal with which witness was connected. Never heard the name of John H. Surratt mentioned before. The Judge Advocate exhibited to the witness a list of localities upon which drafts had been made by the Ontario Bank, and requested him to give the dates and amounts of drafts which as shown by the paper, had been drawn on New York. The witness stated that the following were among the number of drafts drawn on the 3d of October last:—A draft for $10,000 in gold; on the 11th of October one of $3000 in gold; on November 3d. 4th and 5th, bills for about $6000 in United States currency; on the 14th and 21st of March last, small drafts were also drawn.

Testimony of George Wilkes.

By Judge Advocate Holt,—I am acquainted with Benjamin Wood, of New York, and know his handwriting.

The indorsement of "B. Wood" on the back of the bill of exchange given above was exhibited to the witness, and the handwriting identified by him as that of Hon. Benjamin Wood, of New York.

The witness stated further that at the time at which the paper appeared to have been dated Wood was a member of the Congress of the United States, and, he believed, editor and proprietor of the *Daily News*.

Testimony of Mr. Abram D. Russell.

By Judge Advocate-General Holt.—I am acquainted with Benjamin Wood, of the city of New York, and know his handwriting; the indorsement on the bill of exchange exhibited to the previous witness was identified by this witness to be the handwriting of Mr. Wood; at the time of the date of that bill of exchange Mr. Wood was a member of the Congress of the United States and editor and proprietor of the *New York Daily News*; the witness had been in the habit of receiving letters from Mr. Wood.

The Court then took a recess until two o'clock. Upon reassembling, Judge Advocate Holt suggested that if the argument of the counsel for the defense was now commenced, in the absence of Colonel Tompkins, a member of the Court, who was indisposed, it would have to be read over to him during a subsequent session of the Court. He thought there would be no loss of time to the Court if an adjournment was taken till Monday. The Court adjourned till Monday, at ten o'clock.

WASHINGTON, June 19.—Mr. Aiken stated to the Court that he should not be prepared until Wednesday to read the argument in the case of Mrs. Surratt. The delay was attributable to the voluminous evidence previously to he examined by him,

Reverdy Johnson's Argument.

Mr. Clampitt read the argument addressed to the President and gentlemen of the Commission, signed by Reverdy Johnson and concurred in by Frederick A. Aiken and John W. Clampitt as associate counsel for Mrs. Mary E. Surratt.

Mr. President and Gentlemen of the Commission:—Has the Commission jurisdiction of the cases before it is the question which I propose to discuss. That question, in all courts, civil, criminal and military, must be considered and answered affirmatively before judgment can be pronounced. And it must be answered correctly, or the judgment pronounced is void. Every an interesting and vital inquiry, it is of engrossing interest and of awful importance, when error may lead to the unauthorized taking of human life. In such a case, the court called upon to render, and the officer who is to approve its judgment and have it executed, have a concern peculiar to themselves. As to each a responsibility is involved, which, however conscientiously and firmly met, is calculated and cannot fail to awaken a great solicitude and induce the most mature consideration. The nature of the duty is such that even honest error affords no impunity. The legal personal consequences, even in a case of honest, mistaken judgment, cannot be avoided. That this is no exaggeration, the Commission will, I think, be satisfied before I shall have concluded. I refer to it now and shall do. In, with no view to shake your firmness. Such an attempt would be alike discourteous and unprofitable. Every member composing the commission will, I am sure, meet all the responsibility that belongs to it as becomes gentlemen and soldiers. I therefore repeat, that my sole object in adverting to it is to obtain a well-considered and matured judgment. So far, the question of jurisdiction has not been discussed. The pleas which specially present it, as soon as filed, were overruled. But that will not, because, properly, it should not prevent your considering it with the deliberation that its grave nature demands. And it is for you to decide it, and at this time, for you alone. The commission you are acting under of itself does not and could not decide it. If unauthorized, it is a mere nullity, the usurpation of a power not vested in the Executive, and conferring no authority whatever upon you. To hold otherwise would be to make the Executive the exclusive and conclusive judge of its own powers, and that would be to make that department omnipotent. The powers of the President under the Constitution are great, and amply sufficient to give all needed efficiency to the office. The Convention that formed the Constitution, and the people who adopted it, considered those powers sufficient, and granted no others. In the minds of both (and subsequent history has served to strengthen the impression), danger to liberty is more to be dreaded from the Executive than from any other department of the Government. So far, therefore, from meaning to extend its powers beyond what was deemed necessary to the wholesome operation of the Government, they were studious to place them beyond the reach of abuse. With this view, before entering upon the execution of his office," the President is required to take an oath "faithfully" to discharge its duties, and to the best of his "ability preserve, protect and defend the Constitution of the United States." He is also liable to "be removed from office on impeachment for and conviction of treason, bribery, or other high crimes and misdemeanors." If he violates the Constitution, if he fails to preserve it, and, above all if he usurps powers not granted, he is false to his official oath, and liable to be indicted and convicted, and to be impeached. For such an offense his removal from office is the necessary consequence. In such a contingency "he shall be removed" is the command of the Constitution. What stronger evidence could there be that his powers, all of them, in peace and in war, are only such as the Constitution confers? But if this was not evident from the instrument itself, the character of the men who composed the Convention, and the spirit of the American people at that period would prove it. Hated of a monarchy, made the more intense by the conduct of the monarch from whose Government they had recently separated, and a deep-seated love of constitutional liberty, made the more keen and active by the sacrifices which had illustrated their revolutionary career, constituted them a people who could never be induced to delegate any executive authority not so carefully restricted and guarded as to render its abuse or usurpation almost impossible. If these observations are well founded, and I suppose they will not be denied, it follows that an executive act beyond executive authority can furnish no defense against the legal consequences of what are done under it. I have said that the question of jurisdiction is ever open. It may be raised by counsel at any stage of the trial, and if it is not the Court not only may but is bound to notice it. Unless jurisdiction, then, exists, the authority to try does not exist, and whatever is done is "*oram non judice,*" and utterly void. This doctrine is as applicable to military as to other courts. O'Brien tells us that the question may be raised by demurrer if the facts charged do not constitute an offense, or if they do, not an offense cognizable by a military court, or that it may be raised by a special plea, or under the general one of not guilty. (O'Brien, 248.) Delfort says: "The Court is the judge of its own competency at any stage of its proceedings, and is bound to notice questions of jurisdiction whenever raised." (DeHart, 111.)

The question, then, being always open, and its proper decision essential to the validity of its judgment, the Commission must decide before pronouncing such judgment whether it has jurisdiction over these parties and the crimes imputed to them. That a tribunal like this has no jurisdiction over other than military offenses, is believed to be self-evident. That offenses defined and punished by the civil law, and whose trial is provided for by the same law, are not the subjects of military jurisdiction, is, of course, true. A military, as contradistinguished from a civil offense, must, therefore, be made to appear, and when it is, it must also appear that the military law provides for its trial and punishment by a military tribunal.

If that law does not furnish a mode of trial, or affix a punishment, the case is unprovided for, and, as far as the military power is concerned, is to go unpunished. But, as either the civil, common or statue law embraces every species of offense that the United States or the States have deemed it necessary to punish, in all such cases the civil courts are clothed with every necessary jurisdiction. In a military court, if the charge does not state a "crime provided for generally or specifically by any of the articles of war," the prisoner must be discharged. (O'Brien p. 235.) Nor is it sufficient that the charge is of a crime known to the military law. The offender, when he commits it, must be subject to such law or he is not subject to military jurisdiction. The general law has "supreme and undisputed jurisdiction over all. The military law puts forth no such pretension; it aims solely to enforce on the soldier the additional duties he has assumed. It constitutes tribunals for the trial of breaches of military duty only." (O'Brien. pp. 26, 27.) "The one code (the civil) embraces all citizens, whether soldiers or not; the other (the military) has no jurisdiction over any citizen as such. (Ib.)

The provisions of the Constitution clearly maintain the same doctrine. The Executive has no authority "to declare war, to raise and support armies, to provide and maintain a navy," or to make "rules for the government and regulation" of either force. These powers are exclusively in Congress. The army cannot be raised or have laws for its government and regulation except as Congress shall provide. This power of Congress was granted by the Convention without objection. In England the King, as the generalissimo of the whole kingdom, has this sole power, though Parliament has frequently interposed and regulated for itself. But with us it was thought safest to give the entire power to Congress, "since otherwise summary and severe punishment might be inflicted at the mere will of the Executive." (3 Story's Com., sec. 1192.) No member of the Convention or any commentator on the Constitution since has intimated that even this Congressional power could be applied to citizens not belonging to the army or navy. In respect, too, to the latter class, the power was conferred exclusively on Congress to prevent that class being made the objects of abuse by the Executive, to guard them especially from "summary and severe punishments," inflicted by mere executive will. The existence of such a power being vital to discipline, it was necessary to provide for it; but no member suggested that it should be or could be made to apply to citizens not in the military or naval service, or be given to any other department in whole or in part than Congress. Citizens not belonging to the army or navy were not made liable to military law, or under any circumstances to be deprived of any of the guaranties or personal liberty provided by the Constitution. Independent of the consideration that the very nature of the Government is inconsistent with such a pretension, the power is conferred upon Congress in terms that exclude all who do not belong to the "land and naval forces." It is a rule of interpretation coeval with its existence that the Government in no department of it possesses powers not granted by express delegation, or necessarily to be implied from those that are granted. This would be the rule incident to the very nature of the Constitution; but to place it beyond doubt, and to make it an imperative rule, the tenth amendment declares that "the powers not delegated to the United States by the Constitution, nor prohibited by it to the States, are reserved to the States respectively, or to the people." The power given to Congress is "to make rules for the government and regulation of the land and naval forces." No artifice of ingenuity can make these words include those who do not belong to the army and navy. And they are therefore to be construed to exclude all others as if negative words to that effect had been added.

And this is not only the obvious meaning of the terms, considered by themselves, but is demonstrable from other provisions of the Constitution. So jealous were our ancestors of ungranted power, and so vigilant to protect the citizen against it, that they were unwilling to leave him to the safeguards which a proper construction of the Constitution, as originally adopted, furnished. In this they resolve that nothing should be left in doubt. They determined, therefore, not only to guard him against executive and judicial, but against Congressional abuse. With that view, they adopted the fifth Constitutional amendment which declares that "no person shall be held to answer for a capital, or otherwise infamous crime, unless on a presentment, or indictment of a Grand Jury, except in cases arising in the land or naval forces, or in the militia when in active service in time of war or public danger."

This exception is designed to leave in force, not to enlarge, the power vested in Congress by the original Constitution, "to make rules for the government and regulation of the land and naval forces." "The land or naval forces" are the very terms used in both, have the same meaning, and until lately have been supposed by every commentator and judge to exclude from military jurisdiction offenses committed by citizens not belonging to such forces. Kent, in a note to his 1 Com., p. 341, states, and with accuracy, that "military and naval crimes and offenses committed while the party is attached to and under the immediate authority of

the army and navy of the United States, and in actual service, are not cognizable under the common law jurisdiction of the Courts of the United States." According to this great authority, every other class of persons, and every other species of offense are within the jurisdiction of the civil Courts, and entitled to the protection of the proceeding by presentment or indictment, and a public trial in such a Court. If the Constitutional amendment has not that effect, it it does not secure that protection to all who do not belong to the army or navy, then the provisions in the sixth amendment are equally inoperative. They, "in all criminal prosecutions," give the accused a right to a speedy and public trial a right to be informed of the nature and cause of the accusation; to be confronted with the witnesses against him; to compulsory process for his witnesses, and the assistance of counsel. The exception in the fifth amendment of cases arising in the land or naval forces applies, by necessary implication at least, in part to this. To construe this as not containing the exception would defeat the purpose of the exception. For the provisions of the sixth amendment, unless they are subject to the exceptions of the fifth, would be inconsistent with the fifth. The sixth is, therefore, to be construed as if it in words contained the exception.

It is submitted that this is evident. The consequence is, that if the exception can be made to include those who, in the language of Kent, are not, when the offense was committed, "attached to and under the immediate authority of the army or navy, and in actual service," the securities designed for other citizens by the sixth article are wholly nugatory. If a Military Commission, created by the mere authority of the President, can deprive a citizen of the benefit of the guaranties secured by the fifth amendment, it can deprive him of those secured by the sixth; it may deny him the right to "a speedy and public trial." Information "of the nature and cause of the accusation," of the right "to be confronted with the witnesses against him," of "compulsory process for his witnesses," and of "the assistance of counsel for his defense." That this can be done no one has, as yet maintained. No opinion, however latitudinarian, of executive power, of the effect of public necessity in war or in peace, to enlarge its sphere, and authorize a disregard of its limitations—no one, however convinced he may be of the policy of protecting accusing witnesses from a public examination under the idea that their testimony cannot otherwise be obtained, and that consequently crime may go unpunished, has to this time been found to go to that extent. Certainly no writer has ever maintained such a doctrine. Argument to refute it is unnecessary. It refutes itself. For, if sound, the sixth amendment, which our fathers thought so vital to individual liberty, when assailed by governmental prosecution, is but a dead letter, totally inefficient for its purpose whenever the Government shall deem it proper to try a citizen by a military commission. Against such a doctrine the very instincts of freemen revolt. It has no foundation but in the principle of unrestrained, tyrannic power, and passive obedience. If it be well founded, then are we indeed a nation of slaves and not of freemen.

If the Executive can legally decide whether a citizen is to enjoy the guarantee of liberty afforded by the Constitution, what are we but slaves? If the President, or any of his subordinates, under any pretense whatever, can deprive a citizen of such guaranties, liberty with us, however loved, is not enjoyed. But the Constitution is not so fatally defective. It is subject to no such reproach. In war and in peace it is equally potential for the promotion of the general welfare, and as involved in and necessary to such welfare for the protection of the individual citizen. Certainly, until this Rebellion, this has been the proud and cherished conviction of the country. And it is to this conviction and the assurance that it could never be shaken that our past prosperity is to be referred. God forbid that mere power, dependent for its exercise on Executive will (a condition destructive of political and social happiness), shall ever be substituted in its place. Should that unfortunately ever occur, unless it was soon corrected by the authority of the people, the objects of our Revolutionary struggle, the sacrifices of our ancestors and the design of the Constitution will all have been in vain.

I proceed now to examine with somewhat of particularity the grounds on which I am informed your jurisdiction is maintained.

1. That it is an incident of the war power.

That power, whatever be its extent, is exclusively in Congress. War can only be declared by that body. With its origin, the President has no concern whatever. Armies, which are necessary, can only be raised by the same body. Not a soldier, without his authority, can be brought into service by the Executive. He is as impotent to that end as a private citizen.

And armies, too, when raised by Congressional authority, can only be governed and regulated by "rules" prescribed by the same authority. The Executive possesses no power over the soldier, except such as Congress may, by legislation, confer upon him. If, then, it was true that the creation of a military commission like the present is incidental to the war power, it must be authorized by the Department to which that power

TRIAL OF THE ASSASSINS AT WASHINGTON.

belongs, and not by the Executive, to whom no portion belongs.

And if it be said to be involved in the power "to make rules for the government and regulation of the land and naval forces," the result is the same. It must be done by Congress, to whom that power, also, exclusively belongs, and not by the Executive. This Congress, then, under either power, authorized such a Commission as this to try such cases as these? It is confidently asserted that it has not. If it has, let the statute be produced. It is certainly not done by that of the 10th of April, 1806, "establishing articles for the government of the armies of the United States." No military courts are there mentioned or provided for but courts-martial and courts of inquiry. And their mode of appointment and organization and of proceeding, and the authority vested in them, are also prescribed. Military Commissions are not only not authorized, but are not even alluded to. And, consequently, the parties, whoever these may be, who, under that act, can be tried by courts-martial or courts of inquiry, are not made subject to trial by a military commission. Nor is such a tribunal mentioned in any prior statute, or in any subsequent one, until those of the 17th of July, '62, and of the 3d of March, '63. In the 5th section of the first, the records of "military commissions" are to be returned for revision to the Judge Advocate-General, whose appointment it also provides for. But how such commissions are to be constituted, what powers they are to have, how their proceedings are to be conducted, or what cases and parties they are to try, are not provided for. In the 38th section of the second, they are mentioned as competent to try persons "lurking or acting as spies." The same absence in the particulars stated in respect to the first are true of this.

And as regards this act of 1863, this reflection forcibly represents itself. If military commissions can be created, and from their very nature possess jurisdiction to try all alleged military offenses (the ground on which your jurisdiction is said to part to rest), why was it necessary to give them the power, by express words, to try persons "lurking or acting as spies?" The military character of such an offense could not have been doubted. What reason, then, can be suggested for conferring the power by express language than that without it it would not be possessed? Before these statutes were passed a commission called a Military Commission, had been issued by the Executive to Messrs. Davis, Holt and Campbell, to examine into certain military claims against the Western Department, and Congress, by its resolution of the 11th of March, 1863, (No. 18), provided for the payment of its awards. Against a commission of that character no objection can be made. It is but auxiliary to the auditing of demands upon the Government, and in no way interferes with any constitutional right of the citizen. But, until this Rebellion, a military commission like the present, organized in a loyal State or territory, where the courts are opened and their proceedings unobstructed, clothed with the jurisdiction attempted to be conferred upon you, a jurisdiction involving not only the liberty but the lives of the parties on trial, it is confidently stated is not to be found sanctioned or the most remotely recognized or even alluded to by any writer on military law in England or the United States, or in any legislation of either country. It has its origin in the Rebellion, and, like the dangerous heresy of secession, out of which that sprung, nothing is more certain, in my opinion, than that, however pure the motives of its origin, it will be an almost equally dangerous heresy to constitutional liberty, and, the Rebellion ended, perish with the other, then and forever.

But to proceed. Such commissions were authorized by Lieutenant-General Scott in his Mexican campaign. When he obtained possession of the City of Mexico, he, on the 17th of September, 1847, republished, with additions, his order of the 19th of February preceding, declaring martial law. By this order he authorized the trial of certain offenses by military commissions, regulated their proceedings, and limited the punishments they might inflict. From their jurisdiction, however, he excepts cases "clearly cognizable by court-martial," and in words limits the cases to be tried to such as are (I quote) "not provided for in the act of Congress establishing rules and articles for the Government of the armies of the United States," of the 10th of April, 1806.

And he further tells us that even this order, so limited and so called for by the greatest public necessity, when handed to the then Secretary of War (Mr. Marcy) "for his approval," "a startle at the title (martial-law order) was the only comment he then, or ever made on the subject," and that it was "soon silently returned on too explosive for safe handling." "A little later (he adds) the Attorney-General (Mr. Cushing) called and asked for a copy, and the law officer of the Government, whose business it is to speak on all such matters, was stricken with *legal dumbness*," (Ib.) How much more startled and more paralyzed would these great men have been had they been consulted on such a commission as this! A Commission not to sit in another country, and to try offenses not provided for by any law of the United States, civil or military, then in force, but in their own country, and in a part of it

where there are laws providing for their trial and punishment, and civil courts clothed with ample powers for both, and in the daily and undisturbed exercise of their jurisdiction and where, if there should be an attempt at disturbance by a force which they had not the power to control, they could invoke (and it would be his duty to afford it) the President to use the military power as his command, and which everybody knows to be ample for the purpose.

The second clause of the order mentions, among other offenses to be so tried, "assassination, murder, poisoning," and in the fourth (correctly, as I submit, with all respect for a contrary opinion) he states that "the rules and articles of war" do not provide for the punishment of any one of the designated offenses, "even when committed by individuals of the army upon the persons or property of other individuals of the same, except in the very restricted case of the ninth of the articles." The authority for even this restricted commission, Scott, not more eminent as a soldier than civilian, placed entirely upon the ground that the named offenses, if committed in a foreign country by American troops, could not be punished under any law of the United States then in force. "The Constitution of the United States and the rules and articles of war," he said, and said correctly, provided no court for their trial or punishment, "no matter by whom or on whom" committed. (Scott's Autobiography, 392.)

If it be suggested that the civil courts and juries of this District could not safely be relied upon for the trial of these cases, because either of incompetency, disloyalty or corruption, it would be an unjust reflection upon the judges, upon the people, upon the Marshal, an appointee of the President, by whom the juries are summoned, and upon our civil institutions themselves, the very institutions on whose integrity and intelligence the safety of our property, liberty, and lives our ancestors thought could not only be safely vested, but would be safe nowhere else. If it be suggested that a secret trial, in whole or in part, as the Executive might deem expedient, could not be had before any other than a military tribunal, the answer is that the Constitution, "in all criminal prosecutions," gives the accused the "right" to a "public trial." So abhorrent were private trials to our ancestors, so fatal did they deem them to individual security, that they were denounced, and as they no doubt thought, so guarded against as in all future time to be impossible. If it be suggested that witnesses may be unwilling to testify, the answer is that they may be compelled to appear and made to testify.

But the suggestion upon another ground is equally without force. It rests on the idea that the guilty only are ever brought to trial; that the only object of the Constitution and the laws in this regard is to afford the means to establish the alleged guilt. That accusation, however made, is to be esteemed *prima facie* presumption of guilt, and that the Executive should be armed, without other restriction than his own discretion, with all the appliances deemed by him necessary to make the presumption conclusive. Never was there a more dangerous theory. The peril to the citizen from a prosecution so conducted, as illustrated in all history, the very elementary principles of constitutional liberty, the spirit and letter of the Constitution itself, repudiate it.

Innocent parties, sometimes by private malice, sometimes for a more partisan purpose, sometimes from a supposed public policy, have been made the subjects of criminal accusation. History is full of such instances. How are such parties to be protected, if a public trial, at the option of the Executive, can be denied them, and a secret one, in whole or in part, substituted? If the names of the witnesses and their evidence are not published, what obstacle does it not interpose to establish their innocence?

The character of the witnesses against them may be all-important to that end. Kept in prison, with no means of consulting the outer world, how can those who may know the witnesses be able to communicate with them on the subject? A trial so conducted, though it may not, as no doubt is the case in the present, be intended to procure the punishment of any but the guilty, it is obvious subjects the innocent to great danger. It partakes more of the character of the Inquisition, which the enlightened civilization of the age has driven almost wholly out of existence than of a tribunal suited to a free people. In the palmiest days of that tribunal, kings as well as people stood abashed in its presence and dreaded its power. The accused was never informed of the names of his accusers. Heresy suspected was ample ground for arrest; accomplices and criminals were received as witnesses, and the whole trial was secret, and continued as long since denounced by the civilized world, not because it might at times punish the heretic (then, in violation of all rightful human power, deemed a criminal), but because it was as likely to punish the innocent as the guilty. A public trial, therefore, by which the names of witnesses and the testimony are given, even in monarchical and despotic governments, is now esteemed amply adequate to the punishment of guilt, and essential to the protection of innocence. Can it be that this is not true of us? Can it be that a secret trial, wholly or partially, if the Executive so decides,

TRIAL OF THE ASSASSINS AT WASHINGTON.

is all that an American citizen is entitled to? Such a doctrine, if maintained by an English monarch, would shake his government to its very centre, and if persevered in would lose him his crown. It will be no answer to these observations to say that this particular trial has been only in part a secret one, and that secrecy will never be resorted to except for purposes of justice. The reply is that the principle itself is inconsistent with American liberty as recognized and secured by constitutional guaranties. It supposes that whether these guaranties are to be enjoyed in the particular case, and to what extent, is dependent on Executive will. The Constitution in this regard is designed to secure them in spite of such will.

Its patriotic authors intended to place the citizen, in this particular, wholly beyond the power, not only of the Executive, but of every department of the Government. They deemed the right to a public trial vital to the security of the citizen, and especially and absolutely necessary to his protection against Executive power. A public trial of all criminal prosecutions they therefore secured in general and unqualified terms. What would these great men have said had they been asked so to qualify the terms as to warrant its refusal under any circumstances, and make it dependent upon Executive discretion? The member who made the inquiry would have been deemed by them a traitor to liberty or insane. What would they have said if told that without such qualification the Executive would be able legally to impose it as incidental to Executive power? If not received with derision, it would have been indignantly rejected as an imputation upon those who at any time thereafter should legally fill the office.

II. Let me present the question in another view. If such a commission as this, for the trial of cases like the present, can be legally constituted, can it be done by mere Executive authority?

1. You are a court, and, if legally existing, endowed with a momentous power, the highest known to man, that of passing upon the liberty or life of the citizen. By the express words of the Constitution, an army can only be raised and governed, and regulated by laws passed by Congress. In the exercise of the power to rule and govern it, the act before referred to of the 10th of April, 1806, establishing the articles of war, was passed. That act provides only for courts-martial and courts of inquiry, and designates the cases to be tried before each, and the laws that are to govern the trial.

Military commissions are not mentioned, and, of course, the act contains no provision for their government. Now, it is submitted as perfectly clear that the creation of a court, whether civil or military, is an exclusive legislative function, belonging to the department upon which the legislative power is conferred. The jurisdiction of such a court, and the laws and regulations to guide and govern it, is also exclusively legislative. What cases are to be tried by it, how the judges are to be selected, and how qualified; what are to be the rules of evidence, and what punishments are to be inflicted, all solely belong to the same department. The very element of constitutional liberty, recognized by all modern writers on government as essential to its security, and carefully incorporated into our Constitution, is a separation of the legislative, judicial and executive powers.

That this separation is made in our Constitution no one will deny. Article 1st declares that "all legislative powers herein granted shall be vested in a Congress." Article 2d vests "the executive power" in a President, and article 3d, "the judicial power in certain designated courts, and in courts to be thereafter constituted by Congress." There could not be a more careful segregation of the three powers. If, then, courts, their laws, modes of proceeding and judgments, belong to legislation (and this, I suppose, will not be questioned,) in the absence of legislation in regard to this court and its jurisdiction to try the present cases, it has for that purpose no legal existence or authority. The Executive, whose functions are altogether executive, cannot confer it. The offenses to be tried by it, the laws to govern its proceedings, the punishment it may award, cannot, for the same reason, be prescribed by the Executive. These, as well as the mere constitution of the court, all exclusively belong to Congress.

If it be contended that the Executive has the powers in question, because by implication they are involved in the war power or in the President's constitutional function as Commander-in-Chief of the army, then this consequence would follow, that they would not be subject to Congressional control, as that department has no more right to interfere with the power of the Executive than that power has a right to interfere with that of Congress. If this be so, if by implication the powers in question belong to the Executive, he may not only constitute and regulate military commissions and prescribe the laws for their government, but all legislation upon the subject by Congress would be usurpation. That the proposition leads to this result would seem to be clear, and if it does, that result itself is so inconsistent with all previous legislation and all Executive practice, and so repugnant to every principle of constitutional liberty, that it demonstrates its utter unsoundness.

Under the power given to Congress "to make rules for the government and regulation of the land forces," they have, from time to time, up to and including the act of the 10th of April, 1806, and since, enacted such rules as they deemed to be necessary, as well in war as in peace, and their authority to do so has never been denied. This power, too, to govern and regulate, from its very nature, is exclusive. Whatever is not done under it is to be considered as purposely omitted. The words used in the delegation of the power "govern and regulate," necessarily embrace the entire subject, and excluded all like authority in others. The end of such a power cannot be attained except thorough uniformity of government and regulation, and this is not to be attained, if the power is in two hands.

To be effective, therefore, it must be in one, and the Constitution gives it to one, to Congress, in express terms, and nowhere intimates a purpose to bestow it, or any portion of it, upon any other department. In the absence, then, of all mention of military commissions in the Constitution, and in the presence of the sole authority it confers on Congress by rules of its own enacting, to govern and regulate the army, and in the absence of all mention of such commissions in the act of the 10th of April, 1806, and of a single word in that act, or in any other, how can the power be considered as in the President? Further, upon what ground, other than those I have examined, can his authority be placed.

It is stated that the constitutional guaranties referred to are designed only for a state of peace. There is not a syllable in the instrument that justifies, even plausibly, such a qualification. These are secured by the most general and comprehensive terms, wholly inconsistent with any restriction. They are also not only not confined to a condition of peace, but are more peculiarly necessary to the security of personal liberty in war than in peace. All history tells us that war, at times, maddens the people, inflames the Government, and makes both regardless of constitutional limitations of power. Individual safety at such periods is more in peril than at any other. Constitutional limitations and guaranties are then also absolutely necessary to the protection of the Government itself. The maxim "salus populi suprema est lex" is but fit for a tyrant's use. Under its pretence the grossest wrongs have been committed, the most awful crimes perpetrated, and every principle of freedom violated, until at last, worn down by suffering, the people, in very despair, have acquiesced in a resulting despotism. The safety which liberty needs, and without which it sickens and dies, is that which law, and not mere unlicensed human will, affords. The Aristotelian maxim, salus publica suprema est lex, "let the public weal be under the protection of the law," is the true and only safe maxim. Nature without law would be chaos, government without law, anarchy, or despotism. Against both, in war and in peace, the Constitution happily protects us.

If the power in question is claimed under the authority supposed to be given the President in certain cases to suspend the writ of habeas corpus and to declare martial law, the claim is equally if not more evidently untenable. Because the fact of these powers, if given to the President at all, is even "when in cases of rebellion or invasion," he deems the public safety requires it. I think he has this power, but there are great and patriotic names who think otherwise. But if he has it, or if it be in Congress alone, it is entirely untrue that its exercise works any other result than the suspension of the writ—the temporary suspension of the right or having the cause of arrest passed upon at once by the civil judges. It in no way impairs or suspends the other rights secured to the accused.

In what court he is to be tried, how he is to be tried, what evidence is to be admitted, and what judgment pronounced, are all to be what the Constitution secures, and the laws provided in similar cases, when there is no suspension of the writ. The purpose of the writ is merely, without delay, to ascertain the legality of the arrest. If adjudged legal, the party is detained; if illegal, discharged. But in either contingency, when he is called to answer any criminal accusation, and he is a civilian and not subject to the articles of war, constitutionally enacted by Congress, it must be done by presentment or indictment, and his trial be had in a civil court, having, by State or Congressional legislation, jurisdiction over the crime, and under laws governing the tribunal and defining the punishment.

The very fact, too, that express power is given in a certain condition of things, to suspend the writ referred to, and that no power is given to suspend, or deny any of the other securities for personal liberty provided by the Constitution, is conclusive to show that all the latter were designed to be in force "in cases of rebellion or invasion," as well as in a state of perfect peace and safety.

III. I have already referred to the act of 1806, establishing the articles of war, and said, what must be admitted, that it provides for no military court like this; but, for argument's sake, let it be admitted. And I then maintain, with becoming confidence and the respect for a different opinion, that it does not embrace the crimes charged against these parties or the parties themselves.

First. The charge is a traitorous conspiracy to take

the lives of the designated persons, "in aid of the existing armed Rebellion." Second. That is the execution of the conspiracy the actual murder of the late President and the attempted murder of the Secretary of State occurred. Throughout the charge and its specifications the conspiracy and its attempted execution are alleged to have been traitorous. The accusation, there ore, is not one merely of murder, but of murder designed and part accomplished with traitorous purpose. If the charge is true and the intent (which is made a substantial part of it) be also true, then the crime is treason and not simple murder.

Treason against the United States, as defined by the Constitution, can "cons.st only in levying war against them or in adhering to their enemies, giving them a d and comfo t." (3d article.) This definition not only tells us what treason is, but that no other crime than the defined one should be considered the offense. And the same section provides that "no person shall be convicted of treason except on the testimony of two witnesses to the same overt act, or on confession in open court," and gives to Congress the power to declare what its punishment shall be. The offense in the general is the same as in England. In that country, at no period since its freedom became settled, has any other treason been recognized. In the pendency of this Rebellion (never be ore) it has been alleged that there exists with us the offense of military treason, punishable by the laws of war.

It is so stated in the instructions of General Halleck to the then commanding officer in Tennessee, of the 8th of March, 1863. (Lawrence's Wheaton, suppt., p. 41.) But Halleck confines it to acts committed against the army of a belligerent, when occupying the territory of the enemy. And he says, what is certainly true, if such an offense can be committed, that it "is broadly distinguished from the treason defined in the constitutional and statutory laws and made punishable by the civil courts." But the term *military treason* is not to be found in any English work or military order, or, before this Rebellion, in any American authority. It has evidently been adopted during the Rebellion as a doctrine of military law, on the authority of continental writers in governments less free than those of England and the United States, and in which, because they are less free, treason is not made to consist of specific acts, and no others.

But if Halleck is right, and all our prior practice, and that of England, from whom we derive ours, is to be abandoned, the cases before you are not cases of "military treason," as he defines it. When the offenses alleged in these cases are stated to have occurred in this District, the United States were not and did not claim to be in its occupation as a belligerent, nor was it pretended that the people of this District were, in a bel ligerent sense, enemies. On the contrary, they were citizens, entitled to every right of citizenship. Nor were the parties on trial enemies. They were either citizens of the District or of Maryland, and under the protection of the Constitution. The offense charged, then, being treason, it is treason as known to the Constitution and laws, and can only be tried and punished as they provide.

To consider these parties belligerents, and their alleged offense military treason, is not only unwarranted by the authority of Halleck, but is in direct conflict with the Constitution and laws, which the President and all of us are bound to support and defend. The offense, then, being treason, as known to the Constitution, its trial by a military court is clearly illegal. And this for obvious reasons. Under the Constitution no conviction of such an offense can be had "unless on the testimony of two witnesses to the overt act, or on confess on in open court." And under the laws the parties are entitled to have "a copy of the indictment and a list of the jury and witnesses, with the names and places of abode of both, at least three entire days be ore the trial." They also have the right to challenge peremptorily thirty-five of the jury, and to challenge for cause without limitation.

And, finally, unless the indictment shall be found by a grand jury within three years next after the treason done or committed, they shall not be persecuted, tried or punished (act 30th April, 1790, 1 Stat. at large, pp. 118, 119). Upon what possible ground, therefore, can this Commission possess the jurisdiction claimed for it? It is not alleged that it is subject to the provisions stated, and in its very nature it is impossible that it should be. The very safeguards designed by the Constitution, if it has such jurisdiction, are wholly unavailing. Trial by jury in all cases our English ancestors deemed (as Story correctly tells us) "the great bulwark of their civil and political liberties, and watched with an unceasing jealousy and solicitude." It constituted one of the fundamental articles of Magna Charta, "*nullus liber homo capiatur nec imprisonetur aut exulet, aut aliquo modo, destruatur*" &c., *nisi per legale judicium parium suorum, vel per legem terrae.*" This great right the American colonists brought with them as their birthright and inheritance. It landed with them at Jamestown and on the rock of Plymouth, and was equally prized by Cavalier and Puritan, and ever since, to the breaking out of the Rebellion, has been enjoyed and esteemed the protection and proud privilege of their posterity. At times during the Rebellion it has been disregarded and denied. The momentous nature of the crisis brought about by that stupendous crime, involving us as it did the very life of the nation, has caused the people to tolerate such disregard and denial. But the crisis, thank God! has passed. The authority of the Government throughout our territorial limits is reinstated so firmly that rebelling men here and elsewhere are convinced that the danger has passed never to return.

The result proves that the principles on which the Government rests have imparted to it a vitality that will cause it to endure for all time, in spite of foreign invasion or domestic insurrection; and one of those principles, the choicest one, is the right in cases of "criminal prosecutions to a speedy and public trial by an impartial jury," and in cases of treason to the additional securities before adverted to. The great purpose of Magna Charta and the Constitution was (to quote story again) "to guard against a spirit of oppression and tyranny on the part of rulers, and against a spirit of violence and vindictiveness on the part of the people." The appeal for safety can, under such circumstances, scarcely be made by innocence, in any other manner than by the severe control of courts of justice, and be firm and impartial verdict of a jury sworn to do right, and guided solely by legal evidence and a sense of duty. In such a course there is a double security against the prejudices of judges who may partake of the wishes and opinions of the Government, and against the passions of the multitude, who may demand their victim with a clamorous precipitancy."

And Mr. Justice Backstone, with the same deep sense of its value, meets the prediction of a foreign writer, "that because Rome, Sparta, Carthage have lost their liberties, those of England in time must perish," by reminding him "that Rome, Sparta, and Carthage, at the time when their liberties were lost, were *strangers to the trial by jury.*" (3 Bla., p. 379.) That a right so valued and esteemed by our fathers to be necessary to civil liberty, so important to the very existence of a free government, was designed by them to be made to depend for its enjoyment upon the war power, or upon any power intrusted to any department of our Government, is a reflection on their intelligence and patriotism.

IV. But to proceed. The articles of war, if they provided for the punishment of the crimes on trial, and authorized such a court as this, do not include such parties as are on trial; and, until the Rebellion, I am not aware that a different construction was ever intimated. It is the exclusive fruit of the Rebellion.

The title of the act declaring the articles is "an act for establishing rules and articles for the government of the *armies of the United States.*"

The first section states that "the following shall be the rules and articles by which the armies of the United States shall be governed," and every other article, except the 56th and 57th, are in words confined to persons belonging to the army in some capacity or other. I understand it to be held by some that because such words are not used in the two articles referred to, it was the design of Congress to include persons who do not belong to the army. In my judgment, this is a wholly untenable construction; but if it was a correct one, it would not justify the use sought to be made of it. It would not bring these parties, for their alleged crimes, before a military court, known to the act, certainly not before a military commission, a court unknown to the act. The offenses charged are a traitorous conspiracy, and murder committed in pursuance of it. Neither offense, if indeed two are charged, is embraced by either the 56th or 57th articles of the statute. The 56th prohibits the relieving the enemy with money, victuals, or ammunition, or knowingly harboring and protecting him. Sophistry itself cannot bring the offenses in question under this article. The 57th prohibits only the "holding correspondence with, or giving intelligence to, the enemy, either directly or indirectly." It is equally clear that the offenses in question are not within this provision.

But, in fact, the two articles relied upon admit of no such construction as is understood to be claimed. This is thought obvious, not only from the general character of the act, and of all the other articles it contains, but because the one immediately preceding, like all those preceding and succeeding it, other than the fifty-sixth and fifty-seventh, include only persons belonging to the "armies of the United States." Its language is, "whosoever belonging to the arm.es of the United States, employed in foreign parts," shall do the act prohibited, shall suffer the prescribed punishment. Now, it is a familiar rule of interpretation, perfectly well settled in such a case, that unless there be something in the following sections that clearly shows a purpose to make them more comprehensive than their immediate predecessors, they are to be construed as subject to the same limitation. So far from there being in this instance any evidence of a different purpose, the declared object of the statute, evidenced by its title, its first section, and its general contents, are all inconsistent with any other construction.

And when to this it is considered that the power exercised by Congress in passing the statute was merely the constitutional one to make rules for the government and regulation of the army, it is doing great injustice to that department to suppose that, in exercising it, they designed to legislate for any other class,

The words, therefore, in the 5th article, "belonging to the Unfted State(," qualifying the immediate preceding word, "whosoever," are applicable to the 5th and 57th, and equa ly qualify the same word "whosoever" also used in each of them. And, finally, upon this point I am supported by the authority of Lieutenant-General Scott. The Commission have seen from my previous reference to his "Autobiography," that he placed his right to issue his martial-law order, establishing, amongst other things, military commissions to try certain offenses in a foreign country, upon the ground that otherwise they would go unpunished, and his army become demoralized. One of these offenses was murder committed or attempted, and for such an offense he tells us that the articles of war provided no court for their trial and punishment, "no matter by whom or on whom committed." And this opinion is repeated in the fourth clause of his order, as true of all the designat d offenses, "except in the very restricted case in the ninth of the articles."

V. There are other views which I submit to the serious attention of the Commission:—The mode of proceeding in a court like this, and which has been pursued by the p ro ecution with your approval, because deemed legal by both, is so inconsistent with the proceedings of civil courts, as regulated for ages by established law, that the fact, I think, demonstrates that persons not belonging to the army cannot be subjected to such a jurisdiction. 1. The character of the pleadings. The oatn use charged is a conspiracy with persons not within the reach of the court, and some of them in a foreign country, to commit the alleged crime. To give you juris liction, the design of the accused and their co-conspirators is averred to have been to aid the Rebellion, and to perfect that end, not only by the murder of the President and Lieutenant-General Grant, but of the Vice President and Secretary of State. It is further averred that the President being murdered, the Vice President becoming thereby President, and as such Commander-in-Chief, the purpose was to murder him, and, as in the contingency of the death of both, it would be the duty of the Secretary of State to cause an election to be held for President and Vice President, he was to be murdered in order to prevent a "lawful election" of these officers, and that by all these means "aid and comfort" were to be given "the insurgents engaged in armed Rebellion against the United States," and "the subversion and overthrow of the Constitution and laws of the United States" thereby effected.

That such pleadings as this would not be tolerated in a civil court, I suppose every lawyer will concede. It is argumentative, and even in that character unsound. The continuance of our Government does not depend on the lives of any or all of its public servants. As fact or law, therefore, the pleading is fatally defective. The Government has an inherent power to preserve itself, which no conspiracy to murder or murder can in the slightest degree impair. And the result which we have just witnessed proves this, and shows the folly of the madman and fiend by whose hands our late lamented President fell. He doubtless thought that he done a deed that would subvert the "Constitution and laws." We know that it had no even a tendency to that result. Not a power of the Government was suspended. All progressed as before the dire catastrophe. A cherished and almost idolized citizen was snatched from us by the assassin's arm, but there was no halt in the march of the Government. That continued in all its majesty, wholly unimpeded. The only effect was to place the nation in tears and drape it in mourning, and to awake the sympathy and excite the indignation of the world.

But this mode of pleading renders impossible the rules of evidence known to the civil courts. It justifies, in the opinion of the Judge Advocate and the Court (or what has been would not have allowed it, as in the latitude that no civil Court would allow, as in the judgment of such a court the accused, however innocent, could not be supposed able to meet it. Proof has been received not only of distinct offenses from those charged, but of such offenses committed by others than the parties on trial. Even in regard to the party himself, other offenses alleged to have been previously committed by him cannot be proved. At one time a different practice prevailed in England, and does now, it is believed, in some of the Continental Governments. But since the days of Lord Holt (a name venerated by lawyers and all admirers of enlightened jurisprudence) it has not prevailed in England. In the case of Harrison, tried before that Judge for murder, the counsel for the Government offered a witness to prove some felonious design of the prisoner three years before. Holt indignantly exclaimed, "Hold! hold! what are you doing now? How can he defend himself from charges of which he has no notice? And how many issues are to be raised to perplex me and the jury? Away! away! that ought not to be—that is nothing to the matter."—[12 State Trials, 883, 874.] I refer to this case not to assail what has been done in these cases contrary to this rule, because I am bound to infer that before such a commission as this the rule has no legal force. If in a civil court, then, these parties would be entitled to the benefit of this rule, one never departed from in such courts, they would not have had proved against them crimes alleged to have been committed by others, and having no necessary or legal connection with those charged. With the same view, and not denying the right of the Commission in the particular case I am about to refer to, but to show that the Constitution could not have designed to subject citizens to the practice, I cite the same judge to prove that in a civil court these parties could not have been legally fettered during their trial.

In the case of Cranburn, accused as implicated in the "assassination plot" on trial before the same judge, if it put an end to what Lord Campbell terms "the revolting practice of trying criminals in fetters." Fearing the clank of chains, though no complaint was made to him, he said:—' I should like to know why the prisoner is brought in ironed. Let them be instantly knocked off.' When prisoners are tried they should stand at their ease." (13 State Trials, 221, ?d Campbell Lives Chief Justices, 140). Finally, I deny the jurisdiction of the Commission, not only because me ther Constitution nor laws justify, but on the contrary repudiate it, but on the ground that all the experience of the past is against it. Jefferson, ardent in the prosecution of Burr, and solicitous for his conviction, from a firm belief of his guilt, never suggested that he should be tried before any other than a civil court. And in that trial, so ably presided over by Marshall, the prisoner was allowed to "stand at his ease," was granted every Constitutional privilege, and no evidence permitted to be given against him but such as a civil court recognizes; and in that case as in this, the overthrow of the Government was the alleged purpose; and yet it was not intimated in any quarter that he could be tried by a military tribunal.

In England, too, the doctrine on which this prosecution is placed is unknown. Attempts were made to assassinate George the Third and the present Queen, and Mr. Percival, then Prime Minister, was assassinated as he entered the House of Commons. In the two first instances the design was to murder the commander-in-chief of England's army and navy, in whom, too, the whole war power of the Government was also vested. In the last, a Secretary, clothed with powers as great at least as those that belong to our Secretary of State. And yet, in each, the parties accused were tried before a civil court, no one suggesting any other. And during the period of the French Revolution, when its principles, if principles they can be termed, were being inculcated to an extent that alarmed the Government, and caused it to exert every power it possessed to frustrate their effect, when the writ of habeas corpus was suspended, and arrests and prosecutions resorted to almost without limit, no one suggested a trial except in the civil courts.

And yet the apprehension of the Government was that the object of the alleged conspirators was to subvert its authority, bring about its overthrow, and subject the kingdom to the horrors of the French Revolution, then shocking the nations of the world. Hardy, Foster and others were tried by civil courts, and their names remembered for the principles of freedom that were made triumphant mainly by the efforts of "that great (in the words of a modern English statesman) genius, Lord Russell, whose sword and buckler protected justice and freedom during the disastrous period," having "the tongue of Cicero and the soul of Hampden, an invincible orator and an undaunted patriot"—Erskine. As it was these trials were conducted with so relentless a spirit, and, it was thought, with such disregard of the rights of the subject, that the administration of the day were not able to withstand the torrent of the people's indignation. What would have been the fate, individually as well as politically, if the cases had been taken before a military commission and life taken.

Can it be that an American citizen is not entitled to all the rights that belong to a British subject? Can it be that, with us, Executive power at times casts into the shade and renders all other power subordinate? An American statesman, with a world-wide reputation, long since gave an answer to these inquiries. In a debate in the Senate of the United States, in which he assailed what he deemed an unwarranted assumption of Executive power, he said, "the first object of a free people is the preservation of their liberties, and liberty is only to be maintained by constitutional restraints and just divisions of political power." It does not trust the amiable weaknesses of human nature, and therefore will, not permit power to overstep its prescribed limits, though benevolence, good intent and patriotic intent came along with it. And he added, "Mr. President, the contest for ages has been to rescue liberty from the grasp of executive power." "In the long list of the champions of human freedom there is not one name dimmed by the reproach of advocating the extension of Executive authority.

Though, eloquently expressed, appeal with subduing power to every patriotic heart, and demonstrate that Webster, if here, would be heard raising his mighty voice against the jurisdiction of this Commission—a jurisdiction placed upon Executive authority alone. But it has been urged, also, that martial law warrants such a commission and that such law prevails here. The doctrine is believed to be alike indefensible and dangerous. It is not, however, necessary to inquire whether martial law, if it did prevail, would maintain your jurisdiction, as it does not prevail. It has never been declared by any competent authority, and the civil courts, we know, are in full and undisturbed exercise of all their functions. We learn, and the fact is doubtless true, that one of the parties, the very chief of the alleged conspiracy, has been indicted and is about to be tried before one of those Courts. If this, the alleged head and front of the conspiracy, is to be, and can be so tried, upon what ground of right, of fairness, or of policy, can the parties who are charged to have been his mere instruments, be deprived of the same mode of trial? It may be said that, in acting under this commission, you are but conforming to an order of the President, which you are bound to obey. Let me examine this for a moment. If that order merely authorizes you to investigate the cases and report the facts to him, and not to pronounce a judgment, and if to that extent legal, then it is because the President has the power himself, without such proceeding, to punish the crime, and has only invoked your assistance to enable him to do it the more justly.

Can this be so? Can it be that the life of a citizen, however humble, depends in any case on the mere will of the President? And yet it does, if the doctrine be sound. What more dangerous one can be imagined? Crime is defined by law, and is to be tried and punished under the law. What is murder, treason or conspiracy, and what is admissible evidence to prove either, are all legal questions, and many of them oftimes difficult of correct solution. What the facts are may also present difficult inquiries. To pass upon the first the Constitution provides courts, consisting of judges selected for legal knowledge, and made independent of Executive power. Military judges are not so selected, and, so far from being independent, are absolutely dependent on such power. To pass upon the latter it provides juries, as not being likely to "partake of the wishes and opinions of the Government." But if your function is only to act as aids to the President, to enable him to exercise his function of punishment, and, as he is under no obligation, by any law, to call for such aid, he may try and punish upon his own unassisted judgment, and without even the form of a trial. In conclusion then, gentlemen, I submit that your responsibility, whatever that be, for error, in a proceeding like this, can find no protection in Presidential authority. Whatever it be, it grows out of the laws and may through the laws be enforced. I suggested in the outset of these remarks that that responsibility in one contingency may be momentous. I recur to it again, disclaiming as I did at first the wish or hope that it would cause you to be wanting in a single particular of what you may believe to be your duty, but to obtain your best and most matured judgment. The wish and hope disclaimed would be alike idle and discourteous; and I trust the Commission will do me the justice to believe that I am incapable of falling into either fault.

Responsibility to personal danger can never alarm soldiers who have faced, and will ever be willing in their country's defense to face death on the battlefield. But there is a responsibility that every gentleman, be he soldier or citizen, will constantly hold before him and make him ponder, responsibility to the Constitution and laws of his country and an intelligent public opinion, and prevent his doing anything knowingly that can justly subject him to the censure of either. I have said that your responsibility is great. If the commission under which you act is void and confers no authority, whatever you do may involve the most serious personal liability. Cases have occurred that prove this. It is sufficient to refer to one. Joseph Wall, at the time of the offence charged against him was committed, was Governor and Commander of the garrison of Goree, a dependency of England, in Africa. The indictment was for the murder of Benj. Armstrong, and the trial was had in January, 1802, before a special court, consisting of Sir Archibald McDonald, chief baron of the Exchequer, Lawrence, of the King's Bench; and Rooke, of the Common Pleas. The prosecution was conducted by Law, then Attorney General, afterwards Lord Ellenborough. The crime was committed in 1782, and under a military order of the accused and the sentence of regimental court-martial. The defense relied upon was that at the time the garrison was in a state of mutiny, and that the deceased took a prominent part in it. That because of the mutiny the order for the court-martial was made, and that the punishment which was inflicted, and said to have caused the death, was under its sentence. The offense was purely a military one, and belonged to the jurisdiction of a military court. If the facts relied upon by the accused were true, and its judgment constituted a valid defense.

The court, however, charged the jury that if they found that there was no mutiny to justify such a court-martial, or its sentence, they were void and furnish no defence whatever. The jury so finding, found the accused guilty, and he was soon after executed. (2 St. Tr. 16.75). The application of the principle of this case to the question I have considered is obvious. In that instance, want of jurisdiction in the court-martial was held to be fatal to its judgment as a defence for the death that ensued under it. In this, if the Commission has no jurisdiction, its judgment, for the same reason, will be of no avail, either to Judges, Secretary of War, or President, if either shall be called to a responsibility for what may be done under it.

Again, upon the point of jurisdiction I beg leave to add that the opinion I have endeavored to maintain is believed to be the almost unanimous opinion of the profession, and certainly is of every judge or court who has expressed any.

In Maryland, where such commissions have been and are held, the Judge of the Criminal Court of Baltimore recently made it a matter of special charge to the grand jury. Judge Bond told them:—"It has come to my knowledge that here, where the United States Court, presided over by Chief Justice Chase, has always been unimposed, and where the Marshal of the United States, appointed by the President, selects the jurors, irresponsible and unlawful military commissions attempt to exercise criminal jurisdiction over citizens of this State, not in the military or naval service of the United States, nor in the militia, who are charged with offenses either not known to the law, or with crimes for which the mode of trial and punishment are provided by statute in the courts of the land. That it is not done by the paramount authority of the United States, your attention is directed to Article V of the Constitution of the United States, which says:—'No person shall be held to answer for a capital or otherwise infamous crime unless on a presentment or indictment of a grand jury, except in cases arising in the land or naval forces, or in the militia, when in actual service in time of war or public danger. Such persons, exercising such unlawful jurisdiction, are liable to indictment by you as well as responsible in civil actions to the parties.' In New York, Judge Peckman, of the Supreme Court of that State, and speaking for the whole bench, charged their Grand Jury as follows:—

'The Constitution of the United States, Article 5, of the amendments, declares that 'no person shall be held to answer for a capital or otherwise infamous crime, unless on presentment or indictment of a grand jury, except in cases arising in the land or naval forces, or in the militia, when in actual service, in time of war or public danger.'

'Article 6 declares that in all criminal prosecutions the accused shall enjoy the right to a speedy and public trial.'

'Article 3, Section 2, declares that 'the trial of all crimes, except in cases of impeachment, shall be by jury,' &c.

'These provisions were made for occasions of great excitement, no matter from what cause, when passion rather than reason might prevail.

'In ordinary times there would be no occasion for such guards, as there would be no disposition to depart from the usual and established modes of trial.

'A great crime has lately been committed, that has shocked the civilized world. Every right-minded man desires the punishment of the criminals; but he desires that punishment to be administered according to law, and through the judicial tribunals of the country. No star-chamber court, no secret inquisition in this nineteenth century, can ever be made acceptable to the American mind.

'If none but the guilty could be accused, then no trial could be necessary; execution should follow accusation.

'It is almost a necessary that the public should have undoubted faith in the purity of criminal justice, as it is that justice should in fact be administered with integrity.

'Grave doubts, to say the least, exist in the minds of intelligent men as to the constitutional right of the per cent military commissions at Washington to sit in judgment upon the persons now on trial for their lives before that tribunal. Thoughtful men feel aggrieved that such a commission should be established in this free country when the war is over, and when the common law courts are open and accessible to administer justice according to law, without fear or favor.

'What remedy exists? None whatever, except through the power of public sentiment.

'As citizens of this free country, having an interest in its prosperity and good name, we may, as I desire to do, in all courtesy and kindness, and with all proper respect, express our disapprobation of this course in our rulers at Washington.

'The unanimity with which the leading press of our land has condemned this mode of trial ought to be gratifying to every patriot.

'Every citizen is interested in the preservation, in their purity, of the institutions of his country, and you, gentlemen, may make such presentment on this subject, if any, as your judgment may dictate.'

The reputation of both of these judges is well and favorably known, and their authority entitled to the greatest deference.

Even in France, during the Consulship of Napoleon, the institution of a military commission for the trial of the prisoner, Duc d'Enghien, for an alleged conspiracy against his life, was, to the irreparable injury of his reputation, ordered by Napoleon. The trial was had, and the Prince at once convicted and executed. It brought upon Napoleon the condemnation of the world, and is one of the blackest spots in his character. The case of the Duke, says the eminent historian of "The Consulate and the Empire," furnished Napoleon "a happy opportunity of saving his glory from a stain," which he lost, and adds, with philosophic truth, that it was "a deplorable consequence of violating the ordinary powers of justice." And further adds:—"To defend social order by conforming to the strict rules and powers of justice, without allowing any feeling of revenge to operate, is the great lesson to be drawn from these tragical events." (Vol. 4, Thiers' History, &c., pp. 318, 322).

Upon the whole, then, I think I shall not be considered obtrusive if I again invoke the court to weigh well all that I have thought it my duty to argue upon them. I feel the duty to be upon me as a citizen sworn to do all that I can to preserve the Constitution and the principles on which it rests. As counsel of one of the parties, I should esteem myself dishonored if I attempted to rescue my client from a proper trial for the offense charged against her by denying the jurisdiction of the Commission upon grounds that I did not conscientiously believe to be sound; and in what I have done I have not more had in view the defense of Mrs. Surratt than of the Constitution and the laws. In my view in this respect her cause is the cause of every citizen; and let it not be supposed that I am seeking to secure impunity to any who may have been guilty of the horrid crimes of the night of the 14th of April. Over these the civil courts of this District have ample jurisdiction and will faithfully exercise it if the cases are remitted to them, and, if guilt is legally established, will surely award the punishment known to the laws. God forbid that such crimes should go unpunished.

In the black catalogue of offenses, these will forever be esteemed the darkest and deepest ever committed by sinning man. And, in common with the civilized world, do I wish that every legal punishment may be legally inflicted upon all who participated in them. A word more, gentlemen, and thanking you for your kind attention, I shall have done. As you have discovered, I have not remarked on the evidence in the case of Mrs. Surratt, nor is it my purpose. But it is proper that I refer to her case in particular for a single moment. That a woman, well educated, and, as far as we can judge from all her past life, as we have it in evidence, a devout Christian, ever kind, affectionate, and charitable, with no motive disclosed to us that could have caused a total change in her very nature, could have participated in the crimes in question it is almost impossible to believe.

Such a belief can only be forced upon a reasonable unsuspecting, unprejudiced mind by direct and uncontradicted evidence, coming from pure and perfectly unsuspected sources. Have we these? Is the evidence uncontradicted. Are the two witnesses, Weichman and Lloyd, pure and unsuspected. Of the particulars of their evidence I say nothing. They will be brought before you by my associates. But this conclusion in regard to those witnesses must have in the minds of the court, and is certainly strongly impressed upon my own, that if the facts which they themselves state as to their connection and intimacy with Booth and Payne are true, their knowledge of the purpose to commit the crimes and their participation in them, is much more satisfactorily established than the alleged knowledge and participation of Mrs. Surratt. As for, gentlemen, as I am concerned, her case is now in your hands. REVERDY JOHNSON.

June 16, 1865.

As associate counsel for Mrs. Mary E. Surratt, we concur in the above.

FREDERICK A. AIKEN,
JOHN W. CLAMPITT.

Mr. F. Stone's Argument.

F. Stone, Esq., counsel for Harold, being necessarily absent, the argument prepared by him was read by Mr. James J. Murphy, one of the official reporters of the Court. It commences by saying that at the earnest request of the widowed mother and estimable sisters of the accused he had consented to act as counsel. After denying the jurisdiction of this Court the counsel says the charge in this case consists of several distinct and separate offenses embodied in one charge. The parties accused are charged with a conspiracy in aid of the Rebellion, with murder, with assault with intent to kill, and with lying in wait. It is extremely doubtful, from the language of the charge and the specification, under which or the following crimes the accused, Harold, is arraigned and now on his trial, viz.:

First. Whether he is on trial for the crime of conspiracy to overthrow the Government of the United States, or punishable by the Act of the Congress of the United States, passed the 31st of July, 1861; or, second, whether he is on his trial for giving aid and comfort to the Rebellion as punishable by the Act of Congress passed the 13th of July, 1862; or, third, whether he is on trial for aiding or abetting the murder of Abraham Lincoln, President of the United States. His counsel well understands the legal definition of the crimes above mentioned, but does not understand that either to the common law or to the laws of war is known any one offense composed of the three crimes mentioned in the charge. He knows of no one crime of a conspiracy to murder and an actual murder, all in aid of the Rebellion, distinct and separate from the well-known and defined crimes of murder, of conspiracy in aid of the Rebellion as defined by the Act of Congress. It is extremely doubtful from the language of this charge, whether the murder of the President of the United States is not referred to as to the mere means by which the conspirators gave aid and comfort to the Rebellion; whether it was not merely the overt act by which the crime of aiding the Rebellion was completed.

First. As to the crime of conspiracy, the counsel, after reviewing the testimony for the Government, says:—These facts would probably convict fifty people, but they do not give either separately or collectively the slightest evidence that this boy, Harold, ever conspired with Booth and others in aid of the Rebellion and for the overthrow of the Government of the United States. They show nothing that might not have occurred to any one perfectly innocent.

The term "confidential communication" is the witness' (Weichman's) own construction. He meant only to say that the three were talking together that after leaving the theatre, where they had been, they stopped and went into a restaurant, and that he felt then there talking together near a store. So much for the conspiracy. Of the fact that this boy Harold was an aider and abettor in the escape of Booth there is no rational or reasonable doubt. He was clearly guilty of that crime, and must abide by its consequences; but the accused, by his counsel, altogether denies that he was guilty of the murder of Abraham Lincoln, or that he aided or abetted in such murder, as set forth in the specification and charge; but though Booth exercised unlimited control over this miserable boy, body and soul, he found him unfit for deeds of blood and violence. He was cowardly; he was too weak and trifling, but still he could be made useful.

He knew some of the roads through lower Maryland and Booth persuaded him to act as a guide, postboy and companion. This accounts for their companionship. There was one piece of evidence introduced by the Government that should be weighed by the Commission. It is the declaration of Booth made at the time of his capture. "I declare before my Maker this man is innocent." Booth knew well enough at the time he made that declaration that his hours, if not his minutes, were numbered. There is no evidence that Harold procured, counseled, commanded or abetted Booth to assassinate the President of the United States. The feeble aid that he could render to any enterprise was rendered in accompanying and aiding Booth in his flight, and nothing beyond. That itself is a grave crime and it carries with it appropriate punishment.

The counsel concludes the defense with a quotation from "Burnett on Military Law and Courts-martial," where the punishment for particular offenses are not fixed by law, but left discretionary with the Courts. The above mandate of the Constitution must be directly kept in view, and the benign influence of a mandate from a still higher law ought not to be ignored, and that justice should be tempered with mercy.

The elaborate argument, of which the above is a mere notice, is signed by F. Stone, counsel for D. C. Harold.

Mr. Cox next offered his argument in behalf of Arnold and O'Laughlin.

Mr. Cox's Argument.

He said that for himself, execrating as he did the odious crime wrought upon the Chief Magistrate of the nation, he would not have been willing to connect his name with this defense until he felt assured that the accused was merely the victim of compromising appearances, and was wholly innocent of the great offense. The evidence, he contended, showed that even if these two accused were even beguiled for a moment to listen to the suggestions of this restless schemer, Booth, yet there is no blood on their hands, and they are wholly guiltless of all previous knowledge of the participation in that "arch demon of malice" which plunged the nation into mourning.

Both the accused and their counsel have in this trial labored under disadvantages not incident to the civil courts and courts-martial. The accused receives not only a copy of the charge or indictment in time to prepare his defense, but also a list of the witnesses with whom he is to be confronted; and in the civil courts it is usual for the prosecution to state in advance the general nature of the charge he expects to establish and the general scope of the evidence he expects to adduce.

The crime was laid at Washington. The purlieus of Montreal and Toronto had been searched; the city of New York was examined; the sea had been encompassed, and Western waters and yellow fever hospitals had been visited, and this eccentric career had terminated in a New York wood. (Laughter.)

In this case the accused were aroused from their slumbers on the night before their arraignment, and for the first time presented with a copy of the charge. For the most part they were unable to procure counsel until the trial had commenced; and when counsel were admitted they came to the discharge of their duties in utter ignorance of the whole case which they were to combat, except as they could gather from the general language of the charge, as well as for the most part wholly unacquainted with the prisoners and their antecedents; and the consequence is that the earlier witnesses for the Government were allowed to depart with little or no cross-examination, which subsequent events showed was of vital importance to elicit the truth and reduce their vagaries of statements to more of accuracy; and he would add that this testimony has consisted of statements of informer s and accomplices, always suspicious, brought from remote places, whose antecedents and character it is impossible for the prisoners to trace. He was constrained further to notice the manner in which the trial has been conducted. The accused were arraigned upon a single charge. It described one offense of some kind, but however specific in form it seems to have been intended to fit every conceivable form of crime which the wickedness of men can devise. The crime is located at Washington, yet we have been carried to the purlieus of Toronto and Montreal, have skirted the borders of New York and Vermont, touching at Ogdensburg and St. Albans, have passed down the St. Lawrence, and out to sea, inspected our ocean shipping, have visited the fever hospitals of the British isles, and have returned to the prison pen of Andersonville, and seen the camp at Belle Isle, and the historical Libby, and penetrated the secret councils of Richmond, have passed thence to the hospitals of the West, and ascended the Mississippi, and at length terminated this eccentric career in the *woods* of New York. Under a charge against the prisoners of conspiring to kill the President and others, in Washington, Jefferson Davis and his associates have been tried, and in the judgment of many, convicted of starving, poisoning, arson, and other crimes too numerous to mention. He had apprehended that the counsel for the accused would appear in a false position by their apparent acquiescence in this wide range of inquiry, and, therefore, felt it due to himself, at least, to explain. For his part, he felt no interest whatever in insisting on the exposure of the misdeeds of the Rebel authorities and agents. His only concern has been to show that his clients had nothing to do with the conspiracy set forth in the charge. To the best of his ability he had scrutinized the evidence of that conspiracy so far as necessary to their defense. With regard to other matters foreign to this issue, he had to say, in the first place, the charge was artfully framed with a view to admit them in evidence. It imputes that the accused conspired with Jefferson Davis and others, to kill and murder the President, &c., with intent to aid and comfort the insurgents, &c., and thereby aid in the subversion and overthrow of the constitution and laws of the United States; and on the principle that other acts constituting distinct offenses, were sometimes admitted as proof of intent, these subjects, foreign to the main issue, have been put in evidence. By no possible ingenuity can these foreign matters be used to the prejudice of the accused. He had supposed that the object of introducing them was to bring to the public, in the shape of sworn testimony, information of the practices of the Rebel leaders, to which, however irregular the proceedings, he had no objection to interpose. He could not, for a moment, suppose that the object was to inflame prejudice against the accused, because of their supposed remote connection with the authors of all these evils, and, for want of higher victims, to make them the scape goats for all the other atrocities imputed to the Rebellion; to annihilate them, to hush the clamors of the public for a victim, or to appease the Nemesis that has recorded the secrets of the Southern prison houses, or the deadly deeds wrought by fire and pestilence.

In regard to the issue before the Commission he had intended to confine himself to a simple review of the evidence, but the anomalous character of the charge, the uncertainty with which they were left with reference to the positions to be taken by the Government, and the general course of the investigation pursued, admonished him that he should present some legal considerations at least of a general character.

Assuming for argument sake that the Court has jurisdiction to try the accused upon this charge, he proceeded to discuss the power and limits of that jurisdiction and the mode in which it is to be executed, submitting some general reflections upon the character of the offenses set forth in the charge and specification, as they are known to and punishable by the civil law of the land; and proceeded to argue how far this Commission in dealing with them was to be guided and restrained by that law.

Mr. Cox, in his analysis of the crimes charged, said that below the grade of treason crimes are ranged under two general heads, viz., felonies and misdemeanors, and proceeded to point out in the question of a conspiracy to commit a felony and then with a conspiracy to commit treason, and the nice proceeded to take up the question of unexecuted conspiracy and the case of a party involved in a conspiracy who shall withdraw from it, contending that he is not responsible for any act done by the others in prosecution of the objects of the conspiracy.

Afterwards these and other points in this connection were presented by Mr. Cox, with a large array of citations from legal authorities. The question how far tribunals sitting by virtue of martial law, can depart from the established law of the land, in its distinction between crime and its scale of punishments, was dealt with at considerable length. Mr. Cox then proceeded

to examine the evidence so far as was material to his case, and claimed in b's analysis of proof that no active design against the life of the President was on foot between January and the early part of April, and further, from the evidence of the Government, that during that interval, Booth was contriving an entirely different project, the capture of the President and others.

It further appeared that the project was abandoned, and that the abandonment is fixed by facts referred to by Booth, to wit—the defection of some of the parties, the sale of horses, &c; and that the date is ascertained to have been about the middle of March. Now, it is clear that if any connection is shown between Booth on one hand, and O'Laughlin and Arnold on the other, it existed only during the period when the absurd project of capture was agitated, and terminated with that. Their fitful stay in Washington was only between February 10 and March 18. By Arnold's confession it would appear that if he is not mistaken, O'Laughlin attended one meeting about the middle of March, to consider the plan of capture; but so inimaterial was the plan, and so slight his connection with it, that he did not even know the names of the others at the meetings—two in number—besides Booth, Surratt and Atzeroth.

At that meeting the scheme fell through, and he and O'Laughlin immediately afterwards left for Baltimore. Booth told him he might sell the arms he had given him; and in fact it is proved that he gave part of them away shortly after this. His confession as to O'Laughlin proves nothing but his presence at this single meeting. This was the beginning and end of their connection with Booth in any scheme whatever of a political character, and in this it is evident that he was the arch contriver and they the dupes; and when they had escaped his influence, although he still evidently clung to his design, and telegraphed, and wrote, and called to see them, it is evident that they refused to heed the voice of the charmer, "charm he never so wisely." From O'Laughlin he received no response at all; from Arnold only the letter offered in evidence. There are expressions in the letter which look to a continued renewal of their relations in the future, but they were employed to party his importunities for the present. Certainly all connection ceased from that time. If, therefore, any conspiracy at all be proved by the utmost latitude of evidence against those two accused, it was a mere unenacted, stillborn scheme, scarce conceived before it was abandoned; of a nature wholly different from the offense described in this charge. the proof of which does not sustain this charge, and of which the accused could not be convicted upon this trial. For this Court is bound by the rules of evidence which prevails in others; and one of the most important is that the proof must correspond with the charge of indictment, and show the same offense, or the accused is entitled to acquittal; and there is no evidence which connects these two accused with that dreadful conspiracy which forms the subject of this charge. There is nothing to show that during their brief intercourse with Booth, at Washington, that nefarious design was agitated at all; certainly none that it was ever disclosed to them. And if such conspiracy had any existence it was in a state of slumbered suspense, awaiting that sanction without which it had no motive, end, aim or life.

Mr. Cox contended that the following conclusions were established, viz:—

First. That the accused, Samuel Arnold and Michael O'Laughlin, had no part whatever in the execution of the conspiracy set forth in this charge and its specifications.

Second. That if they were implicated in such conspiracy, they withdrew from and abandoned it, while yet wholly unexecuted and resting merely in intention, and are not responsible for any of the acts subsequently done in pursuance of it.

Third. That there is no legal and competent evidence implicating O'Laughlin in any conspiracy whatever, and implicating either O'Laughlin or Arnold in the conspiracy charged.

Fourth. That if there is any evidence against them of any conspiracy, it is of one wholly different from that set forth in the charge and specification, and upon these they must be wholly acquitted.

He therefore claimed for them an absolute and unqualified acquittal. That the accused were wrong in ever joining the Rebellion against their Government no one will deny. But it would be to insult the intelligence of this Court to waste time in showing that this Court are not sitting in judgment on all the errors in the lives of these accused, but to decide the single question, whether they are guilty of conspiring to kill and murder the President, Vice President, Secretary of State and the General in command of the armies of the United States, and of the acts charged against them severally in purauance of said conspiracy.

The Court adjourned till to-morrow afternoon, when it is expected arguments in the case of Spangler and others will be read.

Early in the day Mrs. Surratt was compelled to be taken from the Court-room, owing to severe sickness.

WASHINGTON, June 20.—The Court met at 2 o'clock, when Mr. Ewing read his argument in favor of the accused, Edward Spangler, reviewing at length all the testimony bearing upon the particular case filed. Spangler, it had been shown, seemed to have a great admiration for Booth, who excelled in all the manly sports, and witnesses had also testified that Spangler's character was that of a peaceful, good-natured, kind and harmless man. Spangler was the drudge for Booth, sometimes taking care and feeding the latter's horse. Booth, out of courtesy, had access to the theatre whenever it was open. In calling attention to the relations between Spangler and Booth, Mr. Ewing desired to mark the fact that in all the testimony as to the latter's meetings, associations and acts done and things said, there was not the slightest indication that Spangler ever met Booth except in the theatre, and there was nothing to show that Spangler had any intimation of Booth's purpose, or even innocently helped him to effect it.

It appeared from the testimony for the prosecution that there were found in Spangler's carpet-bag a rope eighty-one feet long, some letter paper and a shirt collar. It was shown that just such ropes were used at the theatre for hoisting borders to scenes, hauling up timber to the top dressing rooms, etc. This rope had been produced by the Government as proof against Spangler, but from the testimony of persons employed in the theatre it appeared that Spangler stole the rope for a crab-line. In the devilish scheme of Booth his rope certainly was not to be used as a lariat or a halter. If it was intended for such a purpose it would have been kept at the theatre, and not at his boarding house in a carpet-bag.

Mr. Ewing was not bound to show what Spangler was going to do with the shirt collar and letter paper.

The counsel next examined the testimony in relation to the box occupied by the late President, relating by a reference to the evidence things which had been said concerning Spangler in that connection. The acts of preparation for the assassination were performed by Booth himself, when he had previously occupied the same box. If Booth had a confederate in Spangler, the boring of the hole in the door and the door brace would have been made with Spangler's carpenter tools. The hole had first been bored with a gimlet and then enlarged with a penknife; these acts of preparation were mere drudgery, which Spangler would have been called upon to do if he had been in conspiracy with Booth. That Booth did both and Spangler neither, showed that Spangler was not in the plot when the preparations were made. Mr. Ewing alluded to the testimony that Booth came to the back of the theatre at nine o'clock on the night of the 14th of April, and said, "Ned, you help me all you can't to which Spangler is represented as answering, "Oh, yes!"

This testimony was contradicted by the responsible utility man and other witnesses. But grant that Spangler did make the reply, it must have been in a loud tone to be heard by the witness. As there was no previous testimony showing the slightest act or arrangement of conspiracy on the part of Spangler, the reply of Spangler should be treated as nothing but the reply of a drudge to his superior and not knowing the intent of the question. If Spangler was to have helped Booth, he would have got a substitute to shove the scenes, and after the pistol shot to have opened the door for the escape of the assassin. If Spangler had been in league with Booth, would he, as has been testified, have stood motionless and leave Booth to the hazard of flight unaided? And would Spangler himself have run for water after he heard that somebody had been shot? If Booth made use of that language to Spangler and Spangler thus replied, the latter could have known nothing of a criminal purpose. If Spangler had any specific part to play, it was to hold Booth's horse. He failed to do that and remained on the stage. The evidence did not show that he was a party to the crime. Booth came to the house with his horse but once that night, and thus Booth could have had no previous opportunity to communicate with him, that night. Weichman's testimony is unsupported by the other evidence and is inconsistent with it. The fact that Booth knocked the horse holder down on emerging from the theatre shows that Booth, who naturally supposed it was Spangler he was thus striking, had no complicity with Spangler. Booth thought it was Spangler, and not "Peanuts," who held his horse, for Booth had just rushed out from the glare of gaslight into the darkness. Another item was produced to show that Spangler knew of Booth's purposes. Sergeant Dye testified as to seeing a roughly dressed man in front of the theatre with whom Booth whispered before entering the theatre and previous to the assassination of the President. This man, it was said, had a black moustache, but it had been proven that Spangler on that night wore no such moustache. If he had been in front of the theatre with a black moustache, red as his hair is, the visitors to the theatre would have had their attention drawn to his grotesque appearance.

Spangler could not have been absent from the stage from twenty-five to thirty minutes past nine to ten minutes past ten without being missed, for it was his business to shove the scenes. If he could not have been absent three quarters of an hour without attracting attention, and an alibi was clearly proved he was not only not in front of the theatre, but, at half-past nine o'clock, was opposite the door at which the murderer escaped, and least able to help the villian's flight. Spangler was on the stage for an hour up to the time of the assassination. Having presented all the evidence bearing upon the acts done and words spoken by Spangler up to that time, Mr. Ewing proceeded to discuss his conduct until his arrest, on the 17th of April, at his boarding house, where he had lived for five or six months, during the three days and nights intervening between the assassination and the arrest nothing was done by Spangler which did not indicate a conscious sense of innocence.

He felt confident in the assertion that Booth had no accomplice. He did not need any. Booth had pl'yed at that theatre, and by courtesy had free admittance; therefore he had made his own preparations. The leap from the box to the stage was one which might have been made by any man with safety. Had not his spur caught in the flag Booth would have made the leap with ease. The counsel was confident that Booth needed no help, but some one to hold his horse, which "Peanut John" did and he opened and shut the door for himself. It appeared from the testimony of Mr. Hess, the manager of a rival theatre, that Booth inquired particularly of him whether Grover's theatre was to be illuminated, and whether the President was invited on the occasion. From the testimony as to Booth's inquiries it seems clear that the assassination of the President would have been attempted at Grover's theatre had the President attended that house on the night of the illumination.

Mr. Ewing examined at length other parts of the testimony, and concluded by saying he could see in the evidence no such suspicion as would induce a grand jury to present Spangler for trial, and he believed a candid review of the entire subject would leave in the minds of but very few a reasonable doubt of his innocence.

Colonel Doster stated that he would be prepared to read the argument for Payne to-morrow.

General Howe said that the Court has already extended the time for the arguments. If they were all not present to-morrow let the remainder be filed. With these delays they might not get through till autumn.

General Aiken said he was willing to grant all the time the counsel asked to prepare their arguments on subjects of this importance.

General Hunter said the testimony was very voluminous.

Mr. Ewing remarked the labor of preparation was greater than was supposed; it would be out of his power to prepare Dr. Mudd's defense before Friday, as there were two hundred and fifty pages of evidence in that case.

The Court voted to grant an extension of time for the preparation of the remaining arguments, and then adjourned till noon to-morrow.

WASHINGTON, June 21.—Court being called to order Mr. Doster, counsel for Payne and Atzeroth, proceeded to read his argument in behalf of Payne. There are three things, he said, in the case of the prisoner Payne, which are admitted beyond cavil or dispute:—

1st. That he is the person who attempted to take the life of the Secretary of State.

2d. That he is not within the medical definition of insanity.

3d. That he believed what he was doing was right and justifiable.

The questions as to his identity and sanity are therefore settled, and among the things of the past, and the sole remaining question is, "How far shall his convictions serve to mitigate his punishment?" He used the word punishment deliberately, and with the consciousness that in so doing he admitted that if the prisoner is a responsible being, he ought to be punished, and he said it because he could not allow his duties as counsel to interfere with his convictions as a man so far as to make him blind to the worth of the life of a distinguished citizen, and to the awful consequences of an attempt to take it away. If, indeed, such an attempt should be allowed to go without rebuke, then it seemed to him the office is but a perilous exposure to violence, the highest compensation for public service is the distinction which follows assassination, and then our public servants are but pitiable and defenseless offerings to sedition; and surely if any public servant deserved to be excepted from that fate it was the illustrious and sagacious statesman who, during a long life of arduous service, has steadfastly checked all manner of faction and public discontent; who, in the darkest days of discord, has prophesied the triumph of concord, and who at all times has been more ready to apply antidotes than the knife to the nation's wounds. That we may accurately and as fully as the occasion demands understand the convictions of the prisoner, the counsel proceeds to give a sketch of his life, the customs under which he was reared, and the education which he received.

Lewis Payne Powell is the son of Rev. George C Powell, a Baptist minister, at present supposed to live at Live Oak Station, on the railroad between Jacksonville and Tallahassee, in the State of Florida, and was born in Alabama, in the year 1845. Besides himself his father had six daughters and two sons. He lived for some time in Worth and Stewart counties, Georgia, and in 1859 moved to Florida. At the breaking out of the war, but four years ago, the prisoner was a lad of sixteen engaged in superintending his father's plantation and a number of slaves.

We may safely presume that, occupied in the innocent pursuits of country life, he daily heard the precepts of the Gospel from his father, and that in the society of his sisters the hardy life of a planter was softened by the charms of a refined and religious circle, and that in the natural course of events he would be to-day as he was then, a farmer and an honest man. But in 1861 war broke out—war, the scourge and pestilence of the race. The signal, which spread like a fire, was not long in reaching Live Oak station.

His two brothers enlisted, and Lewis, though but sixteen, enlisted in Captain Stuart's Company, in the Second Florida Infantry, commanded by Colonel Ward, and was ordered to Richmond. Mr. Doster proceeded to consider what, in the eyes of this Florida boy, was the meaning of the war, and what the thoughts that drove him from a pleasant home to the field of arms.

The Counsel pictured in vivid language, the auspices under which Powell was trained in a slave community, where it was the custom to defend the institution of slavery in meeting-houses, at political gatherings, and in family prayers, where it was the practice to whip and burn men who preached against the institution, and to hunt fugitives with bloodhounds, and also those who helped them to freedom. In the eyes of the lad the war meant to abolish this custom and upheave society from its foundations. His inheritance was to be dissipated, his vassals equal, his laws invaded, his religion confounded, his politics a heresy. For this the lad was going to fight: in the defense of a social system. He was going to fight in behalf of the traditional precept of the State—to defend State rights. For a third reason, he was going to fight to show that he was a better man than the Northerners, under the deep conviction prevailing in his section that their blood and breeding were better than that of Northerners. The fourth reason was to repel invasion. These were his incentives. But he had been schooled and trained to war by the bowie-knife and pistol code of honor prevalent there.

The counsel asks whether in the wide world there is another school in which the prisoner could so well have been trained for assassination as in this slavaocracy? Mr. Doster proceeds to argue that in this prisoner is to be found the legitimate moral offspring of slavery, State Rights, chivalry and delusion, and then goes on to inquire if we, as the American people, are not responsible for the wicked school in which he was educated, and if we will determine to destroy him because he learned but as we instructed.

But there is another school before him; the school of war at Richmond. His regiment joined the army of General Lee, and was joined to A. P. Hill's Corps. With it he passed through the Peninsula campaign and the battles of Chancellorsville and Antietam. Here he heard that his two brothers had been killed at the battle of Murfreesboro'. Finally, on the 3d of July, 1863, in the charge upon the Federal centre at Gettysburg, he was wounded, taken prisoner, and detailed as a nurse in a Pennsylvania Hospital. The demoralizing effect of his two years' campaigning as a private in the army, which he entered as a boy of sixteen, is shown.

He is one of that army who made baskets and cups out of the bones of Union soldiers, who starved their prisoners, who plundered the dead, who slew men after surrender, and who were commanded by officers who had violated their oaths to the United States; an army that believed any means justifiable that helped the cause of Southern Independence; and, finally, an army that held the person and Cabinet of the President of the United States in holy execration.

This is the horrible demoralization of civil war, and on those responsible for this war should rest the responsibility of the acts of this plastic boy, who came into the world in the year of the annexation of Texas, has lived but four administrations, and is younger than the last compromise with slavery. He is the moral product of the war, and belongs to those who first begun it. How does he differ from the other Rebel soldiers?

The best Rebel soldiers have fired at Mr. Lincoln and Mr. Seward; have approached the city by stealth from Baltimore, and aimed to destroy the Government by a sudden blow; so did he. The best Rebel soldiers have picked off high officers of the Government—Kearney, Stevens, Baker, Wadsworth, Lyon, Sedgwick; so did he. What, then, has he done that every Rebel soldier has not tried to do?

Only this; he has ventured more, he has shown a higher courage and a better hate; a more ready sacrifice. He has aimed at the head of a Department instead of the head of a Corps. To us the President appeared as the savior of a nation from civil war, and Mr. Seward as the great pacificator, the savior from foreign war. But to this boy, and five millions of his fellow countrymen, the one appeared as a usurper, invader and violator of laws, and destroyer of life, liberty and property. The other as an adviser in oppression and a slippery advocate of an irrepressible conflict. He differed from the Southern army simply because he surpassed it in courage, and he differed from a patriot and martyr simply because he was mistaken in his duty.

But there is a third school before him. From Gettysburg he was sent to West's Buildings Hospital, Pratt street, Baltimore, and remained until October, 1863, when, seeing no hope of exchange, he deserted with a view to rejoin his regiment. Not being able to get through our lines, he joined a regiment of cavalry at Fauquier, and remained in that service until January 6, 1865. On that day, as we see by the narrative of Mrs. Grant, he saved the lives of two Union soldiers. About the same time he, like many other Southern soldiers, began to despair of the Confederacy, came to Alexandria, sold his horse, gave his name as Payne, took the oath of allegiance as a refugee from Fauquier, and went to Baltimore and took a room at the house of Mrs. Branson, the lady he had met at Gettysburg, and resolved to wait for the return of peace. In this third school, the Rebel cavalry service, he received further damaging training, and amongst the people of Loudon and Fauquier, who had suffered most from the war, gained an added acrimony and hate for those deemed their oppressors. But there is a fourth school before him, the school of necessity.

He was in Baltimore without trade or profession. He was unused to manual labor. In perplexity about his future, for the little money he got for his horse was fast going. He whiled away the time in reading medical works and brooding in his chamber. While in this condition, the fracas occurred at his boarding house, by which he was arrested, brought before the Provost Marshal and ordered north of Philadelphia. Everywhere the sky is dark to him. He is proscribed amongst Northern men as a Rebel, despised amongst Southern men in Baltimore as a recreant Southerner, and a by-word among Southern men at home as a deserter. Penniless and friendless, the earth seems to reject him and God and man to be against him: This is the work of civil war. His education is now completed. Slavery has taught him to wink at murder. The Southern army has taught him to practice and justify murder. Guerrilla warfare has taught him to love murder. Necessity has taught him resolution to commit murder. He needs no further education; his four terms are complete, and he graduates an assassin. And of this college we the reunited people of the United States have been the stern tutors, guides and professors. It needs now only that some one should employ him. At the beginning of the war Powell one night went to the theatre at Richmond; it was the first play that Powell ever saw, and he was spell-bound with the magical influence of the stage, but was chiefly attracted by the voice and manner of one of the actors—J. Wilkes Booth.

Although only a private soldier, Powell considered himself the equal of any man, and, after the play was over, sought and gained an introduction to the actor. Never were two natures thrown together so different yet so well calculated to rule the other and be ruled. The soldier was tall, awkward, rough, frank, generous and illiterate. The actor was of delicate mould, polished, graceful, subtle, with a brilliant fancy and an abundant stock of reading. They saw enough of one another to form a close intimacy, sufficient to complete the control of Booth over the prisoner, and parted not to meet for nearly four years. In the twilight of that memorable day in March just depicted, Powell was dragging himself slowly along the street past Barnum's Hotel, a poor creature, overcome by destiny. Suddenly a familiar voice hailed him. Looking up the steps, he saw the face of the Richmond actor. The actor, on his side, expressed astonishment to find Powell in such a plight.

Powell answered him in few words—"Booth, I want food; I am starving." Under other circumstances Booth might have given him bread, but he was filled with a mighty scheme, for he had just come from Canada, and was lying in wait for agents. He seized with eagerness this poor man's hunger to wind about him his toils, saying, "I will give you as much money as you want, but you must swear to stick by me; it is in the oil business." A hungry stomach is not cautious of oaths, and Powell then swore that fatal oath binding his soul as firmly to Booth as Faust to Mephistophiles, and went in and feasted. Next morning Booth gave him money enough to buy a change of clothing and keep him for a week.

Powell now grew anxious to know what plan it was that was to make him rich, but Booth answered evasively that it was in the "oil business." He knew well enough that he had to do with a desperate man, but he knew also that any proposition of a guilty character might as yet be rejected.

TRIAL OF THE ASSASSINS AT WASHINGTON.

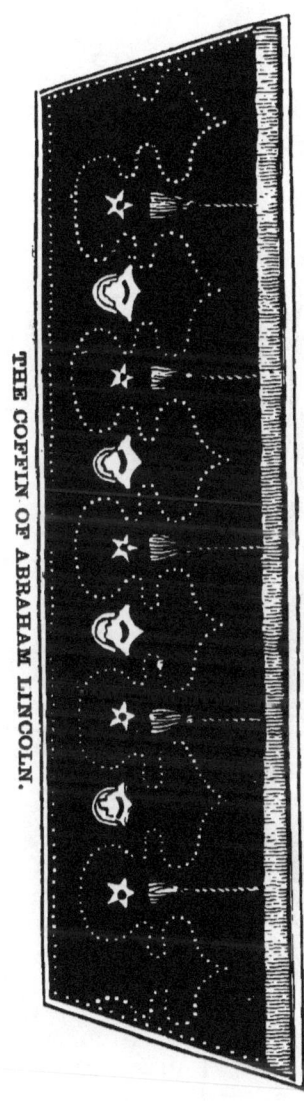

THE COFFIN OF ABRAHAM LINCOLN.

Mr Doster proceeded to describe and narrate in animated language the manner in which Booth, step by step, worked on the mind of his victim, depicting to the prisoner the wrongs of the South and the guilt of her oppressors, and wrought him up to a pitch of purposed passion to avenge the wrongs of his country and set himself right with his countrymen, who despised him as a recreant. Booth saw his victim was ready, and hastened to impart his mysterious plans.

The plan was to go to Washington, take a ride with confederates on horseback to the Soldier's Home, capture the President and deliver him to the Rebel authorities. On the evening of the 14th of April, at 8 o'clock, Booth told him the hour had struck, placed in his hands the knife, the revolver and the bogus package of medicine, and told him to do his duty, and gave him a horse, with directions to meet him at the Anacosta Bridge; and he went and did the deed.

Said Mr. Doster.—I have asked him why he did it. His only answer is, "because I believed it my duty."

Mr. Doster argued that Payne at the time he committed this deed had no will of his own, but had surrendered his will completely to Booth, under that influence, that complete supremecy of one mind over another, that has gone by various names amongst various nations, and which we call "mesmerism."

Booth was a person peculiarly gifted with this unaccountable influence, and the prisoner was further held to Booth by the ties of gratitude, by his oath, by ties of interest, and by ties of sympathy in a common cause. Hence the explanation why, when informed of Booth's plans, he did not inform the authorities and break away from Booth. Mr. Doster drew a distinction between the hired assassin who kills for gold, and the fanatical assassin who deems it his duty to offer up his own life in exchange for the life he believes to be a public enemy, and contended that Payne was of the latter class.

The erect bearing, the patience, the smiling self-possession of the prisoner, were referred to as indicating the political lanatic, a monomaniac on the subject of his duty. He urged that this man wishes to die in order to gain the full crown of martyrdom, and therefore if we gratify him he will triumph over us, but if we spare him we will triumph over him. If suffered to live, he will receive the worst punishment, obscurity, and the public will have nothing to admire.

He has killed no man, and if he be put to death we shall have the anomaly of the victim surviving the murderer, and, under the laws, he can be punished only for assault and battery, with intent to kill, and therefore imprisoned. Mr. Doster proceeded with other considerations why the prisoner's life should be saved, and before concluding spoke of the many good qualities he had found in the prisoner by his intercourse with him, his frank, manly bearing, his disinclination for notoriety, and his indisposition to screen himself from punishment. His only prominent anxiety was lest people should think him a hired assassin or a brute, an aversion to being made a public spectacle of, and a desire to be tried at the hands of his fellow citizens.

After an hour's recess taken by the Court, Mr. Doster entered upon the argument on behalf of Atzeroth, commencing by offering a statement by his client as follows:—

The prisoner, Atzeroth, submits the following statement to the Court:—

"I am one of a party who agreed to capture the President of the United States, or any member of the Cabinet, or General Grant, or Vice President Johnson. The first plot, to capture, failed; the second, to kill, I broke away from the moment I heard of it. This is the way it came about.

On the evening of the 14th of April I met Booth and Payne at the Herndon Hotel, in this city, at 8 o'clock; he (Booth) said he himself would take charge of Mr. Lincoln and General Grant, Payne should take Mr. Seward, and I should take Mr. Johnson. I told him I would not do it; that I had gone into the thing to capture, but that I was not going to kill. He told me I was a fool, that I would be hung any how, that it was death for every man that backed out, and so we parted. I wandered about the streets until about two o'clock in the morning, and then went to the Kimmell House, and from there I procured my pistol at George own, and went to my cousin's house, in Montgomery county, where I was arrested the 19th following. After I was arrested I told Provost Marshal Wells and Provost Marsual McPhail the whole story; I also told it to Captain Monroe, and Colonel Wells told me if I pointed out the way Booth had gone I would be reprieved, and so I told him I thought he had gone down Charles county, in order to cross the Potomac.

The arms which were found in my room at the Kirkwood House and a black coat, do not belong to me. On the afternoon of the 14th of April Harold called to see me, and left the coat there. It is his coat. All of it belongs to him, as you can see by the handkerchief, marked with his initial and with the name of his sister, Mrs Naylor. Now I will state how I passed the whole of the evening of the 14th of April. In the afternoon, about two o'clock, I went to the livery stable on Eighth street, near D, and hired a dark bay mare, and rode into the country for pleasure, and on my return put her up at Naylor's stable. The dark bay mare which I had kept at Naylor's before, on or about the 3d of April, belonged to Booth, and, also, the saddle and bridle, and I had charge of her to sell her, and I do not know what become of her.

At about six in the evening I went to Naylor's again and took out the mare, rode out for an hour and returned her to Naylor's. It was then nearly eight o'clock, and I told him to keep the mare ready at ten o'clock, in order to return her to the man I hired her from. From there I went to the Herndon House. Booth sent a message to Oyster Bay, where I was, saying he wanted to see me, and I went. Booth wanted me to murder Mr. Johnson. I refused; I then went to the Oyster Bay, on the Avenue, above Twelfth street, and whiled away the time until near ten.

At ten I got the mare, and having taken a drink with the hostler, galloped about town and went to the Kimmell House; from there I rode down to the depot, and returned with very hard riding up Pennsylvania avenue to Kelcher's. From Kelcher's I went down to the Navy Yard to get a room with Wash. Briscoe. He had none, and by the time I got back to the Kimmell House it was near two. The man Thomas was a stranger I met on the street. The next morning, as stated, I went to my cousin Kechler's in Montgomery county. GEORGE A. ATZEROTH.

Mr. Doster, proceeding with his argument, quoted the specification under which the prisoner Atzeroth is charged, as follows:—

"And in further prosecution of said conspiracy and its traitorous and murderous designs, the said George A. Atzeroth did, on the night of the 14th of April, Anno Domini 1865, and about the same hour of the night aforesaid, within the military department and military lines aforesaid, lie in wait for Andrew Johnson, then Vice President of the United States aforesaid, with the intent unlawfully and maliciously to kill and murder the said Andrew Johnson.

In support of this specification the Government has submitted the testimony of Welchman and Miss Surratt that he was frequently at Mrs. Surratt's, in company with Booth; of Greenwalt, that he had interviews with Booth at the Kimmell House, and that he said on the 1st of April, "Greenwalt, I am pretty near broke, though I have friends enough to give me as much money as will keep me all my lifetime. I am going away one of these days, but will return with as much money as will keep me all my lifetime."

Of Marcus P. Norton, that he overheard him in conversation with Booth, in which it was said, about the evening of the 3d of March, that "if the matter succeeded as well with Johnson as it did with old Buchanan, the party would be sold;" and also, "that the character of the witnesses would be such that nothing could be proved by them." Of Colonel Nevins, that he was asked by the prisoner, between four and five of the afternoon of the 12th of April, at the Kirkwood House, to point out Mr. Johnson while at dinner.

Of John Fletcher, that on or about April 3d the prisoner owned a horse and saddle, which he afterwards said was sold in Montgomery county, and which was afterward found near Camp Baring Hospital on the night of the 14th of April, and also that he got a dark bay mare at Naylor's, on the evening of the 14th, which he had brought there in the morning and rode her away at half-past six. Brought her back at eight returned again at ten, ordered his mare, took a drink, said "if this thing happens to-night you will hear of a present," and said of the mare, "she is good on a retreat." That then he rode to the Kirkwood House, came out again, went along D Street and turned up Tenth.

Of Thomas L. Gardner, that the same dark bay one-eyed horse found near Camp Barry was sold by his uncle to George Gardner. Of John Toffey, that the same horse was found at 12½ A. M., Saturday, 15th of April, near Camp Barry. Of Wash. Briscoe, that on the night of the 14th of April, between 12 and 12½ o'clock, the prisoner got out of the cars near the Navy Yard and asked him three times to let him sleep in the store; that he was refused and said he would return to the Kimmell House. Of Greenwalt, that he came to the Kimmell House at 2 A. M. with a man named Thomas and hesitated to register his name and went away in the morning without paying his bill. Of Lieut. Keim, that he stopped in the same room with the prisoner at the Kimmell House, and when he (witness) spoke of the assassination Atzeroth said "It was an awful affair;" and that on the Sunday before he saw a knife in his possession, a large bowie knife in a sheath, and that he, Atzeroth, remarked, "if one fails I want the other." Of Wm. Clendenin, that he found a knife similar to the one seen by Keim, on F, between Eighth and Ninth streets, on the morning after the assassination. Of Robert Jones and John Lee, that Atzeroth took a room at the Kirkwood, No. 126, and that in the room on the morning of the 15th, was found a coat containing a pistol loaded, and bowie knife, and handkerchief marked with the name of J. Wilkes Booth. Of Provost Marshal McPhail, that Atzeroth confessed to him that he threw his knife away near the Herndon House; that he pawned his pistol at Caldwell's store, in Georgetown, and borrowed ten dollars, and that the coat and arms at the Kirkwood belonged to Harold.

TRIAL OF THE ASSASSINS AT WASHINGTON.

Of Sergeant Gemmill, that he denied having left Washington recently, or having anything to do with the assassination.

Of Hezekiah Metts, that on Sunday following the murder Atzerodt said at his house, "If the man had followed General Grant who was to have followed him, he would have been killed." To negative this specification the defense had submitted the testimony of Somerset Leaman that the prisoner said at Metts' house, when asked if Grant was killed, "no, I do not suppose he was." If he had been killed, it would have been done probably by a man that got on the same train of cars that he did, and that he never used the language imputed to him by Mr. Metts. That he was confused; that the daughter of Metts, to whom he was paying his addresses, was throwing him the cold shoulder that day. Of James E. Leaman to the same effect. Of James Killiker, that Atzerodt had a dark bay mare at his stable at half-past two o'clock on the afternoon of the 14th; wrote his name in a large hand and willingly gave references, and said he lived in Port Tobacco, and was a coachmaker by trade: of Samuel Smith, that the mare was returned about eleven o'clock on the evening of the 14th: of Samuel McAllister, that Atzerodt rode up to the Kimmell House about ten, and called the black boy to hold his mare, that the knife found near the Herndon House, and the revolver found at Caldwell's, had been in Atzerodt's possession, but he could not identify the coat, or its contents, found at the Kirkwood House: of Provost Marshal McPhail, going to show that the watch belonged to Harold; of Mrs. Naylor, that the handkerchief picked up in Atzerodt's room was marked with the name of Harold's sister: of Hartman Richter, that the prisoner came to his house, in Montgomery county, and made no effort to escape; of Somerset Damon that he is of respectable family; of Samuel McAllister, that he was generally considered a coward; of Washington Briscoe, that he is a noted coward; of George Farwell, that he saw no one lying in wait about Vice President Johnson's room at the Kirkwood immediately after the assassination, nor did he see any one attempt to enter for half an hour; of W. C. Browning, Private Secretary, that the Vice President was in his room till 5 o'clock, the balance of the evening: of M. J. Pope, that on the 12th the prisoner was at the stable endeavoring to sell a horse; that he went off with John Barr; of the latter, that the prisoner was at Pope's; of Henry Branner and L. C. Hawkers, that on the 3d of March he was in Port Tobacco; of Judge Olin and Henry Burden, that they would not believe Marcus Norton on oath.

The prisoner submits that the testimony adduced by the prosecution fails utterly to support the specification, but corroborates the prisoner's own statement in every particular.

The specification charges him with lying in wait for Andrew Johnson, etc., and on this point the evidence is circumstantial. Colonel Nevins says Atzerodt inquired for the President on the afternoon of April 12, between four and five o'clock, and acknowledges that he saw him only for a moment at the time. Pope says that the prisoner came to his stable some day in April to sell a horse, and thinks they fixed by John Barr as the 12th of April, because he made an entry in his book at the time. Colonel Nevins' testimony must, therefore, fall to the ground, and while it is concluded that some one at the Kirkwood had asked Colonel Nevins this common question, it is certain that Atzerodt is not the man.

The second point brought in support of the specification is by Marcus P. Norton, whose declaration is to the effect that he saw Atzerodt in company with Booth on the evening of March 3d, he thinks, and heard it said, "If the matter succeeds as well with Johnson as it did with old Buchanan the party would be sold;" also, the words "the character of the witnesses would be such that nothing could be proved by them." The prisoner says this is a deliberate falsehood, as he proved that he was not in Washington on the 2d and 3d of March by Henry Branner, of Port Tobacco, and Louis F. Hawkins, who testify that about that time he was at home. This would be sufficient to disprove Norton's statement, but there is other evidence that he was deliberately making testimony, for he says on the same day he saw Dr. Mudd, who was asking for Booth. Dr. Mudd has shown that he was not at the Kirkwood or in Washington on that day.

This ingenious fabricator of testimony chose the 3d of March to give his story probability, and he appears before he wove this line of perjury in, to have omitted reading the testimony of Conover, who says the name of Andrew Johnson was not joined in the plot until after the inauguration, and that at that time the name of Mr. Hamlin was on the list, and so perpetrated an egregious blunder. How singular that he should remember exact words for three months, and faces when he is so short sighted as might be inferred. He is a notable false witness. He takes patent cases, and if he cannot urge by argument, he takes the witness stand and swears them through.

Mr. Henry Burden, a wealthy citizen of Troy, and Judge E. Olin, testify that they would not believe him on his oath. From internal evidence of his testimony, its falsity in the matter of Dr. Mudd, its proven falsity in the time of Atzerodt's visits to the Kirkwood, and his known reputation as a false witness, leaves no shadow of doubt that his testimony is the offspring of a desire to distinguish himself on the witness stand, and that Atzerodt never met Booth at the National on the 3d of March, or had the alleged conversation with him. The third strong point of the prosecution is that Atzerodt left room No. 126 at the Kirkwood, taking the key with him, and in his room was found a coat, containing a bowie knife, pistol, handkerchief marked "J. Wilkes Booth," together with notes on the Ontario Bank, in the name of Booth, and memoranda, showing that they coat belonged to Booth.

The coat and contents were disposed of by the prosecution. McPhail swears that Atzerodt told him that the coat and arms belonged to Harold. The clerk swears that some one called to see Atzerodt in the afternoon. It was Harold, and he left his coat in the room. The handkerchief is marked with the name of Mary E. Naylor, sister of Harold. Another is marked H, for Harold. But why did Atzerodt suffer his coat and arms to be in his room? Because he was in a plot to capture the President, in so far he was the colleague of Harold and Booth; no further. Because for this purpose to capture the President, to be used in defense, he carried the knife and pistol, which McAllister used to keep for him. The same knife he threw away, the same pistol he pawned, and therefore he suffered Harold to leave his armor for the same reason he carried his own. But why did Atzerodt go away with the key and never come back? Because he did not want to be arrested; because he was not guilty of aiding in the assassination of Mr. Lincoln because he was in the plot so far as to capture the President, and when he was ordered to kill the Vice President and refused, he was unable to resolve either to inform the authorities for fear of Booth, or to do the deed for fear of being hung: and so just abandoned the room as he abandoned every thing connected with the conspiracy. Had he been able to resolve to carry out his allotted duty he would naturally have taken the coat of Harold and put it on and used the arms.

Had he been able to resolve to flee at once he would have removed all traces of his participation. One reason for leaving without paying Wash was because he had no money, and the reason for leaving the coat was because they did not belong to him; but the main reason was because he was between two fires, which brought out his native irresolution, and so he cut the gordian knot by running away. We shall see that he left the Kimmell House the next morning without paying his bill. It was for the same reason he had no money until after he had pointed his pistol at Georgetown. The fourth point of the prosecution is that Atzerodt lodged in the same house with the Vice President, and the relative situation of the rooms was favorable to assassination. The room of the Vice President was one which no one could help passing in going down or up, and room 126 was as remote from it as possible, in a different wing. It is evident that any one desirous of lying in wait for the Vice President would have taken a room on the same floor, but the actual fact is better than suppositions.

Mr. Browning says the Vice President was in his room from 5 to 10, during which time the deed could have been done. There is no evidence that Atzerodt was at the house during that time, except that of Fletcher, who says that Atzerodt went there and stayed five minutes. What was he doing there? He was taking a drink at the bar. If he tried to kill Mr. Johnson why was it not shown? No one was seen lying in wait; the lock had not been tampered with; the Vice President was undisturbed even by a knock on the door—and why? Because Atzerodt refused to do it. Because he kept up appearances but backed out. Because the instrument which was to have assassinated the Vice President was too conscientious, or afraid to do it.

The fifth point is, that on his arrest he gave a false name, denied having left Washington recently, and said he had nothing to do with the assassination. For the last statement he told the truth. Assassination and murder were things for which he was not by nature intended, and he had nothing to do with it; as for the false name, it appeared that Sergeant Gemmill understood his name to be Atwood; knowing that he had been in colleague with others to capture the President, he was afraid to confess his part, and then and there denied having recently left Washington.

The sixth point is that he said to Fletcher, after ten on the 14th, "If this thing happens to-night you will hear of a present." And also in reference to the mare, "she is good on a retreat;" and to Lieutenant Keim, on the Sunday before, "if one fails I shall want the other." On the first occasion, Atzerodt was about half drunk, while the other remark was made after the parties had taken their cocktails, so that even if we credit the drunken memories of the witnesses, we cannot do more than credit it to pot valor, pointing to the possible desperate meice of an attempt to capture.

There is only one assumption that will make every thing agree. Atzerodt backed out. He arrived here; he liked the money, but did not like to be hung. He never heard of murder before that evening at eight o'clock, or he would long before have hid himself. When he did hear it he had firmness enough to object. Coward conscience came to his rescue. But Booth

TRIAL OF THE ASSASSINS AT WASHINGTON. 171

threatened to kill, and he knew well enough he was the man to close the mouth of any one who troubled him, so he went off, driven like a poor frail being between irresolution and fear; took drinks, feigned to be doing his part, talked valiantly while the rum was in his throat, promised gloriously, galloped round fiercely, talked daggers, and when the hour struck did nothing and ran.

The specification charges that about 10:15 he was lying in wait to murder, &c., and the counsel contends that all the circumstances can be accounted for. The prisoner had opportunity to lie in wait, and as there was no proof that he did, he should be considered guiltless of the attempt to murder. If the theory of his attempting to murder be adopted, it is met with denial at every point. He tried to become a hero, but was only a coachmaker, absolutely without courage. The plain, unvarnished statement is that during the latter part of February, John Surratt and Booth wanted a man who understood boating, and would both get a boat and ferry a party over the Potomac on a capture. Surratt knew Atzeroth, and under the influence of great promises of a fortune, consented to furnish the boat and do the ferrying over.

This plot was attempted on the 18th of March and failed. Booth, however, kept his subordinates uninformed of his plans, except that it was understood the President was to be captured. Meanwhile everybody was waiting for Booth. On the 18th of March Atzeroth went to the Kimmel House. On the 1st of April he talked of future wealth; on the 6th he spoke to Lieutenant Kelm, over their liquor, of using one if the other failed. On the 12th he stopped at the Kirkwood, and tried to sell the bay horse to Pope; on the 14th Booth unfolded his plans at the Herndon House, and Atzeroth refused; from the Herndon House he went to Oyster Bay till ten, and took drinks; at ten he took a drink with Fletcher; at ten minutes past ten he took a drink at the Kirkwood House; at twenty minutes past ten ditto at Kimmel, and rode about the city; at eleven returned his horse; at twelve he was at the Navy Yard; at two he went to bed.

Next morning at five he got up and went to Georgetown, pawned his pistol, and went to Mr. Mott's; on the 10th, took dinner at Mett's; on Sunday evening he went to Hartman Richter's; on the 19th he was arrested. This ends this history, which might have become a tragedy, but which the prisoner has turned to a farce. He was riding round from bar-room to bar-room while Payne was at Seward's, and it is plain he was drunk. After his peregrinations, to charge him with lying in wait, &c., is paying him an undeserved compliment. There is not a particle of use specification proved, but the immediate contrary. During the whole of the evening, so far as the evidence throws any light on his conduct, instead of lying in wait near to the Vice President, he was standing at the different bars from the Union House to the Kimmel House, with the intent then and there unlawfully and maliciously to make Atzeroth drunk.

Booth employed him for an emergency. He was especially competent to perform in the plan to capture, to furnish the boat, and to carry the party across the Potomac. For participating in the President's murder he never could have been intended. Booth was, as his conduct shows, anxious to carry off the glory of the thing. He remarked that he wanted "no botching with General Grant." He must have known when he told Atzeroth to take charge of the Vice President, that he had not the courage and did not care particularly whether he accomplished it or not.

The charge is divisible in two separate and distinct parts, "with combining, confederating," etc., "on or before the 6th of March," etc. And even suppose he was proven guilty of the charge and specification, he has already turned State's evidence to the Provost Marshal, and therefore his punishment would fall under the practice usual in all courts of justice, that one confessing has an equitable right to the leniency of the Court. His case, however, rests on no such slender ground. Instead of conspiring to kill, he refused to kill; instead of lying in wait to murder, he intoxicated himself at the appointed hour, and the next morning ran away.

He is guilty solely of what he confesses, of conspiring to abduct the President, and of that he can be found guilty only under a new indictment.

Mr. Aiken read the argument in behalf of Mrs. Surratt, commencing as follows:—

For the lawyer, as well as the soldier, there is an equally pleasant duty, an equally imperative command. That duty is to shelter from injustice and wrong the innocent; to protect the weak from oppression, and to rally, at all times and on all occasions when necessity demands it, to the special defense of those whom nature, custom or circumstances may have placed in dependence upon our strength, honor and cherishing regard. That command emanates and reaches each class from the same authoritative source. It comes from a Superior whose right to command none dare question, and none dare to disobey.

In this command there is nothing of that *lex lationis* which nearly two thousand years ago enjoined to us cross its Divine Author. "Therefore all things whatsoever ye would that men should do to you, do ye even so unto them, for this is the law and the prophets."

God has not only given us life but he has filled the world with everything to make life desirable, and when we sit down to determine the taking away of that which we did not give, and which, when once taken, we cannot restore, we consider a subject the most solemn within the range of human thought and human action. Profoundly impressed with the innocence of our client, we enter upon this last duty in her case with the heartfelt prayer that her honorable judges may enjoy the satisfaction of not having a single doubt left on their minds in granting her an acquittal, either as to the testimony affecting her or by the surrounding circumstances of the case.

After alluding to the argument of the Hon. Reverdy Johnson, whom he styled the "*grande dress columnque*" of his profession, Mr. Aiken discussed with much particularity the plea of reasonable doubt, and in applying the rules which obtain in civil courts to courts-martial, and that they must be governed in the acceptance and analysis precisely by these reasonable rules of evidence, that time and experience *ab autico*, surviving many ages of judicial wisdom, have unalterably fixed as guides in the administration of the criminal law. Mr. Aiken here quoted many authorities sustaining his positions. He claimed that if Mrs. Surratt could be found guilty in a civil court she might be convicted here. He then stated that for private and public reasons it was highly desirable that the findings of the Court should be sustained by sufficient evidence. If they were, the public would overlook any irregularity that might be supposed to exist.

He stated that the case was wonderfully barren of even circumstantial evidence against Mrs. Surratt; but all that was circumstantial by no means connected her with guilty knowledge or guilty intent. He then inquired what these facts were, the character of this evidence in support of them, and of the witness, and whether they were consistent with a reasonable theory by which guilt is excluded.

The character, scope and tone of the argument can be gathered from the remarks near the close, viz:—A mother and son, associated in crime, and such a crime as this had of the civilized world never saw matched in all its dreadful bearings. Our judgments can have hardly recovered their unprejudiced poise since the shock of the late horrors; if we can contemplate with credulity such a picture conjured by the unjust spirits of indiscriminate accusation and revenge; a crime which in private misery would have driven even the gifts haunted heart of a Medici, a Borgia, or a Madame Bocarini to wild confusion before its accomplishment, and daunted even that soul, of all the recorded world, the most eager for novelty in license and most unshrinking in sin the industried soul of Christianism of Sweden; such a crime as profoundest plotters within padded walls would scarcely dare whisper; the words forming the expression of which spoken aloud in the upper air would convert all listening boughs to aspens, and all glad sounds of nature to shuddering wails, and this made known even surmised to a woman a "mater familias." The good genius, the "*places uxor*" of a home where children had gathered all the influences of purity and the reminiscences of innocence, where religion watched and the Church was minister and watcher, who were circumstantial evidence strong and conclusive, such as only time and the slow-weaving fates could elucidate, and deny. Who will believe, when the mists of uncertainty which cloud the present shall have dissolved, that a woman born and bred in respectability and competence, a Christian mother and a citizen who never offended the laws of civil propriety; whose unfailing attention to the most sacred duties of life has won for her the name of "a proper Christian matron;" whose hearth was ever warmed by charity; whose door was unbarred to the poor, and whose Penates has never cause to veil their faces, who will believe that she could so suddenly and fully have learned the intricate arts of sin?

Mr. Aiken closed with the following remarks:—"Let not this first state tribunal in our country's history, which involves a woman's name, be blazoned before the world with the harsh hints of intolerance which permits injustice, but as the benignant heart and kindly judging hand of the world-lamented victim of a crime which would, in its ramifications of woe, aroused so many fates, would himself have counselled you. Let the heralds of peace and charity, with their wool-bound slaves, follow the fasces and axes of judgment and law, and without the sacrifice of any innocent subjecents, let the ship of state launch with dignity of unstained sails into the unruffled sea of union and prosperity.

The Court adjourned over till Friday.

Proceedings of Friday.

WASHINGTON, June 23.—George B. Hutchinson, a witness called by the Government, testified that he was an enlisted man during the recent war, for a year and a half he saw Clement C. Clay on or about the 12th or 13th of February last, at the Queen's Hotel, Toronto; he did not think he was mistaken in seeing Clay then and there; he also saw Sanders, Beverly Tucker, and others, at Montreal, on the 16th or 17th of the same month.

The witness was present at a conversation at the St. Lawrence Hall, Montreal, on the 2d or 3d of June, when the present trial was the subject discussed by Dr. Merritt, Beverly Tucker, General Carroll, of Tennessee, and ex-Governor Wescott, of Florida. Beverly Tucker said he had burned all the letters, for fear the Yankee sons of —— would steal them. The witness had knowledge that Dr. Merritt enjoyed the confidence of Tucker and the others.

Mr. Ewing's Argument.

Mr. Ewing then proceeded to read the argument in the prisoner Arnold's case. He remarked that the evidence was not voluminous, and it was all in harmony as to the main facts. Mr. Burner, the detective, said that Arnold after his arrest gave an account of a meeting held at the Lichen House in Washington, the effect of which was to capture the President and take him South for the purpose of compelling the Government to an exchange of prisoners. After announcing his intention of having nothing to do with it if not performed within the week, Arnold withdrew from it. When Booth said for this he ought to be shot. Booth had previously furnished the conspirators with arms, and so perfectly satisfied did he become that Arnold had withdrawn from the plot, that he told Arnold to dispose of the arms placed in the prisoner's hands just as he pleased.

This statement of Arnold was truthful and ingenuous, and all the evidence corroborated and conformed to it. In Booth's trunk was found a letter from Arnold, dated from Hookstown, March 27, in reply to one from Booth, who had endeavored to reclaim and again enlist him in his scheme. This letter showed that the rupture between them was complete, never to be healed. During Arnold's stay at Mrs. Van Tyne's in this city it was not denied that he was engaged in the plot for the capture of President Lincoln. Arnold remained in Maryland from the 21st to the 31st of March, when he proceeded to Fortress Monroe for the purpose of entering upon a situation as clerk with Mr. Wharton. About the 20th of March occurred the meeting which resulted in the quarrel of the accused with Booth, when Arnold gave up his room at Mrs. Van Tyne's and never saw Booth afterwards.

The evidence established only that at one time Arnold was a party to a plot to capture or abduct the President. If on the 11th of April the President had been abducted, instead of assassinated, Arnold could not be punished, because he had withdrawn from the conspiracy, as the prisoner countermanded the intention to abduct, and altogether withdrew from it. There was no crime committed, and as a consequence no punishment should follow.

Mr. Ewing quoted from various legal authorities to show that after Arnold had terminated his association with the conspirators, he was not responsible for what was done afterwards. No one act of the conspirators could affect him. There was not the remotest testimony to connect Arnold with the commission of the murderous deed. He repeated, that the original plot in which Arnold bore a part was abandoned, and an entirely new one, with which Arnold was in no way connected was substituted. Although he had conspired with the same parties for a different purpose, he certainly was not responsible with the wicked men who did the wicked deed of murder. The prisoner, the counsel argued, could not be an accessory before the fact of a crime he did not know was to be committed. At the time of the assassination Arnold was not in Washington. He was not nearer the scene than Fortress Monroe, nor did he give any guilty aid or partici. pation to the murder after the crime had been committed.

After a Recess

Mr. Ewing addressed the Court upon the subject of jurisdiction, arguing that neither the Constitution of the United States nor the laws passed under it gives them power to try the prisoners for the crime with which they are charged. As there was no Constitutional or legal provision for trial in such a Court, it must have been authorized by some mandate from the Executive, which the Constitution prohibits. If his clients were to be tried for treason and murder, it must be proved that they aided in or abetted the acts, for either of them, on conviction, was punishable with death. The Judge Advocate would not say on what law and authority he rested the conviction of these parties and for what crime. The civil Courts were open, without impediment, for impartial trial, and hence, in the absence of other considerations, there was no necessity for this trial before a military Court. If such a precedent he set we may have fastened upon us a military despotism. It might be this arraignment before a military Court was more convenient and conviction more certain than before a civil tribunal.

The Judge Advocate had said that the parties were tried under the common military law. This was a *quiddity*, and might make a fictitious crime, and attach an arbitrary punishment, and who may gainsay it? Our rules and articles of war are familiar to us all. We never heard of the common laws of war having juris-diction not conferred by express enactment or constitutional grant. If the laws govern, he (Mr. Ewing) felt satisfied that his clients were safe. One of them, Dr. Mudd, had committed no crime known to the law. He could not be charged with treason, nor as aiding and abetting in the murder of the President, for, at the time of the tragedy, Dr. Mudd was at his residence, thirty miles from the place of the crime. He certainly could not be charged with the commission of the overt act. There were not two witnesses to show it, but there was abundant evidence to show he did not commit the overt act. Dr. Mudd never by himself, or with others, levied war against the United States or gave aid and comfort to the enemy.

Mr. Ewing then proceeded to comment on the evidence, claiming that there was nothing which in the remotest degree connected Dr. Mudd with the conspiracy. He ventured to say, that rarely in the annals of the civil trials, has the life of accused been assailed by so much false testimony, as had been exhibited in this case, and rarely has it been the good fortune of an innocent man to so confute and overwhelm his false accusers by a preponderance of undisputed truth. There was no reliable evidence to show that Dr. Mudd met Booth more than twice, and that was last November, in Charles county, on a mere matter of trade. He had never met Booth in this city. The counsel then reviewed the evidence relative to Dr. Mudd, having set Booth's leg and other events in that connection, arguing that from all this there was nothing to lead to a conclusion unfavorable to the accused. Dr. Mudd voluntarily, not on compulsion, gave in'ormation concerning the route by which Booth with Harold had escaped, and instead of thanking him for this, as a good and loyal citizen, an effort was made to punish him. Truly the ways of military justice, like those of Providence, are inscrutable and past finding out. In the course of his defense Mr. Ewing said that in all the writings which had been seized there is not a scratch of a pen implicating Dr. Mudd, nor is there anything whatever to show that he had the least intimation or knowledge either of assassination or of abduction. He concluded that his client could not be punished either as a principal or as an accessory before the fact, for the evidence fails to show either knowledge, or intimation or suspicion to commit the crime. If the prisoner was to be held responsible at all, it was as an accessory after the fact, and beyond all controversy there was no proof on this point.

All the arguments for the accused having been read, Associate Judge Advocate Bingham said that on Tuesday next he would be ready with so much of his summing up as touches the question of the jurisdiction of the Court. and he hoped, by the next day, to deliver the conclusion of his argument.

The Court then adjourned until Tuesday morning, at 11 o'clock.

WASHINGTON, June 27.—The Court met at 11 o'clock, when Judge Advocate-General Holt recalled Sandford Conover, alias J. W. Wallace, as a witness for the Government.

Judge Holt said he held in his hand a volume containing the judicial proceedings in the case of the St. Albans raid, and asked the witness whether his evidence therein was truthfully reported. The witness said the testimony to which General Holt had especially referred was partly his, but associated with that of another person named Wallace.

Q. Do you remember how many persons named Wallace gave testimony on that trial? A. There were three so far as I know; William Pope Wallace, J. Watson Wallace, and J. Wallace; what was read from the work just now was the report of the Montreal *Telegraph*, printed from the type of that newspaper; the report which appeared in the Montreal *Witness* was correct. This was read as follows:—

"James Watson Wallace said:—I reside at present in this city and have been here since October; I formerly resided in the Confederate States; I know James A. Seddon; he occupied the position o Secretary of War; I should say the signatures to the papers M, N, and O, are those of the said Seddon; I have on several occasions seen the signature of James A. Seddon and have seen him on several occasions write his name. He has signed documents in my presence, and handed them to me after signing; I never belonged to the Confederate army, but have seen many commissions issued by the Confederate Government; the commission of Lieutenant Young, marked M,, is in the usual form; the army commissions are always signed by the Secretary of War; I have never seen a commission with the name of the President or with the seal of the Government; the Confederate States at the time I left the country had no seal; one had been designed, but not prepared."

The witness remarked that the above was substantially what he did say; it was clipped either from the Montreal *Witness* or the *Herald*.

Q. State whether, after you gave your testimony in this Court, you visited Montreal. A. I left here perhaps the same day.

TRIAL OF THE ASSASSINS AT WASHINGTON. 173

Q. Whom did you meet there of those spoken of as refugees? A. I met Tucker, Carroll, Dr. Pallen, ex-Governor Wescott, George Sanders, Lewis Sanders, his son, and a number of others; I had a free conversation with some of them, especially with Tucker and Sanders.

Q. What did Tucker say, so far as the purpose of those men was concerned? A. They had not the slightest idea that I had testified before this Commission, and received me with great cordiality; the subject of this trial was generally discussed; Tucker, after denouncing Secretary Stanton and President Johnson as scoundrels, spoke of Judge Holt as a bloodthirsty old villain; he said they must protect themselves by a guard at present; "but, by the Eternal, the day of reckoning will come, and they would have a long account to settle;" Sanders did not make such violent threats as Tucker did; William S. Cleary, whom he also met, made similar violent threats; he said that Beale would have been pardoned by the President had it not been for Judge Holt; he also said blood should follow blood; he reminded me of what he had formerly remarked concerning President Lincoln, "That retributive justice had come, and the assassination of the President was the beginning of it."

Q. After giving your testimony here did you not go to Canada for me? A. I did, to get a certified copy of the record; at Montreal I met these conspirators; I had not been there long when they discovered that my testimony had been published; I received a message from Sanders, Tucker, Carroll and O'Donnell, a Virginian, sometimes called McDonnell.

Q. The man who boasted of setting fire to houses in New York? A. He so boasted; I went into the saloon to wait until the public offices were opened; while sitting there about ten minutes a dozen Rebels surrounded me; they accused me of having betrayed their secrets; not knowing at the time that my testimony had been published I denied it; they said if I would give them a letter to that effect it would be well; just as I was about to get away Beverly Tucker came in; he said a mere letter would not do, because I had testified before the Court, therefore I must give some paper under oath to make my denial sufficiently strong; about a dozen of these men assailed me in a furious manner; O'Donnell took out his pistol and said unless I did so I should never leave the room alive; at last Sanders said, "Wallace, you see what kind of hands you are in;" I at length consented; it was understood that I was to prepare the paper in my own way; I intended, however, not to prepare the paper but to escape from them at the most convenient opportunity; Mr. Kerr was then sent for to prepare the paper; two of Morgan's men were there; a pistol was again drawn on me; Kerr came and the affidavit was prepared and I signed it and went through the ceremony of an oath.

Q. Did you know that Kerr had knowledge of these menaces? A. It must have so appeared to him, for Tucker said if I did not sign the paper I should never leave the town alive, and that they would follow me to ——

Q. Did that paper appear in the *Telegraph*, and was it afterwards copied into the New York *World*? A. It did (the paper was read); it appeared in the Montreal *Evening Telegraph*, of June 10th, and is to the effect that if President Johnson will send to Washington and to return to Montreal, he would proceed hither and go before the Military Court and make proffer of himself in order that they may see whether he was the same Sandford Conover who swore as stated; this is dated June 8th, 1865, and is signed James W. Wallace; to this the affidavit before referred to is appended namely:—

"I am the same James W. Wallace who gave evidence on the subject of the St. Alban's raid, which evidence appears in page 212 of the printed report of the case; I am a native of London county, Virginia; I resided in Montreal in October; I have seen and examined the report of what is called the suppressed evidence before the court-martial now being holden at Washington on Mrs. Surratt, Payne and others, and I have looked carefully through the report of the evidence in the New York papers of a person calling himself Sandford Conover, who referred to the fact that whilst in Montreal he went by the name of James Watson Wallace, and gave evidence in the St. Alban's raid investigation; that said Conover evidently personated me before the said court-martial; that I never gave any testimony whatsoever before the said court-martial; I have never given any testimony whatsoever before the said court-martial at Washington City; that I never had knowledge of John Wilkes Booth, except seeing him on the stage, and did not know he was in Montreal until I saw it published after the murder of President Lincoln; that I never was a correspondent of the New York *Tribune*; that I never went under the name of Sandford Conover; that I never had any confidential conversation with George N. Sanders, Beverly Tucker, Hon. Jacob Thompson, General Carroll, of Tennessee, Dr. M. N. Paller, or any of the others therein mentioned; that, my acquaintance with every one of these gentlemen was slight, and in fine, I have no hesitation in stating that the evidence of the said Conover personating me is false, untrue and un-

founded in fact, and is, from beginning to end, a tissue of falsehoods.

I have made this deposition voluntarily, and in justice to my own character and name.

(Signed) "J. WATSON WALLACE."

This was sworn to before G. Smith, Justice of the Peace, at Montreal, on the 8th of June, last; Alfred Terry testified that Wallace subscribed to the paper of his own free will, &c.

By Judge Advocate Holt.—Q. I understand this is the paper sworn and subscribed to by you under the circumstances which you have detailed, with pistols pointed at your face, and that the statements in this paper are false. A. Yes sir; I never heard of Alfred Terry, who said I swore to it voluntarily; the advertisement appended to the deposition, and which is as follows, was also induced by the same threats.

"Five hundred dollars reward will be given for the arrest, so that I can bring to punishment in Canada, the infamous and perjured scoundrel who recently personated me under the name of Sandford Conover, and deposed to a tissue of falsehoods before the Military Commission at Washington.

(Signed) "J. W. WALLACE."

Q. You have stated that you were never in the Confederate army; what did you mean? A. I meant that I never served as a soldier after I was conscripted; I was detailed as a clerk in the Rebel War Department.

Q. By Judge Holt.—Was any attempt made by those men to detain you in Canada? A. I believe so, by friends of theirs, and I was relieved through the influence of General Dix.

Testimony of Nathan Auser.

By Judge Holt.—Witness said he had known Sandford Conover for eight or ten years; his character for integrity was good; recently witness had accompanied Conover to Montreal and was present at the interview with Tucker and Sanders; after they went into O'Donnell's room Mr. Cameron came there with a paper containing an account of Conover's testimony; Conover had the paper shown to him, but denied he had so testified; he was told he must sign a writing to that effect or he should not leave the room alive; they would shoot him like a dog; they all went into the St. Lawrence Hall, but would not let the witness follow them; there were twelve or fifteen persons in the party, including Sanders, Tucker, O'Donnell, Carroll, Dr. Pallen and Cameron. The witness said he did not see any weapons on their persons.

Testimony of John Cantly.

By Judge Holt.—I reside at Selma, Alabama, and am a printer in the office of the Selma *Dispatch*.

Judge Holt said, I will read the following which purports to have been clipped from that newspaper, namely:—"A million dollars wanted, to have peace by the 1st of March. If the citizens of the Southern Confederacy will furnish me with the cash or good securities for the sum of $1,000,000, I will cause the lives of Abraham Lincoln, Wm. H. Seward, and Andrew Johnson to be taken by the 1st of March next. This will give us peace and satisfy the world that cruel tyrants cannot live in a land of liberty. If this is not accomplished nothing will be claimed beyond the sum of $50,000 in advance, which is supposed to be necessary to reach and slaughter the three villains. I will give, myself, $1000 towards the patriotic purpose. Every one wishing to contribute will address 'X,' Cahawba, Alabama, December 1st, 1864."

Q. Will you state whether this advertisement was published in the Selma *Dispatch* in December 1864? A. As far as I recollect it was November, and was published four or five times; I saw the manuscript, which was in the handwriting of G. W. Gale, of Cahawba, Alabama; his name was signed at the bottom of the sheet simply to indicate the author and who was responsible for it; the *Dispatch* had a circulation of eight hundred copies, and exchanged with the Richmond papers; Gale is a lawyer of considerable reputation, and is distinguished for his extreme views on the subject of slavery; I never saw Gale before his arrest.

Watkins D. Graves, also a printer, who had been employed in the Selma *Dispatch* office, remembered to have seen the advertisement signed X; it was in Mr. Gale's handwriting, which the witness had frequently seen.

Dr. Merritt was recalled for the Government with reference to a statement made by Mr. Hutchinson that he overheard a conversation on the 2d of June. The Doctor said on that day he saw General Carroll at St. Lawrence Hall, and introduced himself as Dr. Merritt, of Memphis. As there was a large family of that name at Memphis, from which vicinity General Carroll came, he expressed to the witness great gratification at meeting him.

General Carroll introduced him to Tucker and others as Dr. Merritt. On Tuesday, the 6th of June, the testimony was published in Canada, when Tucker said they were perfectly posted as to everything on this trial, and Tucker said they had burned the papers from the Confederate Government for fear some Yankee would steal them for evidence. Ex-Governor Westcott was present during the interview with witness, but he did not hear the latter utter any disloyal sentiments, although it must be inferred he was playing into his friends' hands.

By General Wallace.—Q. By whom were they being ----? He said, we have friends in Court; who, I don't know; I did not take for granted it was any member of the Court. (Laughter.)

Judge Holt said the Government was now through with its testimony.

Assistant Judge-Advocate Bingham then delivered his argument, as follows:—

Argument of John A. Bingham,

SPECIAL JUDGE ADVOCATE, IN REPLY TO THE SEVERAL ARGUMENTS IN DEFENSE OF MARY E. SURRATT AND OTHERS, CHARGED WITH CONSPIRACY AND THE MURDER OF ABRAHAM LINCOLN, LATE PRESIDENT OF THE UNITED STATES.

May it please the Court—The conspiracy charged and specified, and the acts alleged to have been committed in pursuance thereof, and with the intent laid, constitute a crime the atrocity of which has sent a shudder through the civilized world. All that was agreed upon and attempted by the alleged inciters and instigators of this crime constitutes a combination of atrocities with scarcely a parallel in the annals of the human race. Whether the prisoners at your bar are guilty of the conspiracy and the acts alleged to have been done in pursuance thereof, as set forth in the charge and specification, is a question the determination of which rests solely with this honorable court, and in passing upon which this court are the sole judges of the law and the fact.

In presenting my views upon the question of law raised by the several counsel for the defense, and also on the testimony adduced for and against the accused, I desire to be just to them, just to you, just to my country, and just to my own convictions. The issue joined involves the highest interests of the accused, and, in my judgment, the highest interests of the whole people of the United States.

It is a matter of great moment to all the people of this country that the prisoners at your bar be lawfully tried and lawfully convicted or acquitted. A wrongful and illegal conviction or a wrongful and illegal acquittal upon this dread issue would impair somewhat the security of every man's life, and shake the stability of the republic.

The crime charged and specified upon your record is not simply the crime of murdering a human being, but it the crime of killing and murdering on the 14th day of April, A. D. 1865, within the military department of Washington and the intrenched lines thereof, Abraham Lincoln, then President of the United States, and Commander-in-Chief of the army and navy thereof; and then and there assaulting, with intent to kill and murder, William H. Seward, then Secretary of State of the United States; and then and there lying in wait to kill and murder Andrew Johnson, then Vice President of the United States, and Ulysses S. Grant, then Lieut.-General and in command of the armies of the United States, in pursuance of a treasonable conspiracy, entered into by the accused with one John Wilkes Booth, and John H. Surratt, upon the instigation of Jefferson Davis, Jacob Thompson, George N. Sanders and others, with intent thereby to aid the existing Rebellion and subvert the Constitution and laws of the United States.

The Rebellion, in aid of which this conspiracy was formed and this great public crime committed, was prosecuted for the vindication of no right, for the redress of no wrong, but was itself simply a criminal conspiracy and gigantic assassination. In resisting and crushing this Rebellion the American people take no step backward, and cast no reproach upon their past history. That people now, as ever, proclaim the self-evident truth that whenever Government becomes subversive of the ends of its creation, it is the right and duty of the people to alter and abolish it; but during these four years of conflict they have as clearly proclaimed, as was their right and duty, both by law and by arms, that the Government of their own choice, humanely and wisely administered, oppressive of none and just to all, shall not be overthrown by privy conspiracy or armed Rebellion.

What wrong had this Government or any of its duly constituted agents done to any of the guilty actors in this atrocious Rebellion? They themselves being witnesses, the Government, which they assailed had done no act, and attempted no act, injurious to them, or in any sense violative of their rights as citizens and men and yet for four years, without cause of complaint or colorable excuse, the inciters and instigators of the conspiracy charged upon your record have, by armed Rebellion, resisted the lawful authority of the Government, and attempted by force of arms to blot the republic from the map of nations. Now that their battalions of treason are broken and flying before the victorious legions of the republic, the chief traitors in this great crime against our Government secretly conspire with their hired confederates to achieve by assassination, if possible, what they have in vain attempted by wager of battle, the overthrow of the Government of the United States and the subversion of its Constitution and laws. It is for this secret conspiracy in the interest of the Rebellion, formed at the instigation of the chiefs of that Rebellion, and in pursuance of which the acts charged and specified are alleged to have been done and with the intent laid, that the accused are upon trial.

The Government in preferring this charge does not indict the whole people of any State or section, but only the alleged parties to this unnatural and atrocious conspiracy and crime. The President of the United States, in the discharge of his duty as Commander-in-Chief of the Army, and by virtue of the power vested in him by the Constitution and laws of the United States, has constituted you a military court. To hear and determine the issue joined against the accused, and has constituted you a court for no other purpose whatever. To this charge and specification the defendants have pleaded, first, that this court has no jurisdiction in the premises; and, second, not guilty. As the court has already overruled the plea to the jurisdiction, it would be passed over in silence by me but for the fact that a grave and elaborate argument has been made by counsel for the accused, not only to show the want of jurisdiction, but to arraign the President of the United States before the country and the world as a usurper of power over the lives and the liberties of the prisoners. Denying the authority of the President to constitute this commission is an averment that this tribunal is not a court of justice, has no legal existence, and therefore no power to hear and determine the issue joined. The learned counsel for the accused, when they make this averment by way of argument, owe it to themselves and to their country to show how the President could otherwise lawfully and efficiently discharge the duty enjoined upon him by his oath to protect, preserve, and defend the Constitution of the United States, and to take care that the laws be faithfully executed.

An existing Rebellion is alleged and not denied. It is charged that in aid of this existing Rebellion a conspiracy was entered into by the accused, incited and instigated thereto by the chiefs of this Rebellion, to kill and murder the executive officers of the Government, and the commander of the armies of the United States, and that this conspiracy was partly executed by the murder of Abraham Lincoln, and by a murderous assault upon the Secretary of State; and counsel reply, by elaborate argument, that although the facts be as charged, though the conspirators be numerous and at large, able and eager to complete the horrid work of assassination already begun within your military encampment, yet the successor of your murdered President is a usurper if he attempts by military force and martial law, as Commander-in-Chief, to prevent the consummation of this traitorous conspiracy in aid of this treasonable Rebellion. The civil Courts, say the counsel, are open in the District, I answer, they are closed throughout half the Republic, and were only open in this District on the day of this confederation and conspiracy, on the day of the traitorous assassination of your President, and are only open at this hour, by force of the bayonet. Does any man suppose that if the military forces which garrison the intrenchments of your capital, fifty thousand strong, were all withdrawn, the Rebel bands who this day infest the mountain passes in your vicinity would allow this Court, or any Court, to remain open in this District for the trial of these their confederates, or would permit your executive officers to discharge the trust committed to them, for twenty-four hours?

At the time this conspiracy was entered into, and when this Court was convened and entered upon this trial, the country was in a state of civil war. An army of insurrectionists have, since this trial began, shed the blood of Union soldiers in battle. The conspirator, by whose hand his co-conspirators, whether present or absent, jointly murdered the President on the 14th of last April, could not be and was not arrested upon the order of any civil magistrate, but was pursued by the military power of the Government, captured and slain. Was this an act of usurpation, a violation of the right guarantied to that fleeing assassin by the very Constitution against which and for the subversion of which he had conspired and murdered the President? Who in all this land is weak enough or base enough to assert it?

I would be glad to know by what law the President, by a military force, acting only upon his military orders, is justified in pursuing, arresting, and killing one of these conspirators, and is condemned for arresting in like manner, and by his order subjecting to trial, according to the laws of war, any or all of the other parties to this same damnable conspiracy and crime, by a military tribunal of justice, a tribunal, I may be pardoned for saying, who-e integrity and impartiality are above suspicion, and pass unchallenged even by the accused themselves.

The argument against the jurisdiction of this court rests upon the assumption that even in time of insurrection and civil war, no crimes are cognizable and punishable by military commission or court-martial, save crimes committed in the military or naval service of the United States, or in the militia of the several States when called into the actual service of the United States. But that is not all the argument; ultimate that under this plea to the jurisdiction, the accused have the right to demand that this court at decide that it is not a judicial tribunal and has no existence.

This is a most extraordinary proposition: that the President, under the Constitution and laws of the United States, was not only not authorized but absolutely forbidden to constitute this court for the trial of the accused, and, therefore, the act or the President is void, and the gentlemen who compose the tribunal without judicial authority or power, and are not in fact or in law a court.

That I do not mistake what is claimed and attempted to be established on behalf of the accused, I ask the attention of the Court to the following as the gentleman's (Mr. Johnson's) propositions:—

That Congress has not authorized, and, under the Constitution, cannot authorize the appointment of this Commission.

That this Commission has, "as a Court, no legal existence or authority," because the President, who alone appointed the Commission, has no such power.

That his act "is a mere nullity, the usurpation of a power not vested in the Executive, and conferring no authority upon you."

We have had no common exhibition of law learning in this defense, prepared by a Senator of the United States; but with all his experience, and all his learning, and acknowledged ability, he has failed, utterly failed, to show how a tribunal constituted and sworn, as this has been, to duly try and determine the charge and specification against the accused, and by its Commission not authorized to hear or determine any other issues whatever, can rightfully entertain, or can by any possibility pass upon, the proposition presented by this argument of the gentleman for its consideration.

The members of this Court are officers in the army of the United States, and by order of the President, as Commander-in-Chief, are required to discharge this duty, and are authorized in this capacity to dis harge no other duty, to exercise no other judicial power. Of course, if the commission of the President constitutes this a Court for the trial of this case only, as such Court it is competent to decide all questions of law and fact arising in the trial of the case. But this Court has no power, as a Court, to declare the authority by which it was constituted null and void and the act of the President a mere nullity, a usurpation. Has it been shown by the learned gentleman who demands that this Court shall so decide, that officers of the army may lawfully and constitutionally question in this manner the orders of their Commander-in-Chief, disobey, set them aside or declare them a nullity and a usurpation? Even if it be conceded that the officers thus detailed by order of the Commander-in-Chief may question and utterly disregard his order and set aside his authority, is it possible, in the nature of things, that any body of men, constituted and qualified as a tribunal of justice, can sit in judgment upon the proposition that they are not a Court for any purpose, and finally decide judicially, as a Court, that the Government which appointed them was without authority? Why not crown the absurdity of this proposition by asking the several members of this Court to determine that they are not men, living intelligent, responsible men? This would be no more irrational than the question upon which they are asked to pass. How can any sensible man entertain it? Before he begins to reason upon the proposition he must take for granted, and therefore decide in advance the very question in dispute, to wit, his actual existence.

So with the question presented in this remarkable argument for the defense. Before this Court can enter upon the inquiry of the want of authority in the President to constitute them a Court, they must take for granted and decide the very point in issue, that the President had the authority; and that they are, in law and in fact, a judicial tribunal; and, having assumed this, they are gravely asked, as such judicial tribunal, to finally and solemnly decide and declare that they are not in fact or in law a judicial tribunal, but a mere nullity and nonentity. A most lame and impotent conclusion!

As the learned counsel seems to have great reverence for judicial authority, and requires precedent for every opinion, I may be pardoned for saying that the objection which I urge against the possibility of any judicial tribunal, after being officially qualified as such, entertaining, much less judicially deciding, the proposition that it has no legal existence as a Court, and that the appointment was a usurpation and without authority of law, has been solemnly ruled by the Supreme Court of the United States.

That Court say:—"The acceptance of the judicial office is a recognition of the *authority* from which it is derived. If a court should enter upon the inquiry (whether the *authority* of the Government which established it existed), and should come to the conclusion that the Government under which it acted had been put aside, it would cease to be a court and be *incapable* of pronouncing a judicial decision upon the question it undertook to try. If it decides at all, as a court, it necessarily affirms the existence and *authority* of the Government under which it is exercising judicial power."—(*Luther vs. Borden*, 7 *Howard*, 40.)

That is the very question raised by the learned gentleman in his argument, that there was no *authority* in the President, by whose act alone this tribunal was constituted, to vest it with judicial power to try this issue, and by the order upon your record, as has already been shown, if you have no power to try this issue for want of authority in the Commander-in-Chief to constitute you a Court, you are no Court and have no power to try any issue, because his order limits you to this issue, and this alone.

It requires no very profound legal attainments to apply the ruling of the highest judicial tribunal of this country just cited, to the point raised, not by the pleadings, but by the argument, This Court exists as a judicial tribunal by authority only of the President of the United States; the acceptance of the office is an acknowledgment of the validity of the authority conferring it, and if the President had no authority to order, direct and constitute this Court to try the accused, and, as is claimed, did, in so constituting it, perform an unconstitutional and illegal act, it necessarily results that the order of the President is void and of no effect, and has created no court; therefore this a tribunal of justice, and therefore its members are incapable of pronouncing a judicial decision upon the question presented.

There is a marked distinction between the question here presented and that raised by a plea to the jurisdiction of a tribunal whose existence as a Court is neither questioned nor denied. Here it is argued, through many pages, by a learned Senator and a distinguished lawyer, that the order of the President, by whose authority alone this Court is constituted a tribunal of military justice is unlawful; if unlawful it is void and of no effect, and has created no court; therefore this body, not being a court, can have no more power as a court to decide any question whatever than have its individual members power to decide that they as men do not in fact exist.

It is a maxim of the common law—the perfection of human reason—that what is impossible the law requires of no man.

How can it be possible that a judicial tribunal can decide the question that it does not exist any more than that a rational man can decide that he does not exist?

The absurdity of the proposition so elaborately urged upon the consideration of this Court cannot be saved from the ridicule and contempt of sensible men by the pretense that the Court is not asked judicially to decide that it is not a court, but only that it has no jurisdiction; for it is a fact not to be denied that the whole argument for the defense on this point is that the President had not the lawful authority to issue the order by which alone this Court is constituted, and that the order for its creation is null and void.

Gentlemen might as well ask the Supreme Court of the United States, upon a plea to the jurisdiction, to decide as a Court that the President had no lawful authority to nominate the Judges thereof severally to the Senate, and that the Senate had no lawful authority to advise and consent to their appointment, as to ask this Court to decide as a Court that the order of the President of the United States constituting it a tribunal for the sole purpose of this trial was not only without authority of law, but against and in violation of law. If this Court is not a lawful tribunal, it has no existence, and can no more speak as a court than the dead, much less pronounce the judgment required at its hands, that it is not a court, and that the President of the United States, in submitting it such to try the question upon the charge and specification preferred, has transcended his authority, and violated his oath of office.

Before passing from the consideration of the proposition of the learned Senator that this is not a court, it is fit that I should notice that another of the counsel for the accused (Mr. Ewing) has also advanced the same opinion, certainly with more directness and candor, and without any qualification. His statement is, "You," gentlemen, "are no court under the Constitution." This remark of the gentleman cannot fail to excite surprise, when it is remembered that the gentleman, not many months since, was a General in the service of the country, and as such, in his Department in the West, proclaimed and enforced martial law by the constitution of military tribunals for the trial of citizens not in the land or naval forces, but who were guilty of military offenses, for which he deemed them justly punishable before military courts, and accordingly he punished them. Is the gentleman quite sore, when that account comes to be rendered for these alleged unconstitutional assumptions of power, that he will not have to answer for more of these alleged violations of the rights of citizens by illegal arrests, convictions and executions than any of the members of this Court? In support of his opinion that this is no Court, the gentleman cites the 3d article of the Constitution, which provides "that the judicial power of the United States shall be vested in one supreme court, and such inferior courts as Congress may establish," the judges whereof "shall hold their offices during good behavior."

It is a sufficient answer to say to the gentleman, that the power of this Government to try and punish military offenses by military tribunals is no part of the judicial power of the United States," under the 3d article of the Constitution, but a *power conferred* by the 8th section of the 1st article, and so it has been ruled by the Supreme Court in *Dyres vs. Hoover*, 20 Howard 78. If this power is so conferred by the 8th section, a military court authorized by Congress, and constituted as this has been to try all persons for military crimes in time of war, though not exercising "the judicial power" provided for in the 3d article, is nevertheless a court as constitutional as the Supreme Court itself. The gentleman admits this to the extent of the trial, by courts-martial, of persons in the military or naval service, and by admitting it, he gives up the point. There is no *express* grant for any such tribunal, and the power to establish such a court, therefore, is *implied* from the provisions of the 8th section, 1st article, that "Congress shall have power to provide and maintain a navy," and also "to make rules for the government of the land and naval forces." From these grants the Supreme Court infer the power to establish courts-martial, and from the grants in the same 8th section, as I shall notice hereafter, that "Congress shall have power to declare war," and "to pass all laws necessary and proper to carry this and all other powers into effect," it is necessarily implied that in time of war Congress may authorize military commissions to try all crimes committed in aid of the public enemy, as such tribunals are necessary to give effect to the power to make war and suppress insurrection.

Inasmuch as the gentleman (General Ewing) for whom, personally, I have a high regard, as the military commander of a Western Department made a liberal exercise, under the order of the Commander-in-Chief of the army, of this power to arrest and try military offenders not in the land or naval forces of the United States, and indicted upon them, as I am informed, the extreme penalty of the law by virtue of his military jurisdiction, I wish to know whether he proposes, by his proclamation of the personal responsibility awaiting all such usurpations of judicial authority, that he himself shall be subjected to the same stern judgment which he invokes against others; that, in short, he shall be drawn and quartered for inflicting the extreme penalties of the law upon citizens of the United States in violation of the Constitution and laws of his country? I trust that his error of judgment in pronouncing this military jurisdiction a usurpation and violation of the Constitution may not rise up in judgment to condemn him, and that he may never be subjected to pains and penalties for having done his duty heretofore in exercising this rightful authority, and in bringing to judgment those who conspired against the lives and liberties of the people.

Here I might leave this question, committing it to the charitable speeches of men, but for the fact that the learned counsel has been more careful in his extraordinary argument to denounce the President as a usurper than to show how the Court could possibly decide that it has no judicial existence, and yet that it has judicial existence.

A representative of the people and of the rights of the people before this Court, by the appointment of the President, and which appointment was neither sought by me nor desired, I cannot allow all that has here been said by way of denunciation of the murdered President and his successor to pass unnoticed. This has been made the occasion by the learned counsel, Mr. Johnson, to volunteer, not to defend the accused, Mary E. Surratt, not to make a judicial argument in her behalf, but to make a political harangue, a partisan speech against his Government and country, and thereby swell the cry of the armed legions of sedition and rebellion that but yesterday shook the heavens with their infernal enginery of treason and filled the habitations of the people with death. As the law forbids a Senator of the United States to receive compensation, or fee, for defending, 'n cases before civil or military commissions, the gentleman volunteers to make a speech before this Court, in which he denounces the action of the Executive Department in proclaiming and executing martial law against Rebels in arms, their aiders and abettors, as a usurpation and a tyranny. I deem it my duty to reply to this denunciation, not for the purpose of presenting thereby any question for the decision of this Court, for I have shown that the argument of the gentleman presents no question for its decision as a Court, but to repel, as far as I may be able, the unjust aspersion attempted to be cast upon the memory of our dead President and upon the official conduct of his successor.

I propose now to answer fully all that the gentleman (Mr. Johnson) has said of the want of jurisdiction in this Court, and of the alleged usurpation and tyranny of the Executive, that the enlightened public opinion, to which he appeals, may decide whether all this denunciation is just; whether, indeed, conspiring against the whole people, and confederation and agreement in aid of insurrection to murder all the executive officers of the Government, cannot be checked or arrested by the executive power. Let the people decide this question, and in doing so, let them pass upon the action of the Senator as well as upon the action of those whom he so arrogantly arraigns. His plea in behalf of an expiring and shattered rebellion is a fit subject for public consideration and for public condemnation.

Let that people also note, that while the learned gentleman (Mr. Johnson), as a volunteer, without pay, thus condemns as a usurpation the means employed so effectually to suppress this gigantic insurrection, the New York *News*, whose proprietor, Benjamin Wood, is shown, by the testimony upon your record, to have received from the agents of the Rebellion twenty-five thousand dollars, rushes into the lists to champion the cause of the Rebellion, its aiders and abettors, by following to the letter his colleague (Mr. Johnson), and with greater plainness of speech, and a fervor intensified, doubtless, by the twenty-five thousand dollars received, and the hope of more, denounces the Court as a usurpation, and threatens the members with the consequences!

The argument of the gentleman to which the Court has listened so patiently and so long is but an attempt to show that it is unconstitutional for the Government of the United States to arrest upon military order, and try before military tribunals, and punish upon conviction, in accordance with the laws of war and the usages of nations, all criminal offenders acting in aid of the existing Rebellion. It does seem to me that the speech in its tone and temper is the same as that which the country has heard for the last four years, uttered by the armed Rebels themselves and by their apologists, averring that it was unconstitutional for the Government of the United States to defend by arms its own rightful authority and the supremacy of its laws.

It is as clearly the right of the Republic to live and to defend its life until it forfeits that right by crime as it is the right of the individual to live so long as God gives him life, unless he forfeits that right by crime. I make no argument to support this proposition. Who is there here or elsewhere to cast the reproach upon my country that for her crimes she must die? Youngest born of the nations! is she not immortal by all the dread memories of the past, by that sublime and voluntary sacrifice of the present, in which the bravest and noblest of her sons have laid down their lives that she might live, giving their serene brows to the dust of the grave, and lifting their hands for the last time amidst the consuming fires of battle! I assume, for the purposes of this argument, that self-defense is as clearly the right of nations as it is the acknowledged right of men that the American people may do in the defense and maintenance of their own rightful authority against organized armed rebels, their aiders and abettors, whatever free and independent nations anywhere upon this globe, in time of war, may of right do.

All this is substantially denied by the gentleman in the remarkable argument which he has here made. There is nothing further from my purpose than to do injustice to the learned gentleman or to his elaborate and ingenious argument. To justify what I have already said, I may be permitted here to remind the Court that nothing is said by the counsel touching the conduct of the accused, Mary E. Surratt, as shown by the testimony; that he makes confession at the end of his arraignment of the Government and country, that he has not made such argument, and that he leaves it to be made by her other counsel. He does take care, however, to arraign the country and the Government for conducting a trial with closed doors and before a secret tribunal, and compares the proceedings of this Court to the Spanish Inquisition, using the strongest words at his command to intensify the horror which he supposes his announcement will excite throughout the civilized world.

Was this dealing fairly by this Government? Was there anything in the conduct of the proceedings here that justified any such remark? Has this been a secret trial? Has it not been conducted in open day, in the presence of the accused, and in the presence of seven gentlemen learned in the law, who appeared from day to day as their counsel? Were they not informed of the accusation against them? Were they deprived of the right of challenge? Was it not secured to them by law, and were they not asked to exercise it? Has any part of the evidence been suppressed? Have not all the proceedings been published to the world? What, then, was done, or intended to be done, by the Government which justifies this clamor about a Spanish Inquisition?

That a people assailed by organized treason over an extent of territory half as large as the continent of Europe, and assailed in their very capital by secret assassins banded together and hired to do the work of murder by the instigation of those conspirators, may not be permitted to make inquiry, even with closed doors, touching the nature and extent of the organization, ought not to be asserted by any gentleman who makes the least pretensions to any knowledge of the law, either common, civil or military. Who does not know that at the common law all inquisition touching crimes and misdemeanors, preparatory to indictment by the grand inquest of the State, is made with closed doors?

In this trial, no parties accused, nor their counsel, nor the reporters of this Court, were at any time excluded from its deliberations when any testimony was being taken; nor has there been any testimony taken in the case with closed doors, save that of a few witnesses, who testified, not in regard to the accused or either of them, but in respect to the traitors and conspirators not on trial, who were alleged to have incited the crime. Who is there to say that the American people, in time of armed Rebellion and civil war, have not the right to make such examination as secretly as they may deem necessary, either in a military or civil court?

I have said this, not by way of apology for anything the Government has done or attempted to do in the progress of this trial, but to expose the animus of the argument, and to repel the accusation against my country sent out to the world by the counsel. From anything that he has said, I have yet to learn that the American people have not the right to make their inquiries secretly, touching a general conspiracy in aid of an existing rebellion, which involves their nationality and the peace and security of all.

The gentleman then enters into a learned argument for the purpose of showing that, by the Constitution, the people of the United States cannot, in war or in peace, subject any person to trial before a military tribunal, whatever may be his crime or offense, unless such person be in the military or naval service of the United States. The conduct of this argument is as remarkable as its assaults upon the Government are unwarranted, and its insinuations about the revival of the inquisition and secret trials are inexcusable. The Court will notice that the argument, from the beginning almost to its conclusion, insists that no person is liable to be tried by military or martial law before a military tribunal, save those in the land and naval service of the United States. I repeat, the conduct of this argument of the gentleman is remarkable. As an instance, I ask the attention, not only of this Court, but of that public whom he has ventured to address in this tone, and temper, to the authority of the distinguished Chancellor Kent, whose great name the counsel has endeavored to press into his service in support of his general proposition, that no person save those in the military or naval service of the United States is liable to be tried by for any crime whatever, either in peace or in war, before a military tribunal.

The language of the gentleman, "after citing the provision of the Constitution, "that no person shall be held to answer for a capital or otherwise infamous crime unless on a presentment or indictment of a grand jury, except in cases arising in the land or naval forces, or in the militia, when in actual service in time of war or public danger," is "that this exception is designed to leave in force, not to enlarge, the power vested in Congress by the original Constitution to make rules for the government and regulation of the land and naval forces; that the land or naval forces are the terms used in both, have the same meaning, and until lately have been supposed by every commentator and judge to exclude from military jurisdiction offenses committed by citizens not belonging to such forces." The learned gentleman then adds: "Kent, in a note to his 1st Commentaries, 341, states, and with accuracy, that 'military and naval crimes and offenses, committed while the party is attached to and under the immediate authority of the army and navy of the United States and in actual service, are not cognizable under the common law jurisdiction of the courts of the United States.'" I ask this Court to bear in mind that this is the only passage which he quotes from this note of Kent in his argument, and that no man possessed of common sense, however destitute he may be of the exact and varied learning in the law to which the gentleman may rightfully lay claim, can for a moment entertain the opinion that the distinguished Chancellor of New York, in the passage just cited, intimates any such thing as the counsel asserts that the Constitution excludes from military jurisdiction offenses committed by citizens not belonging to the land or naval forces.

Who can fail to see that Chancellor Kent, by the passage cited, only decides that military and naval crimes and offenses committed by a party attached to and under the immediate authority of the Army and Navy of the United States and in actual service, are not cognizable under the common law jurisdiction of the Courts of the United States? He only says they are not cognizable under its common law jurisdiction; but by that he does not say or intimate, what is attempted to be said by the counsel for him, that "all crimes committed by citizens are by the Constitution excluded from military jurisdiction," and that the perpetrators of them can under no circumstances be tried before military tribunals. Yet the counsel ventures to proceed, standing upon this passage quoted from Kent, to say that, "according to this great authority, every other class of persons and every other species of offenses are within the jurisdiction of the civil Courts, and entitled to the protection of the proceeding by presentment or indictment and the public trial in such a Court."

Whatever that great authority may have said elsewhere, it is very doubtful whether any candid man in America will be able to come to the very learned and astute conclusion that Chancellor Kent has asserted in the note or any part of the note which the gentleman has just cited. If he has said it elsewhere, it is for the gentleman, if he relies upon Kent for authority, to produce the passage. But was it fair treatment of this "great authority"—was it not taking an unwarrantable privilege with the distinguished Chancellor, and his great work, the enduring monument of his learning and genius, to so mutilate the note referred to, as might leave the gentleman at liberty to make his deductions and assertions under cover of the great name of the New York chancellor, to suit the emergency of his case, by omitting the following passage, which oc-

curs in the same note, and absolutely excludes the conclusion so defiantly put forth by the counsel to support his argument? In that note Chancellor Kent says:—

"Military law is a system of regulations for the government of the armies in the service of the United States, authorized by the act of Congress of April 10, 1806, known as the Articles of War, and naval law is a similar system for the government of the navy, under the act of Congress of April 23, 1800. But martial law is quite a distinct thing, and is founded upon paramount necessity, and proclaimed by a military chief."

However unsuccessful, after this exposure, the gentleman appears in maintaining his monstrous proposition, that the American people are by their own Constitution forbidden to try the aiders and abettors of armed traitors and rebellion before military tribunals, and subject them, according to the laws of war and the usages of nations to just punishment for their great crimes, it has been made clear from what I have already stated that he has been eminently successful in mutilating this beautiful production of that great mind; which act of mutilation every one knows is violative alike of the laws of peace and war. Even in war the divine creations of art and the immortal productions of genius and learning are spared.

In the same spirit, and it seems to me with the same unfairness as that just noted, the learned gentleman has very adroitly pressed into his service, by an extract from the autobiography of the war-worn veteran and hero, General Scott, the names of the late Secretary of War Mr, Marcy, and the learned ex-Attorney General, Mr. Cushing. This adroit performance is achieved in this way: after stating the fact that General Scott in Mexico proclaimed martial law for the trial and punishment by military tribunals of persons guilty of "assassination, murder, and poisoning," the gentleman proceeds to quote from the Autobiography, "that this order, when handed to the then Secretary of War (Mr. Marcy) for his approval, 'a startle at the title (martial law order) was the only comment he then or ever made on the subject,' and that it was 'soon silently returned as too explosive for safe handling.' A little later (he adds) the Attorney-General (Mr. Cushing) called and asked for a copy, and the law officer of the Government, whose business it is to speak on all such matters, was stricken with legal dumbness.'" Thereupon the learned gentleman proceeds to say: "How much more startled and more paralyzed would these great men have been had they been consulted on such a commission as this! A commission not to sit in another country, and to try offenses not provided for in any law of the United States, civil or military, then in force, but in their own country and in a part of it where there are laws providing for their trial and punishment, and civil courts clothed with ample powers for both, and in the daily and undisturbed exercise of their jurisdiction."

I think I may safely say, without stopping to make any special references, that the official career of the late Secretary of War (Mr. Marcy) gave no indication that he ever doubted or denied the constitutional power of the American people, acting through their duly constituted agents, to do any act justified by the laws of war, for the suppression of a rebellion or to repel invasion. Certainly there is nothing in this extract from the Autobiography which justifies any such conclusion. He was startled, we are told, it may have been as much the admiration he had for the boldness and wisdom of the conqueror of Mexico as any abhorrence he had for the trial and punishment of "assassins, poisoners, and murderers," according to the laws and usages of war.

But the official utterances of the ex-Attorney-General Cushing, with which the gentleman doubtless was familiar when he prepared this argument, by no means justify the attempt here made to quote him as authority against the proclamation and enforcement of martial law in time of rebellion and civil war. That distinguished man, not second in legal attainments to any who have held that position, has left an official opinion of record touching this subject. Referring to what is said by Sir Matthew Hale in his History of the Common Law concerning martial law, wherein he limits it, as the gentleman has seemed by the whole drift of his argument desirous of doing, and says that it is "not in truth and in reality law, but something indulged rather than allowed as a law—the necessity of government, order and discipline in an army," Mr. Cushing makes this just criticism: "This proposition is a mere composite blunder, a total misapprehension of the matter. It confounds martial law and law military; it ascribes to the former the uses of the latter; it erroneously assumes that the government of a body of troops is a necessity more than of a body of civilians or citizens. It confounds and confuses all the relations of the subject, and is an apt illustration of the incompleteness of the notions of the common law jurists of England in regard to matters not comprehended in that limited branch of legal science. * * * Military law, it is now perfectly understood in England, is a branch of the law of the land, applicable only to certain acts of a particular class of persons and administered by special tribunals; but neither in that nor in any other respect essentially differing as to foundation in constitutional reason from admiralty, ecclesiastical, or indeed chancery and common law. * * * It is the system of rules for the government of the army and navy established by successive acts of Parliament. * * * * * Martial law, as exercised in any country by the commander of a foreign army, is an element of the *jus belli.*

"It is incidental to the state of solemn war, and appertains to the law of nations. * * Thus, while the armies of the United States occupied different provinces of the Mexican Republic, the respective commanders were not limited in authority by any local law. They allowed, or rather required, the magistrates of the country, municipal or judicial, to continue to administer the laws of the country among their countrymen, but in subjection, always to the military power, which acted summarily and according to discretion, when the belligerent interests of the conqueror required it, and which exercised jurisdiction, either summarily or by means of military commissions for the protection or the punishment of citizens of the United States in Mexico."—*Opinions of Attorneys-General,* vol. viii, 366, 369.

Mr. Cushing says, "That, it would seem, was one of the forms of martial law;" but he adds, that such an example of martial law administered by a foreign army in the enemy's country "does not enlighten us in regard to the question of martial law in one's own country, and was administered by its military commanders. That is a case which the law of nations does not reach. Its regulation is of the domestic resort of the organic laws of the country itself, and regarding which, as it happens, there is no definite or explicit legislation in the United States, as there is none in England.

"Accordingly, in England, as we have seen, Earl Grey assumes that when martial law exists it has no legal origin, but is a mere fact of necessity, to be legalized afterward by a bill of indemnity, if there be occasion. I am not prepared to say that, under existing laws such may not also be the case in the United States."—*Ibid.* 370.

After such a statement, wherein ex-Attorney-General Cushing very clearly recognizes the right of this Government, as also of England, to employ martial law as a means of defense in time of war, whether domestic or foreign, he will be as much surprised when he reads the argument of the learned gentleman, wherein he is described as being struck with *legal dumbness* at the mere mention of proclaiming martial law, and its enforcement by the commander of our army, in Mexico, as the late Secretary of War was startled with even the mention of its title.

Even some of the reasons given, and certainly the power exercised by the veteran hero himself would seem to be in direct conflict with the propositions of the learned gentleman.

The Lieutenant-General says he "excludes from his order cases already cognizable by court-martial, and limits it to cases not provided for in the act of Congress establishing rules and articles for the government of the armies of the United States." Has not the gentleman who attempts to press General Scott into his service argued and insisted upon it that the commander of the army cannot subject the soldiers under his command to any control or punishment whatever, save that which is provided for in the articles?

It will not do, in order to sustain the gentleman's hypothesis, to say that these provisions of the Constitution, by which he attempts to fetter the power of the people to punish such offenses in time of war within the territory of the United States, may be disregarded by an officer of the United States in command of its armies in the trial and punishment of its soldiers in a foreign war. The law of the United States for the government of its own armies follows the flag upon the sea and in every land.

The truth is that the right of the people to proclaim and execute martial law is a necessary incident of war, and this was the right exercised, and rightfully exercised by Lieutenant-General Scott in Mexico. It was what Earl Grey has justly said was a "fact of necessity," and, I may add, an act as clearly authorized as was the act of fighting the enemy when they appeared before him.

In making this exception, the Lieutenant-General followed the rule recognized by the American authorities on military law, in which it is declared that "many crimes committed even by military officers, enlisted men, or camp retainers, cannot be tried under the rules and articles of war. Military commissions must be resorted to for such cases, and these commissions should be ordered by the same authority, be constituted in a similar manner, and their proceedings be conducted according to the same general rules as general courts-martial."—*Benet,* 15.

There remain for me to notice, at present, two other points in this extraordinary speech; first, that martial law does not warrant a military commission for the trial of military offenses, that is, offenses committed in time of war in the interests of the public enemy, and by concert and agreement with the enemy; and second, that martial law does not prevail in the United States, and has never been declared by any competent authority.

It is not necessary, as the gentleman himself has declined to argue the first point, whether martial law authorizes the organization of military commissions by order of the commander-in-chief, to try such offenses, that I should say more than that the authority just cited by me shows that such commissions are authorized under martial law, and are created by the commander for the trial of all such offenses, when their punishment by court-martial is not provided for by the express statute law of the country.

The second point, that martial law has not been declared by any competent authority, is an arraignment of the late murdered President of the United States for his proclamation of September 24, 1862, declaring martial law throughout the United States, and of which, in Lawrence's edition of Wheaton on International Law, p. 522, it is said.,"Whatever may be the inference to be deduced either from constitutional or international law, or from the usages of European Governments, as to the legitimate depository of the power of suspending the writ of *habeas corpus,* the virtual abrogation of the judiciary in cases affecting individual liberty, and the establishment as *matter of fact* in the United States, by the Executive alone, of martial law, not merely in the insurrectionary districts, or in cases of military occupancy, but throughout the entire Union, and not temporarily, but as an institution as permanent as the insurrection on which it professes to be based, and capable on the same principle of being revived in all cases of foreign as well as civil war, are placed beyond question by the President's proclamation of September 24, 1862." That proclamation is as follows:—

"By the President of the United States of America.
"A PROCLAMATION.

"Whereas, It has become necessary to call into service not only volunteers, but also portions of the militia of the States, by a draft, in order to suppress the insurrection existing in the United States, and disloyal persons are not adequately restrained by the ordinary processes of law from hindering this measure, and from giving aid and comfort in various ways to the insurrection; Now, therefore, be it ordered, that during the existing insurrection, and as a necessary means for suppressing the same, all Rebels and insurgents, their aiders and abettors, within the United States, and all persons discouraging volunteer enlistments, resisting militia drafts, or guilty of any disloyal practice, affording aid and comfort to Rebels, against the authority of the United States, shall be subject to martial law, and liable to trial and punishment by courts-martial or military commission.

"Second. That the writ of *habeas corpus* is suspended in respect to all persons arrested, or who are now, or hereafter during the Rebellion shall be imprisoned in any fort, camp, arsenal, military prison or other place of confinement, by any military authority, or by the sentence of any court-martial or military commission.

"In witness whereof I have hereunto set my hand and caused the seal of the United States to be affixed.

"Done at the city of Washington, this 24th day of September, A. D. 1862, and of the independence of the United States the eighty-seventh.

"ABRAHAM LINCOLN.

"By the President:
"WILLIAM H. SEWARD, Secretary of State."

This proclamation is duly certified from the War Department to be in full force and not revoked, and is evidence of record in this case; and but a few days since a proclamation of the President, of which this court will take notice, declares that the same remains in full force.

It has been said by another of the counsel for the accused (Mr. Stone) in his argument, that, admitting its validity, the proclamation ceases to have effect with the insurrection, and is terminated by it. It is true the proclamation of martial law only continues during the insurrection; but inasmuch as the question of the existence of an insurrection is a political question, the decision of which belongs exclusively to the political department of the Government, that department alone can declare its existence, and that department alone can declare its termination, and by the action of the political department of the Government every judicial tribunal in the land is concluded and bound. That question has been settled for fifty years in this country by the Supreme Court of the United States: First, in the case of Brown vs. The United States (8 Cranch); also in the prize cases (2 Black., 641). Nothing more, therefore, need be said upon this question of an *existing* insurrection than this; The political department of the Government has heretofore proclaimed an insurrection, that department has not yet declared the insurrection ended, and the event on the 14th of April, which robbed the people of their chosen Executive, and clothed this land in mourning, bore sad but overwhelming witness to the fact that the Rebellion is not ended. The fact of the insurrection is not an open question to be tried or settled by parol, either in a military tribunal, or in a civil court.

The declaration of the learned gentleman who opened the defense (Mr. Johnson), that martial law has never been declared by any competent authority, as I have already said, arraigns Mr. Lincoln for a usurpation of power. Does the gentleman mean to say that, until Congress authorizes it, the President cannot proclaim and enforce martial law in the suppression of

TRIAL OF THE ASSASSINS AT WASHINGTON.

armed and organized Rebellion? Or does he only affirm that this act of the late President is a usurpation?

The proclamation of martial law in 1862 a usurpation, though it armed the people in that dark hour of trial with the means of defense against traitorous and secret enemies in every State and district of the country; though by its use some of the guilty were brought to swift and just punishment, and others deterred from crime or driven to flight; though by this means the innocent and defenseless were protected; though by this means the city of the gentleman's residence was saved from the violence and pillage of the mob and the torch of the incendiary. But, says the gentleman, it was a usurpation, forbidden by the laws of the land!

The same was said of the proclamation or blockade issued April 19 and 27, 1861, which declared a blockade of the ports of the insurgent States, and that all vessels violating the same were subjects of capture, and, together with the cargo to be condemned as prize. Inasmuch as Congress had not then recognized the fact of civil war, these proclamations were denounced as void. The Supreme Court decided otherwise, and affirmed the power of the Executive thus to subject the property on the seas to seizure and condemnation. I read from that decision.

"The Constitution confers upon the President the whole executive power; he is bound to take care that the laws be faithfully executed; he is commander-in-chief of the army and navy of the United States, and of the militia of the several States when called into the actual service of the United States. * * Whether the President, in fulfilling his duties as commander-in-chief in suppressing an insurrection, has met with such armed hostile resistance, and a civil war of such alarming proportions as will compel him to accord to them the character of belligerents is a question to be decided by him, and this court must be governed by the decisions and acts of the political department of the Government to which this power was intrusted. He must determine what degree of force the crisis demands.

"The proclamation of blockade is itself official and conclusive evidence to the court that a state of war existed which demanded and authorized a recourse to such a measure under the circumstances peculiar to the case." (2 Black, 670.)

It has been solemnly ruled by the same tribunal, in an earlier case, "that the power is confided to the Executive of the Union to determine when it is necessary to call out the militia of the States to repel invasion," as follows:—"That he is necessarily constituted the judge of the existence of the exigency in the first instance, and is bound to act according to his belief of the facts. If he does so act, and decides to call forth the militia, his orders for this purpose are in strict conformity with the provisions of the law; and it would seem to follow as a necessary consequence, that every act done by a subordinate officer, in obedience to such orders, is equally justifiable. The law contemplates that, under such circumstances, orders shall be given to carry the power into effect; and it cannot therefore be a correct inference that any other person has a just right to disobey them. The law does not provide for any appeal from the judgment of the President, or for any right in subordinate officers to review his decision, and in effect defeat it. Whoever a statute gives a discretionary power to any person, to be exercised by him upon his own opinion of certain facts, it is a sound rule of construction, that the statute constitutes him the sole and exclusive judge of the existence of those facts." (12 Wheaton, 31).

In the light of these decisions it must be clear to every mind that the question of the existence of an insurrection, and the necessity of calling into requisition for its suppression both the militia of the States and the army and navy of the United States, and of proclaiming martial law, which is an essential condition of war whether foreign or domestic, must rest with the officer of the Government who is charged by the express terms of the Constitution with the performance of this great duty for the common defense and the execution of the laws of the Union.

But it is further insisted by the gentleman in this argument that Congress has not authorized the establishment of military commissions, which are essential to the judicial administration of martial law and the punishment of crimes committed during the existence of a civil war, and especially that such commissions are not so authorized to try persons other than those in the military and naval service of the United States, or in the militia of the several States, when in the actual service of the United States. The gentleman's argument assuredly destroys itself, for he insists that the Congress, as the legislative department of the Government, can pass no law which, either in peace or war, can constitutionally subject any citizen not in the land or naval forces to trial for crime before a military tribunal, or otherwise than by a jury in the civil courts.

Why does the learned gentleman now tell us that Congress has not authorized this to be done, after declaring just as stoutly that by the fifth and sixth amendments to the Constitution no such military tribunals can be established for the trial of any person not in the military or naval service of the United States, or in the militia when in actual service, for the commission of any crime whatever in time of war or insurrection? It ought to have occurred to the gentleman when commenting upon the exception in the fifth article of the Constitution, that there was a reason for it very different from that which he saw fit to assign, and that reason, manifestly upon the face of the Constitution itself, was, that by the eighth section of the first article, it is expressly provided, that Congress shall have power to make rules for the government of the land and naval forces, and to provide for organizing, arming, and disciplining the militia, and for governing such part of them as may be employed in the service of the United States, and that, inasmuch as military discipline and order are as essential in an army in time of peace, as in time of war, if the Constitution would leave this power to Congress in peace, it must make the exception, so that rules and regulations for the government of the army and navy should be operative in time of peace as well as in time of war; because the provisions of the Constitution give the right of trial by jury IN TIME OF PEACE, in all criminal prosecutions by indictment, in terms embracing every human being that may be held to answer for crime in the United States; and therefore if the eighth section of the first article was to remain in full force IN TIME OF PEACE, the exception must be made, and accordingly, the exception was made. But by the argument we have listened to, this court is told, and the country is told, that in time of war, a war which involves in its dread issue the lives and interests of us all, the guaranties of the Constitution are in full force for the benefit of those who conspire with the enemy, creep into your camps, murder in cold blood, in the interests of the invader or insurgent, the commander-in-chief of your army, and secure to him the slow and weak provisions of the civil law, while the soldier who may when overcome by the demands of exhausted nature, which cannot be resisted, have slept at his post, is subject to be tried upon the spot by a military tribunal and shot. The argument amounts to this:—That as military courts and military trials of civilians in time of war are a usurpation and tyranny; and as soldiers are liable to such arrests and trial, Sergeant Corbett, who shot Booth, should be tried and executed by sentence of a military court, while Booth's co-conspirators and aiders should be saved from any such indignity as a military trial. I confess that I am too dull to comprehend the logic, the reason, or the sense of such a conclusion. If there is any one entitled to this privilege of a civil trial, it is remote period, and by a jury of the District, in time of civil war, when the foundations of the Republic are rocking beneath the earthquake tread of armed Rebellion, that man is the defender of the Republic. It will never do to say, as has been said in this argument, that the soldier is not liable to be tried in time of war by a military tribunal for any other offense than those prescribed in the rules and articles of war. To my mind, nothing can be clearer than that citizen and soldier alike, in time of civil or foreign war, after a proclamation of martial law, are triable by military tribunals for all offenses of which they may be guilty, in the interests of, or in concert with, the enemy.

These provisions, therefore, of your Constitution, for indictment and trial by jury in civil courts of all crimes are, as I shall hereafter show, silent and inoperative in time of war when the public safety requires it.

The argument to which I have thus been replying, as the Court will not fail to perceive, nor that public to which the argument is addressed, is a labored attempt to establish the proposition, that, by the Constitution of the United States, the American people cannot, even in a civil war the greatest the world has ever seen, employ martial law and military tribunals as a means of successfully asserting their authority, preserving their nationality, and securing protection to the lives and property of all, and especially to the persons of those to whom they have committed, officially, the great trust of maintaining the national authority. The gentleman says, with an air of perfect confidence, that he denies the jurisdiction of military tribunals for the trial of civilians in time of war, because neither the Constitution nor laws justify, but on the contrary repudiate them, and that all the experience of the past is against it. I might content myself with saying that the practice of all nations is against the gentleman's conclusion. The struggle for our national independence was aided and prosecuted by military tribunals and martial law, as well as by arms. The contest for American nationality began with the establishment, very soon after the firing of the first gun at Lexington, on the 19th day of April, 1775, of military tribunals and martial law. On the 30th of June, 1775, the Continental Congress provided that "whosoever, belonging to the continental army, shall be convicted of holding correspondence with, or giving intelligence to the enemy, either indirectly or directly, shall suffer such punishment as by a court-martial shall be ordered." This was found not sufficient, inasmuch as it did not reach those civilians who, like certain civilians of our day, claim the protection of the civil law in time of war against military arrests and military trials for military crimes. Therefore, the same Congress, on the 7th of November, 1775, amended this provision by striking out the words "belonging to the continental army," and adopting the article as follows:—

"*All persons* convicted of holding a treacherous correspondence with, or giving intelligence to the enemy, shall suffer death or such other punishment as a general court-martial shall think proper."

And on the 17th of June, 1776, the Congress added an additional rule—

"That all persons, not members of, nor owing allegiance to, any of the United States of America, who should be found lurking as spies in or about the fortifications or encampments of the armies of the United States, or any of them, shall suffer death, according to the law and usage of nations, by the sentence of a court-martial, or such other punishment as a court-martial shall direct."

Comprehensive as was this legislation, embracing as it did soldiers, citizens, and aliens, subjecting all alike to trial for their military crimes by the military tribunals of justice, according to the law and the usage of nations, it was found to be insufficient to meet that most dangerous of all crimes committed in the interests of the enemy by citizens in time of war, the crime of conspiring together to assassinate or seize and carry away the soldiers and citizens who were loyal to the cause of the country. Therefore, on the 27th of February, 1778, the Congress adopted the following resolution:—

"*Resolved*, That whatever inhabitants of these States shall kill, or seize, or take any loyal citizen or citizens thereof and convey him, her, or them to any place within the power of the enemy, or shall enter into any combination for such purpose, or attempt to carry the same into execution, or hath assisted, or shall assist therein; or shall, by giving intelligence, acting as a guide, or in any manner whatever, aid the enemy in the perpetration thereof, he shall suffer death by the judgment of a court-martial as a traitor, assassin, or spy, if the offense be committed within seventy miles of the head-quarters of the grand or other armies of these States where a general officer commands."—*Journals of Congress*, vol ii, pp. 459, 460.

So stood the law until the adoption of the Constitution of the United States. Every well informed man knows that at the time of the passage of these acts, the courts of justice having cognizance of all crimes against persons, were open in many of the States, and that by their several constitutions and charters, which were then the supreme law for the punishment of crimes committed within their respective territorial limits, no man was liable to conviction but by the verdict of a jury. Take, for example, the provisions of the Constitution of North Carolina, adopted on the 10th of November, 1776, and in full force at the time of the passage of the last resolution by Congress above cited, which provisions are as follows:—

"That no freeman shall be put to answer any criminal charge but by indictment, presentment or impeachment."

"That no freeman shall be convicted of any crime but by the unanimous verdict of a jury of good and lawful men in open court, as heretofore used."

This was the law in 1778 in all the States, and the provision for a trial by jury every one knows meant a jury of twelve men, empannelled and qualified to try the issue in a civil court. The conclusion is not to be avoided, that these enactments of the Congress under the Confederation set aside the trial by jury within the several States, and expressly provided for the trial by court-martial of "any of the inhabitants" who, during the revolution, might, contrary to the provisions of said law, and in aid of the public enemy, give them intelligence, or kill any loyal citizens of the United States, or enter into any combination to kill or carry them away. How comes it, if the argument of the counsel be true, that this enactment was passed by the Congress of 1778, when the constitutions of the several States at that day as fully guaranteed trial by jury to every person held to answer for a crime, as does the Constitution of the United States at this hour? Notwithstanding this fact, I have yet to learn that any loyal man ever challenged, during all the period of our conflict for independence and nationality, the validity of that law for the trial, for military offenses, by military tribunals, of all offenders, as the law, not of peace, but of war, and absolutely essential to the prosecution of war. I may be pardoned for saying that it is the accepted common law of nations, that martial-law is, at all times and everywhere, essential to the successful prosecution of war, whether it be a civil or a foreign war. The validity of those acts of the Continental and Confederate Congress I know was challenged, but only by men charged with the guilt of their country's blood.

Washington, the peerless, the stainless, and the just, with whom God walked through the night of that great trial, enforced this just and wise enactment upon all occasions. On the 30th of September, 1780, Joshua H. Smith, by the order of General Washington, was put upon his trial before a court-martial, convened in the State of New York, on the charge of there aiding and assisting Benedict Arnold, in a combination with the enemy, to *take*, *kill*, and *seize* such loyal citizens or soldiers of the United States as were in garrison at West Point. Smith objected to the jurisdiction, averring that he was a private citizen, not in the military or naval service, and therefore was only amenable to the civil authority of the State, whose Constitution had guaranteed the right of trial by jury to all persons held to answer for crime. (Chandler's Criminal Trials, vol. 2, p. 187). The Constitution of New York then in force had so provided; but, notwithstanding that, the Court overruled the plea, held him to answer, and tried him. I repeat that, when Smith was thus tried by court-martial, the Constitution of New York as fully guaranteed trial by jury in the civil courts to all civilians charged and held to answer for crimes within the limits of that State, as does the Constitution of the United States guarantee such trial within the limits of the District of Columbia. By the second of the Articles of Confederation each State retained "its sovereignty," and every power, jurisdiction and right not *expressly* delegated to the United States in Congress assembled. By those articles there was no express delegation of judicial power, therefore the States retained it fully.

If the military courts constituted by the commander of the army of the United States under the Confederation, who was appointed only by a resolution of the Congress, without any *express* grant of power to authorize it, his office not being created by the act of the people in their fundamental law, had jurisdiction in every State to try and put to death "any inhabitant" thereof who should *kill* any loyal citizen or enter into "any combination" for any such purpose therein in time of war, notwithstanding the provisions of the constitution and laws of such States, how can any man conceive that, under the Constitution of the United States, which is the supreme law over every State, anything in the constitution and laws of such State to the contrary notwithstanding, and the supreme law over every Territory of the republic as well, the Commander-in-Chief of the army of the United States, who is made such by the Constitution, and by its supreme authority clothed with the power and charged with the duty of directing and controlling the whole military power of the United States in time of rebellion or invasion, has not that authority?

I need not remind the Court that one of the marked differences between the Articles of Confederation and the Constitution of the United States was, that under the Confederation the Congress was the sole depository of all Federal power. The Congress of the Confederation, said Madison held "the command of the army," (Fed., No. 38). Has the Constitution, which was ordained by the people the better "to insure domestic tranquility and to provide for the common defense," so fettered the great power of self-defense against armed insurrection or invasion that martial law, so essential in war, is forbidden by that great instrument? I will yield to no man in reverence for or obedience to the Constitution of my country, esteeming it, as I do, a new evangel to the nations, embodying the democracy of the New Testament, the absolute equality of all men before the law, in respect of those rights of human nature which are the gift of God, and therefore as universal as the material structure of man. Can it be that this Constitution of ours, so divine in its spirit of justice, so beneficent in its results, so full of wisdom and goodness and truth, under which we be came one people, a great and powerful nationality, has in terms, or by implication, denied to this people the power to crush armed rebellion by war, and to arrest and punish, during the existence of such rebellion, according to the laws of war and the usages of nations, secret conspirators, who aid and abet the public enemy?

Here is a conspiracy, organized and prosecuted by armed traitors and hired assassins, receiving the moral support of thousands in every State and district, who pronounced the war for the Union a failure, and your now murdered but immortal Commander-in-Chief a tyrant; the object of which conspiracy, as the testimony shows, was to aid the tottering Rebellion which struck at the nation's life. It is in evidence that Davis, Thompson, and others, chiefs in this Rebellion, in aid of the same, agreed and conspired with others to poison the fountains of water which supply your commercial metropolis, and thereby murder its inhabitants; to secretly deposit in the habitations of the people and in the ships in your harbors inflammable materials, and thereby destroy them by fire; to murder by the slow and consuming torture of famine your soldiers, captive in their hands; to import pestilence in infected clothes to be distributed in your capital and camps, and thereby murder the surviving heroes and defenders of the Republic, who, standing by the holy graves of your unreturning brave, proudly and defiantly challenge to honorable combat and open battle all public enemies, that their country may live; and, finally, to crown this horrid catalogue of crime, this sum of all human atrocities, conspired, as charged upon your record, with the accused and John Wilkes Booth and John H. Surratt, to kill and murder in your capital the executive officers of your Government and the commander of your armies. When this conspiracy, entered into execution, and the foul and brutal murder of your President in the capital, you are told that it is unconstitutional, in order to arrest the further execution of the conspiracy, to interpose the military power of this Government for the arrest, without civil process, of any of the parties thereto and for their trial by a military tribunal of justice. If any such rule had obtained during our struggle for Independence, we never would have been a nation. If any such rule had been adopted and acted upon now, during the fierce struggle of the past four years, no man can say that our nationality would have thus long survived.

The whole people of the United States, by their Constitution, have created the office of President of the United States and Commander-in-Chief of the Army and Navy, and have vested, by the terms of that Constitution, in the person of the President and Commander-in-Chief, the power to enforce the execution of the laws, and preserve, protect and defend the Constitution.

The question may well be asked, If, as Commander-in-Chief, the President may not, in time of insurrection or war, proclaim and execute martial law, according to the usages of nations, how he can successfully perform the duties of his office—execute the laws, preserve the Constitution, suppress insurrection, and repel invasion?

Martial law and military tribunals are as essential to the successful prosecution of war, as are men, and arms, and munitions. The Constitution of the United States has vested the power to declare war and raise armies and navies exclusively in the Congress, and the power to prosecute the war and command the army and navy exclusively in the President of the United States. As under the Confederation, the commander of the army, appointed only by the Congress, was by the resolution of that Congress empowered to act as he might think proper for the good and welfare of the service; subject only to such restraints or orders as the Congress might give; so, under the Constitution, the President is, by the people who ordained that Constitution and declared him Commander-in-chief of the army and navy, vested with full power to direct and control the army and navy of the United States, and employ all the forces necessary to preserve, protect and defend the Constitution and execute the laws, as enjoined by his oath and the very letter of the Constitution, subject to no restriction or direction save such as Congress may from time to time prescribe.

That these powers for the common defense, intrusted by the Constitution exclusively to the Congress and the President, are, in time of civil war or foreign invasion, to be exercised without limitation or restraint, to the extent of the public necessity, and without any intervention of the Federal judiciary or of State constitutions or State laws, are facts in our history not open to question.

The position is not to be answered by saying you make the American Congress thereby omnipotent, and clothe the American Executive with the asserted attribute of hereditary monarchy—the king can do no wrong. Let the position be fairly stated—that the Congress and President, in war as in peace, are but the agents of the whole people, and that this unlimited power for the common defense against armed rebellion or foreign invasion is but the power of the people intrusted exclusively to the legislative and executive departments as their agents, for any and every abuse of which, these agents are directly responsible to the people; and the demagogue cry of an omnipotent Congress and an Executive invested with royal prerogatives, vanishes like the baseless fabric of a vision. If the Congress, corruptly or oppressively or wantonly abuse this great trust, the people by the irresistible power of the ballot hurl them from place. If the President so abuse the trust, the people by their Congress withhold supplies, or by impeachment transfer the trust to better hands, strip him of the franchises of citizenship and of office, and declare him forever disqualified to hold any position of honor, trust or power under the Government of his country.

I can understand very well why men should tremble at the exercise of this great power by a monarch whose person, by the constitution of his realm, is inviolable, but I cannot conceive how any American citizen, who has faith in the capacity of the whole people to govern themselves, should give himself any concern on the subject. Mr. Hallam, the distinguished author of the Constitutional History of England, has said:—

"Kings love to display the divinity with which their flatterers invest them in nothing so much as in the instantaneous execution of their will, and to stand revealed, as it were, in the storm and thunderbolt when their power breaks through the operation of secondary causes and awes a prostrate nation without the intervention of law."

How just are such words when applied to an irresponsible monarch! how absurd when applied to a whole people, acting through their duly appointed agents, whose will, thus declared, is the supreme law, to awe into submission and peace and obedience, not a prostrate nation, but a prostrate rebellion! The same great author utters the fact which all history attests, when he says:—

"It has been usual for all Governments during actual Rebellion to proclaim martial law for the suspension of civil jurisdiction; and this anomaly, I must admit," he adds, "is very far from being less indispensable at such unhappy seasons where the ordinary mode of trial is by jury than where the right of decision resides in the court."—*Const. Hist.*, vol. 1, ch. 5, p. 326.

That the power to proclaim martial law and fully or partially suspend the civil jurisdiction, Federal and State, in time of Rebellion or civil war, and punish by military tribunals all offenses committed in aid of the public enemy, is conferred upon Congress and the Executive, necessarily results from the unlimited grants of power for the common defense to which I have already briefly referred. I may be pardoned for saying that this position is not assumed by me for the purposes of this occasion, but that early in the first year of this great struggle for our national life I proclaimed it as a representative of the people, under the obligation of my oath, and as I then believed, and still believe, upon the authority of the great men who formed and fashioned the wise and majestic fabric of American Government.

Some of the citations which I deemed it my duty at that time to make, and some of which I now reproduce, have, I am pleased to say, found a wider circulation in books that have since been published by others.

When the Constitution was on trial for its deliverance before the people of the several States, its ratification was opposed on the ground that it conferred upon Congress and the Executive unlimited power for the common defense. To all such objectors, and they were numerous in every State, that great man, Alexander Hamilton, whose words will live as long as our language lives, speaking to the listening people of all the States and urging them not to reject that matchless instrument which bore the name of Washington, said:—

"The authorities essential to the care of the common defense are these—To raise armies; to build and equip fleets; to prescribe rules for the government of both; to direct their operations; to provide for their support. These powers ought to exist WITHOUT LIMITATION; because it is impossible to foresee or define the extent and variety of national exigencies, and the correspondent extent and variety of the means which may be necessary to satisfy them.

"The circumstances that endanger the safety of nations are infinite, and for this reason no constitutional shackles can wisely be imposed on the power to which the care of it is committed. * * * This power ought to be under the direction of the same councils which are appointed to preside over the common defense. * * * It must be admitted, as a necessary consequence, that there can be no limitation of that authority, which is to provide for the defense and protection of the community, in any manner essential to its efficacy; that is, in any manner essential to the formation, direction, or support of the national forces."

He adds the further remark:—"This is one of those truths which, to a correct and unprejudiced mind, carries its own evidence along with it, and may be obscured, but cannot be made plainer by argument or reasoning. It rests upon axioms as simple as they are universal the *means* ought to be proportioned to the *end;* the persons from whose agency the attainment of any *end* is expected ought to possess the means by which it is to be attained."—*Federalist*, No. 23.

In the same great contest for the adoption of the Constitution Madison, sometimes called the Father of the Constitution, said:—

"Is the power of declaring war necessary? No man will answer this question in the negative. * * * Is the power of raising armies and equipping fleets necessary? * * * It is involved in the power of self-defense. * * * With what color of propriety could the force necessary for defense be limited by those who cannot limit the force of offense. * * * The means of security can only be regulated by the means and the danger of attack. * * * It is in vain to oppose constitutional barriers to the impulse of self-preservation. It is worse than in vain, because it plants in the Constitution itself necessary usurpations of power."—*Federalist*, No. 41.

With this construction proclaimed both by the advocates and opponents of its ratification, the Constitution of the United States was accepted and adopted, and that construction has been followed, and acted upon by every department of the Government to this day.

It was as well understood then in theory as it has since been illustrated in practice, that the judicial power, both Federal and State, had no voice and could exercise no authority in the conduct and prosecution of a war, except in subordination to the political department of the Government. The Constitution contains the significant provision, "The privilege of the writ of *habeas corpus* shall not be suspended, unless when in cases of rebellion or invasion the public safety may require it.

What was this but a declaration that in time of rebellion or invasion, the public safety is the highest law? that so far as necessary the civil courts (of which the Commander-in-Chief, under the direction of Congress, shall be the sole judge) must be silent, and the rights of each citizen, as secured in time of peace, must yield to the wants, interests, and necessities of the nation? Yet we have been gravely told by the gentleman, in his argument, that the maxim *salus populi suprema est lex,* is but fit for a tyrant's use. Those grand men, whom God taught to build fabric of empire, thought otherwise, when they put that maxim into the Constitution of their country. It is very clear that the Constitution recognizes the great principle which underlies the structure of society and of all civil government, that no man lives for himself alone, but each for all; that, if need be, some must die, that the State may live, because at best the individual is but for to-day, while the commonwealth is for all time. I agree with the gentleman in the maxim which he borrows from Aristotle, "Let the public weal be under the protection of the law;" but I claim that in war, as in peace. by the very terms of the Constitution of the country, the public safety is under the protection of the law; that the Constitution itself has provided for the declaration of war for the common defense, to suppress rebellion, to repel invasion, and, by express terms, has declared that whatever is necessary to make the prosecution of the war successful, may be done, and ought to be done, and is therefore constitutionally lawful.

Who will dare to say that in time of civil war "no person shall be deprived of life, liberty, and property, without due process of law?" This is a provision of your Constitution than which there is none more just or sacred in it; it is, however, only the law of peace, not of war. In peace, that wise provision of the Constitution must be, and is, enforced by the civil courts; in war, it must be, and is, to a great extent, inoperative and disregarded. The thousands slain by your armies in battle were deprived of life "without due process of law." All spies arrested, convicted and executed by your military tribunals in time of war, are deprived of liberty and life "without due process of law;" all enemies captured and held as prisoners of war are deprived of liberty "without due process of law;" all owners whose property is forcibly seized and appropriated in war are deprived of their property "without due process of law." The Constitution recognizes the principle of common law, that every man's house is his castle; that his home, the shelter of his wife and children, is his most sacred possession; and has therefore specially provided, "that no soldier shall *in time of peace* be quartered in any house without the consent of its owner, nor in time of war, but in a manner to be prescribed by law (III Amendment), thereby declaring that in time of war Congress may by law authorize, as it has done, that without the consent and against the consent of the owner, the soldier may be quartered in any man's house, and upon any man's hearth. What I have said illustrates the proposition, that in time of war the civil tribunals of justice are wholly or partially silent, as the public safety may require; that the limitations and provisions of the Constitution in favor of life, liberty and property are therefore wholly or partially suspended. In this I am sustained by an authority second to none with intelligent American citizens, Mr. John Quincy Adams than whom a purer man or a wiser statesman never ascended the chair of the chief magistracy in America, said in his place in the House of Representatives, in 1836, that:—

"In the authority given to Congress by the Constitution of the United States to declare war, all the powers incident to war are by necessary implication conferred upon the Government of the United States. Now the powers incidental to war are derived, not from their internal municipal source, but from the laws and usages of nations. There are, then, in the authority of Congress and of the Executive two classes of powers altogether different in their nature and often incompatible with each other, the war power and the peace power. The peace power is limited by regulations and restricted by provisions prescribed within the Constitution itself. The war power is limited only by the laws and usage of nations. This power is tremendous; it is strictly constitutional, but it breaks down every barrier so anxiously erected for the protection of liberty, of property, and of life."

If this be so, how can there be trial by jury for military offences in time of civil war? If you cannot, and do not, try the armed enemy before you shoot him, or the captured enemy before you imprison him, why should you be held to open the civil courts and try the spy, the conspirator, and the assassin, in the secret service of the public enemy, by jury, before you convict and punish him? Why not clamor against holding imprisoned the captured armed Rebels, deprived of their liberty without due process of law? Are they not citizens? Why not clamor against slaying for their crime of treason, which is cognizable in the civil courts, by your rifled ordnance and the iron hail of your musketry in battle, these public enemies, without trial by jury? Are they not citizens? Why is the clamor confined exclusively to the trial by military tribunals of justice of traitorous spies, traitorous conspirators and assassins hired to do secretly what the armed Rebel attempts to do openly, murder your nationality by assassinating its defenders and its executive officers? Nothing can be clearer than that the Rebel captured prisoner, being a citizen of the republic, is as much entitled to trial by jury before he is committed to prison as the spy, or the aider and abettor of the treason by conspiracy and assassination, being a citizen, is entitled to such trial by jury before he is subjected to the just punishment of the law for his great crime. I think that in time of war the remark of Montesquieu, touching the civil judiciary, is true, that " it is next to nothing." Hamilton well said, "The Executive holds the sword of the community; the judiciary has no direction of the

strength of society; it has neither force nor will; it has judgment alone, and is dependent for the execution of that upon the arm of the Executive." The people of these States so understood the Constitution, and adopted it, and intended thereby, without limitation or restraint, to empower their Congress and Executive to authorize by law, and execute by force, whatever the public safety might require to suppress rebellion or repel invasion.

Notwithstanding all that has been said by the counsel for the accused to the contrary the Constitution has received this construction from the day of its adoption to this hour. The Supreme Court of the United States has solemnly decided that the Constitution has conferred upon the Government authority to employ all the means necessary to the faithful execution of all the powers which that Constitution enjoins upon the Government of the United States, and upon every department and every officer thereof, speaking of that provision of the Constitution which provides that "Congress shall have power to make all laws that may be necessary and proper to carry into effect all powers granted to the Government of the United States, or to any department or officer thereof," Chief Justice Marshall, in his great decision in the case of McCulloch vs. State of Maryland, says:—

"The powers given to the Government imply the ordinary means of execution, and the Government, in all sound reason and fair interpretation, must have the choice of the means which it deems the most convenient and appropriate to the execution of the power. * * * The powers of the Government were given for the welfare of the nation; they were intended to endure for ages to come, and to be adapted to the various crises in human affairs. To prescribe the specific means by which Government should, in all future time, execute its power, and so confine the choice of means to such narrow limits as should not leave it in the power of Congress to adopt any which might be appropriate and conducive to the end, would be most unwise and pernicious." (4 Wheaton, 420.)

Words fitly spoken! which illustrated at the time of their utterance the wisdom of the Constitution in providing this general grant of power to meet every possible exigency which the fortunes of war might cast upon the country, and the wisdom of which words, in turn, has been illustrated to-day by the gigantic and triumphant struggle of the people during the last four years for the supremacy of the Constitution, and in exact accordance with its provisions. In the light of these wonderful events the words of Pinckney, uttered when the illustrious Chief Justice had concluded this opinion, "The Constitution of my country is immortal!" seem to have become words of prophecy. Has not this great tribunal, through the chief of all its judges, by this luminous and profound reasoning, declared that the Government may by law authorize the Executive to employ, in the prosecution of war, the ordinary means, and all the means necessary and adapted to the end? And in the other decision, before referred to, in the 8th of Cranch, arising during the late war with Great Britain, Mr. Justice Story said:—

"When they legislative authority, to whom the right to declare war is confided, has declared war in its most unlimited manner, the executive authority, to whom the execution of the war is confided, is bound to carry it into effect. He has a discretion vested in him as to the manner and extent, but he cannot lawfully transcend the rules of warfare established among civilized nations. He cannot lawfully exercise powers or authorize proceedings which the civilized world repudiates and disclaims. The sovereignty, as to declaring war and limiting its effects, rests with the legislature. The sovereignty as to its execution rests with the President." (Brown vs. United States, 8 Cranch, 153.)

Has the Congress, to whom is committed the sovereignty of the whole people to declare war, by legislation restricted the President, or attempted to restrict him in the prosecution of this war for the Union from exercising all the "powers" and adopting all the "proceedings" usually approved and employed by the civilized world? It would, in my judgment, be a bold man who asserted that Congress has so legislated; and the Congress which should by law fetter the executive arm when raised for the common defense would, in my opinion, be false to their oath. That Congress may prescribe rules for the Government of the army and navy and the militia when in actual service, by articles of war, is an express grant of power in the Constitution, which Congress has rightfully exercised, and which the Executive must and does obey. That Congress may aid the Executive by legislation in the prosecution of a war, civil or foreign, is admitted. That Congress may restrain the Executive, arraign, try and condemn him for wantonly abusing the great trust, is expressly declared in the Constitution. That Congress shall pass all laws necessary to enable the Executive to execute the laws of the Union, suppress insurrection and repel invasion, is one of the express requirements of the Constitution, for the performance, of which the Congress is bound by an oath.

What was the legislation of Congress when treason fired its first gun on Sumter? By the act of 1795, it is provided that whenever the laws of the United States shall be opposed, or the execution thereof obstructed

TRIAL OF THE ASSASSINS AT WASHINGTON.

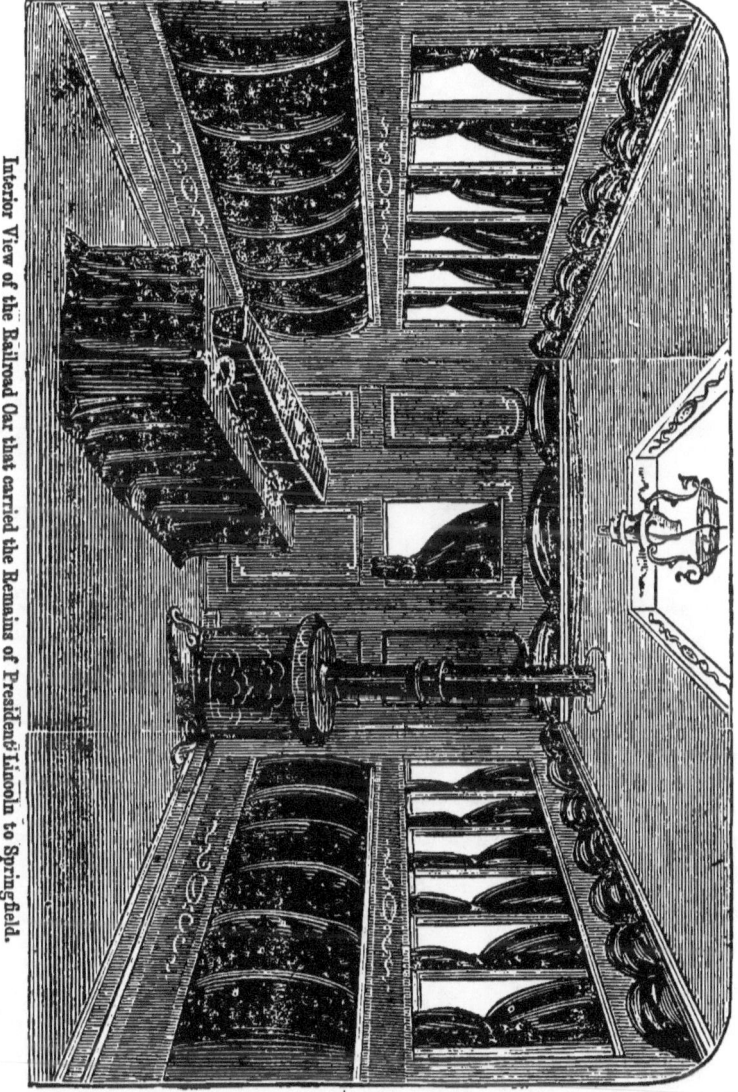

Interior View of the Railroad Car that carried the Remains of President Lincoln to Springfield.

TRIAL OF THE ASSASSINS AT WASHINGTON. 183

in any State by combinations too powerful to be suppressed by the ordinary course of judicial proceeding, or by the powers vested in the marshals, it shall be lawful by this act for the President to call forth the militia of such State, or of any other State or States, as may be necessary to suppress such combinations and to cause the laws to be executed. (1st Statutes at Large, 424.) By the act of 1807 it is provided that in case of insurrection or obstruction to the laws, either of the United States or of any individual State or Territory, where it is lawful for the President of the United States to call forth the militia for the purpose of suppressing such insurrection, or of causing the laws to be duly executed, it shall be lawful for him to employ for such purpose such part of the land or naval forces of the United States as shall be judged necessary. (2d Statutes at Large, 443.)

Can any one doubt that by these acts the President is clothed with full power to determine whether armed insurrection exists in any State or Territory of the Union, and if so, to make war upon it with all the force he may deem necessary or be able to command? By the simple exercise of this great power it necessarily results that he may, in the prosecution of the war for the suppression of such insurrection, suspend, as far as may be necessary, the civil administration of justice by substituting in its stead martial law, which is simply the common law of war. If, in such a moment, the President may make no arrests without civil warrant, and may inflict no violence or penalties on persons (as is claimed here) for the accused), without first obtaining the verdict of juries and the judgment of civil courts, then is this legislation a mockery, and the Constitution, which not only authorized but enjoined its enactment, but a glittering generality and a splendid bauble. Happily the Supreme Court has settled all controversy on this question. In speaking of the Rhode Island insurrection, the court say:—

"The Constitution of the United States, as far as it has provided for an emergency of this kind and authorized the general Government to interfere in the domestic concerns of a State, has treated the subject as political in its nature and placed the power in the hands of that department."

"By the act of 1795, the power of deciding whether the exigency has arisen upon which the Government of the United States is bound to interfere, is given to the President."

The court add:—

"When the President has acted and called out the militia, is a Circuit Court of the United States authorized to inquire whether his decision was right? If it could, then it would become the duty of the court, provided it came to the conclusion that the President had decided incorrectly, to discharge those who were adrested or detained by the troops in the service of the United States." * * * "It the judicial power extends so far, the guarantee contained in the Constitution of the United States is a guarantee of anarchy and not of order." * * * "Yet if this right does not reside in the courts when the conflict is raging, if the judicial power is at that time bound to follow the decision of the political, it must be equally bound when the contest is over. It cannot, when peace is restored, punish as offenses and crimes the acts which it before recognized and was bound to recognize as lawful." Luther vs. Borden, 7 Howard, 42, 43.

If this be law, what becomes of the volunteer advice of the volunteer counsel, by him given without money and without price, to this Court, of their responsibility, their personal responsibility, for obeying the orders of the President of the United States in trying persons accused of the murder of the chief magistrate and commander-in-chief of the army and navy of the United States in time of Rebellion, and in pursuance of a conspiracy entered into with the public enemy? I may be pardoned for asking the attention of the Court to a further citation from this important decision, in which the Court say, the employment of military power to put down an armed insurrection "is essential to the existence of every Government, and is as necessary to the States or to this Union as to any other Government, and if the Government of the State deem the armed opposition so formidable as to require the use of military force and the power to declare MARTIAL LAW, we see no ground upon which this Court can question its authority."—Ibid. This decision in terms declared that under the act of 1795 the President had power to decide and decided the question so as to exclude further inquiry whether the State Government which thus employed force and proclaimed martial law was the Government of the State, and therefore was permitted to act. If a State may do this, to put down armed insurrection, may not the Federal Government as well? The reason of the man who doubts it may justly be questioned. I but quote the language of that tribunal, in another case before cited, when I say the Constitution confers upon the President the whole executive power.

We have seen that the proclamation of blockade made by the President was affirmed by the Supreme Court as a lawful and valid act, although its direct effect was to dispose of the property of whoever violated it, whether citizen or stranger. It is difficult to perceive what course of reasoning can be adopted, in the light of that decision, which will justify any man in saying that the President had not the like power to proclaim martial law in time of insurrection against the United States, and to establish, according to the customs of war among civilized nations, military tribunals of justice for its enforcement, and for the punishment of all crimes committed in the interests of the public enemy.

These acts of the President have, however, all been legalized by the subsequent legislation of Congress, although the Supreme Court decided, in relation to the proclamation of blockade, that no such legislation was necessary. By the act of August 6th, 1861, ch. 63, section 3, it is enacted that—

"All the acts, proclamations and orders of the President of the United States, after the 4th of March, 1861, respecting the army and navy of the United States, and calling out, or relating to the militia or volunteers from the States, are hereby approved in all respects, legalized and made valid to the same extent, and with the same effect as if they had been issued and done under the previous express authority and direction of the Congress of the United States."—(12 Stat. at Large, 326.)

This act legalized, if any such legalization was necessary, all that the President had done from the day of his inauguration to that hour, in the prosecution of the war for the Union. He had suspended the privilege of the writ of habeas corpus, and resisted its execution when issued by the Chief Justice of the United States; he had called out and accepted the services of a large body of volunteers for a period not previously authorized by law; he had declared a blockade of the southern ports; he had ordered the armies to invade them and suppress it; thus exercising, in accordance with the laws of war, power over the life, the liberty, and the property of the citizens. Congress ratified it and affirmed it.

In like manner and by subsequent legislation did the Congress ratify and affirm the proclamation of martial law of September 25, 1862. That proclamation, as the Court will have observed, declares that during the existing insurrection all Rebels and insurgents, their aiders and abettors within the United States, and all persons guilty of any disloyal practice affording aid and comfort to the Rebels against the authority of the United States, shall be subject to martial law and liable to trial and punishment by courts-martial or military commission; and second, that the writ of habeas corpus is suspended in respect to all persons arrested, or who are now or hereafter during the Rebellion shall be imprisoned in any fort, &c., by any military authority, or by the sentence of any court-martial or military commission.

One would suppose that it needed no argument to satisfy an intelligent and patriotic citizen of the United States that, by the ruling of the Supreme Court cited, so much of this proclamation as declares that all rebels and insurgents, their aiders and abettors, shall be subject to martial law, and be liable to trial and punishment by court-martial or military commission, needed no ratification by Congress. Every step that the President took against rebels and insurgents was taken in pursuance of the rules of war and was an exercise of martial law. Who says that he should not deprive them, by the authority of this law, of life and liberty? Are the aiders and abettors of these insurgents entitled to any higher consideration than the armed insurgents themselves? It is against these that the President proclaimed martial law, and against all others who were guilty of any disloyal practice affording aid and comfort to rebels against the authority of the United States. Against these he suspended the privilege of the writ of habeas corpus; and these, and only such as these, were by that proclamation subjected to trial and punishment by court-martial or military commission.

That the Proclamation covers the offense charged here, no man will, or dare, for a moment deny. Was it not a disloyal practice? Was it not aiding and abetting the insurgents and Rebels to enter into a conspiracy with them to kill and murder, within your Capital and your intrenched camp, the Commander-in-Chief of our army, your Lieutenant-General, and the Vice President, and the Secretary of State, with intent thereby to aid the Rebellion, and to subvert the Constitution and laws of the United States? But it is said that the President could not establish a court for their trial, and therefore Congress must confirm and affirm this Proclamation. I have said before that such an argument comes with ill grace from the lips of him who declared as solemnly that neither by the Congress nor by the President, could either the Rebel himself or his aider or abettor be lawfully and constitutionally subjected to trial by any military tribunal, whether court-martial or military commission; but the Congress did ratify, in the exercise of the power vested in them, every part of this Proclamation. I have said, upon the authority of the fathers of the Constitution, and of its judicial interpreters, that Congress has power by legislation to aid the Executive in the suppression of rebellion, in executing the laws of the Union when resisted by armed insurrection, and in repelling invasion.

By the act of March 3, 1863, the Congress of the

United States, by the first section thereof, declared that during the present Rebellion the President of the United States, whenever in his judgment the public safety may require it, is authorized to suspend the writ of habeas corpus in any case throughout the United States or any part thereof. By the fourth section of the same act it is declared that any order of the President, or under his authority, made at any time during the existence of the present Rebellion, shall be a defense in all courts to any action or prosecution, civil or criminal, pending or to be commenced, for any search, seizure, arrest or imprisonment made, done or committed, or acts omitted to be done, under and by virtue of such order. By the fifth section it is provided that if any suit or prosecution, civil or criminal, has been or shall be commenced in any State Court against any officer, civil or military, or against any other person, for any arrest or imprisonment made or other trespasses or wrongs done or committed, or any act omitted to be done at any time during the present Rebellion, by virtue of or under color of any authority derived from or exercised by or under the President of the United States, if the defendant shall, upon appearance in such Court, file a petition stating the facts ⟨…⟩ on affidavit, &c., as aforesaid, for the removal of the cause for trial to the Circuit Court of the United States, it shall be the duty of the State Court, upon his giving security, to proceed no further in the cause or prosecution. Thus declaring that all orders of the President made at any time during the existence of the present Rebellion and all acts done in pursuance thereof shall be held valid in the courts of justice. Without further inquiry, these provisions of this statute embrace Order No. 141, which is the proclamation of martial law, and necessarily legalize every act done under it, either before the passage of the act of 1863 or since. Inasmuch as that proclamation ordered that all rebels, insurgents, their aiders and abettors and persons guilty of any disloyal practice, affording aid and comfort to rebels against the authority of the United States at any time during the existing insurrection should be subject to martial law and liable to trial and punishment by *military commission*, the sections of the law just cited declaring lawful all acts done in pursuance of such order, including of course the trial and punishment by military commission of all such offenders as directly legalized this order of the President as it is possible for Congress to legalize or authorize any executive act whatever. 12 Stat. at Large. 755-6.

But after assuming and declaring with great earnestness in his argument, that no person could be tried and convicted for such crimes by any military tribunal, whether a court-martial or a military commission, save those in the land or naval service in time of war, the gentleman makes the extraordinary statement that the creation of a military commission must be authorized by the legislative department, and demands, if there be any such legislation, "let the statute be produced." The statute has been produced. The power so to try, says the gentleman, must be authorized by Congress, when the demand is made for such authority. Does not the gentleman thereby give up his argument, and admit that, if the Congress has so authorized the trial of all aiders and abettors of rebels or insurgents, for whatever they do in aid of such rebels and insurgents, during the insurrection, that the statute and proceedings under it are lawful and valid? I have already shown that the Congress have so legislated, by expressly legalizing order No. 141, which directed the trial of all Rebels, their aiders and abettors, by military commission. Did not Congress expressly legalize this order, by declaring that the order shall be a defense in all courts, to any action or prosecution, civil or criminal, for acts done in pursuance of it? No amount of argument could make this point clearer than the language of the statute itself. But, says the gentleman, if there be a statute authorizing trials by military commission, "Let it be produced."

By the act of March 3, 1863, it is provided in section thirty that in time of war, insurrection or rebellion, murder and assault with intent to kill, &c., when committed by persons in the military service, shall be punishable by the sentence of a court-martial or *military commission*, and the punishment of such offences shall never be less than those inflicted by the laws of the State or District in which they have been committed. By the thirty-eighth section of the same act it is provided that all persons who in time of war or rebellion against the United States, shall be found lurking or acting as spies in or about the camps, &c., of the United States, or elsewhere, shall be triable by a *military commission*, and shall, upon conviction, suffer death. Here is a statute which expressly declares that all persons, whether citizens or strangers, who in time of rebellion shall be found acting as spies shall suffer death upon conviction by a military commission. Why did not the gentleman give us some argument upon this law? We have seen that it was the existing law of the United States under the Confederation. Then and since men not in the land or naval service of the United States have suffered death for this offense upon conviction by courts-martial. If it was competent for Congress to authorize their trial by courts-martial, it was equally competent for Congress to authorize their trial by military commission, and accordingly they have done so. By the same authority the Congress may extend the jurisdiction of military commissions over all military offenses or crimes committed in time of rebellion or war in aid of the public enemy; and if certainly stands with right reason that if it were just to subject to death by the sentence of a military commission all persons who should be guilty merely of lurking as spies in the interests of the public enemy in time of rebellion, though they obtained no information, though they inflicted no personal injury, but were simply overtaken and detected in the endeavor to obtain intelligence for the enemy, those who enter into conspiracy with the enemy; not only to lurk as spies in your camp, but to lurk there as murderers and assassins, and who, in pursuance of that conspiracy, commit assassination and murder upon the Commander-in-Chief of your army, within your camp, and in aid of rebellion, should be subject in like manner to trial by military commission.—Stat. at Large. 12, 736-7, ch. 8.

Accordingly, the President having so declared, the Congress, as we have stated, have affirmed that his order was valid, and that all persons acting by authority, and consequently as a court pronouncing such sentence upon the offender as the usage of war requires, are justified by the law of the land. With all respect, permit me to say, that the learned gentleman has manifested more acumen and ability in his elaborate argument, by what he has omitted to say, than by anything which he has said. By the act of July 2, 1864, cap. 215, it is provided that the commanding General in the field, or the commander of the department, as the case may be, shall have power to carry into execution all sentences against guerrilla marauders for robbery, arson, burglary, &c., and for violation of the laws and customs of war, as well as sentences against spies, mutineers, deserters and murderers.

From the legislation I have cited, it is apparent that military commissions are expressly recognized by the law-making power; that they are authorized to try capital offenses against citizens not in the service of the United States, and to pro ounce the sentence of death upon them; and that the commander of a department, or the commanding general in the field, may carry such sentence into execution. But, says the gentleman, grant all this to be so, Congress has not declared in what manner the court shall be constituted. The answer to that objection has already been anticipated in the citation from Benet, wherein it appeared to be the rule of the law martial that in the punishment of all military offenses not provided for by the written law of the land, military commissions are constituted for that purpose by the authority of the commanding officer or the Commander-in-Chief, as the case may be, who selects the officers of a court-martial; that they are similarly constituted, and deal their proceedings conducted according to the same general rules. That is a part of the very law martial which the President proclaimed, and which the Congress has legalized. The proclamation has declared that all such offenders shall be tried by military commissions. The Congress has legalized the same by the act which I have cited, and by every intendment it must be taken that as martial law is, by the proclamation, declared to be the rule by which they shall be tried, the Congress, in affirming the act of the P esident, simply declared that they should be tried according to the customs of martial law: that the Commission should be constituted by the Commander-in-Chief according to the rule of procedure known as martial law, and that the penalties inflicted should be in accordance with the laws of war and the usages of nations. Legislation no more definite than this has been upon your statute book since the beginning of the century, and has been held by the Supreme Court of the United States valid for the punishment of offenders.

By the thirty-second article of the act of 23d April, 1800, it is provided that "all crimes committed by persons belonging to the navy which are not specified in the foregoing articles shall be punished according to the laws and customs in such cases at sea." Of this article the Supreme Court of the United States say, that when offenses and crimes are not given in terms or by definition, the want of it may be supplied by a comprehensive enactment, such as the thirty-second article of the rules for the government of the navy; which means that courts-martial have jurisdiction of such crimes as are not specified, but which have been recognized to be crimes and offenses by the usages in navies of all nations, and that they shall be punished according to the laws and customs of the sea.—(Dynes vs. Hoover, 20 Howard, 82.)

But it is a fact that must not be omitted in the reply which I make to the gentleman's argument, that an effort was made by himself and others in the Senate of the United States, on the 3d of March last, to condemn the arrests, imprisonments, &c., made by order of the President of the United States in pursuance of his proclamation, and to reverse, by the judgment of that body, the law which had been before passed affirming his action, which effort most signally failed.

Thus we see that the body which, by the Constitution, if the President had been guilty of the misdemeanors alleged against him in this argument of the gentleman, would, upon presentation of such charge in legal form against the President, constitute the high court of impeachment for his trial and condemnation, has decided the question in advance, and declared upon the occasion referred to, as they had before declared by solemn enactment, that this order of the President declaring martial law and the punishment of all rebels and insurgents, their aiders and abettors, by military commission, should be enforced during the insurrection as the law of the land, and that the offenders should be tried as directed by military commission. It may be said that this subsequent legislation of Congress, ratifying and affirming what had been done by the President, can have no validity. Of course, it cannot if neither the Congress nor the Executive can authorize the proclamation and enforcement of martial law in the suppression of rebellion for the punishment of all persons committing military offenses in aid of that rebellion. Assuming, however, as the gentleman seemed to assume, by asking for the legislation of Congress, that there is such power in Congress, the Supreme Court of the United States has solemnly affirmed that such ratification is valid. (2 Black, 671.)

The gentleman's argument is full of citations of English precedent. There is a late English precedent bearing upon this point—the power of the legislature, by subsequent enactment, to legalize executive orders, arrests and imprisonment of citizens—that I beg leave to commend to his consideration. I refer to the statute of 11 and 12 Victoria, ch. 35, entitled "An act to empower the Lord Lieutenant, or other chief governor or governors of Ireland, to apprehend and detain until the 1st day of March, 1849, such persons as he or they shall *suspect* of conspiring against her Majesty's person and Government," passed July 25, 1848, which statute in terms declares that all and every person and persons who is, are, or shall be, within that period, within that part of the United Kingdom of England and Ireland called Ireland at or on the day the act shall receive her Majesty's royal assent, or after, by warrant for high treason or treasonable practic s, or suspicion of high treason or treasonable practices, signed by the Lord Lieutenant, or other chief governor or governors of Ireland for the time being, or his or their chief secretary, for such causes as aforesaid, may be detained in safe custody, without bail or main prize, until the first day of March, 1849; and that no Judge or justice shall bail or try any such person or persons so committed, without order from her Majesty's privy counsel, until the said first day of March, 1849, any law or statute to the contrary notwithstanding. The second section of this act provides that, in cases where any persons have been, *before* the passing of the act, arrested, committed or detained for such cause by warrant or warrants signed by the officers aforesaid, or either of them, it may be lawful for the person or persons to whom such warrants have been or shall be directed, to detain such person or persons in his or their custody in any place whatever in Ireland: and that such person or persons to whom such warrants have been or shall be directed shall be deemed and taken, to all intents and purposes, lawfully authorized to take into safe custody and be the lawful jailers and keepers of such persons so arrested, committed, or detained.

Here the power of arrest is given by the act of Parliament to the Governor or his Secretary; the process of the civil courts was wholly suspended; bail was denied and the parties imprisoned, and this not by process of the courts, but by warrant of a Chief Governor or his Secretary, not for crimes charged to have been committed, but for being *suspected* of treasonable practices. Magna charta it seems opposes no restraint, notwithstanding the parade that is made about it in this argument upon the power of the Parliament of England to legalize arrests and imprisonments made before the passage of the act upon an executive order, and without colorable authority of statute law; and to authorize like arrests and imprisonments of so many as six million of people as such executive officers might *suspect* of treasonable practices.

But, says the gentleman, whatever may be the precedents English, or American, whatever may be the provisions of the Constitution, whatever may be the legislation of Congress, whatever may be the proclamations and orders of the President as Commander-in-chief, it is a usurpation and a tyranny in time of rebellion and civil war to subject any citizen to trial for any crime before military tribunals, save such citizens as are in the land or naval forces, and against this usurpation, which he asks this Court to rebuke by solemn decision, he appeals to public opinion. I trust that I set as high value upon enlightened public opinion as any man. I recognize it as the reserved power of the people which creates and dissolves armies, which creates and dissolves legislative assemblies, which enacts and repeals fundamental laws, the better to provide for personal security by the due administration of justice. To that public opinion upon this very question of the usurpation of authority, of unlawful arrests, and unlawful imprisonments, and unlawful trials, condemnations and executions by the late President of the United States, an appeal has already been taken to public opinion. On this very issue the President was tried before the tribunal of the people, that great nation of freemen who cover this continent, looking out upon Europe from their eastern and upon Asia from their western homes. That people came to the consideration of this issue not unmindful of the fact that the first struggle for the establishment of our nationality could not have been, and was not successfully prosecuted without the proclamation and enforcement of martial law, declaring, as we have seen, that any inhabitant who, during that war, should kill any loyal citizen, or enter into any combination for that purpose, should, upon trial and conviction before a military tribunal, be sentenced as an assassin, traitor or spy, and should suffer death, and that in this last struggle for the maintenance of American nationality the President but followed the example of the illustrious Father of his Country. Upon that issue the people passed judgment on the 8th day of last November, and declared that the charge of usurpation was false.

From this decision of the people there lies no appeal on this earth. Who can rightfully challenge the authority of the American people to decide such questions for themselves? The voice of the people, thus solemnly proclaimed, by the omnipotence of the ballot, in favor of the righteous order of their murdered President, issued by him for the common defense, for the preservation of the Constitution, and for the enforcement of the laws of the Union, ought to be accepted, and will be accepted, I trust, by all just men, as the voice of God.

Mr. Ewing said, I ask permission of the Court to say in response to the allusion of the Assistant Judge Advocate to any acts as military commander, that he will find in the Bureau of Military Justice no records of the trial in my former commands of any persons not in the military service of the United States or in the Confederate service, except guerillas, robbers and others, *hostes humani generis* taken *flagrante bello*, with arms in their hands, or in acts of hostility, and if he will do me the favor to refer to my argument on the jurisdiction, he will see that I not only did not deny, but conceded the power of arrest and summary punishment by the commanding general in the field of all such persons, restricted only by the laws and the orders of military superiors.

The Court adjourned until to-morrow, at 1 o'clock.

WEDNESDAY, June 28.—The Court met at 1 P. M. when Associate Judge Bingham resumed his argument as follows:—

May it please the Court; I have said thus much concerning the right of the people under their Constitution, in time of civil war and rebellion, to proclaim through their Executive, with the sanction and approval of their Congress, martial law, and enforce the same according to the usage of nations.

I submit that it has been shown that, by the letter and spirit of the Constitution, as well as by its contemporaneous construction, followed and approved by every department of the Government, this right is in the people; that it is inseparable from the condition of war, whether civil or foreign, and absolutely essential to its vigorous and successful prosecution; that, according to the highest authority upon constitutional law, the proclamation and enforcement of martial law are "usual under all Governments in time of rebellion;" that our own highest judicial tribunal has declared this and solemnly ruled that the question of the necessity for its exercise rests exclusively with Congress and the President; and that the decision of the political departments of the Government, that there is an armed rebellion and a necessity for the employment of martial force and martial law in its suppression, concludes the judiciary.

In submitting what I have said in support of the jurisdiction of this honorable Court and of its constitutional power to hear and determine this issue, I have uttered my own convictions, and for their utterance in defense of my country and its right to employ all the means necessary for the common defense against armed rebellion, and secret treasonable conspiracy in aid of such Rebellion, I shall neither ask nor offer apology. I find no words with which more fitly to conclude all I have to say upon the question of the jurisdiction and constitutional authority of this Court than those employed by the illustrious Lord Brougham to the House of Peers, in support of the bill referred to, which empowered the Lord Lieutenant of Ireland and his deputies to apprehend and detain, for the period of seven months or more, all such persons within that Island as they should *suspect* of conspiracy against Her Majesty's person and Government. Said that illustrious man, "A friend of liberty I have lived, and such will I die; nor care I how soon the latter event may happen, if I cannot be a friend of liberty without being a friend of traitors at the same time, a protector or criminals of the deepest dye, an accomplice of foul rebellion and of its concomitant civil war, with all its atrocities and all its fearful consequences." (Hansard's Debates, 3d series, vol. 100, p. 653.)

May it please the Court:—It only remains for

me to sum up the evidence, and present my views of the law arising upon the facts in the case on trial. The questions of fact involved in the issue are—

First, Did the accused, or any two of them, confederate and conspire together as charged? and

Second, Did the accused, or any of them, in pursuance of such conspiracy, and with the intent alleged, commit either or all of the several acts specified?

If the conspiracy be established, as laid, it results that whatever was said or done by either of the parties thereto, in the furtherance or execution of the common design, is the declaration or act of all the other parties to the conspiracy; and this whether the other parties, at the time such words were uttered, or such acts done by their confederates, were present or absent, here, within the intrenched lines of your Capital, or crouching behind the intrenched lines of Richmond, or awaiting the results of their murderous plot against their country, its Constitution and laws, across the border, under the shelter of the British flag.

The declared and accepted rule of law in cases of conspiracy is that—

"In prosecutions for conspiracy it is an established rule that where several persons are proved to have combined together for the same illegal purpose, any act done by one of the party, in pursuance of the original concerted plan, and in reference to the common object, is, in the contemplation of law, as well as in sound reason, the act of the whole party; and therefore, the proof of the act will be evidence against any of the others, who were engaged in the same general conspiracy, without regard to the question whether the prisoner is proved to have been concerned in the particular transaction." (Phillips on Evidence, p. 210.)

"The same rule obtains in cases of treason:—"If several persons agree to levy war, some in one place and some in another, and one party domestically appear in arms, this is a levying of war by all, as well those who were not in arms as those who were, if it were done in pursuance of the original concert, for those who made the attempt were emboldened by the confidence inspired by the general concert, and therefore these particular acts are in justice imputable to all the rest." (1 East., Pleas of the Crown, p. 97; Roscoe, 84).

In ex parte Bollman and Swartwout, 4 Cranch, 126, Marshall, Chief Justice, rules:—"If war be actually levied, that is, if a body of men be actually assembled, for the purpose of effecting, by force, a treasonable purpose, all those who perform any part, however minute or however remote, from the scene of action, and who are actually leagued in the general conspiracy are to be considered as traitors."

In United States vs. Cole et al., 5 McLean, 601, Mr. Justice McLean says:—"A conspiracy is rarely if ever proved by positive testimony. When a crime of high magnitude is about to be perpetrated by a combination of individuals, they do not act openly, but covertly and secretly. The purpose formed is known only to those who enter into it. Unless one of the original conspirators betray his companions and give evidence against them, their guilt can be proved only by circumstantial evidence. * * It is said by some writers on evidence that such circumstances are stronger than positive proof. A witness swearing positively, it is said, may misapprehend the facts or swear falsely, but that circumstances cannot lie.

"The common design is the essence of the charge; and this may be made to appear when the defendants steadily pursue the same object, whether acting separately or together, by common or different means, all leading to the same unlawful result. And where prima facie evidence has been given of a combination, the acts or confessions of one are evidence against all. * * It is reasonable that where a body of men assume the attribute of individuality, whether for commercial business or for the commission of a crime, that the association should be bound by the acts of one of its members in carrying out the design.

It is a rule of the law, not to be overlooked in this connection, that the conspiracy or agreement of the parties, or some of them, to act in concert to accomplish the unlawful act charged, may be established either by direct evidence of a meeting or consultation for the illegal purpose charged, or more usually, from the very nature of the case, by circumstantial evidence. (2 Starkie, 232.)

Lord Mansfield ruled that it was not necessary to prove the actual fact of a conspiracy, but that it might be collected from collateral circumstances. (Parson's Case, 1 W. Blackstone, 392.)

"It," says a great authority on the law of evidence, "on a charge of conspiracy, it appear that two persons by their acts are pursuing the same object, and often by the same means, or one performing part of the act, and the other completing it, for the attainment of the same object, the jury may draw the conclusion there is a conspiracy. If a conspiracy be formed and a person join in it afterwards, he is equally guilty with the original conspirators." (Roscoe, 415.)

The rules of the admissibility of the acts and declarations of any one of the conspirators, said or done in furtherance of the common design, applies in cases as well where only part of the conspirators are indicted, or upon trial, as where all indicted and upon trial. Thus, upon an indictment for murder, if it appear that others, together with the prisoner, conspired to commit the crime, the act of one, done in pursuance of that intention, will be evidence against the rest." (2 Starkie, 237.)

They are all alike guilty as principals. (Commonwealth vs Knapp, 9 Pickering, 496; 10 Pickering, 477; 6 Term Reports, 528; 11 East, 584.)

What is the evidence, direct and circumstantial? That the accused, or either of them, together with John H. Surratt, John Wilkes Booth, Jefferson Davis, George N. Sanders, Beverly Tucker, Jacob Thompson, William C. Cleary, Clement C. Clay, George Harper and George Young, did combine, confederate and conspire in aid of the existing Rebellion, as charged, to kill and murder within the military department of Washington, and within the fortified and intrenched lines thereof, Abraham Lincoln, late, and, at the time of the said combining, confederating and conspiring, President of the United States of America, and Commander-in-Chief of the Army and Navy thereof; Andrew Johnson, Vice President of the United States; William H. Seward, Secretary of State of the United States, and Ulysses S. Grant, Lieutenant-General of the armies thereof, and then in command, under the direction of the President.

The time, as laid in the charge and specification, when this conspiracy was entered into, is immaterial, so that it appears by the evidence that the criminal combination and agreement were formed before the commission of the acts alleged. That Jefferson Davis, one of the conspirators named, was the acknowledged chief and leader of the existing Rebellion against the Government of the United States, and that Jacob Thompson, George N. Sanders, Clement C. Clay, Beverly Tucker, and others named in the specification, were his duly accredited and authorized agents to act in the interests of said Rebellion, are facts established by the testimony in this case, beyond all question. That Davis, as the leader of said Rebellion, gave to those agents, then in Canada, commissions in blank, bearing the official signature of the war minister, James A. Seddon, to be by them filled up and delivered to such agents as they might employ to act in the interests of the Rebellion within the United States, and intended to be a cover and protection for any crimes they might there commit in the service of the Rebellion, are also facts established here, and which no man can gainsay. Who doubts that Kennedy, whose confession made in view of immediate death as proved here was commissioned by these accredited agents of Davis to burn the city of New York? that he was to have attempted it on the night of the Presidential election, and that he did, in combination with his confederates, set fire to four hotels in the city of New York on the night of the 25th of November last? Who doubts that, in like manner in the interests of the R R'lion and by the authority of Davis, the e his agents also commissioned Bennett H. Young to commit arson, robbery, and the murder of unarmed citizens in St. Albans, Vermont? Who doubts, upon the testimony shown, that Davis, by his agents, deliberately adopted the system of starvation for the murder of our captive soldiers in his hands, or that, as shown by the testimony, he sanctioned the burning of hospitals and steamboats, the property of private persons, and paid therefor from his stolen treasure the sum of thirty-five thousand dollars in gold?

By the evidence of Joseph Hyams it is proved that Thompson—the agent of Jefferson Davis—paid him money for the service he rendered in the infamous and fiendish project of importing pestilence into our camps and cities to destroy the lives of citizens and soldiers alike, and into the house of the President for the purpose of destroying his life. It may be said, and doubtless will be said, by the practiced advocates of this Rebellion, that Hyams, being infamous, is not to be believed. It is admitted that he is infamous, as it must be conceded that any man is infamous who either participates in such a crime or attempts in any way to extenuate it. But it will be observed that Hyams is supported by the testimony of Mr. Sandford Conover, who heard Blackburn and the other Rebel agents in Canada speak of this infernal project, and by the testimony of Mr. Wall, the well-known auctioneer of this city, who se character is unquestioned, that he received this importation of pestilence (of course without any knowledge of the purpose), and that Hyams consigned the goods to him in the name of J. W. Harris—a fact in itself an acknowledgment of guilt; and that he received afterwards a letter from Harris, dated Toronto, Canada West, December 1, 1864, wherein Harris stated that he had not been able to e nter the States since his return to Canada, and asked for an account of the sale. He identifies the Joseph Godfrey Hyams who testified in Court as the J. W. Harris who imported the pestilence. The very transaction shows that Hyams' statement is truthful. He gives the names of the parties connected with this infamy (Clement C. Clay, Dr. Blackburn, Rev. Dr. Stuart Robinson, J. C. Holcomb—all refugees from the Confederacy in Canada), and states that he gave Thompson a receipt for the fifty dollars paid to him, and that he was by occupation a shoemaker; in none of which facts is there an attempt to discredit him. It is not probable that a man in his position in life would be able to buy five trunks of clothing, ship them all the way from Halifax to Washington, and then order them to be sold at auction, without regard to price, solely upon his own account. It is a matter of notoriety, that a part of his statement is verified by the results at Newbern, North Carolina, to which point, he says, a portion of the infected goods were shipped, through a sutler; the result of which was, that nearly two thousand citizens and soldiers died there about that time, with the yellow fever.

That the Rebel Chief, Jefferson Davis, sanctioned these crimes, committed and attempted, through the instrumentality of his accredited agents in Canada, Thompson, Clay, Tucker, Sanders, Cleary, &c., upon the persons and property of the people of the North, there is positive proof on your record. The letter brought from Richmond, and taken from the archives of his late pretended Government there, dated February 11, 1865, and addressed to him by a late Rebel Senator from Texas, W. S. Oldham, contains the following significant words:—"When Senator Johnson, of Missouri, and myself waited on you a few days since, in relation to the project of annoying and harrassing the enemy by means of burning their shipping, towns, &c., &c., there were several remarks made by you upon the subject, which I was not fully prepared to answer, but which, upon subsequent conference with parties proposing the enterprise, I find cannot apply as objections to the scheme. First, the 'combustible materials' consist of several preparations, and not one alone, and can be used without exposing the party us.ng them to the least danger of detection whatever.

* * *

"Second, there is no necessity for sending persons in the military service into the enemy's country, but the work may be done by agents. * * * I have seen enough of the effects that can be produced to 'satisfy me that in most cases, without any danger to the parties engaged, and in others but very slight, we can, first, burn every vessel that leaves a foreign port for the United States; second, we can burn every transport that leaves the harbor of New York, or other Northern port, with supplies for the armies of the enemy in the South; third, burn every transport and gun-boat on the Mississippi River, as well as devastate the country of the enemy', and fill his people with terror and consternation. * * * For the purpose of satisfying your mind upon the subject, I respectfully but earnestly request that you will give an interview with General Harris, formerly a member of Congress from Missouri, who, I think, is able, from conclusive proofs, to convince you that what I have suggested is perfectly feasible and practicable."

No one can doubt, from the tenor of this letter, that the Rebel Davis only wanted to be satisfied that this system of arson and murder could be carried on by his agents in the North successfully and without detection. With him it was not a crime to do these acts, but only a crime to be detected in them. But Davis, by his endorsement on this letter, dated the 20th of February, 1865, bears witness to his own complicity and his own infamy in this proposed work of destruction and crime for the future, as well as to his complicity in what had before been attempted without complete success. Kennedy, with his confederates, had failed to burn the city of New York. "The combustibles" which Kennedy had employed were, it seems, defective. This was "a difficulty to be overcome." Either had he been able to consummate the dreadful work without subjecting himself to detection. This was another "difficulty to be overcome." Davis, on the 29th of February, 1865, endorsed upon this letter these words:—"Secretary of State, at his convenience, see General Harris and learn what may be he has for overcoming the difficulties heretofore experienced. J. D."

This indorsement is unquestionably proved to be the handwriting of Jefferson Davis, and it bears witness on its face that the monstrous proposition met his approval, and that he desired his Rebel Secretary of State, Benjamin, to see General Harris, and learn how to overcome the difficulty heretofore experienced, to wit: the inefficiency of "the combustible materials" that had been employed, and the liability of his agents to detection. After this, who will doubt that he had endeavored, by the hand of incendiaries, to destroy by fire the property and lives of the people of the North, and thereby "fill them with terror and consternation;" that he knew his agents had been unsuccessful; that he knew his agents had been detected in their villany and punished for their crime; that he desired through a more perfect "chemical preparation," by the science and skill of Professor McCulloch, to accomplish successfully what had been unsuccessfully attempted?

The intercepted letter of his agent, Clement C. Clay, dated St. Catherine's, Canada West, November 1, 1864, is an acknowledgment and confession of what they had attempted, and a suggestion made through J. P. Benjamin, Rebel Secretary of State, of what remained to be done, in order to make the "chemical preparations" efficient. Speaking of this Bennett H. Young, he says:—"You have doubtless learned through the press of the United States of the raid on St. Albans by about twenty-five Confederate soldiers, led by Lieutenant Bennett H. Young; of their a tempt and failure to burn the town; of their robbery of three banks there

of the aggregate amount of about two hundred thousand dollars; of their arrest in Canada by the United States forces; of their commitment and the pending preliminary trial.

He makes application, in aid of Young and his associates, for additional documents, showing that they acted upon the authority of the Confederate States Government, taking care to say, however, that he held such authority at the time, but that it ought to be more explicit, so far as regards the particular facts complained of. He states that he met Young at Halifax, in May, 1864, who developed his plans for retaliation on the enemy; that he, Clay, recommended him to the Rebel Secretary of War; that after this, "Young was sent back by the Secretary of War with a commission as Second Lieutenant, to execute his plans and purposes, but to report to Hon. —— and myself." Young afterwards "proposed passing through New England, burning some towns and robbing them of whatever he could convert to the use of the Confederate Government. This I approved as justifiable retaliation. He attempted to burn the town of St. Albans, Vermont, and would have succeeded but for the failure of the chemical preparation with which he was armed. He then robbed the banks of funds amounting to over two hundred thousand dollars. That he was not prompted by selfish or mercenary motives I am as well satisfied as I am that he is an honest man. He assured me before going that his effort would be to destroy towns and farm-houses, but not to plunder or rob; but he said if, after firing a town, he saw he could take funds from a bank or any house, and thereby might inflict injury upon the enemy and benefit his own Government, he would do so. He added most emphatically that whatever he took should be turned over to the Government, or its representatives in foreign lands. My instructions to him were to destroy whatever was valuable, not to stop to rob; but if, after firing a town, he could seize and carry off money, or Treasury or bank notes, he might do so upon condition that they were delivered to the proper authorities of the Confederate States," that is, to Clay himself.

When he wrote this letter, it seems that this accredited agent of Jefferson Davis was as strongly impressed with the usurpation and despotism of Mr. Lincoln's Administration as some of the advocates of his aiders and abettors seem to be at this day; and he indulges in the following statement:—"All that a large portion of the Northern people, especially in the Northwest, want to resist th oppressions of the despotism at Washington is a leader. They are ripe for resistance, and it may come soon after the Presidential election. At all events, it must come, if our armies are not overcome, or destroyed, or dispersed. No people of the Anglo-Saxon blood can long endure the usurpations and tyrannies of Lincoln." Clay does not sign the despatch, but indorses the bearer of it as a person who can identify him and give his name. The bearer of that letter was the witness Richard Montgomery, who saw Clay write a portion of the letter, and received it from his hands, and subsequently delivered to the Assistant Secretary of War of the United States, Mr. Dana. That the letter is in Clay's handwriting is clearly proved by those familiar with it, Mr. Montgomery testifies that he was instructed by Clay to deliver this letter to Benjamin, the Rebel Secretary of State. If he could get through to Richmond, and to tell him what names to put in the blanks.

This letter leaves no doubt, if any before existed, in the mind of any one who had read the letter of Oldham, and Davis' indorsement thereon, that "the chemical preparations" and "combustible materials" had been tried and had failed, and it became a matter of great moment and concern that they should be so prepared as, in the words of Davis, "to overcome the difficulties heretofore experienced;" that is to say, complete the work of destruction, and secure the perpetrators against personal injury or detection in the performance of it.

It only remains to be seen whether Davis, the procurer of arson and of the indiscriminate murder of the innocent and unoffending necessarily resultant therefrom, was capable also of endeavoring to procure, and in fact d.d procure, the murder, by direct assassination of the President of the United States and others charged with the duty of maintaining the Government of the United States, and of suppressing the Rebellion in which this arch-traitor and conspirator was engaged.

The official papers of Davis, captured under the guns of our victorious army in his R bel Capital, identified beyond question or shadow of doubt, and placed upon your record, together with the declarations and acts of his co-conspirators and agents, proclaim to all the world that he was capable of attempting to accomplish his treasonable procuration of the murder of the late President, and other chief officers of the United States, by the hands of hired assassins.

In the fall of 1864, Lieutenant W. Alston addressed to "his Excellency" a letter now before the Court, which contains the following words:

"I now offer you my services, and if you will favor me in my designs, I will carry them out as soon as my health will permit, to rid my country of some o' her deadliest enemies, by striking at the very hearts' blood of those who seek to enchain her in slavery. I consider nothing *dishonorable* having such a tendency. All I ask of you is, to favor me by granting me the necessary papers, &c., to travel on. * * * *I am perfectly familiar with the North*, and feel confident that I can *execute* anything I undertake. I was in the raid last June in Kentucky, under General John H. Morgan; * * * was taken prisoner, * * * escaped from them by dressing myself in the garb of a citizen. * * * I went through to the Canadas, from whence, by the assistance of Colonel J. P. Holcomb, I succeeded in working my way around and through the blockade. * * * I should like to have a *personal* interview with you in order to perfect the arrangements before starting."

Is there any room to doubt that this was a proposition to *assassinate*, by the hand of this man and his associates, such persons in the North as he deemed the "deadliest enemies" of the Rebellion? The weakness of the man who, for a moment, can doubt that such was the proposition of the writer of this letter, is certainly an object of commiseration. What had Jefferson Davis to say to this proposed assassination of the "deadliest enemies" in the North of his great treason? Did the atrocious suggestion kindle in him indignation against the villain who offered, with his own hand, to strike the blow? Not at all. On the contrary, he ordered his private secretary, on the 29th of November, 1864, to indorse upon the letter these words:— "Lieutenant A. W. Alston, accompanied raid into Kentucky, and was captured; but escaped into *Canada*, from whence he found his way back. None offers his services to rid the country of some of his *deadliest enemies*; asks for papers, &c. Respectfully referred, by direction of the President, to the honorable Secretary of War." It is also indorsed, for attention, "By order." Signed "J. A. Campbell, Assistant Secretary of War."

Note the fact, in this connection, that Jefferson Davis himself, as well as his subordinates, had, before the date of this indorsement, concluded that Abraham Lincoln was "the deadliest enemy" of the Rebellion. You hear it in the Rebel camp in Virginia, in 1863, declared by Booth, then and there present, and assented to by Rebel officers, that "Abraham Lincoln must be killed." You hear it in that slaughter-pen in Georgia, Andersonville, proclaimed among Rebel officers, who, by the slow torture of starvation, inflicted cruel and untimely death on ten thousand of your defenders, captives in their hands whispering, like demons, their horrid purpose, "Abraham Lincoln must be killed," And in Canada, the accredited agents of Jefferson Davis, as early as October, 1864, and afterward, declared that "Abraham Lincoln must be killed," if this re-election could not be prevented. These agents in Canada, on the 13th of October, 1864, delivered, in cipher, to be transmitted to Richmond by Richard Montgomery, the witness whose reputation is unchallenged, the following communication:—

"OCTOBER 13, 1864.—We again urge the immense necessity of our gaining immediate advantages. Strain every nerve for victory. We now look upon the re-election of *Lincoln* in November as almost certain, and we need to whip these hirelings to prevent it. Besides, with *Lincoln* re-elected and his armies victorious, we need not hope even for recognition, much less the help mentioned in our last. Holcomb will explain this. Those figures of the Yankee armies are correct to a unit. *Our friends shall be immediately set to work as you direct.*"

To which an official reply, in cipher, was delivered to Montgomery by an agent of the State Department in Richmond, dated October 19, 1864, as follows:—

"Your letter of the 13th inst. is at hand. There is yet time enough to colonize many voters before November. A blow will shortly be stricken here. It is not quite time. General Longstreet is to attack Sheridan without delay, and then move North as far as practicable toward unprotected points. This will be made instead of movement before mentioned. He will endeavor to assist the *Republicans in collecting their ballots*. Be watchful and assist him."

On the very day of the date of this Richmond despatch Sheridan was attacked, and with what success history will declare. The Court will not fail to notice that the *re-election of Mr. Lincoln* is to be prevented, if possible, by any and every means. Nor will they fail to notice that *Holcomb* is to "explain this"—the same person who, in Canada, was the friend and adviser of *Alston*, who proposed to Davis the assassination of the "deadliest enemies" of the Rebellion.

In the despatch of the 13th of October, which was borne by Montgomery, and transmitted to Richmond in October last, you will find these words:—"Our friends shall be immediately set to work as you direct." Mr. Lincoln is the subject of that despatch. Davis is therein notified that his agents in Canada look upon the re-election of Mr. Lincoln in November as almost certain. In this connection he is assured by these agents that the *friends* of their cause are to be set to work as *Davis had directed*.

The conversations which are proved by witnesses, whose character stands unimpeached, disclose what "work" the "friends" were to do under *the direction* of Davis himself. Who were these "friends," and what was "the work which his agents, Thompson, Clay, Tucker, and Sanders, had been directed to set them at? Let Thompson answer for himself. In a conversation with Richard Montgomery, in the summer of 1864, Thompson said "he *had his friends*, Confederates, all over the Northern States, who were ready and willing to go any length for the good of the cause of the South, and he could at any time have the *tyrant Lincoln, or any other of his advisers* that he chose, *put out of his way;* that they would not consider it *a crime* when done for the cause of the Confederacy." This conversation was repeated by the witness in the summer of 1864 to Clement C. Clay, who immediately stated:— "That is so; we are all devoted to our cause, and ready to go any length—to do anything under the sun."

At and about the time that these declarations of Clay and Thompson were made, *Alston*, who made the proposition, as we have seen, to Davis, to be furnished with papers *to go North* and rid the Confederacy of some of its "deadliest enemies," was in Canada. He was, doubtless, one of the "friends" referred to. As appears from the testimony of Montgomery, Payne, the prisoner at your bar, was about that time in Canada, and was seen standing by Thompson's door, engaged in a conversation with Clay, between whom and the witness some words were interchanged, when Clay stated he (Payne) was one of *their friends*, "we trust him." It is proved beyond a shadow of doubt, that in October last, John Wilkes Booth, the assassin of the President, was also in Canada and upon intimate terms with Thompson, Clay, Sanders, and other Rebel agents. Who can doubt, in the light of the events which have since transpired, that he was one of the "friends" to be "set to work," as Davis had already directed: not, perhaps, as yet to assassinate the President, but to do that other work which is suggested in the letter of Oldham, indorsed by Davis in his own hand, and spread upon your record, the work of the secret incendiary, which was to "fill the people of the North with terror and consternation."

The other "work" spoken of by Thompson, putting the *tyrant Lincoln* and *any of his advisers out of the way*, was work doubtless to be commenced only after the re-election of Mr. Lincoln, which they had already declared in their despatch to their employer, Davis, was with them a foregone conclusion. At all events, it was not until after the Presidential election in November that Alston proposed to Davis to *go North* on the work of assassination; nor was it until after that election that Booth was found in possession of the letter which is in evidence, and which discloses the purpose to assassinate the President. Being assured, however, when Booth was with them in Canada, as they had already declared in their despatch, that the re-election of Mr. Lincoln was certain, in which event there would be no hope for the Confederacy, they doubtless entered into the arrangement with Booth as one of their "friends," that as soon as that fact was determined he should go "to work," and as soon as might be "rid the Confederacy of the tyrant Lincoln and of his advisers."

That these persons named upon your record, Thompson, Sanders, Clay, Cleary and Tucker, were the agents of Jefferson Davis, is another fact established in this case beyond a doubt. They made affidavit of it themselves, of record here, upon the examination of their "friends," charged with the raid upon St. Albans, before Judge Smith, in Canada. It is in evidence also by the letter of Clay, before referred to.

The testimony, to which I have thus briefly referred, shows, by the letter of his agents, of the 13th of October, that Davis had before directed those agents to set his *friends at work*. By the letter of Clay, it seems that his direction had been obeyed, and his friends had been at St. Albans, in the attempt to burn the city of New York, and in the attempt to introduce pestilence into this Capital and into the house of the President. It having appeared, by the letter of Alston, and the indorsement thereon, that Davis had in November entertained the proposition of sending agents, that is to say, "friends," to the North, to not only "spread terror and consternation among the people," by means of his "chemical preparations," but also, in the words of that letter, "to strike," by the hands of assassins, "at the heart's blood" of the deadliest enemies in the North to the confederacy of traitors: it has also appeared by the testimony of many respectable witnesses, among others the attorneys who represented the people of the United States and the State of Vermont, in the preliminary trial of the raiders in Canada, that Clay, Thompson, Tucker, Sanders and Cleary, declared themselves the agents of the Confederacy. It also clearly appears by the correspondence referred to and the letter of Clay, that they were holding, and at any time able to command blank commissions from Jefferson Davis to authorize *their friends* to do whatever work they appointed them to do, in the interest of the Rebellion, by the destruction of life and property in the North.

If *a prima facie* case justifies, as we have seen by the law of evidence it does, the introduction of all declarations and acts of any of the parties to a conspiracy, uttered and done in the prosecution of the common design, as evidence against all the rest, it results, that whatever was said or done in furtherance of the common design, after this month of October, 1864, by either of these agents in Canada, is evidence not only against themselves, but against Davis as well, of his complicity with them in the conspiracy.

Mr. Montgomery testifies that he met Jacob Thompson in January, at Montreal, when he said that "a proposition had been made to him to rid the world of the tyrant, Lincoln. Stanton, Grant, and some others; that he knew the men who had made the proposition; were bold, daring men, able to execute what they undertook; that he himself was in favor of the proposition, but had determined to defer his answer until he had consulted his Government at Richmond; that he was then only awaiting their approval." This was about the middle of January, and, consequently, more than a month after Alston had made his proposition direct to Davis, in writing, to go North and rid their Confederacy of some of its "deadliest enemies." It was at the time of this conversation that Payne, the prisoner, was seen by the witness standing at Thompson's door in conversation with Clay. This witness also shows the intimacy between Thompson, Clay, Cleary, Tucker and Sanders.

A few days after the assassination of the President, Beverly Tucker said to this witness "that President Lincoln deserved his death long ago; that it was a pity he didn't have it long ago; and it was too bad that the boys had not been allowed to act when they wanted to."

This remark undoubtedly had reference to the propositions made in the fall to Thompson, and also to Davis, to rid the South of its deadliest enemies by their assassination. Cleary, who was accredited by Thompson as his confidential agent, also stated to this witness that Booth was one of the party to whom Thompson had referred in the conversation in January, in which he said he knew the men who were ready to rid the world of the tyrant Lincoln, and of Stanton and Grant. Cleary also said, speaking of the assassination, "that it was a pity that the whole work had not been done," and added "they had better look out, we are not done yet;" manifestly referring to the statement made by his employer, Thompson, before in the summer, that not only the tyrant Lincoln, but Stanton and Grant, and others of his advisers, should be put out of the way. Cleary also stated to this witness that Booth had visited Thompson twice in the winter, the last time in December, and had also been there in the summer.

Sanford Conover testified that he had been for some time a clerk in the War Department in Richmond; that in Canada he knew Thompson, Sanders, Cleary, Tucker, Clay and other Rebel agents; that he knew John H. Surratt and John Wilkes Booth; that he saw Booth there upon one occasion, and Surratt upon several successive days; that he saw Surratt (whom he describes) in April last, in Thompson's room, and also in company with Sanders; that about the 6th or 7th of April last Surratt delivered to Jacob Thompson a despatch, brought by him from Benjamin, at Richmond, inclosing one in cipher from Davis. Thompson had before this proposed to Conover to engage in a plot to assassinate President Lincoln and his Cabinet, and on this occasion he laid his hand upon these despatches and said, "This makes the thing all right." referring to the assent of the Rebel authorities, and stated that the Rebel authorities had consented to the plot to assassinate Lincoln, Johnson, the Secretary of War, Secretary of State, Judge Chase and General Grant. Thompson remarked further that the assassination of these parties would leave the Government of the United States entirely without a head; that there was no provision in the Constitution of the United States by which they could elect another President, if these men were put out of the way.

In speaking of this assassination of the President and others, Thompson said that it was only removing them from office; that the killing of a tyrant was no murder. It seems that he had learned precisely the same lesson that Alston had learned in November, when he communicated with Davis, and said, speaking of the President's assassination, "he did not think anything dishonorable that would serve their cause." Thompson stated at the same time that he had conferred a commission on Booth, and that everybody engaged in the enterprise would be commissioned, and if it succeeded, or failed, and they escaped into Canada, they could not be reclaimed under the extradition treaty. The fact that Thompson and other Rebel agents held blank commissions, as I have said, has been proved, and a copy of one of them is on record here.

This witness also testifies to a conversation with William C. Cleary, shortly after the surrender of Lee's army, and on the day before the President's assassination, at the St. Lawrence Hotel, Montreal, when speaking of the rejoicing in the States over the capture of Richmond, Cleary said, "they would put the laugh on the other side of their mouth in a day or two." These parties knew that Conover was in the secret of the assassination, and talked with him about it as freely as they would speak of the weather. Before the assassination he had a conversation also with Sanders, who asked him if he knew Booth well, and expressed some apprehension that Booth would "make a failure of it; that he was desperate and reckless, and he was afraid the whole thing would prove a failure."

Mr. James D. Merritt testifies that George Young, one of the parties named in the record, declared in his presence, in Canada, last fall, that Lincoln should never be inaugurated; that they had friends in Washington, who, I suppose, were some of the same friends referred to in the despatch of October 14, and which Davis had directed them "to set to work." George N. Sanders also said to him "that Lincoln would keep himself mighty close if he did serve another term;" while steels and other Confederates declared that the tyrant never should serve another term. He heard the assassination discussed at a meeting of these Rebel agents in Montreal in February last. "Sanders said they had plenty of money to accomplish the assassination, and named a number of persons who were ready and willing to engage in undertaking to remove the President, Vice President, the Cabinet, and some of the leading Generals. At this meeting he read a letter which he had received from Davis, which justified him in making any arrangements that he could to accomplish the object." This letter the witness heard read, and it, in substance declared that if the people in Canada and the Southerners in the States were willing to submit to be governed by such a tyrant as Lincoln, he did not wish to recognize them as friends. The letter was read openly; it was also handed to Colonel Steele, George Young, Hill and Scott to read. This was about the middle of February last. At this meeting Sanders named over the persons who were willing to accomplish the assassination, and among the persons thus named was Booth, whom the witness had seen in Canada in October; also George Harper, one of the conspirators named on the record, Caldwell, Randall, Harrison and Surratt.

The witness understood, from the reading of the letter, that if the President, Vice-President, and Cabinet could be disposed of, it would satisfy the people of the North that the Southerners had friends in the North; that a peace could be obtained on better terms than the Rebels had endeavored to bring about a war between the United States and England, and that Mr. Seward, through his energy and sagacity, had thwarted all their efforts; that was given as a reason for removing him. On the 5th or 6th of April last, this witness met George Harper, Caldwell, Randall, and others, who are spoken of in this meeting at Montreal as engaged to assassinate the President and Cabinet, when Harper said they were going to the States to make a row such as had never been heard of, and added that "if I (the witness) did not hear of the death of Old Abe, of the Vice-President, and of General Dix, in less than ten days, I might put him down as a fool. That was on the 5th of April. He mentioned that Booth was in Washington at that time. He said they had plenty of friends in Washington, and that some fifteen or twenty were going."

This witness ascertained on the 8th of April that Harper and others had left for the States. The proof is that these parties could come through to Washington from Montreal or Toronto in thirty-six hours. They did come, and within the ten days named by Harper the President was murdered. Some attempts have been made to discredit this witness (Dr. Mott), not by the examination of witnesses in court, not by any apparent want of truth in the testimony, but by the ex parte statements of these Rebel Agents in Canada and their hired advocates in the United States. There is a statement upon record, verified by an official communication from the War Department, which shows the truthfulness of this witness, and that is, that before the assassination, learning that Harper and his associates had started for the States, informed as he was of their purpose to assassinate the President, Cabinet and leading Generals, Merritt deemed it his duty to call, and did call, on the 10th of April, upon a justice of the peace in Canada, named Davidson, and gave him the information that he might take steps to stop these proceedings. The correspondence on this subject with Davidson has been brought into court. Dr. Merritt testifies, further, that after this meeting in Montreal he had a conversation with Clement C. Clay, in Toronto, about the letter from Jefferson Davis, which Saunders had exhibited, in which conversation Clay gave the witness to understand that he knew the nature of the letter perfectly, and remarked that he thought "the end would justify the means." The witness also testifies to the presence of Booth with Sanders in Montreal last fall, and of Surratt in Toronto in February last.

The Court must be satisfied, by the manner of this and other witnesses to the transactions in Canada, as well as by the fact that they are wholly uncontradicted in any material matter that they state, that they speak the truth, and that the several parties named on your record—Davis, Thompson, Cleary, Tucker, Clay, Young, Harper, Booth and John H. Surratt—did combine and conspire together in Canada to kill and murder Abraham Lincoln, Andrew Johnson, William H. Seward and Ulysses S. Grant. That this agreement was substantially entered into by Booth and the agents of Davis in Canada as early as October, there cannot be any doubt. The language of Thompson at that time and before was that he was in favor of the assassination. His further language was, that he knew the men who were ready to do it, and Booth, it is shown, was there at that time, and, as Thompson's Secretary says, was one of the men referred to by Thompson.

The fact that others, besides the parties named on

the record, were, by the terms of the conspiracy, to be assassinated, in nowise affects the case now on trial. If it is true that these parties did conspire to murder other parties as well as those named upon the record, the substance of the charge is proved.

It is also true that if, in pursuance of that conspiracy, Booth, confederated with Surratt and the accused, killed and murdered Abraham Lincoln, the charge and specification is proved literally as stated on your record, although their conspiracy embraced other persons. In law the case stands, though it may appear that the conspiracy was to kill and murder the parties named in the record, and others not named in the record. If the proof is that the accused, with Booth, Surratt, Davis, &c., conspired to kill and murder one or more of the persons named, the charge of conspiracy is proved.

The declaration of Sanders, as proved, that there was plenty of money to carry out this assassination, is very strongly corroborated by the testimony of Mr. Campbell, cashier of the Ontario Bank, who states that Thompson, during the current year preceding the assassination, had upon deposit in the Montreal branch of the Ontario Bank, six hundred and forty-nine thousand dollars, besides large sums to his credit in other banks in the Province.

There is a further corroboration of the testimony of Conover as to the meeting of Thompson and Surratt in Montreal, and the delivery of the despatches from Richmond, on the 6th or 7th of April, first, in the fact which is shown, by the testimony of Chester, that in the winter or spring Booth said he himself or some other party must go to Richmond; and, second, by the letter of Arnold, dated 27th of March last, that he preferred Booth's first query, that he would first go to Richmond and see how they would take it, manifestly alluding to the proposed assassination of the President.

It does not follow because Davis had written a letter in February which, in substance, approved the general object that the parties were fully satisfied with it, because it is clear there was to be some arrangement made about the funds, and it is also clear that Davis had not before as distinctly approved and sanctioned this act as his agents either in Canada or here desired. Booth said to Chester, "We must have money; there is money in this business, and if you will enter into it I will place three thousand dollars at the disposal of your family, but I have no money myself, and must go to Richmond," or one of the parties must go, "to get money to carry out the enterprise." This was one of the arrangements that was to be "made right in Canada." The funds at Thompson's disposal, the banker testifies, were exclusively raised by drafts of the Secretary of the Treasury of the Confederate States upon London, deposited in their bank to the credit of Thompson.

Accordingly, about the 27th of March, Surratt d'd go to Richmond. On the 3d of April he returned to Washington, and the same day left for Canada. Before leaving, he stated to Weichman, that when in Richmond he had a conversation with Davis and with Benjamin. The fact in this connection is not to be overlooked, that on or about the day Surratt arrived in Montreal, April 6, Jacob Thompson, as the cashier of the Ontario Bank states, drew of these Confederate funds the sum of one hundred and eighty thousand dollars in the form of certificates, which, as the bank officer testifies, "might be used anywhere."

What more is wanting? Surely no word further need be spoken to show that John Wilkes Booth was in this conspiracy; and that Jefferson Davis and his several agents named in Canada, were in this conspiracy. If any additional evidence is wanting to show the complicity of Davis in it, let the paper found in the possession of his hired assassin Booth come to bear witness against him. That paper contained the secret cipher which Davis us d in his State Department in Richmond, which he employed in communicating with his agents in Canada, and which they employed in the letter of October 13, notifying him that "their friends would be set to work as he had directed."

The letter in cipher found in Booth's possession is translated here by the use of the cipher machine now in Court, which, as the testimony of Mr. Dana shows, he brought from the rooms of Davis' State Department in Richmond. Who gave Booth this secret cipher? Of what use was it to him if he was not in confederation with Davis?

But there is one other item of testimony that ought, among honest and intelligent people at all conversant with this evidence, to end all further inquiry as to whether Jefferson Davis was one of the parties with Booth, as charged upon this record, in the conspiracy to assassinate the President and others. That is, that on the fifth day after the assassination, in the city of Charlotte, North Carolina, a telegraphic despatch was received by him, at the house of Mr. Bates, from John C. Breckinridge, his Rebel Secretary of War, which despatch is produced here, identified by the telegraph agent, and placed upon your record in the words following:—

"CHARLESSTOWN, April 19, 1865.—His Excellency President Davis,—Presid nt Lincoln was assassinated in the theatre at Washington on the night of the 14th, lost. Seward's house was entered on the same night, and he was repeatedly stabbed, and is probably mortally wounded. JOHN C. BRECKINRIDGE."

At the time this despatch was handed to him, Davis was addressing a meeting from the steps of Mr. Bates' house, and after reading the despatch to the people he said:—"If it were to be done, it were better it were well done." Shortly afterward, in the house of the witness, in the same city, Breckinridge, having come to see Davis, stated his regret that the occurrence had happened, because he deemed it unfortunate for the people of the South at that time. Davis replied, referring to the assassination, "Well, General, I don't know; if it were to be done at all, it were better that it were well done; and if the same had been done to Andy Johnson, the beast, and Secretary Stanton, the job would then be complete."

Accomplished as this man was in all the arts of a conspirator, he was not equal to the task—as, happily, in the good providence of God, no mortal man is—of concealing, by any form of words, any great crime which he may have meditated or perpetrated either against his Government or his fellow-man. It was doubtless furthest from Jefferson Davis' purpose to make confession, and yet he did make confession. His guilt demanded utterance; that demand he could not resist; therefore his words proclaimed his guilt, in spite of his purpose to conceal it. He said, "if it were to be done, it were better it were well done." Would any man ignorant of the conspiracy be able to devise and fashion such a form of speech as that? Had not the President been murdered? Had he not reason to believe that the Secretary of State had been mortally wounded? Yet he was not satisfied but was compelled to say, "it were better it were well done;" that is to say, all that had been agreed to be done had not been done.

Two days afterwards, in his conversation with Breckinridge, he not only repeats the same form of expression, "If it were to be done it were better it were well done," but adds these words:—"And if the same had been done to Andy Johnson, the beast, and to Secretary Stanton, the job would then be complete." He would accept the assassination of the President, the Vice President, of the Secretary of State, and the Secretary of War as a complete execution of the "job," which he had given out upon contract, and which he had "made all right," so far as the pay was concerned, by the despatches he had sent to Thompson by Surratt, one of his hired assassins.

Whatever may be the convictions of others, my own conviction is that Jefferson Davis is as clearly proven guilty of this conspiracy as is John Wilkes Booth, by whose hand Jefferson Davis inflicted the mortal wound upon Abraham Lincoln. His words of intense hate, and rage, and disappointment are not to be overlooked—that the assassins had not done their work well; that they had not succeeded in robbing the people altogether of their constitutional Executive and his advisers; and hence he exclaims, "if they had killed Andy Johnson, the beast!" Neither can he conceal his chagrin and disappointment that the war minister of the republic, whose energy, incorruptible integrity, sleepless vigilance, and executive ability had organized day by day, month by month, and year by year, victory for our arms, had escaped the knife of the hired assassins. The job, says this procurer of assassination, was not well done; it had been better if it had been well done! Because Abraham Lincoln had been clear in his great office, and had saved the nation's life by enforcing the nation's laws this traitor declares he must be murdered; because Mr. Seward, as the foreign Secretary of the country, had thwarted the purposes of treason to plunge his country into a war with England, he must be murdered; because, upon the murder of Mr. Lincoln, Andrew Johnson would succeed to the Presidency, and because he had been true to the Constitution and Government, faithful found among the faithless of his own State, clinging to the falling pillars of the Republic when others had fled, he must be murdered: and because the Secretary of War had taken care, by the faithful discharge of his duties, that the Republic should live and not die, he must be murdered. Inasmuch as these two faithful officers were not also assassinated, assuming that the Secretary of State was mortally wounded, Davis could not conceal his disappointment and chagrin that the work was not "well done;" that "the job was not complete."

Thus it appears by the testimony, that the proposition made to Davis was to kill and murder the deadliest enemies of the Confederacy—not to kidnap them, as is now pretended here; that by the declaration of Sanders, Tucker, Thompson, Clay, Cleary, Harper and Young, the con-pirators in Canada, the agreement and combination among them was to kill and murder Abraham Lincoln, Wm. H. Seward, Andrew Johnson, Ulysses S. Grant, Edwin M. Stanton, and others of his advisers, and not to kidnap them; it appears from every utterance of John Wilkes Booth, as well as from the Charles Selby letter, of which, mention w ll presently be made, that, as early as November, the proposition with him was to kill and murder, not to kidnap.

Since the first examination of Conover, who testified, as the court will remember, to many important facts against these conspirators and agents of Davis in Canada, among others the terrible and fiendish plot disclosed by Thompson, Pallen and others, that they had ascertained the volume of water in the reservoir supplying New York city, estimated the quantity of poison required to render it deadly, and intended thus to poison a whole city—Conover returned to Canada, by direction of this court, for the purpose of obtaining certain documentary evidence. There, about the 8th of June, he met Beverly Tucker, Sanders and other conspirators, and conversed with them. Tucker declared that Secretary Stanton, whom he denounced as "a scoundrel," and Judge Holt, whom he called "a bloodthirsty villain," "could protect themselves as long as they remained in office by a guard, but that would not always be the case, and, by the Eternal, he had a large account to settle with them."

After this, the evidence of Conover here having been published, these parties called upon him and asked him whether he had been to Washington, and had testified before this Court. Conover denied it; they insisted, and took him to a room, where, with drawn pistols, they compelled him to consent to make an affidavit that he had been falsely personated here by another, and that he would make that affidavit before a Mr. Kerr, who would witness it. They then called in Mr. Kerr to certify to the public that Conover had made such a denial. They also compelled this witness to furnish for publication an advertisement offering a reward of five hundred dollars for the arrest of the "infamous and perjured scoundrel" who had recently personated James W. Wallace under the name of Sandford Conover, and testified to a tissue of falsehoods before the Military Commission at Washington, which advertisement was published in the papers.

To these facts Mr. Conover now testifies, and also discloses the fact that these same men published, in the report of the proceedings before Judge Smith an affidavit purporting to be his, but which he never made. The affidavit which he in fact made, and which was published in a newspaper at that time, produced here, is set out substantially upon your record, and agrees with the testimony upon the same point given by him in this Court.

To suppose that Conover ever made such an affidavit voluntarily as the one wrung from him as stated is impossible. Would he advertise for his own arrest, and charge himself with falsely impersonating himself? But the fact cannot evade observation that, when these guilty conspirators saw Conover's testimony before this Court in the public prints, revealing to the world the atrocious plots of these felon conspirators, conscious of the truthfulness of his statements, they cast about at once for some defense before the public, and devised the foolish and stupid invention of compelling him to make an affidavit that he was not Sandford Conover, was not in this Court, never gave this testimony, but was a practicing lawyer at Montreal! This infamous proceeding, coupled with the evidence before detailed, stamps these ruffian plotters with the guilt of this conspiracy.

John Wilkes Booth having entered into this conspiracy in Canada, as has been shown, as early as October, he is next found in the city of New York, on the 11th day, as I claim, of November, in disguise, in conversation with another, the conversation disclosing to the witness, Mrs. Hudspeth, that they had some matter of personal interest between them; that upon one of them the lot had fallen to go to Washington; upon the other to go to Newbern. This witness upon being shown the photograph of Booth swears "that the face is the same" as that of one of those men, who she says was a man of education and culture, as appeared by his conversation; and who had a scar like a bite near the jaw bone. It is a fact proved here by the Surgeon-General, that Booth had a scar on the side of his neck. Mrs. Hudspeth heard him say he would leave for Washington the day after to-morrow. His companion appeared angry because it had not fallen on him to go to Washington. This took place after the Presidential election in November. She cannot fix the precise date, but says she was told General Butler left New York on that day. The testimony discloses that General Butler's army was on the 11th of November leaving New York. The register of the National Hotel shows that Booth left Washington on the early morning train, November 11, and that he returned to this city on the 14th. Chester testifies positively to Booth's presence in New York early in November.

This testimony shows most conclusively that Booth was in New York on the 11th of November. The early morning train on which he left Washington would reach New York early in the afternoon of that day. Chester saw him there early in November, and Mrs. Hudspeth not only identifies his picture, but describes his person. The scar upon his neck near his jaw was peculiar, and is well described by the witness as like a bite. On that day Booth had a letter in his possession which he accidentally dropped in the street car in the presence of Mrs. Hudspeth, the witness, who delivered it to Major-General Dix the same day, and by whom, as his letter on file before this Court shows, the same was transmitted to the War Department November 17, 1864. That letter contains these words:—

"DEAR LOUIS:—The time has at last come that we have all so wished for, and upon you every thing depends. As it was decided before you left, we were to cast lots. We accordingly did so, and you are to be the Charlotte Corday of the nineteenth century. When you remember the awful, solemn vow that was taken by us, you will feel there is no drawback. Abe must die, and now. You can choose your weapons—the cup, the knife, the bullet. The cup failed us once, and might again. Johnson, who will give this, has been like an enraged demon since the meeting, because it has not fallen on him to rid the world of a monster. * * You know where to find your friends. 'Your disguises are so perfect and complete, that without one knew your face, no police telegraphic despatch would catch you. The English gentleman, Harcourt, must not act hastily. Remember, he has ten days. Strike for your home, strike for your country; bide your time, but strike sure. Get introduced; congratulate him; listen to his stories; cat many more with the bruto tell to earthly friends;) do anything but fail, and meet us at the appointed place within the fortnight. You will probably hear from me in Washington. Sanders is doing us no good in Canada. CHAS. SELBY."

The learned gentleman (Mr. Cox), in his very able and carefully considered argument in defense of O'Laughlin and Arnold, attached importance to this letter, and doubtless very clearly saw its bearing upon the case, and, therefore, undertook to show that the witness, Mrs. Hudspeth, must be mistaken as to the person of Booth. The gentleman assumes that the letter of General Dix, of the 17th of November last, transmitting this letter to the War Department, reads that the party who dropped the letter was heard to say that he would start to Washington on Friday night next, although the word "next" is not in the letter, neither is it in the quotation which the gentleman makes, for he quotes it fairly; yet he concludes that this would be the 18th of November.

Now the fact is, the 11th of November last was Friday, and the register of the National Hotel bears witness that Mrs. Hudspeth is not mistaken; because her language is, that Booth said he would leave for Washington day after to-morrow, which would be Sunday, the 13th, and if in the evening, would bring him to Washington on Monday, the 14th of November, the day on which the register shows he did return to the National Hotel. As to the improbability which the gentleman raises, on the conversation happening in a street car, crowded with people, there was nothing that transpired, although the conversation was earnest, which enabled the witness, or could have enabled any one, in the absence of this letter, or of the subsequent conduct of Booth, to form the least idea of the subject-matter of their conversation.

The gentleman does not deal altogether fairly in his remarks touching the letter of General Dix; because, upon a careful examination of the letter, it will be found that he did not form any such judgment as that it was a hoax for the Sunday Mercury, but he took care to forward it to the Department, and asked attention to it; when, as appears by the testimony of the Assistant Secretary of War, Mr. Dana, the letter was delivered to Mr. Lincoln, who considered it important enough to indorse it with the word "Assassination," and file it in his office, where it was found a.ter the commission of this crime, and brought into this Court to bear witness against his assassins.

Although this letter would imply that the assassination spoken of was to take place speedily, yet the party was to bide his time. Though he had entered into the preliminary arrangements in Canada, although conspirators had doubtless agreed to co-operate with him in the commission of the crime, and lots had been cast for the chief part in the bloody drama, yet it remained for him as the leader and principal of the hired assassins, by whose hand their employers were to strike the murderous blow, to collect about him and bring to Washington such persons as would be willing to lend themselves, for a price, to the horrid crime, and likely to give the necessary aid and support in its consummation. The letter declares that Abraham Lincoln must die, and now, meaning as soon as the agents can be employed and the work done. To that end you will bide your time.

But, says the gentleman, it could not have been the same conspiracy charged here to which this letter refers. Why not? It is charged here that Booth, with the accused and others, conspired to kill and murder Abraham Lincoln; that is precisely the conspiracy disclosed in the letter. Granted that the parties on trial had not then entered into the combination; if they at any time afterward entered into it they became parties to it, and the conspiracy was still the same. But, says the gentleman, the words of the letter imply that the conspiracy was to be executed within the fortnight. Booth is directed, by the name of Louis, to meet the writer within a fortnight. If by no means follows that he was to strike within the fortnight because he was to meet his co-conspirator within that time, and any such conclusion is excluded by the words, "Bide your time."

Even if the conspiracy was to be executed within the fortnight, and was not so executed, and the same party, Booth, afterwards by concert and agreement with the accused and others, did execute it by "striking sure" and killing the President, that act, whenever done, would be but the execution of this same conspiracy. The letter is conclusive evidence of so much of this conspiracy as relates to the murder of President Lincoln. As Booth was to do anything but fail, he immediately thereafter sought out the agents to enable him to strike sure, and execute all that he had agreed with Davis and his co-confederates in Canada to do—to murder the President, the Secretary of State, the Vice-President. General Grant and Secretary Stanton.

Even Booth's co-conspirator, Payne, now on his trial, by his defense admits all this, and says Booth had just been to Canada, "was filled with a mighty scheme, and was lying in wait for agents." Booth asked the co-operation of the prisoner Payne, and said:—"I will give you as much money as you want; but first you must swear to stick by me. It is in the oil business." This you are told by the accused was early in March last. Thus guilt bears witness against itself.

We find Booth in New York in November, December and January, urging Chester to enter into this combination, assuring him that there was money in it; that they had "friends on the other side;" that if he would only participate in it, he would never want for money while he lived, and all that was asked of him was to stand at and open the back door of Ford's Theatre. Booth, in his interview with Chester, confesses that he is without money himself, and allows Chester to reimburse him the fifty dollars which he (Booth) had transmitted to him in a letter for the purpose of paying his expenses to Washington as one of the parties to this conspiracy. Booth told him, although he himself was penniless, "there is money in this, we have friends on the other side," and if you will but engage, I will have three thousand dollars deposited at once for the use of your family.

Failing to secure the services of Chester, because his soul recoiled with abhorrence from the foul work of assassination and murder, he found more willing instruments in others whom he gathered about him. Men to commit the assassinations, horses to secure speedy and certain escape were to be provided, and to this end Booth, with an energy worthy of a better cause, applies himself. For this latter purpose he told Chester he had already expended $5000. In the latter part of November, 1864, he visits Charles county, Maryland, and is in company with one of the prisoners, Dr. Samuel A. Mudd, with whom he lodged over night, and through whom he procures of Gardner one of the several horses which were at his disposal, and used by him and his co-conspirators in Washington on the night of the assassination.

Some time in January last, it is in testimony, that the prisoner Mudd introduced Booth to John H. Surratt and the witness Weichmann; that Booth invited them to the National Hotel; that when there, in the room which Booth took them, Mudd went out into the passage, called Booth out and had a private conversation with him, leaving the witness and Surratt in the room. Upon their return to the room Booth went out with Surratt, and upon their coming in all three, Booth, Surratt, and Samuel A. Mudd, went out together and had a conversation in the passage, leaving the witness alone. Up to the time of this interview it seems that neither the witness nor Surratt had any knowledge of Booth, as they were then introduced to him by Dr. Mudd. Whether Surratt had in fact previously known Booth it is not important to inquire. Mudd deemed it necessary, perhaps, a wise precaution, to introduce Surratt to Booth; he also deemed it necessary to have a private conversation with Booth shortly afterwards, and directly upon that to have a conversation together with Booth and Surratt alone.

Had this conversation, no part of which was heard by the witness, been perfectly innocent, it is not to be presumed that Dr. Mudd, who was an entire stranger to Weichman, would have deemed it necessary to hold the conversation secretly, nor to have volunteered to tell the witness, or rather pretend to tell him, what the conversation was; yet he did say to the witness, upon their return to the room, by way of apology, I suppose, for the privacy of the conversation, that Booth had some private business with him, and wished to purchase his farm. This silly device, as is often the case in attempts at deception, failed in the execution; for it remains to be shown how the fact that Mudd had private business with Booth, and that Booth wished to purchase his farm, made it at all necessary or even proper that they should both volunteer to call out Surratt, who up to that moment was a stranger to Booth. What had Surratt to do with Booth's purchase of Mudd's farm? And, if it was necessary to withdraw and talk by themselves secretly about the sale of the farm, why should they disclose the fact to the very man from whom they had concealed it?

Upon the return of these three parties to the room, they seated themselves at a table, and upon the back of an envelope Booth traced lines with a pencil, indicating, as the witness states, the direction of roads. Why was this done? As Booth had been previously in that section of country, as the prisoner in his defense has taken great pains to show, it was certainly not necessary to anything connected with the purchase of Mudd's farm that at that time he should be indicating the direction of roads to or from it; nor is it made to appear by anything in this testimony, how it comes

that Surratt, as the witness testifies, seemed to be as much interested in the marking out of these roads as Mudd or Booth. It does not appear that Surratt was in any wise connected with or interested in the sale of Mudd's farm. From all that has transpired since this meeting at the hotel, it would seem that this plotting the roads was intended, not so much to show the road to Mudd's farm, as to point out the shortest and safest roads for flight from the Capital, by the houses of all the parties in this conspiracy, to their "friends on the other side."

But, says the learned gentleman (Mr. Ewing), in his very able argument in defense of this prisoner, why should Booth determine that his flight should be through Charles county? The answer must be obvious, upon a moment's reflection, to every man, and could not possibly have escaped the notice of the counsel himself, but for the reason that his zeal for his client constrained him to overlook it. It was absolutely essential that his murderers should have his co-conspirators at convenient points along his route, and it does not appear in evidence that by his route to his friends, who had then fled from Richmond, which the gentleman (Mr. Ewing) indicates as the more direct, but of which there is not the slightest evidence whatever, Booth had co-conspirators at an equal distance from Washington. The testimony discloses further, that on the route selected by him for his flight, there is a large population that would be most likely to favor and aid him in the execution of his wicked purpose, and in making his escape. But it is a sufficient answer to the gentleman's question, that Booth's co-conspirator, Mudd, lived in Charles county.

To return to the meeting at the hotel. In the light of other facts in this case, it must become clear to the Court that this secret meeting between Booth, Surratt and Mudd was a conference looking to the execution of this conspiracy. It so impressed the prisoner, it so impressed his counsel, that they deemed it necessary and absolutely essential to their defense to attempt to destroy the credibility of the witness Weichman.

I may say here, in passing, that they have not attempted to impeach his general reputation for truth by the testimony of a single witness, nor have they impeached his testimony by calling a single witness to discredit one material fact to which he has testified in this issue. Failing to find a breath of suspicion against Weichman's character, or to contradict a single fact to which he testified, the accused had to fly to the last resort, an alibi, and very earnestly did the learned counsel devote himself to the task.

It is not material whether this meeting in the hotel took place on the 23d of December or in January. But, says the counsel, it was after the commencement or close of the Congressional holiday. That is not material: but the concurrent resolution of Congress shows that the holiday commenced on the 22d December, the day before the accused spent the evening in Washington. The witness is not certain about the date of this meeting. The material fact is, did this meeting take place—either on the 23d of December or in January last? Were the private interviews there held, and was the apology made, as detailed, by Mudd and Booth after the secret conference to the witness? That the meeting did take place, and that Mudd did explain that these secret interviews, with Booth first, and with Booth and Surratt directly afterward, had relation to the sale of his farm, is confessedly admitted by the endeavor of the prisoner, through his counsel, to show that negotiations had been going on between Booth and Mudd for the sale of Mudd's farm.

If no such meeting was held, if no such explanation was made by Mudd to Weichman, can any man for a moment believe that a witness would have been called here to give any testimony about Booth having negotiated for Mudd's farm? What conceivable connection has it with this case, except to show that Mudd's explanation to Weichman for his extraordinary conduct was in exact accordance with the fact? Or was this testimony about the negotiations for Mudd's farm intended to show so close an intimacy and intercourse with Booth that Mudd could not fail to recognize him when he came flying for aid to his house from the work of assassination? It would be injustice to the able counsel to suppose that.

"I have said that it was wholly immaterial whether this conversation took place on the 23d of December or in January; it is in evidence that in both those months Booth was at the National Hotel; that he occupied a room there; that he arrived there on the 22d and was there on the 23d of December last, and also on the 12th day of January. The testimony of the witness is, that Booth said he had just come in. Suppose this conversation took place in December, on the evening of the 23d, the time when it is proved by J. T. Mudd, the witness for the accused, that he, in company with Samuel A. Mudd, spent the night in Washington city. Is there anything in the testimony of that or any other witness to show that the accused did not have and could not have have had an interview with Booth on that evening?

J. T. Mudd testifies that he separated from the prisoner, Samuel A. Mudd, at the National Hotel, early in the evening of that day, and did not meet him again until the accused came in for the night at the Pennsylvania House, where he stopped. Where was

TRIAL OF THE ASSASSINS AT WASHINGTON.

Dr. Samuel A. Mudd during this interview? What does his witness know about him during that time? How can he say that Dr. Mudd did not go up on Seventh street in company with Booth, then at the National; that he did not, on Seventh street, meet Surratt and Weichman; that he did not return to the National Hotel; that he did not have this interview, and afterwards meet him, the witness, as he testifies, at the Pennsylvania House? Who knows that the Congressional holiday had not, in fact, commenced on that day? What witness has been called to prove that Booth did not on either of those occasions occupy the room that had formerly been occupied by a member of Congress, who had temporarily vacated it, leaving his books there?

Weichman, I repeat, is not positive as to the date, he is only positive as to the fact; and he disclosed voluntarily, to this Court, that the date could probably be fixed by a reference to the register of the Pennsylvania House. That register cannot, of course, be conclusive of whether Mudd was there in January or not, for the very good reason that the proprietor admits that he did not know Samuel A. Mudd; therefore, Mudd might have registered by any other name. Weichman does not pretend to know that Mudd had registered at all. If Mudd was here in January, as a party to this conspiracy, it is not at all unlikely that, if he did register at that time in the presence of a man to whom he was wholly unacquainted, his kinsman not then being with him, he would register by a false name.

But if the interview took place in December, the testimony of Weichman bears as strongly against the accused as if it had happened in January. Weichman says he does not know what time was occupied in this interview at the National Hotel; that it probably lasted twenty minutes; that after the private interviews between Mudd, and Surratt, and Booth, which were not of very long duration, had terminated, the parties went to the Pennsylvania House, where Dr. Mudd had rooms, and after sitting together in the common sitting-room of the hotel, they left Dr. Mudd there about 10 o'clock P. M., who remained during the night. Weichman's testimony leaves no doubt that this meeting on Seventh street and interview at the National took place after dark, and terminated before or about 10 o'clock P. M. His own witness, J. T. Mudd, after stating that he separated from the accused at the National Hotel, says after he had got through a conversation with a gentleman of his acquaintance, he walked down the Avenue, went to several clothing stores, and "after a while" walked round to the Pennsylvania House, and "very soon after" he got there Dr. Mudd came in, and they went to bed shortly afterwards.

What time he spent in his "walk alone" on the Avenue, looking at clothing; what period he embraces in the terms "after a while," when he returned to the Pennsylvania House, and "soon after" which, Dr. Mudd got there, the witness does not disclose. Neither does he intimate, much less testify, that he saw Dr. Mudd when he first entered the Pennsylvania House on that night after their separation. How does he know that Booth and Surratt and Weichman did not accompany Samuel A. Mudd to that house that evening? How does he know that the prisoner and those persons did not converse together some time in the sitting room of the Pennsylvania Hotel? Jeremiah Mudd has not testified that he met Dr. Mudd in that room, or that he was in it himself.

He has, however, sworn to the fact, which is disproved by no one, that the prisoner was separated from him long enough that evening to have had the meeting with Booth, Surratt and Weichman, and the interviews in the National Hotel, and at the Pennsylvania House, to which Weichman has testified. Who is there to disprove it? Of what importance is it whether it was on the 23d day of December or in January? How does that affect the credibility of Weichman? He is a man, as I have before said, against whose reputation for truth and good conduct they have not been able to bring one witness. If this testimony did by possibility take place that night, is there anything to render it improbable that Booth, and Mudd, and Surratt did have the conversation at the National Hotel to which Weichman testifies? Of what avail, therefore, is the attempt to prove that Dr. Mudd was not here during January. If it was clear that he was here on the 23d of December, 1864, and had this conversation with Booth? That the attempt to prove an *alibi* during January has failed, is quite as clear as the proof of the fact that the prisoner was here on the evening of the 23d of December, and present in the National Hotel, where Booth stopped.

The fact that the prisoner, Samuel A. Mudd, went with J. T. Mudd on that evening to the National Hotel, and there separated from him, is proved by his own witness, J. T. Mudd; and that he did not rejoin him until they retired to bed in the Pennsylvania House, is proved by the same witness, and contradicted by nobody. Does any one suppose there would have been such assiduous care to prove that the prisoner was with his kinsman all the time on the 23d of December in Washington, if they had not known that Booth was then at the National Hotel, and that a meeting of the prisoner with Booth, Surratt and Weichman on that day would corroborate and confirm Weichman's testimony in every material statement he made concerning that meeting?

The accused having signally failed to account for his absence after he separated from his witness, J. T. Mudd, early in the evening of the 23d of December, at the National Hotel, until they had again met at the Pennsylvania House, when they retired to rest, he now attempts to prove an *alibi* as to the month of January. In this he has failed, as he failed in the attempt to show that he could not have met Booth, Surratt and Weichman on the 23d of December.

For this purpose the accused calls Betty Washington. She had been at Mudd's house every night since the Monday after Christmas last, except when there at Court, and says that the prisoner, Mudd, has only been away from home three nights during that time. This witness forgets that Mudd has not been at home any night or day since this Court assembled. Neither does she account for the three nights in which she swears to his absence from home. First, she says he went to Gardner's party second, he went to Giesboro', then to Washington. She does not know in what month he was away, the second time, all night. She only knows where he went from what he and his wife said, which is not evidence; but she does testify that when he left home and was absent over night, the second time, it was about two or three weeks after she came to his house, which would, if it were three weeks, make it just about the 13th of January, 1865, because she swears she came to his house on the first Monday after Christmas last, which was the 26th day of December; so that the 13th of January would be three weeks, less one day from that time; and it might have been a week earlier, according to her testimony, as, also, it might have been a week earlier, or more, by Weichman's testimony, for he is not positive as to the time.

What I have said of the register of the Pennsylvania House, the head-quarters of Mudd and Atzerodt, I need not here repeat. That record proves nothing, save that Dr. Mudd was there on the 23d of December, which, as we have seen, is a fact, along with others, to show that the meeting at the National then took place. I have also called the attention of the Court to the fact that if Mudd was at the house again in January, and did not register his name, the fact proves nothing; or, if he did, the register only proves that he registered falsely; either of which facts might have happened without the knowledge of the witness called by the accused from that house, who does not know Samuel A. Mudd personally.

The testimony of Henry L. Mudd, his brother, in support of this *alibi*, is that the prisoner was in Washington on the 23d of March and on the 10th of April, four days before the murder! But he does not account for the absent night in January, about which Betty Washington testifies. Thomas Davis was called for the same purpose, but stated that he was himself absent one night in January, after the 9th of that month and he could not say whether Mudd was there on that night or not. He does testify to Mudd's absence over night three times, and fixes one occasion on the night of the 26th of January; this witness cannot account for the absence of Mudd on the night referred to by Betty Washington.

This matter is entitled to no further attention. It can satisfy no one, and the burden of proof is upon the prisoner to prove that he was not in Washington in January. How can such testimony convince any rational man that Mudd was not here in January, against the evidence of an unimpeached witness, who swears that Samuel A. Mudd was in Washington in the month of January? Who, that has been examined here as a witness, knows that he was not?

The Rev. Mr. Evans swears that he saw him in Washington last winter, and that at the same time he saw Jarboe, the one coming out of, and the other going into, a house on H street, which he was informed, on inquiry, was the house of Mrs. Surratt. Jarboe is the only witness called to contradict Mr. Evans, and he leaves it in extreme doubt whether he does not corroborate him, as he swears that he was here himself last winter or fall; but cannot state exactly the time. Jarboe's silence on questions touching his own credibility leaves no room for any one to say that his testimony could impeach Mr. Evans, whatever he might swear.

Miss Anna H. Surratt is also called for the purpose of impeaching Mr. Evans. It is sufficient to say of her testimony on that point that she swears negatively only, that she did not see either of the persons named at her mother's house. This testimony neither disproves, nor does it even tend to disprove, the fact put in issue by Mr. Evans. No one will pretend, whatever the form of her expression in giving her testimony, that she could say more than that she did not know the fact, as it was impossible that she could know who was, or who was not, at her mother's house, casually, at a period so remote. It is not my purpose, neither is it needful here, to question in any way the integrity of this young woman.

It is further in testimony that Samuel A. Mudd was here on the 3d day of March last, the day preceding the inauguration, when Booth was to strike the traitorous blow; and it was, doubtless, only by the interpo-

TRIAL OF THE ASSASSINS AT WASHINGTON.

sition of that God who stands within the shadow and keeps watch above His own, that the victim of this conspiracy was spared that day from the assassin's hand, that he might complete his work and see the salvation of his country in the fall of Richmond and the surrender of its great army. Dr. Mudd was here on that day (the 3d of March), to abet, to encourage, to nerve his co-conspirator for the commission of this great crime. He was carried away by the awful purpose which possessed him, and rushed into the room of Mr. Norton, at the National Hotel, in search of Booth, exclaiming excitedly. "I'm mistaken; I thought this was Mr. Booth's room." He is told Mr. Booth is above, on the next floor. He is followed by Mr. Norton, because of his rude and excited behavior, and, being followed, conscious of his guilty errand, he turns away, afraid of himself and afraid to be found in concert with his fellow confederate. Mr. Norton identifies the prisoner, and has no doubt that Samuel A. Mudd is the man.

The Rev. Mr. Evans also swears that, after the 1st and before the 4th day of March last, he is certain that within that time, and on the 2d or 3d of March, he saw Dr. Mudd drive into Washington City. The endeavor is made by the accused, in order to break down this witness, by proving another *alibi*. The sister of the accused, Miss Fanny Mudd, is called. She testifies that she saw the prisoner at breakfast in her father's house on the 2d of March, about five o'clock in the morning, and not again until the 3d of March at noon. Mrs. Emily Mudd swears substantially to the same statement. Betty Washington, called for the accused, swears that he was at home all day at work with her on the 2d of March, and took breakfast at home. Frank Washington swears that Mudd was at home all day; that he saw him when he first came out in the morning, about sunrise, from his own house, and knows that he was there all day with them. Which is correct, the testimony of six sisters or the testimony of servants? The sisters say that he was at their father's house for breakfast on the morning of the 2d of March; the servants say he was at home for breakfast with them on that day. If this testimony is followed it proves one *alibi* too much. It is impossible, in the nature of things, that the testimony of all these four witnesses can be true.

Seeing this weakness in the testimony brought to prove this second *alibi*, the endeavor is next made to discredit Mr. Norton for truth; and two witnesses, not more, are called, who testify that his reputation for truth has suffered by contested litigation between one of the impeaching witnesses and others. Four witnesses are called, who testify that Mr. Norton's reputation for truth is very good; that he is a man of high character for truth, and entitled to be believed whether he speaks under the obligation of an oath or not. The late Postmaster-General, Hon. Horatio King, not only sustains Mr. Norton as a man of good reputation for truth, but expressly corroborates his testimony, by stating that in March last, about the 4th of March, Mr. Norton told him the same fact to which he swears here—that a man came into his room under excitement, alarmed his sister, was followed out by himself, and went down stairs instead of going up; and that Mr. Norton told him this before the assassination, and about the time of the inauguration.

What motive had Mr. Norton at that time to fabricate this statement? It detracts nothing from his testimony that he did not at that time mention the name of this man to his friend, Mr. King, because it appears from his testimony, and there is none to question the truthfulness of his statement, that at that time he did not know his name. Neither does it take from the force of his testimony, that Mr. Norton did not, in communicating this matter to Mr. King, make mention of Booth's name; because there, was nothing in the transaction at the time, he being ignorant of the name of Mudd, and equally ignorant of the conspiracy between Mudd and Booth, to give the least occasion for any mention of Booth or of the transaction further than he detailed it. With such corroboration, who can doubt the fact that Mudd did enter the room of Mr. Norton, and was followed by him, on the 3d of March last? Can he be mistaken in the man? Who ever looks at the prisoner carefully once will be sure to recognize him again.

For the present I pass from the consideration of the testimony showing Dr. Mudd's connection with Booth in this conspiracy, with the remark that it is in evidence, and I think established, both by the testimony adduced by the prosecution and that by the prisoner, that since the commencement of this Rebellion John H. Surratt visited the prisoner's house; that he concealed Surratt and other Rebels and traitors in the woods near his house, where for several days he furnished them with food and bedding; that the shelter of the woods by night and by day was the only shelter that the prisoner dare furnish *those friends* of his; that in November Booth visited him and remained over night; that he accompanied Booth at that time to Gardner's, from whom he purchased one of the horses used on the night of the assassination to aid the escape of one of his confederates; that the prisoner had secret interviews with Booth and Surratt, as sworn to by the witness, Weichman, in the National Hotel, whether on the 2d of December or in January, is a matter of entire indifference; that he rushed into Mr. Norton's room on the 3d of March in search of Booth, and that he was here again on the 10th of April, four days before the murder of the President.

Of his conduct after the assassination of the President, which is confirmatory of all this; his conspiring with Booth, and his sheltering, concealing, and aiding the flight of his co-conspirator, this felon assassin, I shall speak hereafter, leaving him for the present with the remark that the attempt to prove his character has resulted in showing him in sympathy with the Rebellion, so cruel that he shot one of his slaves, and declared his purpose to send several of them to work on the Rebel batteries in Richmond.

What others, besides Samuel A. Mudd and John H. Surratt and Lewis Payne, did Booth, after his return from Canada, induce to join him in this conspiracy to murder the President, the Vice President, the Secretary of State and the Lieutenant-General, with the intent thereby to aid the Rebellion and overthrow the Government and laws of the United States?

On the 10th of February the prisoners Arnold and O'Laughlin came to Washington and took rooms in the house of Mrs. Vantyne; were armed; were there visited frequently by John Wilkes Booth, and alone; were occasionally absent when Booth called, who seemed anxious for their return; would sometimes leave notes for them, and, sometimes a request that when they came in they should be told to come to the stable.

On the 18th of March last, when Booth played in *The Apostate*, the witness, Mrs. Vantyne, received from O'Laughlin complimentary tickets. These persons remained there until the 20th of March. They were visited, so far as the witness knows, during their stay at her house only by Booth, save that on a single occasion an unknown man came to see them, and remained with them over night. They told the witness they were in the "oil business." With Mudd, the guilty purpose was sought to be concealed by declaring that he was in the "land business;" with O'Laughlin and Arnold it was attempted to be concealed by pretense that they were in the "oil business." Booth, it is proved, had closed up all connection with the oil business last September. There is not a word of testimony to show that the accused, O'Laughlin and Arnold, ever invested or sought to invest, in any way or to any amount, in the oil business; their silly words betray them; they forgot when they uttered that false statement that the truth is strong, next to the Almighty, and that their crime must find them out was true, the irrevocable and irresistible law of nature and of nature's God.

One of their co-conspirators, known as yet only to the guilty parties to this damnable plot and to the Infinite, who will unmask and avenge all blood-guiltiness, comes to bear witness, unwittingly, against them. This unknown conspirator, who dates his letter at South Branch Bridge, April 6, 1865, mailed and postmarked Cumberland, Maryland, and addressed to John Wilkes Booth, by his initials, "J. W. B., National Hotel, Washington, D. C." was also in the "oil speculation." In that letter he says:—

"Friend Wilkes: I received yours of March 12, and reply as soon as practicable. I saw French, Brady, and others about the oil speculation. The subscription to the stock amounts to eight thousand dollars, and I add one thousand myself, which is about all I can stand. Now, when you sink your well go *deep enough; don't fail;* everything depends upon you and your *helpers*. If you cannot get t.rough on *your (l)ip*, after you strike oil, strike through Thornton Gap and across by Capon, Romney, and down the Branch. I can keep you *safe* from all hardships for a year. I am clear of all surveillance now that infernal Purdy is beat.

* * * * * * *

"I send this by Tom, and, if he don't get drunk, you will get it the 9th. At all events, it cannot be *understood* if lost. * * * * *

"No more, only *Jake* will be at Green's *with the funds*. LON."

That this letter is not a fabrication is made apparent by the testimony of Purdy, whose name occurs in the letter. He testified that he had been a detective in the Government service, and that he had been falsely accused, as the letter recites, and put under arrest; that there was a noted Rebel by the name of Green, living at Thornton Gap; that there was a servant, who drank, known as "Tom," in the neighborhood of South Branch Bridge; that there is an obscure route through the Gap, and as described in the letter; and that a man commonly called "Lon" lives at South Branch Bridge. If the Court were satisfied, and it is for them to judge, that this letter was written before the assassination, as it purports to have been, and on the day of its date, there can be no question with any one who reads it that the writer was in the conspiracy, and knew that the time of its execution drew nigh. If a conspirator every word of its contents is evidence against every other party to this conspiracy.

Who can fail to understand this letter? His words "go deep enough," "don't fail," "everything depends on you and your helpers," "if you can't get through on your *trip* after you *strike oil*, strike through Thornton Gap," &c., and "I can keep you safe from all hardships for a year," necessarily imply that when he "*strikes oil*" there will be an occasion for *a flight;* that *a trip,* or route, has already been determined upon; that he may not be able to go through by that route; in which event he is to strike for Thornton Gap, and across by Capon and Romney, and down the Branch, for the shelter which his co-conspirator offers him. "I am clear of all surveillance now." Does any one doubt that the man who wrote those words wished to assure Booth that he was no longer watched, and that Booth could safely hide with him from his pursuers? Does any one doubt, from the further expression in this letter, "Jake will be at Green's with the funds," that this was a part of the price of blood, or that the eight thousand dollars subscribed by others, and the one thousand additional, subscribed by the writer, were also a part of the price to be paid?

"The oil business" which was the declared business of O'Laughlin and Arnold, was the declared business of the infamous writer of this letter. Was the declared business of John H. Surratt; was the declared business of Booth himself, as explained to Chester and Hess and Payne: was "*the business*" referred to in his telegrams to O'Laughlin, and meant the murder of the President, of his Cabinet, and of General Grant. The first of these telegrams is dated Washington, 13th March, and is addressed to M. O'Laughlin, No. 57 North Exeter street, Baltimore, Maryland, and is as follows: "Don't you fear to neglect your business; you had better come in at once. J. Booth." The telegraph operator, Hoffman, who sent this despatch from Washington, swears that John Wilkes Booth delivered it to him in person on the day of its date; and the handwriting of the original telegram is established beyond question to be that of Booth. The other telegram is dated Washington, March 27, addressed "M. O'Laughlin, Esq., 57 North Exeter street, Baltimore, Maryland," and is as follows:—"Get word to Sam. Come on with or without him on Wednesday morning. We sell that day sure: don't fail. J. Wilkes Booth."

The original of this telegram is also proved to be in the handwriting of Booth. The sale referred to in this last telegram was doubtless the murder of the President and others, the "oil speculation," in which the writer of the letter from South Branch Bridge, dated April 6, had taken a thousand dollars, and in which Booth said there was money, and Sanders said there was money, and Atzeroth said there was money. The words of this telegram, "get word to Sam," meaning Samuel Arnold, his co-conspirator, who had been with him during all his stay at Washington, at Mrs. Vantyne's. These parties to this conspiracy, after they had gone to Baltimore, had additional correspondence with Booth, which the Court must infer had relation to carrying out the purposes of their confederation and agreement. The colored witness, Williams, testifies that John Wilkes Booth handed him a letter for Michael O'Laughlin, and another for Samuel Arnold, in Baltimore, some time in March last; one of which he delivered to O'Laughlin at the theatre in Baltimore, and the other to a lady at the door where Arnold boarded in Baltimore.

Their agreement and co-operation in the common object having been thus established, the letter written to Booth by the prisoner Arnold, dated March 27, 1865, the handwriting of which is proved before the Court, and which was found in Booth's possession after the assassination, becomes testimony against O'Laughlin, as well as against the writer, Arnold, because it is an act done in furtherance of their combination. That letter is as follows:—

"Dear John:—Was business so important that you could not remain in Baltimore till I saw you? I came in as soon as I could, but found you had gone to Washington. I called also to see *Mike*, but learned from his mother that he had gone out with you and had not returned. I concluded, therefore, he had gone with you. How inconsiderate you have been! When I left you, you stated that *we would not meet* in a month or so, and therefore I made application for employment, an answer to which I shall receive during the week. I told my parents I had ceased with you. Can I, then, under existing circumstances, act as you request? You know full well that the Government suspicions something is going on there, therefore the *undertaking* is becoming more complicated. Why not, *for the present,* desist? For various reasons, which, if you look into, you can readily see without my making any mention thereof, you, nor any one, can censure me for my present course. You have been its cause, for how can I now come after telling them I had left you? Suspicion rests upon me now from my whole family and even parties in the country.

"I will be compelled to leave home any how, and how soon I care not. None, no not one, were more in favor of the enterprise than myself, and to-day would be there, had you not done as you have. By this, I mean manner of proceeding. I am, as you well know, in need. I am, you may say, in rags, whereas, to-day, I ought to be *well clothed.* I do not feel right stalking about with *means,* and more from appearances a beggar. I feel my dependence. But, even all this would have been, and was, forgotten, for *I was one with you.* Time more *propitious* will arrive yet. Do not act rashly or in haste. I would prefer your, first, query, "Go and see how it will be taken in Richmond," and, *ere long,* I shall

he better prepared *to again be with you.* I dislike writing. Would sooner verbally make known my views. Yet your now waiting causes me thus to proceed. Do not in anger peruse this. Weigh all I have said, and, as a rational man and a *friend,* you cannot censure or upbraid my conduct. I sincerely trust this, nor aught else that shall or may occur, will ever be an obstacle to obliterate our former friendship and attachment. Write me to Baltimore, as I expect to be in about Wednesday or Thursday; or, if you can possibly come on, I will Tuesday meet you at Baltimore at B.

"Ever, I subscribe myself, your friend,
"SAM."

Here is the confession of the prisoner Arnold, that he was one with Booth in this conspiracy; the further confession that they are suspected by the Government of their country, and the acknowledgment that, *since they parted,* Booth had communicated, amongst other things, a suggestion which leads to the remark in this letter, "I would prefer your first query, 'Go see how it will be taken at Richmond,' and *ere long* I shall be better prepared *to again be with you.*" This is a declaration that affects Arnold, Booth and O'Laughlin alike. If the court are satisfied, and it is difficult to see how they can have doubt on the subject, that the matter to be referred to Richmond is the matter of the assassination of the President and others, to effect which these parties had previously agreed and conspired together. It is a matter in testimony, by the declaration of John H. Surratt, who is as clearly proved to have been in this conspiracy and murder as Booth himself, that about the very date of this letter, the 27th of March, upon the suggestion of Booth, and with his knowledge and consent, he went to Richmond, not only to see "how it would be taken there," but to get funds with which to carry out the enterprise, as Booth had already declared to Chester in one of his last interviews, when he said that he or 'some one of the party" would be constrained to go to Richmond for funds to carry on the conspiracy. Surratt returned from Richmond, bringing with him some part of the money for which he went, and was then going to Canada, and, as the testimony discloses, bringing with him the despatches from Jefferson Davis to his chief agents in Canada, which, as Thompson declared to Conover, made the proposed assassination "all right," Surratt, after seeing the parties here, left immediately for Canada, and delivered his despatches to Jacob Thompson, the agent of Jefferson Davis. This was done by Surratt upon the suggestion, or in exact accordance with the suggestion, of Arnold, made on the 27th of March, in his letter to Booth, just read, and yet you are gravely told that four weeks before the 27th of March Arnold had abandoned the conspiracy.

Surratt reached Canada with these despatches, as we have seen, about the 6th or 7th of April last, when the witness, Conover, saw them delivered to Jacob Thompson, and heard their contents stated by Thompson, and the declaration from him that these despatches made it "all right." That Surratt was at that time in Canada, is not only established by the testimony of Conover, but it is also in evidence that he told Weichman, on the 3d of April, that he was going to Canada, and on that day left for Canada, and afterwards, two letters addressed by Surratt, over the fictitious signature of John Harrison, to his mother and to Miss Ward, dated at Montreal, were received by them on the 14th of April, as testified by Weichman and by Miss Ward, a witness called for the defense. Thus it appears that the condition named by Arnold in his letter had been complied with. Booth had "gone to Richmond" in the person of Surratt, "to see how it would be taken." The Rebel authorities at Richmond had approved it, the agent had returned; and Arnold was, in his own words, thereby the better prepared to rejoin Booth in the prosecution of this conspiracy.

To this end Arnold went to Fortress Monroe. As his letter expressly declares, Booth said when they parted, "we would not meet in a month or so, and *therefore* I made application for employment—an answer to which I shall receive during the week." He did receive the answer that week from Fortre s Monroe, and went there to await the "more propitious time," hearing with him the weapon of death which Booth had provided, and ready to obey his call, as the act had been approved at Richmond, and been made "all right." Acting upon the same fact that the conspiracy had been approved in Richmond, and the *funds* provided, O'Laughlin came to Washington to identify General Grant, the person who was to become the victim of his violence in the final consummation of this crime—General Grant whom, as is averred in the specification, it had become the part of O'Laughlin, by his agreement in his conspiracy, to kill and murder.

On the evening preceding the assassination, the 13th of April, by the testimony of three reputable witnesses, against whose truthfulness not one word is uttered here or elsewhere, O'Laughlin went into the house of the Secretary of War, where General Grant then was, and placed himself in position in the hall where he could see him, having declared before he reached that point to one of these witnesses that he wished to see General Grant. The house was brilliantly illuminated at the time; two, at least, of the witnesses conversed with the accused, and the other stood very near to him, took special notice of his conduct, called attention to it, and suggested that he be put out of the house, and he was accordingly put out by one of the witnesses. These witnesses are confident and have no doubt, and so swear upon their oaths, that Michael O'Laughlin is the man who was present on that occasion.

There is no denial on the part of the accused that he was in Washington during the day and during the night of April 13, and also during the day and during the night of the 14th; and yet, to get rid of this testimony, recourse is had to that common device—an *alibi*: a device never, I may say, more frequently resorted to than in this trial. But what an *alibi*! Nobody is called to prove it, save some men who, by their own testimony, were engaged in a drunken debauch through the evening. A reasonable man who reads their evidence can hardly be expected to allow it to outweigh the united testimony of three unimpeached and unimpeachable witnesses, who were clear in their statements, whose opportunities to know were full and complete, and who were constrained to take special notice of the prisoner by reason of his extraordinary conduct.

These witnesses describe accurately the appearance, stature and complexion of the accused, but, because they describe his clothing as dark or black, it is urged that as part of his clothing although dark, was not black, the witnesses are mistaken. O'Laughlin and his drunken companions (one of whom swears that he drank ten times that evening) were strolling in the streets and in the direction of the house of the Secretary of War up the avenue; but you are asked to believe that these witnesses could not be mistaken in saying they were not off the Avenue, above Seventh street, or on K street. I venture to say that no man who reads their testimony can determine satisfactorily all the places that were visited by O'Laughlin and his drunken associates that evening from seven to eleven P.M. All this time, from seven to eleven P. M., must be accounted for satisfactorily before an *alibi* can be established. Laughlin does not account for all the time, for he left O'Laughlin after seven o'clock, and rejoined him, as he says, "I suppose about eight o'clock." Grillet did not meet him until half-past ten, and then only casually saw him in passing the hotel. May not Grillet have been mistaken as to the fact, although he did meet O'Laughlin after eleven o'clock, the same evening, as he swears? Purdy swears to seeing him in the bar with Grillet about half-past 10, but, as we have seen by Grillet's testimony it must have been after 11 o'clock. Morphy contradicts, *as to time*, both Grillet and Purdy, for he says it was half-past 11 or 12 o'clock when he and O'Laughlin returned to Hullman's from Platz's; and Early swears the accused went from Hullman's to Second street to a dance about a quarter past 11 o'clock, when O'Laughlin took the lead in the dance, and stayed about one hour. I follow these witnesses no further. They contradict each other, and do not account for O'Laughlin all the time from 7 to 11 o'clock. I repeat that no man can read their testimony without finding contradictions most material *as to time*, and coming to the conviction that they utterly fail to account for O'Laughlin's whereabouts on that evening. To establish an *alibi* the witnesses *must know the fact* and *testify* to it. O'Laughlin, Grillet, Purdy, Murphy and Early utterly fail to prove it, and only succeed in showing that t..cy did not know where O'Laughlin was all this time, and that some of them were grossly mistaken in what they testified, both as to *time and place*.

The testimony of James B. Henderson is equally unsatisfactory. He is contradicted by other testimony of the accused as *to place*. He says O'Laughlin went up the avenue above Seventh street, but that he did not go to Ninth street. The other witnesses swear he went to Ninth street. He swears he went to the Canterbury at about o'clock, after going back from Seventh street to Hullman's. Laughlin swears that O'Laughlin was with him at the corner of the avenue and Ninth street at 9 o'clock, and went from there to Canterbury, while Early swears that O'Laughlin went up as far as Eleventh street, and returned and took supper with him at Welcker's about 8 o'clock. If these witnesses prove an *alibi*, it is really against each other. It is folly to pretend that they prove facts which make it impossible that O'Laughlin could have been at the house of Secretary Stanton, as three witnesses swear he was, on the evening of the 13th of April, looking for General Grant.

It is not, by the testimony, thus reviewed, been established *prima facie* that O'Laughlin had combined, confederated and agreed with John Wilkes Booth and Samuel Arnold to kill and murder Abraham Lincoln, William H. Seward, Andrew Johnson and Ulysses S. Grant? Is it not established, beyond a shadow of doubt, that Booth had so conspired with the Rebel agents in Canada as early as October last; that he was in search of agents to do the work *on pay*, in the interests of the Rebellion, and that in this speculation Arnold and O'Laughlin had joined us as early as February; and then,

and after, with Booth and Surratt, they were in the "oil business," which was the business of assassination by contract as a speculation? If this conspiracy on the part of O'Laughlin with Arnold is established even *prima facie*, the declarations and acts of Arnold and Booth, the other conspirators, in furtherance of the common design, is evidence against O'Laughlin as well as against Arnold himself or the other parties. The rule of law is that the act or declaration of one conspirator, done in pursuance or furtherance of the common design, is the act or declaration of all the conspirators. (1 Wharton, 706).

The letter, therefore, of his co-conspirator, Arnold, is evidence against O'Laughlin, because it is an act in the prosecution of the common conspiracy, suggesting what should be done in order to make it effective, and which suggestion, as has been stated, was followed out. The defense has attempted to avoid the force of this letter by reciting the statement of Arnold, made to Horner at the time he was arrested, in which he declared, among other things, that the purpose was to abduct President Lincoln and take him South; that it was to be done at the theatre by throwing the President out of the box upon the floor of the stage, when the accused was to catch him. The very announcement of this testimony excited derision that such a tragedy meant only to take the President and carry him gently away! This pigmy to catch the giant as the assassins hurled him to the floor from an elevation of twelve feet!

The Court has viewed the theatre, and must be satisfied that Booth, in leaping from the President's box, broke his limb. The Court cannot fail to conclude that this statement of Arnold was but another silly device, like that of "the oil business" which, for the time being, he employed to hide from the knowledge of his captor the fact that the purpose was to murder the President. No man can, for a moment, believe that any one of these conspirators hoped or desired, by such a proceeding as that stated by this prisoner, to take the President alive, in the presence of thousands assembled in the theatre, after he had been thus thrown upon the floor of the stage, much less to carry him through the city, through the lines of your army, and deliver him into the hands of the Rebels. No such purpose was expressed or hinted at by the conspirators in Canada, who commissioned Booth to let these assassinations on contract. I shall waste not a moment more in combatting such an absurdity.

Arnold does confess that he was a conspirator with Booth in this purposed murder; that Booth had a letter of introduction to Dr. Mudd; that Booth, O'Laughlin, Atzerodt, Surratt, a man with an alias, "Mosby," and another whom he does not know, and himself were parties to this conspiracy, and that Booth had furnished them all with arms. He concludes this remarkable statement to Horner with the declaration that at that time, to wit: the first week of March, or four weeks before he went to Fortress Monroe, he left the conspiracy, and that Booth told him to sell his arms if he chose. This is sufficiently answered by the fact that four weeks *afterwards*, he wrote his letter to Booth, which was found in Booth's possession after the assassination, suggesting to him what to do in order to make the conspiracy a success, and by the further fact that at the very moment he uttered these declarations, part of his arms were found upon his person, and the rest not disposed of, but at his father's house.

A party to a treasonable and murderous conspiracy against the Government of his country cannot be held to have abandoned it because he makes such a declaration as that, when he is in the hands of the officer of the law; arrested for his crime, and especially when his declaration is in conflict with and expressly contradicted by his written acts, and unsupported by any conduct of his which becomes a citizen and a man.

If he abandoned the conspiracy, why did he not make known the fact to Abraham Lincoln and his constitutional advisers that these men, armed with the weapons of assassination, were daily lying in wait for their lives? To pretend that a man who thus conducts himself for weeks after the pretended abandonment, volunteering advice for the successful prosecution of the conspiracy, the evidence of which is in writing, and about which there can be no mistake, has, in fact, abandoned it, is to insult the common understanding of men. O'Laughlin having conspired with Arnold to do this murder, is, there ore, as much concluded by the letter of Arnold of the 27th of March as is Arnold himself.

The further testimony touching O'Laughlin, that of Strett, establishes the fact that about the 1st of April he saw him in confidential conversation with J. Wilkes Booth, in this city, on the Avenue. Another man, whom the witness does not know, was in conversation. O'Laughlin called Streett to one side, and told him Booth was on ly engaged with his friend, was *talking privately* to his friend. This remark of O'Laughlin's attempt to be accounted for, but the attempt failed; his counsel taking the pains to ask what induced O'Laughlin to make the remark, received the lit reply—"I did not see the interior of Mr. O'Laughlin's mind; I cannot tell." It is the province of this Court to infer why that remark was made, and what it signified.

That John H. Surratt, George A. Atzerodt, Mary E.

TRIAL OF THE ASSASSINS AT WASHINGTON.

Remains of President Lincoln, as they lay in state, in "Old Independence Hall," Philadelphia, on Sunday, April 23d, 1865.

Surratt, David E. Harold, and Lewis Payne, entered into this conspiracy with Booth, is so very clear upon this testimony, that little time need be occupied in bringing again before the Court the evidence which establishes it. By the testimony of Weichman we find Atzeroth in February at the house of the prisoner, Mrs. Surratt. He inquired for her or for John when he came, and remained over night. After this, and before the assassination, he visited there frequently, and at that house bore the name of "Port Tobacco," the name by which he was known in Canada among the conspirators there. The same witness testifies that he met him on the street, when he said he was going to visit Payne at the Herndon House, and also accompanied him, along with Harold and John H. Surratt to the theatre in March, to see Booth play in the *Apostate*.

At the Pennsylvania House, one or two weeks previous to the assassination, Atzeroth made the statement to Lieutenant Keim, when asking for his knife which he had left in his room, a knife corresponding in size with the one exhibited in Court, "I want that; if one fails I want the other," wearing at the same time his revolver at his belt. He also stated to Greenawalt, of the Pennsylvania House, in March, that he was nearly broke, but had friends enough to give him as much money as *would see him through*, adding, "I am going away some of these days, but will return with as much gold as will keep me all my lifetime." Mr. Greenawalt also says that Booth had frequent interviews with Atzeroth, sometimes in the room, and at other times Booth would walk in and immediately go out, Atzeroth following.

John M. Floyd testifies that some six weeks before the assassination, Harold, Atzeroth and John H. Surratt came to his house at Surrattsville, bringing with them two Spencer carbines, with ammunition, also a rope and wrench. Surratt asked the witness to take care of them and to conceal the carbines. Surratt took him into a room in the house, it being his mother's house, and showed the witness where to put the carbines, between the joists on the second floor. The carbines were put there according to his directions and concealed. Marcus P. Norton saw Atzeroth in conversation with Booth at the National Hotel about the 2d or 3d of March; the conversation was confidential, and the witness accidentally heard them talking in regard to President Johnson, and say that "the class of witnesses would be of that character that there could be little proven by them." This conversation may throw some light on the fact that Atzeroth was found in possession of Booth's bank book!

Colonel Nevens testifies that on the 12th of April last he saw Atzeroth at the Kirkwood House; that Atzeroth there asked him, a stranger, if he knew where Vice President Johnson was, and where Johnson's room was. Colonel Nevens showed him where the room of the Vice President was and told him that the Vice President was then at dinner. Atzeroth then looked into the dining-room, where Vice President Johnson was dining alone. Robert R. Jones, the clerk at the Kirkwood House, state; that on the 14th, the day of the murder, two days after this, Atzeroth registered his name at the hotel. G. A. Atzeroth, and took No. 126, retaining this room that day, and carrying away the key. In this room, after the assassination, were found the knife and revolver, with which he intended to murder the Vice President.

The testimony of all these witnesses leaves no doubt that the prisoner, George A. Atzeroth, entered into this conspiracy with Booth; that he expected to receive a large compensation for the services that he would render in its execution; that he had undertaken the assassination of the Vice President for a price; that he, with Surratt and Harold, rendered the important service of depositing the arms and ammunition to be used by Booth and his confederates as a protection to their flight after the conspiracy had been executed, and that he was careful to have his intended victim pointed out to him, and the room he occupied in the hotel, so that, when he came to perform his horrid work, he would know precisely where to go and whom to strike.

I take no further notice now of the preparation which this prisoner made for the successful execution of this part of the traitorous and murderous design. The question is, did he enter into this conspiracy? His language, overheard by Mr. Norton, excludes every other conclusion. Vice President Johnson's name was mentioned in that secret conversation with Booth, and the very suggestive expression was made between them that "little could be proved by the witnesses." His confession to his defense is conclusive of his guilt.

That Payne was in this conspiracy is confessed in the defense made by his counsel, and is also evident from the facts proved, that when the conspiracy was being organized in Canada, by Thompson, Sanders, Tucker, Cleary, and Clay, this man Payne stood at the door of Thompson; was recommended and endorsed by Clay with the words, "We trust him;" that after coming hither he first reported himself at the house of Mrs. Mary E. Surratt, inquired for her and for John H. Surratt, remained there for four days, having conversation with both of them; having provided himself with means of disguise, was also supplied with pistols and a knife, such as he afterwards used, and spurs, preparatory to his flight; was seen with John H. Surratt, practicing with knives such as those employed in this deed of assassination, and now before the Court; was afterwards provided with lodging at the Herndon House, at the instance of Surratt; was visited there by Atzeroth, attended Booth and Surratt to Ford's Theatre, occupying with those parties the box, as I believe and which we may readily infer, in which the President was afterwards murdered.

If further testimony be wanting that he had entered into the conspiracy, it may be found in the fact sworn to by Weichman, whose testimony no candid man will discredit, that about the 20th of March Mrs. Surratt, in great excitement, and weeping, said that person John had gone away not to return, when about three hours subsequently, in the afternoon of the same day, John H. Surratt reappeared, came rushing in a state of frenzy into the room, in his mother's house, armed, declaring he would shoot whoever came into the room, and proclaiming that his prospects were blasted and his hopes gone; that soon Payne came into the same room, also armed and under great excitement, and was immediately followed by Booth, with his riding whip in his hand, who walked rapidly across the floor from side to side, so much excited that for some time he did not notice the presence of the witness. Observing Weichman, the parties then withdrew, upon a suggestion from Booth, to an upper room, and there had a private interview. From all that transpired on that occasion it is apparent that when these parties left the house that day it was with the full purpose of completing some act essential to the final execution of the work of assassination, in conformity with their previous confederation and agreement. They returned foiled, from what cause is unknown, dejected, angry and covered with confusion.

It is almost imposing upon the patience of the Court to consume time in demonstrating the fact, which none conversant with the testimony of this case can for a moment doubt, that John H. Surratt and Mary E. Surratt were as surely in the conspiracy to murder the President as John Wilkes Booth himself. You have the frequent interviews between John H. Surratt and Booth; his intimate relations with Payne; his visits from Atzeroth and Harold; his deposit of the arms to cover their flight after the conspiracy should have been executed; his own declared visit to Richmond to do what Booth himself said to Chester must be done to wit:—That he or some of the party must go to Richmond in order to get funds to carry out the conspiracy; that he brought back with him gold, the price of blood, confessing himself that he was there; that he immediately went to Canada, delivered despatches in cipher to Jacob Thompson from Jefferson Davis, which were interpreted and read by Thompson in the presence of the witness Conover, and in which the conspiracy was approved, and in the language of Thompson the proposed assassination was "made all right."

One other fact, if any other fact be needed, and I have done with the evidence which proves that John H. Surratt entered into this combination; that is, that it appears by the testimony of the witness, the cashier of the Ontario Bank, Montreal, that Jacob Thompson, about the day that these despatches were delivered, and while Surratt was then present in Canada, drew from that Bank of the liked funds there on deposit, the sum of one hundred and eighty thousand dollars. This being done, Surratt finding it safer, doubtless, to go to Canada for the great bulk of funds, which were to be distributed amongst these hired assassins than to attempt to carry it through our lines direct from Richmond, immediately returned to Washington, and was present in this city, as is proven by the testimony of Mr. Reid, *on the afternoon of the 14th of April*, the day of the assassination, booted and spurred, ready for the flight whenever the fatal blow should have been struck.

If he was not a conspirator and a party to this great crime, how comes it that from that hour to this no man has seen him in the Capital, nor has he been reported anywhere outside of Canada, having arrived at Montreal, as the testimony shows, on the 18th of April, four days after the murder. Nothing but his conscious cowardly guilt could possibly induce him to absent himself from his mother, as he does, upon her trial. Being one of these conspirators, as charged, every act of his in the prosecution of this crime is evidence against the other parties to the conspiracy.

That Mary E. Surratt is as guilty as her son of having thus conspired, combined and confederated to do this murder, in aid of this Rebellion, is clear. First, her house was the head-quarters of Booth, John H. Surratt, Atzeroth, Payne and Harold. She is inquired for by Atzeroth: she is inquired for by Payne, and she is visited by Booth, and holds private conversations with him. His picture, together with that of the chief conspirator, Jefferson Davis, is found in her house. She sends to Booth for a carriage to take her, on the 11th of April, to Surrattsville, for the purpose of perfecting the arrangement deemed necessary to the successful execution of the conspiracy, and especially to facilitate and protect the conspirators in their escape from justice. On that occasion Booth, having disposed of his carriage, gives to the agent she employed ten dollars with which to hire a conveyance for that purpose.

And yet the pretence is made that Mrs. Surratt went on the 11th to Surrattsville exclusively upon her own private and lawful business. Can any one tell, it that be so, how it comes that she should apply to Booth for a conveyance, and how it comes that he, of his own accord, having no conveyance to furnish her, should send her ten dollars with which to procure it? There is not the slightest indication that Booth was under any obligation to her, or that she had any claim upon him, either for a conveyance or for the means with which to procure one, except that she was bound to contribute, being the agent of the conspirators in Canada and Richmond, whenever money might be necessary to the consummation of this infernal plot. On that day, the 11th of April, John H. Surratt had not returned from Canada with the funds furnished by Thompson.

Upon that journey of the 11th, the accused, Mary E. Surratt, met the witness, John M. Floyd, at Uniontown. She called him, be got out of his carriage and came to her, and she whispered to him in so low a tone that her attendant could not hear her words, though Floyd, to whom they were spoken, did distinctly near them, and testifies that she told him he should have those "shooting irons" ready, meaning the carbines which her son and Harold and Atzeroth had deposited with him, and added the reason, "for they would soon be called for." On the day of the assassination she again sent for Booth, had an interview with him in her own house, and immediately were again to Surrattsville, and then, at about 9 o'clock in the afternoon, she delivered to Floyd a field-glass, and told him to "have two bottles of whisky and the carbines ready, as they would be called for that night."

Having thus perfected the arrangement, she returned to Washington to her own house, at about half past eight o'clock in the evening to await the final result. How could this woman anticipate on Friday afternoon, at six o'clock, that these arms would be called for and would be needed that night, unless she was in the conspiracy and knew that the blow was to be struck, and the light of the assassins attempted, and by that route? Was not the private conversation which Booth held with her in her parlor on the afternoon of the 14th of April, just before she left on this business, in relation to the orders she should give to have the arms ready?

An endeavor is made to impeach Floyd. But the Court will observe that no witness has been called who contradicts Floyd's statement in any material manner, neither has his general character for truth been assailed. How then is he impeached? Is it claimed that his testimony shows that he was a party to the conspiracy? Then it is conceded by those who set up any such pretence that there was a conspiracy. A conspiracy between whom? There can be no conspiracy without the co-operation or agreement of two or more persons. Who were the other parties to it? Was it Mary E. Surratt? Was it John H. Surratt, George A. Atzeroth, David E. Harold? These are the only persons, so far as his own testimony or the testimony of any other witness discloses, with whom he had any communication whatever or any subject immediately or remotely touching this conspiracy before the assassination. His receipt and concealment of the arms are, unexplained, evidence that he was in the conspiracy.

The explanation is that he was dependent upon Mary E. Surratt; was her tenant; and his declaration given in evidence by the accused himself, is that "she had turned him, and brought this trouble upon him." But because he was weak enough, or wicked enough, to become the guilty depository of these arms, and to deliver them on the order of Mary E. Surratt to the assassins, it does not follow that he is not to be believed on oath. It is said that he concealed the facts that the arms had been left and called for. He so testifies himself, but he gives the reason that he did it only from apprehension of danger to his life. If he were in the conspiracy, his general credit being unchallenged, his testimony being uncontradicted in any material matter, he is to be believed, and cannot be disbelieved. If his testimony is substantially corroborated by other reliable witnesses. Is he not corroborated, touching the deposit of arms by the fact that the arms are produced in Court? one of which was found upon the person of Booth at the time he was overtaken and slain, and which is identified as the same which had been left with Floyd by Harold, Surratt and Atzeroth? Is he not corroborated in the fact of the first interview with Mrs. Surratt by the joint testimony of Mrs. Offut and Lewis J. Weichman, each of whom testified, and they are contradicted by no one, that on Tuesday, the 11th day of April, at Uniontown, Mrs. Surratt called Mr. Floyd to come to her, which he did, and she held a secret conversation with him? Is he not corroborated as to the last conversation on the 14th of April by the testimony of Mrs. Offut, who swears that upon the evening of the 14th of April she saw the prisoner, Mary E. Surratt, at Floyd's house, approach and hold conversation with him? Is he not corroborated in the fact to which he swears, that Mrs. Surratt delivered to him at that time the field-glass wrapped in paper, by the sworn statement of Weichman, that Mrs. Surratt took with her on that

occasion two packages, both of which were wrapped in paper, and one of which he describes as a small package, about six inches in diameter? The attempt was made by calling Mrs. Offut to prove that no such package was delivered but it failed; she merely states that Mrs. Surratt delivered a package wrapped in paper to her after her arrival there, and before Floyd came in, which was laid down in the room. But whether it was the package about which Floyd testifies, or the other package of the two about which Weichman testifies, as having been carried there that day by Mrs. Surratt, does not appear. Neither does this witness pretend to say that Mrs. Surratt, after she had delivered it to her, and the witness had laid it down in the room, did not again take it up, if it were the same, and put it in the hands of Floyd. She only knows that she did not see that done; but she did see Floyd with a package like the one she received in the room before Mrs. Surratt left. How it came into his possession she is not able to state; nor what the package was that Mrs. Surratt first handed her; nor which of the packages it was she afterwards saw in the hands of Floyd.

But there is one other fact in this case that puts forever at rest the question of the guilty participation of the prisoner, Mrs. Surratt, in this conspiracy and murder; and that is that Payne, who had lodged four days in her house; who during all that time had sat at her table, and who had often conversed with her; when the guilt of his great crime was upon him, and he knew not where so he could so safely go to find a co-conspirator, and he could trust none that was not like himself, guilty, with even the knowledge of his presence; under cover of darkness, after wandering for three days and nights, skulking before the pursuing officers of justice, at the hour of midnight, found his way to the door of Mrs. Surratt, rang the bell, was admitted, and upon being asked, "whom do you want to see?" replied, "Mrs. Surratt." He was then asked by the officer, Morgan, what he came at that time of night for? to which he replied, "to dig a gutter in the morning. Mrs. Surratt had sent for him." Afterwards he said "Mrs. Surratt knew he was a poor man, and came to him."

Being asked where he last worked, he replied, "sometimes on I street;" and where he boarded, he replied, "he had no boarding-house, and was a poor man who got his living with the pick," which he bore upon his shoulder, having stolen it from the intrenchments of the capital. Upon being pressed again why he came there at that time of night to go to work, he answered that he simply called to see what time he should go to work in the morning. Upon being told by the officer who fortunately had preceded him to this house that he would have to go to the Provost Marshal's office, he moved and did not answer, whereupon Mrs. Surratt was asked to step into the hall and state whether she knew this man. Raising her right hand she exclaimed, "Before God, sir, I have not seen that man before; I have not hired him; I do not know anything about him." The hall was brilliantly lighted.

If not one word had been said, the mere act of Payne in flying to her house for shelter would have borne witness against her strong as proofs from Holy Writ. But when she denies, after hearing his declarations that she had sent for him, or that she had gone to him and hired him, and calls her God to witness that she had never seen him, and knew nothing of him, when, in point of fact, she had seen him for four successive days in her own house, in the same clothing which he then wore, who can resist for a moment the conclusion that these parties were alike guilty?

The testimony of Spangler's complicity is conclusive and brief. It was impossible to hope for escape after assassinating the President, and such others as might attend him in Ford's Theatre, without arrangements being first made to aid the flight of the assassin, and to some extent prevent immediate pursuit.

A stable was to be provided close to Ford's Theatre, in which the horses could be concealed and kept ready for the assassin's use whenever the murderous blow was struck. Accordingly, Booth secretly, through Maddox, hired a stable in rear of the theatre and connecting with it by an alley, as early as the 1st of January last; showing that at that time he had concluded, notwithstanding all that has been said to the contrary, to murder the President in Ford's Theatre and provide the means for immediate and successful flight. Conscious of his guilt he paid the rent for this stable through Maddox, month by month, giving him the money. He employed Spangler, doubtless for the reason that he could trust him with the secret, as a carpenter to fit up this shed, so that it would furnish room for two horses and provided the door with lock and key. Spangler did this work for him. Then it was necessary that a carpenter, having access to the theatre, should be employed by the assassin to provide a bar for the outer door of the passage leading to the President's box, so that when he entered upon his work of assassination, he would be secure from interruption from the rear.

By the evidence, it is shown that Spangler was in the box in which the President was murdered on the afternoon of the 14th of April, and when there damned the President and General Grant, and said the President ought to be cursed, he had got so many good men killed; showing not only his hostility to the President, but the cause of it, that he had been faithful to his oath and had resisted that great Rebellion in the interest of which his life was about to be sacrificed by this man and his co-conspirators. In performing the work which had doubtless been intrusted to him by Booth, a mortice was cut in the wall. A wooden bar was prepared, one end of which could be readily inserted in the mortice and the other pressed against the edge of the door on the inside so as to prevent its being opened. Spangler had the skill and opportunity to do that work and all the additional work that was to be done.

It is in evidence that the screws in "the keepers" to the locks on each of the inner doors of the box occupied by the President were drawn. The attempt has been made, on behalf of the prisoner, to show that this was done some time before, accidentally, and with no bad design, and had not been repaired by reason of in-advertence; but that attempt has utterly failed, because the testimony adduced for that purpose relates exclusively to but one of the two inner doors, while the fact is, that the screws were drawn in both, and the additional precaution taken to cut a small hole through one of these doors through which the party approaching and while in the private passage would be enabled to look into the box and examine the exact posture of the President before entering. It was also deemed essential, in the execution of this plot, that some one should watch at the outer door, in the rear of the theatre, by which alone the assassin could hope for escape. It was for this work Booth sought to employ Chester in January, offering $500 down of the money of his employers, and the assurance that he should never want.

What Chester refused to do Spangler undertook and promised to do. When Booth brought his horse to the rear door of the theatre, on the evening of the murder, he called for Spangler, who went to him, when Booth was heard to say to him, "Ned, you'll help me all you can, won't you." To which Spangler replied, "Oh, yes."

When Booth made his escape, it is testified by Col. Stewart, who pursued him across the stage and out through the same door, that as he approached it some one slammed it shut. Ritterspaugh, who was standing behind the scenes when Booth fired the pistol and fled, saw Booth run down the passage toward the back door, and pursued him; but Booth drew his knife upon him and passed out, slamming the door after him. Ritterspaugh opened it and went through, leaving it open behind him, leaving Spangler inside, and in a position from which he readily could have reached the door. Ritterspaugh also states that very quickly after he had passed through this door he was followed by a large man, the first who followed him, and who was, doubtless, Colonel Stewart. Stewart is very positive that he saw this door slammed that he himself was constrained to open it, and had some difficulty in opening it.

He also testifies that as he approached the door a man stood near enough to have thrown it to with his hand, and this man, the witness believes, was the prisoner Spangler. Ritterspaugh has sworn that he left the door open behind him when he went out, and that he was followed by the large man, Colonel Stewart. Who slammed that door behind Ritterspaugh? It was not Ritterspaugh; it could not have been Booth, for Ritterspaugh swears that Booth was mounting his horse at the time, and Stewart swears that Booth was upon his horse when he came out. That it was Spangler who slammed the door after Ritterspaugh may not only be inferred from Stewart's testimony, but it is made very clear by his own conduct afterward upon the return of Ritterspaugh to the stage. The door being then open and Ritterspaugh being asked which way Booth went, had answered, Ritterspaugh says: "Then I came back on the stage, where I had left Edward Spangler; he hit me on the face with his hand, and said, 'Don't say which way he went.' I asked him what he meant by slapping me in the mouth? He said, 'For God's sake, shut up.'"

The testimony of Withers is adroitly handled to throw doubt upon these facts. It cannot avail, for Withers says he was knocked in to the scene by Booth, and when he "come to" he got a side view of him. A man knocked down and senseless, on "coming to" might mistake anybody by a side view, for Booth.

An attempt has been made by the defense to discredit this testimony of Ritterspaugh, by showing his contradictory statements to Gifford, Carlan and Lamb, neither of whom do in fact contradict him, but substantially sustain him. None but a guilty man would have met the witness with a blow for stating which way the assassin had gone. A like confession of guilt was made by Spangler when the witness, Miles, the same evening, and directly after the assassination, came to the back door, where Spangler was standing with others, and asked Spangler who it was that held the horse, to which Spangler replied:—"Hush; don't say anything about it." He confessed his guilt again when he denied to Mary Anderson the fact, proved here beyond all question, that Booth had called him when he came to that door with his horse, using the emphatic words, "No, he did not; he did not call me."

The rope comes to bear witness against him, as did the rope which Atzeroth and Harold and John H. Surratt had carried to Surrattsville and deposited there with the carbines.

It is only surprising that the ingenious counsel did not attempt to explain the deposit of the rope at Surrattsville by the same method that he adopted in explanation of the deposit of this rope, some sixty feet long, found in the carpet-sack of Spangler, unaccounted for save by some evidence which tends to show that he may have carried it away from the theatre.

It is not needful to take time in the recapitulation of the evidence, which shows conclusively that David E. Harold was one of these conspirators. His continued association with Booth, with Atzeroth, his visits to Mrs. Surratt's, his attendance at the theatre with Payne, Surratt and Atzeroth, his connection with Atzeroth on the evening of the murder, riding with him on the street in the direction of and near to the theatre at the hour appointed for the work of assassination, and his final flight and arrest, show that he, in common with all the other parties on trial, and all the parties named upon your record not upon trial, had combined and conspired to kill and murder in the interest of the Rebellion, as charged and specified against them.

That this conspiracy was entered into by all these parties, both present and absent, is thus proved by the acts, meetings, declarations and correspondence of all the parties, beyond any doubt whatever. True it is circumstantial evidence, but the Court will remember the rule before recited that circumstances cannot lie; that they are held sufficient in every court where justice is judiciously administered to establish the fact of a conspiracy.

I shall take no further notice of the remark made by the learned counsel who opened for the defense, and which has been informed by several of his associates, that, under the Constitution, it requires two witnesses to prove the overt act of high treason, than to say, this is not a charge of high treason, on but of a treasonable conspiracy, in aid of a rebellion, with intent to kill and murder the Executive officer of the United States, and commander of its armies, and of the murder of the President in pursuance of that conspiracy, and with the intent laid, &c. Neither by the Constitution, nor by the rules of the common law, is any fact connected with this allegation required to be established by the testimony of more than one witness. I might say, however, that every substantial averment against each of the parties named upon this record has been established by the testimony of more than one witness.

That the several accused did enter into this conspiracy with John Wilkes Booth and John H. Surratt to murder the officers of this Government, named upon the record in pursuance of the wishes of their employers and instigators in Richmond and Canada, and with intent thereby to aid the existing Rebellion, and subvert the Constitution and laws of the United States, as alleged, is no longer an open question.

The intent as said, was expressly declared by Sanders in the meeting of the conspirators at Montreal, in February last, by Booth in Virginia and New York, and by Thompson to Conover and Montgomery; but if there were no testimony directly upon this point, the law would presume the intent, for the reason that such was the natural and necessary tendency and manifest design of the act itself.

The learned gentleman (Mr. Johnson) says the Governor has survived the assassination of the President, and thereby would have you infer that this conspiracy was not entered into and attempted to be executed with the intent laid. With as much show of reason it might be said that because the Government of the United States has survived this unmatched Rebellion, it therefore results that the Rebel conspirators waged war upon the Government with no purpose or intent thereby to subvert it. By the law we have seen that without any direct evidence of previous combination and agreement between these parties, the conspiracy might be established by evidence of the acts of the prisoners, or of any others with whom they co-operated, concurring in the execution of the common design. (Roscoe, 416.)

Was there co-operation between the several accused in the execution of this conspiracy? That there was is as clearly established by the testimony as is the fact that Abraham Lincoln was killed and murdered by John Wilkes Booth. The evidence shows that all of the accused, save Mudd and Arnold, were in Washington on the 14th of April, the day of the assassination, together with John Wilkes Booth and John H. Surratt; that on that day Booth had a secret interview with the prisoner, Mary E. Surratt; that immediately thereafter she went to Surrattsville to perform her part of the preparation necessary to the successful execution of the conspiracy, and did make that preparation; that John H. Surratt had arrived here from Canada, notifying the parties that the price to be paid for this great crime had been provided for, at least in part, by the deposit receipts of April 6, for $180,000, procured by Thompson, of the Ontario Bank, Montreal, Canada; that he was also prepared to keep watch, or strike a blow, and ready for the contemplated flight; that Atzeroth on the afternoon of that day, was seeking to obtain a horse, the better to secure his own safety by flight after he should have performed the task which he had voluntarily undertaken, by contract, in the conspiracy—the murder of Andrew Johnson, then Vice President of the United States; that he did procure a horse for that purpose at Naylor's, and was seen, about nine o'clock in the evening, to ride to the Kirkwood House, where the Vice President then was, dismount and enter.

At a previous hour Booth was in the Kirkwood House, and left his card, now in evidence, doubtless intended to be sent to the room of the Vice President, and was in these words: "Don't wish to disturb you. Are you at home? J. Wilkes Booth." Atzeroth, when he made application at Brooks' in the afternoon for the horse, said to Weichman, who was there, he was going to ride to the country, and that "he was going to get a horse and send for Payne." He did get a horse for Payne, as well as for himself; for it is proven that on the 12th he was seen in Washington, riding the horse which had been procured by Booth, in company with Mudd, last November, from Gardner. A similar horse was tied before the door of Mr. Seward on the night of the murder, was captured after the flight of Payne, who was seen to ride away, and which horse is now identified as the Gardner horse. Booth also procured a horse on the same day, took it to his stable in the rear of the theatre, where he had an interview with Spangler, and where he concealed it. Harold, too, obtained a horse in the afternoon, and was seen between nine and ten o'clock, riding with Atzeroth down the Avenue from the Treasury, then up Fourteenth and down F street, passing close by Ford's Theatre.

O'Laughlin had come to Washington the day before, had sought out his victim (General Grant) at the house of the Secretary of War, that he might be able with certainty to identify him, and to the very hour when these preparations were going on, was lying in wait at Rullman's, on the Avenue, keeping watch and declaring, as he did at about ten o'clock P. M., when told that the fatal blow had been struck by Booth, "I don't believe Booth did it." During the day, and the night before, he had been visiting Booth, and doubtless encouraging him, and at that very hour was in position, at a convenient distance, to aid and protect him in his flight, as well as to execute his own part of the conspiracy by inflicting death upon General Grant, who happily was not at the theatre nor in the city, having left the city that day. Who doubts that Booth, having ascertained in the course of the day that General Grant could not be present at the theatre, O'Laughlin, who was to murder General Grant, instead of entering the box with Booth, was detailed to lie in wait, and watch and support him.

His declarations of his reasons for changing his lodgings here and in Baltimore, after the murder, so ably and so ingeniously presented in the argument of his learned counsel (Mr. Cox), avail nothing before the blasting fact, that he did change his lodgings, and declared "he knew nothing of the affair whatever." O'Laughlin, who lurked here, conspiring daily with Booth and Arnold for six weeks to do this murder, declares "he knew nothing of the affair." O'Laughlin, who says he was "in the oil business," which Booth and Surratt, and Payne and Arnold, have all declared meant this conspiracy, says "he knew nothing of the affair." O'Laughlin, to whom Booth sent the despatches of the 13th and 27th of March; O'Laughlin, who is named in Arnold's letter as one of the conspirators, and who searched for General Grant on Thursday night, laid in wait for him on Friday, was defeated by that Providence "which shapes our ends," and laid in wait to aid Booth and Payne, declares "he knew nothing of the matter." Such a denial is as false and inexcusable as Peter's denial of our Lord.

Mrs. Surratt had arrived at home from the completion of her part of the plot, about half-past eight o'clock in the evening. A few moments afterwards she was called to the parlor, and there had a private interview with some one unseen, but whose retreating footsteps were heard by the witness Weichman. This was doubtless the secret and last visit of John H. Surratt to his mother, who had instigated and encouraged him to strike this traitorous and murderous blow against his country.

While these preparations were going on, Dr. Mudd was awaiting the execution of the plot, ready faithfully to perform his part in securing the safe escape of the murderer. Arnold was at his post at Fortress Monroe, awaiting the meeting referred to in his letter of March 27th, wherein he says they were not to "meet for a month or so, which month had more than expired on the day of the murder, for his letter and the testimony disclose that this month of suspension began to run from about the first week in March.

He stood ready with the arms which Booth had furnished him to aid the escape of the murderers by that route, and secure their communication with their employers. He had given the assurance to that letter to Booth, that, although the Government "suspicioned them" and the undertaking was "becoming complicated," yet "a time more propitious would arrive" for the consummation of this conspiracy, in which he "was one" with Booth, and when he would "be better prepared to again be with him."

Such were the preparations. The horses were in readiness for the flight; the ropes were procured, doubtless for the purpose of tying the horses at whatever point they might be constrained to delay and secure their boats to their moorings in making their way across the Potomac. The five murderous camp-knives, the two carbines, the eight revolvers, the Derringer, in Court and identified, all were ready for the work of death. The part that each had played has already been in part stated in this argument, and needs no repetition.

Booth proceeded to the theatre about nine o'clock in the evening, at the same time that Atzeroth, and Payne and Harold were riding the streets, while Surratt, having parted with his mother at the brief interview in her parlor, from which his retreating steps were heard, was walking the Avenue, booted and spurred, and doubtless consulting with O'Laughlin. When Booth reached the rear of the theatre, he called Spangler to him (whose denial of that fact, when charged with it, as proven by three witnesses, is very significant), and received from Spangler his pledge to help him all he could, when with Booth he entered the theatre by the stage door, doubtless to see that the way was clear from the box to the rear door of the theatre, and look upon their victim, whose exact position they could study from the stage. After this view Booth passes to the front of the theatre, where on the pavement, with other conspirators yet unknown—among them one described as a low-browed villain—he awaits the appointed moment. Booth himself, impatient, enters the vestibule of the theatre from the front, and asks the time. He is referred to the clock, and returns. Presently, as the hour of ten o'clock approached, one of his guilty associates called the time; they wait; again, as the moments elapsed, this conspirator upon watch called the time; again, as the appointed hour draws nigh, he calls the time; and finally, when the fatal moment arrives, he repeats in a under tone, "Ten minutes past ten o'clock." Ten minutes past ten o'clock! The hour has come when the red right hand of these murderous conspirators should strike, and the dreadful deed of assassination be done.

Booth, at the appointed moment, entered the theatre, ascended to the dress circle, passed to the right, paused a moment, looking down, doubtless to see if Spangler was at his post, and approached the outer door of the close passage leadin to the box occupied by the President; pressed it open, passed in, and closed the passage door behind him. Spangler's bar was in its place, and was readily adjusted by Booth in the mortice, and pressed against the inner side of the door, so that he was secure from interruption from without. He passes on to the next door, immediately behind the President, and there stopping, looks through the aperture in the door into the President's box, and deliberately observes the precise position of his victim, seated in the chair which had been prepared by the conspirators as the altar for the sacrifice, looking calmly and quietly down upon the glad and grateful people, whom, by his fidelity, he had saved from the peril which had threatened the destruction of their Government, and all they held dear this side of the grave, and whom he had come upon invitation to greet with his presence, with the words still lingering upon his lips which he had uttered with uncovered head and uplifted hand before God and his country, when on the 4th of last March he took again the oath to preserve, protect, and defend the Constitution, declaring that he entered upon the duties of his great office "with malice toward none, with charity for all." In a moment more, strengthened by the knowledge that his co-conspirators were all at their posts, seven at least of them present in the city, two of them, Mudd and Arnold, at their appointed places, watching for his coming, this hired assassin moves stealthily through the door, the fastenings of which had been removed to facilitate his entrance, fires upon his victim, and the martyr spirit of Abraham Lincoln ascends to God.

Treason has done his worst; nor steel, nor poison,
Malice domestic, foreign levy, nothing
Can touch him further.

At the same hour, when these accused and their co-conspirators in Richmond and Canada, by the hand of John Wilkes Booth inflicted this mortal wound which deprived the Republic of its defender, and filled this land from ocean to ocean with a strange, great sorrow, Payne, a very demon in human form, with the words of falsehood upon his lips, that he was the bearer of a message from the physician of the venerable Secretary of State, sweeps by his servant, encounters his son, who protests that the assassin shall not disturb his father, prostrate on a bed of sickness, and receives for answer the assassin's blow from the revolver in his hand, repeated again and again, rushes into the room, is encountered by Major Seward, inflicts wound after wound upon him with his murderous knife, is encountered by Hansell and Robinson, each of whom he also wounds, springs upon the defenseless and feeble Secretary of State, stabs first on one side of his throat, then on the other, again in the face, and is only prevented from literally hacking out his life by the persistence and courage of the attendant Robinson. He turns to flee, and his giant arm and murderous hand for a moment paralyzed by the consciousness of guilt, he drops his weapons of death, one in the house, the other at the door, where they were taken up, and are here now to hear witness against him. He attempts escape on the horse which Booth and Mudd had procured of Gardner, with what success has already been stated.

Atzeroth, near midnight, returns to the stable of Naylor the horse which he had procured for this work of murder, having been interrupted in the execution of the part assigned him at the Kirkwood House by the timely coming of citizens to the defense of the Vice-President, and creeps into the Pennsylvania House at 2 o'clock in the morning with another of the conspirators, yet unknown. There he remained until 5 o'clock, when he left, found his way to Georgetown, pawned one of his revolvers, now in Court, and fled northward into Maryland.

He is traced to Montgomery county, to the house of Mr. Metz, on the Sunday succeeding the murder, where, as is proved by the testimony of three witnesses, he said that if the man that was to follow General Grant had followed him, it was likely that Grant was shot. To one of these witnesses (Mr. Leyman) he said he did not think Grant had been killed; or if he had been killed he was killed by a man who got on the cars at the same time that Grant did; thus disclosing most clearly that one of his co-conspirators was assigned the task of killing and murdering General Grant, and that Atzeroth knew that General Grant had left the city of Washington, a fact which is not disputed, on the Friday evening of the murder, by the evening train. Thus this intended victim of the conspiracy escaped, for that night, the knives and revolvers of Atzeroth, and O'Laughlin, and Payne, and Harold, and Booth, and John H. Surratt, and, perchance, Harper and Caldwell, and twenty others who were then here lying in wait for his life.

In the meantime, Booth and Harold, taking the route before agreed upon, make directly after the assassination for the Anacostia bridge. Booth crosses first, gives his name, passes the guard, and is speedily followed by Harold. They make their way directly to Surrattsville, where Harold calls to Lloyd, "Bring out those things," showing that there had been communication between them and Mrs. Surratt after her return. Both the carbines being in readiness, according to Mary E. Surratt's directions, both were brought out. They took but one; Booth declined to carry the other, saying that his limb was broken. They then declared that they had murdered the President and the Secretary of State. They then made their way directly to the house of the prisoner Mudd, assured of safety and security. They arrived early in the morning before day, and no man knows at what hour they left. Harold rode toward Bryantown with Mudd about three o'clock that afternoon, in the vicinity of which place he parted with him, remaining in the swamp, and was afterward seen returning the same afternoon in the direction of Mudd's house; about which time, a little before sundown, Mudd returned from Bryantown toward his home.

This village at the time Mudd was in it was thronged with soldiers in pursuit of the murderers of the President, and although great care has been taken by the defense to deny that any one said in the presence of Dr. Mudd, either there or elsewhere on that day, who had committed the crime, yet it is in evidence by two witnesses whose truthfulness no man questions, that upon Mudd's return to his own house, that afternoon, he stated that Booth was the murderer of the President, and Boyle the murderer of Secretary Seward, but took care to make the further remark, that Booth had brothers, and he did not know which of them had done the act. When did Dr. Mudd learn that Booth had brothers? And what is still more pertinent to this inquiry, from whom did he learn that either John Wilkes Booth or any of his brothers had murdered the President? It is clear that Booth remained in his house until some time in the afternoon of Saturday; that Harold left the house alone, as one of the witnessestates' being seen to pass the window; that he alone of these two assassins was in the company of Dr. Mudd on his way to Bryantown. It does not appear when Harold returned to Mudd's house. It is a confession of Dr. Mudd himself, proven by one of the witnesses, that Booth left his house on crutches, and went in the direction of the swamp.

How long he remained there, and what became of the horses which Booth and Harold rode to his house, and which were put into his stable, are facts nowhere disclosed by the evidence. The owners testify that they have never seen the horses since. The accused give no explanation of the matter, and when Harold and Booth were captured they had not these horses in their possession. How comes it that on Mudd's return from Bryantown, on the evening of Saturday, in his conversation with Mr. Hardy and Mr. Farrell, the witnesses before referred to, he gave the name of Booth as the murderer of the President and that of Boyle as the murderer of Secretary Seward and his son, and carefully avoided intimating to either that Booth had come to his house early that day and had remained there until the afternoon; that he left him in his house and had furnished him with a razor with which Booth attempted to disguise himself by shaving

off his moustache? How comes it, also, that, upon being asked by these two witnesses whether the Booth who killed the President was the one who had been there last fall, he answered that he did not know whether it was that man or one of his brothers, but he understood he had some brothers, and added, that if it was the Booth who was there last fall, *he knew that one*, but concealed the fact that this man had been at his house on that day and was then at his house, and had attempted, in his presence, to disguise his person?

He was sorry, very sorry, that the thing had occurred, but not so sorry as to be willing to give any evidence to these two neighbors, who were manifestly honest and upright men, that the murderer had been harbored in his house all day, and was probably at that moment, as his own subsequent confession shows, lying concealed in his house or near by, subject to his call. This is the man who undertakes to show by his own declaration, offered in evidence against my protest, of what he said afterward, on Sunday afternoon, the 16th, to his kinsman, Dr. George D. Mudd, to whom he then stated that the assassination of the President was a most damnable act, a conclusion in which most men will agree with him, and to establish which his testimony was not needed. But it is to be remarked that this accused did not intimate that the man whom he knew the evening before was the murderer had found refuge in his house, had disguised his person, and sought concealment in the swamp upon the crutches which he had provided for him.

Why did he conceal this fact from his kinsman? After the church services were over, however, in another conversation on that way home, he did tell Dr. George Mudd that two suspicious persons had been at his house, who had come there a little before daybreak on Saturday morning; that one of them had a broken leg, which he handaged; that they got something to eat at his house; that they seemed to be laboring under more excitement than probably would result from the injury; that they said they came from Bryantown, and inquired the way to Parson Wilmer's; that while at his house one of them called for a razor and shaved himself. The witness says: "I do not remember whether he said that this party shaved off his whiskers or moustache, but he altered somewhat or probably materially his features." Finally, the prisoner, Dr. Mudd, told this witness that he, in company with the younger of the two men, went down the road toward Bryantown in search of a vehicle to take the wounded man away from his house.

How comes it that he concealed in his conversation the fact proved that he went with Harold toward Bryantown, and left Harold outside of the town? How comes it that in this second conversation, on Sunday, insisted upon here with such pertinacity as evidence for the defense, but which had never been called for by the prosecution, he concealed from his kinsman the fact which he had disclosed the day before to Hardy and Farrell, that it was Booth who assassinated the President, and the fact which is now disclosed by his other confessions given in evidence for the prosecution, that it was Booth whom he had sheltered, concealed in his house, and aided to his hiding place in the swamp? He volunteers as evidence his further statement, however, to this witness, that on Sunday evening he requested the witness to state to the military authorities that two suspicious persons had been at his house, and see if anything could be made of it. He did not tell the witness what became of Harold and where he parted with him on the way to Bryantown. How comes it that when he was in Bryantown on the Saturday evening before, when he knew that Booth was then at his house, and that Booth was the murderer of the President, he did not himself state it to the military authorities then in that village, as he well knew? It is difficult to see what kindled his suspicions on Sunday, if none were in his mind on Saturday, when he was in possession of the fact that Booth had murdered the President, and was then secreting and disguising himself in the prisoner's own house.

His conversation with Gardner on the same Sunday at the church is also introduced here, to relieve him from the overwhelming evidences of his guilt. He communicates nothing to Gardner of the fact that Booth had been in his house; nothing of the fact that he knew the day before that Booth had murdered the President; nothing of the fact that Booth had disguised or attempted to disguise himself; nothing of the fact that he had gone with Booth's associate, Harold, in search of a vehicle, the more speedily to expedite their flight; nothing of the fact that Booth had found concealment in the woods and swamp near his house, upon the crutches which he had furnished him. He contents himself with merely stating "that we ought to raise immediately a home guard to hunt up all suspicious persons passing through our section of country, and arrest them, for there were two suspicious persons at my house yesterday morning."

It would have looked more like aiding justice and arresting felons if he had put in execution his project of a home guard on Saturday, and made it effective by the arrest of the man then in his house who had lodged with him last fall; with whom he had gone to purchase one of the very horses employed in his flight after the assassination; whom he had visited last winter in

TRIAL OF THE ASSASSINS AT WASHINGTON.

Washington, and to whom he had pointed out the very route by which he had escaped by way of his house; whom he had again visited on the 3d of last March, preparatory to the commission of this great crime; and who he knew, when he sheltered and concealed him in the wood on Saturday, was not merely a suspicious person, but was, in fact, the murderer and assassin of Abraham Lincoln. While I deem it my duty to say here, as I said before, when these declarations, uttered by the accused on Sunday, the 16th, to Gardner and George D. Mudd, were attempted to be offered on the part of the accused, that they are in no sense evidence, and by the law wholly inadmissible, yet I state it as my conviction, that, being upon the record upon motion of the accused himself, so far as these declarations to Gardner and George D. Mudd go, they are additional indications of the guilt of the accused, in this, that they are manifestly suppressions of truth and suggestions of falsehood and deception; they are but the utterances and confessions of guilt.

To Lieutenant Lovett, Joshua Lloyd and Simon Gavican, who, in the pursuit of the murderer, visited his house on the 18th of April, the Tuesday after the murder, he denied positively, upon inquiry, that two men had passed his house, or had come to his house on the morning after the assassination. Two of these witnesses swear positively to his having made the denial, and the other says he hesitated to answer the question he put to him; all of them agree that he afterwards admitted that two men had been there, one of whom had a broken limb, which he had set; and when asked by this witness who that man was, he said he did not know; that the man was a stranger to him, and that the two had been there but a short time. Lloyd asked him if he had ever seen any of the parties, Booth, Harold and Surratt; he said he had never seen them while it is positively proved that he was acquainted with John H. Surratt, who had been in his house; that he knew Booth, and had introduced Booth to Surratt last winter. Afterwards, on Friday, the 21st, he admitted to Lloyd that he had been introduced to Booth last fall, and that this man who came to his house on Saturday, the 15th, remained there from about four o'clock in the morning until about four in the afternoon; that one of them left his house on horseback and the other walking. In the first conversation he denied ever having seen these men.

Colonel Wells also testifies that, in his conversation with Dr. Mudd on Friday, the 21st, the prisoner said that he had gone to Bryantown, or near Bryantown, to see some friends on Saturday, and that as he came back to his own house he saw the person he afterwards supposed to be Harold passing to the left of his house towards the barn, but that he did not see the other person at all after he left him in his own house, about one o'clock. If this statement be true, how did Dr. Mudd see the same person leave his house on crutches? He further stated to this witness that he returned to his own house about 4 o'clock in the afternoon; that he did not know this wounded man said he could not recognize him from the photograph which is of record here, but admitted that he had left Booth some time in November, when he had some conversation with him about lands and horses; that Booth had remained with him that night in November, and on the next day had purchased a horse. He said he had not again seen Booth from the time of the introduction in November up to his arrival at his house on the Saturday morning after the assassination. Is not this a confession that he did see John Wilkes Booth on that morning at his house, and knew it was Booth? If he did not know him, how came he to make this statement to the witness that "he had not seen Booth after November prior to his arrival there on the Saturday morning?"

He had said before to the same witness he did not know the wounded man. He said further to Colonel Wells, that when he went up stairs after their arrival, he noticed that the person he supposed to be Booth, had shaved off his moustache. It is not inferable from this declaration that he then supposed him to be Booth? Yet he declared the same afternoon, and while Booth was in his own house, that Booth was the murderer of the President. One of the most remarkable statements made to this witness by the prisoner was that he heard for the first time on Sunday morning, or late in the evening of Saturday, that the President had been murdered. From whom did he hear it? The witness (Colonel Wells) inquired his "impression" that Dr. Mudd had said he had heard it after the person had left his house. If the "impression" of the witness thus volunteered is to be taken as evidence, and the counsel for the accused, judging from their manner, seem to think it ought to be, let this question be answered, how could Dr. Mudd have made that impression upon any body truthfully, when it is proved by Farrell and Hardy that on his return from Bryantown, on Saturday afternoon, he not only stated that the President, Mr. Seward and his son had been assassinated, but that Boyle had assassinated Mr. Seward. And Booth had assassinated the President? Add to this the fact that he said to this witness that he left his own house at one o'clock, and, when he returned, the men were gone; yet it is in evidence, by his own declarations, that Booth left his house at four o'clock

on crutches, and he must have been there to have seen it, or he could not have known the fact.

Mr. Williams testified that he was at Mudd's house on Tuesday, the 18th of April, when he said that strangers had not been that way, and also declared that he heard, for the first time, of the assassination of the President on Sunday morning, at church; afterwards, on Friday, the 21st, Mr. Williams asked him concerning the men who had been at his house, one of whom had a broken limb, and he confessed they had been there. Upon being asked if they were Booth and Harold, he said they were not; that he knew Booth. I think it is fair to conclude that he did know Booth, when we consider the testimony of Weichman, of Norton, of Evans, and all the testimony just referred to, wherein he declares, himself, that he not only knew him, but that he had lodged with him, and that he had himself gone with him when he purchased his horse from Gardner last fall, for the very purpose of aiding the flight of himself, or some of his confederates.

All these circumstances taken together, which, as we have seen upon high authority, are stronger as evidences of guilt than even direct testimony, leave no further room for argument, and no rational doubt that Doctor Samuel A. Mudd was as certainly in the conspiracy as were Booth and Harold, whom he sheltered and entertained; receiving them under cover of darkness on the morning after the assassination, concealing them throughout that day from the hand of offended justice, and aiding them by every endeavor, to pursue their way successfully to their co-conspirator, Arnold, at Fortress Monroe, and which direction he fled until overtaken and slain.

We next find Harold and his confederate, Booth, after their departure from the house of Mudd, across the Potomac, in the neighborhood of Port Conway, on Monday, the 24th of April, conveyed in a wagon. There Harold, in order to obtain the aid of Captain Jett, Ruggles and Bainbridge, of the Confederate army, said to Jett, "We are the assassinators of the President;" that this was his brother with him, who, with himself, belonged to A. P. Hill's Corps; that his brother had been wounded at Petersburg; that their names were Boyd. He requested Jett and his Rebel companions to take them out of the lines. After this, Booth joined these parties, was placed on Ruggles' horse, and crossed the Rappahannock River.

They then proceeded to the house of Garrett, in the neighborhood of Port Royal, and nearly midway between Washington City and Fortress Monroe, where they were to have joined Arnold. Before these Rebel guides and guards parted with them, Harold confessed that they were travelling under assumed names; that his own name was Harold, and that the name of the wounded man was John Wilkes Booth, "who had killed the President." The Rebels left Booth at Garrett's, where Harold revisited him from time to time, until they were captured. At two o'clock on Wednesday morning, the 26th, a party of United States officers and soldiers surrounded Garrett's barn, where Booth and Harold lay concealed, and demanded their surrender. Booth cursed Harold, calling him a coward, and bade him go, when Harold came out and surrendered himself, was taken into custody, and is now brought into Court. The barn was then set on fire, when Booth sprang to his feet, amid the flames that were kindling about him, carbine in hand, and approached the door, seeking, by the flashing light of the fire, to find some new victim for his murderous hand, when he was shot, as he deserved to be, by Sergeant Corbett, in order to save his comrades from wounds or death by the hands of this desperate assassin. Upon his person was found the following bill of exchange:

"No. 1492. The Ontario Bank, Montreal Branch Exchange for £61 12s. 10d. Montreal, 27th October, 1864. Sixty days after sight of this first of exchange, second and third of the same tenor and date, pay to the order of J. Wilkes Booth £61 12s. 10d. sterling, value received, and charge to the account of this office, H. Starnes, manager. To Messrs. Glynn, Mills & Co., London."

Thus fell, by the hands of one of the defenders of the Republic, this hired assassin, who, for a price, murdered Abraham Lincoln, bearing upon his person, as this bill of exchange testifies, additional evidence of the fact that he had undertaken, in aid of rebellion, this work of assassination by the hands of himself and his confederates, for such sum as the accredited agents of Jefferson Davis might pay him or them, out of the funds of the Confederacy, which, as is in evidence, they had in "any amount" in Canada for the purpose of rewarding conspirators, spies, poisoners and assassins, who might take service under their false commissions, and do the work of the incendiary and the murderer upon the lawful representatives of the American people, to whom had been entrusted the care of the Republic, the maintenance of the Constitution and the execution of the laws.

The Court will remember that it is in the testimony of Merritt, and Montgomery, and Conover, that Thompson and Sanders, and Cay, and Cleary, made their boast that they had money in Canada for this very purpose. Nor is it to be overlooked or forgotten that the officers of the Ontario Bank at Montreal testify that during the current year of this conspiracy and assassination Jacob Thompson had on deposit in that bank the sum of six hundred and forty-nine thousand dollars, and that these deposits to the credit of Jacob Thompson, accrued from the negotiation of bills of exchange drawn by the Secretary of the Treasury of the so-called Confederate States or Fraser, Trenholm & Co., of Liverpool, who were known to be the financial agents of the Confederate States. With an undrawn deposit in this bank of four hundred and fifty-five dollars, which has remained to his credit since October last, and with an unpaid bill of exchange drawn by the same bank upon London, in his possession and found upon his person, Booth ends his guilty career in this work of conspiracy and blood in April, 1865, as he began it in October, 1864, in combination with Jefferson Davis, Jacob Thompson, George N. Sanders, Clement C. Clay, William C. Cleary, Beverly Tucker and other co-conspirators, making use of the money of the Rebel Confederation to aid in the execution and in the flight, bearing at the moment of his death upon his person their money, part of the price which they paid for his great crime, to aid him in its consummation, and secure him afterwards from arrest and the just penalty which by the law of God and the law of man is denounced against treasonable conspiracy and murder.

By all the testimony in the case, it is, in my judgment, made as clear as any transaction can be shown by human testimony, that John Wilkes Booth and John H. Surratt, and the several accused, David E. Herold, George A. Atzerodt, Lewis Payne, Michael O'Loughlin, Edward Spangler, Samuel Arnold, Mary E. Surratt, and Samuel A. Mudd, did, with intent to aid the existing Rebellion and to subvert the Constitution and laws of the United States, in the month of October last and thereafter, combine, confederate and conspire with Jefferson Davis, George N. Sanders, Beverly Tucker, Jacob Thompson, William C. Cleary, Clement C. Clay, George Harper, George Young, and others unknown, to kill and murder, within the military department of Washington, and within the intrenched fortifications and military lines thereof, Abraham Lincoln, then President of the United States and Commander-in-Chief of the army and navy thereof; Andrew Johnson, Vice President of the United States; William H. Seward, Secretary of State; and Ulysses S. Grant, Lieutenant-General in command of the armies of the United States; and that Jefferson Davis, the chief of this Rebellion, was the instigator and procurer, through his accredited agents in Canada, of the treasonable conspiracy.

It is also submitted to the Court that it is clearly established by the testimony that John Wilkes Booth, in pursuance of this conspiracy, so entered into by him and the accused, did, on the night of the 14th of April, 1865, within the military department of Washington, and the intrenched fortifications and military lines thereof, and with the intent laid, inflict a mortal wound upon Abraham Lincoln, then President and Commander-in-Chief of the army and navy of the United States, whereof he died; that in pursuance of the same conspiracy and within the said department and intrenched lines, Lewis Payne, assaulted, with intent to kill and murder, William H. Seward, then Secretary of State of the United States; that George A. Atzerodt, in pursuance of the same conspiracy, and within the said department, laid in wait, with intent to kill and murder Andrew Johnson, then Vice-President of the United States; that Michael O'Laughlin, within said department, and in pursuance of said conspiracy, laid in wait to kill and murder Ulysses S. Grant, then in command of the armies of the United States; and that Mary E. Surratt, David E. Harold, Samuel Arnold, Samuel A. Mudd, and Edward Spangler did encourage, aid and abet the commission of said several acts in the prosecution of said conspiracy.

If this treasonable conspiracy has not been wholly executed; if the several executive officers of the United States and the commander of its armies, to kill and murder whom the said several accused thus confederated and conspired, have not each and all fallen by the hands of these conspirators, thereby leaving the people of the United States without a President or Vice President; without a Secretary of State, who alone is clothed with authority by the law to call an election to fill the vacancy, should any arise, in the offices of President and Vice President, and without a lawful commander of the armies of the Republic, it is only because the conspirators were deterred by the vigilance and fidelity of the executive officers, whose lives were mercifully protected on that night of murder by the care of the Infinite Being, who has thus far saved the Republic and crowned its arms with victory.

If this conspiracy was thus entered into by the accused; if John Wilkes Booth did kill and murder Abraham Lincoln in pursuance thereof; if Lewis Payne did, in pursuance of said conspiracy, assault with intent to kill and murder William H. Seward, as stated; and if the several parties accused did commit the several acts alleged against them in the prosecution of said conspiracy, then it is the law that all the parties to that conspiracy, whether present at the time of its execution or not, whether on trial before this Court or not, are alike guilty of the several acts done by each in the execution of the common design. What these conspirators did in the execution of this conspiracy by the hand of one of their co-conspirators, they did themselves; his act, done in the prosecution of the common design, was the act of all the parties to the treasonable combination, because done in execution and furtherance of their guilty and treasonable agreement.

As we have seen, this is the rule, whether all the conspirators are indicted or not; whether they are all on trial or not. "It is not material what the nature of the indictment is, provided the offense involve a conspiracy. Upon indictment for murder, for instance, if it appear that others, together with the prisoner, conspired to perpetrate the crime, the act of one done in pursuance of that intention, would be evidence against the rest." (1 Whar., 706.) To the same effect are the words of Chief Justice Marshall, before cited, that whoever leagued in a general conspiracy, performed any part, however MINUTE, or however REMOTE from the scene of action, are guilty as principals. In this treasonable conspiracy, to aid the existing armed Rebellion, by murdering the executive officers of the United States and the commander of its armies, all the parties to it must be held as principals, and the act of one, in the prosecution of the common design, the act of all.

I leave the decision of this dread issue with the Court, to which alone it belongs. It is for you to say, upon your oaths, whether the accused are guilty. I am not conscious that in this argument I have made any erroneous statement of the evidence, or drawn any erroneous conclusions; yet I pray the Court, out of tender regard and jealous care for the rights of the accused, to see that no error of mine, if any there be, shall work them harm. The past services of the members of this honorable Court give assurance that, without fear, favor, or affection, they will discharge with fidelity the duty enjoined upon them by their oaths. Whatever else may befall, I trust in God that in this, as in every other American Court, the rights of the whole people will be respected, and that the Republic in this its supreme hour of trial, will be true to itself and just to all, ready to protect the rights of the humblest, to redress every wrong, to avenge every crime, to vindicate the majesty of law, and to maintain inviolate the Constitution—whether it be secretly or openly assailed by hosts, armed with gold or armed with steel. JOHN A. BINGHAM,
Special Judge Advocate.

WASHINGTON, June 28.—The Military Commission met this day, with closed doors, in secret session, to deliberate on the testimony and finding of a verdict for or against the conspirators, and after a session of six hours duration, not coming to a decision in all the cases, adjourned till the next day, Thursday, June 29th.

WASHINGTON, June 29.—The Military Commission met this morning in secret session, with closed doors, and after being in session some hours found a verdict in the case of each of the conspirators, when a record was made up and forwarded to the War Department for review, from whom it will be sent to the President, who will examine the whole of the voluminous testimony closely before rendering his decision on the findings of the Military Commission.

WASHINGTON, July 6.—In accordance with the findings and sentences of the Military Commission, which the President approved yesterday, David E. Harold, Lewis Payne, Mrs. Surratt and George A. Atzerodt are to be hung to-morrow, by the proper military authorities.

Dr. Mudd, Arnold and O'Laughlin are to be imprisoned for life, and Spangler for six years, all at hard labor, in the Albany Penitentiary.

The Official Order.

WASHINGTON, July 6.—The following important order has just been issued:—
WAR DEPARTMENT, ADJUTANT-GENERAL'S OFFICE, WASHINGTON, July 5, 1865.—To Major-General W. S. Hancock, United States Volunteers, commanding the Middle Military Division, Washington, D. C.

Whereas, By the Military Commission appointed in paragraph 4, Special Orders No. 211, dated War Department, Adjutant-General's Office, Washington, May 6, 1865, and of which Major-General David Hunter, United States Volunteers, was President, the following persons were tried, and, after mature consideration of evidence adduced in their cases, were found and sentenced as hereinafter stated, as follows:—

Harold's Sentence.

First, David E. Harold.—Finding of the specification, guilty, except combining, confederating and conspiring with Edward Spangler, as to which part thereof, not guilty; of the charge guilty, except the words of the charge, that he combined, confederated and conspired with Edward Spangler, as to which part of the charge not guilty.

Sentence.—And the Commission does, therefore, sentence him, the said David E. Harold, to be hanged by the neck until he be dead, at such time and place as the President of the United States shall direct, two-thirds of the Commission concurring therein.

Atzeroth's Sentence.

Second. George A. Atzeroth.—Finding of specification, guilty, except combining, confederating and conspiring with Edward Spangler; of this, not guilty. Of the charge, guilty, except combining, confederating and conspiring with Edward Spangler; of this, not guilty.

Sentence.—And the Commission does therefore sentence him, the said George A. Atzeroth, to be hung by the neck until he be dead, at such time and place as the President of the United States shall direct, two-thirds of the Commission concurring therein.

Payne's Sentence.

Third. Lewis Payne.—Finding of the specification, guilty, except combining, confederating and conspiring with Edward Spangler; of this, not guilty. Of the charge, guilty, except combining, confederating and conspiring with Edward Spangler; of this, not guilty.

Sentence.—And the Commission does therefore sentence him, the said Lewis Payne, to be hung by the neck until he be dead, at such time and place as the President of the United States shall direct, two-thirds of the Commission concurring therein.

Mrs. Surratt's Sentence.

Fourth. Mary E. Surratt.—Finding of the specification guilty, except as to receiving, sustaining, harboring and concealing Samuel Arnold and Michael O'Laughlin, and except as to combining, confederating and conspiring with Edward Spangler; of this not guilty. Of the charge guilty, except as to combining, confederating and conspiring with Edward Spangler; of this not guilty.

Sentence.—And the Commission does, therefore, sentence her, the said Mary E. Surratt, to be hung by the neck until she be dead, at such time and place as the President of the United States shall direct, two-thirds of the members of the Commission concurring therein.

President Johnson's Approval.

And Whereas, The President of the United States has approved the foregoing sentences in the following order, to wit:—

EXECUTIVE MANSION, July 5, 1865.—The foregoing sentences in the cases of David E. Harold, G. A. Atzeroth, Lewis Payne and Mary E. Surratt, are hereby approved; and it is ordered that the sentences in the cases of David E. Harold, G. A. Atzeroth, Lewis Payne and Mary E. Surratt be carried into execution by the proper military authority, under the direction of the Secretary of War, on the 7th day of July, 1865, between the hours of 10 o'clock A. M. and 2 o'clock P. M. of that day.   (Signed)
ANDREW JOHNSON, President.

Therefore you are hereby commanded to cause the foregoing sentences in the cases of David E. Harold, G. A. Atzeroth, Lewis Payne and Mary E. Surratt to be duly executed, in accordance with the President's order.

By command of the President of the United States.   E. D. TOWNSEND,
Assistant Adjutant-General.

In the remaining cases of O'Laughlin, Spangler, Arnold and Mudd, the findings and sentences are as follows:—

O'Laughlin's Sentence.

Fifth. Michael O'Laughlin.—Finding of the specification guilty, except the words thereof, as follows:—

And in the words thereof as follows:—And in the further prosecution of the conspiracy aforesaid, and of its murderous and treasonable purposes aforesaid, on the nights of the 13th and 14th of April, 1865, at Washington City, and within the military department and military lines aforesaid, the said Michael O'Laughlin did there and then lie in wait for Ulysses S. Grant, then Lieutenant-General and Commander of the armies of the United States, with intent then and there to kill and murder the said Ulysses S. Grant, of said words not guilty, and except combining, confederating and conspiring with Edward Spangler, of this not guilty. Of the charge, guilty, except combining, confederating and conspiring with Edward Spangler; of this not guilty.

Sentence.—The Commission sentence O'Laughlin to be imprisoned at hard labor for life.

Spangler's Sentence.

Sixth. Finding.—Edward Spangler, of the specification, not guilty, except as to the words "the said Edward Spangler, on said 14th day of April; A. D. 1865, at about the same hour of that day, as aforesaid, within said military department and the military lines aforesaid, did aid and abet him (meaning John Wilkes Booth) in making his escape after the said Abraham Lincoln had been murdered in manner aforesaid," and of these words, guilty.

Of the charge not guilty, but guilty of having feloniously and traitorously aided and abetted John Wilkes Booth in making his escape after having killed and murdered Abraham Lincoln, President of the United States, he, the said Edward Spangler, at the time of aiding and abetting as aforesaid, well knowing that the said Abraham Lincoln, President as aforesaid, had been murdered by the said John Wilkes Booth as aforesaid. The Commission sentenced Spangler to hard labor for six years.

Arnold's Sentence.

Seventh. Samuel Arnold.—Of the specifications guilty, except combining, confederating, and conspiring with Edward Spangler, of this not guilty. Of the charge guilty, except combining, confederating and conspiring with Edward Spangler, of this not guilty. The Commission sentenced him to imprisonment at hard labor for life.

Dr. Mudd's Sentence.

Eighth. Samuel A. Mudd.—Of the specification guilty, except combining, confederating and conspiring with Edward Spangler; of this not guilty; and excepting receiving and entertaining and harboring and concealing said Lewis Payne, John H. Surratt, Michael O'Laughlin, George A. Atzeroth, Mary E. Surratt and Samuel Arnold, of this not guilty. Of the charge guilty, except combining, confederating and conspiring with Edward Spangler, of this not guilty. The Commission sentenced Mudd to be imprisoned at hard labor for life.

The President's order in these cases is as follows:—

It is further ordered that the prisoners, Samuel Arnold, Samuel A. Mudd, and Michael O'Laughlin, be confined at hard labor in the Penitentiary at Albany, New York, during the period designated in their respective sentences.
ANDREW JOHNSON, President.

WASHINGTON, July 6.—The announcement and findings of the Military Commission in the cases of the conspirators, made to-day about noon, completely absorbed public attention during the remainder of the day. Scarcely anything else was talked of in the streets, hotels and in every place where citizens mostly congregate.

The general sentiment seemed to justify the findings of the Commission, but the short period of time allowed the prisoners between the announcement of the sentence and their execution did not generally appear to meet the public approval. This, however, is in accordance with the practice of courts-martial, sentences in such cases being executed almost immediately after the findings are officially published.

Judge Holt with the President.

The President having nearly recovered from his indisposition, yesterday invited Judge Advocate-General Holt to the White House, and after mature deliberation, the President approved the findings and sentences in each case as rendered by the Commission.

The Sentences Read to the Prisoners.

About noon to-day General Hancock, who is charged with the execution of the sentences, proceeded to the Penitentiary, and in company with Major-General Hartranft visited the cell of each prisoner and informed each what verdict had been rendered. No one was present at this interview but the two Generals and the turnkey.

Mrs. Surratt.

On learning her fate, was extremely depressed, and wept bitterly. She was alone, her daughter having left her a short time before, not knowing the sentence was to be announced to her mother to-day.

Payne.

Seemed to regard it as a foregone conclusion, and manifested little or no emotion. He has evidently nerved himself to meet his death with firm resolution.

Atzeroth

Was violently agitated and almost paralyzed with fear. He evidently hoped for a different result, but it is difficult to see how he could have expected it to have been otherwise.

Harold

Listened to the reading of the order in his case with boyish indifference, but soon after became impressed with the solemnity of his situation and appeared more serious, asking that his sisters might be allowed to visit him.

Payne asks for a Baptist Clergyman.

Payne asked that Dr. Stracker, a Baptist clergyman of Baltimore, be sent for, which was done, and that gentleman arrived here this evening, and is in attendance upon the prisoner.

Mrs. Surratt's Spiritual Advisers.

Mrs. Surratt asked that Fathers Walter and Wiget, Catholic priests of Baltimore, be sent for. Her wish was immediately complied with, and both the clergymen arrived this evening, and were admitted to her cell.

Rev. Dr. Butler Attends Atzeroth.

Atzeroth could name no clergyman he wished to attend him; but upon General Hartranft naming Rev. Mr. Butler, a Lutheran clergyman of Washington city, the prisoner desired he might be sent for, and he was in attendance upon the prisoner early this afternoon.

Harold's Sisters Visit Him.

Five of Harold's sisters visited him this afternoon at the prison and the scene was truly distressing. After they left him they wept bitterly, in the entrance room down stairs. Two are grown ladies and the others young misses. But they all seemed to realize the dreadful situation of their brother.

One of them brought a small basket of cakes and little delicacies for the prisoner, which was left in charge of General Hartranft to be examined before being given to him. One of the elder sisters sat down and wrote a note to her brother, which was also left in charge of General Hartranft to give Harold.

The Scaffold

Is being built this afternoon, in the south yard of the prison, and will be large enough to execute all at one time. The coffins and burial clothes are being prepared this afternoon and evening at the arsenal.

A False Rumor.

An impression appears to prevail throughout the city that Mrs. Surratt will not be executed, that the President will commute her sentence to imprisonment.

In less than an hour after the findings had been announced this rumor was on the street, and it was asserted that many who had been most strenuous in asking for severe punishment upon the conspirators were willing to unite in an effort to have the sentence in Mrs. Surratt's case changed to imprisonment. This rumor was wide spread, but had no foundation in fact, The wish was evidently father to the thought.

No Executive Clemency.

Harold's sisters called at the White House this afternoon, pleading for mercy, and Father Walker and Mr. Aiken, one of Mrs. Surratt's counsel, also called on behalf of Mrs. Surratt, but the President declined to see any of them, and referred them all to Judge Holt. It would seem to be the determination of the President to decline interfering in the matter, and there is no doubt but all those condemned to death will be executed to-morrow, Mrs. Surratt among the number.

Aiken says he has some after-discovered testimony to offer, favorable to her case. But it is not probable the President will relent to-morrow.

Payne, Atzeroth, Harold and Mrs. Surratt are hung!

WASHINGTON, July 9, 1865.—To-day the last scene of the terrible tragedy of the 14th of April took place. Lewis Payne, David E. Harold, George A. Atzeroth, and Mary E. Surratt, the ringleaders in the murderous plot to assassinate the heads of the Government, and throw the land into anarchy and confusion, paid the penalty of their crime upon the gallows.

The execution was comparatively a private one. The following is the form of order which was imperatively required to secure admission to the scene of the execution:—

HEAD-QUARTERS, MIDDLE MILITARY DIVISION, WASHINGTON, D. C., July 7, 1865.—Major-General J. F. Hartranft, Military Governor of Military Prisons:—Admit ——, Reporter of THE PHILADELPHIA INQUIRER, to the Military Prison this day.
WINFIELD S. HANCOCK,
Major-General Volunteers Commanding.

On the reverse was written "between 10 and 1 P. M." Each pass was registered with the rank and station of the officer and the paper to which the representative belonged.

Only one hundred were issued, and one-fourth of these were to representatives of the press. Over a thousand applications were made to General Hancock for passes from various sources, but he conducted the whole affair with the most commendable propriety, and squelched completely the "secesh" sympathizers who wished to witness the execution. Those who came from mere personal curiosity were all denied.

The Weather.

The sun shone with its intensest rays, and had it not been for a breeze at intervals the thermometer would have stood at 100.

Early in the Morning.

At as early an hour as eight A. M. people commenced to wend their way down to the prison, and the boats to Alexandria, which ran close by the jail, were crowded all day by those who took the trip in hopes of catching a glimpse of the gallows, or of the execution, but it was all in vain. The only position outside of the jail that could be used as an observatory, was the large building upon the left side of the Arsenal, which had about fifty spectators upon it, who had a good view of the whole.

The Army Officers.

Between nine and ten o'clock in the morning the three ante-rooms of the prison, on the first floor, were thronged with army officers, principally of Hancock's corps, anxious to get a view of the execution from the windows, from which the scaffold could be plainly seen.

The Newspaper Reporters

Soon began to congregate there also, and in a few minutes not less than a score were in attendance, waiting to pick up the smallest item of interest. No newspaper man was allowed to see the prisoners in their cells before they were led out to execution, and General Hartranft was very decided on this point.

The Clergy.

While waiting here for over two hours, the clergymen passed in and out through the heavily riveted doors leading to the prisoners' cells, which creaked heavily on its hinges as it swung to and fro, and the massive key was turned upon the inner side with a heavy sound as a visitor was admitted within its portals.

Mrs. Surratt's Daughter

Passed into the ante-room, accompanied by a lady, who remained seated, while the daughter rapidly entered the hall, and, passing through the heavy door, is soon in the corridor where her mother is incarcerated

The Counsel for the Prisoners.

Messrs. Cox, Doster, Aiken and Clampitt, counsel for the prisoners, are specially passed in for a short interview, and in a few minutes they return again to the ante-rooms. Time flies rapidly, and not a moment is to be lost. No useless words are to be spoken, but earnest, terse sentences are from necessity employed when conversing with the doomed prisoners, whose lives are now measured by minutes.

Aiken and Clampitt are both here. They walk impatiently up and down the room, whispering a word to each other as to the prospects of Mrs. Surratt's being reprieved through the operations of the habeas corpus, which, Aiken confidently tells us, has been granted by Justice Wylie, and from which he anticipates favorable results. Strange infatuation! It was the last straw to which, like drowning men, they clutched with the fond hope that it was to rescue their client from her imminent peril.

Atzerodt in His Cell.

Atzerodt passed the night previous to the execution without any particular manifestations. He prayed and cried alternately, but made no other noise that attracted the attention of his keeper. On the morning of the execution he sat most of the time on the floor of his cell in his shirt sleeves.

A Mysterious Visitant.

He was attended by a lady dressed in deep black, who carried a prayer book, and who seemed more exercised in spirit than the prisoner himself. Who the lady was could not be ascertained. She left him at half-past twelve o'clock, and exhibited great emotion at parting.

During the morning Atzerodt was greatly composed, and spent part of the time in earnest conversation with his spiritual adviser, Rev. Mr. Butler, of St. Paul's Lutheran Church, Washington. He occupied cell No. 151 on the ground floor to-day, which was directly in view of the yard, where he could see the gathering crowd and soldiery, although he could not see the scaffold. He sat in the corner of his cell on his bed, and when his spiritual adviser would go out for a few minutes and leave his testament in his hands, his eyes would be dropped to it in a moment, and occasionally wander with a wild look towards the open window in front of his cell.

His Costume.

He wore nothing but a white linen shirt and a grey pair of pants. The long irons upon his hands, which he had worn during the trial, were not removed.

A Partial Confession.

Atzerodt made a partial confession to the Rev. Mr. Butler, a few hours before his execution. He stated that he took a room at the Kirkwood House on Thursday afternoon, and was engaged in endeavoring to get a pass to Richmond. He then heard the President was to be taken to the theatre and there captured. He said he understood that Booth was to rent the theatre for the purpose of carrying out the plot to capture the then President. He stated that Harold brought the pistol and knife to the Kirkwood House, and that he (Atzerodt) had nothing to do with the attempted assassination of Andrew Johnson.

Harold to Have Murdered Mr. Johnson.

Booth intended that Harold should assassinate Johnson, and he wanted him, Atzerodt, to back him up and give him courage. Booth thought that Harold had more pluck than Atzerodt.

The Original Plot.

He alluded to the meeting at the restaurant about the middle of March. He said Booth, Harold, Payne, Arnold and himself were present and it was then concerted that Mr. Lincoln should be captured and taken to Richmond.

They heard that Lincoln was to visit a camp near Washington, and the plan was that they should proceed there and capture the coach and horses containing Lincoln, and run him through Prince George's county and Old Fields to G. R. There they were to leave the coach and horses and place the President in a buggy which Harold would have on hand, and thus convey him to a boat to be in readiness, and run him by some means to Richmond. He denies that he was in favor of assassinating Lincoln, but was willing to assist in his capture.

His Knowledge of the Assassination.

He stated, however, that he knew Lincoln was to be assassinated about half-past eight o'clock on the evening of the occurrence, but was afraid to make it known as he feared Booth would kill him if he did so.

The Influence of Slavery.

He said that slavery caused his sympathies to be with the South. He had heard a sermon preached which stated that a curse on the negro race had turned them black. He always hated the negroes, and thought they should be kept in ignorance.

Booth had promised him that if their plan succeeded for the capture of Lincoln they should all be rich men, and they would become great. The prisoners would all be exchanged, and the independence of the South would be recognized and their cause be triumphant. He had never received any money as yet.

Eleven O'clock.

The crowd increases. Reporters are scribbling industriously. A suppressed whisper is audible all over the room and the hall as the hour draws nearer, and the preparations begin to be more demonstrative.

The rumbling sound of the trap as it falls in the course of the experiments which are being made to test it, and to prevent any unfortunate accident occurring at the critical moment, is heard through the windows, and all eyes are involuntarily turned in that direction, for curiosity is excited to the highest pitch to view the operations of the fatal machinery. There are two or three pictorial papers represented. One calmly makes a drawing of the scaffold for the next issue of his paper, and thus the hours till noon passed away.

Twelve O'clock.

The bustle increases. Officers are running to and fro calling for orderlies and giving orders. General Hartranft is trying to answer twenty questions at once from as many different persons. The sentry in the hall is becoming angry because the crowd will keep intruding on his beat, when suddenly a buggy at the door, announces the

Arrival of General Hancock.

He enters the room hurriedly, takes General Hartranft aside, and a few words pass between them in a low tone, to which Hartranft nods acquiescence; then, in a louder voice, Hancock says, "Get ready, General; I want to have everything put in readiness as soon as possible." This was the signal for the interviews of the clergymen, relatives and friends of the prisoners to cease, and for the doomed to prepare for execution.

The bustle increases. Mr. Aiken approaches Gen. Hancock and a few minutes' conversation passes between them. Aiken's countenance changes perceptibly at Gen. Hancock's words. The reason is plain; there is no hope for Mrs. Surratt. The habeas corpus movement, from which he expected so much, has failed, and Aiken, in a voice tremulous with emotion, said to your correspondent, "Mrs. Surratt will be hung."

The bright hopes he had cherished had all vanished, and the dreadful truth stood before him in all its horror. Clampitt, too, till General Hancock arrived, indulged the hope that the habeas corpus would effect a respite for three or four days.

One O'Clock.

Three or four of Harold's sisters, all in one chorus of weeping, come through the prison door into the hall. They had left their brother and spoken to him the last words, and heard his voice for the last time.

At fifteen minutes after one o'clock General Hartranft blandly informs the "press gang" to be in readiness for the prison doors to be opened, when they can pass into the prison yard, from whence a good view of the procession can be obtained as it passes by to the scaffold. About 11 A. M. the prison yard was thrown open to those having passes, and about fifty entered. The first object in view was

The Scaffold,

Which was erected at the northeast corner of the Penitentiary yard, and consisted of a simple wooden structure of very primitive appearance, faced about due west. The platform was elevated about twelve feet from the ground, and was about twenty feet square. Attached to the main platform were

The Drops, &c.,

Two in number, on which the criminals stood. At the moment of execution these drops were connected with the main platform by means of large hinges, four to each drop.

The drops were supported by a post which rested on a heavy piece of timber placed on the ground, and so arranged that two soldiers stationed at the rear of the scaffold instantaneously detached the supports from their positions by means of pressing two poles, which occupied a horizontal position, the action of which dislodged the props of the scaffold and permitted the drops to fall.

The gallows proper was divided into two parts by means of a perpendicular piece of timber, resting on the platform and reaching up to the cross-beam of the gallows. Two ropes hung on either side of the piece of timber mentioned. They were wound around the cross-beam, and contained large knots and nooses at the lower end. The platform was ascended by means of a flight of steps, thirteen in number, erected at the rear of the scaffold, and guarded on either side by a railing, which also extended around the platform. The platform was sustained by nine heavy uprights, about which rose the two heavy pieces of timber which supported the cross-beam and constituted the gallows. The entire platform was capable of holding conveniently about thirty people, and was about half full at the time of the execution.

TRIAL OF THE ASSASSINS AT WASHINGTON. 207

The Executioners.

Wm. Coxbell, D. F. Shoupe, G. F. Taylor and F. B. Haslett, all of Company F, Fourteenth Veteran Reserves, were detailed to act as executioners. They were all fine stalwart specimens of Union soldiers and did their work well. The rope was furnished from the Navy Yard, and was one-and-a-half inches in circumference and composed of twenty strands.

The Graves.

Four in number, were dug close to the scaffold and next to the prison wall. They were four in number, and were about three feet and a half deep. In a dry clayey soil, and about seven feet long and three wide. Four pine boxes, similar to those used for packing guns in, stood between the graves and the scaffold. These were for coffins, both being in full view of the prisoners as they emerged from their cells, and before them until they commenced the dreadful ascent of those thirteen steps.

About a thousand soldiers were in the yard and upon the high wall around it, which is wide enough for sentries to patrol it. The sun's rays made it very oppressive, and the walls kept off the little breeze that was stirring. There was no shade, and men huddled together along the walls and around the pump to discuss with one another the prospect of a reprieve or delay for Mrs. Surratt. But few hoped for it, though some were induced by Mrs. Surratt's counsel to believe she would not be hung to-day. When one of them came out and saw the four ropes hanging from the beam he exclaimed to one of the soldiers, "My God, they are not going to hang all four, are they?"

But there are times when it is mercy to hang criminals, and that time was drawing nigh, it seemed, for those who have been used for years to apologizing for the Rebellion, and its damning acts, to be brought to believe that any crime is to be punished. Of such material were the prisoners' counsel.

Eleven-thirty.

The drops, at eleven-thirty, are tried with three hundred pound weights upon them, to see if they will work. One falls all right; one hangs part way down, and the hatchet and saw were brought into play. The next time they were all right. The rattle echoes around the walls, it reaches the prisoners' cells close by, and penetrates their inmost recesses. All is quiet in the yard save the scuffle of the military, and the passing to and fro of a few civilians.

Twelve-forty.

Four arm chairs are brought out and placed upon the scaffold, and the moving around of General Hartranft indicates the drawing near of the time. The newspaper correspondents and reporters are admitted to a position about thirty feet from the gallows, and about one o'clock and ten minutes, the heavy door in front of the cells is swung upon its hinges for the hundredth time within an hour, and a few reporters, with Gen. Hancock, pass in and through to the yard, and the big door closes with a slam behind them. All take positions to get a good view. Gen. Hancock for the last time takes a survey of the preparations, and being satisfied that everything is ready, he re-enters the prison building, and in a few minutes

The Solemn Procession

Marched down the steps of the back door down into the yard, in the following order:—The condemned, Mrs. Surratt, supported by Lieutenant-Colonel McCall, Two-hundredth Pennsylvania Regiment, on her left side, and Sergeant W. R. Keeney, Company A, Twelfth Veteran Reserve Corps; Fathers Walker and Weigel walking together. Harold, accompanied by Sergeant Thomas, Company B, Eighteenth Veteran Reserve Corps, and an officer attached to Col. Baker's Detective force. Payne, accompanied by Sergeant Grover. Company D, Eighteenth Veteran Reserve Corps. and one of Colonel Baker's detectives. Atzeroth, attended by Sergeant White, Fourteenth Veteran Reserve Corps, and one of Baker's detectives. Mrs. Surratt, on emerging from the back door, cast her eyes upward upon the scaffold for a few moments with a look of curiosity, combined with dread. One glimpse, and her eyes fell to the ground, and she walked along mechanically, her head drooping, and if she had not been supported would have fallen.

Appearance and Demeanor of Mrs. Surratt.

She ascended the scaffold, and was led to an armchair, in which she was seated. An umbrella was held over her by the two holy fathers, to protect her from the sun, whose rays shot down like the blasts from a fiery furnace. She was attired in a black bombazine dress, black alpaca bonnet, with black veil, which she wore over her face till she was seated on the chair. During the reading of the order for the execution by General Hartranft, the priests held a small crucifix before her, which she kissed fervently several times.

She first looked around at the scene before her, then closed her eyes and seemed engaged in silent prayer. The reading and the announcement of the clergymen in behalf of the other prisoners having been made, Colonel McCall, assisted by the other officers, proceeded to remove her bonnet, pinion her elbows, and tie strips of cotton stuff around her dress below the knees. This done, the rope was placed around her neck and her face covered with a white cap reaching down to the shoulders.

When they were pinioning her arms she turned her head and made some remarks to the officers in a low tone, which could not be heard. It appeared they had tied her elbows too tight, for they slackened the bandings slightly, and then awaited the final order. All the prisoners were prepared thus at the same time, and the preparations of each were completed at about the same moment, so that when Mrs. Surratt was thus pinioned she stood scarcely ten seconds, supported by those standing near her, when General Hartranft gave

The Signal,

By clapping his hands twice for both drops to fall, and as soon as the second and last signal was given both I'll and Mrs. Surratt, with a jerk, fell to the full length of the rope. It was done as quick as lightning. She was leaning over when the drop fell, and this gave a swinging motion to her body, which lasted several minutes before it assumed a perpendicular position. Her death was instantaneous; she died without a struggle. The only muscular movement discernable was a slight contraction of the left arm, which she seemed to try to disengage from behind her as the drop fell.

After being suspended thirty minutes, she was cut down and placed in a square wooden box or coffin, in the clothes in which she died, and was interred in the prison yard. The rope made a clean cut around her neck fully an inch in diameter, which was black and discolored with bruised blood. The cap was not taken off her face, and she was laid in the coffin with it on, and thus has passed away from the face of the earth Mary E. Surratt. Her body, it is understood, will be given to her family for burial.

The Bearing of Payne on the Scaffold.

Payne died as he has lived, at least as he has done since his arrest, bold, calm and thoroughly composed. The only tremor exhibited by this extraordinary man during the terrible ordeal of the execution was an involuntary vibration of the muscles of his legs after the fatal drop fell. He was next in order to Mrs. Surratt in the procession of the criminals from their cells to the place of execution.

He was supported on one side by his spiritual adviser and on the other by a soldier, although he needed no such assistance, for he walked erect and upright and retained the peculiar piercing expression of the eye that has never characterized him. He was dressed in a blue flannel shirt and pants of the same material. His brawny neck was entirely exposed, and he wore a new straw hat. He ascended the steps leading to the scaffold with the greatest ease, and took his seat on the drop with as much sang froid as though he was sitting down to dinner.

Once or twice he addressed a few words in an undertone to persons close by him, and occasionally glanced at the array of soldiers and civilians spread out before him. A puff of wind blew off his hat, and he instantly turned around to see where it went to. When it was recovered and handed to him, he intimated by gesturing that he no longer required it, and it was laid aside.

During the reading of the sentence by General Hartranft, just previous to the execution, he calmly listened, and once or twice glanced upwards, at the gallows as if inspecting its construction. He submitted to the process of binding his limbs very quietly, and watched the operation with attention.

His spiritual adviser, Rev. Dr. Gillette, advanced, a few minutes previous to the execution, and made some remarks in Payne's behalf. He thanked the different officials for the attention and kindness bestowed on Payne, and exhorted the criminal in a few impassioned words to give his entire thoughts to his future state. Payne stood immovable as a statue when this was said. Although next to Harold who died the hardest, he exhibited more bodily contortions than the others while suspended. While the noose was being adjusted to his neck Payne raised his head and evidently desired to assist the executioner in that delicate operation.

The Last Moments of Harold.

Probably no one of the criminals felt as great a dread of the terrible ordeal through which they were to pass as young Harold. From the time he left his cell until his soul was sent into the presence of the Almighty, he exhibited the greatest emotion, and seemed to thoroughly realize his wretched condition. His face wore an indefinable expression of anguish, and at times he trembled violently. He seemed to desire to engage in conversation with those around him while sitting in the chair awaiting execution, and his spiritual adviser,

Rev. Mr. Old, was assiduous in his attentions to the wretched man.

Harold was dressed in a black cloth coat and light pants, and wore a white shirt without any collar; he wore also a black slouch hat, which he retained on his head until it was removed to make room for the white cap. At times he looked wildly around and his face had a haggard, anxious, inquiring expression. When the drop fell he exhibited more tenacity of life than any of the others, and he endeavored several times to draw himself up as if for the purpose of relieving himself from the rope by which he was suspended.

Atzeroth on the Scaffold.

He ascended the steps of the scaffold without difficulty and took his seat at the south end of the drop without exhibiting any particular emotion. He was dressed in a dark grey coat and pants and black vest and white linen shirt without any collar; on his feet he wore a pair of woolen slippers and socks. He sat in such a position that he could see the profiles of his fellow prisoners, and he had his hands pinioned behind him. He wore no hat, had a white handkerchief placed over his head, with a tuft of hair protruding from it and spreading over his forehead.

Directly behind him stood his spiritual adviser, who held an umbrella over him to keep off the burning rays of the sun. During the reading of the sentence by General Hartranft he kept perfectly quiet, but his face wore an expression of unutterable woe, and he listened attentively. He wore a thin moustache and small goatee and his face was pale and sallow. Once and once only he glanced around at the assembled throng, and occasionally muttered incoherent sentences, but he talked, while on the scaffold, to no one immediately around him.

Just before his execution his spiritual adviser, Mr. Butler, advanced and stated that Atzeroth desired to return his sincere thanks to General Hartranft and the other officials for the many acts of kindness extended towards him. He then called on God to forgive George A. Atzeroth for his many sins, and, turning to Atzeroth, reminded him that while the wages of sin were death, that whomsoever placed their hope in the Lord Jesus Christ were not forgotten. He hoped that God would grant him a full and free forgiveness, and ended by saying "May the Lord God have mercy on you and grant you his peace."

The handkerchief was then taken from his head, and he stood up, facing the assembled audience, directly alongside of the instrument of his death. His knees slightly trembled, and his legs were bent forward. He stood for a few moments the very embodiment of wretchedness, and then spoke a few words in an undertone to General Hartranft, after which he shook hands with his spiritual adviser and a few others near him; while he was being secured with bands tied around his legs and arms he kept muttering to himself as if engaged in silent prayer.

Suddenly he broke forth with the words, "Gentlemen, beware who you—" and then stopped as if with emotion; as the white cap was being placed over his head, he cried, Then he said, "Good bye, gentlemen, who are before me now, may we all meet in the other world; God take me now." He muttered something loud enough for them close by him to hear, just as the drop fell, evidently not anticipating such an event at that moment. He died without apparent pain, and his neck must have been instantly broken.

After hanging a few seconds his stomach heaved considerably, and subsequently his legs quivered a little. His death appeared to be the easiest of any of the criminals, with the exception of Mrs. Surratt, who did not apparently suffer at all. After hanging a half an hour, Atzeroth's body was taken down, it being the first one lowered, and an examination made by Surgeons Otis, Woodward and Porter.

Incidents at the White House.

About half-past eight o'clock this morning, Miss Surratt, accompanied by a female friend, again visited the White House, having been there last evening for the purpose of obtaining an interview with the President, President Johnson having given orders that he would receive no one to-day, the door-keeper stopped Miss Surratt at the foot of the steps leading up to the President's office, and would not permit her to proceed further. She then asked permission to see General Mussey, the President's Military Secretary, who promptly answered the summons, and came down stairs where Miss Surratt was standing.

As soon as the General made his appearance, Miss Surratt threw herself upon her knees before him, catching him by the coat, with loud sobs and streaming eyes, implored him to assist her in obtaining a hearing with the President.

General Mussey, in as tender a manner as possible, informed Miss Surratt that he could not comply with her request, as President Johnson's orders were inoperative, and he would receive no one.

Upon General Mussey's returning to his office Miss Surratt threw herself upon the stair steps, where she remained a considerable length of time, sobbing aloud in the greatest anguish, protesting her mother's innocence, and imploring every one who came near her to intercede in her mother's behalf. While thus weeping she declared her mother was too good and kind to be guilty of the enormous crime of which she was convicted, and asserted that if her mother was put to death she wished to die also.

The scene was heart-rending, and many of those who witnessed it, including a number of hardy soldiers, were moved to tears. Miss Surratt having become quiet was finally persuaded to take a seat in the East Room, and here she remained for several hours, jumping up from her seat each time the front door of the mansion was opened, evidently in hopes of seeing some one other who could be of service to her in obtaining the desired interview with the President, or that they were the bearers of good news to her.

Two of Harold's sisters, dressed in full mourning and heavily veiled, made their appearance at the White House shortly after Miss Surratt, for the purpose of interceding with the President in behalf of their brother. Failing to see the President, they addressed a note to Mrs. Johnson, and expressed a hope that she would not turn a deaf ear to their pleadings. Mrs. Johnson being quite sick it was thought expedient by the ushers not to deliver the note, when, as a last expedient, the ladies asked permission to forward a note to Mrs. Patterson, the President's daughter, which privilege was not granted, as Mrs. Patterson is also quite indisposed to-day.

How the Prisoners Spent the Night.

Payne, during the night, slept well for about three hours, the other portion of the night being spent in conversation with Rev. Dr. Gillette, of the First Baptist Church, who offered his services as soon as he was informed of the sentence. Payne, without showing any particular emotion, paid close attention to the advice of Dr. Gillette. Up to ten o'clock this morning, no relations or friends had been to see Payne.

Atzeroth was very nervous throughout the night, and did not sleep, although he made several attempts. His brother was to see him yesterday afternoon, and again this morning. His aged mother, who arrived during the night, was also present. The meeting of the condemned man and his mother was very affecting, and moved some of the officers of the prison, who have become used to trying scenes, to tears.

Rev. Dr. Butler, of the Lutheran Church, was sent for last night, and has been all night ministering to Atzeroth. Harold was visited yesterday by Rev. Mr. Olds, of Christ Episcopal Church, and five of his sisters, and this morning the minister and the entire family of seven sisters were present with him. Harold slept very well several hours during the night.

Miss Surratt was with her mother several hours last night, as also Rev. Fathers Wiget and Walter, and Mr. Brophy, who were also present this morning. She slept very little if any, and required considerable attention, suffering with cramps and pains the entire night, caused by her nervousness. The breakfast was sent to the prisoners at the usual hour this morning, but none eat, excepting Payne, who ate heartily.

Disposition of the Military.

Major-General Hartranft made the following dispositions of the military on the occasion:—The Sixth Regiment Veteran Volunteers, Major Lavner, were stationed on Four-and-a-half street, from the gate of Penitentiary grounds to Pennsylvania avenue; the First Regiment Veteran Volunteers, Colonel Bond, were on duty inside the Penitentiary yard, and formed the guard around the gallows.

The Fourth Regiment Veteran Volunteers were stationed on the wall surrounding the yard, and the Eighth Regiment Veteran Volunteers, Colonel Price, were stationed along the Potomac River, to prevent the landing of boats on the grounds of the Penitentiary grounds. The Sixteenth New York Cavalry were also on duty near the Penitentiary building. About three thousand troops were employed in guarding the building and its surrounding.

The Execution Ground

Was a large square inclosure, called the Old Penitentiary jail yard, directly south of the Old Penitentiary building. It comprises probably three acres of ground, surrounded by a brick wall, about twenty feet in height.

This wall is capped with white stone and surmounted with iron stakes and ropes to prevent the guard from falling off while patrolling the tops of the wall. The Sixth Regiment Veteran Volunteers were formed on the summit of the wall during the execution, and they presented quite a picturesque appearance in their elevated position.

The gallows occupied a position in the angle of the inclosure formed by the east wall and the Penitentiary building on the north. The First Regiment Veteran Volunteers were posted around the gallows, two sides being formed by the east wall and the Penitentiary building.

The Spectators,

About two hundred in number, were congregated directly in front of the gallows, the soldiers forming a barrier between them and the place of execution. The criminals were led to the scaffold from a small door about one hundred feet from the place of execution. But for a small projection that runs south of the Peni-

TRIAL OF THE ASSASSINS AT WASHINGTON.

tentiary building, the gallows would be in plain view of the prisoners' cells, which are all on the first floor of the building.

It was a noticeable incident of the execution that scarcely any Government officials or citizens were present, the spectators being nearly all connected with the trial in some capacity, or else representatives of the press.

A Heart-rending Scene.

By permission of the authorities, the daughter of Mrs. Surratt passed the night previous to the execution with her mother, in her cell. The entire interview was of a very affecting character. The daughter remained with her mother until a short time before the execution, and when the time came for separation the screams of anguish that burst from the poor girl could be distinctly heard all over the execution ground.

During the morning the daughter proceeded to the Metropolitan Hotel, and sought an interview with General Hancock. Finding him, she implored in pitible accents to get a reprieve for her mother. The General, of course, had no power to grant or obtain such a favor, and informed the distressed girl in as gentle a manner as possible.

General Hancock, with the kindness that always characterizes his actions apart from the stern duties of his noble profession, did his best to assuage the mental anguish of the grief-stricken girl.

The Remaining Prisoners,

Arnold, Dr. Mudd, O'Laughlin and Spangler have not yet been informed of their respective sentences, nor do they know that their companions have been executed.

The After Discovered Testimony.

The alleged important after discovered testimony which Aiken, counsel for Mrs. Surratt, stated would prove her innocence, was submitted to Judge Advocate-General Holt last night, and after a careful examination, he failed to discover anything in it having a bearing on the case. This was communicated to the President and doubtless induced him to decline to interfere in the execution of Mrs. Surratt.

Scenes at the Surratt House.

The residence of Mrs. Surratt, on H street, north, near Sixth, remained closed yesterday after the announcement of her fate had become known.

In the evening but a single dim light shone from one of the rooms, while within the house all was as quiet as death up to about eight o'clock, at which hour Miss Annie E. Surratt, who has been in constant attendance upon her mother, drove up to the door in a hack, accompanied by a gentleman.

She appeared to be perfectly crushed with grief, and as she alighted from the carriage some ladies standing near were moved to tears of sympathy with the unfortunate girl whose every look and action betrayed her anguish.

Miss Surratt, after gaining admittance to the house fainted several times, causing great bustle and excitement among the inmates, who were untiring in their efforts to console the almost heart-broken young lady.

From early in the evening until a late hour at night, hundreds of persons, old and young, male and female, visited the vicinity of Mrs. Surratt's residence, stopping upon the opposite side of the street, glancing over with anxious and inquiring eyes upon the house in which the conspirators met, commenting upon the fate of the doomed woman, and the circumstances connected therewith.

During the evening not less than five hundred persons visited the spot.

THE HABEAS CORPUS APPLICATION.

At about 7½ o'clock this morning the counsel for Mrs. Surratt applied to Judge Wylie, of the Supreme Court of the District of Columbia, for a writ of habeas corpus, to be directed to Major-General W. S. Hancock, to bring into Court the body of the prisoner.

The Petition.

The following is a copy of the petition:—
To the Hon. Andrew Wylie, one of the Justices of the Supreme Court of the District of Columbia.—The petition of Mary E. Surratt, by her counsel, F. A. Aiken and John W. Clampitt, most respectfully represents unto your Honor, that on or about the 17th day of April, A. D. 1865, your petitioner was arrested by the military authorities of the United States, under the charge of complicity with the murder of Abraham Lincoln, late President of the United States, and has ever since that time been and is now confined on said charge, under and by virtue of the said military power of the United States, and is in the special custody of Major-General W. S. Hancock, commanding Middle Military Division; that since her said arrest your petitioner has been tried, against her solemn protest, by a military commission, unlawfully and without warrant, convened by the Secretary of War, as will appear from paragraph 9, special orders, No. 211, dated War Department, Adjutant-General's Office, Washington, May the 6th, 1865, and by said Commission, notwithstanding her formal plea to the jurisdiction of the said Commission, is now unlawfully and unjustifiably detained in custody and sentenced to be hanged on to-morrow, July 7, 1865, between the hours of ten A. M. and two P. M.; your petitioner shows unto your Honor that at the time of the commission of the said offense she was a private citizen of the United States, and in no manner connected with the military authority of the same, and that said offense was committed within the District of Columbia, said District being at the time within the lines of the armies of the United States, and not enemy's territory, or under the control of a military commander for the trial of civil causes. But on the contrary, your petitioner alleges that the said crime was an offence simply against the peace of the United States, properly and solely cognizable under the Constitution and laws of the United States, by the Criminal Court of this District, and which said court was and is now open for the trial of such crimes and offenses. Wherefore, inasmuch as the said crime was only an offense against the peace of the United States, and not an act of war, inasmuch as your petitioner was a private citizen of the same, and not subject to military jurisdiction, or in any wise amenable to military law; inasmuch as said District was the peaceful territory of the United States, and that all crimes committed within such territory are, under the Constitution and laws of the United States, to be tried only before its criminal tribunals, with the right of public trial by jury. Inasmuch as said Commission was a Military Commission, organized and governed by the laws of Military Court-Martial, and unlawfully convened without warrant or authority, and when she had not the right of public trial by jury as guaranteed to her by the Constitution and laws of the United States, that, therefore, her detention and sentence are so without warrant against positive law and unjustifiable; wherefore she prays your honor to grant unto her the United States, most gracious writ of habeas corpus commanding the said Major-General W. S. Hancock to produce before your Honor the body of your said petitioner, with the cause and day of her said detention, to abide, &c., and she will ever pray. MARY E. SURRATT,

By FREDERICK A. AIKEN, JNO. W. CLAMPITT.

Indorsement by the Court.

Indorsed—"Let the writ issue as prayed, returnable before the Criminal Court of the District of Columbia, now sitting, at the hour of ten o'clock A. M., this seventh day of July, 1865.

"ANDREW WYLIE,
"A Justice of the Supreme Court of the District of Columbia, July, 7th, 1865."

The writ was accordingly issued and at 8½ o'clock A. M. the Marshal returned the same served. The Marshal reported that General Hancock had not yet appeared and it was now past the hour for his appearance. The District Attorney suggested certain objections to the proceedings.

The counsel for Mrs. Surratt stated that if his client was guilty of any crime, it was cognizable by this Court, and not by a military tribunal. District Attorney Carrington, after reading the certificate of the Marshal, setting forth that he had served the writ at half-past eight o'clock, said he was only to defend the act of the Marshal, and the duty required of him by direction of the Court, and he found that the Marshal had performed his duty.

The Court said:—The case is now here on its merits on the petition of the party. This morning at an early hour I directed this writ of habeas corpus to issue. The writ was issued, and was served on General Hancock, who has the custody of Mrs. Surratt, the party on whose behalf the writ was obtained. The writ required him to have the body of Mrs. Surratt, with the cause of her detention, before this Court this morning at ten o'clock. He has neglected to obey the order of the Court, and the question now before us is, "what is the Court to do under the circumstances?"

That is the only question before the Court at this time. Any discussion on the merits involved would now be out of place. The Court acknowledges that its powers are inadequate to meet the military power possessed by General Hancock. If the Court were to decide at this moment that General Hancock was in contempt the only process which it would issue would be an attachment for the disregard of its authority. But why issue an attachment against the whole military power of the United States? This Court acknowledges that the laws are silent, and that it is without power in the premises, and therefore declines to make any order whatever.

If there be a disposition on the part of the military power to respect the authority of the civil courts they will respect the writ which has already been served. If, on the other hand, it is their determination to treat the authority of this Court with contempt in this matter, they have the power and will to treat with equal contempt any other process which the Court might order. The Court, therefore, must submit to the supreme physical force which now holds the custody of the petitioner, and decline to issue an attachment or to make any other order in this case.

General Hancock Appears.

At 11½ o'clock Major-General Hancock, to whom the writ was addressed, came into Court accompanied by Attorney-General Speed. The trial of Miss Mary Harris, charged with the murder of Mr. Burroughs, a clerk in the Treasury Department, which was then pending, was immediately suspended, when Attorney-General Speed addressed the Court as follows:—

Address of Attorney-General Speed.

May it please the Court:—In regard to the writ of habeas corpus directed to General Hancock, I desire to say, by way of apology for his not sooner making a return, that the process was not served upon him until about breakfast time this morning, and that owing to his having a great many persons to see, a great many important matters requiring immediate attention, and his distance from the court house, he was not able to get here at an earlier hour.

I wish to assure the Court that no disrespect was intended to it by the delay to which it has been unavoidably subjected. The Court declined to make any order in the case. The Attorney-General and General Hancock, in obedience to the writ, makes the following return:—

HEAD-QUARTERS MIDDLE MILITARY DIVISION, WASHINGTON, D. C., July 7, 1865.—To Hon. Andrew Wylie, Justice of the Supreme Court of the District of Columbia:—I hereby acknowledge the service of the writ hereto attached, and return the same, and respectfully say that the body of Mary E. Surratt is in my possession, under and by virtue of an order of Andrew Johnson, President of the United States and Commander-in-Chief of the Army and Navy, for the purposes in said order expressed, a copy of which is hereto attached and made part of this return; and that I do not produce said body by reason of the order of the President of the United States, indorsed upon said writ, to which reference is hereby respectfully made, dated July 7, 1865.

WINFIELD S. HANCOCK,
Maj.-Gen. U. S. Vols., Commanding Middle Div.

The President's Indorsement.

EXECUTIVE OFFICE, July 7, 1865, 10 A. M.—To Major-General W. S. Hancock, Commander, &c.—I, Andrew Johnson, President of the United States, do hereby declare that the writ of habeas corpus has been heretofore suspended in such cases as this, and I do hereby especially suspend this writ, and direct that you proceed to execute the order heretofore given upon the judgment of the Military Commission, and you will give this order forthwith to the writ.

ANDREW JOHNSON, President.

The Court.—This Court finds itself powerless to take any further action in the premises, and therefore declines to make orders which would be vain for any practical purpose. As regards the delay, it having been fully accounted for, the Court has no fault to attach to the respondent in that respect.

Attorney-General Speed.—It may not be out of order for me to say here, that this whole subject has, of course, had most earnest and anxious consideration of the Executive, and of the war making power of the Government.

Every man upon reflection, and particularly every lawyer knows that war cannot be fought by due process of law, and armies cannot be maintained by due process of law. There must be armies There must be battles: if war comes the law of war, and usage permits battles to be fought, permits human life to be taken without the judgment of the court, and without the process of the court. It permits prisoners to be taken, and prisoners to be held, and your honor will not undertake to discharge them, although the Constitution says that human life shall not be taken, or man be deprived of his liberty or property without due process of law. Conflict of necessity comes up when war comes between the Executive and the Judicial, if the war power or war does not transcend the civil. War is made for the maintenance of the civil power, that is when peace comes for the purpose of giving us the benefit of the civil.

This country is now in the midst of a great war, and the Commander-in-Chief of the armies of the United States was slain in the discharge of his duties, and if the armies of the United States cannot, under the laws of war protect their Commander-in-Chief from assassination, and if the laws and usages of war cannot protect, by military law, the Commander-in-Chief from assassination and destruction, what has the Government come to?

The thing appears to me to be too plain for consideration. But as your Honor has disposed of the case, I only make these remarks for the purpose of satisfying your Honor that we have anxiously, and I think most maturely considered this matter, giving your Honor credit for having done what you regard to be your duty in this matter, and are very glad to bear that your Honor gives us credit for having done what we have done, and regarded to be our duty.

The Court—The writ was applied for, and I had no authority to refuse to grant it. It is a writ dear and sacred to every lover of liberty, indispensable to the protection of citizens, and can only be constitutionally set aside in times of war and insurrection, when the public safety requires it, and in regard to offenses committed in connection with the army or the militia when called into active service.

With reference to the merits of this case, which has occupied so much of the attention of the public, and in fact of the whole civilian world, it would be out of place for the Court to express any opinion. The case is not before it. The Court can only say that it has no doubt that the gentlemen connected with the Government who have had the duty of conducting this trial, are truly convinced in their own minds as to the manner in which they have performed their duties. I do not feel at liberty; I could not; I dared not refuse to grant the writ.

The return which has been made to the writ is from the President of the United States, and declares that the writ of habeas corpus is to be suspended in this case as has been in other and similar cases. The Court has no further power in the case; if the Government desires to carry out its purpose in regard to the petitioner, the Court cannot prevent it; and I do not know that it would be possible, ever hereafter, to bring the case for argument in this Court, for if the petitioner be executed this day, as designed, the body cannot be brought into Court, and therefore is an end to the case. The jurisdiction of this Court yields to the suspension of the writ of habeas corpus from the President of the United States.

General Hancock then asked leave to retire, which was granted, and he left in company with Attorney-General Speed.

THE END.

T. B. PETERSON & BROTHERS' PUBLICATIONS.

The Books on this page will be found to be the very Best and Latest Publications in the world, and are Published and for Sale by T. B. PETERSON & BROTHERS, Philadelphia.

CAPT. MARRYATT'S WORKS.
Jacob Faithful,	50	Newton Foster,	50
Japhet Search of Father,	50	King's Own,	50
Phantom Ship,	50	Pirate & Three Cutters,	50
Midshipman Easy,	50	Peter Simple,	50
Pacha of Many Tales,	50	Percival Keene,	50
Naval Officer,	50	Poor Jack,	50
Snarleyow,	50	Sea King,	50

LIVES OF HIGHWAYMEN.
Life of John A. Murrel,	25	Biddy Woodhull,	25
Life of Joseph T. Hare,	25	Eveleen Wilson,	25
Life of Monroe Edwards,	50	Diary of a Pawnbroker,	50
Life of Helen Jewett,	25	Silver and Pewter,	25
Life of Jack Rann,	25	Sweeney Todd,	25
Life of Jonathan Wild,	25	Life of Mother Brownrig,	25
Life of Henry Thomas,	25	Dick Parker, the Pirate,	25
Life of Dick Turpin,	50	Life of Mary Bateman,	25
Life of Arthur Spring,	25	Life of Captain Blood,	25
Life of Jack Ketch,	25	Life of Galloping Dick,	25
Ninon De L'Enclos,	25	Sixteen-Stringed Jack's Fight for Life,	25
Desperadoes New World,	25		
Mysteries of N. Orleans,	50	Highwayman's Avenger,	25
The Robber's Wife,	25	Life of Raoul De Surville	25
Obi, or 3 Fingered Jack,	25	Life of Sybil Grey,	50
Kit Clayton,	25	Life of Rody the Rover,	25
Lives of the Felons,	25	Captain Blood and the Beagles,	25
Tom Waters,	25	Life of Grace O'Malley,	50
Life of Mrs. Whipple & Jesse Strang,	25	Life of Jack Sheppard,	50
Nat Blake,	25	Life of Davy Crockett,	50
Bill Horton,	25	Life of Guy Fawkes,	75
Galloping Gus,	25	Memoirs of Vidocq,	1 50
Ned Hastings,	25		

SEA TALES.
Adventures Ben Brace,	50	Morgan, the Buccaneer,	25
Jack Adams, Mutineer,	75	Jack Junk,	25
Jack Ariel's Adventures,	50	Davis, the Pirate,	25
Petrel, or Life on Ocean,	50	Valdez, the Pirate,	25
Cruising in Last War,	50	The Iron Cross,	25
Life of Paul Periwinkle,	50	Gallant Tom,	25
Percy Effingham,	75	Yankee Jack,	25
Life of Tom Bowling,	75	Harry Helm,	25
The Pirate's Son,	25	Harry Tempest,	25
The Doomed Ship,	25	Red Wing,	25
The Three Pirates,	50	Rebel and Rover,	25
The Flying Dutchman,	25	Jacob Faithful,	50
Life of Alexander Tardy,	25	Phantom Ship,	50
The Flying Yankee,	25	Midshipman Easy,	50
The Yankee Middy,	25	Pacha of Many Tales,	50
The Gold Seekers,	25	Naval Officer,	50
The River Pirates,	25	Snarleyow,	50
The King's Cruisers,	25	Newton Foster,	50
Man-of-Wars-Man,	25	King's Own,	50
Dark Shades City Life,	25	Japhet,	50
The Mate of the Seine,	25	Pirate & Three Cutters	50
Yankees in Japan,	25	Peter Simple,	50
Red King,	25	Percival Keene,	50
The Corsair,	50	Poor Jack,	50
Charles Ransford,	25	Sea King,	50

AINSWORTH'S GREAT WORKS.
Life of Jack Sheppard,	50	Dick Turpin,	50
Life of Davy Crockett,	50	Life of Henry Thomas,	25
Guy Fawkes,	75	Life of Mr. Whipple	25
The Star Chamber,	75	Desperadoes New World,	25
Old St. Paul's,	75	Ninon De L'Enclos,	25
Mysteries of the Court of Queen Anne,	50	Life of Arthur Spring,	25
		Life of Grace O'Malley,	50
Mysteries Court Stuarts,	75	Tower of London, 2 vls.	1 00
Windsor Castle,	75	Miser's Daughter, do.	1 00

GEORGE SAND'S WORKS.
Consuelo,	75	The Corsair,	50
Countess of Rudolstadt,	75	Indiana, 2 vols., paper,	1 50
First and True Love,	75	or in 1 vol., cloth	2 00
Consuelo and Countess of Rudolstadt, 1 vol, cloth, $2.00			

HARRY COCKTON'S WORKS.
Sylvester Sound,	75	The Sisters,	75
Valentine Vox, the Ventriloquist,	75	The Steward,	75
		Percy Effingham,	75

MAXWELL'S WORKS.
Wild Sports of the West,	75	Brian O'Lynn,	75
Stories of Waterloo,	75		

MILITARY AND ARMY BOOKS.
Ellsworth's Zouave Drill,	25	The Soldier's Companion,	25
U.S. Light Infantry Drill,	25	Volunteer's Text Book,	50
U.S. Government Infantry & Rifle Tactics,	25	The Soldier's Guide,	25

DR. HOLLICK'S WORKS.
Dr. Hollick's great work on Anatomy and Physiology of the Human Figure, with plates, - - 1 50
Dr. Hollick's Family Physician, - - - 25

EUGENE SUE'S WORKS.
Wandering Jew,	1 50	Man-of-War's-Man,	25
Mysteries of Paris,	1 50	Female Bluebeard,	25
Martin, the Foundling,	1 50	Life and Adventures of Raoul De Surville,	25
First Love,	25		
Woman's Love,	25		

SMITH'S WORKS.
The Usurer's Victim; or Thomas Balscombe,	50	Adelaide Waldgrave, or Trials of a Governess,	50

REVOLUTIONARY TALES.
Seven Bros. of Wyoming,	25	Wau-nan-gee,	25
The Brigand,	25	Legends of Mexico,	50
The Rebel Bride,	25	Grace Dudley; or Arnold at Saratoga,	25
Ralph Runnion,	50		
The Flying Artillerist,	25	The Guerilla Chief,	75
Old Put,	25	The Quaker Soldier,	1 50

EMERSON BENNETT'S WORKS.
The Border Rover,	1 50	Bride of Wilderness,	1 50
Clara Moreland,	1 50	Ellen Norbury,	1 50
Viola; or Adventures in Far South-West,	1 50	Forged Will,	1 50
		Kate Clarendon,	1 50

Above are each in paper cover. Each book is also published in one volume, cloth, price $2.00 each.

Heiress of Bellefonte, and Walde-Warren,	50	Pioneer's Daughter and Unknown Countess,	50

T. S. ARTHUR'S WORKS.
The Two Brides,	25	Agnes, or the Possessed,	25
Love in a Cottage,	25	Lucy Sandford,	25
Love in High Life,	25	The Banker's Wife,	25
Year after Marriage,	25	The Two Merchants,	25
The Lady at Home,	25	Insubordination,	25
Cecelia Howard,	25	Trial and Triumph,	25
Orphan Children,	25	The Iron Rule,	25
Debtor's Daughter,	25	Lizzie Glenn; or, The Trials of a Seamstress. Cloth,	2 00
Mary Moreton,	25		
The Divorced Wife,	25		
Pride and Prudence,	25	1 vol., paper,	1 00

MRS. GREY'S WORKS.
Cousin Harry,	1 50	The Little Beauty,	1 50

The above are each in one volume, paper cover. Each book is also in one volume, cloth, price $2.00 each.

Gipsey's Daughter,	25	Old Dower House,	25
Lena Cameron,	25	Hyacinthe,	25
Belle of the Family,	25	Alice Seymour,	25
Sybil Lennard,	25	Mary Seaham,	75
Duke and Cousin,	25	Passion and Principle,	75
The Little Wife,	25	The Flirt,	75
Manoeuvring Mother,	50	Good Society,	75
Baronet's Daughter's,	50	Lion-Hearted,	50
Young Prima Donna,	50		

SIR WALTER SCOTT'S NOVELS.
Ivanhoe,	50	St. Ronan's Well,	50
Rob Roy,	50	Red Gauntlet,	50
Guy Mannering,	50	The Betrothed,	50
The Antiquary,	50	The Talisman,	50
Old Mortality,	50	Woodstock,	50
Heart of Mid Lothian,	50	Highland Widow, etc.,	50
Bride of Lammermoor,	50	The Fair Maid of Perth,	50
Waverly,	50	Anne of Geierstein,	50
Kenilworth,	50	Count Robert of Paris,	50
The Pirate,	50	The Black Dwarf and Legend of Montrose,	50
The Monastery,	50		
The Abbot,	50	Castle Dangerous and Surgeon's Daughter,	50
The Fortunes of Nigel,	50		
Peveril of the Peak,	50	Moredun, A Tale of 1210,	50
Quentin Durward,	50		
Tales of a Grandfather,	50	Life of Scott, cloth,	1 00

A complete set of the novels of Walter Scott will be sent to any one, to any place, free of postage, for Ten Dollars; or another edition of Waverly Novels, in five volumes, in cloth, for $12.00; or the Complete Prose and Poetical Works of Sir Walter Scott, in ten vols, cloth, for $24.00.

GEORGE LIPPARD'S WORKS.
The Empire City,	75	The Entranced,	25
Memoirs of a Preacher,	75	Washington and his Generals, or Legends of the American Revolution,	1 50
The Quaker City,	1 50		
Paul Ardenheim,	1 50		
Blanche Brandywine,	1 50	Legends of Mexico,	25
Mysteries of Florence,	75	Bank Director's Son,	25
The Nazarene,	75	The Robbers,	25
Washington and his Men	75		

LIEBIG'S WORKS ON CHEMISTRY.
Agricultural Chemistry,	25	Liebig's celebrated Letters on Potato Disease,	25
Animal Chemistry,	25		

Liebig's Complete Works on Chemistry. Containing everything written by Professor Liebig, is also issued in one large volume, bound in cloth. Price $2.00.

☞ Copies of any of the above Works will be sent by Mail, free of Postage, to any part of the United States, on receipt of the retail price, by T. B. Peterson & Brothers, Philadelphia.

CHEAPEST BOOK HOUSE IN THE WORLD.

T. B. PETERSON AND BROTHERS,
306 Chestnut Street, Philadelphia, Penna.

Publish the most Saleable Books in the World, and supply all Books at the Lowest Rates.

The cheapest place in the world to buy all kinds of Books, suitable for all persons whatever, for the Family, Army or Railroad Reading, is at the Publishing House of T. B. PETERSON & BROTHERS, Philadelphia, Penna. Any person wanting any books at all, in any quantity, from a single book to a dozen, a hundred, thousand, or larger quantity of books, had better send an their orders at once to the "CHEAP BOOKSELLING AND PUBLISHING HOUSE" of T. B. PETERSON & BROTHERS," No. 306 Chestnut Street, Philadelphia, who publish over One Thousand Books, and have the largest stock in the country, and will supply them and sell them cheaper than any other house in the world. We have just issued a new and complete catalogue, which we send gratuitously to any one on application.

Enclose one, two, five, ten, twenty, fifty or a hundred dollars, or more, to us in a letter, and write what kind of books you wish, and they will be packed and sent to you at once, per first express or mail, or in any other way you may direct, just as well assorted, and the same as if you were on the spot, with circulars, show bills, &c., gratis.

Booksellers, News Agents, Sutlers, and all others, will please address all orders for any books they may want, to the "PHILADELPHIA CHEAP PUBLISHING AND BOOKSELLING HOUSE" of

T. B. PETERSON & BROTHERS, 306 Chestnut Street, Philadelphia.

Publishers of "Petersons' Detector." A Business Journal. Price $1.50 a year.

And the Books will be sent to you at once, per first express after receipt of order, or in any other way you may direct.

CHARLES DICKENS' WORKS.

Great Expectations,	75	Old Curiosity Shop,	75
Lamplighter's Story,	75	Sketches by "Boz,"	75
David Copperfield,	75	Oliver Twist,	75
Dombey and Son,	75	Little Dorrit,	75
Nicholas Nickleby,	75	Tale of Two Cities,	75
Pickwick Papers,	75	New Years' Stories,	75
Christmas Stories,	75	Dickens' Short Stories,	75
Martin Chuzzlewit,	75	Message from the Sea,	75
Barnaby Rudge,	75	Holiday Stories,	75
Dickens' New Stories,	75	American Notes,	75
Bleak House,	75	Pic Nic Papers,	75
Somebody's Luggage,	25	Christmas Carols,	25

Above are each in one large octavo volume, paper cover.

We also publish twenty-eight other editions of Dickens' Works, comprising the Library, the People's and the Illustrated editions, in both octavo and duodecimo form, at prices varying from $15.00 to $100.00 a set, according to the edition and style of binding.

G. W. M. REYNOLDS' WORKS.

Mysteries of the Court of London,	1 00	Rosa Lambert,	1 00
		Mary Price,	1 00
Rose Foster,	1 50	Eustace Quentin,	1 00
Caroline of Brunswick,	1 00	Joseph Wilmot,	1 00
		Banker's Daughter,	1 00
Venetia Trelawney,	1 00	Kenneth,	1 00
Lord Saxondale,	1 00	The Rye-House Plot,	1 00
Count Christoval,	1 00	The Necromancer,	1 00

Above each in paper cover. Each one of a finer edition, is also bound in cloth, for $2.00 each.

The Opera Dancer,	50	Duke of Marchmont,	75
The Ruined Gamester,	50	The Soldier's Wife,	75
Child of Waterloo,	50	May Middleton,	75
Ciprina, or Secrets of a Picture Gallery,	50	Massacre of Glencoe,	75
		Queen Joanna, or the Court of Naples,	75
Robert Bruce,	75	Loves of the Harem,	50
Discarded Queen,	75	Ellen Percy,	75
The Gipsey Chief,	75	Agnes Evelyn,	50
Mary Stuart, Queen of Scots,	75	Pickwick Abroad,	75
Wallace, Hero Scotland,	75	Parricide,	50
Isabella Vincent,	75	Life in Paris,	50
Vivian Bertram,	75	Countess and the Page,	50
Countess of Lascelles,	75	Edgar Montrose,	50

CHARLES LEVER'S WORKS.

Charles O'Malley,	75	Arthur O'Leary,	75
Harry Lorrequer,	75	Con Cream,	75
Jack Hinton,	75	Davenport Dunn,	75
Tom Burke of Ours,	75	Horace Templeton,	75
Knight of Gwynne,	75	Kate O'Donoghue,	75

We also publish a Military Edition of Lever's Novels, with Illuminated covers in colors, price 75 cents each.

A finer edition of the above are also published, each one complete in one volume, cloth, price $2.00 a volume.

Ten Thousand a Year, one vol., paper,	1 50	The Diary of a Medical Student,	75

ALEXANDER DUMAS' WORKS.

Count of Monte Cristo,	1 50	Memoirs of a Physician,	1 00
The Iron Mask,	1 00	Queen's Necklace,	1 00
Louise La Valliere,	1 00	Six Years Later,	1 00
Memoirs of a Marquis,	1 00	Countess of Charny,	1 00
Diana of Meridor,	1 00	Andree de Taverney,	1 00
The Three Guardsmen,	75	Forty-five Guardsmen,	75
Twenty Years after,	75	The Iron Hand,	75
Bragelonne,	75	The Chevalier,	1 00

A finer edition of each of the above are also published, bound in one volume, cloth, price $2.00 each.

The Conscript,	1 50	Camille,	1 50

Above are each in one volume, paper cover. Each book is also published in one vol., cloth. Price $2.00.

The Fallen Angel,	50	Sketches in France,	50
Edmond Dantes,	75	Isabel of Bavaria,	75
George,	50	Mohicans of Paris,	50
Felina de Chamburs,	75	Man with Five Wives,	75
The Horrors in Paris,	50	Twin Lieutenants,	75
Annette, Lady of Pearls,	50		

MRS. SOUTHWORTH'S WORKS.

The Bridal Eve,	1 50	Wife's Victory,	1 50
The Fatal Marriage,	1 50	Retribution,	1 50
Love's Labor Won,	1 50	India, Pearl River,	1 50
Deserted Wife,	1 50	Curse of Clifton,	1 50
The Gipsy's Prophecy,	1 50	Discarded Daughter,	1 50
The Mother-in-Law,	1 50	The Initials,	1 50
Haunted Homestead,	1 50	The Jealous Husband,	1 50
The Lost Heiress,	1 50	Self-Sacrifice,	1 50
Lady of the Isle,	1 50	Belle of Washington,	1 50
The Two Sisters,	1 50	Kate Aylesford,	1 50
The Three Beauties,	1 50	Courtship & Matrimony	1 50
Vivia; Secret Power,	1 50	Family Pride,	1 50
The Missing Bride,	1 50	The Woman in Black,	1 50

The above each in one volume, paper cover. Each book is also published in one volume, cloth, price $2.00.

Hickory Hall,	50	Broken Engagement,	25

CAROLINE LEE HENTZ'S WORKS.

The Lost Daughter,	1 50	Rena; or Snow-bird,	1 50
The Planter's Northern Bride,	1 50	Marcus Warland,	1 50
		Love after Marriage,	1 50
Linda,	1 50	Eoline,	1 50
Robert Graham,	1 50	The Banished Son,	1 50
Courtship & Marriage,	1 50	Helen and Arthur,	1 50
Ernest Linwood,	1 50	Planter's Daughter,	1 50

The above are each in one volume, paper cover. Each book is also published in one volume, cloth, price $2.00.

FREDRIKA BREMER'S WORKS.

Father and Daughter,	1 50	The Neighbors,	1 50
The Four Sisters,	1 50	The Home,	1 50

The above are each in one volume, paper cover. Each one is also published in one volume, cloth, price $2.00. Life in the Old World; or Two Years in Switzerland and Italy, by Miss Bremer; in 2 vols., cloth, price $4.00.

MRS. ANN S. STEPHENS' WORKS.

The Wife's Secret,	1 50	Fashion and Famine,	1 50
The Rejected Wife,	1 50	The Old Homestead,	1 50
Mary Derwent,	1 50	The Heiress,	1 50

The above are each in one volume, paper cover. Each one is also published in one volume, cloth, price $2.00.

CATHARINE SINCLAIR'S, Etc.

Flirtations in Fashionable Life,	1 50	The Pride of Life,	1 50
		The Devoted Bride,	1 50
The Rival Belles,	1 50	Love and Duty,	1 50
The Lost Love,	1 50	Bohemians in London,	1 50
Family Secrets,	1 50	The Woman in Red,	1 50

The above are each in one volume, paper cover. Each book is also published in one volume, cloth, price $2.00.

DOESTICKS' WORKS.

Doesticks' Letters,	1 50	The Elephant Club,	1 50
Plu-Ri-Bus-Tah,	1 50	Witches of New York,	1 50

The above are each in one volume, paper cover. Each one is also published in one volume, cloth, price $2.00.

NOVELS ON THE WAR.

The Coward,	1 50	Days of Shoddy,	1 50
Shoulder-Straps,	1 50		

The above are each in one volume, paper cover. Each book is also published in one volume, cloth, price $2.00.

BEST COOK BOOKS PUBLISHED.

Petersons' New Cook Book, never before issued,	2 00
Miss Leslie's New Cookery Book,	2 00
Widdifield's New Cook Book,	2 00
Mrs. Hale's Receipts for the Million,	2 00
Miss Leslie's New Receipts for Cooking,	2 00
Mrs. Hale's New Cook Book,	2 00
Francatelli's Celebrated Cook Book. The Modern Cook, with 62 illustrations, 600 large octavo pages,	5 00

GREEN'S WORKS ON GAMBLING.

Gambling Exposed,	1 50	The Reformed Gambler	1 50
The Gambler's Life,	1 50	Secret Band Brothers,	1 50

Above are in paper cover, or in cloth at $2.00 each.

☞ Copies of any of the above works will be sent by Mail, free of Postage, to any part of the United States, on receipt of the retail price, by T. B. Peterson & Brothers, Philadelphia."

www.ingramcontent.com/pod-product-compliance
Lightning Source LLC
Chambersburg PA
CBHW020813230426
43666CB00007B/989